MAHABHARATA

MAHABHARATA

A Modern Retelling

Carole Satyamurti

W. W. NORTON & COMPANY

NEW YORK • LONDON

For information about permission to reproduce selections from
this book, write to Permissions, W. W. Norton & Company, Inc.,
500 Fifth Avenue, New York, NY 10110

For information about special discounts for bulk purchases,
please contact W. W. Norton Special Sales at
specialsales@wwnorton.com or 800-233-4830

Manufacturing by Courier Westford
Book design by Brooke Koven
Production manager: Louise Parasmo

Library of Congress Cataloging-in-Publication Data

Satyamurti, Carole.
Mahabharata : a modern retelling / by Carole Satyamurti. —
First edition.
pages cm
Includes bibliographical references.
ISBN 978-0-393-08175-6 (hardcover)
1. India—History—To 324 B.C.—Poetry. I. Mahabharata.
English II. Title.
PR6069.A776M34 2015
821'.914—dc23
2014033595

W. W. Norton & Company, Inc.
500 Fifth Avenue, New York, N.Y. 10110
www.wwnorton.com

W. W. Norton & Company Ltd.
Castle House, 75/76 Wells Street, London W1T 3QT

1 2 3 4 5 6 7 8 9 0

In memory of T. V. Sathyamurthy
(1929–1998)

My gateway to India

Contents

Map   xix

Foreword by Wendy Doniger: xxi
The *Mahabharata*, a Text for All Seasons

Preface by Carole Satyamurti   xxxi

MAHABHARATA

Prologue   3
Introduction to the poem and its main storytellers: Vyasa,
Vaishampayana, and Ugrashravas.

I • THE BOOK OF THE BEGINNING

1. The ancestors: 13
The Bharata lineage; the story of Satyavati and the birth of
Vyasa; Shantanu marries the goddess Ganga, and Bhishma
is born. Shantanu later marries Satyavati and they have
two sons, Chitrangada and Vichitravirya. Chitrangada
dies in battle. Bhishma abducts three royal sisters, Amba,
Ambika, and Ambalika, as brides for Vichitravirya. Amba
had already chosen another husband, and leaves the court.
Vichitravirya dies childless, and Vyasa fathers two sons on
the royal widows—Dhritarashtra (born blind) and Pandu
(born pale)—as well as a son, Vidura, by a maid-servant.

2. Dhritarashtra and Pandu: 25
Bhishma, as regent, arranges marriages for the Bharata
princes: Dhritarashtra marries Gandhari, who chooses to
wear a blindfold lifelong; Pandu marries Kunti and Madri;
Vidura, being born of a shudra mother, marries a woman
of equivalent parentage. Pandu is cursed by a brahmin to
die during the sexual act, so has to remain celibate. Kunti

deploys a boon she has received previously, and gives birth
to three sons, fathered by different gods. Madri gives birth
to two sons in the same way. These five sons—Yudhishthira,
Bhima, Arjuna, Nakula, and Sahadeva—are known as the
Pandavas. Gandhari, blessed by Vyasa, gives birth to one
hundred sons (the Kauravas), and a daughter. Evil omens
attend the birth of the eldest, Duryodhana. Pandu gives way
to temptation and dies in the act of love with Madri. Madri
climbs on his funeral pyre, and Kunti takes the five boys to
Hastinapura, the capital of the Bharata kingdom.

3. Cousins: 38
The five Pandavas and the hundred Kaurava boys get
on badly together. Encouraged by his uncle, Shakuni,
Duryodhana makes an unsuccessful attempt on Bhima's
life. The young princes are trained in the arts of war, first
by Kripa and then by Drona—both brahmins. Drona plans
vengeance on his former friend, Drupada, king of Panchala.

4. Learning the arts of war: 50
Drona trains the royal princes in his weapons school.
Arjuna becomes an outstanding archer, and Drona's
favorite. Drona's son, Ashvatthaman, also receives special
attention. Karna, foundling son of a suta, joins the weapons
school, and is despised. He becomes deeply envious of
Arjuna. Ekalavya, a tribal boy, is turned away by Drona, but
becomes a great archer through diligent practice.

5. Karna: 60
We learn Karna's real parentage. He seeks out the great
weapons teacher, Rama Jamadagnya, and acquires celestial
weapons but, finally, is cursed by his teacher for deception.

6. The tournament: 70
Drona organizes a public display to show the young princes'
skills. Karna arrives and humiliates Arjuna. Duryodhana
befriends Karna.

7. Revenge: 81
Drona mounts an attack on Drupada's city, Kampilya.
Drupada is humiliated. Through prayer and austerity, he
acquires a son, Dhrishtadyumna, born to avenge his father,
and a daughter, Draupadi, who will, he hopes,
marry Arjuna.

8. The lacquer house: 88
Duryodhana persuades his father to send the Pandavas and
Kunti off on a visit to Varanavata. Duryodhana plots the

death of his cousins, but the plot is unsuccessful and they
escape into the forest.

9. Flight: 98
In the forest, the Pandavas encounter the ogre Hidimba
and his sister, whom Bhima marries. She gives birth to their
son, Ghatotkacha. At Vyasa's prompting, the Pandavas move
to the city of Ekachakra, where Bhima kills the ogre Baka.

10. Draupadi's bridegroom choice: 111
The Pandavas, disguised as brahmins, go to Kampilya
where Arjuna wins the contest for Draupadi's hand. Owing
to a misunderstanding, all five brothers become her
husbands. They meet their cousins, Krishna (an incarnation
of Vishnu) and Balarama, for the first time.

11. Acquiring a kingdom: 123
Duryodhana is enraged by the Pandavas' good fortune.
His father, the king, agrees to divide the kingdom in half.
Yudhishthira will be king of the barren Khandava tract.
In time, the Pandavas transform it, building the beautiful
city of Indraprastha. The brothers make an agreement to
avoid jealousy arising between them over Draupadi. Arjuna
transgresses, and insists on going into exile.

12. Arjuna's exile: 136
Arjuna visits sacred sites, has liaisons with Ulupi and
Chitrangadaa, visits Krishna's city, Dvaraka, and marries
Krishna's sister, Subhadra. Back at Indraprastha, Subhadra
gives birth to Abhimanyu, and Draupadi to five sons, one by
each brother.

13. The burning of the Khandava Forest: 144
Walking in the forest, Arjuna and Krishna encounter the
god Agni, who wishes to burn down the forest, but is being
thwarted by the god Indra (Arjuna's father). They agree to help
him, and are given celestial weapons. Through their efforts,
the forest is burned down, only a few creatures escaping.

II • THE BOOK OF THE ASSEMBLY HALL

14. The decision: 153
The divine architect, Maya, builds a beautiful assembly hall
for Yudhishthira. The seer Narada suggests that Yudhishthira
make an attempt to become king of kings. The king of
Magadha, Jarasandha, stands in the way of this ambition, and
Krishna and Bhima challenge him and defeat him.

15. King of kings: 164

Yudhishthira's brothers take armies to other kingdoms throughout the land, and secure the fealty of a number of other kings. A great consecration sacrifice takes place, to which the Kauravas are invited. The king of Chedi, Shishupala, challenges Yudhishthira's choice of Krishna as guest of honor, and Krishna kills him. After the ceremony, Duryodhana tours the assembly hall and is consumed by envy and despair.

16. Duryodhana's despair: 176

Back in Hastinapura, Shakuni suggests that Yudhishthira be invited to a gambling match, which he is sure to lose. Dhristarashtra agrees to this. Yudhishthira, despite misgivings, accepts the invitation.

17. The dice game: 186

Due to Shakuni's sleight of hand, Yudhishthira loses everything he owns, including his brothers, himself, and his wife. Draupadi challenges the elders to say whether her husband could have lost her, when he had already lost himself, and therefore had no right to property. Duhshasana, second eldest Kaurava, tries to strip Draupadi, but fails. Duryodhana lewdly insults Draupadi, and Bhima vows to kill both him and his brother. Draupadi's question remains unresolved, but Dhritarashtra cancels Yudhishthira's losses and allows the Pandavas to leave.

18. The dice game resumes: 203

Duryodhana and Shakuni devise a new basis for a dice game, and the Pandavas are brought back. Whoever loses this time will go into exile for thirteen years, while the winner takes possession of their lands. Only if they remain unrecognized during the thirteenth year will their lands be returned. Yudhishthira agrees, plays, and loses. The Pandavas depart for their forest exile.

III • THE BOOK OF THE FOREST

19. Exile begins: 211

The Pandavas, accompanied by devoted brahmins, settle in a pleasant spot in the forest. Back at court, the seer Maitreya curses Duryodhana. He and Dhritarashtra learn that Bhima

has killed an ogre in the forest, and fear for the future.
Krishna and other allies visit the Pandavas in the forest.

20. Discord: 223
Draupadi and Bhima urge Yudhishthira to ignore the terms
of the dice game and attack the Kauravas. Yudhishthira
refuses. Vyasa appears and counsels them. He advises that
Arjuna should go on a quest to acquire celestial weapons.
Arjuna departs.

21. Quest: 235
Arjuna travels to the Himalaya where he is tested by Indra,
and embarks on a period of strict austerities. He is tested by
the god Shiva, who promises to give him the terrible divine
weapon *Pashupata*. He spends five years in Indra's heaven.
In the forest, Yudhishthira is disconsolate, and the sage
Brihadashva tells him the story of Nala and Damayanti.

22. Pilgrimage: 248
The seer Lomasha, sent by Indra, visits the Pandavas who
are restless, missing Arjuna. He proposes that they go with
him on a pilgrimage to sacred sites, and as they travel, he
tells them enlightening stories—the tales of Rishyashringa,
King Shibi and the hawk, and King Yuvanashva. The
party journeys into the Himalayan mountains, and Bhima
encounters Hanuman, the great ape of the *Ramayana*, and
does battle with yakshas. The Pandavas are reunited with
Arjuna. Bhima has an encounter with the snake Nahusha.
After some years, the Pandavas begin their slow descent to
the forest on the plain.

23. Duryodhana's mistake: 267
The exile enters its twelfth year. The Pandavas are visited by
the ascetic Markandeya, who tells them marvelous stories,
and offers them wise advice. Krishna visits with his chief
wife, Satyabhama. She asks Draupadi what is the secret that
keeps her husbands devoted to her, and Draupadi says there
is no secret; only her own assiduous devotion as a wife. With
the period of exile soon coming to an end, the Kauravas
become increasingly apprehensive. They undertake a huge
expedition into the forest with the aim of intimidating the
Pandavas with a show of strength. Their rash encounter
with the king of the gandharvas results in Duryodhana
being beaten and humiliated. Karna vows that he will grind
Arjuna into the dust.

24. The end in sight: 283

The Pandavas are visited by Vyasa. He advises Yudhishthira and tells the story of Mudgala the gleaner. Jayadratha, Duryodhana's brother-in-law, attempts to abduct Draupadi and is punished and humiliated by Bhima. He vows to have revenge. Markandeya visits and tells the story of Savitri and Satyavat. Karna's father, Surya the sun god, warns him that Indra will try to obtain the protective armor he was born with. Karna encounters Indra disguised as a brahmin. He gives him the armor and receives Indra's spear in exchange. The Pandavas begin to prepare for their thirteenth year of exile. The god Dharma, Yudhishthira's father, tests them and promises that they will succeed in remaining unrecognized until their exile expires.

IV • THE BOOK OF VIRATA

25. Virata's court: 299

The Pandavas plan the disguises they will assume during their thirteenth year. They travel to the kingdom of King Virata and obtain employment in the royal court. Bhima protects Draupadi from the lustful advances of Kichaka.

26. The cattle raid: 313

The Kauravas mount a raid on King Virata's cattle. Arjuna, still disguised as a eunuch, defeats them, with Virata's son, Uttara, as his charioteer. The Kauravas recognize him, but the thirteenth year is up. Virata offers Arjuna his daughter, Uttaraa, in marriage, but Arjuna suggests that his son, Abhimanyu, marry her instead.

V • THE BOOK OF PERSEVERANCE

27. Suing for peace, preparing for war: 331

Duryodhana refuses to return Yudhishthira's kingdom and the Pandavas, expecting war, meet with their main allies. In the hope of achieving a resolution, Drupada sends his household priest to Hastinapura. Both Arjuna and Duryodhana seek Krishna's support; Krishna will act as Arjuna's charioteer, and Krishna's army will join the Kaurava side. Shalya, Madri's brother, takes the side of the Kauravas. Dhritarashtra sends Sanjaya to urge the Pandavas not to make war.

28. Diplomacy continues: 345
Dhritarashtra is extremely agitated, and Vidura tries to
soothe him with stories and wise words. The council meets
to hear a report from Sanjaya. Duryodhana is confident of
victory and refuses to make any concessions.

29. Krishna's mission: 360
The Pandavas are pessimistic about the chances of peace.
Krishna decides to make one last attempt, and travels to
Hastinapura. He addresses Duryodhana in the council, but
the Kaurava insists that he is in the right. Krishna reveals
his divine power.

30. The temptation of Karna: 375
Before leaving Hastinapura, Krishna reveals to Karna the
truth about his origins—he is really the eldest brother of
the Pandavas—in the hope of persuading him to change
sides and share the kingdom with the Pandavas. Kunti
makes the same attempt, but Karna refuses on principle.

31. Marshaling the armies: 384
Huge forces are assembled on the plain of Kurukshetra.
Bhishma is appointed commander of the Kauravas, but he
and Karna declare that they will not fight alongside each
other; and Bhishma will not fight Shikhandin because he
was born a woman, Shikhandini, and, in a previous life,
was Amba, whose goal was to have revenge on Bhishma for
ruining her life.

VI • THE BOOK OF BHISHMA

32. The song of the Lord: 395
Through the gift of divine sight, Sanjaya will report every
stage of the war to the blind king. Arjuna suddenly sinks
down in his chariot declaring that he will not fight, that
he cannot commit the sin of killing his kinsmen. Krishna,
through teachings and through revelation, persuades him
that his attitude is wrong (the "Bhagavad Gita").

33. The war begins: 421
Yudhishthira approaches the Kaurava elders to ask for their
blessing. Battle begins. The first day brings heavy losses for
the Pandavas.

34. Bhishma in command: 431
The second day goes better for the Pandavas. On the third

day Arjuna engages in combat with Bhishma, but so half-heartedly that Krishna intervenes. The fourth day favors the Pandavas; several Kaurava princes are killed. Duryodhana starts to worry. Bhishma urges him to make peace but he refuses. On the fifth day, many thousands of troops are killed. Bhima fights heroically and, on day six, wounds Duryodhana severely.

35. Bhishma implacable: 448
Bitter fighting involves many named warriors, including Arjuna's son Iravat. Ghatotkacha inflicts huge damage on the Kauravas. Duryodhana is discouraged and suspects Bhishma of favoring the Pandavas. Next day, Bhishma scorches the allies of the Pandavas. Again, Arjuna is reluctant to fight him.

36. The fall of Bhishma: 461
Bhishma is felled by Arjuna, using Shikhandin as a shield. Bhishma has been given the boon that he can choose the time of his death, and this is not an auspicious time. He will lie on the field of Kurukshetra, pierced by arrows, but alive, until the winter solstice.

VII • THE BOOK OF DRONA

37. Drona leads the Kauravas: 471
Karna and Bhishma are reconciled. Drona fails to capture Yudhishthira. Arjuna is challenged by the Trigartas. Death of Bhagadatta.

38. The death of Abhimanyu: 490
Arjuna is drawn away to fight the Trigartas. Jayadratha's revenge leads to Abhimanyu being trapped by the Kauravas and killed. Arjuna vows to kill Jayadratha the next day.

39. In pursuit of Jayadratha: 505
Arjuna and Krishna make every effort to reach Jayadratha before nightfall, but he is heavily defended. Bhurishravas is killed by Satyaki in dubious circumstances. Thanks to a ruse of Krishna's, Arjuna succeeds in killing Jayadratha, fulfilling his vow.

40. Battle at night: 526
General fighting continues through the night. Karna is an outstanding warrior, but the Pandavas do well. Duryodhana suspects Drona of favoring the Pandavas. Discord

among the Kauravas, whose forces are hard pressed by
Ghatotkacha. Karna uses the celestial spear he was keeping
for Arjuna, and kills Ghatotkacha.

41. Drona and Ashvatthaman: 541
The fighting continues, Drona inflicting great damage
on the Pandava forces. Drona is killed through deception
encouraged by Krishna. Drona's son Ashvatthaman swears
vengeance and uses celestial weapons which Krishna and
Arjuna neutralize.

VIII • THE BOOK OF KARNA

42. Karna in command: 557
Karna is consecrated as Kaurava commander, with Shalya as
his charioteer. Arjuna fears Yudhishthira has come to harm,
and seeks him out. They quarrel and Krishna helps them
resolve their differences. Arjuna swears not to return until
he has killed Karna.

43. Tragic Karna: 575
Shalya tries to undermine Karna's morale. Bhima kills
Duhshasana and drinks his blood, fulfilling his vow. Karna's
sons are killed. Arjuna and Karna finally meet in a duel to
the death. Karna is killed.

IX • THE BOOK OF SHALYA

44. Defeat for Duryodhana: 589
Shalya is the Kaurava commander. Bhima kills the last
of Dhritarashtra's sons, apart from Duryodhana who
flees and hides in a lake. The Pandavas track him down
and challenge him to come out and fight. He is narrowly
defeated by Bhima who smashes his thighs, contrary to the
rules of fair fight. The war is over. Krishna takes the news to
Hastinapura.

X • THE BOOK OF THE NIGHT ATTACK

45. Massacre by night: 611
Ashvatthaman vows to avenge Duryodhana and his father.
With Kripa and Kritavarman, he attacks the Pandava
camp and, strengthened by the god Shiva, slaughters the
surviving Pandava and Panchala fighters, including all of

Draupadi's sons. The Pandavas pursue Ashvatthaman and
defeat him, but at great cost.

XI • THE BOOK OF THE WOMEN

46. Dhritarashtra's grief: 631
Dhritarashtra is heartbroken and is consoled by Vidura and
Vyasa. Dhritarashtra, Gandhari, and the Pandavas go to the
battlefield.

47. Gandhari's lament: 642
The field is crowded with women looking for their dead
loved ones. Gandhari is given the gift of divine sight and
describes what she sees. She curses Krishna for his part in
the war. Kunti reveals that Karna was her son.

XII • THE BOOK OF PEACE

48. Yudhishthira, reluctant ruler: 653
Yudhishthira is grief-stricken by the carnage and by Karna's
death. He holds himself responsible and says he will
renounce the kingdom. Only in that way can he atone. His
brothers and Draupadi try to dissuade him.

49. Yudhishthira listens to the seers: 664
Devasthana, Vyasa, and Krishna all speak to Yudhishthira.
Vyasa tells him he should perform the great horse sacrifice.
He sets aside his doubts and enters Hastinapura. Krishna
tells him to learn from Bhishma.

50. The education of the Dharma King (1):   680
Bhishma, lying on his bed of arrows, instructs Yudhishthira
on the duties of a king.

51. The education of the Dharma King (2):   698
Bhishma's teaching continues. He speaks about a person's
moral obligations, as well as the need for a king to exercise
good judgment. He tells instructive stories.

52. Dharma in difficult times: 709
Through parables, Bhishma talks about right action at
times when the kingdom is under threat, or is undergoing
famine. Yudhishthira asks his brothers for their views on
the relative importance of the three goals of kshatriya
dharma—virtue, wealth, and pleasure. He praises a fourth

goal—moksha—and asks Bhishma to talk to him about how
absolute freedom can be achieved.

53. The path to absolute freedom: 724
Through stories, Bhishma teaches the subtleties of karma,
spiritual practice, and the importance of worshiping
Vishnu. He discusses the difficulty of achieving absolute
freedom while still living in the world.

XIII • THE BOOK OF INSTRUCTION

54. The teaching continues: 745
Bhishma's final stories concern the nature of responsibility
for actions; whether Death can be conquered; whether
men or women enjoy sex more; whether one can become a
brahmin within one lifetime; and the nature of compassion.

55. The death of Bhishma: 756
Yudhishthira continues to learn from Bhishma. With the
arrival of the winter solstice, Bhishma composes himself
and dies.

XIV • THE BOOK OF THE HORSE SACRIFICE

56. King Yudhishthira turns to the future: 767
Yudhishthira is again despondent but is heartened by the
prospect of the horse sacrifice through which he can atone
for wrongdoing. Yudhishthira travels to the mountains to
retrieve buried treasure which he will need for the sacrifice.
Arjuna spends time with Krishna and receives spiritual
instruction. Krishna sets off for Dvaraka and encounters
Uttanka, an ascetic to whom he reveals his divine nature.
Uttaraa gives birth to a son but the baby is born dead as a
result of Ashvatthaman's deadly invocation. Krishna brings
him to life and he is named Parikshit.

57. The horse sacrifice: 782
Arjuna accompanies the sacrificial horse throughout
the land in preparation for the great ceremony. He
encounters Chitrangadaa and Ulupi, and his son
Babhruvahana. The elaborate sacrifice takes place. A
mongoose disparages it, and tells the story of the devout
brahmin of Kurukshetra.

XV • THE BOOK OF THE HERMITAGE

58. The retreat of the elders: 797
After fifteen years, Dhritarashtra and the other elders
depart for the forest, to lead an ascetic life. The Pandavas
visit them. Vidura dies and his spirit enters Yudhishthira.
Vyasa arranges an epiphany: for a single night, the heroes
killed at Kurukshetra rise up from the Ganga and are
reconciled, and reunited with their loved ones.

XVI • THE BOOK OF THE CLUBS

59. Krishna's people: 817
Thirty-six years into Yudhishthira's reign, grim portents are
seen. In Dvaraka, Vrishni warriors are cursed by brahmins
for disrespect, and are killed by one another, thus fulfilling
Gandhari's curse. Krishna's time on earth is over; he and
Balarama die. Arjuna escorts the citizens of Dvaraka out of
the city before it is engulfed by the sea. His divine weapons
fail him. Vyasa advises the Pandavas to leave Hastinapura.

XVII AND XVIII • THE BOOKS OF THE FINAL JOURNEY AND THE ASCENT TO HEAVEN

60. The final journey: 829
Yudhishthira abdicates in favor of Parikshit. The Pandavas
and Draupadi circumambulate the kingdom and make for
the Himalaya. One by one, they fall dead and their spirits
go to heaven, except for Yudhishthira who enters heaven in
his body as a mark of his extraordinary virtue. In heaven his
virtue is tested. He sheds his earthly body and is reunited
with those he loves.

Epilogue   841
Ugrashravas has come to the end of Vyasa's epic poem. He
takes his leave from the forest ascetics, and goes on his way.

Afterword by Vinay Dharwadker: 845
The Poetry of the *Mahabharata*

Acknowledgments   864

Genealogies   866

Suggestions for Further Reading   870

Glossary   873

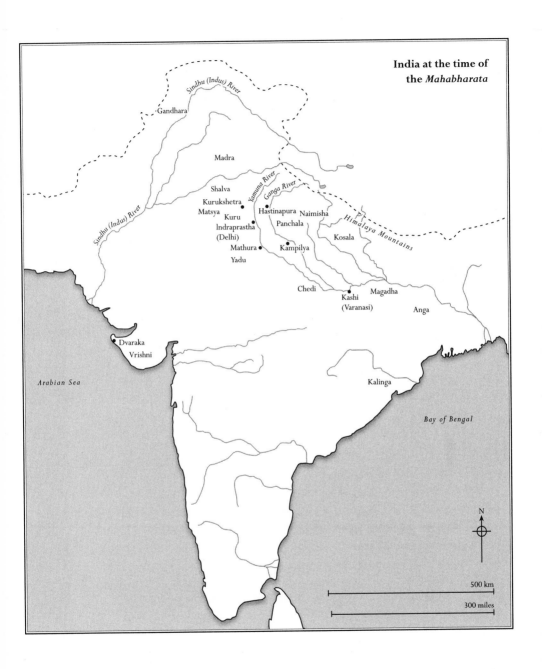

**India at the time of
the *Mahabharata***

Gandhara

Sindhu (Indus) River

Madra

Shalva

Kurukshetra

Matsya

Kuru

Indraprastha
(Delhi)

Hastinapura

Naimisha

Panchala

Kosala

Himalaya Mountains

Yamuna River

Ganga River

Mathura

Yadu

Kampilya

Chedi

Kashi
(Varanasi)

Magadha

Anga

Dvaraka

Vrishni

Arabian Sea

Kalinga

Bay of Bengal

Sindhu (Indus) River

N

500 km

300 miles

FOREWORD

The *Mahabharata*, a Text for All Seasons[1]

WENDY DONIGER

THE TEXT: VARIATIONS ON A THEME

THE *Mahabharata* is a text of about 75,000 verses—sometimes rounded off to 100,000—or three million words, some fifteen times the combined length of the Hebrew Bible and the New Testament, or seven times the *Iliad* and the *Odyssey* combined, and a hundred times more interesting. More interesting both because its attitude to war is more conflicted and complex than that of the Greek epics and because its attitude to divinity is more conflicted and complex than that of the Jewish and Christian scriptures. It resembles the Homeric epics in many ways (such as the theme of the great war, the style of its poetry, and its heroic characters, several of them fathered by gods), but unlike the Homeric gods, many of the *Mahabharata* gods were then, and still are, worshiped and revered in holy texts, including parts of the *Mahabharata* itself. It has remained central to Hindu culture since it was first composed. It is thus "great" (*Maha*), as its name claims, not only in size but in scope. Hindus from the time of the composition of the *Mahabharata* to the present moment know the characters in the texts just as Christians and Jews and Muslims, even if they are not religious, know Adam

---

1. Some portions of this essay are reworked from my book *The Hindus: An Alternative History* (New York: Penguin Books, 2009), pp. 252–76.

and Eve. To this day, India is called the land of Bharata, and the *Mahabharata* functions much like a national epic.

The story may have been told in some form as early as 900 BCE; its resemblance to Persian, Scandinavian, Greek, and other Indo-European epic traditions suggests that the core of the tale may reach back to the time when these cultures had not yet dispersed, well before 2000 BCE. But the *Mahabharata* did not reach its present form until the period from about 300 BCE to 300 CE—or half a millennium; it takes a long time to compose three million words.

The *Mahabharata* marks the transition from the corpus of Sanskrit texts known as *shruti*, the unalterable Vedic canon of texts (dated to perhaps 1500 BCE) that the seers "heard" from divine sources, to those known as *smriti*, the human tradition, constantly revised, the "remembered texts" of human authorship, texts that could be altered. It calls itself "the fifth Veda" (though so do several other texts) and dresses its story in Vedic trappings (such as ostentatious Vedic sacrifices). It looks back to the Vedic age, and may well preserve many memories of that period, and that place, up in the Punjab. The Painted Gray Ware artifacts discovered at sites identified with locations in the *Mahabharata* may be evidence of the reality of the great *Mahabharata* war, which is usually supposed to have occurred around 950 BCE. But the text is very much the product of its times, the centuries before and after the turn of the first millennium.

The *Mahabharata* was retold very differently by all of its many authors in the long line of literary descent. It is so extremely fluid that there is no single *Mahabharata*; there are hundreds of *Mahabharata*s, hundreds of different manuscripts and innumerable oral versions (one reason why it is impossible to make an accurate calculation of the number of its verses). The *Mahabharata* is not *confined to* a text; the story is there to be picked up and found, salvaged as anonymous treasure from the ocean of story. It has been called "a work in progress,"[2] a literature that "does not belong in a book."[3]

2. Alf Hiltebeitel, *The Ritual of Battle* (Ithaca, N.Y.: Cornell University Press, 1976), pp. 14–15.
3. Milton Singer, *When a Great Tradition Modernizes* (Chicago: University of Chicago Press, 1972), pp. 75–76.

The *Mahabharata* (1.1.23)[4] describes itself as unlimited in both time and space—eternal and infinite: "Poets have told it before, and are telling it now, and will tell it again. What is here is also found elsewhere, but what is *not* here is found nowhere else." And in case you missed that, it is repeated elsewhere and then said yet again in slightly different words toward the end of the epic: "Whatever is here about dharma, profit, pleasure, and release [from the cycle of death and rebirth] is also found elsewhere, but what is *not* here is found nowhere else . . ." (18.5.38).

The *Mahabharata* grew and changed in numerous parallel traditions spread over the entire subcontinent of India, constantly retold and rewritten, both in Sanskrit and in vernacular dialects. It grows out of the oral tradition and then grows back into the oral tradition; it flickers back and forth between Sanskrit manuscripts and village storytellers, each adding new gemstones to the old mosaic, constantly reinterpreting it. The loose construction of the text gives it a quasi-novelistic quality, open to new forms as well as new ideas, inviting different ideas to contest one another, to come to blows, in the pages of the text. It seems to me highly unlikely that any single author could have lived long enough to put it all together, but that does not mean that it is a miscellaneous mess with no unified point of view, let alone "the most monstrous chaos," "the huge and motley pile," or "gargantuan hodge-podge" and "literary pile-up" that some scholars have accused it of being. European approaches to the *Mahabharata* often assumed that collators did not know what they were doing and, blindly cutting and pasting, accidentally created a monstrosity.

But the *Mahabharata* is not the head of a brahmin philosophy accidentally stuck onto a body of non-brahmin folklore, like the heads and bodies of people in several Indian myths, or the mythical beast invoked by Woody Allen, which has the body of a lion and the head of a lion, but not the same lion.[5] True, it was somewhat like

4. All of the translations are my own, from the Critical Edition of the *Mahabharata* (Poona, Maharashtra, India: Bhandarkar Oriental Research Institute, 1933–69).

5. Woody Allen, "Fabulous Tales and Mythical Beasts," in *Without Feathers* (New York: Random House, 1976).

an ancient Wikipedia, to which anyone who knew Sanskrit, or who knew someone who knew Sanskrit, could add a bit here, a bit there. But the powerful intertextuality of Hinduism ensured that anyone who added anything to the *Mahabharata* was well aware of the whole textual tradition behind it and fitted his or her own insight, or story, thoughtfully into the ongoing conversation. However diverse its sources, for several thousand years the tradition has regarded it as a conversation among people who know one another's views and argue with silent partners. It is a contested text, a brilliantly orchestrated hybrid narrative with no single party line on any subject. It was contested not only within the Hindu tradition, where concepts of dharma were much debated, but also by the rising rival traditions of Buddhism and Jainism. These challenges to the brahmin narrators are reflected in the text at such places as Bhishma's teachings in Books 12 and 13. But the text has an integrity that the culture supports (in part by attributing it to a single author) and that it is our duty to acknowledge. The contradictions at its heart are not the mistakes of a sloppy editor but enduring cultural dilemmas that no author could ever have resolved.

The great scholar and poet A. K. Ramanujan used to say that no Indian ever hears the *Mahabharata* for the first time. For centuries Indians heard it in the form of public recitations, or performances of dramatized episodes, or in the explanations of scenes depicted in stone or paint on the sides of temples. More recently, they read it in India's version of Classic Comics (the *Amar Chitra Katha* series) or saw it in the hugely successful televised version, based largely on the comic book; the streets of India were empty (or as empty as any street ever is in India) during the broadcast hours on Sunday mornings, from 1988 to 1990. Or they saw various Bollywood versions, or the six-hour film version (1989) of Peter Brook's nine-hour theatrical adaptation (1985).

In 1989, Shashi Tharoor (Indian Minister of State for External Affairs) retold the *Mahabharata* as *The Great Indian Novel*, in which the heroes are recast as thinly veiled forms of Mahatma Gandhi, Jawaharlal Nehru, Indira Gandhi, and others. (The hero Karna, who, in the Sanskrit version, slices off the armor that grows on his body and fights against his brothers, appears as Mohammed Ali

Karna, who, when he goes over from the Hindu to the Muslim side, seizes a knife and circumcises himself.) Chitra Banerjee Divakaruni, in her 2009 novel *The Palace of Illusions*, retells the *Mahabharata* from the standpoint of the heroine, Draupadi, who is, in this telling, in love with Karna and close to the transsexual heroine Shikhandin/Shikhandini, who is, in the Sanskrit text, too, Draupadi's brother/sister but never meets her. And now there is Chindu Sreedharan's "Epicretold," posted on Twitter, so that we can read the *Mahabharata* one 140-character tweet at a time (www.time.com/time/world/article/0,8599,1917882,00.html). Reintepretations of this sort have been going on from the moment the *Mahabharata* began to be composed. Whenever the *Mahabharata* is told or retold, the ethical and religious questions it raises are given new, contemporary meanings.

And this new verse retelling by Carole Satyamurti takes its place in this honorable lineage. It is not, technically, a new translation, since Satyamurti worked not from the Sanskrit original but from other translations, particularly the Ganguli and van Buitenen/Fitzgerald translations. Nor is it a freely rendered retelling, since she sticks very close to the content, if not the wording, of the translations she used. Her abridgment, too, is different from that of the many other available versions, including that of John Smith; Satyamurti has made her own choices, and has included several episodes that Ganguli, van Buitenen/Fitzgerald, and Smith leave out, popular stories such as the episode in which Vyasa dictates the text to Ganesha. And most significantly, she has told the story not in prose but in blank verse.

THE STORY OF THE HEROES, AND THE STORIES OF WOMEN

The bare bones of the central story (and there are hundreds of peripheral stories, too) could be summarized like this, for our purposes:

The five sons of King Pandu, called the Pandavas, were fathered by gods: Yudhishthira by Dharma (the moral law incarnate), Bhima by the Wind, Arjuna by Indra (king of the gods), and the twins by the Ashvins. All five of them married Draupadi. When Yudhishthira lost the kingdom to his cousins in a game of dice, the Pandavas and Draupadi went into exile for twelve years, at the end of which—with the help of their cousin, the incarnate god Krishna, who befriended the Pandavas and whose counsel to Arjuna on the battlefield is the *Bhagavad Gita*—they regained their kingdom through a cataclysmic battle in which almost everyone on both sides was killed. They all went to heaven and died happily ever after.

But the story of the Pyrrhic victory of the Pandava princes constitutes just a fifth of the epic, its skeleton. Many episodes, including some about women, are hooked on fairly securely to the fabric of the plot: a question about the ancestors of the Pandavas inspires the narrator to tell the story of the birth of their ancestor Bharata, from Shakuntala, the innocent maiden whom King Dushyanta seduced and abandoned (a story that captivated Goethe); Yudhishthira is consoled, after his own gambling disaster, by the tale of Nala, whose compulsive gambling lost him his kingdom and his wife Damayanti, until she managed to reunite them. Other stories are told as moral lessons to the human heroes and heroines, such as the tale of King Shibi, who chopped off his own flesh to save a dove fleeing from a hawk (both birds turned out to be gods disguised to test him); and Savitri, whose steadfastness persuaded the god of death to spare her doomed husband. Philosophical and legal questions also arise out of the aporias of the plot and are answered in discourses that sometimes go on for hundreds of verses. Hindu tradition attributes the work to a single author, named Vyasa, but Vyasa is also the author (that is, the father) of the two fathers of the warring heroes, Pandu and his brother Dhritarashtra. Thus Vyasa, the author, is himself a character in his own story.

The text depicts women with powers and privileges they would seldom have again in Hindu literature. Women with multiple sexual partners appear with surprising frequency in the *Mahabharata;* the text offers us, in four consecutive generations, positive images of women who had several sexual partners (sometimes premarital) seriatim. Satyavati has two sexual partners (her legitimate husband Shantanu and the sage who fathers Vyasa on the island). Ambika and Ambalika have two legitimate partners (the king who dies and Vyasa, through the Levirate). Kunti has one husband (Pandu, legitimate but unconsummated) and four sexual partners (gods, quasi-legitimate). Madri has three partners (Pandu, legitimate and fatally consummated, and two quasi-legitimate gods). The prize goes to Draupadi, who has five legitimate husbands, simultaneously—the five Pandavas. Her pentad is truly extraordinary, for though men could have several spouses throughout most of Hindu history (and a number of men in the *Mahabharata* do have several wives, most famously the Pandava hero Arjuna and the incarnate god Krishna), women most decidedly could not. It is always possible that the *Mahabharata* was recording a time when polyandry (multiple husbands) was the custom (as it is nowadays in parts of the Himalaya), but there is no evidence to support this contention. Since there is no other evidence that women at this time actually had multiple sexual partners, these stories can only be suggestive, evidence either of women's greater sexual freedom or, perhaps, of men's fears of what might happen were women to have that freedom, of the male redactors' nightmare vision of where all that autonomy might lead. Draupadi's hypersexuality may simply have validated an ideal that was understood to be out of reach for ordinary women—imagined precisely in order to be disqualified as a viable option. King Pandu tells his wife Kunti a story explicitly remarking upon an archaic promiscuity that is no longer in effect, pointedly reminding her, and any women who may have heard (or read) the text, that female promiscuity was an ancient option no longer available to them, even though he tells her this story in order to persuade her to have sex with someone other than himself—admittedly, a god.

The lineage of the heroines is therefore a remarkably positive fantasy of female equality. True, Draupadi doesn't choose to have five husbands, and though she has a sharp tongue at times, she generally exerts her power through subtlety and manipulation—as subservient women always have—not exactly a model of equality. But many of the *Mahabharata* women are a feminist's dream (or a sexist's nightmare): smart, aggressive, steadfast, eloquent, tough as nails, and resilient. Other women in the *Mahabharata* show remarkable courage and intelligence, too, but their courage is often used in subservience to their husbands. The wives of the two patriarchs,

Pandu and the blind Dhritarashtra, are paradigms of such courage. Gandhari, the wife of Dhritarashtra, keeps her eyes entirely blindfolded from the day of her marriage to him, in order to share his blindness. Pandu's two widows vie for the privilege of dying on his pyre.

THE *MAHABHARATA* AS A RELIGIOUS TEXT

But the *Mahabharata* is not just a story. It is a religious text, foundational for Hinduism. At moments scattered through the text, the Pandavas' cousin, the incarnate god Krishna, intervenes, most famously in his counsel to the hero Arjuna on the battlefield of Kurukshetra, which many Hindus revere as the *Bhagavad Gita,* "the song of god." Krishna straddles the line between a human prince and an incarnation of Vishnu. Other gods, however, appear in unambiguous full divinity throughout the epic. Throughout the *Mahabharata,* we encounter people who say they worship a particular god, the start of sects and therefore of sectarianism. It includes a "Hymn of the Thousand Names of Shiva" and tells a story about the circumstances under which Shiva came to be worshiped. Shiva appears to Arjuna in the form of a naked tribal hunter and occasionally goes in human disguise among mortals. Pilgrimage is described at length, particularly but not only in the "Tour of the Sacred Fords" (3.80–140).

Many chapters are devoted to disquisitions on the nature of spiritual peace (*shanti*) and liberation (*moksha*) from the wheel of transmigration (*samsara*). And the text not only describes several great sacrifices—a triumphal horse sacrifice after the great war near the end of the story, and a grotesque sacrifice of snakes at the beginning—but often describes the battle itself as a great sacrifice, in which the warriors offer themselves as victims. The great battle on the field called Kurukshetra—a name as familiar to Hindus as Armageddon to the Abrahamic religions—is also an eschatological conflict at the moment when the universe is about to self-destruct. For the end of that battle marks the beginning of the Kali age, the fourth of the four degenerating ages, or yugas. Even within this moment of degeneration, Krishna is said to descend to earth (as an avatar of the god Vishnu) to restore dharma (the moral law) when it has declined in the course of the cycle.

Many passages end with the "fruits of hearing" them ("Anyone who hears this story [about snakes] will never die of snakebite," etc.). And the book as a whole declares, at the very end:

> This auspicious story, called a history, is the supreme purifier. Whatever wise man recites this constantly at every lunar fort-night, his evils are shaken off, he wins heaven, and he goes to the state of brahman. Whatever sin one commits by day in the senses or even in the mind-and-heart, he is set free from that at that evening's twilight by narrating the *Mahabharata*. This history, called "Victory," should be heard by anyone who wants power, and also by a king, and by the king's sons, and by a pregnant woman. A person who desires heaven would get heaven, and one who desires victory would get victory. A preg-nant woman gets a son or a well-married daughter. Whoever recites this worthy history that has great meaning and value and is Veda-made, that man becomes free from evil, achieves fame here on earth and will achieve supreme success; I have no doubt about this. If a man of faith studies even a line by means of this worthy study of the Bharatas, he is purified of all his evils, with-out exception. Whoever recites the story of the *Mahabharata*, with his mind well collected, achieves supreme success; I have no doubt about this. Whoever thoroughly understands, as it is being spoken, the *Bharata* that slipped out of the cup of the lips of Vyasa and is immeasurable, worthy, purifying, auspicious, and removes all evils, what use has he for ablutions with the waters of lake Pushkara? (18.5.31–46, 52–54)

Above all, the *Mahabharata* is an exposition of dharma, the moral and religious law of Hinduism, including the proper conduct of a king, of a warrior, of an individual living in times of calamity, and of a person seeking to attain freedom from rebirth. The text debates the clash between, on the one hand, the growing doctrine of non-violence toward all creatures (*ahimsa*) and, on the other, both the justice of war and the still dominant tradition of animal sacrifice. It both challenges and justifies the entire class structure.

Many other deep philosophical questions, too, grow out of the human dilemmas that tangle the protagonists in their coils. Dharma continued to denote the sort of human activity that leads to human prosperity, glory, and victory ("Where there is dharma, there is victory," the text famously proclaims), but now it also had much more to do. For now the text was often forced to acknowledge the impossibility of maintaining any sort of dharma at all in a world where every rule seemed to be canceled out by another. The gods, too, were sometimes tripped up by the subtlety of dharma. Time and again when a character finds that every available moral choice is the wrong choice, or when one of the good guys does something obviously very wrong, he will mutter, or be told, "Dharma is subtle" (*sukshma*), thin and slippery as a fine silk sari, elusive as a will-o'-the-wisp, internally inconsistent as well as disguised, hidden, masked. People try again and again to do the right thing, and fail and fail, until they no longer know what the right thing is.

The *Mahabharata* deconstructs dharma, exposing the inevitable chaos of the moral life. The narrators kept painting themselves into a corner with the brush of dharma. Their backs to the wall, they could only reach for another story. And this is the epic tale that Carole Satyamurti now retells in a new form.

Preface

L OVE, LOSS, RAGE, envy, loyalty, heroism, spiritual aspiration, ethical and political dilemmas—the *Mahabharata* brings to life all these timeless human experiences, and more. I had been familiar with the story in outline for many years, but there came a point, in about 2007, when dissatisfaction with the various translations, abridgments, and versions of it in English prose crystallized into a wish to try to retell it myself—in the form of a poem, as the original is a poem. The sheer scale and grandeur of the epic were both daunting and exhilarating—the literary equivalent of the soaring Himalayan peaks which are a reference point for so many of its characters.

In some ways, it is a strange and distant world the *Mahabharata* conjures up, a strangeness that can show us something about the variety and breadth of human experience, about thought and behavior that otherwise we might never have imagined. And yet I am repeatedly struck by parallels, both at individual and at societal levels, between that world and our own. Perhaps most striking is the epic's moral complexity. Although it is clear who is in the right in the violent struggle for possession of the kingdom, each one of the "heroes," and the divine Krishna himself, engages at some point in morally dubious action, while the main "villain," Duryodhana, is true to his principles, and is blessed by heaven on his death.

The question of what constitutes right action (dharma) for a particular actor in particular circumstances is the central preoccupation of the poem—and of human beings in every time and place—as is the question of how to reconcile right action with self-interest. Throughout, the *Mahabharata* wrestles with these problems. Yudhishthira after his victory in the internecine war at the center of the poem is, as it were, the battleground on which incompatible desires, and seemingly irreconcilable conflicts between desire and dharma, are played out.

The concept of dharma focuses mainly on action. This is Krishna's concern in the *Bhagavad Gita* (Chapter 32), but he is also concerned, in that passage, with the state of mind that gives rise to action. If action is undertaken in a spirit of right understanding, and of devotion to the deity, then the consequences of it are not the responsibility of the actor. There are parallels here with the position of the modern soldier, whose duty (dharma) is to obey, whose training prepares him or her to hand over responsibility to the commanding officer, and whose devotion, if not to God, is to country and comrades.

The *Mahabharata* says of itself that it is addressed to women as well as to men, and one of its unusual features, in the context of other ancient epics, is the importance given to women characters. For instance, what Homeric (mortal) women have to say has very little impact on events. In the *Odyssey*, Penelope is told by her son, Telemachos, that power, including the power of speech, is the business of men, and she is sent off to her room! In the *Mahabharata*, by contrast, women—notably the Pandavas' wife, Draupadi—often refuse to be silenced. A number of female characters have their own, distinctive points of view and are seen to engage in debate and comment on an equal footing with men, especially, but not only, in matters of war and peace.

The poem is also explicitly addressed to people of all social positions, and although the importance is recurrently asserted of maintaining the distinct identities of the top two ranks in the social order, there are also places where, implicitly or explicitly, we are reminded of the worth, and the suffering, of people at the bottom of the social hierarchy—suffering whose relevance transcends time and place. The story of lowborn Ekalavya (Chapter 4), whose luminous gifts as an archer are destroyed by Arjuna's jealousy, has been adopted by the Dalit movement in India as an iconic instance of the injustice to which their community continues to be subjected. The burning of the Khandava Forest (Chapter 13), in which snakes and other forest dwellers are slaughtered in huge numbers, could be taken as a symbolic representation of the way that, always and everywhere, the powerful can oppress the weak.

Many retellings give rather scant attention to Bhishma's teachings to Yudhishthira, centered on the subject of how to be a good ruler (Books 12 and 13). These constitute over twenty-five percent of the whole, and it is true that there are elements in these books that can be omitted as being tangential to the central narrative, and of little interest to the modern reader. But timeless political concerns, and notably questions of how rulers can retain power, feature strongly in the *Mahabharata*. And like Machiavelli's *The Prince*, to which it bears a striking resemblance, what Bhishma has to say about how the ruler should operate, and what mistakes he should avoid, has direct relevance today and should not be treated in a perfunctory way. Nor, in my view, should Bhishma's teaching on spiritual matters. Although some of the beliefs about life and the afterlife, for example, may seem alien to many readers, when considered with an open mind they may be seen to have parallels with ideas that are commonplace in many religious traditions.

The *Mahabharata* also gives us plenty to think about from an ontological point of view. Its sense of the enormous scale of the cosmos, for instance, is very different from the depiction featured in the Greek and Roman myths, and prefigures modern understandings. And although one should be wary of drawing facile parallels between ancient Indian cosmology and modern physics, the idea that "every coherent thing tends inherently toward dissolution" (Chapter 53) is reminiscent of the concept of entropy.

Central to the epic is the prolonged account of the great war at Kurukshetra (Books 6–10), where we are invited to imagine the theater of war as a series of set-piece duels and battles, as though we were looking at an unfurling tapestry. The descriptions, and the vast numbers of combatants cited, are clearly not meant to be realistic, but rather to conjure up huge scale and grotesque detail in order to imprint the excesses of war on the imagination. At a time when arrows were the most lethal weapons known, the poets imagine celestial weapons which anticipate the mass-murderous capability of modern warfare—weapons which create pure victims, rather than losers in even-handed combat. As the First World War is commemorated a century on, we know how difficult it is to absorb, from facts alone, what war means for those affected by it. We need images; and we need language.

The *Mahabharata* gives us these, by piling detail upon detail, story upon story, and often by mobilizing formulaic turns of phrase—stock epithets, vocatives, and descriptions—key features of the oral epic poetry which probably was part of the Sanskrit *Mahabharata* tradition. One of the aspects of the way the poem is narrated is repetition or recurrence, as if to remind us, across its enormous canvas, of what it is important for us to remember.

Indeed, *within* the epic, the characters do not always remember what they have been told, or what they really know—or else they are unable to take it in and act on it. Dhritarashtra is repeatedly warned that his son will bring catastrophe on the Bharata clan; he believes it and yet he cannot bring himself to take the necessary preventive measures. Yudhishthira knows that gambling can be disastrous, but continues to engage in it anyway. Arjuna appears to have been persuaded by Krishna's great sermon and revelation on the battlefield (the *Bhagavad Gita*) that he has no alternative but to fight and kill his cousins and his teachers (Chapter 32). Yet he repeatedly makes only halfhearted efforts. And in fact, later on (Chapter 56) he declares that he does not remember what Krishna told him. It is as if Krishna's words graze past him and out into the wider world, where generations of Hindus and others have taken them to heart.

Fate, or the gods' design, is often invoked to explain such paradoxical behavior, and the tension between fate and human effort, free will and determinism, is a recurrent theme—and a continuing preoccupation for us today. How freely do we really choose between one course of action and another?

Much more could be said, but I want to mention a final aspect of the *Mahabharata*—its psychological plausibility. As just one example, I am interested in the fact that, for different reasons, neither Duryodhana's parents nor Karna's birth mother *see* them as children. Duryodhana's mother, by choosing to be blindfolded so as to have no advantage over her blind husband, is depriving her son of the affirmation and visible love that a baby would normally find in his/her mother's eyes. She is putting her husband first. Kunti, by abandoning Karna at birth to the vagaries of the river, is choosing to value respectability over the welfare of her baby. Although Duryodhana and Karna are loved and cherished during their upbringing, as adults they are both characterized by extreme enviousness. It may seem fanciful, but it is as if nothing but the actual experience of the loving maternal gaze can convince them that they possess enough of value, and that the wealth or skill of others is not a diminishment of their own. No wonder they become soul mates!

Despite the availability of various versions of the *Mahabharata,* on page, screen, and in live performance, I am assuming that it will be less familiar to the average American or European reader than the *Iliad* or the *Aeneid,* for instance. I have seen my task as one of trying to open the reader's eyes—as my own were opened—to the richness of a literary masterpiece they may hardly have heard of until now.

I do not read Sanskrit, and have worked from scholarly translations (not other people's retellings) in order to come as close as possible to the original. Given its size (roughly 5,000 closely packed prose pages in the only complete English translation to date, by K. M. Ganguli,[1] published in the late nineteenth century), any version of the *Mahabharata* intended for the general reader is necessarily an abridgment. When I got to grips with Ganguli's translation, as well as with other (partial) translations,[2] I wanted to try to convey the epic's extraordinary qualities in as vivid and accessible a way as possible. My guiding principle throughout has been faithfulness to the original, as I have become yet another meta-narrator, though I have included some widely loved stories that do not figure in the Poona Critical Edition, or in Ganguli's translation. In my version, as in the original, the register is that of a storyteller addressing an audience.

In constructing my abridgment, I was guided by my sense of the outline and architecture of the epic, informed by my reading. My method was to read Ganguli and other translations, section by section, and then to put them aside, and give myself time to digest what I had read, intellectually, emotionally, and aesthetically. Out of this would come a decision about what to include and what could

1. There is a complete translation by M. N. Dutt, also published in the late nineteenth century, but it is said to be heavily dependent on Ganguli.
2. See Suggestions for Further Reading at the back of the book.

be excluded; what must be foregrounded and what could be mentioned briefly. I then wrote my own version, checking what I had written against the original (translated) source, and doing this repeatedly throughout the entire writing process.

The Sanskrit *Mahabharata* is mainly composed in *shlokas*, a verse form with specific metrical requirements and stanzaic arrangement, used in ancient India for a wide variety of texts, some imaginative, some religious, some practical. It is the wide applicability of the form that has led some people to the view that it was, for ancient India, what prose is for us, arguing that prose is the best medium in which to render the epic for a modern readership. But the *Mahabharata* is composed in patterned language, designed to be recited, or chanted, and I wanted something of that quality to come across in my version. For this reason, I have chosen a flexible form of blank verse, which arguably occupies a place in the English literary tradition analogous to that of the *shloka* in ancient Sanskrit. It is the meter of Shakespeare's plays, of Milton's *Paradise Lost*, and Wordsworth's *Prelude*. In saying this, I am not setting myself up as being on a par with the greats of English literature, but rather saying that the meter of blank verse is laid down in the mind's ear of anyone even slightly familiar with English poetry. It is a form particularly well suited to narrative verse, and is still widely used. It is also the basic meter of natural English speech. Listen to anyone speaking English, and you will soon pick up the rhythm of iambic pentameter.

Blank verse is an unrhymed form, with ten or eleven syllables, and five beats, or stresses, to the line. Of course no one would adhere rigidly to this description; that would make for a very mechanical and numbing effect. Rather, the rhythm of a five-beat line is laid down in the mind's ear as a template against which the reader or listener receives the line—which may stretch or contract the number of syllables, and which will not be composed entirely of iambs. For that reason, in this retelling, I would like the reader to imagine the names of at least the main people and places in their approximately correct pronunciation (AR-ju-na, for instance, not Ar-JOO-na). Many of the names may be unfamiliar, and the Glossary at the back of the book provides a guide to pronunciation, showing in each case where the stress or stresses should fall.

In choosing blank verse, I have allowed the number of syllables per line to vary slightly—that is, with very few exceptions, each line has nine, ten, or eleven syllables. Because I have imagined the poem being spoken, I have exercised some license as to what constitutes a syllable. In English speech, there are "half-syllables," as when syncope is used. So "chariot," for instance, does not have the same unequivocal three syllables as "destiny." Although the basic meter is pentameter, this too has been used with a certain latitude. Rather than every line having an audible five beats, I have heard the meter as allotting the same amount of *time* to each line, with syllables and stresses having the freedom to dispose themselves variously within that amount of time. Many lines do, in fact, have five beats, so I trust the reader to have that rhythm in mind as a benchmark, against which he/she receives those lines which seem not to conform metrically, and assigns them their due portion of time.[3] In the end, though, the reader should not be put off by thinking about these technical considerations, but should read as comes naturally to them.

Vinay Dharwadker points out in his Afterword that the *shloka* verse form is meant to be chanted or sung. English blank verse does not inhabit the same tradition, but it is meant to be *heard,* as well as read, and my version is composed for the ear, for reading aloud, as well as for the intelligence and the imagination. I have used internal rhyme, alliteration, and assonance—not in a systematic way, but as aural threads that run through the poem.

The diction of the Sanskrit epic is relatively plain. There are many similes, but relatively little use of extended metaphors or heightened language, so in rendering the epic in language that does not draw attention to itself—that is, does not divert attention from the narrative drive—I am not betraying the original. Furthermore, as Coleridge argued,[4] many of the linguistic resources one

3. The difficulty readers may have in accommodating different metrical principles, and the need for them to be open to the musicality of a line, is discussed by Ted Hughes in his essay "Myths, Metres, Rhythms," in *Winter Pollen* (London: Faber and Faber, 1994).

4. A poem of any length neither can be, nor ought to be, all poetry" (Samuel Coleridge, *Biographia Literaria,* Chapter 14).

looks for in a lyric poem are not appropriate in a long narrative one. The intensity of expression that is possible over a fairly short span could probably neither be sustained nor tolerated over 800 pages.

I have thought hard about the issue of gendered language. It has been common in English until relatively recently to refer to a non-specific human being as "he." This is no longer acceptable—and the *Mahabharata* is meant for everyone. I have therefore tried to use gender-neutral language where appropriate, and where it can be done without clumsiness.

As is explained more fully in the Afterword, the *Mahabharata* is structured as a series of narrative frames, one inside another, "authored" by a series of different speakers. Apart from the assumed anonymous meta-narrator, the entire epic consists of one character speaking to one or more others. There is a danger, in trying to reproduce this, of confusing the reader, and I have tried to deal with it partly by explicitly flagging who is speaking, and partly through the device of using prose when characters within the story are themselves telling a story.

At the center of any of the ancient epics is the quest for honor, glory, and fame. The afterlife of heroes depends on their being remembered. For the Pandavas, for tragic Karna, for Bhishma, for the single-minded Duryodhana, the great *Mahabharata* is that commemoration.

CAROLE SATYAMURTI

MAHABHARATA

Prologue

First, I acknowledge the eternal being,
Brahman, essence of everything that is,
source of all, the inconceivable;
bliss-bestowing Vishnu, Hari Krishna.

And I bless the name of Sarasvati,
goddess of deep learning and of art,
she who can touch a poet's tongue with silver.
To her I dedicate my epic poem.

This is the tale of a tragic dynasty;
a narrative of hatred, honor, courage,
of virtue, love, ideals and wickedness,
and of a war so terrible, it marked
the threshold between one age and the next.

We approach the story through Ugrashravas,
singer of ancient songs, a traveling poet
who wandered the world free of encumbrances,
worshiping at sacred bathing places;
welcome at every court and hermitage
where people loved spellbinding tales.

                                He told it
to a community of brahmin seers

at their ashram in the Naimisha Forest.
Engaged in a twelve-year-long sacrifice,
they were, no doubt, avid for entertainment
of an improving kind. They gathered round him
clamorous with questions. "Distinguished bard,"
they said, "tell us where you have traveled from.
What have you seen? What news have you brought us?"

"Not long ago, I spent time at the court
of the great King Janamejaya
of the house of Bharata. You may know
that the king is the direct descendant
of the world-renowned Pandavas—great-grandson
of Arjuna, the legendary archer.

"I happened to be present at the time
when the king was holding a snake sacrifice
to avenge King Parikshit, his father,
who was poisoned by the snake, Takshaka,
and died a premature and painful death.
While there, I listened, rapt, day after day
to an unforgettable narration
of the monumental Mahabharata—
the history of the royal lineage,
storehouse of wisdom, and much more besides.

"Then I made a solemn pilgrimage
to sacred Kurukshetra, site of war.
And now, full of respect, wishing to see you,
I have come to visit. So, holy sages,
say what stories you would like to hear."

"Tell us in detail about the sacrifice."

"First, a huge fire was built. The flames leapt high,
mantras were recited by the brahmins
as ritual oblations, no cost spared,

were poured into the blaze by black-robed priests.
Then snakes appeared, drawn irresistibly
toward their death. Serpents by the million,
of every color, some as thin as threads,
others thick as trunks of elephants;
snakes from the dark recesses of the earth,
snakes from the forest, snakes from ponds and rivers
fell hissing, terrified, into the furnace.
Wildly they writhed, fruitlessly they screeched
as the flames devoured them. The race of snakes
would have been entirely extinguished
but for the fulfillment of a prophecy:
a brahmin will disrupt the sacrifice.

"Astika, devout son of a snake woman,
implored by his mother to save her kin,
came to the court of Janamejaya.
He was a brahmin child of great sweetness
and he praised the king so eloquently
that Janamejaya offered him a boon.
'Then stop the sacrifice,' said Astika.
The king tried to persuade the boy to choose
another favor, since the snake Takshaka,
Parikshit's killer, had not yet been thrown
into the boiling flames. But Astika
declined. So it was that Takshaka
survived, to the great joy of his relatives.

"Guests had come from the remotest corners
of the land, to witness the event.
Among them was the ancient seer Vyasa—
noblest of men, greatest of all scholars,
widely revered poet and ascetic—
together with his most advanced disciples.
King Janamejaya received Vyasa
with lavish honors, and the seer was pleased.
'Sir,' said the king, 'you witnessed at first hand

all that happened to my ancestors,
all their actions, all their vicissitudes.
Please tell me everything, as it occurred.'

"Vyasa smiled. 'That is a large request.
I have composed the story of your lineage
in a poem so long, so all-embracing,
that it will take a whole lunar cycle,
and more, to recite in its entirety.
The poem was born, grew, and took its shape
in the presence of my five disciples
—my son Shuka, Vaishampayana,
Paila, Jaimini and Sumantu—
and, while they attended to my needs,
they took it in, and learned my words by heart.'

"Vyasa turned to his most able student,
seated beside him. 'Vaishampayana,
please tell the king the story of his forebears,
the epic poem of the Bharatas,
as you have heard it from me, word for word.'

"'Gladly!' said the disciple. 'I am honored
to be the channel of Vyasa's thought,
for anyone who speaks these marvelous lines,
and anyone who hears them, is purified,
cleansed even of their worst iniquity.
What the poem contains concerning dharma,
pursuit of wealth, pleasure, and final freedom,
may be found elsewhere. But you can be sure
that what it does not contain is found nowhere.

"'Although the poem tells of huge events,
battles, armies of a million men,
and though it speaks of gods and demons acting
directly in the human world, the gist—
the conflicts and dilemmas, the regrets,
the way that good and bad, wisdom, delusion,

strive for dominance in each of us—
is still played out in every human heart
and always will be. As you will soon see,
the poem contains much more than epic action.'

"First, Vaishampayana outlined the story
of how the Bharata lineage began.
'Many generations back, Duhshanta,
a powerful king, was hunting in the forest
when he came upon the lovely hermitage
of the seer Kanva. The seer was not at home
but his adopted daughter, Shakuntala,
made the king welcome. Duhshanta was smitten
with desire for the beautiful young woman
and urged her to marry him. She consented
on one condition: that her future son
would become the heir to Duhshanta's kingdom.
They lay together. Then the king departed,
promising to send for her. Months passed
and Shakuntala gave birth to a boy.
No word came from Duhshanta. After six years,
Kanva sent Shakuntala and her son
to Hastinapura, where the king held court.
But Duhshanta claimed to have no memory
of Shakuntala, or of his promise,
and with harsh insults told her to be gone.
Shakuntala reproached him, reminding him
of their meeting. But the king was adamant.
As Shakuntala left, a heavenly voice
told Duhshanta to fulfill his promise.
The king then joyfully called Shakuntala
and told her he had only rejected her
to deflect the suspicions of his people.
The boy was acknowledged as his son and heir
and named Bharata. When he grew to manhood
he became a great and benevolent king
and your lineage descends from him.'

"Vaishampayana then traced the subsequent
history of the distinguished clan, naming
the heroes and their qualities, describing
how bitter enmity arose among them
resulting in a cataclysmic war.
For on the part-forested and fertile plain
nourished by the Ganga and the Yamuna
scalding events occurred which, ever since,
have been a lesson and a light to those
able to see something of themselves
within the lives the story animates.

"'I wish to hear the tale in much more detail,'
said Janamejaya. 'But first, tell me
how those heroic men, those ancestors
who spilled so much blood on the battlefield,
came to be born. What divine destiny
were they fulfilling when they walked the earth?'

"'Long, long ago,' said Vaishampayana,
'no kshatriyas roamed the land causing havoc;
the brahmin warrior Rama Jamadagnya
had wiped them out many times over.
Kshatriya women, lacking warrior husbands,
lay with brahmins, and new kshatriya children
were born, to repopulate their kind.
Then the world passed through a golden time.
Brahmins headed the whole social order.
There was respect for dharma; people behaved
harmoniously, without lust or anger.
They lived long lives in peace and kindness, free
of all disease. Plants and animals
also flourished, each in the proper season.

"'But this would change. Unseen, in the cosmos,
gods and demons fought for supremacy.
Demons, defeated, forced out by the gods,

began to take birth in the human world
as kshatriyas. They thought they should be gods.
They despised lawful ways and moderation;
the beautiful resources of the world
were theirs to plunder, squander, smash, defile.
Ravaging the earth, they multiplied,
sowing hate, mistrust and fear, oppressing
and slaughtering gentler creatures, so that life
became a misery.

        "'Earth went to Brahma,
lord of creation, and bowed down before him.
O Lord Brahma, I am overwhelmed
by so much wickedness. I shall be destroyed!
She described to him what was taking place.
Of course, omniscient Brahma knew already
every corner of the created world.
He assured her he would bring together
the mighty powers of heaven to support her.

"'Then Brahma summoned all the gods, and spoke:
Earth is in danger. You must each be born
as humans, using a portion of yourselves
to endow a human being with god-like power.
Employ your attributes as you see fit.
Pitch your strength against the demonic forces
which threaten to engulf the entire earth.
The gods were eager to begin their mission
and they exhorted the supreme being,
Vishnu himself, to take on human form.

"'So it was that your splendid great-grandfather
and his brothers, the five sons of Pandu,
were partial incarnations of deities.
And Krishna Vasudeva, their supporter
in all things, was the knowing avatar
of the great lord Vishnu, the all-powerful.

Their cousins, sons of Pandu's sightless brother,
the hundred Kauravas, were of demon stock.'

"Vaishampayana gave the king details
of the cosmic origins of many more
heroes who figure in this history—
a roll call of courageous warriors
whose fame lives on in legend, drama, song.
'Their story, made immortal by Vyasa,
is the tale of the eternal struggle fought
between opposing forces, good and evil,
the powers of darkness and the power of light.'

"'Now tell me everything,' said Janamejaya,
'exactly as you heard it from Vyasa.'
So, day after day, at the king's behest,
and as Vyasa listened, silently,
Vaishampayana, chosen disciple,
recited Vyasa's poem. No one who heard it
could forget the sense of being carried
off to another time and place. And I,
Ugrashravas, was one of those fortunates."

※

Soon you will hear the tale Ugrashravas
told the forest brahmins. But first, learn
how the ancient seer Krishna Dvaipayana,
known as Vyasa, master of cosmic knowledge,
composed this poem, the longest in the world,
a poem-compendium. It first took shape
silently, in his mind, a panorama
spreading out before him. He himself
was both author and actor in his story—
as we are in our own lives and, besides,
all is permitted to the storyteller.

Wise Vyasa had already arranged
the Vedas, but conceived this masterpiece
not just for the highborn, but for all.
Those of humble birth, laborers, women
should hear his poem and be enriched by it.
As he had spoken it to his disciples,
and as he heard it told by Vaishampayana
to a hushed gathering, he clearly saw
how it could enlighten all who heard it.
The poem was a map of the labyrinth,
the moral maze, that is our life on earth.
It told of choices and of mortal error,
of how even the saintly go astray
while, even in the worst, glimmers of gold
reveal themselves to a compassionate eye.

All should have access to the edifice
that was his narrative. But he realized
that for his poem to last for ages hence,
it must be written down.

Picture him
standing, bearded, rake thin, his eyes closed,
his head and body smeared with ash and ochre,
rags for covering, a visionary,
the entire epic cradled in his head.

He approached Brahma, lord of creation,
his inspiration all along, who happened
to be paying him a visit. Vyasa spoke:
"Lord, I have composed a mighty poem.
My work will open eyes dulled by ignorance
as the sun scatters darkness, as the moon's
subtle beams illumine the lotus buds.
All the wisdom of the world is in it.
But who will write it down, so that people
in the far future may read and learn from it?"

Lord Brahma praised the seer. "You have done well.
Your poem will awaken all who hear it;
and it should be written. You have my blessing."
Then he cast his mind over a number
of candidates, all worthy scribes, and said,
"Ask Ganesha, the elephant-headed god,
master of all things intellectual,
god of beginnings. He it is who guards
thresholds, the boundaries of time and space,
who removes obstacles. Yes, ask Ganesha.
He is best fitted for this gargantuan task."

"I'll do it," said Ganesha, "but only if
you speak your poem at my writing speed.
I won't put up with hesitations, false starts
and other tedious practices, too common
in those who dictate."
                              "Agreed!" replied Vyasa,
"but you in turn must undertake to write
only those things you have fully understood."
So, by inserting knotty passages,
the seer would win himself some thinking time.

Hardly pausing for breath, Vyasa spoke;
Ganesha wrote with equal energy.
When his pen failed, he broke off his tusk tip
and scribbled on, and on.

                              In this way
was written the story of a noble line
divided against itself.

                    Now, listen . . .

I

THE BOOK OF
THE BEGINNING

1.

THE ANCESTORS

Long before the ill-fated Bharatas
fought the great war on the crack of ages;
years before that dreadful sacrifice
squandered the blood of warriors in their millions,
young and old, on the plain of Kurukshetra,
there lived the foundling daughter of a fisherman
(really the daughter of a royal seer)
whose name was Satyavati. It could be said
that the whole tragic tale began with her
and her ambitious foster father.

                              Each day
she rowed a boat across the Yamuna
ferrying travelers from bank to bank.
One morning, the great sage Parashara,
on a tour of sacred bathing places,

boarded her boat. As they glided gently,
her beautiful arms pulling easily,
bare feet braced against the sturdy timbers,
he desired her—though she smelled unpleasant
(not only did she live with fishermen
but she had been born from a fish's belly).

Parashara made his intention known.
The girl was horrified, "O blessed one,
those rishis standing on the banks can see us!"
The sage summoned a mist to envelop them.
"But I am a virgin—how could I return
home to my father's house if I lay with you?"
He reassured her: her virginity
would remain intact. "And furthermore,
lovely smiling girl, you may choose a boon."
"I wish my body had a heavenly fragrance,"
replied Satyavati. And it was so.

That same day, she gave birth to a son
on an island in the river. Instantly,
he became a grown man, dedicated
to an ascetic life. Before departing,
he told his mother she could summon him
in time of need, merely by thinking of him:
"Remember me when things are to be done."
This was the author of our epic poem,
Vyasa Dvaipayana, "the island-born."

༄

Hastinapura, on the river Ganga,
a well-ordered, large and prosperous city,
was the stronghold of the lineage
of Bharata. Its ruler at the time
was Shantanu, known for his hunting prowess.
One day, riding near the riverbank,
stalking buffalo and antelope,

he saw a woman. She was so beautiful
the king stood still, staring in amazement
at her flawless skin, her lovely face.
He did not know she was the river goddess,
Ganga, in human form. "Whoever you are,"
cried Shantanu, "female demon, goddess
or celestial nymph—consent to be my wife!"

Ganga had a vow to fulfill. The Vasus,
eight celestial beings who enjoyed
all the delights of heaven, had been cursed
to be born mortal. Distraught, they begged Ganga
to become human, so she could carry them
in her womb. "And who shall be your father?"
she asked. "It should be Shantanu," they said,
"and once we are born, throw us in the river
to drown. In that way, we shall be released
from the hardships of a mortal life."
Ganga had already marked out Shantanu
to be her husband. In a prior existence,
the two had known each other, although he
did not remember. "O Vasus," she replied,
"I will do as you ask on this condition:
allow one son to live, so Shantanu
may have an heir." "Agreed," said the Vasus,
"but that son will have no son of his own."

So, when Shantanu pressed her, Ganga said,
"I shall become your queen, Shantanu,
I shall love you dearly, cherish you,
do all I can to please you, but for your part,
you must never question what I do
or I shall leave you instantly." The king
agreed.

They enjoyed happy years together,
and Ganga gave birth to seven healthy sons.
But one by one, she drowned them in the river,

and each time, Shantanu held his tongue.
Finally, with the eighth, he could not bear it.
"I long for my own son—how can you do this,
wicked, unnatural woman!" Ganga laughed.
"I am Ganga, goddess of the river.
Those boys were gods. I was obliged to drown them
as I had promised, to give them release
from human suffering. My task is done.
But you shall have your son. He will return
when he is grown—Ganga's gift to you.
Now I must leave you." And with that, she plunged
into the sparkling waters, and was gone.

Though grief-stricken, Shantanu ruled in peace
for many years, and his kingdom flourished.
One afternoon, wandering by the river,
he noticed that the water level had fallen,
and saw a handsome boy, shooting arrows
with such speed and skill they formed a dam
across the river. As the king stared, the boy
vanished. Then Ganga rose up from the water
leading the boy archer by the hand.
"This is your son," she said. "He is well versed
in the Vedas, trained in the arts of war,
and understands dharma as profoundly
as the most learned sage. Now, take him home."
For some time, Shantanu lived joyfully
with his son, who was all sons to him,
as dutiful as he was talented.
His name was Devavrata, "of god-like vows."

The king often traveled far from home
on hunting expeditions. One spring day,
riding in the forest by the Yamuna,
he noticed an intoxicating fragrance.
Tracking it, he found a dark-eyed girl,
divinely beautiful, a fisher maiden.

"Tell me who you are—what shall I call you?"
"My name is Satyavati," she replied.

The king, of course, knew nothing of her past;
to him, she was the answer to his longing
and, keen to marry her, he sought her father.
The wily fisherman was thrilled, but cautious.
"I know how these things work," said the old man.
"You have a son. In the course of time,
he will ascend the throne, and my poor daughter
and her own children will be cast adrift,
cut off without one coin to call their own.
I see it coming! I'll only consent
if you make her first-born son heir apparent."

Shantanu was shocked. Out of the question
for him to disinherit Devavrata.
But back in Hastinapura, in his heart
he pined for Satyavati. Obsessively,
through every sleepless night, he thought of her,
until his cheeks grew thin, his eyes lackluster;
he was not himself. Devavrata
was concerned, and finally discovered
why his father was so melancholy.
"Father," he told him, "here is the solution,
it's an easy matter—I resign my place
as heir apparent. Satyavati's son
shall be the next king. I will go and speak
to her father."

                But it was not easy.
Satyavati's father, shrewd old fellow,
shook his head at Devavrata's plan.
He had thought of yet another problem.
"Strong-armed one, it's not that I don't trust you.
I know that you would never break a promise,
but how do I know your sons will feel the same?

Suppose they don't respect their father's word?
I think there's every chance that your own sons
will feel entitled to take precedence
over my daughter's. I still withhold consent."

"Then," said Devavrata, "here and now,
in the name of all that I hold sacred,
in the name of my guru, of my mother,
and of dharma, I vow to live a life
of celibacy. I shall never marry."

The old man shook with joy. Then Devavrata
helped the lovely girl into his chariot.
"Come, Mother, we shall go to your new home."
They drove to Hastinapura, where Shantanu
embraced Satyavati as his queen.
From this time onward, Prince Devavrata
was known as Bhishma, meaning "awesome one."

The people were dismayed to think that Bhishma,
whom they loved, would never be their ruler.
But the king was so grateful to his son
for the immense sacrifice he had made
he blessed him, saying, "My son, may your death
only come at the moment of your choosing."

With no wife or children of his own,
no personal ambition to pursue,
Bhishma directed god-like energy
to widening the boundaries of the kingdom.
Tall and strong, a brilliant strategist,
he led forays into neighboring lands
and annexed substantial territories
to the spreading kingdom of the Bharatas.

ॐ

Two sons were born to the royal couple,
Chitrangada and Vichitravirya,
and Bhishma cherished them like his own children.
On the death of Shantanu, Chitrangada
was consecrated king. He was a warrior
par excellence, and defeated every foe,
growing in confidence and self-regard
until he fought the chief of the gandharvas
and lost his life. Vichitravirya
was too young to handle affairs of state
and Bhishma acted for him, as his regent.

Bhishma grew concerned for the young king
to marry, to secure the royal line.
He came to hear that the king of Kashi
had three daughters, each one beautiful,
Amba, Ambika and Ambalika,
who were about to make their choice of husband.
Summoning his chariot and his weapons,
Bhishma set off at speed for Varanasi
where eligible kshatriyas had gathered
for the princesses' joint svayamvara.

Striding into the forum, Bhishma spoke,
his voice like thunder. "There are several ways
by which a kshatriya may claim a bride.
But the one that commands greatest respect
is to bear her off by force. This, I shall do.
I stand here, ready to fight any man
who cares to challenge me!" And with that
he lifted all three girls into his chariot
and raised his sword, which glittered in the sun.

A cry of anger went up. All around,
suitors were casting off their courtly clothes,
struggling to strap on their armor, buckling
their jeweled scabbards, stringing their strong bows.

Then they jostled forward to attack.
Bhishma fought with every kind of weapon,
parrying sword thrusts, intercepting arrows,
showing such skill that even his opponents
cheered him. Last to admit defeat was Shalva.
"Stop, you lecher, stop!" he cried in rage.
These words infuriated Bhishma. Frowning,
he told his charioteer to charge at Shalva
and there followed a duel so dramatic
that everyone laid down their arms to watch.
Bhishma's skill was much the greater; soon
Shalva's charioteer was slumped and bleeding,
and his four horses dead between the shafts.
Bhishma spared Shalva's life, and wheeled away,
pointing his horses toward Hastinapura.

Clattering into the courtyard of the palace,
Bhishma gave the beautiful princesses
to handsome Vichitavirya, as his brides.
The two younger princesses were delighted,
and he with them—their dark shining hair,
voluptuous breasts and buttocks, perfect skin.
But Amba had already made her choice;
she had been about to bestow her garland
on King Shalva. When she told Bhishma this,
formally, in the assembly hall,
he consulted with the brahmins present
and gave her leave to depart from the city
and go to Saubha, where Shalva had his court.

Later, you will hear the fatal consequence
of that decision, for Amba, and for Bhishma.

The pleasure-loving Vichitravirya
left the detailed conduct of the kingdom
to Bhishma, while he dallied with his wives.

He was proud of his elegant, handsome looks
and, with their shapely hips, their graceful bearing,
he felt his wives reflected well on him.
The seasons came and went; no heir was born.

After seven years, the king fell ill
with consumption and, despite the efforts
of the best doctors, he grew weak and sank,
like the setting sun, to the realm of darkness.
His sorrowing young widows were left childless.
This was catastrophe. With no one left
who could provide the next generation,
the thread of the Bharatas would be broken.

Satyavati took to her bed in grief.
Her two dear sons deceased. The lineage
in deep crisis. And she longed for grandsons.
Then she thought—in this extremity
perhaps Bhishma would set aside his vow.

Tactfully, she opened up the subject.
"Bhishma, you know what is right, you know
that the law provides for special measures
in times of distress, such as we have now.
Could you not, within the frame of dharma,
father children on my son's young widows?
You owe it to your ancestors—otherwise
there will be no kin to offer food for them,
none to sustain them in the afterlife."

"Mother," said Bhishma, "it is impossible.
I understand your anguish, but my vow
is more important to me than life itself.
Sun may lose its brilliance, moon its luster,
rain may withhold its blessing from the earth,
fire may grow cold, and color colorless
before I will consent to break my word."

Satyavati did not give up easily.
But however much she argued, pleaded,
wept, invoked the immortal gods, reasoned,
Bhishma was immovable as Mount Meru.

"Dharma for times of distress does not extend
to breaking solemn promises," he said.
"My vow is everything. The words, once uttered,
can never be unsaid without dishonor.
This is my truth, and truth for me is greater
than all the possible rewards of earth
or heaven—even to save the Bharatas.
In the great sweep of time, everything passes.
All we can do is stay faithful to truth.

"But there is an alternative solution—
a brahmin can be asked to plow the fields
of Vichitravirya. That has been done before.
When almost every male kshatriya
had been slaughtered by Rama Jamadagnya,
brahmins lay with kshatriya women. In this way
the kshatriya population was restored."

When Bhishma said this, Satyavati thought
of Vyasa. Shyly, she told Bhishma
the circumstances of Vyasa's birth.
"I was mastered—completely overpowered
by the sage Parashara; I was frozen
with fear that he would curse me if I refused;
and his boons were a consideration.
I can summon Vyasa now, and ask him
to father children on the royal widows."

Bhishma readily approved the plan.
Satyavati bent her mind on Vyasa
and he appeared. He was tall and gaunt
with rusty, matted hair, filthy, foul-smelling,

smeared with earth and ash: a fearful sight.
"I will do it," he said, "but we must wait
for a year, during which the young queens
must observe a vow, to sanctify themselves."
"No! No!" cried Satyavati, "we have no time!
A kingdom without a king cannot flourish;
it must be done at once." "Then," said Vyasa,
"their discipline must be to tolerate
my smell and unkempt looks without flinching."

She prepared Ambika: "In the dead of night
your brother-in-law will come into your room.
Welcome him, so you can bear a son
to save the Bharatas." At night, soft lamps
were placed around the room, and incense burners
wafted pleasant scents. Ambika thought
it would be Bhishma who would come to her.
Instead, she saw a dirty, bearded stranger
whose piercing eyes appeared to blaze at her.
The girl was so appalled and terrified
she kept her eyes closed tightly.

                              "My wise son,"
asked Satyavati, "will a prince be born?"
"He will," replied Vyasa. "He will be
immensely strong, courageous, learned, wise;
he will be the father of a hundred sons,
but because his mother would not look at me
he will be blind."
                    "Alas," said Satyavati,
"a blind man cannot be an effective king."
In due course, as Vyasa had predicted,
Dhritarashtra was born, completely blind.

Satyavati made the same arrangement
with Ambalika. But when Vyasa
stood beside her bed, the girl took fright,

her face drained of color. So it was
that her son was born unnaturally pale,
though well endowed in every other way.
He was named Pandu, "pale one."

                                     Satyavati
asked Vyasa to give Ambika
one more chance to bear a perfect son.
But, her courage failing her, Ambika
put a maidservant in her bed instead.
The girl welcomed Vyasa as a lover
and the seer greatly enjoyed his night with her.
"You will no longer be a servant," he said,
"and your son will be the wisest man on earth."
So Vidura was born, an incarnation
of Dharma, god of virtue, who had been cursed
to be born from a shudra womb. Vidura
would become known for loyalty and wisdom.
But because his mother was lowborn,
he would frequently be disregarded
within the household.

                         After this third birth
the seer vanished, for now no longer needed.
So it happened that the great Vyasa
secured the future of the lineage,
to general rejoicing in the kingdom.

2.

DHRITARASHTRA AND PANDU

Now came a joyful time. It was as if
the coming of the three Bharata princes
conferred a benediction on the land.
The kingdom prospered. Rains were plentiful,
swelling the Ganga, spilling generously
onto the lush green of the paddy fields.
Plump ears of barley, rice, fruits, vegetables
were piled high in the markets; livestock thrived
and granaries were full to overflowing.

People flourished: in countryside and city
calm contentment reigned. There was no crime.
Merchants and craftsmen plied their diverse trades
with honesty and skill. Throughout the land
shrines and sacred monuments were seen.
People were kind and generous to each other
and, under Bhishma's wise and steady hand,
reverence for holy rites prevailed.

Bhishma was like a father to the princes.
He brought to court the best and wisest teachers
to ensure that the boys would be well trained
in Vedic lore, and all the skills and arts
essential to a royal kshatriya.
They learned to fight with every kind of weapon;
Pandu excelled with a bow, Dhritarashtra

at heroic feats of strength, while Vidura's
knowledge of dharma was unparalleled.

༜

Janamejaya said, "Now please tell me
what happened as those princes grew to manhood."
Vaishampayana resumed his tale.

༜

Owing to his blindness, Dhritarashtra
was thought unfit to rule without assistance.
Many of the functions of a king
were held by Bhishma, while the fearless Pandu
took on the protection of the realm.
His successful conquests swelled the coffers
of the treasury, and Hastinapura
teemed with travelers from many lands.
He shared his personal booty with his brothers
and decked their mothers with exquisite jewels.
Dhritarashtra, as the senior brother,
held splendid and elaborate sacrifices,
with fat remuneration for the priests.

With the lineage always in his mind,
Bhishma arranged a marriage for the blind prince
with Gandhari, daughter of King Subala.
On her wedding day, she took a cloth
and bound it around her eyes. This she wore
from that time onward, so she would not enjoy
superiority over her husband.

Bhishma thought hard about a match for Pandu.
Not only must his bride be virtuous,
but the marriage should be advantageous
politically, securing an alliance

with another powerful kingdom. He heard
that Kunti, a lovely Yadava princess,
as spirited as she was virtuous,
and Madri, daughter of the Madra king,
were of an age to marry. Pandu traveled
to Kunti's svayamvara, and was chosen
by her, from many thousands of contenders.
Then Bhishma visited the Madra king
and, at great expense, obtained for Pandu
Madri, celebrated for her beauty.

Last, Bhishma found a bride for Vidura:
the illegitimate daughter of a king,
of mixed descent like him, with whom he found
great happiness, fathering many sons.

Perfect. But all was not quite as it seemed
for Kunti had a secret. She had buried it,
consigned it to a rarely visited
corner of memory and there, she hoped,
it would stay. But acts have consequences.
Karma, the eternal law, plays out
ineluctably, and Kunti's secret
contained the seed of tragedy and grief.

ॐ

When Pandu was not absent on campaigns
he often spent his time deep in the forest
on hunting expeditions, for the chase
was his great passion. One unlucky day,
he saw a deer in the act of mating
with a lovely doe. He aimed; he shot it.
The deer was actually an ascetic
who had assumed the likeness of a deer
because he had renounced all human contact.
With his failing breath, he shouted out,

"Even the vilest sinner would stop short
of doing what you have done! You are highborn
and come from a distinguished lineage
yet you have allowed yourself to act
brutally, out of greed!"

                    "You should not blame me,"
protested Pandu, "I am a kshatriya.
Killing is what we do, whether it be
enemies or animals. Besides,
any deer I kill are consecrated
as sacrifice to the gods."
                  "I don't blame you
for hunting," said the sage, "but it was cruel
to kill an innocent in the act of love.
Because you had no knowledge of who I am
you escape the guilt of brahmin-murder
for which the punishment is terrible.
But you will share my fate—your life will end
when you give way to passionate desire
for a beloved woman." Then he died.

Pandu was desolate—he must become
a celibate. Never to have children!
To live without the comfort of his wives!
The deer-ascetic had revealed to him
the errors of his pleasure-seeking life.
"Better renounce the world, shave my head,
wander the land homeless, without blessings,
without possessions, eating what I beg.
In that way I can expiate my guilt."

Kunti and Madri cried, "We will come too!
What would our lives be worth apart from you
whom we love above all other beings?
We will go together to the wilderness.
Living simply, even this dreadful curse
will not prevent us finding joy together."

Pandu at last agreed. He gave away
his royal robes and all his worldly wealth.
Putting on the roughest, simplest garments,
shouldering a few necessities,
passing through lines of weeping citizens
the three of them set out into the wild.

They traveled north. For many months they walked,
across bleak desert country, through the foothills
of the Himalaya, into the high mountains.
Through austerity and self-denial,
Pandu did penance for his previous life,
only refraining from the harshest pain
out of consideration for his wives.
Compassionate, unselfish, disciplined,
he won great merit, great respect. And yet—
he was still disturbed. "A man's duty
is to beget sons for his ancestors.
Childless, I'm no better than a eunuch.
When I die, I will die forever;
there will be no one to remember me
and I shall never reach the heavenly realms."

This thought came to distress him more and more.
His wives were desperate to ease his sorrow.
At last he said, "Consider—in ancient times,
there were no rules for who could mate with whom.
Long ago, during the golden age,
women were not confined to just one husband.
Even more recently, in times of crisis
rules have occasionally been set aside
to serve the greater good. Beloved Kunti,
you could conceive by a holy man."

"Pandu! You violate me by such talk!
You are proposing to treat me like a whore,
with you as pimp. I am your wife, Pandu,

and that, to me, is sacred. I am devoted
only to you, beautiful husband. Never,
not even in my thoughts, shall I consider
any man but you."

Pandu persisted:
"But reflect for a moment—I myself
am only on this earth through the good deed
of the sage Vyasa." Kunti knew the facts
but, though she wanted to console her husband,
she was adamant. No other man
would ever lie with her.

Then, quietly,
she revealed to Pandu the following:
"When I was young, not much more than a child,
a brahmin taught me how to summon gods
to do my bidding. I shall say no more,
but now, if you agree, cherished husband,
I will call on a god to give us a son."
"Lovely woman!" cried Pandu joyfully,
"summon Dharma, god of righteousness."
Kunti did so and, through the power of yoga,
Dharma took human form to lie with her.
In due time, when she gave birth to a son,
a disembodied voice was heard to say,
He shall be called Yudhishthira; he will be
the Dharma King, defender of right action.

After a year, another son was born—
sturdy Bhima, child of the wind god, Vayu,
he who stirs up cyclones and tornados.
Bhima was built like a block of iron.
Once, he tumbled off his mother's lap
when she was sitting on a mountain ledge.
Down he hurtled, spinning, plummeting
as Kunti screamed in horror. But the rocks

were shattered as his body hit the ground,
while he laughed in delight.

       Pandu reflected:
"Success on earth rests on both fate and effort.
One cannot change the course of destiny
but heroic acts can achieve wonders;
I wish for a son whose deeds will be supreme."
He thought of Indra, chieftain among gods,
he who hurls thunderbolts and lashing rain.
"I will obtain a powerful son from him."

Pandu engaged in strict mortifications,
and Kunti, too, observed stringent vows
to honor Indra. Then she summoned him
and the god favored her with a child.
When Arjuna was born a voice was heard,
rumbling from the clouds: *This child will bring*
joy to his mother. He will be a scourge
to countless enemies. Bull among men,
undefeated, he will save the Bharatas.

Then a joyous clamor was heard—the voices
of heavenly beings, singing in their delight
while gongs clanged, and flowers rained on the earth.

Madri longed to have sons of her own.
Too diffident herself, she asked Pandu
to speak to Kunti for her. So it was
that Kunti gave Madri one use of the boon.
Madri fixed her mind upon the Ashvins,
beautiful twin deities who drive
away the darkness, heralding the dawn.
She gave birth to Nakula and Sahadeva,
twins who would be both beautiful and brave.

༄

When Yudhishthira was born to Kunti
the joyful news soon reached Hastinapura.
Gandhari wept. She herself was pregnant—
had been pregnant for a year already—
but as the seasons came and went, she waited,
and waited. Nothing.

        Some time before, Vyasa
had arrived at court exhausted, famished,
and Gandhari had welcomed and cared for him.
Vyasa had been moved by her compassion,
her piety, the fact that she had chosen
blindness, when she could have had the joy
of seeing the glorious created world.
He blessed her, saying, "You will be the mother
of a hundred strong, courageous sons."

Did the wise and far-seeing Vyasa,
even as he granted her this boon,
know the sorrow that would come of it,
as though he had just cursed her, not wished her joy?
Perhaps. But with his insight he could see
all that had to happen, and how. And why.
He understood the business of the gods;
his task, to be their earthly emissary.

Now, Gandhari nursed her swollen belly
as the months dragged on. It was hard and lifeless.
Despairing, she decided she must act.
Grimacing with pain, to rid herself
of the intolerable load she carried
she struck her belly, pushed, strained, cried aloud
and gave birth to a monstrous mass of flesh,
like a dense and glistening clot of blood.

Horrified, she made to throw the thing
onto the fire, but found Vyasa standing
in the room. "Is this the hundred sons
you promised me?" she asked him bitterly.
"I never lie, not even as a joke,"
said Vyasa, "still less when I am serious.
Have a hundred jars filled up with ghee.
Now, sprinkle the flesh with water." Instantly,
the hideous ball split into a hundred pieces—
embryos, the size of a finger joint—
and one extra. Vyasa took each one,
placed it in a jar, and left instructions
about the tending of the embryos,
and when the vessels should be broken open.
"I would have liked to have a daughter too,"
thought Gandhari. Vyasa read her mind.
Then he departed for the far Himalaya
to perform austerities and prayer.

More months of waiting. In the room of jars,
a dozen nurses tended the embryos
that slowly grew inside the glowing vessels.
One day, Gandhari woke to a loud commotion.
The first baby had been born from his jar
and was brought to her. Her hands encountered
a large, muscular infant, her first-born son.

But those who cared for him became uneasy.
They shuddered as the infant raised his voice,
dismal, ugly, like a braying ass.
This infant, who was born on the same day
as Kunti's Bhima, was named Duryodhana.
Dhritarashtra summoned many brahmins
as well as Vidura and Bhishma. "I know
that Yudhishthira as the eldest prince
will inherit the kingdom. But will my son,
my Duryodhana, come after him?

Give me your best advice." At that moment
a horrible cacophony was heard—
howling wolves, hyenas' insane cackle,
harsh croaks as crows and other carrion-eaters
flapped overhead. The city streets swarmed
with creatures never seen before—familiars
of the strange royal brood born in darkness,
born to remain always invisible
to their blind father, their blindfolded mother.

Dhritarashtra heard the disturbing sounds,
and was apprehensive. Vidura
knew what the portents meant. "Oh, my brother,
this birth portends the ruin of your line.
Your first-born son is destined to destroy
all that we've held sacred through the ages."

Dhritarashtra wept and wrung his hands.
"What can I do to guard against disaster?"
"Only something that you will not do—
kill him! Content yourself with ninety-nine.
Without this eldest, all your other sons
will be harmless, ordinary boys.
But this creature comes from an evil place
to spread pain and destruction everywhere.
Exterminate him so the rest may flourish.
Give him up for the sake of all of us."

But Vidura was right. Though Dhritarashtra
did not doubt his brother spoke the truth,
he could not bring himself to kill the child,
his longed-for first-born, Duryodhana.

Over the next month, the other jars
yielded ninety-nine more infant boys
and one daughter, who was named Duhshala.
The hundred sturdy sons of Dhritarashtra
would come to be known as the Kauravas.

Meanwhile Gandhari, fulfilled at last,
caught up in the delight of motherhood,
did not hear the howling of the wolves,
nor the unearthly predatory birds,
nor the harsh grunting from her children's throats.
She only heard the cries of human babies
demanding to be nourished.

                At this time,
another son was born to Dhritarashtra
by a lowborn woman, sent to serve him
while Gandhari was indisposed. His name
was Yuyutsu, and he would become
a loyal friend to the five sons of Pandu.

༁

In their forest home among the mountains
the Pandavas were happy—running free,
climbing, inventing games, learning the skills
a kshatriya boy should know, protected, cherished
by Pandu and their two devoted mothers.

But their father never saw them grow
to manhood. One spring day, when lovely blossom
and soft unfurling leaves infused his mind
with lustful vigor, Pandu was consumed
by love and passionate desire for Madri.
Despite her screams, her terrified reminders,
destiny deprived him of all sense;
he entered her, and died in the act of love.
Thus was the curse fulfilled.

                Kunti bitterly
blamed Madri and, despite her protestations,
the weeping Madri felt responsible.

As the senior wife, Kunti proposed
to follow Pandu. But Madri held her back:
"Our beloved husband died because of me,
cheated of fulfillment, as was I.
I will follow him to Yama's realm.
Kunti—be a mother to my children
as, I know, I could never be to yours."

With that, she climbed onto the funeral pyre
and, covering Pandu's body with her own,
abandoned herself willingly to the flames.

ॐ

The last rites for Pandu were performed
by the seers among whom he had lived
and who were now entrusted with the care
of his wife and sons. They thought it right
to take the family to Hastinapura,
where Bhishma would look after them. For twelve nights,
wan with sorrow for their beloved father,
the boys slept on the ground outside the walls
while rituals to cleanse them of pollution
were performed. A lavish ceremony
was held for Pandu and, when all was ready,
the Pandavas processed into the city.

The grieving people gladly welcomed them.
Pandu's sons were home where they belonged,
to take their place beside their hundred cousins!
But Vyasa spoke to Satyavati.
"With Pandu's passing, the times of happiness
are over. There is trouble in the offing.
Earth herself is growing old and sick.
If you would avoid a painful sight—
the Bharata clan tearing itself apart—
you should leave now."

Satyavati listened.
She sought out Ambika and Ambalika
and, together, the three aging women
entered the last phase of their earthly life.
After retreating to a forest ashram
they passed their days in great austerity,
before embarking on their final journey.

3.

COUSINS

The Pandavas were awed by Hastinapura.
The main gateway, topped by massive towers,
was tall enough for elephants to enter.
Not far away stood impressive buildings
whose several stories housed the offices
of the foremost state officials, their gables
ornamented with imposing statues.
Just inside the gate, a tall stone column,
its capital ornately carved, proclaimed
the king's authority, and the protection
that his rule extended to his people,
like a father's strong, benevolent arm.
This was the noble City of the Elephant.

A broad, straight avenue, lined with the houses
of the wealthy, led from the entrance gate
to the high ramparts of the royal palace—
soaring, dwarfing even the grandest mansions
of the nobility. Here, the Pandavas,
successors to their father, were received
with every show of joy. They stared around
bewildered as bumpkins. Their mother, of course,
remembered elegance and luxury;
but to her five sons, the spaciousness
of this new life—soft beds, exquisite food
(eating was Bhima's favorite occupation)
servants on every hand—was wonderful.

At first, the two families of cousins
played well together, being close in age,
keen on the same games and daring stunts.
But it is never long before young boys
try to outdo each other, prove who is best.
So it was with these. The Pandavas
excelled in every childish game and contest.
But Duryodhana was used to being
eldest, biggest, strongest, so was shocked,
when he challenged Bhima to a fight,
to find that he was so completely trounced
that he ached for days. Humiliation.
This was just the first of many reasons
that Duryodhana grew to hate Bhima.
Bhima, in fact, gained everyone's affection
(except the Kauravas') by his energy
and his engaging, frank enthusiasm.
His booming voice, his bouncing, boisterous step
and freely given smiles made all who saw him
smile in return.

           But the Kauravas
saw him in another way entirely.
Bhima liked to tease and bully them,
holding them underwater in the river
when they were swimming, until they nearly drowned;
shaking trees they'd climbed, so that they tumbled
down like mangoes, bumping on the ground.
His behavior never sprang from malice
but, because no one had ever beaten him,
he had no idea how being picked on
with no chance of redress can wring the heart.
So he would innocently use his strength
to bait his cousins, and found fun in it.

Month by month, year by bitter year,
in Duryodhana, corrosive hatred

grew like a hidden reservoir of gall.
Most of all, he felt the Pandavas
stood between him and life's advantages—
power, in particular. Yudhishthira
looked very likely, as the eldest prince,
to be the next king. Yet for all the time
that Pandu and his sons were in the forest
Dhritarashtra reigned, and Duryodhana
had thought he would, in time, be king himself.

He was prepared to fight if necessary,
when the time came, but he saw that Bhima
would bar his way: Bhima the undefeated,
Bhima, massive, stout as a mighty tree,
Bhima, brave as a fighting elephant,
Bhima, so devoted to his brothers,
Bhima . . . Bhima . . . with a passionate longing
he wanted Bhima dead. But how? *How?*

At the court, Duryodhana had an ally,
Shakuni, Gandhari's older brother.
His mild demeanor, soft voice, silky manner
concealed a mind quick as a serpent's tongue
and as poisonous. To Duryodhana
this was a kindred soul; and while his parents
made light of his complaints against his cousin,
Shakuni listened, sympathized, caressed
his nephew's seething head. And put in words
the thought the unhappy prince had never dared
voice to anyone: "Bhima must die."

For Duryodhana, this was the moment
when idea, fantasy—to kill a kinsman,
kill him under the very roof they shared—
changed from mere dream to possibility.

Thought became language—that was the alchemy
that led in turn to deeds. And once such words
were spoken, fluent on his uncle's lips,
next came strategy and, after that,
action.
 Action, the tipping point, the turn
that, step by step, and inescapably,
set him on the road to Kurukshetra.

☙

Duryodhana arranged a grand excursion.
All the Pandavas and Kauravas
set out on horseback, elephants or chariots
to a choice spot beside the river Ganga
where all kinds of delight had been devised—
games, music, swimming, wrestling matches
and, to top it all, a splendid feast
specially designed to gladden Bhima's heart.
Duryodhana was all affability.
The Pandavas had never sought to quarrel
with their cousin; now it seemed that he
had put his animosity behind him.
He brought the finest dishes for his friend,
Bhima. He even fed him personally
and repeatedly filled his cousin's wine cup.
Inside the spicy snacks and luscious sweetmeats
that Bhima loved, the Kaurava had smeared
a deadly poison, enough to kill a man
many times over, then more, to be quite sure.

Colossal Bhima seemed to manifest
no instant ill-effects. But in the evening,
as he was sleeping on the riverbank,
tired from the games, drugged with poisoned food,
Duryodhana approached him stealthily,
bound him with tough vines, and bundled him,

still sleeping like a corpse, into the Ganga
where he quickly vanished. Duryodhana,
exulting, slipped away to join the others.

Bhima sank, oblivious, down, down
toward the riverbed. But the Ganga
is a goddess—and, in a sense, was Bhima's
great-grandmother. As he sank, nuzzled
by phosphorescent fishes, she stirred up
the deepest bed, where scarlet and green serpents
awoke, and dug their fangs into his limbs,
injecting him with oleaginous venom.
Mother Ganga knew what she was doing—
rather than killing Bhima, the snake juice,
an antidote to Duryodhana's poison,
was bringing him to life with every sting.

He struck the river bottom, and fell through
into the watery kingdom of the Nagas,
waking to find himself sprawled at the feet
of Vasuki, the reigning Naga king,
erect and magnificently hooded.
The throne he sat on was a single emerald,
and two scaly, jeweled Naga queens
were twined around him.
                                    "This is a welcome guest,"
he hissed—for he recognized that Bhima
was no ordinary youth, but the son
of Vayu, god of the winds and tempests.
"Young man, I know how you come to be here,"
and he described Duryodhana's wicked act,
which he had witnessed. "We have an elixir,
which will make you even stronger than before."
Bhima was given a soporific drink.
"Sleep deeply and sleep long," said Vasuki,
"the longer you sleep, the stronger you will be."
For eight days, Bhima slept, then he awoke

with a huge roar of delight, sensing his limbs
newly energized. Thanking Vasuki,
he left, and rose up through the riverbed,
up through the sunlit sparkling water, stepping
onto dry land—and home to Hastinapura.

All this time, his mother and his brothers
worried frantically. They looked for Bhima
everywhere. Duryodhana, his face
straining to look concerned, had joined the search—
but there had been no trace. Vidura
had warned Yudhishthira about his cousin's
evil intentions, and he feared the worst.

Then Bhima walked through the door! What joy there was
among the Pandavas. What baffled rage
filled Duryodhana's heart, though he pretended
to be as glad as anyone.
                        When Bhima
told his brothers what had happened to him
they were enraged. But wise Yudhishthira
warned them not to show it. While they lived
at Hastinapura, they had to maintain
a friendly manner, though they must keep watch
constantly. In this way, they succeeded
in blocking each attempt on Bhima's life.

Year by year, as the princes grew,
Bhishma oversaw their education.
He himself would gather them together
and tell them stories of their ancestors,
and tales of the immortal gods. He taught them
how the world began, and how the ages

follow one from another in a cycle.
Learned brahmins taught them to know the Vedas;
they studied history, and the science
of statecraft and of how wealth is created.

But, as young kshatriyas, the princes
measured themselves by prowess in the arts
of warfare. At first, Kripa was their teacher,
a brahmin who, for years, had lived at court.
How did a brahmin come to be an expert
in weaponry? The story goes like this:

A worthy sage had a son called Sharadvat
who, as well as dutifully acquiring
Vedic learning, as a young brahmin should,
thought of little else but weaponry,
constantly practicing the arts of war.
In order to enhance his mastery,
he performed severe austerities—
to the point that the gods themselves were worried,
lest he outdo them in discipline and skill.

Indra, chief of the gods, devised a plan.
He sent an apsaras to tempt Sharadvat
to abandon his renunciant ways.
Walking in the forest beside the river,
carrying his bow and arrows, the young man
caught sight of a divinely lovely girl,
half-naked. She came toward him, smiling.
Sharadvat held his ground, but stared and stared
and his bow and arrows slipped from his hand.
A profound shudder shook him, and he spilled
his seed, although he did not notice it.
He turned and walked away.

                              The seed fell
on a reed stalk and, as it fell, it split.

From the two halves, a boy and a girl were born.
Soon after, King Shantanu found the babies
while he was hunting in the forest. Seeing
a bow and arrows on the ground beside them,
as well as a black deer skin, he concluded
that they were the children of a brahmin, skilled
in weaponry. He took them back to court
and cared for them. These were Kripa and Kripi.
Later, Sharadvat came to Hastinapura
and taught Kripa mastery of weapons.

Kripa grew up an asset to the court,
a gifted fighter. He taught the young princes
how to string a bow, to heft a mace,
to feint and thrust with short and long sword.
They learned fast, especially the Pandavas,
and soon Bhishma saw that he must find
another teacher for them, more advanced
in all the branches of the arts of war.

௸

Around this time, a person of importance
arrived in Hastinapura, unannounced.
This was Drona, who had married Kripi,
Kripa's sister. By birth he was a brahmin
but he was also expert in the feats
appropriate to the kshatriya class.
Not only could he wield conventional weapons
with quite outstanding skill but, in addition,
from his teacher, Rama Jamadagnya,
he had acquired rare and powerful astras.
He understood that to become a master
in wielding bow or sword required much more
than physical adroitness, or great strength,
more, even, than perseverance. Qualities

of heart were needed, stillness of mind and body,
complete focus.
                    Never an easy man,
quick to take offense, testy-tempered,
at this time he was nursing a great grievance
and, holed up in his brother-in-law's house,
he brooded, eating little, hardly speaking.

Like Kripa's, Drona's birth had been unusual.
The great seer Bharadvaja once caught sight
of a lovely apsaras, fresh from her bath.
A breeze parted her skirt, and the seer's seed
gushed forth spontaneously. Bharadvaja
placed it in a pot, and in due time
Drona was born (the name meaning "pot").

༄

One day, near the palace, the young princes
were playing catch, throwing a ball around,
when someone missed, and the ball went bouncing
into a deep, dry well. The boys brought sticks
and ropes and tried a dozen ways to lift it
but without success. Then they noticed
a cadaverous and shabby brahmin
standing near. "Call yourselves kshatriyas,
and you can't retrieve a ball out of a well?"
the brahmin laughed. "I will get your ball
using nothing but these blades of grass
and—see this ring?" He took it from his finger
and dropped it nonchalantly down the well.
"I'll rescue that too." The princes were intrigued.
Then Drona (it was he) muttered a mantra
over the blades of grass and, with his bow,
shot one down the well and pierced the ball.
Then he shot another through the first
and a third into the second. In this way

he made a chain of blades, and drew the ball
up into the light—and then he loosed
a single arrow, which swooped into the well
and out again, encircled by the ring.

"Who can you be?" the princes asked, amazed.
"Tell Bhishma what you've seen," Drona replied,
turning away. "He will know who I am."

When Bhishma heard the boys' account, he knew
this must be the great Drona. He had found
the teacher the princes needed. But he saw
that Drona was consumed by rage and grief.
"My friend," said Bhishma, "it seems that some great ill
is troubling you. Let me share your burden—
tell me."

     "Prince," said Drona, "you should know
I come here seething with a great obsession—
revenge! When I was young, I had a friend
so dear to me, and I to him, we were
inseparable. He was Prince Drupada,
eldest son of the Panchala king.
He had been sent to the forest where I lived,
to receive instruction from my father,
Bharadvaja. We spent every day
together—studied, played, practiced archery;
often we fell asleep in the same bed
hating to put an end to conversation
by going to separate rooms. He used to say,
'Drona, when I am king of Panchala,
you will come and join me in my palace.
I'll share with you everything I have.'
I can still hear his words!

     "Not long ago,
I fell on times of crippling poverty.

Kripi, my sweet wife, was uncomplaining
but when we were too poor even to buy
milk for Ashvatthaman, our young son,
and other boys were taunting him—well, then
I thought of Drupada, of our friendship,
and I decided to take Ashvatthaman
and Kripi to Kampilya, where Drupada
has his court, now he is king. We traveled
for many days, and arrived collapsing
with exhaustion, ragged and half-starved.
I asked to see the king, telling the guard
my full name, confident that Drupada
would hurry out to greet me when he heard
his friend was here.

           "But that's not how it was.
Two days he kept us waiting by the gate,
despised and ridiculed by passersby,
hunkered with pye-dogs and foul-smelling beggars.
At last, my heart racing with excitement,
longing to see my friend, I was conducted
into his presence, where he sat, bejeweled,
lolling at ease on his ivory throne.
Emotion cracked my voice as I greeted him,
'My friend!' He didn't smile, nor rise to meet me.
'Scruffy brahmin, how dare you presume
to call me friend! Of course, we knew each other
when we were boys, but that was another life.
Friendship is a bond between equals
and, in those days, your friendship suited me.
But did you delude yourself we could remain
eternal boys, alike in innocence,
forever irresponsible, outside time?
No—time and circumstance change everything.
It's sentimental to think otherwise
and a king should be above mere sentiment.
With time comes experience; with circumstance
comes parting of the ways.' And he dismissed me.

"Bhishma, it was as if an icy hand
clutched at my heart and twisted it. My eyes
struggled to penetrate the scarlet mist
that swirled in front of them. 'Time and circumstance
will give me a chance to speak to you again,'
I muttered; and left, stumbling blindly through
the marble courtyards, scoffed at by the guards,
out through the gates, fleeing that evil place,
never resting until we arrived here
in Hastinapura, where the blessed Kripa
has kindly welcomed us into his house;
and, truth to tell, we've nowhere else to turn.

"Kripi, wiser than I, is not surprised
at how the mighty ruler of Panchala
has treated me—but then, she never saw
how close we once were, Drupada and I.
I just can't reconcile . . . Only revenge
can free me from the rage and hurt I carry
each waking moment, like a burning sore."

Bhishma saw that Drona was a man
with too much pride for his own peace of mind.
Although advanced in spiritual disciplines,
he would not, could not, find it in himself
to overlook such crushing disrespect.
Only by humbling Drupada in turn
would he find rest.

                    "Drona, my friend," said Bhishma,
"please consent to put down roots with us.
You are the teacher our young princes need.
Here, you will be honored as you deserve
and live in comfort with your family.
It seems to me that destiny has sent you."

4.

LEARNING THE ARTS OF WAR

Drona never could have swallowed pity
even for the sake of his wife and child.
But he had been watching the young Bharatas
and, talking with Kripa, had become convinced
that these young men were ripe for the instruction
he could provide. So he agreed, with grace.
He moved into the mansion Bhishma offered,
with his wife and son, and made ready
to become the princes' weapons master.

Drona gathered the royal youths together
and addressed them: "I have a driving passion
gnawing my heart, a task that will stab at me
until it's done. Will you give me your word
that, when the time is right, when you have mastered
all the skills with weapons I can teach you,
you will help me carry out this task?"
The Kauravas shifted uneasily
and stayed silent, but brave Arjuna,
ambidextrous third-born son of Pandu,
promised without hesitation. Drona
embraced him warmly, and shed tears of joy.

☙

Drona was a most exacting master,
demanding discipline from all his pupils.

The hundred Kauravas, five Pandavas
and Ashvatthaman, the stern teacher's son,
were treated all alike in principle—
though now and then, Drona devised ways
of giving his son a little extra time;
and since Arjuna was exceptional
in his dedication, he became
the favorite among all Drona's pupils,
cherished even more than his own son.

As was to be expected from their birth,
almost all the youths were competent,
or excelled, at one weapon or another.
They mastered the basic skills of archery,
of fighting with sword and javelin, with the spear,
dagger, mace, and the small hand-thrown dart.
They learned to fight on horseback and on foot,
and how to steer a chariot; they learned
every earthly weapon, and a few,
according to their inner aptitude,
were taught astras—for the proper use
of these occult weapons was dependent
on the depth of spiritual maturity
attained by the man who would summon them.

Drona arranged frequent competitions
so each boy knew exactly how he ranked
on the scale of skill, for every weapon.
Through this strategy, each prince possessed
something to aspire to, someone to beat.

Ashvatthaman, being his father's son,
had outstanding knowledge of the lore
and mantras of the god-given astras.
Yudhishthira was the best charioteer—
no one could outmaneuver him at speed.
Bhima and Duryodhana, both stronger
by far than any of the others, shone

at wielding the spike-encrusted mace,
swinging its colossal weight with ease.
The twins, Sahadeva and Nakula,
were outstanding swordsmen, and they moved,
elegant as dancers, round each other,
perfectly matched.

           But it was Arjuna,
tall, quick-moving, perfectly proportioned,
who was the best all-round kshatriya:
accomplished at each single form of combat,
and better by far at the art of archery
than all the others. You only had to see
his natural poise—the way he moved and stood,
his one-pointed attention as he drew
back the bowstring, letting the arrow fly
at just the right moment, and no other—
to know that this youth was extraordinary.
In him, natural genius was harnessed
to a fanatical determination.

A master can only teach a pupil
those things he is ready to receive.
Young Arjuna was like a water jug
thirsty for water. He learned everything
from Drona, sometimes indirectly.

               One night,
the lesson went on hour after hour until
it grew quite dark. As Arjuna was eating
his late meal, a sudden gust of wind
blew out the taper light, and yet his hand
found its way to each dish in front of him
unerringly. Suddenly, he rose—
and running out into the moonless night
he flexed his bow, nocked an arrow, let fly,

although the target was invisible;
then, feeling his way through the inky darkness,
he found each arrow clinched into the place
he had intended.

        Now he had understood
what it means to aim, but without straining.
He had a glimpse of how one may become
a channel for the world's natural forces
to play themselves out. How, without striving,
without attachment to the end result,
abandoning desire and memory,
an arrow can be loosed, and find its home.
This he learned that night. It was a lesson
he would have to learn anew in great anguish,
years from now.

        For hours each day, he practiced.
Even Drona, not easily impressed,
was awed by him, and told him privately,
"Arjuna, I shall do all in my power
to see that you become the greatest archer
in the whole world—this I promise you."
The young man swelled with joy and, in time,
came to feel this honor was his right.

One day, Drona held a competition
in archery. He had a small wooden bird
placed high in a tree, and asked each pupil
to shoot it in the head with a single arrow.
One by one they stepped up to the mark.
"Tell me everything you see," said Drona.
Some mentioned the tree, some the topmost limbs,
others the bird itself. Some got distracted

by trying to identify the species
and wondering if it was real. Drona
dismissed each one before he could take aim.
Then Arjuna stepped up. "What do you see?"
"I see the bird's head."
"What else?"
"Nothing, master."
"Then loose your arrow, son."

               Calmly, Arjuna
took aim, released. The tiny bird splintered,
its head shattered, and the painted fragments
floated to earth. Drona praised him warmly.
"When the time comes, Arjuna, you will give
my lost friend Drupada what he deserves!"

Another time, the young Bharata princes
went swimming in the Ganga with their master
who, standing in the shallows, offered up
prayers to the gods, and for his ancestors.
Suddenly, one of the rough-hewn logs
that floated by the bank stirred into life—
a gigantic crocodile! Its cruel jaws
gaped hugely, then locked fast round Drona's leg.
It began to drag him into deeper water.
Almost instantaneously, it seemed,
yet without haste, Arjuna raised his bow
and a stream of well-aimed arrows found their mark
in the monster's eye and neck. Its vicious grip
slackened; it sank, bloodying the water.
Not a thought had ruffled Arjuna's mind.
He had simply acted. For this feat,
Drona bestowed on him the *Brahma Head,*
a weapon so deadly it could not be used
against mere mortals without burning up
the whole world; it was to be reserved
for fighting supernatural enemies.

Ashvatthaman, jealous that his father
had favored Arjuna above himself,
pestered Drona for the supreme weapon,
nagging, wheedling until Drona, worn down,
taught him the mantra he had shown Arjuna,
the mantra that would summon the *Brahma Head*.
But in doing so Drona was uneasy,
suspecting as he did that Ashvatthaman
desired the weapon for ignoble reasons.

֍

To be the favored pupil of one's master
is what each disciple longs for, strives for.
But it may not be the blessing it appears.
Envy feeds the flames of enmity,
and when they heard Drona repeatedly
extolling Arjuna, the Kauravas
choked with resentment; to Duryodhana,
every word of praise for Arjuna
was bitterest wormwood. Great praise may also
lead to great pride, and young Arjuna
was not immune to that.

                        Drona's renown
as a preceptor in the princely arts
spread throughout the kingdom, and beyond.
There was no finer weapons school than his,
and kshatriya boys traveled from near and far
to learn from him. There was a boy called Karna,
son of a driver, whom other boys despised
but feared as well. He was tall, aquiline,
and was distinguished by his gold cuirass
and golden earrings—features he was born with.
Wary of rebuff, he made no friends;
only Duryodhana was kind to him.
He was an archer of exceptional skill.

Seeing that Arjuna was the star pupil,
Karna sought to rival him in all things
and was painfully jealous of his prowess.
Arjuna scorned him, treating him with contempt.

Gathering his nerve, he went to Drona.
"Master, please teach me the *Brahma* weapon."
"That ultimate weapon can only be learned,"
said Drona, "by a brahmin of stringent vows,
or a kshatriya who has undertaken
great austerities; no one else at all."
Karna saw that Drona would never teach
the higher mysteries of a warrior's skill
to one who was of lowly origin.
Angry and sad, he gathered his possessions
determined to seek out another teacher,
vowing that, one day, he would be back;
he would prove himself greater than Arjuna!
He left the city, passing through the gate
unremarked, and was soon forgotten.

❧

One night, as he was walking in his garden,
Drona was startled by a rustling sound—
a boy leapt from the bushes and threw himself
at the guru's feet. He turned his dark face
upward in adoration, and begged Drona
to accept him as one of his disciples.
He was a nishada, a forest tribal,
called Ekalavya, younger than the princes,
lithe, with a strange accent.
                          Drona sighed,
"I have to disappoint you—I only teach
youths who come from highborn families.
You're a nishada. It just wouldn't do."
Ekalavya bowed his head and, springing up,
was gone.

He ran, sure-footed, through the forest.
In a moonlit clearing at its heart,
lush with vigorous vines, there was a pool
lovely with lotuses. The boy scooped up
clay from the water's edge and carefully
modeled a life-size figure of his master.
It took him many days and nights of work,
work informed by pure-hearted commitment.

When the likeness was complete, Ekalavya
slept. Then he rose, gathered perfumed flowers
and made a garland for his master's neck.
"Bless me, Guruji." And having touched
earth with his brow, he began to practice
with faith, devotion, and pure discipline.

Time passed.

       One sparkling afternoon in winter,
the Pandavas rode out into the forest
to hunt wild boar. Their prized dog was with them
snuffling, bounding off ahead of them.
Suddenly they heard it growl, and then
a frenzy of barks, making birds fly upward
in alarm. Then stifled whines. The hound
slunk from the bushes, bleeding and subdued,
and the princes found it had been silenced
by seven evenly spaced arrows clamping
its muzzle shut. They were amazed—surely,
at the first wound, the dog would have bolted.
These arrows must have flown from the bowstring
in unimaginably quick succession.
And so precisely! Even Arjuna
could never have accomplished such a feat.

Following the track the dog had taken
they came upon a clearing in the wood

where a dark-skinned youth, his crude bow raised,
was shooting a cascade of arrows, calmly,
gracefully, and with such dazzling skill
the brothers were astounded.

                  "Who are you?
And where could you have learned to shoot like that?"
The youth replied, "My name is Ekalavya,
my father is the chief of the nishadas,
and I owe my skill to the great Drona,
my master."

        Soberly, the brothers rode
back to the city. Pale with jealousy,
Arjuna took Drona to one side.
"Did you not promise me, not long ago,
that I would be the world's greatest archer?
How, then, can you be teaching, secretly,
that lowborn boy—an archer so accomplished
he makes me look like a mere beginner!"
Drona was mystified, then called to mind
the forest boy he had refused to teach.

With Arjuna, he set off for the forest
and there they came across Ekalavya
calmly practicing, his rough-hewn arrows
clustering in a line of perfect circles
on a straw target.

          He fell at Drona's feet,
surprise and joy lighting his dark face
at seeing his master. Drona, for his part,
had never witnessed such unearthly skill—
he could understand Arjuna's despair.
He framed what he must say. "Ekalavya,
if I am your teacher, you should now
give me my fee."

"Name it—anything!"
the boy cried, flooded with happiness
that he had been acknowledged by his guru.
"There is no gift I shall withhold from you."
"Then," said Drona, "give me your right thumb."

Ekalavya's smile did not falter.
With an arrow's single downward slash
he sliced off his right thumb, and placed it, dripping,
at Drona's feet. From now on, he would never
shoot with such breathtaking speed. And Drona's
words would not be falsified—Arjuna
would be the greatest archer in the world.

The Pandava glowed with confidence restored.
Without a word, the two then strode away
and out of Ekalavya's small story.

But we may imagine this: Ekalavya
bound the throbbing socket of his thumb
with herbs and soothing leaves, then sat in thought.
Sunlight left the forest canopy,
dusk came, then darkness. Still he sat alone.
He listened to the creatures of the night
as they went about their earnest purposes
constrained, and free.

In the dawn light, he rose
and bathed, then stood in front of Drona's statue.
In respect, he touched its feet. Then, straightening,
he took his bow, began again to practice.

5.

KARNA

Who was the extraordinary youth,
the strong young eagle, child of nobodies,
who dared aspire to outclass Arjuna?
Born in sorrow, born to encounter trouble,
even as a child he was a stranger
in his own skin. The shining gold cuirass
he was born with, the luminescent earrings,
seemed incongruous for a driver's son.
And with his tawny eyes, the nobility
of his demeanor, he looked so unlike
his humble parents, he was often mocked
by others, so preferred to walk alone.

To understand who Karna really was
we must now uncover Kunti's secret.

Some time before her birth, Kunti's father,
ruler of the powerful Vrishni clan,
had made a promise to a childless cousin,
"You shall have the first child born to me
to bring up as your own." That child was Kunti,
and she grew up in her foster father's palace
loved and loving, modest and beautiful.
It happened that one day a famous brahmin,

known for his short temper and ready curses,
came to visit. He was tall, formidable,
curt in his demands. Kunti's foster father,
extremely anxious not to give offense,
said to him, "Great brahmin, my house is yours.
My daughter, who is of excellent conduct,
will satisfy your needs in every way.
You only have to ask."

So, night and day,
putting aside all wishes of her own,
Kunti served the brahmin. He tested her
by making rude, unreasonable requests
but at all times, promptly and cheerfully,
she waited on him, and the uncouth guest
grew fond of her. When a full year was up
the brahmin was preparing to move on.
"Lovely one, you have served me perfectly.
You may choose a boon and I shall grant it."
"Sir, that you and my father are pleased with me
is boon enough."
                    "Then," said the great brahmin,
"I shall teach you a mantra; with these words
you can summon any god you like
to give you a son." And, having taught her,
he disappeared, to everyone's relief.

Kunti was curious. Could the brahmin's mantra
really summon the celestials?
At this time, she noticed her first period
and felt ashamed that she was now a woman,
and yet unmarried. One day, as the sun
rose in its glory over the distant hills,
the mantra came into her mind. At once
Surya, the sun god, in human form
blazed before her, the most beautiful
creature she had ever seen. Immense,

armored in gold, he said, "Speak, charming girl,
you summoned me, what shall I do for you?"
Kunti cried out in terror, "Go back, my lord,
back where you came from! I was only playing."
Surya frowned. "You cannot call forth a god
simply to dismiss him. I know your mind—
you wish to lie with me, and to bear a son
who will be unrivaled in his prowess.
Come now—if I simply take my leave
and do not give you the son your heart desires
I shall be ridiculed by all the gods,
and I shall curse you—and your father too."

Kunti sobbed, "But I am just a child,
a virgin. The good name of my family
will be ruined. Spare me! To lie with you
would be a dreadful sin."
                              "Not at all,
sweet and comely woman," said the sun god.
"How could I urge you to do something wrong,
when I have the welfare of the world at heart?
Besides, after we have lain together,
you will remain a virgin."
                              "And will my son
have golden armor as you have?"
                                        "He will,
and, in addition, he will be endowed
with divine earrings to protect him from harm."
"Then," said Kunti, "I will lie with you."

❧

She managed to conceal her state from all
except her nurse, and when she came to term,
Kunti gave birth to a boy, most beautiful,
wearing a cuirass of gold, and earrings
that lit up his face. She wept—with joy,

but with grief too, since she must give him up,
play the part of the innocent, carefree girl
she was before. She placed him in a casket
and, at dead of night, she and her nurse
crept to the riverbank. Holding the casket,
Kunti whispered a blessing to her son:

> *"May the world welcome you.*
> *May no creature harm you,*
> *neither those that walk on land*
> *nor those that lurk in water.*
> *May your shining father guard you.*
> *May you perform heroic deeds.*
> *May you be loved, my son.*

"How fortunate you are to have a father
who will watch over you. How fortunate
is the woman who will nurture you,
hear your first words, guide your first tottering steps
and see you blossom into glorious manhood."

Then, in tears, she floated him adrift
in his casket on the shining water
and he was borne up by the gentle current,
carried on the black breast of the river
drifting onward calmly, silently,
as one river flowed into another
joining, at last, the broad, majestic Ganga.
Eventually, the casket caught in reeds
and there its journey ended.

　　　　　　　　At that time,
a worthy chariot driver, Adhiratha,
went with his wife, Radha, to the Ganga,
to pray and worship at the sacred river,
as they always did when evening came.

They were a devout and devoted couple
but they had no children—a great sorrow.
Radha had tried every remedy,
always disappointed. On that evening,
she saw the casket by the riverbank
and, when Adhiratha brought his tools
and levered off the lid, they were amazed—
they saw a baby, glowing like the sun,
with golden armor and bright, sparkling earrings
that were joined to him. The man and wife
were overcome with joy, "A miracle!"
said Adhiratha. "This is certainly
the child of a god, given us by the gods."

They took the baby home and, after this,
Radha bore other children of her own.
The boy grew strong, devoted to the truth.
They named him Vasusena, "armed with riches,"
later known as Karna. When he was older,
his parents told him how he had come to them.
They would often talk about that day
and speculate about his origins.

ॐ

All through Karna's life, although his birth
was unknown to him, he was attracted
to the sun god as his special deity.
The brazen heat of day, which drove most others
to seek the shade, slapped him on the shoulders
like a call to action. And at evening
the horizontal fingers of the sun,
piercing the forest foliage, appeared
to beckon to him. Every morning, early,
as the ascending sun, breasting the hills,
painted the world blood-red, he stood alone,
facing east, worshiping Surya.
And in the evening, as the sun declined,

he stood in contemplation, his palms joined
in prayer and devotion. At such times,
if brahmins came to him begging for alms,
he would always give them what they asked.
This was his lifelong practice, and his vow.

No parents could have cherished a child more
than Karna's; none were more worthy of respect,
and he in turn loved and revered them.
He was very different from his brothers.
Rather than being a driver like his father,
his natural talents and his inclinations
tended toward a hero's martial calling.
He listened avidly to the old tales
told by his father, of heroic conquest
and courageous deeds. At night, he dreamed
he was the greatest archer in the world.

His father understood what must be done.
When the boy grew old enough, Adhiratha
took him to train at Drona's weapons school—
and you have heard what happened to him there.
At Hastinapura, he learned many skills,
but he also learned humiliation.
His obsession, his defining passion,
was resentment of the Pandavas—
the careless way they seemed to feel entitled
to be, and have, the best of everything.
His envy fixed, above all, on Arjuna.
Wormwood entered his soul; he became
proud and bitter, and these qualities
remained with him, lifelong.

                  After he left
the City of the Elephant, he traveled
to where the legendary weapons teacher,

Rama Jamadagnya, had his home—
a hermitage set in a tranquil forest
close beside the sparkling western sea.
This Bhargava, both divine and human,
belonged to another age. Long, long before,
to avenge his father, killed by kshatriyas,
he had slaughtered the whole warrior race
many times over. But these days, he lived
in peaceable retirement. Karna knew
he still hated kshatriyas—though once,
long ago, he had been Bhishma's teacher.

How would Karna best present himself?
Probably not as a driver's son.
He abased himself at the master's feet,
begging to be taken as his pupil.
"I am a brahmin, master," he declared—
only half a lie since, as a suta,
he was of mixed descent. The weapons master,
touched by the youth's desperate entreaties,
agreed to teach him.

                    So began the years
of training with the celebrated teacher.
Never again would Karna be as happy
as he was then, learning the arts and skills
that most accorded with his deepest nature.
His master loved him, valuing his grace,
his devotion, above all, his truthfulness.
He was a brilliant pupil, more than meeting
every challenge the guru threw at him.
He nurtured in his heart's secret recess,
a goal: "One day, I'll be respected, famous.
One day, I'll show the people who despise me
that I'm as good—no, better than anyone!"

☙

Once, Karna was wandering near the hermitage,
beside the ocean. At his feet, the water
trailed its frothy hem around his ankles.
The sun had kept him steadfast company
from dawn, when the sky was tinged with rose,
to evening, when the final fiery blaze
cast a crimson sheen over the water.
Karna stood, praying beside the ocean
that seemed to stretch out to infinity.

He had his bow with him and, practicing,
he accidentally shot a cow, provider
of milk for the daily ritual offerings
of a devout, Veda-reciting brahmin.
Karna begged forgiveness, "Holy one,
I didn't mean to kill your cow. Forgive me!"
This he said over and over, and offered
compensation, but the furious brahmin
refused to be placated in any way:
"Wicked kshatriya! You have killed the creature
who was my lovely daughter, mother, friend,
who gave milk for my daily sacrifice.
She was everything to me. I curse you!
Since you killed my cow through inattention,
when you meet your enemy in battle
your chariot wheel will get bogged down in mud
and your enemy will kill you then and there
as you are struggling with the wheel, distracted,
unprepared for death." Karna sank down
as if oppressed by an enormous weight.

৬

The master's final teaching to his pupil
was how to bring to mind the arcane mantras
that would invoke the astras, terrifying
weapons of the gods, especially
the death-dealing *Brahma* weapon. To prepare,

Karna performed rigorous austerities.
"Now," said the teacher, "you are unbeatable.
Your genius with the bow far surpasses
that of any pupil I have known;
and you command the astras. But remember,
you should only use these sacred powers
in the service of dharma. Death is the price
of using them for any evil purpose."

One day, the master feeling tired, Karna
made a pillow of his lap, and soon
Rama was sound asleep. Time passed slowly
in peaceful meditation. Suddenly
Karna felt a piercing pain—a worm,
a parasite, feeder on flesh and blood,
was sitting on his thigh, burrowing, biting!
He wanted to leap up and crush the creature
but, fearing to wake his master, he sat still,
enduring agony. When his blood trickled
onto the teacher, Rama sprang up, shouting:
"Aaah! I am polluted! What have you done?
Out with it now—tell me what has happened."
Karna told him.

                    The master was enraged.
"No brahmin could have tolerated pain
so agonizing—you have lied to me,
you must be a kshatriya! I have given
the astras to a lying kshatriya!"
Karna explained—"My passionate desire
to learn the *Brahma* weapon tempted me
to lie about my birth—master, forgive me!"
But the teacher uttered a solemn curse:
"Your selfish craving is at the root of this.
One day, when your very life depends on it,
and you try to invoke the *Brahma* weapon,
your memory will fail you. That is the day
that you will meet your death. Now, go from here!"

☙

On that day, the youth became the man.
From then on, Karna walked through the world
alone. Destiny could not be bargained with.
He would dedicate himself to the pursuit
of truthfulness and virtue for their own sake,
looking for no immediate reward.
The curses always crouched in wait for him.
Living his life according to his nature,
he was crucial to the cosmic drama
the gods had devised for the sake of Earth.

6.

THE TOURNAMENT

Now Vaishampayana regaled the king
with an account of how the royal princes
proved themselves, and came of age as warriors.

Imagine an enormous amphitheater.
To build it, on the outskirts of the city,
hundreds of laborers had toiled for months.
For Drona had decided the young princes
had now learned from him everything they could,
and all their years of effort would be crowned
by a grand demonstration of their skills.
Hastinapura had never seen the like.

Word had traveled fast throughout the kingdom.
Excited crowds had gathered from small towns,
from villages, from fishing settlements;
even ascetics in their forest ashrams
had heard the news and come for the spectacle.
People camped outside the city walls
on land that gently sloped down to the river,
and near the forest's edge, where they could gather
brushwood for cooking. Even before first light,
fragrant woodsmoke from a thousand fires
was already rising, flames leaping

as if impatient, like the jostling people
anxious for the great day to begin.
A crowd formed, pressing toward the gate
which opened when the sun began to rise
above the pinnacles of the king's palace.

How glorious the arena was, far bigger
than anything ever seen, even in dreams:
oval-shaped, and lined with ranks of seats
steeply banked, rising, tier on tier,
and shaded from the sun by colored awnings.

While people waited, drummers and trumpeters
made joyful, stirring music. Crafty tinkers
touted their wares—bangles, lamps, ornaments,
gaudy trinkets that children pestered for—
and snack sellers worked the narrow aisles.

Just as people started to get restless,
deep triumphal notes sounded from conches
positioned all around the stadium.
There was a stir, up at the far end.
All heads turned toward the royal enclosure
splendid with its patterns in gold leaf,
its lattices, its jeweled canopy.
A walkway linked the arena to the palace
and now, emerging into the bright sunlight,
King Dhritarashtra came with careful steps,
guided by the arm of Vidura.
His queen walked beside him, led by Kunti,
then Kripa, and then grandfather Bhishma
with other court notables, all resplendent
in brilliant silks and jewels. And at last
came Drona, the master, dressed in purest white—
white sacred thread, white hair, white beard, white garlands,
white sandal paste smeared across his body.
A roar went up, a salvo of applause:

whatever skills the young princes possessed,
whatever feats they were about to show,
they owed to him.

And now the performance starts.
First the princes each take up a bow
in order of age, led by Yudhishthira
and, mounted on horses, canter round the ring,
then wheel in an elaborate formation,
well-fitting breastplates glittering, dazzling.
They perform amazing feats of archery,
taking aim at a revolving target
hung in the center, shooting, galloping
faster and faster, while not a single arrow
misses its goal. The display only stops
when the bristling target is crammed with arrows.

Next, there are races. The best charioteers
among the princes line up to compete—
which of them will drive his gleaming vehicle
fastest round ten laps of the arena?
One by one, they weave a complex course
round obstacles, cutting through twists and bends
hugging them close, hauling their horses round
without the wheels grazing. Each chariot
is freshly painted and adorned with flowers.
Each one is drawn by four glossy horses
bred for this, superbly schooled, manes braided,
and in each, the driver stands, erect,
magnificent, dressed in burnished armor.

Now, Drona announces a mock fight.
One hundred and five princes brandish weapons
and seem about to slaughter one another
so savage are their shouts, so fierce they look,

their swords and daggers flashing as they thrust,
feint, dance around each other. The huge crowd
is on its feet, shouting the princes' names,
more anxious than encouraging—and yet,
at a slight sign from Drona, it all stops;
not a single drop of blood has been spilled.

In the royal enclosure, Vidura
is describing everything that happens
to Dhritarashtra, and Kunti to Gandhari.
"On a day like this," sighs Dhritarashtra,
"I envy hopelessly those who can see,
who now are witnessing my young sons' triumph."

Now Bhima, built like a colossal boulder,
and the strong and nimble Duryodhana
fight with maces. Drona emphasizes
that this, too, is a mock fight—though quite soon
it is clear they are serious. They will inflict
as much harm as they can, swinging their clubs
with the huge momentum of their powerful arms,
roaring like two rutting elephants,
sparks leaping as the weapons clash, rebound.
The crowd screams support, some for one,
some for the other, starting to trade blows
between themselves. Drona stops the contest,
fearing a bloody riot in the stands.
Each cousin has suffered wounds. Grim-faced, silent,
they stalk off. This has seemed like a rehearsal
for a deadly fight that is to come, one day.

There is loud grumbling on the terraces
at the violent and exciting duel
being cut short. But Drona raises his voice:
"I now present to you Prince Arjuna,
son of Indra, greatest of all archers,
whom I love even more than my own son."

Conches blare, drums beat out a tattoo
in a joyful musical explosion.
The cry goes up—*Ar-ju-na! Ar-ju-na!*
The crowd yearns for the legendary warrior;
they stamp their feet, chanting in ecstasy.
He, above all, is the prince they wish to see.

Wild anticipation often leads
only to disappointment. Not today!
Muscular, graceful, shining hair unbound,
Arjuna steps forward, bows to Drona.
Completely focused, with no hint of strain
he raises his bow, draws back his left arm
and then—

       and then the miracles begin!

First he sends an effortless stream of arrows
into the mouth of a tiny wooden boar
so far off it is almost out of sight.
Not one misses. The crowd roars in delight.
Then he does the same again, blindfolded,
then with his back turned. It looks impossible,
and yet it seems tame when you see what follows.
He stands with his eyes closed, his lips moving
in a silent mantra. He shoots an arrow
straight into the sky. Slowly it rises,
then begins to glow, then blazes, then
the sky is on fire over the arena.
The crowd cringes in terror but, next moment,
a stream of flashing silver arcs upward
and instantly the sky becomes a sea,
an upside-down ocean, quenching the flames.
These are truly weapons of the gods!

More marvels follow. Arjuna moves swiftly
with the panache and poise of a great dancer,
master of his body, never doubting
that he can transcend nature's normal laws.

He changes size at will. He conjures mountains.
He shoots an arrow into the sand, making
the ground split wide open in front of him,
and close when he has walked inside—and then,
when people start to worry, a yawning crack
opens up before the royal stand—
Arjuna steps out and bows to his uncle!

The crowd erupts, delighted and relieved.
They shriek themselves hoarse, blow whistles, stamp their feet
until they are sore. This is the day's climax;
what they have seen will never be surpassed.

୬

When at last the uproar had died down,
and people were preparing to go home,
they became aware of a strange sound,
like thunder, coming from beside the gate.
Someone said, "That sound is a challenge,
some hero is slapping his arms boastfully."

The crowd was hushed, looking toward the gate.
A man strode forward, an imposing figure,
beautiful, tall as a kadamba tree.
A shining gold cuirass encased his body
and in his ears, there sparkled golden earrings,
like two drops of sunlight. He looked forbidding
—serious, remote, stern even, as if
his life had been hard. Anyone could tell
from his bearing, the authority
with which he walked into the arena
holding his bow as though it were a scepter,
that this man was a very great warrior.

He inclined his head to Dhritarashtra,
nodded to Drona, then turned to Arjuna
and, although he did not raise his voice,

his words were heard all over the stadium.
"Pandava, you seem to take great pride
in the facile feats you've just displayed to us.
With the master's permission, I, Karna,
will now match every easy act of yours,
each paltry trick. So don't be too puffed up."

Drona gave consent, probably curious
to see what his former pupil had become
since he left Hastinapura as a boy.
Surely this man would not outdo Arjuna.
The crowd was humming with curiosity.
Who could this be? There was complete silence.
Then, effortlessly, Karna emulated
every feat Arjuna had performed.
Some people thought them even better done,
and felt like fools that they themselves had been
so easily impressed before. As one,
like a surging wave, the crowd rose, cheering.
Karna raised his arms triumphantly.

Drona seemed shocked. Arjuna looked tense
and angry; he considered himself insulted.
But Duryodhana joyfully embraced
Karna. "Welcome to you, strong-armed hero!
Hastinapura is honored by your presence.
You certainly know how to humble pride!
From today, the kingdom of the Bharatas
is home to you; ask of me what you will."
"I choose two things to ask of you," said Karna,
"your friendship, and a duel with Arjuna."

Arjuna addressed the towering Karna:
"How dare you barge in here uninvited!
Karna, I swear to you, when I have killed you
you will sink to the realm reserved for those
who indulge in empty boastful prattling!"

Karna smiled. "This place is open to all.
Strength is what matters here, not whimpering words,
not half-baked insults. A truly great warrior
will rise to any challenge. I, Karna,
challenge you to a contest—no mere display,
but a duel to the death between archers.
I shall behead you in your teacher's presence—
or will you admit I have the greater skill?'

"I'll send you to hell first!" cried Arjuna.

ॐ

As he spoke, the sky grew dark—Indra,
bringer of storms, was gathering his forces
as if to bless his son. But the next moment
a shaft of brilliant sunlight pierced the clouds,
making a golden circle around Karna.

In the royal box, Kunti fainted.
She had realized who Karna was
and was overcome, remembering
the lovely golden infant she had sent
floating down the river, to take his chance.
Now her heart hammered with fear—her sons
fighting to the death! But she said nothing.

Kripa, expert in the etiquette
of dueling, spoke now: "Here stands Arjuna,
third-born son of Pandu of this royal house,
youngest offspring of Kunti, his wife.
It is known that no prince will condescend
to duel with a man of lesser lineage
than his own. You must tell us, hero,
who your father is. Who is your mother?
To what royal clan do you belong?"

Like a drooping flower drenched with rain,
Karna hung his head. Arjuna waited.
Then Duryodhana spoke up forcefully:
"This rigmarole is just old-fashioned nonsense!
But if Arjuna is too punctilious
to fight with anyone except a prince
I have the solution. Our vassal state,
Anga, lacks a ruler. Here and now
I propose that this outstanding man
shall be consecrated king of Anga.
Then there will be no excuse for Arjuna
to dodge away from dueling with him."

Dhritarashtra gave his blessing; brahmins
were summoned, bringing all the ritual objects
needed for consecration—flowers, gold,
roasted rice grains, water from the Ganga,
a white silk parasol, emblem of a king—
and, in the presence of the cheering crowd,
Karna was installed as king of Anga.

He turned to Duryodhana. "How can I
ever repay you for this priceless gift?"
The prince smiled with pleasure. "All I want
from you, Karna, is your lifelong friendship.
I know, together, we shall do great things."
Karna's face lit up. "Here is my promise—
as long as I shall live, while these two arms
have strength and skill in them, I shall defend you.
Your future will be mine, your interests, mine.
All that my head and heart can give are yours."

An old man tottered forward from the crowd
sweating and trembling, leaning on a stick.
The man was Karna's father, Adhiratha.
Seeing him, Karna went over to him
and, in reverence, touched the old man's feet

with his head, still wet from the anointing.
Adhiratha's face was bright with love.
"My son!" he cried, his eyes moist with tears.

The Pandavas laughed. "This man's a wagoner,"
jeered Bhima, "and you're his son! Off with you,
off to the stables—go and muck out horses.
That's where you belong!" Karna breathed hard
and fixed his gaze on the sun, low in the sky.

Immediately, up sprang Duryodhana
and, in a white-hot rage, he said to Bhima,
"Wolf-belly, your rudeness and crass ignorance
are hardly worthy of the kshatriya
you claim to be. The learned texts distinguish
three kinds of king—one of a royal line,
the leader of an army, and a hero.
This man, by his heroic skill, his courage,
has proved himself equal to any of us.
Prowess counts most for a kshatriya.

"As for lineage—just think about it.
It's not unknown for sons of kshatriya mothers
to become brahmins. Drona here was born
from a water pot, Kripa from reeds.
Arjuna calls himself a son of Pandu
but in fact, as we all know, his origins
are murky—and the same goes for his brothers.
Think of Pandu himself, and my father,
and Uncle Vidura—we respect them
and yet their birth was by no means straightforward.

"The most powerful forces in the world
are often born in darkness. Think of fire,
the molten fire that sleeps beneath the ocean
but will erupt at the apocalypse
to engulf the earth. The mightiest rivers

have unimpressive origins; their greatness
grows as they make their journey through the world
joining with others, broadening, deepening,
meeting barriers, overcoming them.
That's how it is with the noblest warriors.
But, of course, a deer can't sire a tiger
and this man is a tiger—so I would guess
his mysterious birth must hold a clue
to his greatness. Karna deserves—hear me out—
our deep respect and, in my eyes at least,
he is a king.

       "Now, tell your little brother
to gather his scattered wits, pick up his bow
and fight the King of Anga—if he dares!"

At this, the audience murmured its approval.
But night had fallen, it was too late to fight.
The crowd drifted away, talking of Karna.

7.

REVENGE

Arjuna's public humiliation
was a setback for the Pandavas.
Even Yudhishthira was now convinced
that no archer on earth could beat Karna.

But Drona had his mind on other matters.
He gathered all the princes. "Listen, young men—
that's what I call you; after yesterday
you are no longer boys. You have made me proud.
What you all achieved in that arena
showed me your education is complete.
But yesterday was circus tricks compared
to the glorious battles you were born for.
The time has come for me to claim my dues.
You know my grievance against Drupada.
Year by year, the craving for revenge
has swelled in me, like a blocked watercourse
longing for release. This will be your fee—
that you shall take an army to Kampilya
and bring Drupada to me as a prisoner."

This prospect was thrilling to the princes.
They cheered and punched the air in exultation
and the elders too supported Drona's cause.
A fighting force was rapidly assembled
and, with the Bharata princes at its head,
and Drona riding with them, they set out.

Entering the land of the Panchalas
the Bharata force crushed all opposition
and reached the fine city of Kampilya.
Outside the city ramparts, they milled about,
keen but disorganized. The Kauravas,
led by Duryodhana, were desperate
to storm the city and tear it apart.
They were consumed by feverish excitement
jostling for the chance to achieve glory.
The Pandavas, calm and more thoughtful, waited
at a distance. While Duryodhana
led the army in a charge, breaching
the city gate through the force of numbers,
the Pandavas stayed well behind, with Drona.
This self-restraint was their first victory.
Arjuna was confident, "You'll see,
Drupada will overpower our cousins—
I've heard he is a formidable archer."

As Duryodhana and his troops rampaged
through the streets of the unfamiliar city,
killing all opponents, they felt triumphant.
The Kaurava prince was opening his mouth
to declare victory, when the palace gates
burst open, to the deep bray of conches,
and Drupada rode out in a white chariot
like a whirling fire. His arrows streamed
in a continuous line, and every one
found its intended mark. Counter-attack
was impossible. At the same time
the citizens bombarded the invaders
with whatever heavy objects came to hand.
The Kauravas were routed. They had learned
that a thirst for victory was not enough.

"Retreat!" cried Duryodhana to his men,
and a ragged line of Kaurava chariots,

many driven by corpses, straggled out
beyond the city walls. Badly battered,
the defeated princes wailed to Drona,
"You pitched us against completely hopeless odds—
it was unfair, Drupada's unbeatable!"

Then the Pandavas came quietly forward
buckling their armor. "We'll attack him now."
It was agreed by Arjuna and Drona
that Yudhishthira, as the future king,
should not join the assault and risk his life.
The four brothers flew into the city
without the army. First went giant Bhima,
swinging his mace like a force of nature
felling men, elephants and horses,
striking such fear into the Panchala troops
that they scattered like a flock of parakeets.
Drupada raised his great bow as before
but this time each arrow of his was blocked
midair by Arjuna's answering cascade,
as dense and accurate as a water jet.
Arjuna was inspired, transfigured, god-like
as he whirled in a shimmering haze of light.

Drupada, half paralyzed with shock,
tried even harder, but found his jeweled bow
split by a silver shaft. It was the end.
He prepared himself for death, but Arjuna
leapt onto his chariot and seized him,
holding him fast so he could not escape,
as an eagle grasps a snake in its talons.
Bhima would have indiscriminately
razed the city, killing all he met,
but Arjuna restrained him, now the purpose
for which they had attacked had been accomplished.

While his brothers covered his retreat
he galloped back to Drona with his prisoner.

The shame he had suffered at the tournament
was dissipated now. In this real battle
he had salvaged his lost honor from the dust
and amply paid his master what he owed.

༄

Drupada, when he had time to think,
was quite astonished by the whole onslaught
since he had no quarrel with the Bharatas.
Now, thrown at Drona's feet, he understood.
He rose in silence, and stood with his head bowed.
For Drona, who had waited long for this,
it was the sweetest moment.

                        "Drupada,
you once said friendship was impossible
except for equals. We are not equals now.
Remember 'time'? Remember 'circumstance'?
You are defeated, and your entire kingdom
is forfeit, given me by my disciples
as my fee. Your very life is mine
if I should choose to take it. But instead,
I choose forgiveness. You should know, we brahmins
are not vindictive. I'll make you my equal
by giving half the kingdom back to you;
as equals, we two may be friends again."

No kshatriya ever would have made
such an unwise proposal—Drupada
allowed to live, humiliated, certainly
would seek revenge at some time in the future.
But Drona was a brahmin, and remembered
the happy times in his father's ashram.

Unbearably insulted, burning with rage
which he concealed with a glassy grin
Drupada swallowed the demeaning terms.

The people were one people—*his* people
as of right, bequeathed by his ancestors.
Now half of them would have to learn to bow
to Drona as their lord. Border families'
lives would be split, kinsmen tilling land
on different sides would slowly grow apart.
The body politic of Panchala
would be deformed beyond all recognition.
He would continue to live in Kampilya
but rule over an amputated kingdom,
while Drona took the city of Ahicchatra
and the extensive countryside around.

Bitter as he was, he thought of Arjuna
with admiration, rather than resentment.
"O mighty gods," he prayed, "give me a son
who will become a formidable warrior
and kill Drona for what he has done to me.
And give me a daughter, who will become
the wife of this noble son of Pandu."

With the insult always gnawing at him,
Drupada became gloomy and thin.
None of his existing sons was capable
of defeating Drona—that he knew.
"Miserable brood!" he thought. He summoned
learned brahmins, hoping to find one
with perfect knowledge of the rituals
that would produce a son. Such a son
would have to be exceptional in his prowess
to be able to avenge his father,
for Drona was unrivaled in his knowledge
both of weapons and of sacred lore.
Above all, he had the *Brahma* weapon.
Drupada knew that, to achieve his purpose,
no ordinary warrior would do.

Finally, he tracked down an ascetic,
Yaja, who would conduct the complex ritual
in return for eighty thousand cows.
A towering sacrificial fire was built
and customary ritual objects brought.
Drupada's queen played her required part.
Yaja offered well-prepared oblations
and from the fire emerged an awesome youth,
the color of fire, crowned with a diadem
and carrying a shield and splendid weapons.
A disembodied voice from heaven announced,
This unrivaled prince of the Panchalas
has been born for the destruction of Drona.

Then from the center of the altar
stepped a girl of such heart-stopping beauty
all were amazed. She was dark-skinned and shapely,
with eyes like pools and lustrous curling hair.
She had the fragrance of a blue lotus.
She was Shri, goddess of royal fortune,
in human form. And, as she emerged,
the same celestial voice was heard proclaiming,
This dark woman will be the occasion
of the destruction of the kshatriyas.
Her birth is one of the events designed
to accomplish the purpose of the gods.

The brahmins bestowed names. "Drupada's son,
bold as flame, shall be called Dhrishtadyumna."
They called the girl Krishnaa, which means "dark,"
but she came to be known as Draupadi.
Dhrishtadyumna afterward became
a pupil in Drona's weapons school, for Drona
knew that there is no avoiding fate.

⚜

After the tournament, Duryodhana
swelled with confidence. At last, in Karna,
he had a friend, a world-class warrior,
who could support him in his fixed obsession:
to eliminate the sons of Pandu.
And when he learned that Karna had acquired
the *Brahma* weapon from the Bhargava,
Duryodhana caught the scent of victory.

Around this time, hundreds of princes gathered
for a svayamvara in a neighboring realm.
The beautiful and fair-complexioned daughter
of the reigning king would choose her husband.
Duryodhana, accompanied by Karna,
vied for the girl's attention, but was ignored.
Incensed, deciding to take her by force,
he grabbed her, lifting her onto his chariot.
There followed a great battle—Duryodhana
against the other, outraged, kshatriyas.
Karna backed him up so skillfully—
destroying the bows and arrows of his rivals,
and killing many of their charioteers—
that the other suitors finally withdrew.
With his hard-won bride, Duryodhana
rode back in triumph to Hastinapura.

One of the rivals had been Jarasandha,
mighty king of Magadha. Impressed
by Karna's outstanding feats, he challenged him
to a chariot duel. The two were well matched.
They fought with bows, with swords, with divine astras,
and finally they fought on foot, bare-handed
wrestling arm to arm. Jarasandha,
tiring sooner, was finally defeated.
He was so pleased with Karna, they became
friends, and the king gave the driver's son
the fine city of Malini. Karna's fame
as a brilliant warrior spread far and wide.

8.

THE LACQUER HOUSE

The wealth and power of the Bharatas
were largely due to Pandu. In his time,
before he had retreated to the forest,
Pandu had been an outstanding warrior
subduing lands for many miles around,
annexing them to the Bharata kingdom,
stuffing the vast vaults of Hastinapura
with wealth of every kind. The people prospered.
Pandu had been loved.

        And now, in turn,
his sons, having acquired at Kampilya
a taste for battle, went on their own campaigns
at least as formidable as their father's,
earning a most glorious reputation.
Hearing reports of the five Pandavas'
prowess and strength, Dhritarashtra became
filled with anxiety. His nights were sleepless
and uneasy.

        He summoned Kanika,
one of his ministers, a man accomplished
in the labyrinthine arts of politics
and intrigue. "Sir, you must be bold," he said.
"A king should strike against his enemies
before they grow in power. Hide your intentions,

then act with single-minded ruthlessness.
Each enemy requires a different tactic.
The timid should be terrorized, the brave
should be conciliated, the covetous
kept sweet with gifts, while equals and inferiors
should be crushed by a powerful show of arms.

"Even close kin, even revered teachers
should be put down if they turn dangerous,
and your nephews are becoming enemies.
You have been kind to them for far too long.
Pretend to love them still, until you find
a way to free yourself. You know, young trees
are easy to transplant. But every day
those brothers, nourished by the people's love,
establish deeper roots."

         Dhritarashtra
listened, but he knew that Vidura
and Bhishma, if asked, would have offered him
a different view. The blind king always wanted
to be seen to act with complete rectitude.
He groped his way toward decision, clinging
to the last advice he had been given.

Young Yudhishthira, the heir apparent,
resembled his father. He was generous,
concerned for the people and their families.
The young prince had a warm and natural manner
and the population loved him, unaccustomed
to having their voices heard. Dhritarashtra,
by incapacity or inclination,
was remote, and Bhishma preoccupied
with large affairs of state.

         Up until now,
Duryodhana had thought that his father's rule
would last for years to come. He had influence

over the king. Meanwhile, partly by dint
of bribery and blackmail, and with support
from Shakuni and Karna, he was busy
weaving a network of alliances,
a secret coterie made up of men
bound to him by ties of obligation;
men of ill will, who felt themselves shut out
from the gilded circle of the Pandavas.

But then the Kaurava, ever vigilant,
started to pick up alarming gossip.
His informants went about the streets
and marketplaces, lingering on corners,
loitering in doorways. So it was
that Duryodhana's spies reported to him
a buzz of restlessness, a new climate.
People were clamoring for change, saying,
"Dhritarashtra isn't up to it.
Due to his blindness, he did not inherit;
why is he king now? What kind of king
can he be, with no eyes in his head?
The eldest Pandava, wise beyond his years,
should be our king immediately, not later.
It's up to us to make our voices heard."
All this, the spies faithfully reported.

Duryodhana sweated and shook with rage.
He rushed to the king. "Father, listen to me.
Out there, beyond the palace walls, unrest
is stirring among the common citizens.
They want Yudhishthira to be their king
instead of you! Think of what this means.
You have allowed your nephews to usurp
the place you and your sons should occupy
in popular esteem. Do you realize
you have condemned your children to penury—

yes, that's what you've done! In a few years from now,
when you are gone, and all the elders too,
we Kauravas—your own sons—will be begging
Yudhishthira even for food and drink!
His son will be king after him, and *his* son—
we will be disinherited for ever.
This is your fault. If you were a strong king
we wouldn't have to heed the people's views."
The prince sank down, weeping angry tears.

The king's heart swithered, hating to hurt his son,
his first-born, first-loved eldest. And he remembered
Kanika's stark warnings. All the same
he would not be accused without a protest.
"Come, my dear—you know Yudhishthira.
He's like Pandu, he'd always treat you fairly.
Even if he weren't the heir apparent
the people would worship him—I myself
have heard the way they ululate and cheer
when he walks out among them. If I now
fail to honor my commitment to him
there'll be a revolution, as you say."

"Enough!" cried Duryodhana. "I can't stand
having to watch those preening Pandavas
strut around—they make my life a torment.
Father, you raised me as a king's first-born;
I should be king in turn. If you don't listen,
if you consign me to subservience,
I'll kill myself!"

                Then Duryodhana
spoke about the network he was forming
of those who would support him when the moment
was right for him to lay claim to the throne.
But he needed time. "I have a plan,"
he said. "At least give me a breathing space—

send the Pandavas on some journey. Meanwhile,
in their absence, I'll build my public base,
do what it takes to become popular.
The people's memories are short, and fickle.
Once they start receiving generous handouts
they'll switch support to me. Then, later on,
the Pandavas can come back."

                    "Yes, my son,
the same maneuver had occurred to me,
although it seemed too devious to mention.
But what about the elders? Would they not
understand this plan as a banishment
and refuse to sanction it?"
                Duryodhana
had been weighing up each of the elders:
how Bhishma would avoid taking sides,
not wanting to divide the dynasty;
how Drona would follow the wishes of his son,
Ashvatthaman, jealous of Arjuna;
how Kripa would side with the two of them;
how Vidura favored the Pandavas
but had no power, being of low status.

"The plan is perfect," said Duryodhana.
"Act on it—remove the dreadful thorn
that's sticking in my heart, this raging grievance."
Now Dhritarashtra's course seemed clearer to him.
Now, at least, the king would sleep at night.
He knew his son would not be satisfied
with a brief respite, but he shut his mind
to what the prince's darker plans might be.

༄

In the city of Varanavata
a festival to honor the god Shiva

would soon take place.
                    "My dear Yudhishthira,"
said Dhritarashtra, smiling at his nephew,
"you should go. Take Kunti and your brothers,
enjoy the festival, relax. Let people
in the provinces see their future king."
Yudhishthira was wary, but said nothing,
prevented from opposing the king's idea
by respect for his father's elder brother.
He made ready for the coming journey;
brahmins chose the most auspicious day
for the departure, performing prescribed rites.

While the preparations were under way
Duryodhana sought out Purochana,
his aide, whose loyalty he counted on.
"There is no ally I trust more than you.
Help me, and you will be well rewarded.
You must rush ahead to Varanavata.
Build a splendid mansion near the armory
specially for the Pandavas, providing
every comfort, every kind of pleasure.
Call it 'the House of Wealth.' No luxury
should be lacking—sumptuous brocades,
couches so soft a man could sleep for ever,
gold cornices, cool, jasmine-scented courtyards.
That will keep my father satisfied.

"But under gorgeous tapestries, the walls
should be stuffed with straw, oil-drenched, and smoothed
with gilded wax; the floors, crushed travertine
blended with resin; and those elaborate couches,
positioned under weighty architraves,
should be softwood, soaked in butter, gleaming
with twenty coats of lac.
                    Let them settle in,

let them enjoy themselves without suspicion,
and then, one windy night, while they're asleep,
an 'accidental' fire should torch the building
and them as well." Purochana understood.

The day arrived for the Pandavas to leave.
As Yudhishthira touched the elders' feet
to receive their blessing, wise Vidura
murmured to him in code: "Be very watchful.
One who understands his enemy
cannot come to harm—be guided by
the jackal, who prepares many bolt-holes."

⚜

The Pandavas arrived in Varanavata
and were made welcome. Canny Yudhishthira,
as soon as he had set foot in the mansion,
picked up a faint odor of ghee and resin.
He guessed. "Smell that!" he muttered to the others,
"but don't betray by the slightest gesture
that we have noticed anything. Our cunning
must equal theirs." Bhima's inclination,
when the brothers talked about it later,
was to leave at once, escape the city.
But Yudhishthira warned, "Duryodhana
has power, allies, keys to the treasury.
We have none of that. If we should show,
by leaving now, that we have realized
what he is plotting, he would have us followed
and killed. We must be patient."

                              He thought hard—
and remembered that in his entourage
was an engineer, a friend of Vidura.
At Varanavata, this man spent time
looking, listening, drawing his own conclusions.
He knew what wickedness was in the offing.

"I am a specialist in digging mines
and tunnels; I propose we sink a pit
beneath the inmost room, and then from there
drive a tunnel, deep under the grounds,
to surface in the woods. Purochana
will not move yet; he wants you to relax.
But you should all sleep underground, in case."

Months passed. The Pandavas spent many hours
exploring the surrounding woods and forests
on the pretext of hunting expeditions.
Then the engineer sent them a message:
"Take care—Purochana intends to act
on the darkest night of the next lunar month."
And, indeed, Yudhishthira had noticed
a new cheerfulness in Purochana.

Yudhishthira discussed the planned escape
with the others. Only one difficulty
occurred to them—their bones would not be found
among the ashes and, by this, their cousin
would know they had survived, and track them down
relentlessly, seeking to have them killed.
No one would ever know.

                          For some time,
Kunti had been providing food and shelter
to a poor tribal woman from the forest
and her sons—five strongly built young men.
But she had lately started to suspect
that they were spying for Purochana.
Before the appointed night, she held a feast
for the townsfolk and, as royal agent,
Purochana was invited. Liquor flowed
lavishly. Most of the guests went home at last,
but Kunti took the forest family
to her room, where they fell into a stupor.

In the hall, Purochana stretched out
and slept as deeply as a sated pig.
He did not hear Bhima's cautious footsteps,
the soft click of the barricaded door.
He never heard the flames gobble the rafters,
nor boiling resin bubble from the floor,
the creak, roar, crash as the roof fell in;
he did not smell the scent of burning rushes—
he breathed the toxic fumes of wax and lacquer
and never woke.
           The fire surged, crackling
from room to room, through corridors and stairways,
tongues of flame greedy for each other
red, yellow, orange, leaping upward,
playful, free. An ecstasy of burning.

Meanwhile, the Pandavas had clambered down
into the pit, covering it behind them.
They ran through the tunnel—out into the air,
and to the forest. They dodged among the trees
making their way south, and soon the uproar
and horror of the city were left behind.

Watching, helpless, hour after anguished hour,
the citizens of Varanavata
witnessed the House of Wealth become a wreck.
Wracking explosions, showers of sparks and cinders
lit the entire sky.
           They flung their garments
over their heads and wept.
                "Oh terrible!
Shiva! Shiva!
           We've lost the Pandavas,
the jewels of the kingdom,

our bright hope!
How could it happen that colossal Bhima,
stronger than any other man on earth,
couldn't escape?
                        And the great Arjuna . . .
the twins—so noble . . . !"

                        But most of all, they wept
for Prince Yudhishthira, and for their future
stripped of the wise ruler he would have been,
a king who would have given them protection
in the difficult conditions of their lives.

With the dawn breeze, the flames exhausted, ash
and stinking smoke were carried everywhere
so that no hovel, courtyard, alleyway
escaped the stench of death.
                        And despite
the deviousness of sly Purochana,
despite the guile of Duryodhana,
the people guessed this was their evil work.
When the bones of a woman and five men
were found jumbled, raked from the noxious debris,
they were convinced—the brothers had been murdered.
"Let us send a message to the king:
'You have succeeded; the Pandavas are dead!'"

When he received the news, Dhritarashtra
was torn, as always. Just as a deep pool
is chilly in its depths, warm on the surface,
so Dhritarashtra's heart was at the same time
hot with instant grief, and deeply cold.
He had not, quite, expected these events.
He and his sons cast off their royal robes
and carried out the proper funeral rites.
He ordered public mourning, kingdom-wide.
No outward show of sorrow was omitted.

9.

FLIGHT

In the forest, the six fugitives
were desperate to put the greatest distance
between them and their possible pursuers.
They ran as fast as they were able, wearily
trying to take their bearings from the stars,
impeded by the leafy canopy.

Nothing had prepared them for experience
this difficult. In Pandu's forest home
they had lived simply, but always had a roof,
plenty to eat, and the certainty
that all who knew them loved them. And at court
they had become accustomed to luxury.
Now all was stripped away. They were bereft
of all the clothing, weapons, pastimes, friendships
that told them who they were.

                      Hunger, thirst,
scratched flesh and bleeding feet afflicted them.
After a while, forest became thick jungle.
This was a threatening place, very different
from forests they had known and hunted in,
inflicting death for sport. Now it was they
whose skin prickled at the strange and menacing
sounds surrounding them. They had no way
of knowing fierce from friendly, friendliness

from mere indifference. Snared at every step
by twining roots and scrub, they had no notion
which plants and animals were safe to eat.

When they were dropping from exhaustion, Bhima,
powerful as an elephant, carried them.
He placed his mother on one brawny shoulder,
the twins rode on his hips, while Yudhishthira
and Arjuna were tucked under his arms.
Hour after hour, Wolf-belly forged ahead,
racing on as if with the wind behind him,
trampling, smashing every obstacle.

They entered a rank wilderness, infested
with slinking beasts and scrawny, raucous birds.
The trees were sparse, with gray and brittle leaves,
but they came across an arching banyan tree
and made a welcome stop under its roots.
All, except Bhima, fell asleep at once.
Bhima thought he heard the sound of herons
and followed it until he found a lake.
He drank long drafts, and bathed, then brought back water
for his family. He sat beside them
through the night, keeping watch, reflecting
on their misfortune: "Ah, my unlucky brothers
and my dear mother, used to comfort, now
stretched on the unyielding ground like beggars.
These vigorous vines and creepers all around
are struggling upward from impoverished soil,
helping each other climb toward the light.
Why is it, if these plants can coexist
in harmony, that all our pampered cousins
so strenuously seek to damage us
when we've done nothing wrong?" And he wept
for the suffering of Kunti and his brothers.

⚜

This jungle was home to a rakshasa,
Hidimba, a vile ogre, and his sister,
Hidimbaa. They were vampire bats writ large,
loathsome, yellow-eyed and tireless gluttons.
They would track and slaughter any animal,
drink its blood, gnaw raw flesh from the bones.
But what they relished above anything
was human meat. Now they were very hungry.
Prowling through the trees, the ogre picked up
the scent of the Pandavas, and growled with pleasure.
"Humans! My favorite! I long to sink my tusks
in their delicious flesh, slice their veins
and guzzle their rich, foaming blood. Hidimbaa,
go and find them, bring them here for me!"

Off went his sister, loping stealthily,
but one glimpse of Bhima, and she fell
besottedly, lustfully in love with him.
"Oh, what a gorgeous man, so strong and upright,
bulging in every place a man should bulge,
tall as a shala tree. Look at that neck!
Those lion-like shoulders! And what lovely eyes!
This is certainly the man for me.
He shall be my husband—and a wife's duty
overrides a sister's any day.
If I kill this family, my appetite
and my brother's will be satisfied
for a mere half hour. But if I marry
this delicious man, I will have pleasure
for years on end!"

                    Then, quicker than a blink
(for rakshasas can change their form at will),
she shed her hideous aspect and appeared
as a shapely girl, casting lascivious looks
at Bhima. She sidled up and stood beside him.
"Who on earth are you, you bull-like man?

And who are these other people, sleeping
on the ground so trustfully? I warn you,
a hungry rakshasa, my wicked brother,
wants to make a meal of you. But, darling,
I shall save you. My body and my heart
are mad with love for you. Be my husband,
and we shall fly to anywhere you choose.
The whole world shall be our paradise!"

"What kind of scoundrel would I be," said Bhima,
"if—alluring as you are, O luscious one—
I left my helpless mother and my brothers
to be gobbled by a ravenous rakshasa?"

"All right, I'll save you all," said Hidimbaa.
"Wake them up now. We can be on our way."
"I won't," said Bhima, "they deserve their rest.
No ill-tempered ogre can frighten me,
sweetheart. The same applies, my gorgeous girl,
to any man or monster on this earth.
Go, or stay, you sexy one—you choose.
But send that evil brother of yours to me."

Hidimbaa sent a signal to her brother
and, before long, the ugly rakshasa
came powering through the trees, sweating with rage
at how his sister had betrayed him, putting
such soppiness as love before a feast.
He had been looking forward to sweet blood,
and sucking brains from foolish human skulls.
"Have you lost your wits, stupid Hidimbaa?
You're a traitor to the race of rakshasas.
I'll kill you now, before I eat these others."

Bhima laughed. "You idiot, fight with me,
not with this woman who has done no wrong—
in fact, she has been wronged herself, smitten
by the god of love, when she saw my beauty!

Come on—fight! Today, you evil beast,
your body will be severed, head from trunk
and scavengers, not you, will eat their fill."

The monster gave a roar, insane with fury.
With claws and fangs and superhuman strength
he tore at Bhima, but he could not crush
the huge son of the wind. Bhima fought
with enormous relish, like a lion
tussling with its prey, dragging, shaking it
as though it were a game. And all the time
Hidimbaa was watching, breathless, weak with love.

At the noise, the others stirred from sleep
and were amazed to see the radiant girl.
"Who are you?" asked Kunti curiously.
"I am the sister of the rakshasa—
that flesh-eating monster over there,
being manhandled by your god-like son.
I have chosen Bhima as my husband—
I love him madly. I have to confess
I tried to get him to elope with me
but he refused to leave you unprotected.
Look at them now, rakshasa and human,
dragging each other through the dust!"

                              Arjuna
sprang up to help Bhima dispatch the monster
but Bhima wanted this to be his fight
and his alone; and, before too long,
the ogre was a mess of skin and blood
smeared on the forest floor. With his death,
birds sang more brightly, and the grayish trees
sprouted new green leaves and scented flowers.

What was to be done with Hidimbaa?
"Kill her," suggested Bhima, "rakshasas

bear grudges and resort to wicked magic."
Yudhishthira opposed him forcefully.
"Even if she is a rakshasa,
never kill a woman. It is contrary
to dharma—and what damage can she do?"
Hidimbaa spoke up. "I love your brother.
For his sake, I have betrayed my kin,
my friends, the code that governs rakshasas.
Am I to be rejected by you all
for having spoken truthfully? Have pity,
let Bhima love me, as I know he can.
You may think me foolish, but I promise
that I shall serve you—I can carry you,
all of you, over any obstacle.
Let me marry Bhima."

        Yudhishthira
softened toward her. "You can marry him,
and you can take him anywhere you wish.
But every day, at sunset, he must return
as we rely on him."

        Now Hidimbaa,
summoning her supernatural powers,
took Bhima off on blissful honeymoons
to secret places where time stopped for them
in their exquisite lovemaking. They traveled
to coral islands, sparkling mountaintops,
lovely glades where trees bent over them
heavy with ripe fruit. And, every night,
she brought him back to guard his family
where they had set up house, by a jungle pool.

Rakshasas give birth the very day
that they conceive, and Hidimbaa produced

a son by Bhima. He was huge and hairless.
"The child's bald as a pot," said Bhima proudly
and that became his name—Ghatotkacha.
He was an awesome sight: cross-eyed, large-mouthed,
beautifully ugly, with pointed ears
and terrifying tusks. In a few short weeks,
he grew up; it was as if he lived
in another time dimension. He became
mountainous, a master with all weapons,
devoted to truth. He loved the Pandavas
and they in turn adored him as their own.

The day arrived when Hidimbaa announced
the end of their idyllic time together.
Then she disappeared. Ghatotkacha
told his father he would always come
when he was needed. Then he too departed.
The Pandavas decided that they, also,
should seek a new life. They tied up their hair
like brahmin students, dressed themselves in deerskins
and, in this disguise, they traveled widely.
As they went, they studied the sacred Vedas
the better to conceal their identity.

Months passed by. One day the sage Vyasa,
the author of them all, arrived to see them.
As a seer, he knew the Pandavas
were alive and well. He spoke gently:
"I have long known the sons of Dhritarashtra
would try to rid themselves of you. Of course,
you and they are equally my kin.
But it is natural that I should favor you
since you are wronged, and living in penury."
Kunti poured out her sorrow, and Vyasa
listened. Worse than anything was knowing
that their own family desired their death.
That hurt her like a never-healing wound.

"Be assured that this distress will pass,"
Vyasa said. "Your son Yudhishthira
will rule the kingdom as the Dharma King.
But, for now, you must be patient. Listen,
near here is the town of Ekachakra.
You should live there quietly, as brahmins,
and wait for better times. I shall return."

Having left the seer, they made their way
toward the undistinguished, one-wheel town.

༄

Vyasa had arranged for them to live
as lodgers with a kind brahmin family,
a couple and their children. Every morning
the five young men collected the day's food,
going from house to house with begging bowls.

When the bowls were full, they hurried home
in case Duryodhana's spies should be around.
Kunti shared out the food—half for Bhima,
half for the rest of them. But even so,
Bhima grew thin, and was always hungry.

One afternoon, when Bhima was at home
keeping Kunti company, loud crying
came from the landlord's quarters. Kunti went in
and found the man lamenting to his wife:
"Since one of us must die, it should be I.
You have always been a loving wife,
dear to me as my friend, my great mainstay,
my children's mother—I can't let you die.
And how could I sacrifice my daughter?
Some say a father loves his son the most;
I don't. She is just as precious to me
as her brother. No, it should be I

who loses his life. But then—how will you all
survive without me to work and protect you?
Better we all die!" And the poor man
gave way to utter anguish.

                              His wife said,
"What is the use of all your education
if you collapse just like a common man
when you meet adversity? Everything ends;
and if an ending is inevitable
grief is pointless. I myself shall go.
A woman's task is always to defend
her husband's welfare, even with her life.
We both will gain great merit from my action.
You're able to protect and feed our children;
I can do neither. How can a widow manage?
How would I prevent unscrupulous men
from sniffing at our daughter? How would I teach
our son good conduct, without your example?
Our children would be left like two small fish
stranded on a dried-up riverbed.
You can find another mother for them;
that is lawful. For me, it is not the same.
My life has brought me happiness; I've borne
two lovely children by you. To die now
will not grieve me." And, with that, the husband
and wife embraced each other, sorrowfully.

But then the daughter spoke. "Listen to me.
I am the one whose life should be surrendered.
You have to lose me sometime—it's the custom
for a bride to live in her husband's house—
so why not now? A child should be like a boat
to save its parents—in life and afterlife.
By my death, I save my father's life
for, if Father dies, my little brother
will surely not survive. Then who will there be

to make the offerings to the ancestors?
Without me, there will still be a family.
As the saying goes, 'A daughter is a burden.'
Without you, Father, I shall be a wretched,
unprotected girl. Do the right thing.
Sacrifice me, who anyway will be
sacrificed sooner or later."

They all wept,
and the little boy, not understanding,
seized a stick and waved it joyfully.
"Me kill nasty monster!" he announced.

"What monster does he mean?" Kunti asked.
Then the landlord's wife told her their trouble.
"Our turn for death has come. There's no escape.
Baka, a rakshasa, lives in the hills
outside the town. We citizens are powerless.
There's just one way to stop him coming down
at will, and killing anyone he likes:
each week, a member of one family
loads up a bullock cart with food, and takes it
up to his lair. He eats the food, the bullocks
and the driver—but at least that buys
a blessed reprieve for the rest of us.
And now it is the turn of our family!
We've talked and talked about which of us should go,
but none of us can bear to lose each other.
The only answer is to die together."
And the poor woman began to shed fresh tears.

Kunti saw at once what could be done.
"You have only one son; I have five.
One of my sons will go on your behalf.
You've been so kind to us—it's only right
that we should show our gratitude."
"No! No!"

exclaimed the landlord. "I could not allow
a brahmin, a guest at that, to die for me,
however fond I am of my own life.
That would make me wickedly complicit
in brahmin murder."

                    "It won't come to that,"
said Kunti. "My son will kill this rakshasa.
He's done it before; he has special powers.
But you must promise not to say a word
lest people become curious." They agreed.

She put her plan to Bhima, who exulted
at the prospect of a square meal—and a fight!
Yudhishthira was appalled. "What mad idea
of duty led you to risk Bhima's life
when our entire survival rests on him?"
But Kunti was firm. She knew that she was right.

The women of the house prepared a cartload
of the most delicious rice and curries.
Bhima set out, driving the bullock cart
and singing loudly. Coming to the foothills,
he stopped and, with enormous appetite,
began to eat the provisions in the cart.
He sat there at his ease, munching peacefully,
and thought no meal could be more delectable,
though all the time the bullocks were bellowing
and straining at their ropes, sensing the presence
of something dreadful.

                    With a thunderous roar,
Baka lumbered out from among the trees,
a ten-foot ogre, filthy and obese,
murderous at seeing the empty cart.
He picked up boulders, throwing them at Bhima
who caught them, laughing, hurling them straight back.
Baka uprooted trees, and came at Bhima
howling curses. A furious tree-fight followed,

then they grabbed each other, and for hours
they wrestled, until Baka began to tire.
Then Bhima bent him backwards, and broke his spine
as one might snap kindling for firewood.
Ekachakra was safe from the rakshasa.

In the afternoon, the brahmin landlord found
his bullocks grazing peacefully, and Baka
a sprawling corpse on the outskirts of the town.
People were agog—who could have done it?
The landlord kept his promise not to tell.

卐

Weeks passed, and more weeks. Then one day, at dusk,
a mendicant came to the door. The landlord,
always hospitable, invited him
to shelter for the night. When he had bathed
and eaten, and all were gathered in the yard,
he began to tell them marvelous stories—
miracles he had seen at holy shrines,
amazing sights encountered on his journeys
throughout the land, from the Himalaya
down to Cape Comorin. "But I'm forgetting—
I'm really on a mission. King Drupada
has asked us wanderers to spread the word—
meant for the ears of one kshatriya.
His daughter Draupadi's svayamvara
is shortly to take place in Kampilya."

The mendicant then started on the story
of Drona and Drupada, and Drona's revenge;
and of how Drupada had then obtained
both a son and daughter, born from fire.
"The son is a fine young man, and Draupadi
is the most beautiful woman in the world."
All this the mendicant told his rapt audience.

A while later, Vyasa visited.
The brothers welcomed him with joined hands.
Having examined them on their behavior,
the blessed sage told them the following tale:

"THERE WAS ONCE a young woman, the daughter of a
distinguished seer. She was of excellent conduct but,
owing to some past action of hers, she was unfortunate in
love. Beautiful though she was, with narrow waist and curving hips, she did not find a husband.

"She embarked on a program of austerities with the aim
of achieving marriage, and impressed the god Shiva with her
extreme self-discipline.

"'Radiant maiden,' he said, 'choose a boon and I will
grant it.'

"'I want a virtuous husband,' said the girl. And, in her
eagerness to be understood, she said it again and again.

"'Dear girl, you shall have your five husbands,' said Shiva.

"'Oh no—I only want one,' she protested.

"'Well, you asked five times, and five husbands you shall
have, when you have been reborn in another body.'

"That maiden was eventually reborn
as the dark and beautiful Draupadi.
She is destined to become your wife."

He smiled, and disappeared. The Pandavas'
blood was racing with the fire of youth
imagining the dazzling Draupadi.
Kunti said, "It seems to me that fate
brought us here to rid the town of Baka.
But it's unwise to stay in one place too long.
Now, perhaps, we should be moving on."

Taking their leave of the brahmin family,
the Pandavas set out for Kampilya.

10.

DRAUPADI'S BRIDEGROOM CHOICE

They traveled southeast, frequently at night
to avoid notice, Arjuna leading them,
holding a firebrand.

           In a lonely spot
at a sacred ford on the river Ganga,
they disturbed the king of the gandharvas
as he sported with his apsarases.
At dusk, rivers belong to the gandharvas;
this was his private place, and he was furious.
"By what right" said Arjuna, "do you keep us
from the Ganga, which belongs to all?"
A fight followed. Arjuna let loose
the *Fire* weapon, and captured the gandharva,
burning up his beautiful chariot.

At Yudhishthira's request, Arjuna
spared his opponent's life and, in return,
he and the gandharva became allies,
exchanging gifts. The gandharva gave horses
of exceptional speed (though Arjuna
thought it wise to leave them behind for now)
and Arjuna presented the grateful king
with the *Fire* weapon. "Now I know who you are,"
said the king. "But let me advise you—
we would not have attacked you in this way

had you been traveling with a household priest
carrying the sacrificial fire
and the objects needed for oblations.
A king can never prosper without a priest."
"How should we find a priest?" asked Arjuna.
The gandharva suggested Dhaumya,
a most renowned scholar of the Vedas,
whose hermitage was nearby. So it was
that the wise Dhaumya became household priest
to the Pandavas, and remained so, lifelong.

☙

Kampilya was buzzing with preparation.
The Pandavas, still disguised as brahmins,
smeared with ash, barefoot, with heavy beards,
were lodging with a potter's family.
Every day, they walked around the city
with their begging bowls, separately, alert
for searching looks. But they noticed none.
Young brahmins, even with a proud demeanor,
attracted no attention—crowds of brahmins
had come to Kampilya, drawn by the prospect
of rich presents. Every evening, Kunti
shared out what the brothers had been given.

The city streets were jostling with strangers
from far and near. In every public space,
entertainers—jugglers, contortionists,
conjurors, dancers, all kinds of musicians—
scrambled for the most strategic pitch.

Gossip was rife. Who was the lucky suitor
who would prove brave and skilled enough to win
the dazzling Draupadi? Some imagined
a warrior of god-like looks and strength
sweeping down in a bejeweled chariot
to win his bride and carry her away.

At last, the auspicious day. The sky was brilliant.
Brahmins had consecrated the event.
Crowds of spectators, fizzing with excitement,
were pressing forward into the arena
where Draupadi's future would be decided.
Surrounded by tall mansions, glistening
white as the sunlit snows of the Himalaya,
and lavishly adorned with costly hangings,
the amphitheater was an impressive sight.

Now, from the massive entrance to the palace,
Draupadi, with her brother, Drishtadyumna,
walked slowly to the dais, head slightly bowed.
She was dressed in scarlet silk; her ornaments
were of the finest jewel-encrusted gold.
Her beauty made those who had never seen her
gasp—her skin with the sheen of a black pearl,
her lovely face, lustrous wavy hair,
her perfect body, fragrant as blue lotus;
while in her eyes, in her calm expression,
there was something that engendered awe.
Surely she was nervous? So much depended
on these few hours.

                Prince Dhrishtadyumna spoke.
"Warriors who are gathered here today
hoping to win the hand of Draupadi,
the task is this: a bow has been provided
together with five arrows. Overhead
is a revolving wheel and, higher still,
a small target. You have to string the bow,
and hit the target with each of the arrows,
aiming through the wheel. My sister, Draupadi,
will choose her husband from those who succeed."

The task had been devised by Drupada.
He was hoping, against all the odds,

that Arjuna might have survived the fire
and could be among the assembled warriors.
King Drupada had witnessed at first hand
what Arjuna could do. Still, he had kept
his great wish to himself. Now, he waited.

Dhrishtadyumna announced the contestants
by name and pedigree. Duryodhana
was here with Karna and Duhshasana
and several more of Dhritarashtra's sons;
Shalya, king of the Madras, with his sons;
Drona's son Ashvatthaman, Shakuni,
Shishupala, known as the Bull of Chedi;
Satyaki, and dozens of other champions
from the Vrishni clan—in sum, there were scores
of royal heroes. Under an ample awning
they sat in silence. Tension was palpable.

Inconspicuous among the brahmins,
the Pandavas were staring at Draupadi,
mesmerized. At a distance, Krishna,
prince of the Vrishnis, turned to Balarama,
his older brother: "Look at those brahmins—there."
Balarama looked; and smiled at Krishna.
Neither of them would compete that day.
Krishna knew why the Panchala princess
had come into the world—the same reason
as he himself: to be an instrument
for the deliverance of the suffering earth.
To carry out their part in the gods' design.

☙

The first contestant stepped up to the mark.
The bow provided had been specially made
for this occasion, crafted like bows of old
when men were men, and kshatriyas, demigods.

It was so stiff and heavy, few could lift it,
let alone string it and take aim with it.
Prince after prince made the attempt, but failed.
As they tried to bend the bow, it sprang back
flinging them to the ground, smashing their limbs.
They limped away, sore, angry and ashamed,
desire for Draupadi evaporated.
Duryodhana tried, so did his brothers,
but none could even begin to bend the bow.
Shishupala, a formidable warrior,
and his powerful friend Jarasandha
each made the attempt, but each of them
was flung onto his knees, humiliated.

Karna stepped forward. He, if anyone,
would have the necessary strength and, yes,
he grasped and bent the bow into a circle
and was about to string it, when he heard
Draupadi exclaim in a clear voice,
"I will not choose a suta for my husband!"
Karna laughed bitterly, laid down the bow
and, glancing at the sun, walked to his place.

Now you could hear a stirring in the stands,
a frisson of surprise. A young brahmin
was striding forward. Some people were scornful;
others said, "Nothing is impossible
to a brahmin of strict vows—and, besides,
that one has the stature of a god!"

Almost casually, as though the task
were child's play to him, the young man raised the bow,
strung it, and shot five arrows through the wheel.
They clustered close around the target's center;
with the fifth, the target fell to earth.
The contest was over. The crowd cheered and stamped.
A rain of flowers fell on the hero's head.

Draupadi took up the ritual garland
of white flowers, and walked toward the victor.
Smiling, she draped the garland round his neck.

Most spectators were happy that the princess
had such a worthy husband, even though
he was not the prince they naturally expected.
But there was uproar from the kshatriyas—
angry shouting from the Kauravas
and many others: "Drupada has cheated!
He has treated us with complete contempt
and broken the rules. The law is very clear—
only a kshatriya should have his daughter.
He should die!" Several of them surged forward
to kill the king. But Bhima and Arjuna
rushed to defend him. Bhima snatched up a tree,
stripped off the leaves and, swinging it like a club,
lunged like Death himself at furious Shalya,
king of the Madras. The assembled brahmins,
shaking their deerskins, banging their water pots,
were all for joining in, but Arjuna
waved them back, and drawing the mighty bow
with which he had won Draupadi, he entered
into the affray.

                    "So, we were right,"
said Krishna to his brother Balarama.
"Those brahmins are, indeed, the Pandavas."
"Oh, what a joy," exclaimed Balarama,
"that the sons of Kunti, our father's sister,
are alive after all!"

                         Meanwhile, the mayhem
continued. The uneventful brahmin life
the Pandavas had led for so many months
had left them hungry for action. Arjuna
found himself fighting against Karna,

Karna not recognizing his opponent.
Arjuna rejoiced to have the chance
to test his warrior's skill against the man
who had caused him shame at the tournament.

They fought like gods. All the other warriors
dropped their weapons so they could observe
the well-matched pair, the lightning exchange
of arrows, the whirling bodies, dancing feet.
This was a duel, but also an expression
of the highest art, and each great archer
was exhilarated by the other's skill.
"Are you the Art of Archery incarnate?"
asked Karna. "I am not," replied Arjuna,
"I am a brahmin, adept at the astras,
master of the divine *Brahma* weapon,
and I shall defeat you. Fight on, hero!"

But Karna withdrew, unwilling to oppose
brahminic power. The brawl started up again—
Bhima against Shalya, pounding each other
like two great elephants in rut. The battle
was starting to turn ugly. And then Krishna
intervened with diplomatic words:
"The bride was righteously and fairly won;
this fighting is unseemly." Reluctantly,
still unappeased, the kshatriyas turned away
and set out on the journey to their kingdoms.

༄

Kunti had stayed at home, restless, enduring,
hour after hour, that dull anxiety
so familiar to mothers everywhere.
She thought of everything that was at stake,
and of the dangers. At last, she heard her sons'
voices in the yard. "Mother! Mother!

we have brought back largesse!"
                                    "Then, my dears,
you will share it equitably between you,"
called Kunti. Then they walked in with Draupadi!

Kunti was startled; then she was overjoyed
and she and Draupadi embraced each other.
But then she wrung her hands. "Oh! I just said
you must share whatever you were bringing.
But how can you share Draupadi without
breaching dharma? Yet, if you don't, my words
will be a lie." The brothers became silent.
Their mother's word was always absolute—
what could they do? They talked into the night,
and as they talked, glancing at Draupadi,
all five brothers fell in love with her.

Suddenly, Yudhishthira remembered
the story told them by the wise Vyasa.
Of course—to avoid making their mother
a liar, they should *all* marry Draupadi.
A heaven-sent solution! Up to now,
nothing had come between the Pandavas;
the marriage of one could have bred jealousy
among the rest. And though Arjuna had won
the Panchala princess, he should not marry
before Yudhishthira, his eldest brother.
When Draupadi looked at these five heroes,
each wonderful in his own way, she knew
the gods had given her a fivefold blessing.

ॐ

Krishna and Balarama came to see them
(the first time the cousins had met each other)
and wished them all good fortune. The young men
were delighted. "But how did you know us,"

asked Yudhishthira, "disguised as we are?"
Krishna smiled. "Who but the Pandavas
would look so powerful and so dignified?
But we should not stay now." And they took their leave.
Dhrishtadyumna, watching secretly,
was now convinced that the brothers were, indeed,
the Pandavas, and went to tell his father.
The king rejoiced. His hopes had been fulfilled:
the brave young brahmin really was Arjuna!

Next day, Drupada sent a splendid chariot
to bring the Pandavas to the royal palace
where they declared their true identities.
He asked the brothers how they had escaped
the dreadful fire, and what had happened since.
The story took some time. Drupada smiled.
"Now you need have no worries—all my wealth
and my fine army is at your disposal.
You will certainly regain your kingdom.
The Kauravas will not oppose you, now
our dynasties are to be joined by marriage."

But five husbands! There he drew the line.
A kshatriya could marry several wives,
that was normal, but he had never heard
of one woman having many husbands.
It was not right. It was at odds with dharma.
Yudhishthira referred to well-known stories
where rishis—not offenders against dharma,
but holy men—had shared the same woman.
"That may be well for brahmins," said Drupada,
"but not for us. How can I give my daughter,
my dark flower, princess of Panchala,
to *five* husbands, and still preserve her honor?"

At this point, Vyasa was announced,
timely as ever. Drupada turned to him,

"Muni, knower of minds, I need your wisdom,"
and he told Vyasa of the strange proposal.
Vyasa took the king to a private room.
"Drupada," said Vyasa, "it is true
that such a thing is rare in recent times.
But in a nobler age, it was quite common.
And the marriage of your fire-born daughter
to these five brothers, was long ago ordained
by Shiva."

Then Vyasa told the story:

"THE GODS WERE once performing a sacrifice in the Nai-misha Forest. Yama, god of death, was fully occupied with sacrificial duties, and had no time to attend to the death of creatures. So human beings lived on and on, and the earth was becoming overcrowded. The immortal gods went to Brahma and complained that nothing now distinguished them from men.

"'Rest assured,' said Brahma, 'that as soon as the sacrifice is over, Yama will resume normal activity and people will die as they always have.'

"The gods returned to the sacrifice, and Indra, chief of gods, noticed a woman washing herself in the Ganga. She was weeping and, as she wept, each tear became a golden lotus that floated on the water.

"'Who are you,' he asked, 'and why are you weeping?'

"'I will show you—come with me,' she said. She led him to a nearby place where a youth was sitting playing dice, so utterly engrossed in the game that he took no notice when Indra spoke to him.

"'Pay attention when I speak to you!' said Indra, 'Don't you know that I am the chief of gods?'

"The youth smiled and glanced at Indra who became paralyzed immediately, for the youth was none other than the great lord Shiva. When he had finished his game, he told the woman to touch Indra, who collapsed on the ground.

" 'You need to be taught a lesson for your overweening pride,' said Shiva. 'Move that great boulder to one side and enter the cave that you will find behind it.' Trembling with fear, Indra did so and, imprisoned in the cave, he found four other Indras exactly like himself.

"The five Indras begged Shiva to set them free. 'You will recover your celestial status,' said Shiva, 'but only after you have been born in the world of mortals.' The Indras asked that they should at least have gods as their fathers. 'Let the gods Dharma, Vayu, Indra and the Ashvins be our begetters.' Shiva agreed to this, and so it was that five remarkable sons were born to Pandu. Shiva also decreed that Shri, goddess of royal fortune, would be their shared wife in the world of men.

"Supreme Vishnu approved this arrangement. He plucked from his own head one white hair and one black hair, and placed them in human wombs. These were born as Krishna and Balarama.

"So, you see," said Vyasa to Drupada,
"what seems to you contrary to dharma
is, in fact, celestially ordained."
Drupada gave in. "If the great Shiva
himself has blessed this marriage, my clear duty
is to make it possible." So it was
that Draupadi became the willing bride
of all five brothers. On successive days,
in order of their age, they married her.
And it is said that, for each one of them,
she came as a virgin to the bridal bed.

⚜

Drupada, having overcome his scruples,
exulted in the fortune that had brought him
five great sons-in-law instead of one.
He gave them all spacious living quarters

and every luxury and entertainment.
Krishna and Balarama spent time with them
and the cousins became deeply attached.
Krishna and Arjuna, in particular,
developed a profound friendship.

                The brothers
were happy in Kampilya. But very often
their thoughts would travel to Hastinapura.
Sitting together in the cool of evening
they wondered what Duryodhana was planning.
They knew their cousin, knew only too well
his vengeful, proud and avaricious nature.
But they had found safety with Drupada
and, though it could not last, although they felt
they would grow slack without the discipline
and challenges that came with their heritage,
they gave themselves, for now, to the delight
of family, of friendship and of love.

11.

ACQUIRING A KINGDOM

By the time Duryodhana and Karna
arrived back in Hastinapura, the news
had flown before them, as great news often does,
mysteriously, as if borne on the wind.
Vidura, filled with joy, informed the king.
At first, Dhritarashtra misunderstood,
and thought it was his son, Duryodhana,
who had triumphed at the svayamvara.
Put right by his brother, the king exclaimed,
"This is a great day—my beloved nephews
alive and well! And beautiful Draupadi
the bride of all five! What great happiness!
What a triumph for the Bharatas!
Drupada will be a splendid ally."
"May you hold this view for a hundred years!"
said Vidura; and he went to his own house.

Duryodhana harangued his smiling father.
"How can you talk like that to Vidura?
This disaster could eliminate us
yet you unctuously praise our enemies!
Somehow, they managed to escape the fire;
the consequence—we're objects of suspicion
having reaped no benefit. My cousins
will never be content to cool their heels
at Kampilya. They must want to see
Yudhishthira enthroned in Hastinapura.

"My son," said the king, "it seemed diplomatic
to say to Vidura what he wants to hear,
not to show, by a single muscle's twitch,
my real emotion. Be sure I share your worries.
Now tell me—what do you and Karna think
we should do? What is our best way forward?"

Duryodhana had thought of little else
as he was traveling back from Kampilya.
He had a dozen proposals. "How about
stirring up rivalry between Kunti's sons
and Madri's twins? Or, what if we employ
courtesans to seduce them, so Draupadi
gets jealous? Or convince them that our army
is so powerful they wouldn't stand a chance?
Or we could bribe Drupada with mounds of wealth.
Or, best of all, kill Bhima—set a trap for him.
Without Bhima, they would be half as strong . . ."

To all of this, Karna and Dhritarashtra
listened, unimpressed. "Duryodhana,"
said Karna, "such tricks never would succeed.
The Pandavas would see through all of them.
The best way forward is the most direct.
We should act swiftly, before Drupada
has a chance to marshal his fighting force.
A surprise attack, before Krishna's army
of Yadavas can reach Kampilya,
will strike a double blow—we will be able
to crush both Pandavas and Panchalas.
We have outstanding warriors in our army;
there's our own prowess, and that of your brothers.
We'll win! Let's defeat them in open battle
and live cleanly, without self-reproach.
That is the honorable way."

The king
reflected. "Your plan does you credit, Karna,
but to go down that road, Bhishma, Vidura
and the council must support you. I myself
have to remain neutral at this stage."

In the great council chamber, ministers
and gray-haired elders gathered for the debate.
Some younger men had also recently
joined the council: cronies of Duryodhana,
several of his brothers and loyal Karna.
First, Dhritarashtra asked for Bhishma's view.
The patriarch rose slowly to his feet.
His tone was equable, but no one doubted
the strength of his opinion. "Dhritarashtra,
you are my much-loved nephew, as was Pandu.
Your sons, and his, have grown up at this court
under my care. I never could support
a war between them. My life is devoted
to the advancement of the Bharatas.
That is why I solemnly say to you
the time has come for justice to be done,
or destiny will turn against this kingdom."

He turned to Duryodhana, knowing well
how influenced the king was by his son.
"The Pandavas have given no offense;
rather, it is they who have been injured.
Yudhishthira's the eldest; there's no question
that he's the rightful heir. But it is clear
that you and your brothers, Duryodhana,
will never live in peace under his rule.

"What I propose, therefore, is that the kingdom
should be divided equally. Agree,

and the deadly conflict, foretold for this clan
and the entire land of Bharatavarsha,
can be averted. You know, a man dies
not only when the last breath leaves his body
but when his precious honor is corrupted.
The people blamed you for your cousins' deaths.
You are fortunate—this is a chance
for you to return to the path of dharma
and to redeem yourself in the people's eyes.
If you respect dharma, if you desire
my blessing, if you want security,
then, O prince, relinquish half the kingdom."

Drona spoke up, agreeing, and the other
elders were signifying their assent, when—
"No!" cried Karna, leaping to his feet,
"Sir, this plan is a sludgy compromise.
Bhishma speaks the language of morality,
but I suspect mere prudence is behind it,
cowardice, even. It is no solution.
Mine is the path of honor—let us attack!
Let us protect ourselves preemptively.
Let us win glory for the Kauravas!"

The king's brother, Vidura, stood up.
Dhritarashtra turned his sightless eyes
toward him. Vidura, more than anyone,
was his conscience. "My brother, ignore Karna.
Your nephews are unbeatable in battle.
They have Krishna as their friend and ally
and where Krishna is, there will victory be.
Bhishma and Drona are unmatched in this hall,
or anywhere, for wisdom and experience;
listen to what they say. Right's on their side.
So are your interests. Did I not tell you,
long ago, that this noble lineage
would come to grief because of Duryodhana?

If you listened to the people, you would know
how low you stand in popular esteem,
how they suspect you of complicity
in the tragic blaze at Varanavata."

Dhritarashtra's spirits plummeted;
he feared the people. He made up his mind.
"I have decided. Yudhishthira should have
half the kingdom. That is the fair solution,
as Bhishma and the elders have proposed."

He asked Vidura to travel to Kampilya,
taking lavish gifts. He was to urge
his nephews to return to Hastinapura
as soon as possible, bringing Draupadi.

At Kampilya, Vidura was received
with honor and affection. Without him,
the Pandavas would certainly have died.
Courteously, he conveyed Dhritarashtra's
greetings, and his warm congratulations.
Krishna smiled. The brothers waited warily
for what their uncle Vidura would say.
"The king has asked me to impart his wish
that you should come home to Hastinapura
with your bride. The people long to see you—
as does he. He says he cannot be happy
without embracing his beloved nephews."

Yudhishthira was caught in painful doubt.
How could he trust the king, and Duryodhana?
On the other hand, to spurn the wishes
of his uncle, to show such disrespect,
was not in his nature. "Sir," he said,
turning to his royal father-in-law,

"What is your view? I shall do what you advise."
Drupada hesitated. Courtesy
forbade him to suggest that his guests depart.

"I think you should go to Hastinapura,"
Krishna said, his eye upon the future,
"and I will go too, to ensure your safety."
Kunti was worried, but Vidura assured her
Dhritarashtra, at least, had learned his lesson.
He would never dare to touch the Pandavas
knowing how the people felt about them—
and about him.

                    So the entourage set out,
accompanied by a large, well-armed escort,
for Hastinapura, City of the Elephant.

ॐ

Never, in its very long history,
had the city seen such celebrations.
On the day the brothers were expected,
every gate and arch was garlanded,
every window hung with colored flags,
streets were swept, washed, strewn with lotus petals,
the scent of incense wafted everywhere.
Since dawn, people had milled about the streets,
and many had walked out of the city gate,
laden with flowers, to meet the homecomers.
And when, at last, they spotted the procession,
the princes on horseback, the royal palanquin
carrying the women, fervent cheers,
braying trumpets, drumrolls, booming conches,
shook the very stones, and made white flocks
of doves rise up, clattering into air
as if they too could not contain their joy.

Like a long wave breaking on the shore,
there was a collective sigh of pleasure
when Draupadi stepped from her palanquin.
How beautiful she was, how suitable
as their princes' bride. And how wonderful
would be their future children.

                 Dhritarashtra
was waiting on the palace steps to welcome
his nephews and their bride.

                 After some days,
the king summoned them to his apartments
and made a grave pronouncement. "My dear nephews,
the prosperity of our noble kingdom
owes a great deal to your father, Pandu,
and to you, of course. Yet, to my sorrow,
you and Duryodhana are constantly
in conflict with each other. I have decided
to put an end to all this disagreement—
the kingdom will be split in half exactly.
You, Yudhishthira, will become king
of one half, and rule from Khandavaprastha.
I myself will continue to rule from here
until such time as Duryodhana
takes on the burden of the monarchy.
This should delight you all—Yudhishthira
will be a king at once, as he deserves."

There was silence. Everybody knew
about the Khandava tract. A barren region,
it was a wilderness of arid scrub
and dense forest, inhospitable country
very different from the delightful plain
whose fertile fields nourished Hastinapura.

Although Yudhishthira could clearly see
that he was being banished, he accepted
Dhritarashtra's plan with dignity.

Duryodhana would never be reconciled
to what he saw as cowardly concession
to the Pandavas. Both he and Karna
bitterly regretted they had been stopped
from riding against Kampilya with their troops.
Bhima, too, would have relished battle.
But he deferred to Yudhishthira
as the eldest. And, now, as his king.

Yudhishthira himself had thought carefully.
There was no future for the Pandavas
at Hastinapura; that he understood.
A life of indolence at Kampilya
was no existence for a kshatriya.
As for the other option—all-out war
against the Kauravas—Yudhishthira
had always treated his uncle with respect,
like a father; he saw that as his duty.
And, unlike most young warriors of his rank,
Yudhishthira had never yearned for battle
for its own sake. Though he was not afraid
to fight, if fighting was the only way,
he did not crave the feverish rush of combat.
In fact, bloodshed made him sorrowful.
So, heartened by knowing that his dark cousin
Krishna would go with them, Yudhishthira
prepared himself for taking on the challenge
of his new kingdom in the wilderness.

Vyasa traveled with them, and performed
the rituals to consecrate the ground.

In time, in that place of devastation,
a large and splendid city rose. They named it
Indraprastha. First, robust, high walls
were built, surrounded by a sparkling moat.
The city gates, deterring all intruders,
were massive, shaped like soaring eagles' wings,
and flanked by sturdy towers, well stocked with weapons.
Inside Indraprastha, streets and avenues
were spaciously laid out, all lined with buildings
of different kinds, that shone white in the sun,
like mountain peaks. The palace of the king
was beautiful beyond compare, and furnished
with every luxury.

          Around the city
were tranquil parks and gardens, planned and planted
with arbors, cooling fountains, lily ponds
and many kinds of tree and flowering shrub—
kadamba, jasmine, mango and rose apple
and others too numerous to name—so all
who strolled there could enjoy bright, scented flowers
and luscious fruit at all times of the year.
Peacocks picked their way beneath the trees
which were a haven for melodious birds.

The city prospered. Drawn by reports of it,
and by their loyalty to Yudhishthira,
people came from all over the kingdom
to live there, bringing with them their hard work
and talents—worthy merchants, shopkeepers,
brahmins, accomplished craftsmen of every kind.
Because Yudhishthira was just and honest
and was concerned with the welfare of his people,
the population lived by his example.

Once he saw Indraprastha flourishing,
Krishna, having other obligations,

departed, to return to Dvaraka,
his city by the sea. The Pandavas
consented, but were sorry to see him go.
Krishna was their mainstay and their guide.

ॐ

A visitor arrived at Indraprastha.
It was Narada, great and subtle seer,
traveler in the worlds of gods and men.
A holy busybody, he enjoyed
stirring the stockpot of the status quo,
creating complications, making trouble
challenging what people took for granted,
but in the interests of what was best.
He was an ally of Narayana,
expert in human nature. And in fact
Krishna had asked him to visit Indraprastha.

Yudhishthira bent to wash his holy feet
and made him sit down in a place of honor.
Then the brothers sat around him, listening
to stories of his endless wanderings.
They talked of this and that, then Draupadi
was brought before him to receive his blessing.
After she left, Narada looked troubled.
"Your queen is so lovely, she reminds me
of the tale of Sunda and Upasunda."
"Who are they?" asked Bhima. "Not are—were.
They're dead," said Narada. The Pandavas
urged the seer to tell them the whole story.

"SUNDA AND UPASUNDA were celestial asuras. They were brothers, and completely devoted to one another, sharing everything they possessed.

They decided that they would conquer the universe and, to this end, they embarked on a life of extreme austerities.

They ate and drank nothing, living on air. Dressed in bark, covered with filth, they stood with their arms raised, balancing on their toes, not blinking. Their discipline was so extraordinary that the gods became afraid, and tried to distract them with various temptations. But without success.

Such was their extreme asceticism that the brothers were granted a boon by Lord Brahma. They would become adept at magic, powerful in weapons and able to change their form at will. They asked him, in addition, that they should become immortal. He refused, but granted them this: that they could be killed by no one, and nothing, except each other.

Sunda and Upasunda then went on the rampage. Ruthless, and lacking all respect, they slaughtered all who crossed their path—kings, brahmins, snakes, barbarians and even celestial beings. The gods ran to Brahma, begging him to save them.

Brahma summoned Vishvakarman, the divine craftsman, and asked him to make a woman of unsurpassed beauty. Vishvakarman assembled all the world's most beautiful materials, and created a woman so lovely that even the gods caught their breath in wonder. Her name was Tilottama and Brahma instructed her to go to where the brothers were, and seduce them.

Having conquered the earth, the brothers had settled in Kurukshetra, living a life of utter depravity and self-indulgence. Bleary with drink, when they set eyes on Tilottama, provocatively dressed in a single red garment, each of them claimed her as his alone—even though they had always shared everything. They set about fighting each other with vicious clubs and, before long—both lay dead."

There was a shocked silence. Narada
allowed his cautionary tale to sink in.
For the Pandavas, brotherhood was sacred,
and had been so from their earliest childhood
in the forest. Though different characters,
Kunti had taught them never to allow

anything to sow dissent between them.
But one wife between five strong young men!
One wife, whose beauty and intelligence
they all adored! It was a real test.
Maybe there were times when the strong ties
between the brothers stretched a little thin?

"Think," said Narada, "how Duryodhana
would exult if the five of you fell out.
You would be doing him the greatest favor—
not that I'm suggesting my sad story
could apply to you in any way.
Nevertheless, you should guard yourselves."

Chastened, the Pandavas made a covenant:
if any of them should, by accident,
observe one of the others as he lay
with Draupadi, then the offending brother
would serve time as a celibate, in exile.

ॐ

In their splendid city, the Pandavas
were as happy with their noble wife
as was she, with her heroic husbands.
Then, one morning, Arjuna heard shouts.
An old brahmin was pacing up and down
in fury. "What's the world coming to
when peaceful men can have their cattle taken
and royalty does nothing to put it right,
but lies around, dreaming in indolence!
Why is no one chasing the wicked thieves?
Isn't that your job?" and the old man
began to hobble away in disgust.

Arjuna ran after him, "Just wait
until I fetch my bow." He knew his weapons

were in the chamber where Yudhishthira
and Draupadi were spending time together.
But he must help the brahmin; royal dharma
required it. He rushed into the apartment,
grabbed the bow and arrows and rode off
in pursuit of the thieves. He scattered them
with a stream of well-aimed arrows, and returned
the stolen cattle to the grateful brahmin.
Then he presented himself before the king.
"Brother, I shall now go into exile,
in accordance with our covenant."
Yudhishthira protested—Draupadi
and he had not been offended in the least.
It was no sin for a younger brother
to invade the privacy of the older.
Exile was unnecessary.

        But Arjuna
insisted. "Dharma has to be respected;
you yourself have taught me that one should not
try shiftily to dodge round its requirements.
We all agreed on what should happen now.
I shall embrace exile for a time."

12.

ARJUNA'S EXILE

Never, in all his life, had Arjuna
been separated from his family.
He would return to them in time. But meanwhile
the world was large, and offered new encounters.

He traveled widely, seeking holy places
on sacred rivers. From time to time, he stayed
in forest ashrams, learning all he could
from wise teachers. He was accompanied
by an entourage of learned brahmins
and they journeyed north to where the Ganga,
taking birth in the snow-peaked Himalaya,
leaps over rocks and tumbles to the plain.
There, he settled for a while.

                        One day,
as Arjuna was bathing in the river,
offering oblations to his ancestors,
he was seized, and pulled beneath the water
by Ulupi, beautiful snake princess.
She whisked him off to the kingdom underground
where snakes live amid sacrificial fires.
She wound herself around him tenderly.
"As soon as I caught sight of you, the love god
churned me with desire. Ah, make me happy,
handsome hero of the Bharatas!"

Arjuna hesitated. "Enchanting one,
I am committed to a celibate life
during my exile; I cannot break my vow.
Believe me—I would truly like to please you . . .
But how can I, without transgressing dharma?"
"Surely your vow," said sensuous Ulupi,
"relates to Draupadi, not other women.
Remember too—the highest form of duty
is to preserve life. And, rest assured,
I shall die unless you slake my thirst."
His course was clear. Arjuna passed the night
in pleasure with the sinuous snake princess,
and returned at sunrise to his lodging.

♣

Soon after this, Arjuna left the mountains
and traveled southeast toward Manalura.
There, he called on King Chitravahana,
an ally of the Bharatas. The king
had a nubile daughter, Chitrangadaa,
plump and graceful. Arjuna desired her.
He spoke to the girl's father. The king said,
"You need to understand: in our line,
in each generation, just one child is born.
Mine is a girl, but I am treating her
as a son for purposes of descent.
You may marry her on one condition:
father a son on her, who will belong
not to you, but to our lineage."

Arjuna acquiesced. Then, after staying
with Chitrangadaa for the next three months,
he continued touring the sacred fords.
Most holy sites thronged with devout pilgrims
bathing, praying, offering oblations,
but he was told of one that was deserted

although it was quite beautiful, with trees,
graceful as dancers, shading the riverbank.
Ascetics told him: lurking in the water
were five huge crocodiles, who were inclined
to make a meal of bathers. Undeterred,
Arjuna dived in and, straight away,
was clamped between the jaws of a great beast.
He wrestled with it, thrashing, twisting, churning,
then managed to stand, holding it in the air.
That instant, it became a lovely woman.
Arjuna was astonished. "Beautiful one,
who are you? And, tell me, why this wickedness,
attacking innocent and pious bathers?"

She explained she was an apsaras,
one of five, as alluring as each other,
who had been cursed by a virtuous brahmin
for trying to seduce him. "Narada
told me you would be traveling nearby
and would help us." The Pandava released
the other nymphs from their curse in the same way.

Then Arjuna returned to Chitrangadaa
to see Babhruvahana, his newborn son.

☙

Despite his energetic pilgrimage,
Arjuna knew that his true destiny
would not be one of wandering the world.
A kshatriya was meant to live a life
as a man of action, and in time
he would rejoin his brothers. But for now
he was free to travel as he wished.
He headed southward, to Cape Comorin,
the tip of the subcontinent, the place
where Hanuman once leaped across the sea
to Lanka. There, he immersed himself at dawn

and at sunset, standing with folded hands,
bowing in homage to the god of light.

Eventually, he turned his footsteps north.
He followed the line of the Western Ghats,
along deserted beaches. As he traveled
the season was changing: the time of monsoon
had arrived. The air was still and heavy
with expectation, earth begging for rain
as though the whole of life were in suspense.

Then the weather broke. First came the wind
whipping the sea to frothy peaks and troughs,
bullying the trees to bow before it.
Then the rain: a few large drops at first
followed by blue forked lightning, which lit up
the lashing sea; and then the deafening crash,
the cannonades of thunder so explosive
it was as if immortal gods were battling
for supremacy. The black clouds burst,
the long-awaited rain swept down in sheets
pounding, sluicing over the thirsty land.
Everything that lived opened itself
to the reviving torrent.

                Krishna learned
that Arjuna was close to Dvaraka
and went to meet him. The two friends rejoiced
to see each other, and Arjuna agreed
to spend time at Dvaraka as Krishna's guest.
Entering the city with his friend,
Arjuna was welcomed by a throng
of citizens, all eager to set eyes
on the handsome and illustrious Pandava.

One day, the cousins went to a festival
and, strolling among the crowds, Arjuna
caught sight of a fair-skinned and graceful girl

in the company of her maids. Krishna
looked at Arjuna, smiling his mocking smile.
"Dressed as you are, in a simple robe,
you look the image of a pious pilgrim.
But are your thoughts really a pilgrim's thoughts?"
He always knew what Arjuna was thinking.
"That is my sister, the gentle Subhadra,
favorite daughter of the king, my father."

Arjuna was desperate to marry her.
How could it be achieved? In Krishna's view
a svayamvara would be too uncertain
in its outcome. Instead, Krishna proposed
that his friend should carry the girl away.
Messengers were sent to Yudhishthira
who consented to the cousins' plan.

So it happened. On a favorable day,
Arjuna seized the beautiful Subhadra
and galloped off with her in Krishna's chariot.
Balarama, Krishna's older brother,
was outraged. "The man has insulted us,
grossly abused our hospitality
after we received him with every honor!"

"My dear brother," said Krishna, "think about it.
There's no sign that Subhadra was unwilling
and, after all, she's gone off with the noblest
kshatriya in the land. To seize her by force
accords well with our warrior tradition.
There's great advantage for us in this match.
Who would not be proud of an alliance
with that hero? The pair should be followed
and brought back for a ceremonial wedding.
Diplomacy is all—we would lose face
if it looked as though he had defeated us."
Once he had calmed himself, Balarama
saw the force of Krishna's argument.

Next day, the couple was escorted back
and, with the blessing of her family,
Subhadra, lovely Yadava princess,
was married to the Bharata prince, Arjuna.
The people of Dvaraka were delighted
to have their princess joined in matrimony
to such a legendary kshatriya.

☙

The time of exile was almost at an end.
Family feeling, strongest of all ties,
was tugging at the heart of Arjuna,
and soon the wedded couple said goodbye
to Dvaraka and, with their retinue,
made their way northeast to Indraprastha.
No doubt there would be great celebrations
at Arjuna's return. But how would Draupadi—
Draupadi, adored princess of Panchala,
called the most beautiful woman in the world—
how would the fiery queen of the Pandavas
receive Subhadra? Though she had five husbands
Arjuna was the brother who had won her.
A great deal would depend on the first meeting.

In proper order, Arjuna paid reverence
to Yudhishthira his king, to the brahmins
and to his other brothers. He presented
Subhadra to his mother, who was pleased
that Arjuna had married her young niece.
Then, he went to Draupadi's apartments.
Haughty, she turned away: "Go to that woman!
Things are changed between us. I'm well aware
that the first knot tied loosens most easily."
Arjuna tried to soothe and reassure her
but after angry looks and proud reproaches,
she swept off into an inner room.

Arjuna, dismayed, spoke to Subhadra.
"Go to Draupadi alone, dressed simply,
not like a queen. Just be your natural self
and I'm sure her heart will warm to you."
Subhadra put on simple peasant clothes
and presented herself with her head bowed
at Draupadi's apartments. "I am Subhadra,
I will be your servant." Draupadi,
softened by the girl's sincerity,
embraced her, appreciating her beauty—
as different from the way she looked herself
as is the moon compared to the velvet dark.
She took Subhadra's hand. "At least," she said,
"may your *husband* never have a rival."
And Subhadra replied, "Let it be so."

༄

Shortly after Arjuna's homecoming
a party arrived from sea-set Dvaraka:
Krishna, Balarama and companions,
come to mark the auspicious alliance
between their clan and that of the Pandavas.
They had brought most sumptuous wedding gifts—
priceless silks, sacks of gold and jewels,
a thousand chariots, hung with little bells,
four thousand horses, ten thousand fine cattle,
a thousand tame mules, speedy as the wind,
some with black manes, some with white, a thousand
choice-bred mares, a thousand fine elephants
trained for battle, their howdahs bright with gold.

Yudhishthira acknowledged the largesse
and gave gifts in return. The visitors
stayed on as guests for many days, and Bhima,
the world's greatest host, arranged such feasts,
such lavish entertainment, such excursions

that the Yadavas, returned to Dvaraka,
probably felt life was rather dull!
But Krishna stayed behind at Indraprastha
and the Pandavas derived great joy
from having their cousin with them for a while.

ॐ

There followed happy years at Indraprastha.
Many other rulers were defeated
by the Pandavas, and their lands annexed.
The population prospered and increased.
King Yudhishthira rejoiced in action
that served the people and his kinsmen too—
he saw no conflict. And his contented subjects
worshiped him as their kind and splendid king.

Subhadra bore a son by Arjuna,
Abhimanyu. From his infancy,
he was Krishna's favorite, affectionate,
quick-witted, mettlesome as a young bull,
loved by all, as a bright star is loved.
Krishna oversaw his initiation.
He would be an exceptional warrior.

Draupadi too gave birth to five strong sons
a year apart, one son by each husband.
Like their fathers, these five boys grew up
devoted to each other. They excelled
to differing degrees, in Vedic knowledge,
and in the arts of war taught by Arjuna.

All seemed perfect in the Pandava kingdom.
Only Krishna, who was a frequent guest,
knew of the trials his beloved cousins
would have to undergo before too long.

13.

THE BURNING OF
THE KHANDAVA FOREST

One day in high summer, when the air
seemed to scorch the skin, and every breath
was an effort, Arjuna proposed
that there should be a grand expedition
to the countryside. It would be cool
under the trees on the shady riverbank.
Arrangements were made. With family and friends,
together with a retinue of cooks,
maids and other servants, they left the city
in palanquins, in chariots, on horseback;
dozens of carts were piled with the provisions
Bhima thought essential for their needs.

Encamped beside the sparkling Yamuna,
some plunged into the refreshing water;
some played games, others brought out flutes,
drums and vinas, and there was dance and song.
Needless to say how plentiful and varied
the food was, how delectable the drink.

Krishna and Arjuna walked off by themselves
among the trees, talking, reminiscing.
They were enjoying each other's company,
seated at their ease in a pleasant grove,
when they were approached by a strange brahmin.
He towered above them, tall as a shala tree.

His hair and beard were red, his skin coppery,
and he was radiant as the morning sun,
blazing with glory. The two kshatriyas
stood up to honor him.

                  "I see," he said,
"the world's greatest heroes standing before me.
I beg you—give me enough to eat. I'm starving."
Arjuna said, "We'll fetch you food, enough
and more than you can possibly consume."
"It is not food I want," said the stranger.
"I am Agni. I am Fire itself.
This Khandava Forest is the feast I crave,
but every time I try to gobble it
with my fiery mouth, Indra sends bank on bank
of voluminous black thunderclouds,
dousing the flames with deluges of rain,
frustrating my voracious appetite.
He does it to protect his friend—the snake,
Takshaka, whose home is in this forest.
But now I have met you, I shall succeed.
I know your mastery of every weapon—
come to my aid! Fend off Indra's rain clouds;
prevent the million creatures of the forest
from escaping death."

                The god of fire
was in poor health, suffering from a surfeit
of clarified butter, which had ceaselessly
been poured into him, in sacrifices
sponsored by an overzealous king.
He had been told that only by consuming
fat from the creatures of the Khandava
would he be cured.

               "It's true," said Arjuna,
"that we know how to summon divine weapons,

but we have come here on a pleasure outing—
we have no bows, or quivers, and have only
ordinary chariots and horses.
If I am to help you as you wish
I need a bow commensurate with my strength,
an inexhaustible supply of arrows,
and a chariot that shakes the ground,
as dazzling as the sun. I want fine horses—
divine white horses, faster than the wind.
Krishna, too, needs weapons to suit his skill.
We'll help you, willingly, but we must have
tools for the task."

        Agni summoned Varuna,
keeper of weapons, one of the world guardians,
lord of waters. Agni paid him homage,
then asked him to provide the two warriors
with the weapons they would need. First Arjuna
received with joy the marvelous bow *Gandiva*,
the indestructible, the shining arc,
a bow so mighty that the cording of it
caused the air to throb, the mind to shudder
of anyone who heard it. Then Varuna
gave ambidextrous Arjuna two quivers
filled with an ever-replenishing supply
of shafts. Krishna received a keen-edged discus
that would always return to the thrower's hand;
and a great club, lethal as a thunderbolt.

Lastly, Varuna summoned for the heroes
a horse-drawn chariot, made by Vishvakarman,
celestial craftsman. It was magnificent—
huge and well-proportioned, flying a banner
marked with the image of a divine monkey
whose terrifying and unearthly roars
could render an enemy insensible.
Four white horses, fast as thought, faster

than the strongest wind, drew the chariot.
Now the heroes were equipped for battle
and eager to engage with the chief of gods.

ॐ

Agni spewed out a ring of fire encircling
the dense forest, to cut off all escape.
Then, working inward, the hungry fire consumed
everything in his path. Insatiable
flames leapt, roared and crackled through the trees,
and billows of smoke, rivaling Mount Meru,
could be seen from scores of miles around.

A dreadful screeching started. Many creatures
were burned immediately. Others ran
blazing, scattering mindlessly, eyes bursting,
pawing the ground until they atomized
in the white heat of the conflagration.
Everywhere, animals ran, struggled, writhed.
Some clung to their mothers, fathers, mates
unable to abandon them. In this way
whole tribes and families met death together.

Anything that managed to break free
was hunted down by Arjuna and Krishna,
guarding the periphery of the forest
so nothing could escape the conflagration.
Birds flew upward, but burst into flames
before they could escape to cooler air
or they were shot by Arjuna, to fall
and perish in the deafening inferno.

As forest pools came to boiling point
fish and tortoises jumped out or crawled
onto the banks, to burn and suffocate.

When Arjuna saw them, he cut them to shreds
and, laughing, threw them into the leaping flames.

The creatures' screams ascended to the heavens
so that the gods themselves were terrified
and cried out to Indra, sacker of cities,
"What is this? Why are these creatures dying?
Are we witnessing the final destruction
of the world?" Indra hurled down immense
volumes of water, pelting the burning trees
with shafts of rain, and a barrage of hailstones
as big as pigeons' eggs. So great was the heat
that they turned into scalding clouds of steam
before they reached the ground. Indra increased
his onslaught. Arjuna, raising his bow,
loosed cascades of shafts, shattering hailstones,
casting a net of arrows, a canopy,
so Indra's rainstorm failed to penetrate.
Agni raged on, in his many fiery forms.

Though frustrated, Indra looked down with pride
at his mortal son, the mighty Arjuna,
then mobilized an army of snakes, demons
and predatory creatures, who converged
on the heroes with an almighty din,
as if the oceans of the world were churning.
They unleashed a storm of iron bolts.
Arjuna shot innumerable arrows.
Krishna hurled his discus, which returned
to his hand, time after time, slick with blood.
The attack was soon repelled, and the searing fire
continued unabated. Agni devoured
rivers of fat and marrow, as the millions
of forest creatures gasped their final breath.
His eyes alight, his scarlet tongue flickering,
his flaming mouth and crackling hair ablaze,
Agni feasted, protected by the heroes.

Then the battle of earth and sky began
in earnest. Indra called upon his allies
among the gods, and Arjuna and Krishna
were soon under assault from every side.
But their weapons, and their skill, prevailed.
The gods retreated. Indra then tore off
a mountain peak and hurled it at the heroes;
but Arjuna's arrows intercepted it
and broke it up into a thousand fragments.
Indra summoned predatory birds,
with razor beaks and claws, to strike the warriors;
and snakes slid all around, their sussuration
filling the air, their scalding venom shooting
from burning mouths. Arjuna's heaven-made arrows
diced them up, to shrivel in the flames.

Krishna knew, though Arjuna did not,
that this hard-fought fight was a rehearsal
for the great annihilating war
that would come—a war they would fight together.

❀

Not all the forest dwellers were devoured.
The king of snakes, Takshaka, was away
in Kaurava country. His son, Ashvasena,
tried to escape the advancing flames, but failed.
His mother, desperate to save him, started
to swallow him, but Arjuna shot an arrow
which sliced off her head. Indra, seeing this,
sent great gusts of wind to save his friend's son
which, for a moment, distracted Arjuna
and, in that moment, Ashvasena fled.

Maya, a gifted demon, dodging the flames,
about to be cut down by Krishna's discus,

cried out, "Arjuna! Save me, Arjuna!"
Appealed to in this way, Arjuna called,
"Have no fear." And Maya was protected.

Four other forest creatures survived the blaze.
These were fortunate young sharngaka birds.

✧

The listening king, Janamejaya,
was amazed at this. "But how could young birds
possibly survive such an inferno?"
Vaishampayana explained as follows:

✧

The celebrated seer Mandapala,
thwarted in his spiritual aspirations
by lack of sons, resolved to be a father.
To expedite the process, he became
a sharngaka bird, mating with a female
called Jarita. Having begotten four sons,
he promptly flew off with another female,
Lapita, abandoning his family.
As he was dallying with his lady love,
he saw Agni arrive to burn the forest
and worshiped the fire god with fulsome praise.
Agni, flattered, offered him a boon.
Mandapala bowed: "Please spare my sons
when you are laying waste to the Khandava."

As the fire advanced, the mother bird
was consumed with terror for her chicks
who could not yet fly. What was she to do?
She could not carry them all—should she take one?
Should she cover all four with her body?
The four young birds said, "You should fly away

and save yourself. You can have more sons
and in that way our line will not die out
though we ourselves will perish in the flames."
Jarita urged them to hide in a rat hole
but they preferred death by fire. Eventually,
she flew away to safety. The fire approached,
and the little birds sang a loud hymn of praise
to Agni. The fire god was delighted,
and remembering Mandapala's request,
he left the young birds alone, and raged onward.

Meanwhile, Mandapala was suffering
sharp pangs of anxiety for his offspring
despite the fire god's promise. He lamented
loudly for his little sons. Lapita
was furious, "It's not your sons you're mourning—
Agni promised to spare them after all.
No, it's that other bird you're hankering for.
You love her more than me—go to her then!"

When the fire had passed, Jarita returned
and found her four young sons alive and well.
Full of joy, she embraced each one, and wept.
Then Mandapala arrived, much relieved
to see his family. They, however,
refused to look at him, although he burbled
to each one in turn. "Uncaring wretch!"
cried Jarita. "You left us unprotected
to frolic with your buxom Lapita!"
"Jealousy really is a dreadful thing,"
said Mandapala. "And when once a woman
has sons, she neglects her wifely duties."
Eventually, the two were reconciled
and the entire family left that forest
and flew to settle in another country.

⚜

After the two heroes had done their work,
after Agni was completely sated
and the Khandava Forest was no more
than a blackened, desolate expanse of earth,
Indra appeared before them. "I am pleased.
You have achieved feats that even the gods
have failed at. I will grant you any boon
you ask for." Arjuna chose divine weapons.
"You shall have them, but only at the time
I think is right," said Indra to his son.
As his boon, Krishna asked that Arjuna
should be his friend lifelong, both in this world,
and in worlds to come. Indra gladly blessed
the friendship which had been ordained by heaven.

II

THE BOOK OF
THE ASSEMBLY HALL

14.

THE DECISION

As Arjuna and Krishna made their way
back to Indraprastha, they saw Maya,
the asura whom Arjuna had spared,
waiting to speak to them. "Sir, I owe you
my life—I wish to do something for you
out of friendship. I am a great artist;
what shall I make for you? Name it—anything."
Arjuna demurred, "Make something for Krishna."

Krishna knew Maya. He was the architect
of the marvelous threefold city in the sky,
the Tripura, once destroyed by Shiva.
What Krishna asked for now would play a part
in shaping the direction of events
he was on earth to foster—great events
designed to realize the gods' intentions.

"Maya, your genius is well known to me.
Here is how you can repay Arjuna—
build a great hall for Yudhishthira
in Indraprastha, an assembly hall
more beautiful than any ever seen
here on earth, one like your great Tripura.
It should be the visible embodiment
of cosmic harmony, divine proportion.
Let it be the envy of the world."

Soon afterward, dark Krishna took his leave
to return to Dvaraka, where he was needed.
To the Pandavas, the separation
was always sad, as though the life-giving sun
were hidden for a time behind the clouds.

ॐ

How to convey, when one has only words,
the transcendental beauty of the building?
Decades afterward, old men would tell
how seeing the great hall at Indraprastha
had changed them, changed the meaning of the word
"beautiful." So, ever afterward,
when something was described with admiration,
they would say, "You don't know what beauty is
unless you saw the hall at Indraprastha."

No expense was spared, nothing wasted.
Maya took his time imagining
every aspect of the inspired work,
choosing the location and materials,
calculating sight lines and symmetries.
He envisioned with consummate artistry
the intricate design of every surface:
how to place each precious stone where sunlight,

piercing through graceful stone tracery,
would best reveal its inner properties;
where to position pools, so as to double
the beauty of what was reflected in them.

For some weeks, he was absent on a journey
to Lake Bindu, where he had secreted
a cache of jewels—jewels he now intended
for his masterpiece. He brought back, too,
a heavy club, embellished with golden eyes,
which he gave to Bhima. And for Arjuna
he brought the marvelous conch *Devadatta*.

It took more than a year to build the hall.
Maya and the colleagues he had brought
worked secretly behind tall woven fences.
On an auspicious day named by Dhaumya,
the new hall was complete, screens swept aside,
and there it stood, in all its magnificence.

The hall had many rooms of different sizes,
for differing purposes, and in between
were corridors and courtyards meant to trick
and captivate the eye in equal measure—
marble that looked like water, artful stairs,
ponds so clear and still they seemed like stone,
painted roses asking to be picked,
jeweled flowers among real lotuses.
In this way, the inspired architect
invited visitors to be alert,
to reflect on the nature of illusion.

Yudhishthira was delighted and amazed
by Maya's work. At once, he set in train
a festival, to inaugurate the hall.
For a week, every kind of entertainer
performed for the pleasure of the citizens.

People of every social rank converged
on Indraprastha, many from far off,
to see the wonderful assembly hall.
All were seized with envy or admiration
according to their diverse temperaments.

⚵

One autumn day, there was a visitor:
the seer Narada, holy troublemaker,
had come again to see the Pandavas.
With perfect courtesy, Yudhishthira
welcomed the exalted wanderer
and sat beside him, listening patiently
to his lengthy strictures on good governance.
For many hours, and in exhaustive detail,
the seer interrogated the Dharma King
on whether at all times, and in all respects,
he was ruling as a ruler should.

At last, Yudhishthira managed to turn
Narada's attention to other matters.
"Sir, you travel throughout the three worlds.
Have you ever seen an assembly hall
as beautiful as mine?" Narada answered,
"Never, in all my extensive journeys
in the world of men, have I seen a hall
to rival yours in beauty and opulence—
though in the worlds of gods . . ." And he proceeded
to describe the halls of Indra, Yama, Varuna,
and the hall of Brahma—self-sustaining,
self-illuminated, completely perfect.

"Tell us more about your epic journeys
in the heavenly realms," said the Pandavas,
hoping he would have news of their father.
But though Narada spoke of Indra's palace

where Harishchandra, a great king of the past,
dwelled perpetually, the name of Pandu
was never mentioned.

                              "Muni, how can it be,"
said Yudhishthira, "that Harishchandra
is Indra's guest in the kingdom of the gods,
while our father, no less a pure kshatriya,
who never lied, or acted selfishly,
languishes with Yama, god of death?"

"Ah," said Narada, "you see, Harishchandra
never rested until he was king of kings,
subduing every other and, finally,
performing the Rajasuya ritual,
the imperial consecration sacrifice,
dispensing vast riches in gifts to brahmins.
Pandu died before he could do the same—
and, then, consider the manner of his death.
His fate now depends on you, his heir.
In fact, I met him in the halls of Death
not long since, and he made clear to me
his ardent wish that, with the help of Krishna
and your strong brothers, you should subjugate
every other kingdom of Bharatavarsha
and perform the Rajasuya sacrifice.
Through you, he can fulfill his destiny
as a kshatriya. And only then,
escaping the dark maze of the underworld,
can he enter Indra's realm of light."

After Narada had taken his leave,
the king sighed heavily, weighed down by doubt.
He wanted to perform the Rajasuya
but how, he wondered, could it be achieved?
The undertaking was an enormous one.
True, the territory he ruled over

already embraced many other kingdoms.
But to perform the imperial consecration
he must be sovereign of the farthest reaches
of the land. He must be emperor.

He thought of his father, Pandu, languishing
in Yama's realm, and longed to release him.
He was wary of being led astray
by impulse. But the faces of his brothers
were alight with pleasure and excitement
at the prospect Narada held out—
the chance of challenge, glory, victory!

He listened to the views of his councillors,
and wise Vyasa. They all approved the plan.
Then he thought of Krishna—what would he advise?
He would consult the prince of Dvaraka
before deciding what was for the best.

Krishna arrived, as he usually did
when his cousins needed him. He listened
quietly to Yudhishthira's concerns.
"My brothers, friends, all my best advisers
tell me I should perform the Rajasuya,
but I'm still hesitant; I doubt my motives—
and theirs. Why would I make this bold attempt?
To release my father? To give Arjuna
and Bhima a chance to fully test themselves
in the clash of battle? Or would it be
just for the sake of personal ambition?
Krishna, you are my wisest counselor;
your view will be untainted by self-interest.
Help me to clear my mind of turbulence
so I can act."

Krishna embraced his cousin.
"Yudhishthira, to become supreme sovereign

of Bharatavarsha is the highest calling
for any kshatriya. One who attempts it
must have powerful allies to depend on,
and must have many qualities of heart
and mind, as well as military strength.
You have those qualities and, like your brothers,
I would be overjoyed to see you, one day,
undertake the Rajasuya rite.

"But there are obstacles. Another king
aspires to be the universal sovereign.
He is my old enemy, Jarasandha
of Magadha. He will never bow to you—
he's proud, he is ambitious; above all,
he knows I am your friend. Furthermore
he has many mighty allies. While he lives
your path to the imperial throne is blocked.

"He has conquered strong and prosperous kingdoms
and captured many royal warriors.
My informants tell me he has imprisoned
eighty-six kshatriya princes in his dungeons.
When he has one hundred, he intends
to bring them out, bind them and slaughter them
offering them as sacrifice to Shiva.
If you free them, you will have their loyalty.
But to do that, you must kill Jarasandha,
otherwise, he will mobilize his allies,
including Duryodhana, to attack you.
Without him, they won't dare, however bitter
their hatred for the Pandavas."

                    Yudhishthira
was still enmeshed in doubt. But Arjuna cried,
"We are kshatriyas! It is our dharma
to win glory on the field of battle,
and it is equally kshatriya dharma

to offer our protection to the oppressed.
I have the peerless bow *Gandiva*, the quivers
that never empty, the wind-swift chariot.
And right is on our side—surely Shiva
does not sanction human sacrifice.
Besides, in Krishna's view, Yudhishthira
should perform the Rajasuya. I propose
that we set out for Magadha at once!"

Then Bhima said, "The three of us should go—
Arjuna, whose skill is without equal,
Krishna, whose judgment is that of God himself,
and I, whose strength is second to no man's."
"Ah!" cried Yudhishthira, "you two are my eyes
and Krishna my mind—what if I should lose you?"

"Yudhishthira," said Krishna with a smile,
"time flows on, day by day, and waits for no one.
We do not know when we will meet our death.
To hesitate, to turn away from dharma,
never prolongs life. But it costs a man
his honor—and that loss is worse than death.
Do not divide your mind against itself
through doubt and paralyzing cogitation.
The great man acts, as time demands of him."

It was agreed that Bhima, Arjuna
and Krishna would go at once to Magadha
and challenge Jarasandha to single combat.
"The man is full of pride in his own strength,"
said Krishna, "so he will choose to pit himself
against Bhima—who is easily his match."
However, Krishna knew how difficult
it would be to kill him. Jarasandha
had been born in two halves, from two mothers.
The female demon Jara had made him whole,
hence his name, and Shiva had blessed him,

given him superhuman strength, and foretold
that he would only die when an opponent
tore him apart again.

> The Pandavas
and Krishna traveled light, disguised as brahmins,
and arrived at Jarasandha's city.
It was large and beautifully laid out
with wide streets, lovely parks and watercourses.
All around it stretched lush pastureland
well stocked with plump and healthy herds of cattle.

They made their way into the king's palace,
entering unannounced, by a back-door route
for, in view of their murderous intentions,
it would not be right to receive the welcome
due to brahmins. Then they sought an audience
with Jarasandha. The king was astonished
when he realized who these "brahmins" were.

"Understand," said Krishna, "we are here
to rescue all those blameless kshatriyas
whom you have wickedly incarcerated
in your dungeons. Either you let them go
or we will force you."

> "What are you thinking of,"
said Jarasandha, "talking such brainless nonsense?
I have never offended you. I have done
nothing wrong—those kings I have imprisoned
were all captured fairly by me, in battle.
Therefore, their lives are now at my disposal.
That is kshatriya dharma—how could I now
quietly let them go when I have vowed
to sacrifice them, in honor of the god?"

"Your view of kshatriya dharma is perverted,"
replied Krishna. "How can you propose

to slaughter brave men as though they were beasts?
It is obscene. We therefore challenge you.
Which of us three do you choose to fight?
Which of us will send you to Yama's realm?"
"Deluded Yadava!" growled Jarasandha.
"I'll take on Bhima—let him fight with me."

Then each warrior put on his battle garments
and, shouting insults, the two massive men
set to, seizing each other with bare hands.
Sweat poured off them as they roared and grunted,
each pounding the other with rock-like fists.
Their cries struck dread into all who heard them.
They grappled, clutched, pulled out each other's hair,
strangled, twisted, kicked. But they were matched
exactly, so the fight went on for day
after day, night after night, until
on the fourteenth day, Jarasandha
was exhausted. The chivalrous way forward
would have been to allow him time to rest
and then resume the fight. But Krishna said
meaningfully to Bhima, "Son of the Wind,
a tired opponent should not be attacked
or he *may even die.*" Bhima resolved
to muster every effort there and then
to finish Jarasandha. He grabbed his ankles
and whirled him in the air a hundred times.
Then he placed the helpless king across his knee
and broke him in two. Jarasandha was dead.

His son succeeded him, and pledged loyalty
to King Yudhishthira. The royal captives
were released from their prison underground;
all swore allegiance to the Dharma King.
Krishna commandeered the dead king's chariot
fast as the wind, drawn by celestial horses—
the very one in which Indra and Vishnu

had once slaughtered ninety-nine danavas.
It shone with dazzling gold, and upon it
was mounted a tall flagpole. With a thought,
Krishna summoned Garuda, terrifying
celestial eagle, scourge of snakes, to be
the living banner for his chariot.
Henceforth, hearing the bird's unearthly cries,
Krishna's enemies would be struck witless,
the blood freezing instantly in their veins.

With Jarasandha dead, Yudhishthira
had to secure tribute and allegiance
from the remaining kings of Bharatavarsha.
Then he could perform the Rajasuya,
becoming emperor, the lord of lords,
freeing his father from the realm of Death.

15.

KING OF KINGS

Northward, eastward, to the south and west
rode Yudhishthira's four younger brothers
with their armies. Their mission: to secure
the acknowledgment of every ruler
in Bharatavarsha that Yudhishthira
was their sovereign lord; and to obtain
wealth from them, in kind, gold or jewels,
by way of loyal tribute. Here and there
they met with opposition. Some with grudges,
and some too proud to bear subordination,
took up arms against the Pandavas.

Arjuna rode north, with a huge army.
The ground shook with the thunder of the drums,
the rumbling chariot wheels, the marching tread
of well-trained infantry. At his approach
many kings gave in without a fight,
and came to meet Arjuna, bringing tribute
and swearing fealty to Yudhishthira.
Others resisted, but were quickly smashed,
often with devastating loss of life.
In this manner, Arjuna pressed on,
then, after subduing the snowy regions
of the Himalaya, slowly traveled back
to Indraprastha.

Bhima journeyed east,
conquering as he went. The king of Chedi,
Shishupala, hearing of his approach,
rode out to meet him and made him most welcome.
He was a cousin both of the Pandavas
and of Krishna. He agreed to honor
Yudhishthira as supreme ruler. Bhima
stayed a month with him as his honored guest.
Then he went on to subjugate the Kashis,
the Vatsas, and many other kingdoms
before arriving back in Indraprastha
laden with tribute.

Sahadeva went south.
The dark-skinned peoples of the peninsula
resisted domination by the north;
so did the tribal peoples of the forests
around the coast. Sahadeva conquered
all those kingdoms, systematically.
Some kings surrendered, knowing their own weakness.
They paid their dues, and promised to attend
the coming consecration at Indraprastha.
Sahadeva came at last to the shore
where two oceans meet, and stared across
to where he knew the isle of Lanka lay
beyond the hazy sweep of the horizon.
He sent a message to King Vibhishana
requiring tribute, and inviting him
to travel to the coming Rajasuya.

Nakula too returned to Indraprastha
with trains of elephants and lumbering oxen
and ten thousand camels heaped with treasure.
He had subdued kingdoms to the west,
and received the formal acknowledgment
of Krishna, on behalf of the Yadavas.

༄

No obstacle remained. Yudhishthira
could now be consecrated king of kings,
all-powerful emperor, lord of the earth.
He asked Dhaumya to appoint the day
most auspicious for the ceremony
and issued invitations to the kings
who owed him fealty. With great forethought,
he made a point of asking Nakula,
tactful and modest as his brother was,
to go to Hastinapura, conveying
his brother's deep respect and to request
each member of his uncle's house by name
to attend the royal consecration—
"Not as ordinary guests," said Nakula,
"but as beloved members of the family
sharing in the sacrifice. Yudhishthira
wanted me to say to you that his wealth
is the wealth of all the Bharatas."

                              Meanwhile,
hectic preparations were in train.
A beautiful enclosure was erected
with a high altar at one end of it.
The sacred fire was burning night and day.
Priests especially expert in the Vedas
were brought in by Vyasa, and appointed
to carry out the several distinct stages
of the ceremony. Ritual implements
were assembled. A wooden jar stood ready
in which waters from many holy rivers
and lakes were blended. The jar had been exposed
to the direct rays of both sun and moon;
the precious liquid would be called upon
at the climax of the great event.

Every arrangement for the well-being
and comfort of the guests was put in place;
not the slightest detail was forgotten.
Splendid pavilions, splendidly equipped,
were built, with sumptuous furnishings, cool gardens.
Each room was made sweet with the scent of flowers.

The scale of the provision was stupendous—
immense amounts of food of every kind;
gifts and meals for the thousands of brahmins
who would assist at the ceremony
over many days; costly new garments
for every phase of the consecration;
rice, ghee, as oblations for the gods;
feasts for the citizens of Indraprastha;
gifts for the kings; and much, much more besides.

The day approached. Guests started to arrive
bringing tribute on an enormous scale
to convey their respect for Yudhishthira,
the Dharma King, he who governed justly,
Ajatashatru, he without enemies,
he whose kingdom prospered, whose people loved him.
Each guest thought of his own gift as crucial
to the success of the great sacrifice.

Duryodhana, his brothers and the elders
arrived, and were warmly welcomed by the king.
What were Duryodhana's thoughts as he surveyed
the city he had heard so widely praised:
the splendid palaces, broad avenues
and lovely parkland—even more impressive
than he had imagined? Whatever they were,
he wore a smile, all affability,
as if delighted by everything he saw.

Yudhishthira invited all his kinsmen
to take posts of responsibility

for different aspects of the huge occasion.
Bhishma and Drona were his chief advisers.
Vidura was paymaster. Duryodhana
was given charge of the receipt of gifts,
and had to witness the cascades of wealth,
the gold and jewels like a glittering stream
pouring and tumbling into the royal coffers.

The ceremony took its stately course.
Narada, observing with contentment
the seal set on Yudhishthira's achievement,
remembered hearing, in the realm of Brahma,
the story of the partial incarnation:
of how the gods would take on human form
to counteract the overweening power
of the kshatriyas. He looked at Krishna,
knowing him to be the embodiment
of great Narayana, the self-created.
He glanced at the Pandavas, each brother
the offspring of a god. He was aware
of what had been ordained for all of them.

It was the last day of the sacrifice.
Yudhishthira would become emperor
at the moment when the sacred water
was poured over his head. But before that,
gifts should be given to the assembled kings.
It was his task to choose and call upon
the most illustrious and worthy guest
to be named formally as guest of honor.
His would be the first guest-offering.
At Bhishma's instigation, he chose Krishna,
friend, blood relative, wise counselor.
"This man," said Bhishma, "is to other men
what the sun is to other heavenly bodies,
outshining them by far in energy,

wisdom and prowess as a kshatriya."
Then Sahadeva solemnly presented
Krishna with the finest guest-offering.

At once, the massive King Shishupala,
the Bull of Chedi, with a face like thunder,
leapt to his feet bellowing in protest,
glaring in fury at Yudhishthira.
"What an outrage! Look around this hall,
just cast your eyes on these illustrious monarchs
sitting here, all slighted by your choice.
Here are the greatest warriors in the land,
the most distinguished elders, wisest gurus.
Here are Drona, Kripa, Vyasa, Vidura—
here is Krishna's father, Vasudeva,
yet you choose to bypass him, to honor
his unworthy son! By any standard
dozens of men sitting beneath your roof
deserve the honor more. Krishna here
is not even a king. By choosing him
you have insulted every one of us,
forfeiting the esteem that brought us here.
Perhaps you see him as your priest, or teacher.
Even so—how can you prefer this man
when Drona and Dvaipayana are present?

"What has he done that's so remarkable?
Killed a vulture when he was a child!
Lifted a mountain no bigger than an anthill!
How does this sinful killer of cows and women
deserve the choicest gift? It's favoritism!
In praising him, you are devaluing dharma.

"And you, Krishna—you should be ashamed
to take the token offered. You're like a dog
that grabs some choice tidbit from the oblation
intended for the gods, and gobbles it!"

Shishupala stalked toward the exit,
followed by several disgruntled kings.

Yudhishthira called after him, "My lord,
what you have said is neither kind nor fair,
and insults Bhishma's judgment—you suggest
he doesn't understand what virtue is.
You do not know Krishna as Bhishma does.
Krishna is our guide; his inspiration
lies behind everything we have achieved.
Through us, he has conquered every king
who sits in the hall today, by force of arms
or by capitulation. For this alone
the highest accolade is due to him."

Bhishma added, "We behold in Krishna
the source of everything that's valuable.
As Mount Meru is the greatest mountain,
as the eagle is the lord of birds,
as the ocean is deepest among waters,
so is Krishna foremost among beings
in all the worlds, past, present and to come.
Good people everywhere pay tribute to him.
Contained within him is the universe,
its origins, its being and its end.

"The King of Chedi wallows in ignorance
and sees only the surfaces of things.
As for those kings he thinks deserve more praise
than Krishna—they are mere straw effigies."

Sahadeva rose to his feet, eyes flashing.
"If there is any person in this place
who still disputes Krishna's entitlement,
let him speak. I place this foot of mine
on his dimwitted and unworthy head!
And if any man desires an early death,
let him challenge Krishna to a duel."

There was a furious muttering in the hall,
a stirring and billowing, like an angry sea.
Many present felt themselves entitled
to the honor of the first guest-offering.
The tide was turning against Yudhishthira,
whose consecration was not yet complete.
Even now, those present might refuse
to acquiesce to his imperial rule.

Shishupala's copper-red eyes flashed
in anger. "Bhishma, you're a senile fool.
How can the Bharatas respect your views
when you have shied away from a man's life?
Celibate, whether it's from impotence
or poor judgment, you have done great harm.
By abducting Amba and refusing
to marry her, you ruined that girl's chances.
You caused the blighted lives of your own kin
when you would not sire sons by your brothers' wives.

"Old, unworthy wretch—you only remember
what's convenient. This Krishna here,
this crook, has grossly violated dharma.
What about my friend Jarasandha,
who never wanted war, yet Krishna killed him?
What about my intended bride, Rukmini,
whom Krishna stole?"

Bhishma exclaimed, "For sure
this foolish man has been marked out by fate
for destruction!" Bhima, incandescent
with rage, was about to fall on Shishupala
but Bhishma held him back. Shishupala
laughed, "Let him go, Bhishma, let these kings
see him destroyed by the fire of my majesty,
like a foolish moth flying into flame."

All this time, Krishna had sat serenely,
saying nothing, paying great attention.
But now he spoke, and not to Shishupala
but to the assembled kings. He told the story
quietly, simply, of how the Pandavas
had freed imprisoned kings from the dank dungeons
of Jarasandha. He told them of the times
Shishupala had offended him, and how,
on each occasion, he had spared his life
to honor a promise given long ago
to Shishupala's mother, Krishna's aunt.
The listening kings started to change allegiance.

Krishna described Shishupala's many acts
of cruelty. "And as for Rukmini—
she spurned him. This man could no more hope
to win her than a shudra can aspire
to hear a recitation of the Vedas.
Today, he has insulted me in public,
before you all. Today, there will be no pardon."

Shishupala jeered, "Do as you like—
pardon me, or not. What harm can you do?"
With that, the glimmering and deadly discus
given by Varuna, the god of waters,
appeared in Krishna's fingers. Instantly,
the Bull of Chedi's massive, angry head
was sliced clean from his shoulders, and he fell
like a great tree struck by a thunderbolt.
A radiance arose from the dead king,
enveloped Krishna and entered his body.
All were awestruck. The sky which, up to then,
had been blue and cloudless grew menacing,
black clouds massed overhead, and violent rain
pelted the awnings over the kings' heads.
Not everybody present, by any means,
was convinced that justice had been done

but they kept silent. Funerary rites
were solemnly performed for Shishupala.

The sacrificial fires were still blazing
and now, at last, the imperial consecration
could be completed. As the lustral water
was poured in a silver stream over his head
Yudhishthira became the king of kings.

⚜

Soon afterward, the guests began to leave
to go back to their kingdoms. Krishna, too,
to the sorrow of the Pandavas, prepared
to set off on the road to Dvaraka.
But as he left he said to Yudhishthira,
"Lord of the earth, you should protect your people.
They depend on you as everything that lives
depends on rain, as the immortal gods
rely on Indra of the thousand eyes."
The cousins solemnly embraced each other.

The seers presented themselves at the palace
to take their leave. Yudhishthira was worried;
the strange weather that had accompanied
Shishupala's death—what did it mean?
Had it been a blessing, or a warning?
And if it was a warning, had the danger
been dispelled by the king of Chedi's death?

Vyasa said, "The freakish sky and downpour
were portents of enormous consequences.
For thirteen years, O king, life will be hard,
and when that time is up, a cataclysm
—a war the like of which was never seen—
will bring destruction to the kshatriyas.
Duryodhana's sins will generate this war

with you, Yudhishthira, as the occasion.
It is ordained. No action on your part
can divert the steady flow of time.
You can only bear it." And Vyasa
said farewell, and set out with his disciples
for his hermitage.

King Yudhishthira
was overcome with horror. His first impulse,
if he was to be the harbinger of death
to the kshatriya order, was to kill himself.
But Arjuna dissuaded him, advising
fortitude. "Then," said Yudhishthira,
"since dissension is the cause of war,
I vow that, for the next thirteen years,
I shall practice virtue, ruling impartially,
so there can be no dispute, in word or deed,
between myself and any other person."

The guests had left. Only Duryodhana
and his uncle, Shakuni, stayed longer,
so they could examine the many marvels
of Maya's great hall, now that the crowds were gone.
Their cousins showed them round, and what amazing
craftsmanship and beauty met their eyes
at every turn. But it seemed Duryodhana
was half blinded by his passionate envy,
seeing what was not there, not seeing what was.
He bumped his head on walls he thought were doors,
lifted his robes to pass over a rill
that turned out to be crystal paving, plunged
into a deep pool he took for crystal,
tumbled through arches, thinking them painted walls.
The servants were beside themselves with laughter,
nor could the Pandavas suppress their mirth—

except Yudhishthira, who had the servants
bring fine, dry clothes for Duryodhana.

Sick with humiliation, the Kaurava
managed to conceal his misery,
but could not bear to stay another hour.
He and Shakuni climbed into their chariot
and fled from hated Indraprastha.

16.

DURYODHANA'S DESPAIR

As they traveled, Duryodhana kept
a baleful silence, sighing frequently
and growling to himself. "Best of Kauravas,
why are you sighing?" asked Shakuni at last.
Pale and haggard, Duryodhana groaned,
"Oh, uncle, I keep seeing that great hall,
my cousin's treasury, bursting with wealth.
And all five brothers rich in the attentions
of radiantly lovely Draupadi—
more beautiful than any other woman.
And that sacrifice, fit for the immortals!
I burn with jealousy—I'm like a river
scorched dry by summer sun. And Shishupala!
What Krishna did was unforgivable
and no one had the courage to object—
those craven kings, cowed by the Pandavas,
only bit their lips and kept their seats.

"Thinking of Yudhishthira ensconced
as emperor of the earth, the sons of Pandu
wallowing in wealth, is agony.
I cannot bear to live! I shall take poison,
or drown myself, or set myself on fire!"
And Duryodhana sank to the chariot floor
in dark despair.

"Come now," said Shakuni,
"the sons of Kunti deserve prosperity;
the wealth their father left to them has been
increased through their own energy and skill.
And they enjoy good fortune—think of the times
you tried to finish them, yet they survived.
The gods are on their side—jealousy's useless.
Accept things as they are."

"Impossible!"
cried Duryodhana. "What man worth the name
who sees his enemies enjoy such splendor,
holding imperial sway over half the world—
what man, knowing that such huge success
is beyond his reach, would not despair?
Seeing that success, remembering
how I tried to erase them from the earth,
I know that effort's fruitless. Fate is supreme."

☙

As soon as he arrived in Hastinapura,
Duryodhana rushed to his apartments.
His silks, brocades, the jeweled necklaces,
chests designed by the most gifted craftsmen
inlaid with ivory and precious stones
seemed insufficient now. If they could not be
more splendid than the riches of the Pandavas,
more voluptuous, colored more vibrantly,
then everything he owned was worse than worthless.

Was there some detail of his cousin's court,
anything in the chambers, cloisters, galleries
he could despise? Some detail cheaply made?
Some carelessness? Some error of proportion?
There was nothing. Everything possessed
by the Pandavas seemed to him perfection.

They owned the world—all that was of value,
all joy, all goodness. What he had was nothing.

He thought of the fire trap he had laid for them
at Varanavata—how had they escaped?
And then, when the kingdom was divided,
and they consigned to a wilderness of thorns,
had he not crushed them? No—they had sprung up
stronger, converted setback into triumph,
his triumph into sharp humiliation.
He ground his teeth to think how gleefully
they must be gloating. He writhed, remembering
how everyone had laughed—Bhima, Draupadi
and her women, speechless with amusement,
his cousins' servants doubled up with laughter—
when he fell into the pool he thought was fake,
and teetered round the crystal marquetry
he'd taken for a pool of lotuses.

Shakuni sought him out, and was dismayed
to see his nephew red-eyed, pale, as if
some parasite was gnawing him within.

"Uncle," he whispered, "I am sick with sorrow.
I think of nothing but the Pandavas
and how they block my path to happiness.
Until they're crushed, I have only death in life.
The whole world has flocked to honor them;
I am alone, with no one to support me."

His uncle tried to comfort him. "My dear,
your position is not so terrible.
You say you are alone, bereft of allies,
but you forget your brothers and your friends—
I myself, with all my kin, Drona,
Ashvatthaman, Karna . . . I could go on."

"You are right!" exclaimed Duryodhana.
"All these men are powerful warriors.
Together we can march on Indraprastha
and defeat my cousins. Then I myself
shall become the emperor of the earth
and possess that great assembly hall!"

"War would be foolishness," said Shakuni.
"You've seen their countless legions. And not only
do they have numerous and powerful allies,
but Krishna is on their side. Even the gods
would hesitate to fight the Pandavas.
But in any case, don't let them trouble you.
They've laid no claim to your half of the kingdom.
Why not forget them? Just enjoy your life."

"They won't let me do that. My bitter hatred
pierces and chokes me every waking minute.
Night and day, I hear them laughing at me.
My one goal is to send them to their deaths.
I'd rather die fighting than live like this,
skulking like a pauper, while they flourish."

"Nephew, I understand," said Shakuni.
"There *is* a way for you to have revenge,
but cleverness and guile are the best tactic,
not unsubtle force. Let Dhritarashtra
invite Yudhishthira to the traditional
game of dice. I'll play on your behalf.
No worse gambler exists than Yudhishthira—
he's far too honest, transparent as a child—
yet he loves to play. I, on the other hand,
have never lost a game—my skill at dice
is widely known. I promise I will win
his wealth from him."

A widening chink of hope
lit up the dark heart of Duryodhana.

He saw the possibility of stripping
the Pandavas of everything they owned,
grinding their faces in the dirt. But first
his father must be talked to and persuaded;
the invitation must come from the king.

༄

"How did that fateful dice game come about?"
asked King Janamejaya. "That dicing match
was the root cause of dreadful tragedy.
How was it allowed to happen? Tell me
in detail."

Vaishampayana proceeded
to describe the events as they unfolded.

༄

When Dhritarashtra learned of the proposal
from Shakuni, he was, as usual, doubtful,
but also wracked with sorrow for his son
whose voice he could hear cracking with distress;
whose trembling and emaciated body
he felt under his hands when he embraced him.

He hesitated.

"Oh! What kind of father,"
cried Duryodhana, "won't agree at once
to do something so simple for his son.
I'm burning, Father, tortured by desire.
Envy twists my entrails—the Pandavas
have made us look like beggarly provincials.
I've seen their heaven-made city, Indraprastha,
I've seen their treasuries, engorged with gold

exceeding every dream—tribute from Sind,
from Kashmir, from Kalinga, sumptuous gifts
from far-flung countries—China, Scythia . . .
the jewels, the splendid horses—I can't bear it.
And the consecration—beyond imagining!
The greatest kings, the fiercest and most valiant,
who adhere most strictly to sacred vows,
who are learned in the Vedas, who practice
all the correct sacrifices—all these,
like merchants queuing up to pay their taxes,
made their obeisance to Yudhishthira.
The most holy rishis were in attendance,
uttering mantras, praying to the gods
for blessings on Yudhishthira. And then
there was the silk parasol, the peacock fan,
there was the great conch of Varuna,
fashioned in the workshops of the gods,
which Krishna used to scoop up sacred water
and anoint Yudhishthira, to seal the rites.
At that sight, I fainted.

                    "Father, Yudhishthira
has had himself raised up to the position
of the legendary Harishchandra.
Seeing this, I have no will to live."

Shakuni spoke up. "Illustrious king,
I urge you to accept this plan of mine.
It is a way to take wealth from the Pandavas
without the loss of blood on either side.
One skilled at dice is able to win battles
by other means—the dice will be my arrows,
the marks on them my bow, and the dice cloth
the chariot carrying me to victory!"

"I will give careful thought to your proposal,"
said the king, "but on such crucial matters

I always seek the advice of Vidura."
"Vidura is bound to disapprove,"
retorted Duryodhana. "He will advise
that you refuse to send the invitation
and if you do refuse, I'll kill myself!"

To placate his son, and because he himself
liked the prospect of the gaming match—
though he well knew where gambling could lead—
Dhritarashtra ordered that work begin
on building an ornate assembly hall
to accommodate the dice game. Then he sent
for Vidura.

When he was told the plan,
Vidura knew this was a fatal step
toward catastrophe. He knew that, now,
the age of Kali was at hand, the age
when dharma is enfeebled, when virtue
struggles to overcome evil. He saw
that his brother was more than half persuaded,
and warned him, "This proposed gaming match
will lead to conflict. I cannot approve."
"But," replied Dhritarashtra, "it will take place
in my presence, and before the elders,
so nothing evil will occur. I feel
this dice game must have been ordained by fate."

Even so, the king sent for Duryodhana.
"Vidura does not approve the plan
and I am inclined to follow his advice
since his counsel is always for my good.
You should give up this idea. Why are you
so unhappy, when you have every luxury?
You're my eldest son, born of my senior wife.

You have the finest clothes, the choicest food,
the swiftest horses, jewels, lovely women—
the best of everything. The sons of Kunti
have their half of the kingdom; we have ours.
Surely that should be enough for you?
One who hates suffers the pangs of hell.
Jealousy brings only misery."

"Father, listen," said Duryodhana,
"you and I are like two boats, fastened
one to the other. My interests should be yours.
Or do you really not want me to flourish?
Discontent and jealousy are good
for a kshatriya. Contentment weakens
the ambitious striving which can bring success;
so does fear, and so does limp compassion.
In pursuit of prosperity, any means,
any means at all, are justified.
Think of Indra, who cut off Namuchi's head
even though he had promised not to kill him.
An enemy is one whose interests,
like the Pandavas', run counter to one's own.
Peaceful coexistence with an enemy
is the way of fools and cowards. As things are,
I do not know if I am strong enough
to defeat the Pandavas. I *have* to know."

His voice rose, "You must listen to me, Father,
I want their kingdom for myself, I want
the Pandavas destroyed—is it too much
for you to give assent, when Shakuni
has such a simple plan? I know you feel
as I do, but you cannot bring yourself
to own it. If you won't do this for me
I swear I'll kill myself! Then you can have
your saintly Pandavas—you can forget
you ever had a son called Duryodhana!"

Finally, the blind king was worn down
by Duryodhana's vehemence and threats—
as a sand dune, soft and shifting in its nature,
is eroded by the waves that break on it.
Besides, he loved his son. Without consulting
his ministers as he was prone to do,
he called for Vidura, and ordered him
to carry an invitation with all speed
to Indraprastha: "Come, my dearest nephews,
honor Hastinapura with a visit.
A splendid gaming hall is being built
where you will be well entertained at dice."

Vidura was horrified. He knew
this course, conceived in malice and deceit,
would bring disaster to the Bharatas.
He pleaded with the king to reconsider,
pointing out the folly of the plan.
"Remember the story of the mountaineer
climbing in search of honey, clambering up
dangerous heights, lusting for the prize
without a thought for how he would return
to solid earth. That's Duryodhana."
But Dhritarashtra, deaf as well as blind,
was adamant. "Dice-playing is a noble
pastime among kshatriyas. No harm
need come of it. And if it does, then fate,
which shapes our lives whatever we may do,
will have its way. Fortune will be bestowed
where the gods decide."

                    With deep foreboding,
Vidura set out for Indraprastha.

༄

Arrived at his nephew's court, Vidura
was received with joy and every honor.
"But, wise Vidura," said Yudhishthira,
"you look forlorn. I hope nothing is wrong
at Hastinapura, that the king is well,
that his noble sons obey him?" Heart sinking
and with a grim expression, Vidura
conveyed Dhritarashtra's invitation.

Yudhishthira was most dismayed. "I know
the Vedas speak of a dice game following
an imperial consecration. But if I
and the Kauravas play dice together,
we may quarrel—as happens over dice."
"I know," said Vidura. "King Dhritarashtra
has built a hall, and many practiced gamblers,
cheats and tricksters, are assembled there.
I tried to stop it. Gambling brings disaster.
But the king, devoted to his son,
insisted that I bring this invitation."

"Who will be there? Who will play against me?"
"The skillful Shakuni will play against you."
And Vidura named other men, notorious
for their sharp practice in the game of dice.
Yudhishthira said, "I understand. A trap
is waiting for me. And yet it is my duty
to fall in with the wishes of my uncle.
If I'm not directly challenged, I'll not play.
If I am, then I am honor bound,
and bound by my own vow not to refuse
a challenge. But what man is there who is not
subject to the blinding power of fate
that dazzles us, depriving us of reason?
What will happen is what time ordains."

17.

THE DICE GAME

Yudhishthira, along with his entourage—
his brothers, wife, servants, many brahmins—
arrived at Hastinapura, and was welcomed
by blind Dhritarashtra and his queen.
The women of the court were not best pleased
by the sight of Draupadi's priceless jewels.

The next day, Yudhishthira and his brothers
were taken to the newly built pavilion.
The whole court had assembled for the game—
gamblers, court officials, nobles, princes.
There was an air of nervous expectation,
though the king described it as "a friendly match,
for the pleasure and amusement of our guests."

"Welcome to all present—let play commence!"
cried Duryodhana with false bonhomie.
"Shakuni will play on my behalf;
I put my entire wealth at his disposal."

"Gambling by proxy," said Yudhishthira,
"seems contrary to honorable practice.
However, if you insist, I shall accept.
Gambling is not a noble pastime,
unlike honest victory in war.
There is no kshatriya valor in it.

Dicing involves deceit—Shakuni,
I exhort you not to win by trickery."

"When a Vedic scholar competes with one
who has no Vedic knowledge, it is deceit,
though no one calls it so," said Shakuni.
"In any sport involving competition,
the effort to defeat one's adversary
could be called ignoble, though it never is.
In playing dice, the stronger player tries
to defeat the weaker—that is the game.
If you are afraid, refuse the challenge."
"I have vowed never to refuse a challenge,"
said the Pandava. "Let the game begin.
We all are in the hands of destiny."

Yudhishthira was the first to name his stake—
"This pearl necklace, richly worked with gold"—
matched by Shakuni. He cast his dice.

Shakuni cast, his supple hands flashing
like lightning. He smiled slightly, "I have won."

Yudhishthira protested, "You confused me
with a trick. But very well, Shakuni,
let us continue. My store of gold:
a hundred finely fashioned silver jars,
each containing one thousand gold pieces."
He threw his dice.

       So did clever Shakuni:
"I have won."

       Yudhishthira grew angry.
"My beautiful and swift royal chariot,
the one that brought us here—it stands outside
hung with bells, furnished with tiger skins—

drawn by eight noble purebred horses
white as moonbeams, all this is my stake."
Again he threw, closing his eyes until
he heard Shakuni's voice,
                              "Look, I have won."

It was as if the world shrank to a script
Yudhishthira must follow. He could not see
how Shakuni was managing to win,
he could not track the other's sinuous moves.
He was consumed by furious desire,
a rage to triumph over his tormenter
and recoup his losses. Nothing else mattered.
"I have a thousand rutting elephants,
well trained, powerful, huge as monsoon clouds;
fit for a king, each one a fearless fighter
with terrible tusks, caparisoned in gold."

"Look, I have won."

                    "A hundred thousand slave girls,
beautiful and finely dressed, accomplished
in all the courtly arts, especially dancing
and singing, used to waiting on celestials,
brahmins, kings—I stake them all." He threw.

"Look, I have won." Shakuni's silken voice
was steady, not a trace of exultation.
Dhritarashtra, though, was feverish,
agog to know each new development,
asking repeatedly, "Has my son won?"

"I have thousands of serving men, well trained
in all the domestic skills, indoors and out."

"All these, I have won," smiled Shakuni.

"Thousands of fine horses, and the same number
of warriors, well trained, well kitted-out,
each with a thousand coins as monthly pay
whether he fights or not. All this I stake."

Shakuni performed his graceful throw
effortlessly. "Look, I have won it all."

"Celestial horses, pretty as partridges,
given to Arjuna by the gandharvas.
I stake them."

Shakuni murmured, "I have won."

"Innumerable chariots, sturdy carts
and their handlers. I hereby stake them all!"

"Won," said Shakuni.

"Four hundred chests
bursting with pure gold!" cried Yudhishthira.

"I have won them all," said Shakuni.

The heat was rising in the assembly hall.
Yudhishthira's four brothers had turned ashen.
Duryodhana was shaking with excitement.
Vidura approached the king quietly:
"O wise king, I beg you—reconsider
what you have set in train. Do you remember
when Duryodhana was born he cried aloud
like a jackal, an ill-omened howling
that echoed through the palace; echoes still.
I urged you then to sacrifice your son—
one son, for the sake of the whole family.

I told you he was sure to bring destruction
to the Bharatas. You would not listen.
Now, see what he is doing.

         "Don't let your son
bring ruin to the blameless Pandavas.
Let the ambidextrous archer, Arjuna,
remove him, for the good of the Bharatas.
I see you in raptures every time he wins.
But really—he is losing. The consequence
of this, for all of us, will be unspeakable.
And to what end are you allowing it?

"There is a story of a foolish hunter
who captured forest birds which spat pure gold
and kept them in his house. He became rich
but, not content with what the birds produced,
he cut them open and, for instant gain,
destroyed the birds on which he could have lived
forever. You have enormous wealth yourself,
far more than you can use. Better to keep
the friendship of the virtuous Pandavas
than to win all they own."

         Duryodhana,
overhearing, sneered at Vidura,
"You've always been partial to the Pandavas.
And yet you stay around here, like a cat
scratching spitefully at those who feed it.
You should get lost, old man, we do not need
your gloomy notions." Vidura replied,
"It is never hard to find a toady
who tells you what you want to hear. Far harder
to find an impartial, honest truth-teller."

Meanwhile, Yudhishthira had staked, and lost,
the vast contents of his treasury,

his palaces, lands, his great assembly hall,
the heaven-inspired city of Indraprastha,
his entire kingdom. Each time he threw,
although he well knew the odds were against him,
he hoped, against reason, for a miracle.
Glassy-eyed, he sat in slumped silence.

"Have you nothing more?" murmured Shakuni.
"Surely your luck will turn—you could win back
everything you've lost."

　　　　　　The Pandavas,
silenced by respect for protocol,
willed Yudhishthira to walk away.
But in a voice not like his own at all,
as if half drunk, or mesmerized, he said,
"My brother Nakula, who is wealth to me,
my young lion with the mighty arms,
I stake him now." A disbelieving gasp
ran through the hall. Shakuni, impassive,
threw his dice.

　　　　　"Look, I have won Nakula."

"My brother Sahadeva, wise and just,
learned in the matters of this world;
even though the last thing he deserves
is to be staked like this—I stake him now."

"Look, I have won your brother Sahadeva.
It seems these youngest two are dispensable,
unlike your brothers Arjuna and Bhima."

"Wretch!" cried Yudhishthira, face drained of blood,
"Never try to put a knife blade between us.
The five of us are of one heart and soul.
He that is the world's greatest warrior,

victorious over every enemy,
the prince who is the hero of the world,
my brother Arjuna—I stake him now!"

"Look, I have won him too," Shakuni smiled.
"Why not stake the last wealth you have left?"

"The strongest mace-bearer that ever lived,
my great-souled prince, massive as a bull,
fearless in war, kindest of sons and brothers,
who would spend his last ounce of strength for us—
how little he deserves this. I stake Bhima."

"Look, I have won!"

    The horrified spectators
might have thought that now that the four brothers
were passing into slavery, the dice game
was over. They were wrong.

     "O Pandava,"
said Shakuni, "have you nothing left to stake?"

"Only I myself," said Yudhishthira,
"am still unwon, still free to leave this hall
and travel where I will. Yet how can I,
having stripped my brothers of their liberty,
count my freedom more valuable than theirs?
I hereby stake myself!"

    "Look, I have won,"
smiled Shakuni. "But in staking your own self
while you still had property, you have done wrong.
There still remains an asset dear to you,
your wife, Draupadi, the dark princess
of Panchala, she of outstanding beauty.
By staking her, you could win back yourself."

"She who is perfect," whispered Yudhishthira,
"neither too tall nor too short, whose eyes
sparkle with love, whose care for us is boundless,
our matchless Draupadi—yes, I stake her!"

At once, there was agitation in the hall.
Nobles, elders, members of the court
were deeply shocked at this turn of events.
Vidura slumped down, wringing his hands.
Drona and Bhishma were silent, bathed in sweat.
Some people fainted. Only Duryodhana
and his friends laughed aloud, and Dhritarashtra,
excited, asked repeatedly, "Is she won?"

"Look," cried Shakuni, "I have won her!
I have won the Panchala princess!"

"Go, retainer," said Duryodhana
to Vidura, "fetch Draupadi from her rooms.
They're too good for her now—let her sweep the floor.
Let her move to the slave women's quarters."

"Wretched prince," said Vidura, "don't you know
that by today's vile and unworthy actions
you are tying a cord round your own neck
and dangling above a dreadful chasm?
In any case, Draupadi is not a slave—
the king staked her when he had lost himself."
"A curse on you!" shouted Duryodhana.
He turned to a lowborn page: "You go and fetch her
to serve the household of the Kauravas."

Trembling, and with reluctant steps,
the messenger approached Draupadi's door.
"O queen, you are summoned to the hall.
King Yudhishthira has lost his reason

and gambled every one of his possessions—
city, wealth, his kingdom and then, madam,
his brothers, and himself and, madam . . . you.
So Prince Duryodhana has ordered me
to escort you to his servants' quarters
where you will be put to menial work."

Draupadi was distraught and deeply shocked
but found the words to say to the page, "Go back,
and ask my husband if he gambled me
before he lost himself, or afterward.
Then come and tell me."

                    The messenger obeyed
but could get no answer from Yudhishthira,
almost demented with despair and guilt.
"Let her be brought to the assembly hall,"
said Duryodhana. "She can ask her question
for herself." And again he sent the page
to Draupadi. "I will not come," she said.
"But say that I am willing to respect
what the venerable men in the assembly
may definitely tell me."

                    Seeing the page
quaking with dread, this time Duryodhana
sent Duhshasana, his closest brother,
bloodthirsty and coarse, to fetch Draupadi.

"Come, my fine girl, you've been lost at dice
and are nothing but a slave. We own you now.
You'll have to learn to love the Kauravas
and show us how you've made our cousins happy!
I'm here to fetch you, you've no choice. Be quick."
She tried to run, hoping to find protection
in the women's quarters. Duhshasana

followed, grabbed her, pushed her, dragging her
by the hair toward the assembly hall.
She whispered that it was her time of the month
when she should not be seen, when she was wearing
a single garment, but he laughed lewdly.
"Let everybody see you have your period—
wear what you like, or come to us stark naked.
Slave! You can't be so particular.
Call on the gods until your voice is hoarse—
'Nara, Narayana . . .' They won't rescue you!"

Soon she was flung in front of the assembly,
her long hair loose, her garment torn, disheveled
and stained with blood. Every decent man
lowered his eyes in shame, but none of them—
not the elders, and not her five husbands—
uttered a word of protest. They were silenced,
for to speak out would have been disrespectful
to Dhritarashtra; and some of those present
feared falling out with Duryodhana.

Draupadi stood upright in their midst,
glowing with anger. She glanced scornfully
at her husbands, and that one glance hurt them
more than the loss of everything they owned.
She addressed Duhshasana, "It is an outrage
for you to drag me here—a virtuous woman—
to a hall of men! I see before me
many elders well versed in propriety
and in dharma—yet not one of them
raises his voice at this disgraceful insult.
Do they lack courage? Or do they condone
your vile behavior? A curse on you!
My husbands will not pardon this offense!"

"Slave! Slave!" jeered Duhshasana, rubbing his hands.
Karna laughed, thinking of how Draupadi

had scorned him at her bridal tournament,
and Shakuni and Duryodhana cheered.
But everybody else was choked with shame
and sorrow, and stayed dumb.

Draupadi spoke.
"My noble husband is the son of Dharma
and follows dharma. Let no word of mine
be heard as blaming him in any way.
I wish to hear an answer to my question."

Bhishma said, "Dharma is a subtle matter.
The answer to your question is not obvious.
One without property has nothing to stake
but, on the other hand, it is accepted
that wives are the chattels of their husbands.
Shakuni is an unsurpassed dice-player;
your husband played him of his own free will.
He himself has not accused Shakuni
of cheating."

Draupadi replied at once,
"Great-spirited Yudhishthira was summoned
to this hall and, having no real choice,
was challenged to a shoddy gambling match
despite the fact that, as is widely known,
he has no skill at dice. Then his opponent,
Shakuni, took vile advantage of him—
how then could he be said to have lost?
My lord was caught up in low exploitation—
only possible because he cleaves
to principle. As I understand it,
when he put me up as his last stake
he had already gambled himself away
into slavery—is that not so?"
Draupadi again looked to Bhishma,

master of every nuance of the law,
for a clear reply. No answer came.

Seeing Draupadi weeping piteously,
Bhima, unable to contain himself,
leapt to his feet, his eyes blood-red with rage,
and shouted wildly at Yudhishthira,
"I never heard of a gambler who staked
even the life of a common prostitute,
let alone that of his *wife*! Oh! Shame on you!"
He made as if he would attack his brother,
but Arjuna restrained him. "Wolf-belly!
Never have you uttered such an insult
to our brother. In playing against his will
when invited by a respected elder,
he acted as a kshatriya should act.
You, though, by this rash outburst, are falling
away from the highest dharma; you're matching
our enemies' dishonor and wickedness."

Then Vikarna, one of the younger sons
of Dhritarashtra, addressed the assembled elders,
urging those present to express a view.
There was silence, so he spoke himself.
"It's deeply shameful for her to be dragged here.
Yudhishthira was under the influence
of an addiction; he had lost control
of his own actions, so should not be seen
as properly responsible. Furthermore,
it was not his own idea, but Shakuni's
to stake his wife—this despite the fact
that Yudhishthira is not her sole husband.
In any case, it's clear that the Pandava
could not lose his wife if he had lost himself,
since slaves can have no right to property.
Draupadi is no slave—it stands to reason."
There were sounds of approbation in the hall.

Karna answered him contemptuously,
"You notice none of the elders speaks for her;
only you, you green, impulsive youth,
are swayed by sentiment. The fact remains,
we clearly heard Yudhishthira stake all,
all his possessions. That includes Draupadi.
As for her being brought into this hall
scantily dressed—if that's what's upsetting you—
that is not an act of impropriety.
Even to strip her naked would be no sin
since she has joined herself to five husbands,
flouting every law of decency,
and therefore is undoubtedly a whore
in the eyes of gods and men. Duhshasana—
make the Pandavas take off their clothes,
and strip this woman."
                    At this, the Pandavas
removed their upper garments and flung them down.
Duhshasana then grabbed at the loose end
of Draupadi's robe, and began to pull . . .

☙

                              . . . Draupadi
closed her eyes in silent concentration.
Duhshasana brayed with triumphant laughter
as he twirled her round, unraveling
yard upon yard of cloth which pooled and pooled
on the marble floor, more and more of it.
His gleeful smile began to fade, as minutes
passed and more minutes, and the garment
covered her as securely as before,
though a stream of silk, a multicolored river,
shimmered and snaked around the assembly hall.
Everyone cried out in utter wonder,
and glowered at the sons of Dhritarashtra.
Duhshasana gave up, tired and angry.

Bull-like Bhima roared, his voice like thunder,
"As the gods are my witnesses, I vow
that, before I enter the halls of Death,
I will tear open this man's wicked breast
and drink his blood, as a lion savages
a helpless deer, its eyes pleading in vain.
If I do not, then let me never reach
the pure and blessed realm of my ancestors!"

All who heard him shivered. The tide of feeling
was now increasingly behind the Pandavas,
and against the weak-willed Dhritarashtra
who was sitting, mute, stroking his chin.
Vidura addressed the gathering:
"Learned men, it is not right that Draupadi
stands here, with no answer to her question.
I urge you to speak." But there was silence.
"Take this slave girl away," ordered Karna.
But as Duhshasana was dragging her,
Draupadi cried, "Stop! I have a duty
which I neglected to perform before
through no fault of mine—to greet the elders
in this assembly in the proper fashion.
My lords, I do not deserve this treatment—
to be forced to stand before this court in shame
by you, members of the honored family
that is now mine. Since my svayamvara,
I have never been paraded in this way
for men to scrutinize. Lords of the earth,
where is honor in this hall? Where is dharma?
Time must be out of joint when such outrages
can be enacted unprovoked, unchallenged.
I am the wife of great Yudhishthira,
equal to him in rank. I am the daughter
of King Drupada, and the friend of Krishna.
I ask again for an answer to my question—
am I won, or not? Am I a lowly slave,

or am I a queen in a distinguished line?
You surely know the law. I will accept
whatever you decide."

Bhishma answered,
"As I've already said, the law is subtle,
so obscure that even Drona slumps
with his head bowed. But this much is certain—
you are blameless. What has been done today
will bring disaster on the Bharatas."

Duryodhana spoke: 'This doom-mongering
is so much old man's talk. Stick to the point.
Draupadi, the answer to your question
lies with your husbands—the four younger ones.
If they disown Yudhishthira and declare
that he is not your lord, then you go free."
Duryodhana's cronies applauded him,
while others shed tears at the Pandavas'
cruel predicament. But strong-armed Bhima,
quite clear on this, said, "Do you really think
that if high-souled and just Yudhishthira
were not our unquestioned lord, your ugly head
would still be sitting on your shoulders? Only
because I bow to his authority,
and because Arjuna tightly holds me back,
do I sit quiet, rather than littering
the floor of this assembly with the corpses
of you and your friends, killed with my bare hands!"

"Dark-skinned Draupadi," said Karna, "notice—
no one here is speaking up to say
you have not been won. In fact Yudhishthira
had lost you when he lost himself. Accept it,
you are a slave's wife—or, rather, former wife,
since slaves own nothing.
                          Go now to the quarters

of the king's relatives; the Kauravas,
and not Kunti's sons, are your masters now.
Choose another husband, one who will not
gamble you away—or shall we share you?
In slaves, a willing, sensual disposition
is always welcome. Show us what you can do."

Duryodhana laughed, and bared his hairy thigh
obscenely to the weeping Draupadi.
At this, Bhima's eyes blazed scarlet, "I swear
the day will come when I will break that thigh
in a great battle, and you will plummet then
into the deepest, darkest pit of Death!"

Duryodhana turned again to the Pandavas:
"Come, reply. I'll abide by your decision."

Arjuna said, "Our brother was our master
when he staked us. But when Yudhishthira
had lost himself, then whose master was he?
No one's master—not even Draupadi's.
It follows, then, he had no right to stake her."
He turned to the assembly, "Now acknowledge
that the blameless Draupadi retains
her freedom, and her status, as before."
Many agreed with Arjuna's solution.

Just then, a jackal began to howl loudly
somewhere in the palace; asses squealed,
and frightful birds croaked. King Dhritarashtra
found the courage to address his son:
"Duryodhana, you have gone too far.
This blameless princess of the Panchalas
has endured the most grievous insults.
Virtuous Draupadi, ask me for a boon
and you shall have it."

           "My lord," said Draupadi,

"free the dutiful Yudhishthira
from servitude, so that his son and mine
can never be taunted with the name of slave."
"Let it be so," conceded Dhritarashtra.
"And now let me grant you a second boon."
"Then, my lord, let my other husbands go,
together with their weapons and chariots."
"It shall be as you say," said Dhritrashtra,
"Now, ask again."

         "My lord," said Draupadi,
"greed is a threat to virtue. These two boons
are enough for me. My noble husbands
will make their own way, through their own good acts."
"This is remarkable," said haughty Karna.
"In Draupadi, the Pandavas have a boat
ferrying them across to their salvation."

Bhima now leapt to his feet, on fire
to unleash on the Kauravas the fury
he had suppressed before. But Yudhishthira
forbade it and, approaching Dhritarashtra,
affirmed his loyalty. "Go now in peace,"
said the king, "and bear no grudge against us.
Look with indulgence on your old, blind uncle.
All you lost, I hereby return to you."

With that, the Pandavas, somber and relieved,
mounted their splendid chariots, and left,
setting out on the road to Indraprastha.

18.

THE DICE GAME RESUMES

"How did the son of Dhritarashtra feel,"
asked Janamejaya, "when the Pandavas
rode away with all their wealth intact?"
Vaishampayana answered readily.

☙

You can imagine Duryodhana's rage
when he heard the king dismantling
everything he and Shakuni had achieved.
He and his uncle formed a simple plan.
He held his peace until the dust had settled
in the wake of the departing chariot wheels,
then went to Dhritarashtra.

                    "Do you think
that by restoring all their wealth and assets
to my cousins, all can be as before?
How wrong you are! The Pandavas will never
forget how Draupadi was insulted.
As we speak, the angry sons of Pandu,
before they have even reached Indraprastha,
are planning their revenge—Arjuna flexing
his bow, *Gandiva*, Bhima whirling his mace,
the others urging on their horses, eager
to gather an invincible fighting force,

summoning their allies from far and near
to march on Hastinapura.

                  "Remember,
a wise ruler deals with his enemies
before they grow in strength. Listen, Father,
our hope lies in the saintly Yudhishthira.
If you summon him to play another
game of dice, his honor won't allow him
to refuse you. He's bound to lose again.
This time round, we will propose new terms:
just one throw each, and let the stake be this—
that whoever loses will relinquish
his kingdom to the other. For twelve years
that loser will be exiled in the forest;
the thirteenth year must be spent in public,
incognito. If he is recognized,
then another thirteen years of exile
must begin. But if he succeeds in hiding
his identity, then his former kingdom
will be returned to him. Those will be the terms
of the wager. But in fact, by then,
we will have used his absence to assemble
a huge and loyal army, and to garner
powerful allies; so, if it comes to war,
we will easily defeat the Pandavas."

Ignoring the advice of wise counselors,
the king, fearing the vengeance of his nephews,
prepared to send after Yudhishthira
with this renewed summons. Queen Gandhari
came and pleaded with him. She loved her son
but she feared the portents, and knew disaster
dwelt in the person of Duryodhana.
"I understand, my lord, why, at his birth,
you could not bring yourself to kill our son,
a helpless infant—despite the prophecy

and worthy Vidura's advice. But now
you must oppose him. Surely it is fathers
who should dictate to sons, not the reverse.
The great-hearted Pandavas agree to peace.
You must lead Duryodhana by example
before he brings down ruin on us all."

"If fate decrees the ruin of our race,"
said Dhritarashtra, "I cannot oppose it.
Let the Pandavas return. Let our son
gamble once more with Yudhishthira."

A messenger pursued the Pandavas
and caught up with them on the road to home.
They were shocked and angry, but Yudhishthira
felt unable to refuse the summons.
"What happens to us, good and bad, depends
on what's ordained. Whether I accept
or refuse, in the end it makes no difference."

Sorrowful, head bowed, Yudhishthira
seated himself before the gaming table,
flanked by his four brothers, oppressed by fate.
In the tense silence before play began
his eyes happened to fall on Karna's feet.
They struck him as familiar. Then he forgot.
Opposite, Shakuni smiled unctuously.
He explained the new terms of the game,
what was at stake. Yudhishthira's face was blank.
He threw. Shakuni threw, and "Look," he said,
"Look, I have won!"

❧

At once, the Pandavas
prepared for exile, shedding their princely clothes,
wrapping themselves in crudely cured deerskins,

Draupadi still wearing her bloodstained robe.
Duhshasana could not contain his glee
and danced around the brothers, taunting them.
"These sons of Pandu are no men, they're eunuchs!
All this time they have been puffed up with pride,
contemptuous of the sons of Dhritarashtra,
but now they are brought crashing to the earth.
Choose a different husband, Draupadi—
the Pandavas are nothing now, mere husks
without substance."

    As they left the hall,
Duryodhana did a grotesque imitation
of Bhima's leonine walk. "You stupid fool,"
said Wolf-belly, "your idiotic antics
will come back to haunt you when I tear you
limb from limb, and break that thigh of yours,
and when I rip open Duhshasana's chest
and drink his blood."

    "Be sure," said Arjuna
"that Bhima's words are true." He turned to Karna.
"More certain than the sun's brightness, more certain
than the moon's coldness is this vow of mine:
that thirteen years from now, I will dispatch you,
son of Radha, to the realm of Death
if, on that day, our kingdom is not returned."

Yudhishthira said farewell to Bhishma
who blessed him. "Son, by your worthy actions
you have surpassed even your ancestors.
Go well. I shall look to your return."

Vidura proposed to Yudhishthira
that Kunti, being frail with age, should stay
in Hastinapura, with him, and not face
the rigors of the forest. Pale, sobbing,

Kunti said goodbye to her mighty sons.
Taking Draupadi aside, she said,
"My dear one, I know you are strong and brave.
You will come through this. Please keep special watch
on Sahadeva, my youngest, favorite son.
Help him to guard against despondency.
Oh, why has this disaster befallen you?
It must be due to my own ill fortune.
If I had known my family would wander
the pathless forest, having lost everything,
I never would have brought my growing sons
to Hastinapura after Pandu's death.
Pandu, I now think, was most fortunate
only to know our sons in times of joy;
he never dreamed of sorrow such as this."

As the Pandavas walked through the city
Yudhishthira draped his shawl across his face
lest his furious glance should cast the evil eye.
Bhima strode with his massive arms outspread
to strike fear in the hearts of his opponents.
Arjuna scattered sand as he walked along,
each grain standing for an enemy
he would one day strike down with his arrows.
Sahadeva had covered up his face,
while Nakula, lest women should weep for him,
had smeared himself with dust from head to foot.

Draupadi said, "As I am stained with blood,
so, thirteen years from now, Kaurava women
will be smeared with the blood of their slaughtered sons
and offer up oblations for their dead."

Crowds of grieving people lined the streets.
Then the Pandavas passed through the city gate
accompanied by devoted brahmins
led by Dhaumya, their household priest,

holding sacrificial kusa grass,
intoning the most somber Vedic verses.

ॐ

Shortly after the unfortunate exiles,
no longer visible to straining eyes,
had disappeared among the forest trees,
the sky became green, and grew strangely dark
as if the forces of the night were coveting
the brilliance of day. There were other portents
and premonitions, dreams and appearances,
so that dread, rather than joy, soon pervaded
Dhritarashtra's court. The seer Narada
appeared and addressed the Kauravas: "Take heed!
In thirteen years, you misguided princes
who hear my words now will die violently
through Duryodhana's actions, and through the might
of the Pandavas." And, having spoken,
the seer strode up into the sky and vanished.

Duryodhana, Karna and Duhshasana
were horrified, and appealed to Drona
to protect them from the wrath to come.
"The Pandavas are sons of gods," said Drona,
"and it is said that they can not be killed.
Nevertheless, when the time comes, I shall not
abandon those who ask for my protection,
even though I know my life is forfeit.
Dhrishtadyumna, prince of the Panchalas,
has sworn to kill me, to avenge his father.
He will surely succeed on the battlefield."

Dhritarashtra, listening, said, "Vidura,
bring back the Pandavas. Or, if it's too late,
at least send them our blessings." And he sat
wringing his hands. His attendant, Sanjaya,

questioned him. "Why do you fret and groan—
you have obtained vast wealth, and the whole kingdom."
"Ah," said Dhritarashtra, "I can only think
of the future, and its terrible punishment."
"My lord, that is your doing," said Sanjaya.
"You would not listen to the words of wisdom
offered by Vidura, nor to the portents.
Through his wickedness, your foolish son
will be the death of all the Kauravas."

"It is the work of fate," sighed Dhritarashtra.
"I always try to make the best decisions,
but when the gods intend someone's defeat
they first make him mad, so that the wrong course
seems to him the right one. The power of fate
can be simply this twisted view of things.
All else follows. The Pandavas will never
forgive the way Draupadi was insulted.
Knowing their strength, and aware that Krishna
is their ally, I have never wanted
conflict with them. Yet my foolishness,
my great love for my son, will bring about
the all-consuming tragedy of war."

III

THE BOOK
OF THE FOREST

19.

EXILE BEGINS

That first evening, they halted at the Ganga
where they would spend their first homeless night.
They found a majestic banyan tree, its roots
drooping to the ground, and earthed like pillars—
a natural temple where they lay down to sleep.
Waking at sunrise, they were ravenous
but had no food other than leaves and berries.
Yudhishthira was worried. How would he
feed his family, let alone the others?
"My friends," he said, turning to the brahmins,
"I'm touched by your devotion, I'm most grateful
that you've come this far with us from the city,
but you must go back—I can't provide for you.
There isn't even a grain of rice to eat
and it will get worse. We shall all starve."

The wise brahmin Shaunaka spoke to him.
"People like you, those with understanding,
should not collapse under a heavy weight
of sorrow of the mind or of the body,
but should dispel it through acquiring insight.
Desire tends to feed upon itself."

Yudhishthira said, "I do not desire wealth
out of greed, for the enjoyment of it,
but to enable me to support brahmins
like yourselves. I am a householder,
it is my duty to give sustenance
to those who live on generosity."

"But make sure," said Shaunaka, "that duty
is not performed in order to store up
merit for the dutiful. The Vedas teach,
'Carry out your duty, and renounce it.'"

Other brahmins said, "Yudhishthira,
do you think we are strangers to privation?
We've chosen to entwine our lives with yours,
reciting prayers for you, comforting you
with teaching from the scriptures. How we eat
is our responsibility, not yours."

Yudhishthira was moved, but still he worried
about the welfare of his followers.
Dhaumya spoke, "Lord Surya, the sun god,
is the source of all foods on this earth.
Pray to him—he will help you feed us all."
Yudhishthira fasted for two days and nights,
never sleeping, mastering his breath,
and, on the third day, walked into the river,
the mighty Ganga, as it was getting light
and raised his face toward the rising sun.
He stood waist deep, with the silky water
flowing all around him.

"O lord Surya
enemy of darkness
origin of all things
you who are the eye of the universe
giver of strength to every living thing
you who are fire
you who are subtle mind
you who are the unlocked door
the comfort of those who thirst for freedom
source of all light
source of all comforting warmth
giver of beauty beyond all imagining
O lord, hear my prayer, enable me
to feed my precious brothers, my wife, my friends
who are suffering in this wilderness
on my account."

So sang Yudhishthira,
reciting the sun's hundred and eight names
in the language of the gods.

Self-luminous
Surya, blazing, beautiful, showed himself
in his incarnate form, over the water.
"I shall grant your prayer. I will provide
nourishment for as many as are hungry—
there will be meat, fruits, roots and vegetables
until the last person is satisfied.
For all your twelve years in the wilderness
I will make sure that your needs are met."
Having spoken, the shining god vanished.

Emerging from the river, Yudhishthira
set himself to cook a meager meal
of all the forest foods that could be found—
insufficient even for a child.
Once cooked, it swelled. He served everyone,

and even Bhima's monstrous appetite
was satisfied. Finally Draupadi
served Yudhishthira, and then she ate
what remained, which was enough, precisely.
Afterward, they continued on their journey
to their new home in the Kamyaka Forest.

ॐ

Meanwhile, in Hastinapura, the blind king
was agitated, in a feverish sweat
of fear and guilt. At night he paced his chambers.
If he slept, he dreamed his splendid city
was overrun by angry citizens
baying for his life. He woke, gasping.

He sent for sagacious Vidura, hoping
for words of consolation. But Vidura
offered no comfort. He condemned outright
the dire proceedings in the gaming hall.
"There's only one way to avoid disaster—
forsake misguided Duryodhana,
restore your nephews to their rightful kingdom,
and banish that troublemaker, Shakuni."

Dhritarashtra turned cantankerous:
"You always take the side of Pandu's sons.
But Duryodhana is flesh of my flesh—
how can I abandon my own body
to favor others, even if it's at fault?
It's simply impossible. And as for you—
Go and join your precious Pandavas.
The forest is where you properly belong!"

Vidura, glad to leave the gloom and sorrow
of the court, took his chariot and, tracking
the Pandavas by asking strangers, crossing

the Yamuna, and then the Sarasvati,
reached their camp, in the Kamyaka Forest
where many devout hermits had made their home.
On seeing him approach, Yudhishthira
wondered if he was bringing a new challenge,
a bid by Shakuni to win their weapons,
but he was soon reassured. The Pandavas
welcomed their uncle, eager for his news.
He told them how things were at Hastinapura,
and what the king had said.

                       Vidura passed
delightful days in the pleasant clearing
beside the Sarasvati. But secretly,
his mind often flew to Hastinapura,
to the brother he had loved and served
since they were boys. He knew Dhritarashtra
must be yearning for his company
and he himself longed to give him comfort.
So he was glad when Dhritarashtra's aide,
Sanjaya, arrived with a message for him:
"The king regrets his words, and is most anxious
for your return. You are his eyes and heart
in a dark world. Without you, he is lost."

❧

Duryodhana was furious when he saw
his blind father closeted once more
with Vidura—afraid that, yet again,
his father would backtrack and vacillate
out of sentimental love for his nephews,
and out of fear. Although the Pandavas
had accepted banishment with bowed heads,
as long as they still walked the earth somewhere
Duryodhana could have no peace of mind.
"Suppose Vidura should persuade my father

to reinstate them? If I see them return
I shall take poison, hang myself—or something!
I cannot bear to see them prosperous."

"Of course they won't come back," said Shakuni.
"You're getting agitated for no reason.
They lost the bet—surely you can't imagine
Yudhishthira reneging on the terms?
Your fears are childishness." Duhshasana
and Karna took the same view. But the prince
remained despondent. "Listen to me," said Karna,
"it seems nothing but action will convince you.
Let us go at once to kill the Pandavas
in the forest, while they are undefended."
The other three were pleased with this idea.
They armed themselves, and made preparations
to start the journey.

                        But great-minded Vyasa,
seeing the plotters with his divine eye,
came to Dhritarashtra. "You should know this—
your wicked fool of a son is making plans
to go and kill your nephews in the forest.
There is no way that he can be successful—
he'll die himself. You must put a stop to it.
Perhaps if he spent time with the Pandavas
without his henchmen, he might grow to love them.
But no—a tiger doesn't change its stripes.
What do you think of all this, Dhritarashtra?
What do the elders think?"
                        "I think it's fate,"
said the unhappy king. "I knew the dice game
was ill-judged—the elders thought the same.
But I love my son—I can't stand against him,
and I cannot bear to see him suffer."
"I understand," said Vyasa. "It is well known
that nothing is more important than one's son.
You, Pandu, Vidura and all your sons

are dear to me. And yet the Pandavas
touch my heart most, as they are most afflicted."

Knowing the king's weakness, how he always
bent before the will of his eldest son,
Vyasa summoned the great sage Maitreya
to speak to Duryodhana and his father.
Maitreya had been to see the Pandavas
and, after greeting him appropriately,
Dhritarashtra asked for news of them.
"This is a bad business, Dhritarashtra,"
said the blunt-speaking sage. "It will not do
that, while you are alive, you let this conflict
be played out between your sons and nephews.
A king is the ultimate authority,
for punishment as well as patronage.
How is it, then, that you allowed your son
to organize that catastrophic dice game?
How could you permit such evil goings-on?"

He turned to sullen-faced Duryodhana.
"Listen, son, I speak for your own good.
Do not offend the blameless Pandavas.
All of them are devoted to the truth,
formidable warriors, every one—
strong as elephants, accomplished fighters.
Think of how Bhima slew Jarasandha
and numerous rakshasas—including one
just recently in the forest, Kirmira.
Think of Arjuna's unrivaled prowess
as an archer; think of their tie with Krishna.
It is pure foolishness for you to think
that you can crush the Pandavas. That way
lies only ignominy, and your own death."

While the sage was speaking, Duryodhana
was looking at the ground with a fixed smile,

drawing patterns in the dust, as though
indifferent to what the sage was saying.
With desperate bravado, he slapped his thigh.
Maitreya, enraged, cursed him. "Since you treat me
with such disrespect, that thigh of yours
will be broken, leading to your death,
when Bhima fights you in the greatest war
the earth has ever seen—entirely caused
by your own wickedness." Duryodhana,
despite his defiant manner, felt his heart
shrivel up in dread. Shaken by hearing
of Kirmira's killing, he left the room.

"May it not happen!" cried the anguished king.
"Unless your son makes peace, then, without doubt,
my curse will be fulfilled," said Maitreya.
"I never wanted it to be like this,"
moaned Dhritrashtra, "but who in this world
can pit their will against fate? Kindly tell me
how Bhima killed the rakshasa Kirmira."
But Maitreya had had enough. "Ask Vidura,
he'll tell you," he snapped. And then departed.

Later, Vidura told the king the story
of Bhima's victory over the ogre
who had been seeking to avenge his kinsmen,
Baka and Hidimba. "Once the forest
was safe, your nephews entered it, and settled.
I myself, when I went to visit them,
saw the loathsome body of Kirmira
sprawled on the path, killed by heroic Bhima."
Dhritarashtra sighed in misery
to think of Bhima's preternatural strength.

༊

Krishna visited the exiles' camp,
bringing with him several powerful allies:
warriors from the kingdoms of Panchala
and Chedi, Bhojas, Vrishnis and Andhakas.
All were filled with rage at what had happened.
Never had the brothers witnessed Krishna
so angry, fire blazing in his black eyes.
"Duryodhana, Shakuni and their cronies
are villains! Here are you and Draupadi
condemned to vegetate, year after year,
in rustic poverty, dull, isolated,
deprived of every comfort you have fought for
and deserve. Be assured—the thirsty earth
will drink their blood! They will not prevail."

To calm his cousin's rage, Arjuna said,
"Krishna, your sojourn in this world has been
a chronicle of most amazing feats."
And, at length, in the presence of everyone
gathered there in the forest encampment,
Arjuna, perfect kshatriya, recited
Krishna's history since the dawn of time:
his fundamental being as Lord Vishnu,
and all his incarnations up to now,
acting to protect the world from harm.

"We are one being, you and I," said Krishna.
"Anyone who hates you hates me; your people
are my people too. You are Nara,
I, Narayana, come from another world
for the good of this one. I am you.
You are me, Arjuna. There is no difference."

The lovely Draupadi addressed Krishna,
tears streaming down like rain onto her breasts.
"Krishna, you are the supreme person,
lord of the world. You know everything that is

and all that is to come. Tell me—how could I,
the most devoted wife, mother, sister,
be dragged from my seclusion by the hair
in front of that assembly, wearing only
one bloodstained garment, and treated like a slave?
The vile Duhshasana insulted me
as no woman should be insulted—still less
one born, as I was, to a royal line.

"Had I no husbands? Even a feeble husband
protects his wife. That is the way of dharma.
And yet the Dharma King and his valiant brothers
sat watching this, motionless and silent
like effigies, while the mother of their sons
was vilely savaged. Even the worthy elders
sat silent, shuffling in their splendid seats.
I despise these men. I have contempt
for skill, heroic strength, for marvelous weapons
that yet allow evil Duryodhana
to live and breathe unpunished, unrepentant.
I won't forgive it. I was not born for this!
I have no husbands if my humiliation
goes unavenged!"

                    Krishna said to her,
"Blameless Draupadi, I make this promise:
you will be queen again. And you will witness
the Kaurava wives shrieking with grief to see
their husbands' corpses sprawled on the battlefield,
cloaked in blood, slain by the Pandavas.

"I wish I had been in that gaming hall!
I never would have held my tongue, as Bhishma
and Drona did, to their eternal shame.
I would have given clear counsel to the king
and, if he persisted, I would have pressed him
to call off the dicing, even to the point

of force if necessary. That dreadful game—
which was no game at all, but perfidy—
brings deferred disaster on the Kauravas,
as well as deprivation upon you."

Yudhishthira inquired, "How was it, Krishna,
that you were absent from the gambling match?"
"I heard too late about it," replied Krishna.
"I was caught up in a desperate fight
with Shalva, the demonic king of Saubha.
He'd heard about the death of Shishupala
who was his brother, and was mad with rage.
While I was still with you at Indraprastha,
he struck Dvaraka from his airborne city
which can travel anywhere, and flattened it.
He destroyed dwellings, wrecked verdant parks,
and killed many brave young Vrishni warriors
before he realized I was not at home.
When I got back and saw the devastation
I went in search of him, and found his city
hovering over the ocean. I attacked,
and a bitter fight followed. He mobilized
his powers of illusion to confuse me.
At one point, I saw my beloved father
being flung out of the flying city,
hurtling to earth like a stricken bird,
his arms and legs flailing. I was appalled
until I realized this was wizardry.

"My charioteer, Daruka, though wounded,
urged me on, and I rallied my army,
mounting an assault with renewed resolve.
The short of it is—I defeated Shalva.
I took my shining bow, aimed it upward,
and cut the heads of Shalva's men clean off.
He pelted me with rocks until I was
submerged under a mountainous pile of stones.

My troops became despondent, but I raised
my thunderbolt and pulverized the rocks.

"Taking my discus, uttering a mantra,
I hurled it at Saubha, cutting it in two,
and the flying city fell to earth. Again
I raised my discus, aiming now at Shalva,
and sliced him through. The demon was no more.
I razed the city. Then I traveled home
and only then did I receive the news
of the dire events at Hastinapura."

Soon the time came for sad leave-taking.
Krishna departed, taking Abhimanyu,
and Dhrishtadyumna took Draupadi's children
back with him to his city of Panchala.
Yudhishthira proposed a change of scene.
Arjuna suggested Dvaitavana,
known as a holy and auspicious site.

20.

DISCORD

Lake Dvaitavana was indeed delightful,
bordered with bright flowers and graceful trees
pendulous with many types of mango
and other fruits. Birds sang among the leaves
of the tall palm, arrac and shala trees—
flocks of doves, linnets and forest cuckoos.
Deer and game were plentiful.

                The Pandavas
made their home there, together with the brahmins,
who had brought their sacrificial fires,
and all the ritual objects necessary
for pious observance.

                The sage Markandeya,
passing on his way to the Himalaya,
smiled to see Yudhishthira and his brothers
living as forest dwellers, like Prince Rama,
his wife, Sita, and his brother, Lakshmana.
He knew inaction could be hard to bear
and counseled patience. "Wait, Yudhishthira,
do not be tempted to depart from dharma
and wage war on the Kauravas too soon.
Keep your promise, tolerate your exile
and you will retrieve your fortune in the end."

Time passed by. Yudhishthira was content.
A life stripped of pomp and ceremony,
of luxury, of complex affairs of state,
was the life his introspective nature
welcomed. He had been an excellent ruler—
firm, judicious, capable and fair—
and would be again, but these were years
when he delighted in simplicity,
practiced meditation, learned all he could
from the rishis whose ashrams in the forest
were a haven for him. He took refuge
in the Vedas, and in their wider vision
that lifted his attention from the sorrow
of his current plight.

                But not everyone
was at peace. Draupadi was restless.
Rage and grief gnawed at her constantly
until, one evening, she could not keep silent.
"Oh, Yudhishthira, it breaks my heart
to see you like this, living a hermit's life
when you should be the all-powerful ruler
of Bharatavarsha. I remember you
on your jeweled throne, dressed in rich silk;
now you are wearing garments made of bark.
Once, your skin was fragrant with sandalwood,
and now it is rough, crusty with mud and ash.

"Now no bard sings of your accomplishments.
Have you forgotten who you are? How can you
happily spend time examining
the finer points of scripture with the brahmins,
performing pujas morning, noon and night?
You're a kshatriya! So are your brave brothers.
Bhima, whose every sinew longs for battle,
who used to be so vigorous and playful,
now droops, despondent. Why, Yudhishthira,
does that not make you angry? Arjuna,

outstanding archer, who could conquer worlds
with his two arms, now sits in idle thought.
Why does the sight of him not rouse your rage?
Tall Nakula, spirited Sahadeva,
accomplished sons of Madri, waste their talents
on chasing birds and shooting animals.
You see me, daughter of a distinguished line,
living like a peasant! Best of Bharatas,
why does all this grief not make you furious?

"Patience may come easily to you
but not to them, and certainly not to me.
We all crave revenge. Have you forgotten
how you were led into a trap, and tricked
so easily? How, then, can you be patient?

"You may be sure that wicked Duryodhana
and his friends take pleasure every day
in contemplating our humiliation.
Do they not deserve harsh punishment?
Don't you remember how Duryodhana
and his vile brother grossly insulted me?
Only Shakuni and cruel Karna
in that whole assembly did not weep
for shame and pity! Why are you not enraged?
It is said there is no kshatriya
who lacks anger. You are the exception!
You seem to have banished anger from your heart,
but the whole world despises a kshatriya
who buckles under insults such as these
without wrath, lacking determination
to strike with the rod of punishment
those who behave wrongfully toward him—
as is required by kshatriya dharma.

"A kshatriya who allows his enemies
to rejoice in the fruits of their wickedness

is reviled throughout the earth, and rightly so.
Every day, I relive those abuses
and boil to think of how the Kauravas
are reveling in luxury and joy
while we, for want of proper fighting spirit,
live out our days wandering among the trees!

"There is a time for patience in this life
and a time for wrath—surely, if ever
anger should guide your actions, it is now!"

Yudhishthira replied, "Oh, Draupadi,
best of wives, I understand your fury.
But do not think there's nothing on my mind
but prayer and philosophy. Yes, it is true
I love to sit with the rishis—they can see
beyond this forest, beyond this life, even.
They have their gaze fixed on eternity
and that helps me achieve a kind of peace
when otherwise I would be overwhelmed
by grief and guilt. I too relive those hours
when I lost everything. I'm keenly aware
of how you suffer now, and how my brothers
waste their manhood here.

                    "But, Draupadi,
as the wise know, sinful acts arise
from overhasty rushing to revenge.
One who is wronged and who responds with anger
is prone to bad judgment, liable to act
impulsively. Good rarely comes of it.
If every person with a sense of grievance
struck back immediately, where would it end?
Unceasing death inflicted, death returned.
An endless round of blow and counter-blow
allows for no reflection or repentance

and only leads to sorrow upon sorrow.
A peaceful world is founded upon patience
and only when a kingdom is at peace
can children flourish, cows grow fat, and farmers
plant seeds with confidence, watch their crops grow,
and gather a rich harvest.

                "I believe
that forbearance is the strength of the strong.
One who is forbearing retains power.
Anger is not strength but, rather, weakness;
it is not the same as authority.
True, I was entrapped, but it was my madness
that lost us every precious thing we owned.
I knew the terms. I played. I lost the game
and agreed to these years of banishment.
If now I were to go back on my word,
I would be as sinful as the Kauravas."

"I think the Almighty has addled you!"
retorted Draupadi. "Rather than follow
the path blazed by your ancestors, your mind
has veered off on a different tack entirely.
There is no justice if a man like you—
the very soul of dharma—can encounter
such misfortune. Until the dreadful day
when the passion for gambling possessed you,
no one was more virtuous than you,
Yudhishthira. You have always served the gods,
the brahmins, the ancestors—and yet
grief is your reward. It makes no sense.
The Almighty is not like a loving parent
but, like a child playing with its toys,
manipulates our limbs, controls the strings
as though we were wooden puppets. I believe
there's no such thing as freedom, no mastery
over ourselves or anybody else.

Well, I utterly condemn a God
who can allow such vile injustices
as have afflicted us! What can he gain
by giving fortune to such wicked wretches
as the Kauravas? If it is true
that acts pursue the actor, the Almighty
must be besmirched by the evil he has done.
And if it is not true—well then, mere might
governs everything; big fish devour
little fish. Oh, I grieve for the powerless!"

"Beloved wife," replied Yudhishthira,
"what you say is blasphemous and wrong.
I choose to follow dharma, and I do it
because it is right, not to obtain rewards.
I follow the example of the wise.
We are human beings, not animals
tussling over a piece of carrion.
I firmly believe that if we follow dharma
it does bear fruit, that every single act
has consequences, though we may not see them.
Do not revile the Almighty, Draupadi."

Draupadi said, "It's misery that makes me
talk in this way. I don't despise dharma.
But one who does nothing in the face of evil
is an unfired pot, worn away by water.
You preach forbearance above everything,
but every living human being must act.
From the infant, sucking its mother's nipple,
to the dying person's final labored breath,
we fight to stay alive. What we achieve
is not just fate, nor is it mere chance
but the fruit of all we try to do.
We have to strive with what strength we possess,
using reason and determination,
to convert our actions to achievement.

That way, we need not reproach ourselves.
A peasant turns the soil and plants the seed.
Then he waits for rain. If the monsoon
fails, and the seedlings wither in the ground,
he will, at least, have acted as he should.
Without fate and chance he cannot prosper.
But without his action, best of husbands,
fate and chance have nothing to work upon.
I learned this from a brahmin long ago
while I still lived in my father's house."

Bhima had been listening. Now he burst out,
impatient with his brother's arguments.
"Yudhishthira, you talk about your word.
But slavishly to cling to an agreement
made under duress? Forgiving wrongdoers
who exult in evil and who themselves
have never sought forgiveness? That is madness
and feebleness of the most craven kind!

"It was respect for you, our eldest brother,
that kept us silent when, in some kind of trance,
you made stake after stake. From loyalty
we sat on our hands while Duryodhana,
like a jackal gobbling another's kill,
snaffled the fruit of Shakuni's sleight of hand—
our kingdom! It is for you that we've endured,
for long months now, this wilderness, this exile,
lacking virtue, pleasure, lacking the glory
our limbs and hearts are made for, ridiculed—
and rightly—by those who should respect us.
This is a pitiful life for kshatriyas;
living like this, you emasculate yourself.
Arjuna and I possess between us
all the skill and strength we need to crush
Duryodhana—and we have our allies.
We should declare war on the Kaurava.

And what if we are slaughtered? Better that
than live like eunuchs, vegetating here!

"You insist on dharma—but for kshatriyas
dharma is threefold—pursuit of virtue, wealth
and pleasure. It requires sacrifices
and gifts to brahmins. For that, one must have wealth.
The Vedas are not enough for men like us.
And, though wealth or pleasure by themselves
will lead to tyranny or slothfulness,
all three are needed in a well-lived life.
Each by itself will lead a man astray—
including virtue.

            "A king should be strong, bold,
a vigilant protector of his people.
By losing your kingdom, you abandoned them.
Our lives are finite; time flows on and on.
If you keep to your word so stubbornly,
we could be dead before our exile ends.
Besides, it may never end! What chance is there
that Draupadi, most beautiful of women,
or I, built like an elephant, can live
unrecognized, when Duryodhana's spies
will be searching for us up and down the land,
and when there'll always be some weasel, anxious
to earn a fat reward from Dhritarashtra?
And if, or when, we're recognized, then starts
another thirteen years! Unbearable!

"Even if our suffering fails to move you
consider your dharma as a kshatriya
and as our king. Rouse up your warrior's heart
and earn the world's respect. Fight, best of Bharatas!
Who can withstand the might of Arjuna?
Who can survive the force of my great club?
With Krishna on our side, how can we fail?"

"Bhima," said Yudhishthira, "listen to me—
I cannot blame you for your impatient wrath.
Nothing you and Draupadi can say
can be as harsh as my own self-reproach.
I took the challenge hoping I could win
Duryodhana's possessions. When I saw
Shakuni's dexterity, and knew
I could never match it, I should have withdrawn.
But I was proud and angry—and obsessed
with winning back what I had lost. I think
I lost my reason; it was preordained.

"I know that my insistence upon patience
seems perverse to you. But, I repeat,
I gave my word. You saw that I agreed
in front of all the elders of the court
to stand by the conditions of the wager.
And my word is more important to me
than any kingdom, even than life itself.
The time for you to intervene was when
you saw how I was gripped by gambling madness.
But you said nothing, I can only think
it was the gods' will. Now it is too late.
Our task is patience."

                    "Oh!" cried Draupadi,
her fresh tears flowing, "your mind's unbendable!
Son of Kunti, you would sacrifice
my life, and the lives of all your brothers,
before you would give up your precious 'word'!"

"Brother, consider it like this," said Bhima,
"I have heard the wise expound the view
that months may be substituted for years.
We have been here thirteen months already.
Think of them as years—rally your forces!
If that's wrongdoing, you can atone later
by paying for a costly sacrifice."

Yudhishthira reflected. Then he said,
"Wolf-belly, that may be. But think about it—
while we have been away, Duryodhana
has not been idle. I cannot imagine
that our cousin and his friends are comfortable
in their possession of our kingdom. I know
he must be consumed by ever-mounting fear
as the time for his enjoyment shortens daily.
He has done wrong and, once a man does that,
he wanders in an inner wilderness
of terror and suspicion. I have learned
that he has assembled enormous forces.
Think—his wealth is almost without limit.
Many kings who bowed to us before
are now rallying to Duryodhana.
Our cousin has distributed such wealth
and privileges that he is surrounded
by strong allies. Bhishma, Drona and Kripa,
although they love us equally, are conscious
of whose food they are eating. In the end,
their skill and their celestial weapons will be
deployed in the service of Duryodhana.
Altogether, we're in no position
to fight against such formidable forces—
and that is without reckoning on Karna,
whose prowess with a bow is unsurpassed.
All these multitudinous factors stand
between us and victory, Wolf-belly."

Bhima was silent. Furious though he was,
he saw the sense in what his brother said.
"Brother, I promise you," said Yudhishthira,
"that if our exile ends successfully,
without our being found in the thirteenth year,
and if Duryodhana then refuses
to give us back our kingdom, then, my Bhima,

we shall fight with all the ferocity,
all the skill and courage, we can muster.
Then you will shatter Duryodhana's thigh,
and rip open his evil brother's breast;
then Arjuna can kill the mighty Karna;
then, Draupadi, you can drench your streaming hair
in the heart's blood of wicked Duhshasana.
And I will fight beside you. Then my wrath
will be as resolute as yours is now."

Presently, Vyasa was seen approaching.
He had sensed discord among the Pandavas
and had come to speak to Yudhishthira.
He took the eldest Pandava aside
and told him the time would come when Arjuna
would overcome the Kauravas in battle.
"For this, he will have need of secret knowledge
in order to obtain celestial weapons—
secret knowledge which I shall teach you now.
After you have passed it on to him,
he should undertake a pilgrimage
to the Himalaya, scaling the snowy peaks
where Shiva may be found. There he must embark
on the most rigorous austerities
in order to become a fit possessor
of Shiva's dreadful weapon, *Pashupata*.
Believe me, he will need it. He will succeed,
for he is Nara, the eternal seer,
companion of Narayana. Meanwhile,
you should move away from here; this place
no longer has enough food to sustain you
and your companions." Then Vyasa imparted
secret wisdom to Yudhishthira
and disappeared.

☧

Later, the Pandavas
moved to their original encampment,
the Kamyaka woods by the Sarasvati.
Some time after that, Yudhishthira
spoke to Arjuna in private, telling him
what Vyasa had said: his crucial task.
Placing his hands gently on Arjuna,
he conveyed Vyasa's secret knowledge,
and Arjuna was fired with new resolve
and energy to carry out his mission.

The family parted from Arjuna
with many blessings, and with fervent hopes.
For the weapon above all other weapons
would bring them victory in the war to come.

Draupadi expressed her ardent wish:
"May your mission be successful, Arjuna.
May whatever Kunti wished for you
at your birth come true. But, in the next life,
may we not be born as kshatriyas,
yoked to war! Go well, beloved husband.
Be safe from every threat and enemy.
May the gods protect you. We shall know no joy
until your safe return."

21.

QUEST

Carrying his sword and his bow *Gandiva*,
Arjuna strode out of the shady forest
into the sparkling light of early morning.
Now his life had purpose. He set his course
toward the mountains and the realm of gods.
He traveled swiftly, through the power of yoga,
faster than the wind, as fast as thought.
The air grew colder when, in just one day,
he reached the towering peaks of the Himalaya,
abode of snow, brilliant and aloof.
He passed over Gandhamadana
mountain of fragrant herbs. Beyond it lay
range after range, clothed in dazzling white.
He traveled, never stopping, never tiring,
under an arching sky of deepest blue.

When he reached the mountain Indrakila,
he heard a voice say, "Stop!" An old ascetic
sat there in a posture of meditation.
"Why do you come armed to this holy place?
There is no conflict here, no enemies—
drop your bow, your arrow-brimming quivers.
In this land, you will find serenity;
this is where your quest ends." The man spoke sternly,
his expression was forbidding. Arjuna
bowed before him, but was unpersuaded—

he would not be staying in this place;
he would need his mighty bow *Gandiva,*
his inexhaustible supply of arrows,
for the great work that lay ahead of him.

Then, laughing, the ascetic revealed himself
as Indra, lionhearted Arjuna's
divine father. "What boon shall I grant you,
what heavenly joys, now you have reached this place
so close to heaven?" Arjuna bowed to him.
"What would I want with all the joys of heaven
while my brothers languish in the wilderness?
I wish to master the celestial weapons.
I hear you say I have no need of them,
that I could stay on in these sacred mountains
for ever. But no conceivable delight,
no sovereignty, no worlds, no happiness,
could deflect me from my chosen path—I must
help my brothers to avenge our wrongs."

"Then," said Indra, "you shall have the weapons,
but only after you encounter Shiva,
the celestial three-eyed trident-bearer."
With that, he disappeared, and Arjuna
traveled onward, calm and resolute,
making for the highest Himalaya.
He settled in a peaceful wood, and started
a life of prayer and fierce austerity
dedicated to all-powerful Shiva.
Night and day, he chanted the thousand names
of the god, and, as week succeeded week,
he ate less and less, until at last
he took in nothing but pure mountain air.
When sitting cross-legged seemed to him too easy,
he prayed standing on his toes, arms raised.

The great seers, fearing the consequences
of Arjuna's punishing austerities,

begged Lord Shiva, "Please put a stop to it.
We do not know what he may want from this."
Shiva smiled and gave them reassurance.

One day, a boar, thick-tusked and ferocious,
really a rakshasa, charged at Arjuna.
Quicker than blinking, he took up his bow
and shot it. Now resuming its true form,
it fell, lifeless. But another arrow
had pierced the creature's thick and hairy hide
at the same moment—an imposing hunter
of radiant appearance was standing there,
surrounded by a crowd of women. "Stranger,"
said Arjuna, "why did you shoot this beast
I had marked out for myself? I challenge you!
You have transgressed the conventions of the chase."
"Fool," said the hunter, "the animal is mine—
I killed it. You have insulted me—for that
I shall kill you!" The stranger loosed a stream
of snake-like darts. Arjuna did the same,
pelting the hunter with a rain of arrows
any one of which should have killed him outright.
The hunter stood, the arrows bouncing off him,
while his women were laughing and applauding
as though the fight were for their entertainment.

Astonished, Arjuna shot even more
lethal iron arrows—to no effect.
Then he found his inexhaustible quivers
were empty. He thrust and jabbed courageously
with his bow's tip, but the towering hunter
snatched the great *Gandiva* from his hands.
Arjuna aimed his spear, which broke in fragments
as it met the stranger's skin. They fought with fists,
and the mountains shuddered with the crack of bone
encountering bone, until at last Arjuna
fell, stunned, to the ground.

                                    "Well, well, Bharata!"
said the hunter in a resounding voice,
"I am pleased with you. No other hero
could have put up such a fearless fight."
And in that moment, Arjuna realized
the hunter was the glorious three-eyed god,
Lord Shiva himself. He made prostrations.
"My lord, I beg you to forgive my violence—
I did not know you." The god laughed in delight.
"You have done well, greatest of mortal warriors.
I have not seen such courage anywhere,
in any world. You may ask a favor from me."

"I wish for the terrible *Pashupata*,
the peerless weapon, known as *Brahma's Head*,
to which my teacher Drona introduced me.
Give me that most dreadful of all weapons,
that spews forth thousands of tridents, deadly clubs,
venomous snake-like missiles, capable
of killing evil spirits, powerful demons—
the weapon that will atomize the world
at the end of time. With it I shall defeat
the evildoers and their misguided allies."

"Arjuna," said Shiva, "you shall have it.
But never forget its power. Never use it
wantonly, but only when every other
strategy is used up—only then
should you unleash the ultimate destroyer.
If it is summoned for some paltry reason,
its force will terminate all life on earth."

Arjuna purified himself, and embraced
Shiva's feet. The god instructed him
in how to use the weapon, how to launch it
with a thought, a glance, a word, or with the bow;
and how to call it back. As Arjuna
received *Pashupata* from Lord Shiva,

the earth convulsed, and gods and demons flinched
at the blinding light of the death-dealing weapon.
Then Shiva handed Arjuna *Gandiva*,
his fractured spear and quivers, all restored
and whole; and, with a gesture, healed his wounds.
He left, to travel with his consort, Uma,
to his eternal dwelling in the skies.

Other gods appeared, the world guardians—
Yama, god of death, came from the south,
Varuna from his ocean realm, Kubera,
lord of treasures, arrived from the glittering snows
of Mount Kailasa. Saluting Arjuna,
each gave weapons to the Pandava
and foretold victory in the coming war.
Last came Indra, proud of his son, insisting
that Arjuna should sample the delights
of Amaravati, his sky domain
above the clouds. He sent his charioteer,
Matali, to transport the Pandava
in a resplendent chariot, fast as wind,
drawn by many thousands of bay horses,
and carrying a lovely night-blue banner.
Only one who had performed austerities
of the most rigorous kind could even see
this glorious vehicle, still less ride in it.

They traveled through worlds where no sun or moon
ever shone, but where perfected seers
and those who had died heroically in war
rode on wonderful free-flying chariots
lit by illumination of their own,
and swooped about the sky, blazing with virtue,
taking delight in each other's company.

When at last they reached Amaravati,
the mighty son of Kunti was amazed

by all he saw—such breathtaking palaces,
shining towers, the garden, Nandana,
with its shade-giving trees, laden with blossom,
where sweet-perfumed breezes caressed his skin.

He was welcomed by thousands of gandharvas
and apsarases. Great Indra himself
placed Arjuna on the throne at his side.
A white parasol was held above him;
Indra stroked his face, and his strong arms
scarred by the frequent lashing of the bowstring.
The lionhearted Pandava was enchanted
by all he saw. But never for a moment
did he forget the purpose of his quest.

☙

Arjuna passed five years in Indra's heaven
enjoying the affection of his father.
He learned to master many divine weapons,
studying their diverse applications
and how to call them back. Indra gave him
his own sacred weapon, the thunderbolt,
placing it solemnly in the hero's hands
and teaching him the esoteric mantra
which would awaken it in time of need.

He learned many forms of skill and wisdom
from the celestial beings of the court.
Gandharvas, the heavenly musicians,
taught him how to sing, and play, and dance—
strange skills for a warrior, but they knew
that he would need them if the Pandavas
were to survive their final exiled year.
Chitrasena was his music teacher,
a gandharva king, who soon became
Arjuna's good friend and close companion.

One day, the great ascetic Lomasha
came to visit Indra, and was astonished
to see Arjuna, a mortal, seated
on Indra's throne. The chief of gods explained,
"Arjuna is the ancient seer Nara,
companion of the seer Narayana,
incarnated as my son, and born
to save Earth from demonic tyranny.
But before he goes back to the world,
I have a task for him. Now, Lomasha,
I wish you to seek out the Pandavas,
give them news of Arjuna, reassure them.
Tell them to undertake a pilgrimage
to the sacred bathing places. You go with them
to keep them safe, for they may encounter
dangers."
     "I shall do it," said Lomasha.

What was the task that Indra now required
of Arjuna? In return for the weapons
he had been taught by his immortal father,
Indra asked him to make war against
powerful Nivatakavacha demons.
Later, when the brothers were reunited,
Arjuna would tell them the whole story,
making their hair stand up, their blood run cold.

♻

Meanwhile, through his spies, Dhritarashtra
had been informed of Arjuna's achievements
and was greatly dismayed. He lamented
over and over to his aide Sanjaya,
dwelling on the terrifying wrath
the Pandavas would certainly unleash
upon the Kauravas. "My witless son,
insane and evil-minded as he is,

has stirred up a holocaust—for war
will surely come, a war we cannot win.
No one on this earth can defeat Arjuna—
not Karna, not Bhishma, and not Drona,
certainly not my son. Already I see
the whole Kaurava army broken, shattered.
How crass it was to summon Draupadi
to the gaming hall, and so insult her
that nothing will appease her husbands' fury
except blood. Oh, why did Duryodhana
not listen to my advice? He seems to think
that my lack of sight also deprives me
of any claim to wisdom. But I have
the eyesight of insight—I foresee it all,
all the consequences of his actions,
in frightful detail. I should have attended
to Vidura's advice, but Duryodhana
pressed me."

          "That is the truth," said Sanjaya.
"You could have stopped the game; but you did not."

༄

At their forest camp in the Kamyaka,
the Pandavas were growing weary, pining
for Arjuna, impatient for his return.
The sky itself seemed empty of the sun;
the forest glades appeared less beautiful.
One day, as they sat together, sighing
to think of Arjuna, and of the kingdom
they had lost, their days of happiness,
Bhima reproached Yudhishthira. "How could you
agree to let him go? Who knows what dangers
he'll encounter on his perilous mission—
perhaps he'll die! How could we live without him?
How will we fight the wicked Kauravas
mightily armed, fully geared up for war

without the Terrifier by our side?
Why should we sit here, endure our rage
fettered, inactive, while every single day
the undeserving sons of Dhritrashtra
grow in strength, led by the powerful Karna.
This is no life at all!"
                    Yudhishthira
tried to soothe his brother. "I promise you
that you will have your chance, but only when
it is the proper time."

                    At that moment,
a visitor arrived, Brihadashva,
a holy man. When he had been welcomed,
Yudhishthira confided in the rishi
all his troubles—how he had lost his kingdom
through rash gambling. "Sir, I do not think
a man was ever as miserable as I."
"Yudhishthira," said the sage, "you're not alone
in having lost all you owned through gambling.
Let me tell you the story of King Nala.

"THERE ONCE WAS a king called Nala, strong, beautiful, thoughtful and virtuous. He was devout, a good friend to brahmins, and fearless in battle. He was generous and fair-minded, and his people loved him. In a neighboring king-dom lived Damayanti, daughter of King Bhima, as renowned for her beauty and good character as Nala was for his. The two had never met but their reputations were carried on the wind, and they fell in love with each other, sight unseen.

"Nala took to haunting the woods near Damayanti's home, hoping, but failing, to get a glimpse of her. One day, he caught a wild goose, and was just about to kill it when the bird spoke up in human language. 'Spare my life,' said the bird, 'and I shall do you a kindness. I shall speak to Dama-yanti about you, so eloquently that she will never even think of another man.'

"The goose did as he had promised, and Damayanti grew

so pale and sad from longing for Nala that her father decided she should be married. He arranged to hold a svayamvara for her, to which kshatriyas from far and wide were invited. So famous was she for her beauty that even some of the gods decided to compete for her hand.

"On his way to the svayamvara, Nala met the world guardian gods—Indra, Yama, Varuna and Agni—traveling in the same direction. They insisted that he act as their envoy in winning Damayanti. When Damayanti came to hear of this, she vowed that she would choose Nala but, on the day, she was confronted with a choice between five identical candidates, all looking like Nala. She begged the gods to honor her commitment to Nala, and they consented, resumed their divine forms and gave their blessing to the couple.

"As the gods made their way back to their celestial abodes, Indra encountered Kali, traveling with Dvapara to the svayamvara. When Indra told him that the event was over, Kali became enraged. After the gods had gone, he swore vengeance on Nala. 'I shall take possession of that fortunate king, and you, Dvapara, must enter the dice and help me.'

"At first, Nala and Damayanti lived in total bliss together, each of them as devoted to duty as they were to love. But one day Nala forgot to wash his feet before performing the evening prayers, and this enabled Kali to enter into him. Driven by Kali, Nala accepted the invitation of his brother, Pushkara, to play at dice. Nala had always been fond of playing, in moderation, but now a madness entered his heart and he became obsessed, addicted to the game. The more he lost, the more passionately he played, and in the fullness of time, he lost everything he possessed, including his kingdom, to his brother. Neither Damayanti's pleas nor those of his subjects were able to put a stop to Nala's folly.

"At last, Nala was destitute. His charioteer, Varshneya, took the couple's two children to live with Damayanti's parents in the city of Vidarbha, and Nala and Damayanti, with only the clothes they stood in, were forced to wander out into the world, friendless and hungry. Soon, tricked by Kali,

Nala lost even his one garment. He was full of remorse at the misery he had brought upon Damayanti and, one night, driven by the demon inside him, and reasoning that, without him, she would find her way back to her family, where she would be better off, he crept away into the forest while she was asleep—having first cut away half of the garment she was wearing, in order to cover himself.

"At first, Damayanti could not believe that he had gone, and searched behind every tree and bush, weeping piteously. For days and weeks she wandered, calling Nala's name. 'Oh, my lord, bull among men, strong-armed ruler of your people, how could you leave me? I am your wife. Remember how you said no one was dearer to you than me? Answer me, beloved husband!' As she wandered, she asked every creature she met whether they had seen Nala. She asked the birds in the trees, the fish in the river, the lordly elephants, even the mountain peaks, and the fierce tiger, king of the forest. She approached the brahmin ascetics who lived in those parts. She asked a passing caravan of merchants. None of them had come across her husband, but the brahmins predicted that she and Nala would be reunited. She begged everyone she met to make inquiries as they went about their travels.

"At last, in her wanderings, she came to a large city, the city of the Chedis, and found a place there as a chambermaid to the king's mother, who was kind to her.

"Nala, meanwhile, wandering in the forest, had come upon a forest fire, in the midst of which was an enormous snake. 'Please save me!' cried the snake. 'I am afflicted by a curse, unable to move from here. Save me, and I will do you good. I will make myself light so you can carry me.' The snake shrank until it was no larger than a thumb, and Nala carried it to a place of safety. He was about to let the snake go when it said, 'Continue walking, and count your steps as you go.' At the tenth step, the snake bit him, whereupon his appearance changed and he became deformed.

" 'My poisonous bite will cause great pain—not to you, but to the creature who dwells inside you. You should now go to the city of Ayodhya, where you should enter the service of King Rituparna, as a charioteer. He knows the arcane secret of the dice game.' Nala traveled to that city, and presented himself to the king as Bahuka, expert with horses. The king engaged him. Nala's own former charioteer, Varshneya, was working there, but did not recognize him, altered as he was.

"By this time, Damayanti's identity had been discovered by the mother of the king of the Chedis, and she had been accepted with great joy. Grateful though she was, Damayanti decided to go back to her father's kingdom, and be reunited with her children. There, she continued to pine for her husband. Search parties were sent out far and wide, inquiring after Nala, everywhere asking the same question:

'Former king whose wits deserted you,
Former ruler whose kingdom was lost to you,
Former husband whose wife now weeps for you,
Will you return to the woman who loves you?'

But, for a long time, there was no news.

"Then a brahmin messenger returned from a visit to Ayodhya, and reported a conversation with a deformed man of the court, who had wept when he heard the question, and the story behind it. Damayanti became convinced that this must be Nala. With her mother, she devised a plan. A message was sent to the king of Ayodhya, announcing that Damayanti was to hold a svayamvara, in order to choose a second husband. The event was to happen on the following day. Eager to attend, the king told Bahuka (Nala) to prepare horses for the journey—horses capable of reaching Vidarbha within a day—though when he saw Bahuka's choice, he doubted that it was possible. Bahuka was confident, however.

"The chariot set off, racing as fast as the wind. As they traveled, the king said, 'See that tree? The difference between the number of leaves and nuts that hang from it and the ones that have fallen to the ground is one hundred and one." Bahuka was astonished, and when he stopped the chariot to count the leaves and nuts, he found that the king was correct.

"'I have a facility with numbers,' said the king. 'And I know the secret of the dice.' Bahuka proposed that the king teach him that secret, in return for his teaching the king the secret of horses. The king agreed. 'Since we are pressed for time, you can teach me the secret of horses later, but I shall teach you the secret of the dice as we travel.' The king did so and, at that moment, Kali left Nala's body, the curse was lifted and Nala resumed his previous handsome form.

"Damayanti, waiting with beating heart, heard the thunder of an approaching chariot. 'It must be my beloved!' she exclaimed, 'No one makes a chariot roar as Nala does.' As she watched from an upper window, she saw her father welcome the king of Ayodhya—as puzzled by this unexpected visit as was the king of Ayodhya, to find that there was no svayamvara.

"Explanations were given, misunderstandings were ironed out, and, at last, Nala and Damayanti were reunited as husband and wife. Two matters remained. Nala taught the king of Ayodhya the secret of horses. And he challenged his brother to a dice game, and won back his kingdom and all his wealth.

"So, Yudhishthira," said Brihadashva,
"even after losing everything,
a person may regain his former fortune.
Now I shall teach you the secret of the dice
so you will never lose a game again."

22.

PILGRIMAGE

On his mission from the chief of gods,
the ancient seer Lomasha, passing freely
from one world to another, came to visit
the Pandavas in the Kamyaka Forest.

"Please explain to me," Yudhishthira asked him,
"why the wicked prosper, while such as I,
who strive to follow virtue, have to suffer?"
Lomasha said, "If you take the long view
the wicked do not flourish. They are like plants
with showy flowers but weak and shallow roots.
The virtuous are well grounded in dharma
and, through devoted discipline, they weather
bad times and good, seeing them as the same.
Like the demons before them, wicked people
lose direction, and fall prey to discord.
Given to restless searching after pleasure,
true and lasting happiness eludes them."

To allay their anxiety and longing,
Lomasha had brought news of Arjuna
and a proposal: while he was away,
his brothers should set out on pilgrimage
touring the fords on the sacred rivers,
and Lomasha would go along with them.
They were all delighted by the plan.

The spiritual benefits of pilgrimage
had been explained to them by Narada.
For those without the means for sacrifices,
and for anyone, of any station,
pilgrimage was a way to free oneself
from the fruits of previous misdeeds—
provided one approached the undertaking
in a spirit of self-discipline.
For the restless and unhappy Pandavas,
a pilgrimage would give a change of scene
and purify them for the times ahead.

Dhaumya, their priest, proposed a route.
First they would travel east, to the Naimisha,
and to Gaya, for the seasonal sacrifice;
then south, where they would visit the great seer
Agastya; then west, to the sacred fords
on the river Narmada; and, finally,
they would travel north to bathing places
on the Sarasvati and Yamuna.
Yudhishthira told most of his entourage—
brahmins and citizens who had stayed with him—
to go back to the city. But some brahmins
wished to remain, to join the pilgrimage.

The party set off eastward. On their way,
wise Lomasha recounted many tales,
some of them serious, some entertaining,
all of them instructive. They encountered
other seers, and drank in their stories too.
At every sacred ford, they bathed and worshiped
and their spirits were wonderfully refreshed.

The party made a stop for several days
beside the sparkling river Kaushiki.

At Yudhishthira's request, Lomasha
told them the story of Rishyashringa,
whose hermitage they could see close at hand.

"A BRAHMIN SEER of great repute was bathing in the water
of Lake Mahahrada when his glance fell upon the
apsaras Urvashi, and his seed spurted from him. It fell into
the water and was swallowed by a doe which was drinking
there. In due time, the doe gave birth to a boy who bore a
horn on his head. He became the ascetic Rishyashringa. He
grew up in the forest and, except for his father, he never set
eyes on another human being. His reputation for austerity
and virtue spread far and wide.

"In the nearby kingdom of Anga, no rain had fallen for
years. Indra, god of rain, had withheld his favor on account
of the bad behavior of the ruler, Lomapada, toward brahmins. Even Lomapada's household priest had left him. He
was advised that if he could persuade Rishyashringa, the
great ascetic, to come to his kingdom, rain would surely
follow.

"Lomapada made his peace with the brahmins, and performed rituals of expiation for his past bad deeds. Then,
with his ministers, he devised a plan: specially chosen courtesans would be sent to the forest to entice the seer to come
to Anga. The courtesans were reluctant to oblige, however,
fearing the ascetic's curse. But an older woman among them
took charge of the enterprise. She prepared a lovely hermitage that floated on the water near the ascetic's home, and
installed herself there with the most beautiful and accomplished of the courtesans, her daughter, who was known for
her cleverness.

"The girl presented herself before Rishyashringa as a student of the Vedas, and inquired after his well-being. 'Sir,' she
said, 'I hope your austerities are proceeding well, and that
nothing is interfering with the performance of your vows.'
The young man was astonished by her appearance. 'Sir,'
he said, 'your radiant looks, almost like a god, must mean

that you yourself are prospering. Tell me what discipline you follow. Where is your hermitage? Let me honor you and give you water to wash your feet.'

"'I should rather honor you,' said the girl. 'In my hermitage we pay respect by enfolding the honored person in our arms.' This she did, and with great gaiety, offered the young man delicious food and drink, and played ball with him, laughing and pressing herself against his body. Then, saying that she had a religious duty to attend to, she walked away. Rishyashringa was left in a state of intoxicated bewilderment. When his father came home he told him what had happened, describing the divine-looking stranger.

"'Father, he looked like a god, with beautiful braided hair, and a curving body. His voice was melodious as a cuckoo's, and in front of him hung two soft globes. When he touched me, I was filled with rapture, and now that he is gone I can think of nothing else. I want to go to him.'

"'Son, that must have been a rakshasa,' said the father, keen to protect his son's innocence. 'They take on beguiling shapes to tempt us away from the right path. They are to be avoided at all costs.' The father went in search of the 'rakshasa,' and was away for three days. But meanwhile, the lovely courtesan returned, and enticed Rishyashringa to accompany her. He did so willingly, and was taken to Anga, where he was housed in the women's quarters. The ruler gave his daughter, Shanta, to him as his wife, and bestowed wealth and lands on him. After this, the rains were plentiful.

"Rishyashringa's father was furious at first, but was then reconciled, on condition that his son would return to the forest once Shanta had given birth to a son. This he did, and he and Shanta lived together in the forest, in great happiness."

ॐ

They journeyed on, following the east coast
south, then round the tip of the peninsula
before turning north. They stopped at Prabhasa,

near the sea-girt city of Dvaraka,
where Yudhishthira performed austerities.
While there, they were visited by Krishna
and his Vrishni kinsmen, who were most distressed
by the Pandavas' reduced condition.

☙

"How did those good men pass time together?"
asked Janamejaya. Vaishampayana
told the king about the friends' discussions:

☙

"What justice is there," exclaimed Balarama,
"if the wise and virtuous Yudhishthira
sits here, filthy and emaciated,
while his enemies enjoy prosperity?"
"The Kauravas should be attacked at once!"
said Satyaki. But Krishna disagreed.
"Neither Yudhishthira nor his brothers
will ever swerve from dharma. The day will come
when they will defeat Duryodhana,
for sure; but that day has not yet arrived."

The Pandavas stopped at many sacred fords
where they paid reverence, gave gifts to priests,
immersed themselves and performed penances.
They reached the place on the river Yamuna
where Mandhatri, the great archer, worshiped,
and Lomasha told the story of his birth:

"A WORTHY KING, Yuvanashva, had no son, despite performing a thousand horse sacrifices, and a great many
other rituals, accompanied by generous gifts to priests. He
retired to the forest and pursued a life of harsh discipline.

"One night, he entered the hermitage of the great seer

Bhrigu, and, finding no one awake, and feeling very thirsty, he drank water from a jar he saw there. It happened that, that very day, the seer and his companions had conducted a ritual whose purpose was to obtain a son for Yuvanashva. They had filled a jar with water and purified it with incantations, with a view to the king's wife drinking it. This was the water which the king had now drunk.

"When Bhrigu discovered what had happened, he was first dismayed, then philosophical. 'It must have been ordained. The water was infused with powerful spells, earned by rigorous discipline. Now you have drunk it, you yourself will bear a virile and god-like son.'

"And so it happened that, after a hundred years, King Yuvanashva's side split open and a splendid infant emerged. Fortunately, the king did not die. Indra came to see him and gave the baby his forefinger to suck. In honor of this, he was named Mandhatri. The boy grew tall and beautiful, and became an accomplished archer."

ॐ

At every ford the Pandavas visited,
Lomasha instructed and entertained them,
pointing out the history of the place
and telling stories. By Lake Manasa,
he told the tale of Indra and King Shibi:

"THE KING OF the Shibis was so devout that his sacrifices rivaled those of the gods. In order to test him, Indra, chief of gods, and Agni, the god of fire, devised a plan. Indra took the form of a hawk and Agni that of a dove which, fleeing from the predatory hawk, took refuge on the king's lap.

"'Give up that dove,' said the hawk. 'By giving it shelter, you are flying in the face of nature, for doves are the natural food of hawks.'

"'The bird has sought my protection,' replied the king. 'It

would be absolutely wrong for me to allow you to eat it. I shall give you something else to eat instead.'

"'Nothing else will do,' said the hawk. 'Hawks eat doves— that's the rule. By depriving me of my proper food, you harm not only me but my dependent family as well.'

"'I won't give up this dove,' said the king, 'so tell me what I can give you in its place.'

"'If you cut off a portion of your own flesh equal to the dove's weight, I shall eat it and be satisfied,' said the hawk.

"The king cut away a piece of his own flesh, but it was not as heavy as the dove. He cut another piece, and added it to the first. The dove was still heavier. Eventually, he cut away all his flesh and, in his mutilated form, climbed onto the scale himself. Then the hawk revealed that he was the god, Indra, and assured the king that he would enjoy everlasting fame for his great sacrifice."

As the group approached the Himalaya,
moving toward Mount Gandhamadana
where they would embrace Arjuna at last,
Lomasha warned that they were entering
dangerous territory, where rakshasas
and sorcerers lay in wait for travelers.
"Take good care," said Lomasha, "proceed
boldly but warily. Be resolute,
knowing that my powers will protect you,
as will Bhima's strength." And the seer chanted
a hymn to Ganga, goddess of the river,
imploring her to watch over the travelers.

"I am worried," said Yudhishthira,
"that Draupadi, Sahadeva and the weaker
brahmins may not be strong enough for this.
Bhima, you turn back with them, and wait
while we—Lomasha, Nakula and I—
go on alone, and then come back for you."
Bhima disagreed, "We should stay together.
I can carry Draupadi, and anyone

who cannot keep up." Draupadi laughed,
"I will manage—don't be concerned for me!"
No one wanted to be left behind.

Alert, with weapons ready in their hands,
the brothers set off, leading the contingent
ever upward, living on roots and berries,
negotiating crags and perilous paths.
As they came close to Gandhamadana,
a violent storm blew up. Rocks split open
with a deafening crack, a whirlwind howled
and lashed the trees, hurling clouds of dust,
branches and rocks, blocking off the sun
as though it were night. Bhima seized Draupadi
and sheltered by a stout tree. All the others
spread-eagled on the ground in trepidation
to wait out the storm. But when the wind died down,
torrential rain began, a deafening deluge,
twisting ropes of water carrying
trees, and any debris in their path,
crashing downward to the plain below.
Battered, terrified, the pilgrims clung
to rocks and to more deeply rooted trees.

At last the clouds dispersed. A cautious sun
sent watery rays to warm the drenched party.
They set off once more, but Draupadi,
unused to strenuous walking, fell, fainting,
quite worn out. The four brothers massaged
her feet until she sighed and revived a little,
but it was clear that she would never manage
to reach their destination by herself.
Bhima had a brainwave—"Ghatotkacha!
My son by Hidimbaa—that mighty fellow
will carry her." Then, by the power of thought,
Bhima summoned him, and he appeared,
accompanied by fellow rakshasas.

"Son, worthy crusher of your enemies,"
said Bhima, "our brave Draupadi's exhausted.
Lift her gently, and carry her through the sky—
fly low, so she will not be alarmed."
"I can carry the whole family,"
said Ghatotkacha, "and my strong companions
will bring the rest." So it was that Bhima's son
took the Pandavas lovingly in his arms,
while the brahmins flew with other rakshasas,
and Lomasha traveled by his mystic power.

They passed over beautiful terrain
rich in mineral wealth, and dappled woods
inhabited by monkeys and bright songbirds.
On they flew, until they saw, ahead,
the fabled and majestic Mount Kailasa
gleaming in the pure air, skirted round
by slopes on which grew trees laden with fruit,
and where many great seers had their homes—
a place free from any stinging creature,
temperate, and lush with many crops.
Prominently placed was the hermitage
of Nara and Narayana, a center
of deep learning. In its gardens grew
the legendary jujube tree, whose fruits
dripped honey constantly. The Pandavas
were welcomed with joy by the holy seers,
and there the party settled for some time.

Strolling one day, Draupadi picked up
a flower, dropped at her feet by the wind,
a flower so exquisite, with a perfume
so intoxicating, that she longed for more—
since she felt that she must offer this one
to Yudhishthira. She asked Bhima
to go in search of them, and bring her some,
so he set off, walking fearlessly

up the mountain. Aided by the wind,
his father, he pursued the heavenly scent
past waterfalls, through groves of graceful trees
threaded with vines, toward the cloud-topped peaks,
crashing through the undergrowth, disturbing
the creatures of those parts, in his concern
to get back to protect his family.

Following a flock of water birds,
he came across a wide and gleaming lake,
fringed by clusters of banana trees,
with blue lotuses floating on the water.
Bhima plunged in like a young elephant,
splashing, slapping his arms most joyfully,
and lions, sleeping in their lairs nearby,
awoke and roared, alarming the whole forest.

Bhima heard a deep reverberation
and, tracking it to a banana grove,
came across a most gigantic ape,
tall and handsome, radiant as lightning,
sitting at his ease on a slab of stone,
beating his tail, like thunder, on the ground.
His mouth was broad, his tongue was red as copper,
and, with eyes the color of golden honey,
he glared down at Bhima. "Stupid fellow,
why are you blundering noisily around
in this forest where no human comes,
waking me from health-restoring sleep
when I am sick? This place is dangerous;
turn back while you still can."

                        Bhima refused.
"Move aside! Let me pass!"
                         "Leap over me
if you must go forward," said the monkey.
But Bhima perceived that this was a great soul

and, from reverence, declined to jump. "Move!"
he cried again. "Were it not for respect,
I would leap over you, as Hanuman,
that brave and god-like ape, that mighty hero,
leapt across the sea to Ravana's kingdom
to find Sita, Rama's blameless wife."
"Who is this Hanuman?" grumbled the ape.
"He is the brother I have never met—
son of the wind, like me—and I'm his equal
in strength and courage. So move aside right now!"

The great ape was amused, "Reckless prince,
I am too old to move—if you must pass,
lift up my tail and proceed underneath it."
Bhima strove and sweated, heaved and pushed,
but found himself unable to lift the tail,
try as he might. "Distinguished ape, who are you?"
he asked in wonder. "I am that Hanuman
of whom you speak," replied the radiant monkey.
"It was I who leapt the hundred leagues
across the sea to Lanka." Hearing this,
Bhima prostrated himself in reverence.
Joyfully he asked his newfound brother
to assume the form in which he made
that spectacular leap. Hanuman laughed,
"That was another era, long ago—
a time when even time itself was different.
Now, strong-armed one, you must go from this place."
But only after Bhima had prevailed
on Hanuman to show his wondrous form—
swelling and stretching until he was as vast
as a mountain, awesome, terrifying—
did the Pandava consent to leave.

The two embraced each other tearfully.
"I bless the day I met you," said Hanuman.
"It reminds me of the time I held
Rama in my arms. I wish you well

in the hard undertaking that lies ahead.
I give you this boon: on the battlefield,
when you utter your war cry, I shall add
my roar to yours. Appearing on the flagpole
of matchless Arjuna, my voice will rob
your enemies of their senses." So saying,
Hanuman disappeared. Bhima continued
to make his way with all speed up the mountain,
always pursuing the divine perfume
of the elusive flower.

                    At last he came
to the luxuriant garden of Kubera,
god of wealth, guarded by many yakshas,
and there he saw a large crystalline pool
where sweet-smelling golden water-flowers
clustered abundantly. Kubera's guardians
tried to prevent him picking them, but he
pressed forward, killing many of the yakshas.
A dust storm blew up, darkening the sky
so that Yudhishthira, far below, saw it,
and learned from Draupadi where Bhima had gone.
He had Ghatotkacha transport them all
up the mountain, and saw the devastation.
Kubera appeared, ready to do battle,
but he softened when he saw the Pandavas.
"Bharata," he said to Yudhishthira,
"you should keep this brother of yours in check."

"Oh, son of Kunti," exclaimed the Dharma King
in dismay, "this violence is uncalled for.
If you love me, never do this again."

⚜

"Tell me more," said King Janamejaya,
"about the Pandavas' long years of exile.

Whom did they encounter on their travels?
How did Bhima curb his restlessness?
And Arjuna's return? Tell me the details."
Vaishampayana took up the story:

☘

For some time, the Pandavas dwelled happily
in the mountains. They moved from hermitage
to hermitage, and were welcomed everywhere.
Then they settled on Mount Gandhamadana
where they waited for Arjuna's return.
The mountains offered so much natural beauty.
They took delight in plants they had never seen,
fruit-bearing trees, interlaced with vines,
flowers of vivid colors. Limpid lakes
reflected the passing clouds. Every morning,
they awoke to an aubade of birdsong,
while, all around, tame creatures played and grazed.
Even Bhima put aside his weapons
and enjoyed the peace and the pure air.
But for the pain of missing Arjuna,
their contentment would have been complete.

Then, one day, they saw a distant object
flashing, shimmering across the sky,
coming closer . . . it was a grand chariot
driven by Matali, Indra's charioteer,
and in it, standing, crowned with a diadem
and holding weapons glittering in the sun—
Arjuna! Soon, following close behind,
Indra himself arrived. Yudhishthira
paid him homage and received his blessing,
then the god left.

It may be imagined
with what joy, with what unending questions,

the Pandavas received the beloved hero.
As if they could wipe out the separation,
they wanted him to tell them every detail
of his quest, and his stay in Indra's realm.
For many days, under the shala trees,
for many nights, seated beneath the stars,
he told them all that had befallen him.
"And what was it that Indra asked of you
in return for weapons?" asked Nakula.

"He asked me to do battle with his enemies,
demons called the Nivatakavachas,
numbering many millions. They had their home
in a well-defended spot beside the ocean.
Their city was most beautiful for, once,
it had belonged to the chief of gods himself.
He had been driven out by the demons.
Long before, they had acquired a boon:
that the gods would never conquer them.
That was why the powerful Indra sent me,
a human, to wage war on the gods' behalf.
He gave me impenetrable armor,
and I was well supplied with all the weapons
I had learned from him. Matali drove me
in Indra's chariot to the demons' stronghold.

"As we approached, I blew my divine conch
Devadatta, and the demons streamed
out of their city, thousands upon thousands,
making an ear-shattering din, screaming,
storming toward us, armed with spikes and clubs.
I cut them down with my bow *Gandiva*,
while, with miraculous skill, Matali
swiftly maneuvered the great chariot,
guiding the hundreds of superb bay horses
so they moved as one. Thousands of demons
fell, their severed limbs streaming with blood.

Then they used their powers of wizardry,
creating rain in torrents, showers of rocks,
breath-stopping wind, a darkness so profound
we were quite blinded. Matali fell forward
and seemed to become confused. 'Surely,' he cried,
'the end of the world has come—I have never
lost my wits before, though I have witnessed
the most furious battles ever fought.'
I was gripped by fear myself but, rallying,
I reassured Matali, then summoned
my own powerful weapons. At one point,
when I was almost overcome with terror,
Matali shouted, 'Use the *Brahma's Head*!'
So I invoked that most extreme of weapons
and managed to defeat the demon hordes.
Matali told me, 'Not even the gods
could have fought as well as you, son of Indra.'

"Soon after we had returned to Indra's realm,
my father crowned me with this diadem.
Then he told me it was time to leave
since you were waiting for me—and with what joy
I am now reunited with those I love!"

The next day Yudhishthira asked Arjuna
to demonstrate the weapons he had used
to conquer the Nivatakavachas.
Arjuna prepared himself, intending
to call up the deadly missiles, one by one.
But hardly had he begun when the ground shook,
the sky grew dull, and everything around
turned icy gray. The Pandavas, appalled,
trembled and covered their faces with their hands.
Then, sent by the gods, the seer Narada
and other seers appeared, with serious faces.
Narada spoke in a voice like thunder,
"Arjuna, you must never do that again.
Those weapons must never be used casually,

on an inappropriate target—or even
one that is suitable, when you could use
some other method to achieve your goal.
Always remember—those missiles, wrongly used,
could mean destruction for the universe."

✤

For four more years, the Pandavas lived in peace
in the mountains. Now ten years had passed
since their exile had begun. And now Bhima
was once again pressing Yudhishthira.
"We have a task—we should get on with it,"
he complained, as always craving action.
"No question—we will definitely win!"
But Yudhishthira refused as, no doubt,
Bhima knew he would. Nevertheless,
the eldest Pandava saw the time had come
for them to journey to the plain below
in readiness for the fight that lay ahead.

Before leaving high Gandhamadana,
Yudhishthira toured the streams, crags and copses
he had come to love. He looked upward.
"I leave you now," he said to the silent mountain,
"but when we have regained our stolen kingdom,
I shall return to you, as a penitent."

The time had come for Lomasha to leave them,
to return to his home in the heavenly realms.
Then, with Ghatotkacha carrying them,
they started their slow descent. Often they camped
for several months in some delightful valley
or mountain ridge. Coming to the foothills,
they dismissed Ghatotkacha and his companions.
The terrain would be easier from now on.

One day, Bhima, who never could stay still,
set off into the woods in search of game.
Rounding a bend, he came upon a snake
larger than any he had ever seen,
yellow as turmeric, with fiery eyes
and fangs that glistened in its hungry jaws.
It seized him in its coils and, though he struggled
with superhuman strength, he could not move.

"Who are you?" he asked the snake, "and how can you
render me helpless as an infant—I,
stronger by far than any mortal man?"
"I am your ancestor Nahusha, doomed
to live as a snake, starving perpetually,
cursed for my woeful disrespect for brahmins.
The curse will only lift when someone answers
the precise questions I shall put to him.
Until that day, I satisfy my hunger
by eating anything I catch—and now,
I shall eat you."

      Wolf-belly replied,
"I don't blame you. We all have to do
as destiny dictates. But I sorely grieve
for my brothers—without my fighting prowess,
how will they defeat the Kauravas?
And how will my poor mother bear my loss?"

Back at the hermitage, Yudhishthira
noticed disturbing portents. A jackal howled
repeatedly, the southern sky grew red
and a one-footed quail of evil aspect
spat blood, screeching as if in urgent warning.
"Caw! Caw! Go! Go!" shouted a dusky crow.
Yudhishthira, with Dhaumya, the priest,
ran off in search of Bhima. It was not hard
to follow the trail of footprints and smashed trees
where Wolf-belly had passed. They came across him

still pinioned by the snake, and he told them
all that had happened. "Dharma King," said the snake,
"your brother is my next meal. Nevertheless,
if you can answer my questions correctly
he shall go free."

     "Ask," said Yudhishthira.

"First, who is a brahmin?" asked the snake.
"Brahmins are those who live by truthfulness,
compassion, generosity, self-control,"
replied Yudhishthira, "those who may attain
knowledge of the supreme Brahman, passing
beyond happiness and unhappiness."
"The qualities you mention," said the snake,
"are found even in shudras. Are you saying
brahmins are brahmins not because of birth
but by virtue of their good behavior?
As for a state that somehow goes beyond
sorrow and joy—I doubt that it exists."

"It is like cold and heat," answered Yudhishthira.
"They are extremes, but there are many states
between, when we feel neither hot nor cold.
A person's parentage cannot be known
for certain, therefore it is by their conduct
that we should judge a person's brahminhood."
"What you say is true," replied the snake,
"and conduct must be judged by its effects.
You have answered well. I hardly think
that I could make a meal of your brother now."
He released Bhima, and Yudhishthira
continued his conversation with the snake
until Nahusha said, "My curse is lifted!
Before, I rode round heaven like a god,
full of pride, drunk with my own importance,
forcing brahmins to pay homage to me.
Now I understand the power of virtue."

Saying that, he shed his serpent body
and, acquiring a celestial form,
went up to heaven.

You may well imagine
with what relief Bhima was welcomed back,
although the brahmins, anxious for his welfare,
rebuked him for his rashness, and exhorted him
never, ever, to take such risks again.

23.

DURYODHANA'S MISTAKE

The long exile entered its twelfth year,
the last in the wilderness. It was the time
of the monsoon, when scorching sun gives way
to bank upon bank of dense, black thunderclouds,
rumbling, clashing, disgorging rain in torrents
to drench the grateful earth. All living beings
feel themselves newborn, and leap, run, fly
more vigorously, according to their natures.
Delighting in the freshness of the earth,
the Pandavas rejoiced to see the lakes
full to the brim with clear and sparkling water,
and fringed with brightly colored water-plants.

Krishna visited them, with Satyabhama,
his chief wife, and, joyfully, the cousins
embraced each other after so long apart.
"Who else but you, Yudhishthira," said Krishna,
"could have endured your loss so patiently,
keeping to the terms of your cruel exile
despite temptation. But now, friend, the time
is rapidly approaching when your promise
will be fulfilled, and then, O Dharma King,
we shall see your kingdom restored to you!"

Markandeya, the revered ascetic,
arrived just then to see them. Yudhishthira

urged him to speak of the nature of existence,
of humankind's relation to the gods,
and how it happens that a person's actions
influence their subsequent rebirth.
The sage spoke to them of the law of karma,
how, when people die, and they are reborn
in another womb, their previous acts
stick to them like a shadow, and determine
whether their next life will be fortunate.

Markandeya told them many stories
from his wealth of knowledge of all the worlds,
and the eldest Pandava, who loved to learn,
sat at his feet. "Tell me the tale," he said,
"of the seer Manu and the enormous fish."

"MANU WAS A great and holy seer," began Markandeya. "His austerities were unparalleled. For ten thousand years, he stood on one foot, arms raised above his bowed head, beside the famous jujube tree on the bank of the river Virini. One day, a small fish swam up and spoke to him.

"'My lord,' it said, 'I am constantly terrified of being eaten by a bigger fish, for that is the way of things in this world, since time immemorial. Please protect me, and I promise that I will reward you.'

"Manu was filled with compassion. He scooped up the little fish and placed it in a jar of water, where he looked after it as though it were his own child. In time, the fish grew too big for the jar, and Manu took it to a pond and threw it in. In time, it grew so big that it could hardly turn without bumping into the sides of the pond, and it begged Manu to take it to the river Ganga, which he did. There, the fish kept growing, until a time came when Manu had to take it to the ocean and release it there.

"'My lord,' said the fish, 'you have cared for me, and I am grateful to you. Here is some good advice: soon the world will be overwhelmed by a mighty flood, and everything that stands will be destroyed. You should build a sturdy and capacious boat and attach a strong rope to its prow. Then, you must collect the seeds of all the different species in the world and take them aboard the boat, together with the seven wisest rishis. Then wait for me. I shall appear to you as a horned animal.'

"Manu did as he was told. Then the fish appeared with a great horn on its head, and Manu made a loop in the rope and fastened it around the horn. The fish set off at great speed over the billowing and roaring ocean, the boat tossed and danced like a drunken whore, and never did they see a speck of land. Water covered the entire earth. After many years, the fish approached the highest peak of the Himalaya, and there Manu moored the boat. To this day, that peak is called *Naubandhana*, the harbor.

"Then the fish revealed itself as Brahma, lord of beings, and he decreed that Manu should create anew all the creatures that had perished in the flood. And so it happened."

"Great muni, you have lived through a thousand ages,"
said Yudhishthira, "and witnessed huge events.
You have seen worlds destroyed and re-created.
Please describe how the ages arise and pass,
how they succeed each other in a cycle."

"I shall do so," replied Markandeya,
"but first I bow to the Supreme Person,
Krishna, the self-created.

                    "At the beginning,
in the era known as the Krita age,
human beings mingle with the gods,
moving from earth to heaven as they wish.
They live long lives, pain-free, harmonious,
their every action shaped by righteousness.
But, in time, people become corrupted;
lust arises, and corrosive envy.

Their lives grow short and full of misery,
they fight among themselves, beset by anger;
the gods desert them. Virtue is diminished
by one quarter. That is the Treta age,
which is said to last for three thousand years.
That gives way to the Dvapara age.
Now vice and virtue are mixed half and half.

"Last is the Kali age, a dreadful time
when every kind of evil stalks the earth.
All sense of the sacred fades away.
Vedas are treated with indifference
as people think of nothing but possessions
and make no offerings to their ancestors.
Social differences are swept aside,
brahmins and shudras doing each other's work.
Greed is universal, with no respect
for morality, or for the natural world.
Sons kill fathers, women butcher husbands.
There is drought, famine, pestilence and death
—until the Krita age comes round again.

"Once, after the end of a Kali age,
in a desolate time between ages,
wandering the earth, and finding nothing
that moved or breathed, only a waste of water,
I came across a towering banyan tree.
On a branch, a tiny child was sitting,
round-faced, radiant and lotus-eyed.
He spoke to me: 'My friend Markandeya,
I know you are very tired. Rest in me,
enter my body and I shall make space for you.'
He opened his mouth wide, and I found myself
entering it, and suddenly I saw
a world spread out before me—kingdoms, cities,
oceans, rivers alive with gleaming fish,
the dazzling peaks of the Himalaya,
the heavens blazing with bright constellations.

I saw plains, forests, every kind of creature—
I roamed in the body of the great spirit
for more than a hundred years, and never reached
the limit of it. At last I called upon
the being whose world this was. A gust of wind
blew me from his mouth, and the dark-skinned child
was sitting as before. 'Have you rested
in this body of mine?' he asked me, smiling.
I took his rosy feet into my hands
and touched them with my head.

                           " 'O lord of gods,'
I said, 'why are you here as a little child?
I have seen things beyond my understanding.
Please explain ultimate reality.'
'I am Narayana,' replied the child,
'creator and destroyer of all creatures.
I am Vishnu, Shiva, Yama and all gods.
I am the Placer; I am the Sacrifice.
To sustain the earth, I manifest
at different times as different incarnations;
I take on human form to combat evil
but no one knows me. Understand, brahmin,
that every human quality and impulse—
anger, lust, fear, joy, confusion
as well as duty, truthfulness, compassion—
is an aspect of me. Human beings act
not from free will, but influenced by me.
I alone control the wheel of time.
At the end of each cycle of ages
I am all-destroying Time itself.'

"I remember these great revelations
in all their vividness," said Markandeya.
"Know that your beloved friend and cousin
is none other than Narayana.
You should place your absolute trust in him."

The Pandavas made obeisance to Krishna
who acknowledged them affectionately.

"Out of catastrophe," the seer went on,
"the cycle of time, inexorably turning,
will give rise to a new Krita age.
Led by a brahmin, people will turn again,
in a spirit of devotion, to the gods."

"What must I do," asked Yudhishthira,
"to rule justly and protect my subjects?"
"Be compassionate," said Markandeya,
"treat the people as if they were your children,
honor the gods, and always uphold dharma.
Be humble, and atone for any wrongdoing
with sacrifices. Furthermore, my son,
be decisive, do not let your heart
be weighed down by doubt and hesitation."

Markandeya gave many more teachings
as his eager listeners sat around him.

When Krishna's party and the Pandavas
were left alone, the conversation flowed.
There was a wealth of news to be exchanged.
"How are my children—tell me everything,"
asked Draupadi eagerly. Krishna told her,
"Your sons are flourishing. They are virtuous,
strong, and keen on mastering every weapon.
Abhimanyu has been training them
and, for a mother, they have had Subhadra,
who has cared for them devotedly."

Draupadi and Satyabhama drew aside
to share news and exchange confidences.

"Tell me, Draupadi," said Satyabhama,
"how do you keep your husbands loyal to you?
They are proud and virile men, yet I notice
that they are never angry with you, always
casting you loving looks. Do you use spells
or potions? Do you practice austerities?
Tell me the secret of your power, so I, too,
may keep Krishna always devoted to me."

"Questions like these are unworthy of you,
as you know yourself," replied Draupadi.
"A wife who conjures spells or uses potions
and other such things to ensnare her husband
will never make him happy, nor will she
live peacefully with him. If he finds out,
he will always be suspicious of her—
not a good basis for domestic bliss.
A woman's husband has to be her god;
that is the law I follow. You know, scripture
teaches us that the way to heaven for women
is simply through obedience to her husband.
Since my marriage, my one and only practice
is to serve my husbands and their other wives
with all my heart and soul. My eyes delight
in no other men but them, in all the world.
From dawn to dusk, I try to meet their needs,
both obvious and subtle. I am always
the first to rise, last to lie down at night.
I do my utmost to cherish each of them
and not to give them cause for irritation.
I pay great attention; I watch over
my reasonable, calm and gentle husbands
as though they were irascible, poisonous snakes.

"When Yudhishthira ruled Indraprastha
I waited daily on my husbands' mother
and spoke not one word of complaint about her,

nor argued with her, even with good cause.
I saw to every detail of the household.
The king had many thousand serving women,
thousands of slave girls, skilled in the courtly arts.
I knew the name, the attributes, the history
of every one of them. I listened to them.
I laid down the servants' daily duties
and saw that they were properly performed.
I managed the finances of the household—
I alone knew the particulars
of what the imperial treasury contained.
I cultivated my husbands' favorites
and blocked the access of their enemies.

"All this is my 'secret,' Satyabhama,
nothing devious. By serving my husbands
every minute of my waking life,
regarding them in the most generous spirit,
we live together in harmony and love,
for they, in their turn, love me most sincerely.
Through my devotion, they become devoted.
So my advice is—follow this example;
and, furthermore, delight your husband's senses
by wearing lovely garments, flowers and perfume.
That is the way to keep Krishna's affection."

⚑

The time drew nearer when the Pandavas
would end their exile, and King Dhritarashtra
grew more and more disturbed. Through a brahmin
who had seen the Pandavas in the forest,
he had had news—he knew that Arjuna
now possessed many celestial weapons;
he knew about the brothers' pilgrimage,
and from whom they had received advice.
The anxious king listened to all the gossip

that came his way, the scraps of information
from travelers passing through Hastinapura.

What he heard gave him no shred of comfort.
And what he did not hear, imagination
supplied in the most terrifying detail.
He thought about the bitter sense of grievance
the Pandavas must be nursing in their hearts
and groaned. "How could they possibly forgive
the insults lovely Draupadi endured
at my sons' hands? There is no way for us
to escape their terrible revenge. Surely
we stand no chance against Bhima's searing wrath.
Our forces will be wiped out by Arjuna!"

All this he was prone to say openly
in the hearing of the entire court,
and Duryodhana fumed, "The craven coward!
Why does my father not believe in me?
Why does he have no faith in all my planning,
the strength I've built up over all these years?"

For Duryodhana had not wasted time.
He had made sure his cronies occupied
the most strategic posts within the court,
so now he held the reins of royal power
in all but name. With the help of Karna,
he had built up a massive fighting force.
He had used wealth to ingratiate himself
with the citizens, and to win support
from neighboring kings, securing promises
that they would fight for him when the time came.
He was resolved: no argument on earth
would make him yield his cousin's former kingdom.

But though he swaggered outwardly, in secret
he was afraid, increasingly oppressed

as the twelfth month of the twelfth year approached.
Karna consoled him, "My prince, you are greater
than anyone on earth. No one can crush you—
the Pandavas should recognize that fact.
Suppose we organize an expedition,
take a huge entourage into the forest
to the beautiful Lake Dvaitavana
near where the Pandavas live out their lives
in squalor and degradation? Let them see
the painful contrast between their pitiful
resources and your own magnificence."

"A good plan!" said Duryodhana. At once,
using the pretext of an official tour
of the cattle stations owned by the king,
a large party set out for the forest—
Kaurava brothers, courtiers and friends,
provisioners, cooks and valets, maidservants,
carpenters; dozens of concubines and wives,
bejeweled and richly dressed; most accomplished
singers, musicians, acrobats, dancing girls,
carried in palanquins and carriages;
laden carts—flanked by a well-armed escort
of a thousand soldiers, their bronze helmets
glittering. Duryodhana inspected
the cattle stations, had the new calves branded,
discussed the breeding program with the herdsmen.

Then they settled, pitched their elaborate camp
a short distance from where the Pandavas
had their dwelling, making such a din
with bonfires, drumming and festivities
the exiles could not fail to notice them.

For many days, they enjoyed themselves—
playing games with the cowherds, chasing deer

and wild boar. One day, hot and tired from hunting,
the prince sent his men to the nearby lake
to prepare a place for him to bathe.
They found it fenced off, guarded by gandharvas.
The peaceful lake was reserved for their king
and his consorts. "Then they must make way,"
said the servants, "our great prince, Duryodhana,
wishes to bathe." The gandharvas were amused.
"Your witless prince is dreaming if he thinks
that he, a mortal, can command celestials!"

Duryodhana approached with his entourage
and a battle followed. The gandharva king
was Chitrasena, Arjuna's close friend
from the five years he had spent in Indra's realm.
The gandharvas took to the air, wheeling,
swooping like birds of prey. Some Kaurava troops,
terrified, ran off in all directions,
but Karna stood his ground and, single-handed,
loosing his arrows with amazing skill,
cut down many hundreds of gandharvas—
who fell, but quickly sprang up once again
until the field was swarming with gandharvas
by the thousand. But the Kaurava princes
rallied and, led by Karna, strongly attacked
the gandharvas. Chitrasena, furious,
summoned up illusion. Courageous Karna
fought stubbornly, showering his attackers
with razor-sharp arrows, killing hundreds
until, his chariot shattered, he was forced
to quit the fight.

On seeing this, the troops
that still remained gave up, and ran in fear
toward the position where Yudhishthira,
having heard the tumult, was observing
all that took place. Duryodhana, though wounded,

did not give in, and fought on, single-handed,
until Chitrasena overpowered him
and captured him alive. He was tied up,
as were his wives and several of his brothers.
The abject troops, Duryodhana's retainers
and the straggling, sobbing camp followers
begged for protection from the Pandavas.

Seeing his cousins captured, and their servants
begging for asylum, bull-like Bhima
crowed in triumph. "They've got what they deserve—
they hoped to see us living in misery;
now let the gandharvas finish them!"
"No vengeance for now," said Yudhishthira.
"They are our kin, we're honor bound to help
no matter what they've done to us. Revenge
will take another form than this, believe me.
To save the life of a humiliated
enemy will be pleasure enough for now.
Arjuna, the twins and you, Bhima,
must set our cousins free. Be mild at first,
but if the gandharvas will not give way
then you must use all necessary means
to release the captives."

The Pandavas
strapped on their shining armor, and leapt onto
their well-made chariots. Fierce battle followed,
with all the gandharvas' skill and wizardry
pitted against the mighty Pandavas.
Arrows and spears rained down. The celestials
tried to break the Pandavas' chariots
as they had smashed those of the Kauravas.
But they were kept at bay successfully.
Arjuna deployed his celestial weapons
to such effect that thousands of gandharvas
fell dead upon the ground. Others attempted

to fly away, but Arjuna created
a net of arrows, so that they were trapped
like linnets in a cage. Then Chitrasena,
seeing his forces beaten and terrified,
joined the fray in disguise, grasping his mace,
and rushed at Arjuna, who parried the blows,
shattering the great club. And whatever
illusions the gandharva king employed
Arjuna penetrated and defused them.
Outmaneuvered, Chitrasena then
revealed himself as Arjuna's old friend.

Arjuna laughed, astonished. "Chitrasena!
Why have you held our cousin and his brothers?"
"Indra instructed me," said Chitrasena.
"He wants to punish that mean-spirited man
who came expressly to intimidate you.
I am to deliver him to Indra."
"But he is our kinsman," said Arjuna.
"Please let him go—Yudhishthira requests it."
"That evildoer does not deserve freedom,"
grumbled Chitrasena. Nonetheless,
Duryodhana and his party were set free.
Yudhishthira thanked him, and Chitrasena,
whose dead gandharvas had been restored to life,
departed for the kingdom of the gods.

The Dharma King turned to Duryodhana
and addressed him in a soothing tone.
"Friend, spiteful gloating's never a good idea,
nor is rash violence. Let me advise you
not to be so impulsive. Now, set off home
in safety and good heart."

               Duryodhana,
his head bowed, walked away in silence.
He was overwhelmed with shame and bitterness.

Karna, knowing nothing of what had happened,
greeted him with joy. "You have survived!
What a warrior you are, defeating
the massed gandharvas—and you have emerged
unscathed!" Duryodhana shed bitter tears.
"Karna, it was not like that, not at all."
He told his friend of his humiliation,
of how the gandharvas had been persuaded
to release him through no skill of his.
"Witnessed by my brothers, by my women,
the very men whom I set out to harm
saved my life! I wish I had died in battle.
What warrior of spirit could bear to live
owing his life to his enemies,
mocked by all? Certainly not I!
I have brought this ignominy on myself;
now I have resolved to fast unto death.
Duhshasana can lead the Kauravas!"

Karna tried to imbue the prince with courage
and, failing, vowed that he would die himself
rather than walk the earth without his friend.
Shakuni rebuked Duryodhana,
"Come, this excessive grief is foolishness.
Think of the humiliation you inflicted
on the Pandavas in the gaming hall,
yet, as you see, they hold their heads high;
you don't see *them* fasting unto death.
Your cousins acted well—they rescued you
and you should thank them, and magnanimously
restore their kingdom to them. That's the way
to earn the respect of friends and enemies."

But Duryodhana was unmoved. "I will die.
Life is joyless to me now, a desert
empty of all delight. Friends, I embrace you.
Leave me here; return to Hastinapura."

The grim-faced prince stripped off his finery
and sat on the hard earth, composed and silent.

⚓

In the dank and gloomy underworld,
demons who had been defeated by the gods
heard with dismay of Duryodhana's vow.
In the ongoing war of gods and demons
they had great hopes of him. With magic spells
they had him brought to appear before them
and, as in a dream, Duryodhana
found himself in a huge and crowded hall,
the smoking sconces bolted to the walls
shedding a lurid light.

               Demons jostled him
on every side, "O mighty Kaurava,
why are you doing violence to yourself?
It is wrong to give way to despair.
You are no mere mortal, but divine,
as we are. Long ago, with Shiva's blessing,
you were formed out of diamonds and flowers,
beautiful to women, invincible.
You will destroy your enemies. We demons
will take possession of the inner souls
of Bhishma, of Drona and of Kripa.
However much they love the Pandavas,
they will fight for you with complete ruthlessness,
and will defeat your cousins and their allies.
As for Arjuna—we have a plan.
The demon Naraka has entered into
Karna, whose mission is to fight and kill
the Left-handed Archer. Knowing this,
Krishna, wielder of the all-slaying discus,
has arranged for Karna to be robbed
of the gold earrings and protective armor

he was born with. But if it should happen
that Karna dies, then demons by the thousand
inhabiting the bodies of your allies,
and sworn to destroy the Left-handed Archer,
will slaughter Arjuna, no doubt about it.
Go now—direct your mind to victory!"

Duryodhana awoke from this encounter
no longer set on death. Immensely heartened,
keeping secret what he had been told,
triumphantly, he rode back to the city.
From that day forward he prepared for war
whole-heartedly, convinced he could not lose.
He set in train a lavish sacrifice
and invited guests from far and wide,
including the Pandavas. Yudhishthira
graciously declined the invitation—
the period of exile was not yet spent.

Karna was full of joy to see his friend
resolute again. "Greatest of kings,
I swear to you, I shall not wash my feet
until I have ground Arjuna in the dust!"

24.

THE END IN SIGHT

When news of Karna's vow reached the Pandavas
Yudhishthira was much cast down, for Karna
was the enemy he feared above all others—
knowing him to be a supreme archer,
passionate in his hatred for Arjuna.

It was a dark time. Again, Yudhishthira,
pained by the privations of his family,
knowing himself to blame, was in despair;
while they in turn, seeing him distressed,
were seized with wrathfulness, and with a passion
to punish those who had caused his misery.

Vyasa arrived and spoke to Yudhishthira.
"Virtuous conduct is always rewarded
in this life or the next. Control your sorrow.
Live each day with a calm and even mind,
treating success and setback equally.
Once, you lived in luxury and wealth;
now you are suffering. To be happy,
one has to suffer first. Each of these states
is simply how things are. The two conditions
succeed each other as the seasons do.
The wheel turns. You will regain your kingdom
after the thirteenth year has run its course.
With your strong brothers and your mighty allies
supporting you, you will be king again.

"The wise, neither mourning nor rejoicing,
take what life brings with equanimity.
But with austerity and discipline
wonders may be achieved."

"Which is greater,"
asked Yudhishthira, "austerity
or giving?" Vyasa answered, "In my view,
nothing is more difficult than giving
in a spirit of pure-heartedness
when wealth has been hard won. Let me tell you
the old story of the gleaner Mudgala.

"MUDGALA WAS A law-abiding man, who subsisted on grains of rice picked up from the fields. Yet he was able to give food generously to others since, by virtue of his austerities, the grains multiplied when a guest visited him.

"The seer Durvasas decided to test his generosity. He appeared in the form of an unkempt madman and demanded food. Mudgala welcomed him, washed his feet and set food before him. The madman gobbled up all the food there was, so there was nothing left for the gleaner to eat. Then he smeared the scrapings on his body and departed. The next day, he turned up again, and so it continued for six days, but Mudgala welcomed him each time, and showed no trace of impatience or discourtesy.

" 'I have never encountered such pure-hearted generosity!' exclaimed the seer, revealing his true identity. 'For this, you will go to heaven in your body.'

"A celestial chariot, drawn by swans and cranes, arrived to take Mudgala to heaven. But the gleaner wanted first to know what heaven was like—who lived there, and what were their qualities? The celestial messenger told him, 'Heaven is inhabited by the virtuous, who enjoy happy and pain-free lives there. But once the merit earned in their previous lives is exhausted, they return to earth and are reborn in another body. Beyond heaven there are other worlds, in the highest of which eternal bliss may be attained, beyond happiness and sorrow, beyond rebirth. That world is very hard to reach, even for the gods. Only those who have transcended desire may go there.'

"Mudgala reflected, and decided that so imperfect a heaven as he was being offered was not for him. He entered a life of extreme self-denial and meditation and, in time, he achieved moksha."

Vyasa then continued on his travels,
leaving Yudhishthira happier than before.
As he slept that night, he had a dream.
A group of weeping deer appeared to him
and stood before him, trembling with terror.
"We are all that's left of the rich stocks
of animals that once lived in this woodland.
All the others have been hunted down
for food, by your party. Now there are barely
enough of us to reproduce our kind."
Yudhishthira was seized by remorse and pity.
The next day, he began to organize
a move to another part of the forest
where they would set up a new hermitage,
and live until the twelve years had expired.

☙

One afternoon, the Pandavas went hunting.
Draupadi remained at the hermitage
with Dhaumya, the priest. A while later,
Jayadratha, king of the Sindhus (husband
of Dhritarashtra's daughter, Duhshala),
happened by with his retinue, and noticed
Draupadi wandering among the trees
gathering flowers, and radiating beauty
as the moon illumines the dark clouds.

He lusted after her—her slender waist,
full breasts and shapely hips, and her lovely face.
He sent a close companion to inquire
who she was. Draupadi was conscious
that to converse with this man was improper
but, since there was no one else to answer,
she spoke, naming her husbands, inviting him
to wait, and be the guest of Yudhishthira,
together with his friend.

               The companion
reported back; Jayadratha approached her,
smitten with desire. "Come, gorgeous one,
let me transport you to a better life
than this, inflicted on you by those husbands,
exiled, down on their luck. I promise you
luxury, wealth, pleasure . . . What do you say?"

Draupadi blazed with anger, "Ignorant fool!
Do you take me for an unprotected woman?
How dare you insult my husbands, famous warriors
unsurpassed anywhere! You can no more
defeat them than an idiot with a stick
could hope to subdue a rutting elephant.
Be on your way!"

            "Mere words won't put me off,"
laughed Jayadratha, and, laying hands on her,
he forced her onto his chariot, and drove off,
flanked by his guards. Dhaumya followed them.
The Pandavas, sensing something was amiss,
hurried back to the hermitage, where they found
Draupadi's maidservant distraught and weeping.
She told them what had happened and, at once,
they set off in pursuit of Jayadratha.

They followed traces left by the abductors
and soon caught up with them. Dhaumya, in the rear,

shouted to the brothers, "Attack! Attack!"
Tiger-like, the Pandavas launched themselves
against the forces of the king of Sindhu.
Bhima's mace, its spikes ablaze with gold,
was whirling, slaughtering the foot soldiers
by the dozen. Nakula, unmatched swordsman,
cut a swath through the mounted enemy,
their heads flying off like seeds in the wind,
while Sahadeva with his spear, Yudhishthira
and Arjuna with their fine, deadly arrows,
reduced the Sindhu soldiers to a rabble,
fleeing in all directions. When Jayadratha
saw that the fight was lost, he too fled,
abandoning Draupadi. "He won't escape,"
shouted Bhima, "I'll catch and kill the villain!"

"No," said Yudhishthira, "for Gandhari's sake,
and Duhshala's, vile scoundrel though he is,
he should not be killed."
                              "That excrescence,"
protested Draupadi, glowing with anger,
"that abortion of the Sindhu race
does not deserve to live!"

                              With difficulty,
Bhima refrained from killing Jayadratha
when he caught him. Instead, he made him grovel,
thrashed him brutally, and shaved his head
so that five tufts remained. Yudhishthira
had him brought, and delivered a homily
which, perhaps, was worst of all. Jayadratha
crept away, aching, badly disgraced,
vowing vengeance. Later he embarked
on severe austerities, with a view
to obtaining a boon from Lord Shiva:
that he would block the Pandavas in battle
—excepting Arjuna, who was protected
by Krishna, supreme master of the discus.

❧

Sitting with Markandeya one afternoon,
Yudhishthira was full of despondency.
"Life here is hard—living as forest dwellers,
forced to kill other forest dwellers for food;
our blameless wife abducted, our close kin
attacking us as enemies—was there ever
anyone more afflicted with misfortune?"

"You are not unique," said Markandeya,
"Rama, too, lost his beautiful wife, Sita,
abducted by the demon Ravana."
Markandeya went on to tell the tale
of Rama and his brother, Lakshmana;
how they and Sita endured forest exile;
how Ravana seized Sita, and transported her
to Lanka; how, with the help of Hanuman
and his fellow monkeys, she was rescued;
how, at first, Rama rejected her;
but how, at last, the couple were united
and Rama installed as king of Ayodhya.

"So, you see, you are not the only prince
to suffer tribulations. You are sustained
by your bull-like brothers. You should not grieve."

"My sorrow is not only for myself,"
said Yudhishthira, "nor even for my brothers,
but for our wife who is so cruelly wronged.
Was there ever a woman so virtuous
and loving as Draupadi?"

                              "Let me tell you,"
said the sage, "the story of another
highborn woman, the princess Savitri.

"In the land of the Madras, there lived a king, named Ashvapati. He was generous, devout, an excellent king and loved by all his subjects. But he had no children and, as the years went by, this troubled him more and more. He entered on a course of strict austerities, dedicated to the goddess Savitri and, after eighteen years had passed, she appeared before him, rising up out of the sacred fire.

"'I am pleased with you, O king. You may choose a boon from me.'

"'I wish for many sons, to maintain my lineage,' said Ashvapati.

"'You shall not have sons,' said Savitri, 'but a lovely daughter will be born to you—no argument. That is how it will be.'

"'May it be soon,' said the king.

"In the fullness of time, a girl was born to his first queen, and the king called her Savitri, after the goddess. She grew up so formidably beautiful that potential suitors were reluctant to seek her hand in marriage. Eventually, her father sent her out into the world, suitably escorted, to find a husband for herself. She was gone for months, touring forests and sacred fords, conversing with sages, giving freely to brahmins. When she returned, she found her father sitting with the seer Narada.

"'Father, I have chosen my husband. In the land of the Shalvas, there is a god-fearing king, Dyumatsena. Some time ago, he went blind, and an old enemy, seeing an opportunity, ousted him and sent him to the forest. It is his son, Satyavat, to whom I have given my heart. He is brave and generous—and he is an artist!'

"'Satyavat is perfect in every way,' said all-seeing Narada. 'But the bad news is that he is destined to die exactly one year from now.'

"'That is bad news indeed!' exclaimed the king. 'My dear one, you had better choose again.'

"'There are some things in life,' Savitri said, 'that happen only once. I have chosen my husband, and I will not choose a second time.'

" 'Savitri has spoken well,' said Narada, and with that he took his leave and flew up into the sky.

"Sad, but resigned, the king visited Dyumatsena, and arranged his daughter's marriage to Satyavat. She lived in the forest with her husband and his family, a devoted wife and daughter-in-law, and everyone who knew her loved her. She mentioned to no one what Narada had told her. As the day approached when Satyavat was due to die, she undertook an act of austerity, standing for three days and nights continually, fasting. Then she poured libations on the sacred fire, her heart aching.

"On the fateful day, she announced that she would go with Satyavat when he went deep into the forest, to gather fruit. 'It will be too hard for you,' he said, 'especially after your severe fast.' But she insisted, and the two set off. All around were flowering trees and sparkling brooks, and Savitri pretended to be light-hearted, though she was watchful, tense with fear.

"Satyavat put the fruit he had collected in a sack, and started to split firewood. Suddenly, he exclaimed, 'Oh, my head is hurting terribly, as if it is pierced with knives! I can't go on,' and he sank to the ground, unconscious. Savitri embraced him, and sat nursing his head in her lap.

"Then she saw a handsome, dark-skinned man approaching through the trees, dressed in saffron, a noose in his hand. Gently laying her husband's head on the ground, she stood and greeted the stranger respectfully.

" 'Please tell me who you are, and what you want,' she said, in a trembling voice.

" 'I am Yama, god of death,' he answered. 'Your husband's life has run its course, and, because he is a virtuous man, I have come myself to fetch him, rather than sending my minions. I have deigned to answer you because I know that you, too, live a blameless and disciplined life.' Yama drew from Satyavat's body a thumb-sized figure and tied it in his noose. As he did so, Satyavat stopped breathing, and his skin lost its luster. Yama turned and walked away, and Savitri followed.

" 'You must turn back, Savitri,' said Yama. 'Return and perform funeral rites for your husband. You have come as far as you can.'

" 'Where my husband goes, I will go,' replied Savitri, 'that is dharma. I look for no other way.'

" 'You speak well,' said Yama. 'You may choose any boon, other than your husband's life, and I shall grant it.'

" 'Then may my father-in-law's sight be restored.'

" 'So be it," said Yama. 'But you are exhausted—you should turn back now.'

" 'How can I be tired when I am with my husband?' said Savitri. 'Wherever he goes, I will go. It is said that friendship with the virtuous is the highest good. I will walk with this virtuous man.'

" 'What you say pleases me,' said Yama. 'Choose another boon—other than the life of Satyavat.'

" 'Then may my father-in-law's kingdom be restored to him.'

" 'It shall be done,' said Yama. 'Now, turn back.'

" 'You carry people away by force, not of their own choosing,' said Savitri. 'Most people in the world are kindly disposed. But only the truly virtuous are compassionate even to their enemies.'

" 'Beautifully put!' exclaimed Yama. 'Choose another boon from me—other than this man's life.'

" 'I am my father's only child,' said Savitri. 'I ask that he should have a hundred sons, to carry his line.'

" 'Granted,' said Yama. 'Now, return home, for you have come a long way down this road.'

"Savitri refused. She continued to walk with Death, talking of dharma with great eloquence, as her husband dangled from Yama's noose.

"Yama grew more and more delighted with her. He granted her the boon that she and Satyavat would have a hundred sons and, as she continued to talk, calmly and wisely, refusing to leave her husband, Yama offered her a final boon, this time without conditions.

" 'Then let my husband live, for without him, my own life is a living death. Without him I have no desire for riches, good fortune, even for heaven. And without him, how can I give birth to a hundred sons?'

"Yama smiled, and untied Satyavat from the noose. 'Look, I have freed your husband, virtuous woman. You will live in peace and happiness together.' Savitri joyfully walked back to where her husband's body lay. She placed his head in her lap, and he awoke, bewildered.

" 'I fell asleep and dreamed—or was it real? I found myself in terrible darkness, and I remember a majestic figure who dragged me away . . .'

" 'Later, I will tell you what happened,' said Savitri, 'but night is falling—we should hurry home.' Soon it was pitch dark and they could hear wild animals rustling menacingly in the undergrowth. But Satyavat knew the forest well, and they safely reached the hermitage.

"They found the whole community in a fever of anxiety at their absence. Search parties had been sent out for them. But King Dyumatsena had regained his sight, to everyone's great joy. The next day, Savitri recounted the whole story— how the seer, Narada, had foretold Satyavat's death, and how, through persistence and eloquence, she had won back his life, as well as other boons.

"Soon afterward, the king regained his kingdom. And, in time, Savitri gave birth to a hundred sons, and so did her mother.

"So you see," said the sage to Yudhishthira,
"Savitri, through her virtue and good sense,
rescued those she loved; and in the same way
Draupadi sustains the Pandavas!"

As the end of the twelfth year approached,
Karna's father, Surya, the sun god,

appeared to Karna in a dream, to warn him.
"Most truthful of men, the mighty Indra,
anticipating war, and keen to favor
the Pandavas, will try to take the earrings
and the golden armor you were born with.
The whole world knows how generous you are,
how you never refuse to give to brahmins
when they ask. So he will come to you
in brahminical disguise, and beg from you
your earrings and your shining gold cuirass.
Offer him something else—give him anything
except those things, for they are your protection.
Wearing them, you cannot be killed in battle;
without them, you are open, vulnerable."

"Lord of light, I know you say this to me
for my own good. I am devoted to you
as to no other deity. I love you
more than my wife, my sons, my friends, myself.
But I do not fear death as I fear untruth;
I would rather die than be dishonored.
Giving to brahmins is my avowed practice
and if I die as a result, so be it;
I shall gain fame thereby."
                              "Posthumous fame,"
said Surya, "is a rather poor reward
if you are reduced to a pile of ashes
and scattered to the winds. A dead man's fame
is as useless as adorning him with jewels.
There is a reason, known only to the gods,
why you should keep the armor you were born with."

"I have my arms, my strength, my hard-won skill,"
said Karna. "I can defeat Arjuna
with those alone."
                    "Then at least," said Surya,
"if your mind is so set on your vow,

ask the wielder of the thunderbolt
for a celestial weapon in exchange."
The dream ended, and Karna remembered it.

Not long afterward, as he was praying
to the lord Surya, standing in the river
with hands joined in devotion, a tall brahmin
approached him begging alms. "What shall I give you?"
asked Karna. "Your earrings and your golden armor,"
replied the holy man. "Respected brahmin,
please ask for something else," said Karna, "wealth,
women, cattle, land . . . I need my armor
to protect me from my enemies."
But the brahmin, as Karna knew he would,
refused all other gifts. "O chief of gods,"
said Karna, laughing, "I know who you are.
Is it not the business of the gods
to give gifts to mortals? That being so,
if I am to mutilate my body
you should give me something in exchange."
"Very well," said Indra, "choose a gift—
Surya must have told you I was coming.
Take anything except my thunderbolt."
Karna chose Indra's javelin, which always
found its mark and flew back to his hand.
Indra said, "You shall have it but, for you,
it will only hit a single target
and then return to me."
                              "A single target
is enough," said Karna: "that mighty hero
I fear above all others."
                              "Be aware,"
said Indra, "that the hero you have in mind
is protected by Narayana himself."
"No matter," Karna said, "give me the spear.
But grant that I will not appear disfigured
when I have cut the armor from my body."
"Karna, because you are a man of truth

your body will be unscarred. You will retain
the radiance you inherit from your father."

Then, having accepted the tall spear,
Karna took a sharp knife, and he cut
and cut until the golden armor peeled
slowly away, and he presented it,
wet with blood, to Indra. As he did so
he did not show the smallest sign of pain.
The heavens echoed with admiring shouts
and flowers rained down on the hero's head.

When the news of Karna's renunciation
reached the Kauravas, they were dismayed.
But the Pandavas rejoiced when they heard.

⚜

Now the Pandavas began to talk
about the final period of their exile:
how and where could they live unrecognized?
One day, an old brahmin approached them, shouting—
a stag had run off with his kindling sticks,
he could not do his daily rites without them.
The Pandavas set off in swift pursuit,
they spread out separately, but none of them
hit the animal. Then they lost sight of it.
Nakula, parched with thirst, came to a lake
and, crouching to drink, he heard a booming voice:
"You may not drink until you give the answers
to the questions I wish to put to you."
Nakula looked around and, seeing no one,
and desperate with thirst, drank anyway.
Instantly, he fell dead on the bank.
One by one, his other brothers came,
heard the voice, drank, and also fell lifeless.

Last came Yudhishthira, horrified to find
his brothers dead and, though he was as thirsty
as they had been, when he heard the voice
he reflected, drew back, and, speaking humbly,
called, "Who are you, mysterious being?
Ask your questions, but please let me see you."
A monstrous figure immediately appeared,
towering over the surrounding landscape.
"I am a yaksha, and this lake is mine;
your brothers foolishly disobeyed me."
Then the yaksha fired riddles at him
and, just as quickly, Yudhishthira replied:

"What is it that makes the sun rise?"
"Brahman."
"Who are the sun's companions?"
"The gods."
"How does a person achieve greatness?"
"Greatness is achieved through austerity."
"What is one's most constant friend?"
"Insight."
"By what means does one acquire insight?"
"Through devotedly serving one's elders."
"What is swifter than the wind?"
"The mind."
"What is the highest gift of heaven?"
"The truth."
"What is the most valuable possession?"
"Knowledge."
"What is the highest dharma?"
"Non-cruelty."
"What can be renounced without regret?"
"Anger."
"What disease is a bar to happiness?"
"Greed."
"What is ignorance?"
"Not knowing one's dharma."

"How does one find bliss in the next world?"
"By acting virtuously in this one."
"What sleeps with its eyes open?"
"A fish."
"What does not move when it is born?"
"An egg."
"What has no heart?"
"A rock has no heart."
"What grows as it rushes on its way?"
"A river grows as it rushes on its way."
"What is the greatest wonder in the world?"
"That, every single day, people die,
yet the living think they are immortal."

The huge being asked many more questions
and smiled with pleasure when Yudhishthira
gave the answers. At last, it was satisfied.
"You have answered well. Now you may choose
one of your brothers to be restored to life."
"I choose Nakula," said Yudhishthira.
The yaksha was surprised, "But surely Bhima
is dearest to you. And you need Arjuna
to fight for you in the war that is to come."
"Yes," said Yudhishthira, "but my father
had two wives—and it is only right
that one of Madri's sons should also live."

There was a searing flash over the lake.
The yaksha disappeared and became Dharma,
god of righteousness, Yudhishthira's father.
He was delighted with his son's replies,
and brought all four brothers back to life.
"I was the stag that took the brahmin's sticks—
here they are. Now ask a favour of me."
"My lord, grant that in our thirteenth year
of exile we will not be recognized."
"It shall happen as you wish," said Dharma.

"And, Father, if I may ask one thing more:
may my mind always lead me toward the truth."

"You ask for what you already have, my son."
And the god Dharma blessed the Pandavas.

IV

THE BOOK OF VIRATA

25.

VIRATA'S COURT

Twelve years were over. Now the Pandavas
must think how best to live unrecognized
during their final year—though, thanks to Dharma,
their success was certain. Where should they go?
After the interminable seclusion
of the forest, they welcomed the prospect
of life in a city—somewhere not too close,
and not too famous, a pleasant backwater.
Arjuna, well-traveled, named a number
of delightful kingdoms with hospitable
rulers who reigned from well-appointed cities,
and of these Yudhishthira chose Matsya,
a wealthy kingdom ruled by King Virata.

He discussed the prospect with his brothers.
"We will take employment with the king.
Now, sons of Kunti, say what kind of work

you are best fitted for. What disguises,
what false identities can you sustain
plausibly until our exile ends?

"I myself will be a brahmin, 'Kanka.'
I have become quite learned in the Vedas;
and I can offer the king my mastery
at dice! Remember, the sage Brihadashva
taught me how to win without cheating.
I shall enjoy rolling my fine dice
made of beryl, ivory, gold, ebony . . .
And if the king asks where I learned my skill
I'll say I was once Yudhishthira's close friend.

"But, Wolf-belly, you'll find disguise a problem.
How many men are there as tall and strong
as you, or with so fiery a temper?"
"It's true," laughed Bhima, "that disguising me
is rather like trying to hide Mount Meru!
But I'll be 'Ballava,' a master cook
experienced in every fine cuisine.
I'll install myself in the royal kitchen
and curry favor with my toothsome curries!
I can give wrestling courses on the side.
I'm sure the king will love me when he samples
what I can do. And if he should ask questions
about my previous experience,
I'll tell him that my expertise was honed
in the kitchens of King Yudhishthira
at Indraprastha—that should satisfy him!"

"And you, Arjuna?" asked Yudhishthira.
"The most distinguished warrior in the world,
eagle among men, brilliant as a god,
won't find it easy to go unremarked."
"These bowstring scars on my arms," said Arjuna,
"may be a problem, but I'll cover them

with bangles, braid my hair, wear women's dress.
I'll teach the ladies in the king's seraglio
dancing, singing and all the female arts
I learned from the gandharvas in Indra's realm.
I can play instruments, entertain the court
with beguiling tales as well as any bard.
I'll pose as a eunuch, a transvestite,
woman with a flute, 'Brihannada'!"

Nakula proposed to seek employment
with the horses in the royal stables.
He excelled at all equestrian skills,
and was a master tamer of wild horses,
no matter how intransigent or vicious.
He loved them; and he had acquired the art
of healing them when they were sick or injured.
He would go by the name of "Granthika."

The region of the Matsyas was well known
for its plump and fertile cattle. Sahadeva
had never been happier than in the days
when he had supervised the royal herds
of Indraprastha. Now he would persuade
King Virata that the cattle stations
would flourish under his good management.
He would call himself "Tantipala."

What of the virtuous Draupadi? Her husbands
hated the thought of their beloved wife
condemned to drudgery. But she was scornful
of their scruples. "Do you really think
I'm too weak for the life of a maidservant
after what I have gone through in the forest?
After what happened in the gambling hall?
I shall play the part of a chambermaid,
'Sairandhri,' a woman free to find her own
employment. But I shall say I have a husband—

five, in fact, gandharvas, strong celestials—
who will fight for my honor if required.
I shall enter the service of Queen Sudeshna,
arrange her hair, mix her creams and lotions,
help to dress her, advise her if required.
If I am questioned, I shall say that, once,
I was a handmaid to Queen Draupadi."

They left their forest camp a few days early
so as to give Duryodhana's spies the slip.
They said their heartfelt farewells to the brahmins
who had been with them for their whole exile,
consoling them and saying prayers for them.
Dhaumya gave them blessings for their journey
and words of wise advice.

                        "You must remember
you have never known a life of servitude
and there are gestures, postures, ways of moving
that will come naturally to you, but which
may cause offense when noticed in a servant.
Be vigilant. Take care not to arouse
envy or resentment. Neither too merry
nor too glum, too eager, too reluctant—
rather, be of even temperament,
wearing a habitual gentle smile.
That is the best way to survive at court.

"Speak to the king only when spoken to.
If he should ask you, 'What is your opinion?'
search your mind for what will give him pleasure
and bring him profit—profit first and foremost.
Pay him compliments judiciously
but never make any reference to his wealth.
Be discreet, never repeat to others
what the king may say to you in confidence.
That is the best way to survive at court.

"A wise courtier knows that the king's favor
is uncertain, and always strives to earn it.
Do not spend time with those whom the king dislikes,
nor be too friendly with the courtiers' wives,
arousing jealousy. If the king gives you
gifts—whether vehicles, clothes or jewels—
be grateful, and make sure he sees you use them.

"The successful courtier emulates the king
but never rivals him. Faced with some errand
he leaps to volunteer; the king's interests
must come before those of his own family.
That is the best way to survive at court."

So saying, Dhaumya blessed them yet again.
Yudhishthira expressed his gratitude
and the Pandavas set out on the long walk
to their new place of refuge. They followed
the winding course of the Kalindi River,
through Dasharna, then south of Panchala,
avoiding any towns or villages
and, after crossing miles of wilderness,
reached the outskirts of their destination,
the handsome capital of Virata's realm.

Yudhishthira gave the brothers secret names,
for an emergency, auspicious names
invoking victory—Jaya, Jayatsena,
Jayanta, Vijaya and Jayadbala.

⚜

Before the Pandavas entered the city
they needed to discard their warriors' weapons.
On a hill outside the city walls,
there was a desolate cremation ground,

a doleful place where no one ever loitered;
and there they saw a towering shami tree,
difficult to climb and with thick foliage.
Nakula shinned up, and stowed away
the brothers' bows that had achieved such feats,
their swords, and other oiled and well-made weapons,
tying them fast with rope to a thick branch
where they could not be seen, and where the rain
would not fall on them. As a precaution,
he tied a stinking corpse to another branch
so people would avoid the tree in horror.
Yudhishthira told curious passersby
this practice was a family tradition,
and the corpse was that of his ancient mother.

Entering the city, Yudhishthira
went straight to the palace and sought audience
with King Virata. "Sir, I am a brahmin
seeking a position at your court
having lost my wealth."
                    Virata was impressed
by his appearance. "Just look at the man—
he does not seem a brahmin, more like a god.
Tell me your name, stranger, and where you come from."
"I was once a friend of King Yudhishthira.
I am an expert gambler—see my dice.
My name is Kanka."
                    "Splendid!" said Virata.
"Make your home here, enjoying every comfort.
You should rule the kingdom by my side!"

Later, Bhima sought an audience.
Broad-shouldered as a lion, dressed all in black,
he carried cook's equipment. "Great king," he said,
"I am Ballava, great master chef.
Once, I was cook to King Yudhishthira
and he would eat my dishes with delight.
On the side, I am a champion wrestler

and my skill in fighting lions and tigers
will entertain you—if you will employ me."

"What an amazing man!" exclaimed Virata.
"You shall certainly rule over my kitchens,
although, judging by the look of you,
you should be ruling Matsya instead!"

Arjuna, Nakula and Sahadeva,
clothed in their false names and histories,
presented themselves in turn, and all were met
with a similarly generous welcome.
Each found his place, as planned, within the court.
All were paid a handsome wage, and no one
thought to challenge their identities.

Dark-eyed Draupadi wandered near the palace
dressed in a single black and dirty garment,
looking troubled. Virata's wife, Sudeshna,
standing on her balcony, noticed her
and had her summoned. "Good heavens, my dear,
what are you doing, hanging about the court
unprotected? You are so beautiful!
Your hair is glossy, your breasts and buttocks round,
your movements graceful, your face like the full moon,
and your eyes and mouth are perfect. Tell me,
who are you?"
                    "I am a chambermaid,"
said Draupadi. "I will work for anyone
who will feed me, clothe me and give me shelter.
I have worked for Satyabhama, Krishna's wife,
and for Queen Draupadi at Indraprastha.
I can dress hair, I can make fine unguents.
But I won't eat leftovers, nor will I wash
the feet of anyone."

                    Sudeshna smiled.
"You look more like a goddess than a maid.

I would like you to enter my own service,
but that might well be marital suicide.
If I took you in, I'd be like the crab
whose embryo destroys her from within.
Once my husband glimpsed your voluptuous shape
he would instantly fall in love with you
and cast me off!"

            "Madam," said Draupadi,
"have no fear of that. I am married
to five strong, invisible gandharvas
who guard me constantly. Any man
who looks at me with lustful disrespect
is dead meat, believe me!" Reassured,
resolving to inform Virata, the queen
happily welcomed Draupadi as her maid,
to dress her hair, and that of her entourage,
prepare her unguents, look after her clothes
and generally become a useful presence.

As the months went by, the Pandavas
were well liked in their various occupations.
Yudhishthira won popularity
with the courtiers, and with Virata,
by entertaining them at games of dice.

Arjuna kept largely out of sight
in the seraglio, where all the women
loved him. During his years in Indra's realm,
he had learned to sing and dance exquisitely
and, as we know, women love nothing more
than a man—or even half a man—
who is a gifted dancer. So Arjuna
danced for them, and taught them skillful steps,
showed them how to undulate seductively,
how to cast their eyes in languorous glances
and invitingly flutter their fingers.

In the royal kitchens, Wolf-belly Bhima
grew even more enormous. He was happy
and so was the whole court. Never before
had they looked forward quite so ardently
to the next meal. And when he was not cooking,
Bhima coached the young men of the court
in wrestling—a sport of special interest
since, every year, at the festival of Brahma,
people flocked to the city from far and wide
to take part in a wrestling championship
hosted by King Virata.

                So in the spring,
some months after the Pandavas' arrival,
huge, powerful men gathered in the arena,
strutting, flexing their oiled and bulging muscles.
One wrestler in particular, Jimuta,
a great hulk, lorded over the event,
so far outclassing all other contestants
that the tournament became quite dull.

The king ordered his cook to challenge him
which put Wolf-belly in a quandary—
he could not ignore the king's command,
but if he beat the champion with ease
people might guess who he really was.
So, although he could have floored the strongman
with one arm tied, he went through all the motions
of girding himself up and oiling his body,
then puffed and heaved and grappled valiantly
before lifting the brute, whirling him round,
flinging him to the ground winded. Defeated.
After that, the king often asked Bhima
to fight, and when no one would stand up with him,
he pitted him against tigers and elephants
and had him entertain the seraglio
by entering the ring with full-grown lions.

❧

Ten months had gone by, and the sons of Pandu
still lived unrecognized, in a condition
of quiet contentment. But not Draupadi.
The queen's lecherous brother, Kichaka
(chief of the army, powerful at court
and throughout the kingdom), had noticed her
and made advances. She rejected him
and he, besotted with her, swore he'd send
all his wives away if she would marry him.
"Out of the question—I am already married.
You're like an infant, crying for the moon.
If you persist, my five gandharva husbands
will destroy you."

      Then lustful Kichaka,
on a flimsy pretext, had Sudeshna
send Draupadi on an errand to his house
where he lewdly assaulted her. She ran
into the hall where the men were gathered,
Kichaka chasing her, grabbing her hair
and kicking her. Yudhishthira and Bhima
were choking with outrage and sympathy
but they held back. They would risk exposure
if they gave the man the beating he deserved—
for saving a mere maid from the attentions
of the marshal of the realm.

      But Draupadi,
still guarding her disguise, spoke for herself:
"Am I, the proud wife of five strong gandharvas,
to be kicked and mauled by this lawless brute?
Where are my husbands? Surely, if they were here
they would defend me, for how could they bear
to see their cherished wife defiled like this?

O king, it is your dharma to protect me—
why do you sit silent? It is an outrage
that I should be manhandled by this lout
here, in your very presence!" The courtiers
applauded her, but Virata looked aside,
dependent as he was on Kichaka.
Yudhishthira, though his temples throbbed with rage,
spoke mildly, "Chambermaid, it is not proper
that you are running here and running there
like some dancing girl. You are disrupting
our game of dice. Seek refuge with the queen.
No doubt your husbands will do what you wish
when it is the right time, in their judgment."

"My husbands are tolerant," snapped Draupadi,
"and yet they are no strangers to misfortune
since the eldest is a *gambler*!"
                                    With that,
Draupadi stormed off to the queen's apartments.
Sudeshna took her side, "That brother of mine
deserves to die for what he did to you!"

In the night, Draupadi could not sleep,
tossed by the furious grievance that consumed her.
She left her bed and went to waken Bhima,
certain of his concern. All her troubles
came pouring out. "Every day I have to see
my husbands eat dust—our Yudhishthira,
once the great emperor, now a gamester
on wages! You, wrestling lions to entertain
the women—I feel faint when I see that,
and they tease me, say I'm sweet on the cook!
And Arjuna—a pathetic dancing master!
Sahadeva . . . and Nakula! Well,
when I see all this, I ask myself
how I can go on living. And my own life—
mixing sandalwood paste for my 'mistress,'

ruining my hands." Then Wolf-belly
placed her roughened hands against his cheeks
and wept for her.

       "But, Bhima, worst of all—
that goat Kichaka won't leave me alone.
I can't endure it! I want you to kill him.
Break him, like a pot hurled onto stone!
Do this for me." Together, they devised
a plan.

       Next day Draupadi forced herself
to smile at Kichaka, and she suggested
that they meet each other secretly
in the dance pavilion when night fell.
The man was thrilled, even more enamored.
He went home, doused himself in fragrant oils,
dressed in fine garments and, at dead of night,
crept unnoticed into the pavilion.
He could just make out the padded couch
and saw Draupadi, lying there already,
her body draped in silk, her head covered.
"My lovely one," Kichaka crooned, approaching,
"I have conferred money and jewels upon you.
I have anointed myself with rare perfume.
Not for nothing do my women say,
'Kichaka, you're the handsomest man alive!' "
"How fortunate," murmured a muffled voice.

"Oh, how voluptuous you are, you handful
of gorgeousness!" and he reached out to squeeze
the ample hips. "Your skin smells so delicious . . ."
And those were the last words he ever spoke.
The covers flew apart and, with a roar,
Bhima leapt up and seized Kichaka's throat
in an iron grip. Kichaka struggled free
and the two men wrestled. But it was not long

before the villain's every rib was cracked,
his head and limbs were crushed inside his body
and his spine folded like a broken reed.

Draupadi was exultant. She called the guards
and Kichaka's kinsmen quickly gathered,
and were appalled. "Here is your flesh and blood,"
said Draupadi, "well punished by my husbands,
my five strong gandharvas, for lusting after
a married woman."

                    The dead man's relatives,
bent on vengeance, made the king agree
that she would burn on Kichaka's funeral pyre—
she would satisfy his lust in death at least.
As she was carried to the cremation ground
Draupadi shrieked her husbands' secret names
and Bhima, bursting from his room, his rage
making him swell to twice his usual size,
ran to the place. Uprooting a massive tree,
roaring mightily, he scattered the mourners.
"A gandharva! A gandharva!" they cried,
unable to see clearly in the dark,
and, releasing Draupadi, they fled
toward the city. But Bhima pursued them
like the god of death himself, and slaughtered
more than a hundred of the marshal's kinsmen.
Then he strolled off to his kitchen work.

The whole city was buzzing with the news
of the massacre at the cremation ground.
A deputation went to see the king.
"Your majesty, the whole court is in danger
from that woman—she is too beautiful,
and men will naturally lust after her.
But her husbands' vengeance is terrifying—
You must do something."

                     Virata was alarmed.
This chambermaid was nothing but disaster,
what with her beauty and her vengeful husbands.
He told his wife to dismiss Draupadi.
But the chambermaid requested a delay
of thirteen days, and Sudeshna agreed
to her request—if she could guarantee
there would be no more visits from gandharvas.

In thirteen days, the thirteenth year would end.

26.

THE CATTLE RAID

At the slaying of Kichaka and his kin
there was rejoicing in Virata's kingdom.
He had won power through his bravery.
In his time he had led Virata's army
to many brilliant victories in forays
against surrounding lands, appropriating
thousands of choice cattle. But at home
the man had been a bully and a lecher
and no one, not even the king himself,
had dared to put a stop to his behavior.

Dhritarashtra's and Duryodhana's spies
had lost sight of the Pandavas, ever since
they had left the forest. For a year
scouts had searched the country near and far
but they never brought back any news;
it seemed the Pandavas had simply vanished.
Some thought they must have died. But the elders
disagreed. "I know the sons of Pandu
are not dead," said Bhishma, "they are protected
by their own virtue. Wherever they may be,
they are keeping the terms of their covenant."
The prince decreed that more efficient agents
should be sent out in a last-ditch attempt
to find the Pandavas; and that, meanwhile,
everything should be done to prepare for war.

Meanwhile, Susharman, ruler of Trigarta,
had a proposal. "I have all too often
been oppressed by raids on my cattle stations
by the Matsya army. But now Kichaka
has been found dead in odd circumstances.
Without their general's leadership and courage
the Matsya force will be in disarray.
Now is the time to mount a cattle raid,
rustle some of their fine, glossy herds."

Karna was delighted. "Blameless prince,"
he said to Duryodhana, "Susharman
is right—let us not waste our energy
thinking about the Pandavas, who either
are dead, or lack the means to challenge us.
Let us quickly mount an expedition
and profit from Kichaka's sudden death."

It was agreed. Susharman would start at once
with his army, on a week-long march
to Matsya lands. With Virata occupied
in fending off the marauding Trigartas,
Kaurava troops would follow a day later
and, approaching from another flank,
carry away thousands of prime cattle.

On the eighth day after this plan was hatched
the Pandavas' long exile would expire.

Virata was sitting with his councillors
when a breathless herdsman ran into the hall.
"Indra among men! Trigarta troops
have turned up in force. We fought with them
but they're too numerous for us to tackle

and, even as I speak, they're rounding up
thousands of your sleek and purebred cattle
and driving them away!"

        At once, the king
mobilized his excellent standing army,
well equipped, well trained, and strengthened by
the cook, the gaming master and the two
stockmen. The chaste and accomplished dancer
was not required to give his services,
and stayed discreetly in the women's quarters.
Virata proudly led his troops to battle,
engaging with the well-equipped Trigartas
before night fell.

        The forces were well matched.
The battlefield was soon awash with blood
and strewn with severed limbs. When the darkness
and dust made it impossible to see,
there was a standoff. But then the moon came up,
casting its eerie light over the land,
and the two sides again flew at each other.

Susharman managed to capture the old king.
Seeing this, the Matsya troops lost heart
and started to retreat. Yudhishthira
called to Bhima, "You must rescue Virata,
we are greatly in his debt." Bhima rejoiced
at the chance to show his prowess in a fight.
"I shall uproot that tree—it will be my club
and I shall drive away the enemies!"
"Let the tree stand," said Yudhishthira,
afraid that Bhima would be recognized.
"Do the job with ordinary weapons.
Nakula and Sahadeva will join you."
Bhima obeyed, and fierce battle followed
during which the Matsya king escaped

and, seizing a club, set upon Susharman
with all the vigor of an impetuous youth.
The Trigarta force was driven off, defeated.
The fat cows and bullocks were brought home.
King Virata cried, "Kanka! Ballava!
I owe you my life, and my kingdom.
All I have is yours—take gold, take dancing girls
bedecked with jewels, take anything you wish!"

With hands joined, Yudhishthira replied,
"To see you safe is all the reward we need.
Let messengers be sent off to the city
to proclaim your victory."

         But meanwhile,
Duryodhana and his men were rounding up
hundreds of cattle a few leagues away,
capturing more than sixty thousand strong.
The herdsmen ran panting to the court
where, in the king's absence, his son Uttara
was in charge. "Prince, you must take action!
We've heard your father talk about your prowess,
how brave you are, how skilled with bow and spear.
Now the time has come to prove his words were true.
Let your bowstring thrum, let your silver horses
be yoked to your splendid chariot, let your arrows
blot out the sun and terrify your foes.
You are our only hope, courageous prince."

"I certainly would do as you suggest,"
said Uttara, "spread terror with my bow,
cut a swath through their ranks of stalwart fighters,
decimate their warhorses and elephants
so they would think that Arjuna himself
was bearing down on them . . . The problem is,
I lack a charioteer with the right skills."

Draupadi overheard, and approached shyly.
"That handsome dancing master, Brihannada,
was at one time Arjuna's charioteer
and learned a lot from that great-hearted man.
I myself saw him when the fire god burned
the Khandava Forest—he drove Arjuna
to victory. If it pleases you, your sister
could fetch him quickly from the women's quarters."

Brihannada was summoned, and was told
what was required of him. "O prince," he simpered,
"ask me to sing or dance for you—I'll do it.
But drive a chariot in the thick of battle?
I'm not so sure that I could manage that."
"You'll dance another time," said Uttara,
"but first, prepare yourself to drive my chariot.
I shall defeat the Kauravas, take back
the stolen cattle, and return in glory."

The prince called for his well-made bows and arrows
and, decked out in his expensive armor,
he looked most elegant and glorious.
Arjuna fumbled with his coat of mail
and put his breastplate on the wrong way up,
making the women laugh. "Oh, Brihannada,"
they cried, "when you defeat the Kauravas,
bring us their bright clothing for our dolls."
Arjuna promised. Then he clambered up
clumsily onto the chariot seat, and drove
helter-skelter toward the battle lines,
Prince Uttara clinging tightly to the rail.

Arjuna called, "O tiger among princes,
how glad I am that we will fight together
against the formidable and bloodthirsty
Kauravas, against unbeaten Karna,
Duryodhana whose prowess with a mace

is unparalleled, and those other heroes!"
Behind him, Uttara was pale with fear.

It was not long before the enemy
could be seen in the distance, warriors
by the thousand, like a moving forest.
The sound reached them of the mass of men,
a distant roar, as of a mighty ocean.
Uttara's hair stood on end. "Stop! Stop!
Turn round—I'm too young for this!" he bleated.
"Drive back to the city."

                 But Arjuna
pressed on. "I'm taking you, my strong-armed hero,
to fight with the marauding Kauravas.
You boasted earlier. If you don't fight now,
if you don't recapture the stolen cows
but creep back to the city empty-handed,
the whole court will laugh at you."

                          "I don't care!"
wailed Uttara. Anything—his father's scorn,
the dancing girls' derision—would be better
than early death! With this, the woeful coward
jumped from the chariot, leaving his bow behind,
and fled. The Pandava ran after him,
his braided hair flying, bright red skirts
flapping round him. Some of the Kauravas
laughed at the spectacle, though others wondered
who was the strange man-woman. Could it be
the Terrifier, Arjuna, in disguise?

Arjuna caught up with Uttara
who was gibbering with fear. "Help! Let me go!
I'll give you anything—gold, elephants;
let me go, Brihannada!" Arjuna
took pity on the poor sap. "Noble prince,

you're a kshatriya. If you can't fight,
then drive the chariot instead, while I do.
Together, we'll defeat the enemy;
I will protect you."

                    They drove to the shami tree
at the cremation ground, where Arjuna
wished to retrieve his weapons. "Quick! Climb up,"
he told Uttara. "Tied to a branch, you'll find
the weapons of the Pandavas. Fetch them down."
"But I've heard there is a body in the tree,"
whined Uttara. "I'm a prince, I'll be exposed
to pollution!"
                    "You will expose yourself
to condemnation if you don't climb up.
Do as I tell you," said Arjuna sternly.
"There are bows there, never mind the body."

When Uttara set eyes on the marvelous weapons,
shining with a celestial radiance,
he was amazed. "Brihannada, what are these—
whose is this superb bow whose smooth back
is inlaid with a hundred golden eyes?
And this, patterned with scintillating fireflies
in pure gold? And this one, gem-encrusted?
And these fine arrows, with gold and silver nocks?
And whose is this long sword with the golden hilt,
and these others in their dazzling scabbards?"

Arjuna explained, "They all belong
to the sons of Pandu."
                    "But where are they now,
those illustrious heroes?" asked Uttara.
Then Arjuna revealed that he was Arjuna,
and disclosed the real identities
of the gaming master and the cook,
cowherd, horse tamer and the chambermaid.

Uttara was utterly astonished.
"Can I believe my ears? Can this be true?
If you are really Arjuna, then tell me
your ten names."

            "Very well," said the Pandava.
"I am Arjuna, also Vijaya,
Phalguna, Jishnu, He of the Diadem,
He of the White Horses, the Terrifier,
Left-handed Archer, Dhanamjaya, Krishna."

Uttara bowed down before Arjuna.
"What good fortune to see you, strong-armed one!
Please pardon me if I have offended you.
My fear has fled away. I only feel
great devotion. Please, give me your orders
and I shall drive you into the thick of battle.
You'll find me an outstanding charioteer!
Only one thing still puzzles me—how can you
be a eunuch, and still be Arjuna?"

Arjuna reassured him on this point.
Then he prepared for action—bound his hair,
tied on his stout wrist guards and strung *Gandiva*.
He took Virata's standard from the chariot
and affixed his own: the monkey banner.
He blew *Devadatta*, the sound of which
caused the enemy to become confused,
and Uttara to crouch down in the chariot.
"Oh!" he cried. "I can't see where I am,
my mind is reeling, I am going deaf!"

Arjuna gave him comfort, tenderly
called him "hero," "lion among men,"
enabling him to summon up some courage.
Again, the conch sounded out its challenge
and this time Uttara held fast the reins.

He planted his feet firmly, whipped the horses,
and the two rode out together into battle.

☙

The Kauravas now knew who they were facing.
They knew the deep bray of that battle conch;
they heard the well-known thundering vibration
of *Gandiva*; they saw the monkey banner.
Drona said, "This bodes no good for us.
The peerless archer is coming to do battle.
The earth is shaking, our men have lost their nerve
and do not want to fight. Let us retreat."

"Teachers are wise," said Duryodhana,
"they're good at telling stories to their pupils
but, faced with danger, do they have good judgment?
Beware a pundit who praises the enemy!
The Pandavas have broken the covenant—
it is not yet the end of the thirteenth year.
Therefore they will have to resume their exile—
another thirteen years in the wilderness.
Meanwhile we should protect our captured cattle
and support our allies, the Trigartas."

Karna addressed Drona. "I at least
have the courage to fight the Pandava
and take the captured cows to Hastinapura.
Today, I shall kill Arjuna. My arrows
will fly toward him like a swarm of locusts.
His monkey standard will tumble in the dust.
Why fear him? I am as good as he is.
With my weapons obtained from Jamadagnya,
I would even fight Krishna himself!"

"Son of Radha, you are always boasting,"
complained Kripa, frowning with irritation.

"Arjuna has great victories to his credit.
What have you ever done single-handed?
Go on—tell me! You must have lost your wits
if you think you are a match for Arjuna."

"Yes, you're full of air," said Ashvatthaman.
"The cows have not yet stirred from the Matsya lands.
What man of sense would brag about achievements
not yet performed? When have you ever triumphed
over an enemy through martial valor?
Through what heroic feats did you subdue
Draupadi at the dice game? The Pandavas
were cruelly wronged—tricked out of their kingdom,
their virtuous wife outrageously insulted.
Certainly they will not forgive such treatment,
and now they will be thirsting for revenge
like raging lions released from captivity.
No one can defeat the Left-handed Archer.
Duryodhana—you can fight him if you wish,
fight as you fought in the gambling hall!
Let cheating Shakuni fight the Pandava!
Even if my father decides to fight
I, for one, refuse to take up arms."

Bhishma said, "What you say is accurate.
But I think the son of Radha spoke those words
not as a mindless boast, but to fire us up
to fight, as is fitting for kshatriyas.
We should not be squabbling amongst ourselves.
Prince—the words you spoke concerning Drona
should not have been said." Duryodhana
apologized; Drona was mollified.
"The sons of Kunti are men of principle,"
said Bhishma. "According to my calculations,
the thirteenth year has passed. They have served their time."
"Grandfather," said Duryodhana, "I shall not
give up the kingdom to the Pandavas."

"I understand," said Bhishma. "But for now,
that is not the issue. We have to fight
as best we can." The son of Ganga quickly
gave orders for a battle strategy.

⚜

Surveying the ranks of the Kauravas
as Uttara drove the chariot ever nearer
at full gallop, Arjuna pointed out
the fine emblazoned flags of his oppponents
fluttering above their chariots: Drona's
with its distinctive water gourd, Karna's
boldly displaying a scarlet elephant.
"And see that tall, impressive white-haired man
standing erect, bow in hand, gauntleted,
a sparkling white umbrella shading him,
whose banner has sun and stars on azure blue?
That is Bhishma, grandfather to us all."

Now that they were within arrow range
Arjuna scanned the field for Duryodhana,
knowing that if he could defeat the prince
the others would give in. He could not see him.
"I think that coward's taking the cattle south
while the others make a stand. Let us skirt round
and find him." Uttara slewed the chariot round.
Drona, guessing Arjuna's intentions,
urged his soldiers to attack his rear,
but the Terrifier pelted them with arrows
so that they scattered in complete confusion.
He blew his conch, his chariot wheels thundered,
the monkey on his standard screeched aloud,
and the great din made the advancing enemy
freeze in their tracks, and the Matsya cattle
bellow, wave their tails and head for home,
calves pitifully bawling for their mothers.

The towering Wearer of the Diadem
fought with each one of the Kaurava heroes,
and although he generally refrained
from inflicting mortal wounds, he overcame
each of them. Having killed Karna's brother,
he engaged Radha's son in a bitter fight
until Karna retreated, badly hurt.

Fierce battle continued. Tireless, Arjuna
unleashed his flights of arrows like a storm
raging through the ranks of the Kauravas
and leaving many dead—young champions
sprawled and bleeding in their finery.
Indra, accompanied by other gods,
arrived on glittering, airborne chariots
to watch the way the weapons they had given
were put to use. Karna advanced again:
"Now is the time, suta's son," said Arjuna,
"for you to verify those boasts of yours.
Reap the reward of the disgraceful insults
you heaped upon the blameless Draupadi!
Just now you fled away from the battlefield,
unlike your brother. That is why you're alive
and he is not. Shame on you, son of Radha!"

Karna fought skillfully, inflicting wounds
on Arjuna, but at last, hit in the chest,
he was forced to withdraw, despite his boasts.
So was Vikarna, Duryodhana's brother,
after a well-aimed arrow from *Gandiva*
shot his elephant from under him.
At this, Duryodhana ran from the field.

All this time, Uttara drove the chariot
with skill and courage. Then Arjuna told him
to catch up with the son of Dhritarashtra
who was running for his life. "Duryodhana!

Remember how kings behave!" shouted Arjuna.
"Turn round and show your miserable face."
Stung by the insult, Duryodhana turned
and found his courage. The other Kauravas,
even though they were bleeding from their wounds,
rallied to his support. Then Arjuna
blew *Devadatta* yet again and, this time,
the Kauravas, stupefied, fell to the ground.

Arjuna, remembering his promise
to Virata's women, told Uttara
to run and strip the rich, colorful robes
from the unconscious heroes. "But keep clear
of Bhishma—he will not have lost his wits,
he knows how to counter this conch of mine."
Uttara quickly obeyed.

                    Duryodhana,
when he revived, blamed the other Kauravas
for the way the Pandava had won the day.
Bhishma laughed, "What did you do yourself?
It is only because he did not wish to kill us
that we are still alive. Now, let us depart."
Seeing them leave, Arjuna paid his respects
to the elders. Then, taking up his bow,
he shot Duryodhana's headdress from his head
by way of farewell.

                "My brave Uttara,"
he said joyfully, "turn the chariot round.
The cows are safe, the enemy is gone.
Now we will rest the horses but, meanwhile,
send messengers with all speed to your father
announcing your outstanding victory."

☙

Returned in triumph to his happy city
after his victory over the Trigartas,
Virata was rejoicing with his court
when he heard that Uttara had ridden out
to fight the Kauravas—with just the eunuch
as charioteer. The king was horrified.
Full of dread, he ordered a pursuit,
but then messengers arrived, announcing
that Uttara was safe, the cattle captured,
the enemy reduced to a shame-faced rout.
Virata was relieved and overjoyed,
full of paternal pride in Uttara.
"Let the whole city be decked out with bunting.
Let my ministers and other notables,
together with drummers, singers, dancing girls,
go out to meet my valiant Uttara!
And let his sister, with her handmaidens,
go to welcome home the dancing master."

While he waited, the king played Yudhishthira
at dice. "Just imagine," said Virata,
"my son has defeated the mighty Kauravas!"
"How could he lose, driven by Brihannada?"
replied the gaming master. Furious,
the king shouted, "How dare you praise the eunuch
in the same breath as my son!"
               "I merely know
that only Brihannada could have taken on
the powerful Kauravas, and beaten them."

Virata, enraged, hurled the heavy dice
which struck Yudhishthira so that his nose
began to bleed. He caught the blood in his hand
and Draupadi, reading his intentions,
brought a bowl, to catch the falling drops
before they reached the ground.

Soon, Uttara
made his triumphal entry to the city.
Seeing the gaming master dripping blood,
and knowing who he really was, he asked
what had happened. "I struck him," said his father.
"When I was praising you, he praised the eunuch."
Uttara was aghast. "You have done wrong!
Please ask his forgiveness, lest the brahmin
exact a terrible revenge." Virata
did so. "I'm not angry," said Yudhishthira.
"Cruelty is easy for the powerful.
But if my blood had fallen on the ground
you and your kingdom would have been destroyed."

"Now, my brave son," said the king, "I wish to hear
everything about your great achievement.
How was your fight with Duryodhana?
How did you conquer Drona? And great Bhishma?
Tell me every single blow, in detail."

Arjuna and the prince had planned beforehand
how the victory would be explained.
"Father," said Uttara, "it was not I
who won back our fine cattle from those thieves.
It was not I who beat the Kauravas.
All this was done by the son of a god.
I was fleeing in terror when that god's son
stopped me, and took my place on the chariot
while I drove him. He did everything.
He sowed panic among the Kauravas.
It was that hero who won victory
and crushed our enemies. It was not I."

"Where is that glorious warrior," asked Virata,
"that god's son who has saved for me my own son
and my cattle?"

> "He has disappeared,
> but he will be here in a day or two."

With the king's permission, Brihannada
presented his daughter, Princess Uttaraa,
with the clothes captured on the battlefield—
beautiful and valuable fabrics.
The princess and her friends laughed in delight.

༃

Three days later, to the king's amazement,
the Pandavas appeared in splendid robes
and revealed their true identities.
Draupadi was with them, far outshining
all the beautiful women of the court.
Virata could not have been more delighted
and was most contrite for any insults
they had received while living at his court.

He offered Arjuna his daughter's hand
in marriage. Arjuna declined with tact.
"All this year, I've lived in close proximity
to the princess. She has placed her trust in me
as her teacher, and I have looked on her
as a daughter. But, to protect her honor,
may she instead be married to my son,
strong-armed Abhimanyu, beloved nephew
of long-haired Krishna?" The king gave glad consent.

The Pandavas stayed in Virata's city,
Upaplavya, and elaborate plans
for a joyful wedding were set in train.
Abhimanyu was brought from Dvaraka
together with his mother, Subhadra.
Drupada and valiant Dhrishtadyumna,
Draupadi's kin, journeyed from Panchala

with Draupadi's now tall and stalwart sons.
Krishna came, of course, with Balarama
and a great retinue of Yadavas.
Many allies came from far and near
to celebrate the Pandavas' survival,
and to attend the splendid royal wedding.

It can be imagined what rejoicing,
what tears, what laughter, what exchange of news
were witnessed at the long-delayed reunion
of all these friends and kinsfolk of the Pandavas.
For many days, there was no thought of anything
but happiness, and heartfelt thanks were offered
to the gods, for their longed-for deliverance.

V

THE BOOK OF PERSEVERANCE

27.

SUING FOR PEACE, PREPARING FOR WAR

After the joyful wedding, the Pandavas
called a council in Virata's hall.
Their sons were there, impressive as their fathers,
as were the kings, Virata and Drupada,
Krishna and his brother Balarama,
and many other heroes. The hall glittered
with their dazzling jewels and fine silk robes.

No longer was Yudhishthira the quiet,
patient ascetic of the forest days,
or even the gaming brahmin of the court.
Now, his natural authority
was obvious to all as he sat erect,
attentive to what Krishna had to say:

"You all know the history. You remember
how Shakuni, a skilled and artful player,
took advantage of Yudhishthira
and stripped him of his kingdom. You know the terms—
how the Pandavas had to endure
thirteen years of exile, now completed.
Yudhishthira would not claim an inch of land,
if he thought that claim at all unlawful.
It's clear for all to see—he is entitled,
as Pandu's heir, and as first-born Bharata,
to the whole kingdom of the Bharatas.
Nevertheless, he asks for only half—
his beautiful domain of Indraprastha.
Nor does he seek revenge for all the times
the Kauravas conspired to do him harm.

"We do not yet know what Duryodhana
intends. So I propose an ambassador
be sent from here, someone wise and calm,
to persuade the Kaurava of the merit
of Yudhishthira's claim. He must approach this
in the most tactful way, not hectoring
but calmly, clearly laying out the case."

Balarama said, "That is important.
After all, Yudhishthira, in gambling
all he possessed, took on Shakuni
whose skill at dice he knew was unsurpassed,
and he did so of his own free will.
He lost his wits, and that was his undoing.
Shakuni was not to blame for that."

Krishna's kinsman Satyaki burst out,
"How is Yudhishthira responsible
when he was entrapped? And now Duryodhana
is pretending that the Pandavas were found
before their agreed exile had expired.

Bhishma has told him it is not the case,
but that's his bluff, his pretext for retaining
what rightfully belongs to Yudhishthira.
He should be taught a lesson! Let sharp arrows
and spears present the arguments for us
rather than soft diplomacy."

                        "Quite right.
Gentleness and tact won't work with that one!"
said Drupada. "It's like trying to reason
with a balky mule who understands nothing
except force. We should be drumming up
as many powerful allies as we can
before they're recruited by the Kauravas.
But there's no harm in doing things decently—
I propose that we send my household priest,
a learned, stately man, to Hastinapura
as ambassador of King Yudhishthira."

Krishna agreed. He emphasized that he
and Balarama were loyal to both sides,
related to both as they were, by kinship.
Then the Yadavas set off for their home.

Yudhishthira sent out well-chosen envoys
to the lords of many neighboring kingdoms,
canvassing their support. And Duryodhana
did the same. In the weeks that followed
the whole land was astir with the mustering
of men—the practiced tread of professionals,
the bustle of recruiting agents, fanning
out into the countryside, to snatch
and cajole men from their fields and herds.
Animals of war were being assembled—
beasts of burden, horses, fighting elephants
trained to charge, trample, wheel in formation.
As they gathered, the armies—fighting forces

hundreds of thousands strong—marched to the base camps
of the protagonists, where they stayed, waiting.
The earth held its breath, anticipating
the feast of blood to come.

ॐ

                    Duryodhana,
hearing that Krishna had gone to Dvaraka,
hurried there, to ask for his allegiance
in the coming war. With the same idea,
Arjuna also went there. They arrived
at a time of day when Krishna was asleep.
They waited quietly, Duryodhana
at his head, and Arjuna at his feet.
When Krishna woke up, each began to speak.
"I was here first," argued Duryodhana.
"But Arjuna was the first one I saw,"
said Krishna. "You are both close to me
and I will give both of you my support
if it should come to war. I have an army
of a million men. And I have myself.
I shall be present on the battlefield
but I will not fight. You can choose.
Arjuna, choose first, as you are the younger."
Without hesitation, Arjuna
chose Krishna, by himself, non-combatant.
"I choose to have you as my charioteer."

Duryodhana was exultant. He visited
Balarama. "Do not ask me to fight,"
said Krishna's brother, "I will not take sides
in a war between noble Bharatas.
Go, and behave like true kshatriyas."

Duryodhana visited Krishna's kinsman
Kritavarman, and gained his support.

Then the Kaurava traveled home, rejoicing.
With Krishna and Balarama out of action,
and with Krishna's army on his side—
how could he lose!

          "What did you have in mind
when you chose me, rather than my army?"
Krishna asked Arjuna when they were alone.
"I know you could win this war single-handed,"
said Arjuna, "and so could I. With you
steering my chariot, we shall gain great glory
together. Best of men, may we prevail!"

☙

Shalya, uncle to the younger Pandavas
(he was their mother's brother, King of Madra),
had been expected to weigh in on the side
of his relatives. And that was his intention.
But, traveling toward Upaplavya,
and finding splendid rest-houses on the way
which he thought Yudhishthira had built for him,
he declared that he would give a boon
to his host—but this turned out to be
Duryodhana, who asked for his allegiance.
So Shalya arrived at Upaplavya
seriously embarrassed and contrite.
"It can't be helped," said Yudhishthira calmly.
"Of course you must keep your word. But, listen,
when Arjuna and Karna face each other,
you'll probably serve as Karna's charioteer,
your skill being famous. As you join the fray
and are in conversation, talk to him
in such a way that he becomes discouraged;
try to undermine his fiery zeal.
I know this is not proper, but please do it
to protect the Left-handed Archer."

Shalya agreed. "You deserve every help
after the sufferings you have endured—
though, as we know, even the gods suffer."

Other kings were arriving with their armies,
gigantic forces which, vast as they were,
merged with the Pandava battalions
as a stream is swallowed by a mighty ocean—
Satyaki the Vrishni, Dhrishtaketu
king of Chedi, the powerful Jayatsena
of Magadha, and more. Altogether,
there were seven armies. With their weapons
primed and polished, glittering in the sun,
they resembled a threatening thundercloud
lit by lightning flashes.

                    At Hastinapura,
the city could not house the mass of men
—even the allied kings and their chief warriors—
who had arrived to join the Kaurava ranks.
There were eleven armies altogether.
The entire terrain between the two rivers
and beyond was covered with a sprawling
overspill of tents, a massive camp
that seethed with furious activity,
though not yet with a purpose or direction.
Their field commanders were fully aware
that they must keep the men well occupied
or else fighting, drunkenness, debauchery
and homesickness would start to dissipate
their fighting ardor.

                    For there was still no word
that war would really happen—the two sides
were still deliberating. Only the massed
armies, and the joyful gallimaufry
of war, were signs of serious intent.

It was this that Drupada's priest saw
from miles away, as he approached the city.

&

The dignified, distinguished priest was welcomed
by Bhishma, and by his fellow brahmins
and, with due ceremony, he was ushered
into the presence of King Dhritarashtra
sitting in council with his ministers.
After the appropriate formalities,
he soon came to the point. He itemized
the sufferings and wrongs the Pandavas
had undergone, caused by the Kauravas:
attempts on their lives, loss of their fine kingdom,
grave insults inflicted upon Draupadi,
the years of hardship in the wilderness.

"However," he said, "the noble Pandavas
have set grievance aside. Yudhishthira
does not want war. He wishes above all things
to be reconciled with the Kauravas.
He does not lay claim to Hastinapura
even though his entitlement is clear.
If Indraprastha is restored to him,
he will rule over his half of the kingdom
in perfect happiness, wanting no more
than close, harmonious relationships
with you and your sons. If this is agreed
he will persuade the kings who are his allies
to demobilize their fighting forces
and send their well-armed men back to their homes.
Great king, I hope you will see the sense in this.
After all, Krishna is with the Pandavas.
Who, knowing that, would want to fight with them?"

"Sir," said Bhishma. "What you say is welcome.
The way you put it is a bit too blunt,
but that can be forgiven in a brahmin.
You speak the truth and, furthermore, Arjuna
could subdue the three worlds single-handed."

"Why keep on saying that?" said angry Karna.
"The fact is, there was a covenant
and the sly sons of Pandu have broken it."
"No," said Bhishma, "by my calculations,
the Pandavas had served their thirteen years
before they revealed themselves. I think the law
supports Yudhishthira's claim."

                        The arguments
went to and fro. Dhritarashtra said nothing,
gnawing his lips; then he said, "After due thought,
weighing the pros and cons, I have decided . . ."
the council held its breath, ". . . I have decided
to send my aide Sanjaya as my envoy.
You, sir," he told the priest, "can now return
to Upaplavya. Tell them to expect him."

"What's to be done, Sanjaya?" said the king
when they were alone (for every ruler
needs a disinterested confidant
whose discretion can be relied upon).
"I can find no fault with the Pandavas.
Exemplary kshatriyas, they act
always in line with dharma and good sense.
It is only my foolish son and Karna
who, stubborn and self-interested as always,
insist that they themselves are in the right.
Duryodhana has always been resentful
and envious, and Karna spurs him on
with his streak of bitterness, and fixed hatred
for Arjuna. Yet they are both deluded
if they think that they can win this war—

against Arjuna, with his divine weapons,
against Krishna, ruler of the three worlds,
and Bhima, stronger than forty elephants!
That son of mine is dreaming! And yet . . . and yet
I want him to be great. Above all,
I want him to cast off this yoke of envy
he wears continually.
                    "Sanjaya,
go to the Pandavas, ask after their health,
say we want peace, say . . . whatever comes
into your mind that you think suitable,
anything likely to avert a war."

ॐ

After elaborate formalities,
inquiries after everybody's health,
down to kitchen-women and household slaves,
Yudhishthira asked Sanjaya to tell him
the state of affairs at Hastinapura—
what was Dhritarashtra's thinking now?

"The old king is grieving," said Sanjaya.
"He has no appetite for war, and fears
the dire consequences. The brahmins tell him
that to seek to do harm to the harmless,
as his son is doing, is a dreadful sin.
You have assembled seven mighty armies
in your support. But Duryodhana
and his allies are also powerful—
there are eleven armies on his side.
In my view—that is to say, the king thinks—
if it comes to war, neither side could win
without enormous bloodshed.
                              Furthermore,
it is unlawful to kill one's kith and kin
and you, Yudhishthira, and your brothers here,
are known to uphold the law in all respects.

For this reason, a sinful act of yours
would be like a dark stain on a pure white cloth.
Victory and defeat would be the same."
And Sanjaya went on in the same vein.

There was a silence. "Friend," said Yudhishthira,
"I know you mean well, but you miss the point.
Not even a fool could wish for war
if peace were to be had by any means.
Tell me—when have you ever heard me utter
warmongering words, in any circumstances?
Even when I was least myself, caught up
in gambling fever, even then, I prayed
that the Kauravas would not destroy themselves.
I knew then, and nothing has changed my view,
that Duryodhana is insatiable.
He wants for nothing, lives in great luxury,
all the pleasures of the earth are his,
yet only the complete elimination
of the Pandavas will satisfy him.

"Dhritarashtra knows all this. His brother,
Vidura, has given him wise advice.
So long as the king listened to Vidura
the Kauravas kept some check on wrongdoing.
But now that good man has been pushed aside,
and Dhritarashtra listens to no voice
except that of his son's rapaciousness
which burns untamed, like a fire fed with butter.

"I honor Dhritarashtra; since Pandu's death
I have venerated him as a father.
But, for him, the wishes of his wayward son
are always paramount. Three times at least
we Pandavas have been the blameless objects
of Duryodhana's boundless enmity,
and have not answered back. He tried to kill us
in the lacquer house. Then, though as first-born prince

I was heir apparent, we were fobbed off
with half the kingdom, desolate scrubland
from which we made a paradise on earth.

"Now we have borne thirteen years of exile—
and, yes, my foolishness played a part in that.
But now they should return our kingdom to us
according to the covenant they made.

"Dhritarashtra and his greedy son
want us gone, and they to rule alone.
The two of them have dreams of a great realm,
unchallenged domination of the earth—
a superpower. That way lies misery.
Such a dream can only be sustained
if they don't hear the thrum of *Gandiva*,
if they can forget the unrivaled strength
of Bhima and the heroic sons of Madri.

"Monstrous ambition breeds unreasoning fear.
The Kauravas need have no fear of me,
I wish them well—but please give them this message:
I must have my kingdom of Indraprastha.
On this point, I am immovable."

"Our earthly life is transient," said Sanjaya.
"If the Kauravas refuse to return
your former kingdom, then it would be better
to beg in the streets than to incur the sin
of killing your kinsfolk. And why did you
spend years in exile, if you meant to fight?
Scrupulously you followed the law, yet now
you propose to commit appalling wrong.
Even if you were ruler of the world
you would grow old and die, like everyone.

"Your every action follows you in death.
You are known for your devotion to dharma.

Why change now, to wage unlawful war?
What happiness could you enjoy, knowing
that you have killed your kinsmen and your teachers?
What happiness, as you approach old age,
in contemplating miserable rebirth?"

"You should tell that to my cousin, Sanjaya!
You judge me prematurely. What is dutiful
and what is sinful is not so straightforward.
In a time of grave emergency,
the ordinary rules may not apply.
If virtue is a victim, then the task
is to restore the world to harmony.
Krishna—advise me; be my guide in this."

"Sanjaya," said Krishna, "both the Kauravas
and the Pandavas are dear to me.
Yet clearly Dhritarashtra and his son
have stolen the kingdom of the Pandavas
by refusing to return it, as agreed.
Stealing is wrong no matter how it's done.
Why should they escape responsibility?

"You speak of the sinfulness of war,
but in a land where everybody prospers
each group has its dharma, its proper duty
to society; and a king should govern
and protect his people. If someone seizes
the land of another out of avarice,
then a king's duty is to go to war
to set things right. Action is the duty
of a kshatriya. You know this, Sanjaya.
Why do you, then, against your better judgment,
speak in favor of the Kauravas?

"You were present in the gambling hall
when Shakuni befuddled Yudhishthira,
when Karna jeered and insulted Draupadi,

when Duhshasana tried to strip her naked.
How, then, can you think that the right course
is simply to do nothing? Mere inertia
in the face of such flagrant wrongdoing
is not virtue. The whole cosmos turns
on action. Just as the sun rises daily,
the moon goes through its cycle, the wind blows,
so action is the law for gods and men—
for brahmins, kshatriyas and commoners.
Kshatriya dharma is to protect what's right.
If Yudhishthira could regain his kingdom
by peaceful means, then he would certainly
make Bhima be as gentle as a brahmin!
But the fact is, Duryodhana thinks himself
above the law. And law must be defended.
I will go myself to Hastinapura
and try to broker a peaceful resolution."

Sanjaya gave way. "O Dharma King,
in my loyalty to Dhritarashtra
I hope I did not offend you."
                              "Sanjaya,"
said Yudhishthira, "there is no offense.
I know you speak as the king's emissary.
Convey my heartfelt greetings to all who live
at Hastinapura, and wish them good health.
Say to Duryodhana that we Pandavas,
in the interests of peace, will overlook
our grievances. Instead of Indraprastha,
we will settle for five villages,
one for each of us." Yudhishthira
named the settlements he had in mind.
"In this way we can live in peace. Our allies
can take their soldiers home to their own kingdoms,
back to the arms of their thankful wives."

☙

Sanjaya rode back to Hastinapura.
He thought deeply about all he had heard
and, on arriving, sought an audience
with Dhritarashtra. "Pandu's sons are well.
Yudhishthira greets you fondly, and inquires
after your health. As he always has,
he pursues the law in all particulars.
He is renowned and honored everywhere
and desires nothing that is not rightly his.
They say a man reaps as he sows, but I say
the Pandavas have suffered more, far more
than they deserve. You, my king, have treated
your brother's sons cruelly and unjustly.
Your reputation is soiled throughout the land,
your name a byword for unlawfulness
and greed. If Yudhishthira returned evil
for evil, the Kauravas would be destroyed
and you, as king, would bear the blame for it.
You have trusted your untrustworthy son
and cast off your nephew, rich in wisdom,
so now you are too enfeebled, foolish king,
to protect your vast and wealthy lands
from utter ruin.

             "But that is enough for now.
The chariot has shaken up my bones
and I must rest. Tomorrow, in the council,
I will lay out Yudhishthira's words in full."

28.

DIPLOMACY CONTINUES

Sanjaya left Dhritarashtra chastened
and appalled, but understanding nothing
he did not know already. He asked himself,
not for the first time, how he could have fallen
into this predicament, this nightmare.

As always, when sleep was impossible,
he sent for Vidura, his wise half-brother,
to keep the watches of the night with him.
"Sanjaya has returned; until I hear
the message he has brought from Yudhishthira,
I cannot sleep. My mind is in a tumult.
Tell me something that will bring me peace."

"Many people are sleepless," said Vidura:
"the anxious lover, one who is destitute,
thieves who fear discovery, householders
nervous of thieves—but none of these, I think,
is your condition. Are you, perhaps, burning
because you covet another's property?"

As if he had not heard, Dhritarashtra
asked Vidura to tell him soothing stories.
The night was black outside, and very quiet.
Only an occasional owl's hooting
disturbed the silence. Hour after wakeful hour,

Vidura discoursed on many topics.
He spoke of wisdom and of foolishness;
the virtues of a good ruler; mastery
of the senses; the value of honesty;
the importance of family; austerity;
moderation; the nature of karma—how
people's actions follow them after death.

All this was leavened by engaging tales
and, here and there, as if to test whether
his brother was still awake, and listening still,
Vidura inserted his own thoughts
on the king's obligations to his nephews.
"What am I supposed to do? Tell me
the best way forward for the Kauravas,"
moaned Dhritarashtra, as if he did not know.

"Try to cultivate clear-sightedness,
think of consequences—not like a fish
which gulps at a fat morsel, oblivious
of the hidden hook. Rather, reflect
on what it is that leads you to act wrongly
and avoid that thing—as a drunkard
must avoid strong liquor. Your doting love
for Duryodhana has made you mad
and you don't realize it—you know, they say
that when the gods wish to destroy a person
they make him see the world the wrong way up.
And those they intend to prosper, they endow
with wisdom. Well, Yudhishthira is wise.
How can you hope to flourish when you listen
to Duryodhana and his deluded friends?
The Pandavas regard you as a father;
do the right thing—treat them as your sons.

"Think of the story of the seer Atreya,
wandering the world in the guise of a swan.

Being accosted by the Sadhya gods
and asked for good advice, he said to them:
'This is our task: be serene at all times,
do not be vengeful, nor scorn your enemy;
speak truthfully, befriend the virtuous,
be equable in the face of disaster.
Be aware that everything must pass,
just as clouds arise, drift, and disperse,
so do not seek to cling to anything.'

"The seer was right," said Vidura, "attachment
is the curse of humankind. It leads to grief,
and grief is the enemy of good sense.
You are too attached to Duryodhana,
not realizing that all that lives will pass.
Happiness and misery arise
for all of us. Neither exult nor grieve
but let it be.

> *Time after time, people die and are born,*
> *Time after time, people rise and decline,*
> *Time after time, people give and are given,*
> *Time after time, people mourn and are mourned.*"

In this vein, thoughtful Vidura talked on,
knowing that his words evaporated
into the night air, knowing Dhritarashtra
was no more willing to accept advice
than is a glutton or a drug addict
but, rather, claimed that he was powerless:
"Man is not master of his destiny
but a mere puppet, swinging from a thread.
I cannot abandon Duryodhana."

"Then, O king, you are set on a course
you'll bitterly regret. Can you imagine
the searing grief of hearing that your sons,

one by one, are killed?"
                 "O Vidura,"
sighed Dhritarashtra, "when I listen to you
my mind inclines toward the Pandavas.
But when I hear Duryodhana, well then
it veers away again. It's time that governs
our human affairs; effort is futile.
But I like to listen to you—are there things
that you have left unsaid? If so, then speak."

"There is teaching more profound than I can give,
being shudra-born. But Sanatsujata,
the divine ancient and eternal youth,
can tell you more, concerning death and non-death."
And by thought alone, Vidura summoned him.

"Sanatsujata," said Dhritarashtra,
"I am told you teach that there is no death,
and yet the world's wise men devote their lives
to avoiding it. How can this be explained?"

"Both are true," answered Sanatsujata.
"There is a part of the eternal Self
in each of us, that is indestructible.
Yet men die constantly through their own folly.
Anger, greed, delusion, envy, lust—
each of these waits to entrap a person
as a hunter stalks a witless antelope,
and each of them is death. Through being attached
to 'I' and 'mine' in every misleading form
we invite death to take up residence,
to seize us in its sharp, tenacious claws;
we die repeatedly to our true nature.
Repeatedly, we undergo rebirth.

"But one who practices simplicity,
who banishes desire and lives in truth,
who does not crave the fruit of their own actions

who is humble and who controls the senses—
that person can cross over death, and live."

As Sanatsujata talked, Dhritarashtra
listened. But he lacked the concentration
that could have made the ancient youth's wise words
a door into a different understanding
of what was right, what he should say and do.
As it was, he noticed the palace stirring,
heard birds begin to sing outside the window,
and knew that the long night must soon be over.

ॐ

The council gathered in the assembly hall,
a splendid space, plastered white and gold,
sprinkled with fragrant water of sandalwood;
the seats, inlaid with ivory and jewels,
covered with silk cushions. Courtiers, princes,
ministers and marshals were on edge,
waiting to hear what Sanjaya would say,
no one more eagerly than Dhritarashtra.

"My lords! I bring greetings from Yudhishthira.
He asked me to convey his earnest wishes
for the good health of everyone in turn,
forgetting no one.
              "Now, to the real business.
These words were delivered by Arjuna,
in front of Yudhishthira and Krishna,
speaking for all the Pandavas. 'Tell the king
our cause is just, and we are more than ready
to fight for it. My bow, mighty *Gandiva*,
vibrates with longing to fulfill its purpose.
We have many seasoned warriors, brave,
skilled and single-minded. We have vast armies,
kept in a state of battle-readiness.

"'We do not want war. But that does not mean
we will opt for peace on despicable terms.
Duryodhana should ponder hard and well
before he decides to break the covenant
made thirteen years ago in the gaming hall.
We have spent those years on a bed of sorrow.
If he defaults, Duryodhana will spend
an eternity of nights in Yama's realm,
pinned to a far more painful bed than ours.

"'When he sees our millions of men deployed,
their tread shaking the earth, our massed elephants
of war, their tusks filed to points, spear-sharp,
Duryodhana will regret this war.

"'When he hears Bhima, the strongest man on earth,
each sinew burning with long-pent-up rage,
roaring with the lust to avenge Draupadi,
Duryodhana will regret this war.

"'When Bhima, deadly club swinging, advances
on the previously complacent enemy
like a lion savaging a herd of cows,
Duryodhana will regret this war.

"'When he sees his huge forces scattered
and consumed like straw by a summer fire,
or a stand of saplings ravaged by lightning,
Duryodhana will regret this war.

"'When he catches sight of all our valiant sons
standing, bows raised, in their chariots
like rearing serpents ready to spit poison,
Duryodhana will regret this war.

"'And when he sees my gold, gem-studded chariot
drawn by white horses, flying the monkey banner,

driven by Krishna, inspired charioteer;
when the dim-witted man picks up the thrum
of *Gandiva*, as the string strikes my wristband;
when, like driving rain, my arrows thresh
the ranks of his infantry, as if they were
ripe corn, severing men's heads from their shoulders;
when he sees his elephants stampede
in terror, blinded by their bloody wounds;
when he sees his valiant horses stumbling,
falling, heaped up, their bright-armored riders
mortally pierced by my searching arrows; then,
then Duryodhana will regret this war.

"'My bow flexes without my holding it;
my arrows in their inexhaustible quivers
yearn to fly. My steeds strain at their yokes.
My dagger springs from its sheath, like a serpent
impatient to escape its outworn skin.
The omens are in place, our learned brahmins
have spelled out the conjunctions of the planets
and find the time auspicious for our purpose.
But we do not want war. We can live content,
with no ambition to extend our power.
Sanjaya, you should show Dhritarashtra
the utter folly of quarreling with those
who made his kingdom what it is today
through their past conquests of his neighbors' lands.
Remind him, we have always fought his foes—
show him how insane Duryodhana is!'

"Those were Arjuna's words," said Sanjaya.

Bhishma stood up, addressing Duryodhana,
"Those words are true. Thanks to the advice you take
from Shakuni, from base Duhshasana
and from Karna, your lowborn companion,
you have veered away from the path of dharma."

"Venerable Bhishma!" Karna cried,
"do not speak of me like that. All I do
is designed to serve the king and his great son,
my friend. You cannot name a single time
when I have acted in any other way."

"This fellow is an evil influence,"
said Bhishma, turning now to Dhritarashtra.
"He boasts that he will beat the Pandavas
and Duryodhana places trust in him,
but where was he when the fine Matsya cattle
were lost? Where was he when the gandharvas
routed your son's retinue and captured him?
Nowhere. It was great-hearted Bhima
who came to the rescue. O king, choose peace,
don't be misled by Karna's puffed-up plans.
You should know—Arjuna and Krishna
are not mere mortal men, but part divine
incarnations of invincible
Nara and Narayana, who take birth
in epochs when dharma needs defending."

Drona said, "Bhishma is right. The law
will be flouted if you refuse to cede
to Yudhishthira his half of the kingdom.
We should negotiate with the Pandavas."

But Dhritarashtra was not listening. Restless,
he was plying Sanjaya with questions
at a tangent. And if there was one moment
when the cause of peace was lost; when it was clear
that Dhritarashtra would not oppose his son;
when the Kauravas were condemned to die;
it was that moment, when King Dhritarashtra
turned away from Bhishma and from Drona,
ignoring their views.

"Sanjaya, what forces
have the Pandavas arrayed against us?
How strong are the Panchalas? And the rest?"
Sanjaya sighed deeply, then he sank,
fainting, to the floor. "He must have seen,
in his mind, my nephews and their forces,
and been overcome," said Dhritarashtra.
Sanjaya revived, and dutifully
listed the allies of the Pandavas,
and which Kauravas had been nominated
as dueling partners of named Pandavas,
to fight with them in duels to the death.
Bhishma had been allotted to Shikhandin,
Shalya marked out for Yudhishthira,
Karna for Arjuna, as also were
Jayadratha and envious Ashvatthaman;
Duryodhana, together with his brothers,
would be the share of Bhima, great mace-warrior.

"Those you have named are great fighters," said the king,
"yet, to my mind, all of them together
are not more strong than Bhima by himself.
I wake at night, thinking of Wolf-belly.
He is the one I dread—and it is his fault
that there's this breach between my sons and nephews.
Bhima would torment Duryodhana
when they were children, and it used to grieve me
when my son suffered at that bully's hands.
Then, there was the disastrous dice game.
But even so—war is a dreadful thing.
Think of the prowess of the Pandavas—
the Kauravas don't stand a chance; they'll be
like moths attracted to a blazing furnace.
There should be every effort to make peace."

"I do not understand you," said Sanjaya.
"You know the strength of the Left-handed Archer,
you know the might of Bhima the destroyer,

you can foresee your hundred sons all slaughtered,
and yet you submit to Duryodhana.
All these laments are pointless—you are the king,
what happens is your responsibility,
yet you act as though you were powerless.
As for the dicing—I remember well
how you exulted like a little boy
when you heard Shakuni had won the game."

"Father, don't fear for us," said Duryodhana.
"Our allies would find you ridiculous
for entertaining such cowardly thoughts.
The Pandavas are only mortal men,
born from human mothers, as we are.
Don't be afraid the gods will take their side.
I have heard Vyasa tell you that the gods
became immortal by being indifferent
to love or hatred, greed or sympathy.
They won't be propping up the Pandavas.
If they were so minded, they would have rescued
my cousins from their miserable exile—
at that time, they might have defeated us.

"But now our strength is unsurpassable.
I have incantations of my own.
I can conjure gales, cause avalanches,
or stop them, as I like. I can freeze rivers
so that heavy chariots can pass over.
You harp on about my cousins' skills
but we have our own strength—think about it:
Bhishma, Drona, Kripa, Ashvatthaman
are formidable warriors. No one on earth
is a stronger fighter with the mace
than I am. And valiant Karna—don't forget
how he shamed Arjuna at the tournament.
We should have some pride! Negotiate?
There's nothing to negotiate. Make peace?
I won't cede even a pinprick of land to them.

"Karna and I have talked about this war
and how we should see it as a sacrifice.
We will consecrate ourselves; Yudhishthira,
bull of the Bharatas, is the ritual victim.
My chariot will be the altar, my sword
the spoon, my club the ladle. My horses
will be the four sacrificial priests.
Having dedicated ourselves in this way,
we shall surely win. I'll kill the Pandavas
and rule the earth. Even the gods could not
deflect my passionate hatred from its path!"

"Sanjaya," said the king, "tell us what happened
when you visited Arjuna and Krishna?"
"I went to see them in their private chamber.
They were sitting together, with their wives,
and were reclining on a golden couch.
Both men were drinking mead. Krishna's feet
rested on Arjuna's lap, and Arjuna's
were supported by Draupadi. When I saw
those two imposing heroes, I was awestruck.
It was as if I were in the presence
of Indra and Vishnu. I could not see then,
nor can I now, how they could fail to conquer
the whole world, if they had the mind for it.

"Arjuna nudged Krishna to speak to me
and he spoke gently, but with such seriousness
that I was terrified on your behalf.
'I owe a debt,' he said, 'to Draupadi.
I was far away when she needed me.
For this alone, I would support Arjuna,
though, as he showed outside Virata's city,
he can crush an enemy single-handed.'"

Sanjaya's account was dismal news
for Dhritarashtra. "My poor deluded son!

Complete destruction looms for the Kauravas.
Let it be known—I reject your crackpot plan.
I don't believe that, without bad advice,
you would have had the appetite for war.
It is Karna and Duhshasana
who spur you onward. But what can I do?
Inscrutable time propels us where it will."

Karna stood up, addressing Duryodhana:
"I propose to conquer the Pandavas
single-handed, and after them, the Matsyas,
Panchalas and Karushas. This I will do
with the divine weapon I was awarded
by my great teacher. He withdrew the weapon
when he was angry with me, but I believe
I placated him. You can stay at home
with Bhishma and Drona. I shall take a force
of the best fighting men—the task is mine!"

Bhishma laughed. "You vain and boastful fool,
how can you dream of killing even Arjuna—
the warrior who has never been defeated,
the man who destroyed the Khandava Forest—
let alone the rest, weapon or no weapon.
The spear which you obtained from the god Indra
will be reduced to ash by Krishna's discus.
You and your weapons will be impotent."

Karna flushed at that insult: "Very well!
This is my response to your contempt—
I will lay down my weapons. I will saunter
around the court until the Kauravas'
generals fall in combat, until you, Bhishma,
lie dead on the field of battle. Only then
will I fight, and the world will see my prowess!"
With that, he strode out of the assembly hall.

Bhishma shrugged. "That all-powerful weapon
the driver's son so loves to boast about
is flawed. The holy sage who gave it to him
put conditions on it, because Karna
had lied to him. That is the man he is."

As discussion continued in the hall,
Vidura told the king an instructive story:

"THIS IS SOMETHING I witnessed once, when I was traveling in the Himalaya. We were visiting Mount Gandhamadana, a beautiful place, with groves of fragrant flowers. There we saw a jar of honey, lying on a rock on the edge of a ravine swarming with poisonous snakes. The honey belonged to Kubera, god of wealth, and it had wonderful properties. If a mortal tasted it, he would live for ever. If a blind man tasted it, he would see again.

"Some mountain men in our party were desperate to get hold of the jar, but, in reaching for it, they toppled into the ravine and were killed.

"In the same way, this stupid son of yours
wishes to seize the earth. He turns his mind
away from the ravine."

                    Now, the council
started to disperse. The king, in an aside,
said to Sanjaya, "Is there something
further that you can tell me? Can you foresee
a certain outcome of this dreadful war?"
"Let Vyasa come here, and Gandhari,"
said Sanjaya, "to witness what I learned
at Upaplavya." By the power of thought
Sanjaya brought Vyasa, and Gandhari
came from her apartments. Duryodhana
turned his back.

"It has been revealed to me,"
said Sanjaya, "that Krishna is the Lord,
the blessed Vishnu, he who alone governs
time and death, he who turns the world.
Where there is law, where there is truth, there
Krishna is. He has taken human form,
with human attributes. But make no mistake,
his power is such that he could destroy the world—
reduce it to ash instantly."

"How is it,"
asked Dhritarashtra, "that you recognize
the Lord, while I perceive only Krishna,
prince of Dvaraka?" Sanjaya answered,
"Though I am not highborn, simple devotion
and mastery of the senses have revealed
the Lord to me—Vishnu, the uncreated."

"Duryodhana," said Dhritarashtra, "hurry!
Go and seek the mercy of the Lord!"

"Nothing in earth or heaven would make me seek
the mercy of that crony of Arjuna."

"You see?" said the king to Gandhari.
"Your son is a lost cause with his wicked soul,
his envy, his contempt for his elders."

"You power-crazy fool!" said Gandhari,
"evil-minded wretch! What interminable
sorrow you inflict upon your parents.
You will remember your father's words too late,
when Bhima crushes you."

Vyasa turned
to Dhritarashtra, "Be guided by Sanjaya.
He can set you free from mortal danger

if you listen to him attentively.
People blunder through the wilderness
bewildered by their lusts. The wise know better."

"Tell me, Sanjaya," said Dhritarashtra,
"how may one reach the path to ultimate peace?"

"Steadfast mastery of all one's senses
is the way to peace. Through relinquishment
of irritable longings and attachments
a person may come to know the blessed Lord."

Dhritarashtra sighed. "Ah, how I envy
those who have eyes to see the divine being
in his wonderful, immortal form!"

29.

KRISHNA'S MISSION

After Sanjaya left, disconsolate,
knowing the Pandavas were in the right,
equally sure the king would support his son,
Yudhishthira sat underneath a tree
talking quietly to his cousin Krishna.
His brothers were there too, with Draupadi,
and Satyaki, Krishna's close companion.

"This is a time when we truly need our friends,"
said Yudhishthira. "You heard Sanjaya;
he conveyed Dhritarashtra's views exactly,
as an envoy should. There seems little hope
of any peaceful settlement. It pains me
that I'm unable to take care of Kunti.
Even with five villages . . . but it's useless
to dwell on that. We are dealing with a man
who has lost all sense of what is right, blinded
by his own ungoverned greed and envy.
I know that dharma for a kshatriya
is to fight. That is our law. And yet
where does killing stop? Killers are themselves
killed in return. Thus a feud develops,
vendetta never ends. No one rests easy.
And does any man, even the worst,
deserve to die? Should we conduct ourselves
like dogs, wrangling over a piece of meat?

Heroism's a malady; the heart
can never know serenity that way.

"And yet, we must act. We are kshatriyas.
We welcome neither war nor surrender—
even capitulation would bring no end
to hatred. Duryodhana will never rest
until he has removed us from the earth.
Krishna, wisest of friends, far-seeing one,
what do you think?"

                        "I think the time has come,"
said Krishna, "for me to be ambassador.
All the portents are pointing toward war.
I have no hope that I will change the mind
either of the king or of your cousin.
But everything that can be done must be done.
Tomorrow, I will go to Hastinapura.
I will not beg on your behalf—a kshatriya
should beg only for victory or death
on the battlefield. I remember hearing
how Duryodhana crowed in the gambling hall,
'The Pandavas are well and truly broken,
they've nothing to call their own, even their names
will disappear in time, leaving no trace!'
Such a man deserves death, there's no question."

Bhima said, "Don't threaten him with war.
Give him every chance, talk gently to him.
His nature is so violent, he'll flare up
at the slightest hint of anger from our side,
and close the door on peace once and for all."

Krishna laughed, "Can this be Bhima speaking?
All these long years, you have never ceased
to seethe in rage against the Kauravas.
How often have you conjured in your mind

acts of violence against Duryodhana?
Now it comes to it, are you gripped by panic?
What you've said is as unnatural to you
as human speech would be to a buffalo!
Have you become a eunuch? Has a torrent
become a docile brook?"

                Bhima was hurt.
"Slayer of demons, you have misunderstood.
You know me, Krishna. Faced with the need to fight,
when have you ever seen me hesitate?
On the contrary, if heaven and earth
were to collide, I would prize them apart
with these strong arms. It is only compassion
that leads me to want peace, if possible."

"I was teasing you," said Krishna, smiling.
"I see you as much greater, a thousand times
greater, than you see yourself, Wolf-belly.
Your strength and courage are beyond question.
I assure you, I shall make every effort.
But human action, however well designed,
may be opposed by the gods. Conversely,
the gods' intentions may be overridden
by the effort of a virtuous individual.
Therefore, we have to act. For even though
we may not succeed, or only partially,
we have to do our best, then accept calmly
whatever happens. That is true wisdom."

Arjuna urged Krishna to do whatever
he thought helpful at Hastinapura,
knowing that both sides were dear to him—
but then to let the Pandava warriors
plunge into battle and do what they did best.
Sahadeva, thinking of Draupadi,
and of the way she had been violated,

wanted to fight at once. But Nakula
believed that Krishna, with his tact and skill,
might yet make the Kauravas see sense.

So the discussion swung this way and that.
Some were driven by revenge, while others
thought more strategically, with the sole aim
of recovering Yudhishthira's kingdom.

There was no doubt what Draupadi was feeling.
Thinking that even Bhima was wavering,
she leapt to her feet, trembling with rage.
"All this talk is driving me mad with grief!
We know everything we need to know.
My five strong husbands, my enemy-burners,
and my brave sons, led by Abhimanyu,
can trounce the Kaurava. But if they hanker
pitifully after peace, then my father,
Drupada, will fight, old as he is,
and my brother, Dhrishtadyumna, will fight too!
I've waited years for this precious moment—
I want to see Duryodhana chewing dust.
I want Karna, that contemptuous man
who told me I should choose another husband,
to be dragged through the mud, a mangled corpse.
I want to see Duhshasana's evil arms
torn from his trunk for what he did to me—
pulling me by this hair of mine, attempting
to strip me, reduce me to a naked slave."
Draupadi gathered up her long black hair,
a shining cascade, clutched in both her fists.
"I conjured you in my heart then, Govinda,
and you helped me—help me again now!"

In her fury, Draupadi's hot tears
showered like liquid fire over her breasts.
Krishna promised her that if his mission

proved as fruitless as he thought it would,
the Kauravas would be gobbled up by Death.

✤

"How was the journey of the blessed lord,
and who did he meet along the way?"
asked Janamejaya. Vaishampayana
described in detail Krishna's undertaking.

✤

Next day, Krishna rose in the early morning.
It was the harvest season, and the fields
stood rich in crops, bathed in gentle sunlight.
After he had performed his morning rites,
he asked Daruka to prepare his chariot,
and to load onto it his well-made weapons—
his bow, discus, mace and javelins—
as well as hoisting his fine flag, adorned
with moons, and animals and lovely flowers,
and the divine standard of Garuda.
Daruka harnessed the four noble horses,
freshly washed and groomed, and well rested.
Then, heartened by prayers and fervent wishes,
Krishna started toward Hastinapura
along with Satyaki and other Vrishnis.
He took a thousand foot soldiers, servants,
and plentiful provisions for the journey.
On the way, he encountered Narada
and other seers, bound for the same city
intent on witnessing this crucial mission.

✤

The Kauravas were afraid of Krishna.
Knowing he was coming, Dhritarashtra

had arranged elaborate hospitality.
Along the way, lavish rest pavilions
had been prepared. But he made his own camp.
Arriving in the city, he was received
with every show of pomp and ceremony.
The king urged many gifts upon him, offering
palatial accommodation. He declined,
preferring to be lodged with Vidura.

Vidura understood the king's motives.
"You are hoping that, by your generous gifts,
you will estrange him from the Pandavas,"
he said to Dhritarashtra. "If your gesture
were sincere, you would be offering him
what he has come for—the settlement he seeks.
Yudhishthira has asked for five villages,
and you refuse to give him even those."

Kunti was overjoyed to see Krishna,
to receive news of each son in turn,
and of Draupadi, whom she dearly loved;
yet sorrowful, to hear of their sufferings.
"My life has been a river of misfortune
ever since my father gave me away
—a little girl, playing with her ball—
to his cousin. A few short happy years,
and then Pandu took us to the forest.
There my sons were born, and I was content
for a brief time, watching them grow in strength.
But then he died, to cast us on the mercy
of this blind king—with all the misery
that's happened since. I've always been a good aunt
to my nephews, but their wickedness
has made me hope and pray they'll meet their end,
killed by my heroic sons. Only then
can we be reunited, and Draupadi—
abused as no woman ever should be,

no matter what her birth—will be avenged."
Krishna told her the day was not far off
when she would be united with her loved ones.

Next, he went to see Duryodhana
in his large and ostentatious palace.
Surrounded by his friends, the Kaurava
pressed Krishna to eat with them. He refused.
"Why won't you accept my hospitality,
offered in friendship?" asked Duryodhana.
"Food," said Krishna, "is to be accepted
either from affection or from need.
I do not feel affection for you, neither
am I in need. Envoys do not accept
homage or hospitality until
their mission has succeeded. Only then
will I eat with you, son of Dhritarashtra.
He who hates the Pandavas hates me.
This food, offered with venom in your heart,
is therefore spoiled for me, inedible.
I prefer to take my meal with Vidura."

That night, after dinner, when the servants
had retired to their beds, and the starry sky
was radiant overhead, Vidura said,
"It was useless for you to come, Krishna.
I fear for you in the assembly hall—
that the prince and his perverse supporters
will insult you. Duryodhana's mind is stone,
nothing will move him. He has complete faith
in his advisers—he really does believe
Karna can kill the Pandavas by himself
just because he says so! He is befogged,
the poor fool. But don't underestimate him.
He has gathered a formidable army;
it will not be easy for the Pandavas."

"My friend, I know all this," said Krishna gently,
"and I appreciate your concern for me.
But because the rewards of a peace treaty
would be so great, I have to strive for it.
If the Pandavas and the Kauravas
could live in harmony, it would be a blessing
for all of them, and I would avoid blame
if I could bring that state of affairs about."

The evening passed in profound conversation.
In the morning, Krishna rose, bathed,
performed his morning puja, and dispensed
gifts to the many brahmins in attendance.
He made sure Daruka had fed the horses,
groomed them and harnessed them, ready to leave.
Then Duryodhana and Shakuni came
to escort him to the assembly hall.
Krishna greeted them with courtesy.

In their chariots, flanked by foot soldiers,
they traveled in procession through the streets
of Hastinapura, past crowds thronging,
jostling to catch a glimpse of Krishna,
cheering in ecstasy. Dark-skinned Krishna,
swathed in a robe of yellow silk, resembled
a sapphire in a setting of bright gold.

The council was assembled. Also present
were kings and generals of the allied armies,
splendid in their sumptuous robes and jewels.
As Krishna entered, all rose to their feet,
and he noticed, hovering in the sky,
several seers, headed by Narada.
At Krishna's prompting, Bhishma welcomed them,
offering them fine seats and worthy guest gifts.
Now, in this assembly of the powerful,
after the usual formalities,

addressing Dhritrashtra, Krishna spoke.
His voice was like a deep and resonant drum,
reaching the furthest corners of the chamber.

"Sir, I bring greetings from Yudhishthira.
He sends respects, and prays for your good health.
He wishes me to say he bears no grudge
for what he and his family have suffered
up to now.

        "But you know why I stand here.
The house of Bharata has been renowned,
always, for its honor and probity,
for its courageous following of dharma,
which has brought it riches and acclaim.
But now your sons, led by Duryodhana,
have brought your great house into disrepute
by straying into greed, and cruelly
stripping your nephews of their patrimony.
This is shameful, king. If you do not check
your wayward son, catastrophe will follow—
a war so terrible, the entire clan
together with their allies on both sides
will be strewn, lifeless, on the field of battle,
with no one left to light their funeral pyres.
I have come here wishing to benefit
both the Kauravas and the Pandavas.
If you now follow the righteous course
it will be for your good as well as theirs."

After Krishna had finished his address,
the eminent seers—Rama Jamadagnya,
Narada and Kanva—also spoke,
making the same point through parables,
stories of pride punished by the gods,
designed to change Duryodhana's resolve.
He sat, stony-faced, quite unmoved.

Dhritarashtra murmured, "You are right,
all of you, but I cannot act alone.
I am powerless—speak to my son."

Krishna turned to Duryodhana,
sitting at his ease, next to Karna,
and spoke kindly to him. "Best of Bharatas,
listen to the wisdom of your father,
and of the elders, not to your misguided
and malevolent advisers. They may say
that you can win a glorious victory.
It is not so. What man on earth but you
would make enemies of your virtuous cousins—
and for what? For slaughter and destruction.
Look at your brothers here, your sons, your allies—
don't make them die for you. For die they will.
You could live in peace with the Pandavas,
each in your own domain, each enhancing
the power and prosperity of the other.
Together, you could be invincible."

The king and all the elders lent their voices
to Krishna's plea. They summoned up a prospect
of peaceful times, certain that Yudhishthira
was sincere in his expressed intention
to put past cruelties out of his mind.
"When Krishna returns to Upaplavya,
why not go with him, son," suggested Bhishma.
"Let Yudhishthira take you by the hands,
and his brothers welcome you with affection."

But when Duryodhana stood up to speak,
his angry breath hissing between his teeth,
it was clear that nothing he had heard
had had the least effect. "Long-haired Krishna,
you are reviling me because you favor

the Pandavas. You always have. These elders
are also hostile to me. The fact is
I have done nothing wrong. Yudhishthira
came freely to the gambling hall, and lost.
He paid; and now he wants us to return
Indraprastha to him.

      "But I maintain
that the hasty carve-up of the kingdom,
long ago, was an ill-judged mistake.
It never should have happened. I was young
and could not prevent it. In recent years
I have ruled the entire kingdom as proxy
for my father here. He is the king.
I am his eldest son, his heir apparent.
That is how it will stay. The Pandavas
will not receive a speck of Bharata land,
not while I'm alive! I'm ready to fight.
Manliness consists in making efforts—
striving, never giving in to pressure.
A kshatriya can have no greater honor
than to die in the glorious heat of battle.
If it comes to death, then heaven awaits me."

Krishna's dark eyes shone with mockery.
"You shall have your wish. You'll find a hero's bed
for certain! There is not a single warrior
who will see his home again once he rides out
to battle with the mighty Arjuna,
unvanquishable even by the gods!
'Nothing wrong'? Don't think it is forgotten
how you tried to burn the Pandavas alive,
how you entrapped them in the gambling hall,
how you subjected virtuous Draupadi
to utter humiliation. And you claim
that you've done nothing wrong? Shame, Duryodhana!

"You say I am partial to the Pandavas
but I seek what is best for them *and* you.
Not one of the wise elders in this hall—
not Bhishma, Drona, Kripa, Vidura,
not even your own father—takes your part
in your intransigent malevolence.
If you act against the best advice
you will put yourself in the gravest danger."

Duhshasana spoke to Duryodhana:
"Brother, if you don't agree to peace
it seems to me that Bhishma and Drona here
will capture you—and me and Karna too—
and hand you over to Yudhishthira."
Duryodhana, black with rage, sprang to his feet
and disrespectfully strode from the hall,
followed by his friends.

                    Krishna turned toward
Bhishma, Drona and the other elders.
"I call on you now to act—it is your duty.
Act now, while there is time. A while ago,
in the prosperous kingdom of the Bhojas,
I removed an upstart prince, Kamsa,
who had usurped the throne while his father lived.
There was civil war. By eliminating
that one prince, the kingdom was returned
to peace, prosperity and lawfulness.
I urge you, revered elders—do the same.
Bind the perverse prince and his friends, before
they bring disaster on an unknown scale.
Sacrifice the few to save the many."

Silence. Dhritarashtra, as though deaf,
made no answer, but sent for Gandhari
hoping his son would listen to his mother.
"Dhritarashtra, you are much to blame,"

said Gandhari. "Out of misplaced love
you have allowed your son to have his way,
and now he is past control. I'll speak to him."

Flanked by his friends, his face dark with resentment,
Duryodhana was brought back to the hall
and stood, shifting sulkily, barely listening
while his mother made familiar arguments.
"This kingdom has always been ruled according
to the law of succession. Yudhishthira,
as the eldest of the Bharata princes,
is generally acknowledged heir apparent.
We all know about the obsessive hatred
you have always harbored for your cousins
and, because you have your father's ear—
a father incapable of saying no—
you have engaged in all kinds of deceit
and trickery to seize the throne yourself.

"But the fact remains—the true succession
rests with Yudhishthira. He is generous,
only claiming that half of the kingdom
he ruled before he was tricked out of it.
Yet, gripped by greed, you stubbornly refuse
to give up even this. I blame your father.
If Dhritarashtra had performed his duty,
and restrained you years ago, would you, my son,
be the stubborn fool who stands here now,
bringing ruin on the Bharatas?"

Again, the prince swept out of the assembly,
followed by loyal Karna and Shakuni.
Together they devised a daring plot:
seeing that Krishna could not be appeased,
and perceiving him as unprotected,
Duryodhana proposed to take him hostage,
keep him prisoner until the Pandavas
agreed to give up all claim to the kingdom.

But observant Satyaki got wind of it
and went to tell Krishna and the elders
in the assembly. Once more, Duryodhana
was forced to listen to their reprimands:
Dhritarashtra said, "You must be deranged!
Do you not grasp the measure of Krishna's power?
If you attempted such a hare-brained scheme,
that would be your final act on earth;
you would be like a moth attacking fire.
Just as no human hand can stop the wind,
or reach the moon, as no man can lift the earth,
so there is no force that can capture Krishna."

Krishna turned his gaze on Duryodhana.
"Half-witted prince, just try to use force on me
and Yudhishthira's problem will be over.
I will capture you and your crass friends
and hand you over to the Pandavas.
You think I am just one man, easy prey,
but with me, on this spot, stand the great seers,
the Pandavas, and all our mighty allies."

He laughed a thunderous laugh and, instantly,
he was surrounded by a blinding light.
His body blazed fire, and from his many arms
sprang thumb-sized Pandavas and countless warriors,
Narada and the other holy seers,
Indra, the Ashvins, and many other gods.
From his mouth and nostrils flickered flames.
Conches, discuses and other weapons
shone around him, held in his many hands.

Dazzled, those assembled shrank away
and covered up their eyes in utter terror.
Only the wisest—Bhishma, Vidura,
Drona, Sanjaya—looked on in wonder.
Krishna resumed his human shape, and walked

out of the hall. The king called after him,
"You've seen what power I hold over my son!
Make sure my nephews know I wish them well.
If Duryodhana stays on this wicked path
there's nothing I can do."

                  "You are indeed
powerless," said Krishna ironically.

He left the hall, bound for Upaplavya.
But before setting out, there were two more
people he must see, to complete his mission.

30.

THE TEMPTATION OF KARNA

Krishna went first to Kunti's residence.
He bent and touched her feet in deep respect.
"Kunti, mother of heroes, I am leaving."
He talked about his unsuccessful mission:
"I and the elders all spoke with one voice
but Duryodhana is immovable.
The whole family is in thrall to him,
heading for the abyss. Now, please tell me,
what should I say to your sons on your behalf?"

"Remind them," said Kunti, "they are kshatriyas.
Tell them to have regard for their dharma—
which is to fight, to protect the people,
to wield authority. Tell Yudhishthira
this is what his father and I prayed for,
not for a son who would gabble the Vedas
parrot-fashion, and pass his time with rishis.
Remind him that a king is the creator
of the times he lives in, not the reverse.

"Tell him this ancient story:

"THERE WAS ONCE a woman of the kshatriya class,
famously strong-willed, whose son, defeated in a battle
with the Sindhus, lay about all day in gloom and apathy. His
mother came to him in his apartments, where he was dallying with his concubines.

"The mother said, 'Whose son are you? Not mine, that's for sure! Are you too cowardly to rouse your anger, too feeble even to cling to a low branch with your fingernails? Have some self-respect! You look like a man, but you behave like a eunuch. Wallow in self-pity if you want to waste the rest of your life.

" 'Get up, coward! You have no pride at all. Your enemies are most delighted with you and think you have forgiven them. Have you? Are you going to grow old like a dog, or are you going to rouse yourself and fight back, even if it means your early death? It is far more honorable to blaze up for an instant than to smolder like a pile of damp chaff. Effort is what counts.'

"The son said, 'Your heart is made of iron, relentless, pitiless, warmongering mother. You can't love me, speaking without compassion as you do.'

"The mother said, 'I was born into a great family, highly honored while your father was alive. Now I am pitied, stripped of wealth, ashamed that I can't give to brahmins as before. Your wife is suffering, your little sons long to have a father they can be proud of. We are at sea—be a harbor to us! We are drowning—be a raft to save us! Stand up tall, find your dignity. Better to break in the middle than to bend. You have it in you to be a heroic king. Unknown to you, we have a hidden treasury which you can draw on to raise an army. Stiffen your spine, rise up, defend yourself, be a terror to your enemies. Why don't you answer me?'

"The son said: 'I have kept silent because I wanted to listen to your every word, mother. Now I have found my manhood! I shall fight and, whether I win victory or not, I shall have lived like a kshatriya!'

"Tell my sons that story, Krishna," said Kunti, "to remind them where their duty lies."

☙

As Krishna left the city, he called on Karna
and asked him to ride with him a little way
in his chariot. Seriously, he addressed him.
"Karna, you are well versed in the Vedas.
You know, then, that a child born to a woman
out of wedlock becomes her husband's child
when she marries. That is the case with you.
You are the first-born son of Kunti, conceived
by Surya, the sun god—in law, therefore,
you are the eldest of the Pandavas,
a Bharata on your father's side, my cousin
on your mother's." Krishna explained to him
the detailed circumstances of his birth.

"Recognize then with joy, son of Kunti,
that you are the rightful heir to the kingdom.
Come with me today, my dear cousin,
to Upaplavya. Greet the Pandavas
as your true brothers. They will be overjoyed.
Yudhishthira will gladly renounce his claim
in your favor. Of all the sons of Pandu
it is you whose skill and temperament,
combining truthfulness with martial zeal,
most fits him to govern a great kingdom.
Your nephews will fall down and clasp your feet,
and you will share Draupadi as your wife.

"You are not the son of a wagoner,
you are a kshatriya. This very day,
you can be crowned. Brahmins will officiate,
I myself shall perform your consecration.
You will be king, with Yudhishthira
as your younger deputy. Bhima will hold
the shining parasol over your head.
Today, let the Pandavas be united!"

Karna had been staring at him, amazed,
as this glorious future was laid before him.

Moments passed. Karna remained silent.
Then he spoke.
                    "Krishna, I have no doubt
you speak out of friendship for me. I believe
what you have just told me. It makes clear
what, all my life, has been a mystery.
I have always felt that I was born to fight.
I am never more at ease within myself
than when I raise my bow, and test my skill
against overpowering odds.

                    "So, Krishna,
under the law I am a kshatriya
and, from what you say, a Pandava.
But this revelation comes too late.
Kunti abandoned me. She cast me out
like rubbish, as if I had been stillborn,
left me to the caprices of the river.
Adhiratha found me, and he and Radha
loved me from the first. Out of love for me
Radha's breasts poured forth milk immediately.
Out of love she cleaned up my excrement.
Adhiratha performed the birth rites for me
as a suta. He taught me all he knew.
I love him and respect him as my father.
When I came of age, he found wives for me.
I have sons and daughters—sutas, Krishna.
My heart is tied to them with bonds of love.
Do you think I would disown them now?

"Furthermore, nothing—not gold, not offers
of all the kingdoms in the world, not fear,
not lust for power—could make me break my word.
And I have promised Duryodhana
that I will be his bosom friend till death.
Duryodhana has raised armies and prepared
for war because I have encouraged him,
and I have vowed to defeat Arjuna

single-handed. Only one of us
will live to walk away.

                    "I know full well
that, with your help, the Pandavas will win.
I can see it now—all their great warriors
in their chariots, banners flying, ranged
on the field of Kurukshetra. It will be
the greatest war sacrifice that the world
has ever seen, with you as the chief priest.
I see the Terrifier, with monkey standard
fluttering boldly above his chariot.
Gandiva will be the ladle, men's courage
the sacrificial ghee. The divine missiles
will be invocations uttered by Arjuna,
and men's blood will be the oblation, Krishna.
So much blood.

                    "I want you to promise
not to tell the Pandavas what you have said.
If Yudhishthira knew I am his brother
he would resign his kingdom to me at once;
and I would give it to Duryodhana,
to whom I owe whatever wealth and honor
I have enjoyed. But I know the kingdom
would best belong to him who has Lord Krishna
as his friend and guide—that is, Yudhishthira.
I regret the insults I have flung
at the Pandavas, to please Duryodhana.
You can tell them that, when the time is right."

Krishna smiled. Then he laughed, and said,
"Can my offer really not persuade you?
Not even when you know that Duryodhana
would probably give up all thought of war
if you changed sides, knowing he could not win?
Not even when I am offering you the earth?

Not even when I tell you that this war
will involve unprecedented carnage?
There will be no more lucky throws at dice.
Arjuna's *Gandiva* throws blazing iron."

"I know it all already," Karna said.
"I had a dream—Yudhishthira ascending
steps to a huge palace, with his brothers.
All wore resplendent robes and white turbans
and Yudhishthira was eating rice and ghee
which you had served him, from a golden platter;
I knew that he was swallowing the earth.
Then I saw the armies of Duryodhana,
all in red turbans, except for Ashvatthaman,
Kripa and Kritavarman, turbaned in white.
There were open tumbrils drawn by camels,
and Bhishma, Drona and the rest of us
were being carried off to Yama's realm.

"So I have no illusions. But my honor
is more precious to me than life itself.
I know the dreadful bloodbath that is coming
has been caused by me and my associates
encouraging the folly of Duryodhana.
But it is too late. I will not betray
those I love, or the Kaurava for whom
I have pledged to die, if die I must."

"Then," said Krishna, "the last hope is gone.
I have seen my mission fail completely.
Tell the elders this month is propitious—
not too hot or cold, plenty of fodder
and fuel in the fields. In seven days
it will be New Moon, the Day of Indra.
Tell them that is the day war should begin."

Karna embraced Krishna long and hard.
"When we next meet," he said, "it will be in heaven."

❦

Vidura was in torment. He could not sleep.
He saw all too clearly what was coming,
as in a nightmare from which one cannot wake.
He spoke to Kunti to relieve his feelings
and she, sick with anxiety herself,
wondered what she could do—and thought of Karna.
"Surely," she thought, "when he knows the truth
he will obey me as his mother, and stand
with his brothers against Duryodhana.
That way, war may be prevented, even now."

She rose early, and went to look for Karna,
finding him where he stood every morning—
on the riverbank, stripped to the waist,
chanting his praises to the god of light.
She waited by a tree, taking shelter
from the sun's already oppressive heat,
until Karna had finished his devotions.

He turned and, seeing her, he bowed, hands joined.
"I, the son of Radha and Adhiratha,
greet you, my lady. How may I be of service?"

She blurted out, "Karna, I have to tell you—
you are *my* son, not the son of Radha
and Adhiratha. The sun god is your father."
And Kunti told the story of Karna's birth,
asking him, as Krishna had before her,
to join his brothers as a true Pandava.
Immediately, Karna heard a voice
that came from the sun: *Kunti speaks the truth;
obey your mother and you will benefit.*

But Karna's mind was steady as he replied,
"Noble lady, I hear what you say.

But you did me irreparable wrong
when you cast me on the river. By that act
you robbed me of the honor and respect
I should have had as a kshatriya.
What enemy could ever have harmed me more
than you have? All these years, you have witnessed me
slighted and abused within the court,
heard me sneered at, called 'the suta's son,'
only the king's sons befriending me.
Yet you said nothing. You have never acted
as my mother—you only speak up now
in your own interest, to protect your sons.

"For all the men who live in comfort here,
enjoying the bounty of the Bharatas,
the time has come to repay what they owe.
For Drona, Bhishma, Ashvatthaman, Kripa,
and for me as well, honor demands
that we be true to our salt. Duryodhana
is entitled to my love and loyalty
and he shall have them—I shall strain every sinew
to defeat the sons of Pandu."
                              Then, softening,
"But here is my word—only Arjuna,
not his brothers, will meet death at my hands.
In that way, when the terrible war ends,
you will still have five sons."
                              Kunti sobbed
in anguish, knowing Karna spoke the truth.
There being neither time nor space for pity,
Karna bowed, and they went their separate ways.

ॐ

That night, Duryodhana sent for his brahmins
and asked them to foretell what was to come.
They shook their heads, "The planets are at odds,

the stars are angry, and hostile animals—
jackals, wolves—prowl the far horizon.
We see meteors falling on your armies
and vultures circling the city. Dumb horses
are seen to weep and lie down in the fields
and foul diseases rake the population."

Duryodhana quaked within, but shrugged it off.
The prince would not be turned from his fatal path.

31.

MARSHALING THE ARMIES

The countdown had begun. From camp to camp
excited rumors spread; even the breeze
stirred differently. Men who for many weeks
and months had grown acclimatized to waiting
so that each camp had become a makeshift town
with its own rules and customs, almost home-like,
now sensed in the vibrations of the air
and self-important scurrying of runners
that battle was approaching. Blacksmiths' fires
were bellowed to white heat, whetstones were tested,
spears and arrows sharpened, armor burnished
until it dazzled like the sun itself.

Even the animals got wind of it.
Elephants fretted, straining at their tethers,
swinging their great heads from side to side;
horses rolled their eyes, their nostrils flaring
in longing for the freedom of the gallop.

Just as bees, preparing for mass flight,
seethe and sing, making the hive throb
with anticipation, so the troops
milled about in what seemed wild confusion
but, in fact, was highly organized,
every man concentrating on his tasks.
In each camp, the shout went out, "Form up!

Form up!" And in the din of chariot wheels,
of roaring elephants, of drums and conches,
the hosts of foot soldiers formed their divisions,
then marched about, practicing fierce war cries,
joking, trying out armor and weapons.

༄

Yudhishthira convened his war council
and asked Krishna to give them a report
on his mission to Hastinapura.
Krishna described his negotiations,
the diplomatic twists and turns—but nothing
of his private talk with the suta's son.
"That man Duryodhana does not want peace.
He scorns the law and, drinking in the words
of Karna, he thinks he has won already!
Only Vidura stands up to him.
The villain is wronging you. There must be war."

Leading each of the seven Pandava armies
was a great and experienced warrior:
Bhima, brave and bull-like Pandava;
Drupada, the father of Draupadi;
Dhrishtadyumna, her brother, born from fire;
Virata, who had sheltered the Pandavas
during their final year of exile, now
joined to them by marriage; Chekitana,
long-standing ally of the Pandavas;
Shikhandin, elder son of Drupada;
and Satyaki, Krishna's friend and kinsman.
Which of them should be commander-in-chief?
There was much discussion. Finally,
Yudhishthira appointed Dhrishtadyumna.

Krishna urged deployment of the troops
with all speed. Since every hope of peace

lay in ashes, only slaughter remained.
Balarama, Krishna's brother, refused
any part in this war between kinsmen.
He had taught the mace both to Bhima
and to Duryodhana, and could not bear
to contemplate the death of either man.
With heavy heart, he prepared to set out
on a pilgrimage, along the Sarasvati.

The young princes took their leave of Draupadi,
who stayed in Upaplavya with the women
of the household and their maids and servants.

Like a slow-moving landmass, the force set off—
hundreds of thousands of armored infantry,
tens of thousands of bullock carts, laden
with food, equipment, every kind of weapon,
making for the plain of Kurukshetra.
With them went servants, cooks, surgeons, craftsmen,
attendants and camp followers. Rank on rank
of glossy horses, harnessed to forty thousand
fine chariots, came next, and then war elephants,
tusks sharpened to lethal points, all trained to stay
calm in the cacophony of battle.

Yudhishthira led his armies onward
day after day, until at last they reached
the river Hiranvati at Kurukshetra,
where he chose the site for their encampment,
avoiding cremation grounds and holy shrines.
The river ran clear and sweet, and provided
easy fording places. Yudhishthira
ordered that a deep defensive moat
be dug round the cantonment, where there were
tents erected for the noble warriors,
well supplied with firewood, food and water.
In each tent stout bows were placed, and plentiful

stocks of iron-tipped arrows, shields, cuirasses,
javelins and animal fodder. Everywhere,
artisans were plying their essential trades.
Enclosed, tethered, elephants by the hundred
were jacketed in plates of spiked armor.

Yudhishthira confided to Arjuna
how he quaked with dread—that things had come
to this, as though no effort had been made!
"Brother," said Arjuna, "you heard the message
our mother sent through Krishna; she is right.
It is our dharma and our destiny
to battle for what is right." Yudhishthira
could not disagree. He would perform
his duty as the king, and yet it seemed
as though a nightmarish, impersonal
force was driving him inexorably
toward a precipice . . .

౿

On the plain around Hastinapura,
stretching far, far into the distance,
the vast allied forces of the Kauravas—
eleven armies—waited in readiness.
Fragrant smoke from a hundred thousand fires
curled upward, hovering as a murky haze
above the city, before dispersing slowly.
For many weeks, the bustle of preparation
had been a constant hubbub in the background
of the citizens' quotidian lives.

Now that the point had come for girls and women
to part from their sons, their brothers and husbands,
were they struck, as if for the first time,
by what it meant—that their dear beloved
might never clasp them in his arms again?

That his voice, so ordinary a strand
in the fabric of their daily lives,
might become a sound bitterly yearned for
so that, for years to come, a distant voice
resembling his would make them turn their heads
and weep?

　　　　Now Duryodhana appointed
the commander-in-chief of all his armies.
He asked Bhishma, incorruptible,
distinguished warrior of enormous skill,
to take that post. "You must know," said Bhishma,
"that the Pandavas are very dear to me,
just as you are. But I have pledged to fight
in your cause. I am experienced
in all the various battle formations;
I know how to deploy an army, how to
plan a battle, I have at my command
weapons which could empty the world of people.
But I shall be judicious. I will be
commander-in-chief—but on this condition:
either I must fight first, or Karna must.
The driver's son always seeks to rival me;
I will not ride out with him."

　　　　Then Karna spoke:
"There is no way I will fight while Bhishma,
that spawn of the river Ganga, is alive!
When he is cut down, I will take up arms
and battle to the death with Arjuna."

"You must also understand," said Bhishma,
"that though I will exert my every nerve,
summon all my expertise to kill
the Pandava forces, I will never fight
Shikhandin."
　　　　"Why is that?" asked Duryodhana.

"Because he was once a woman," Bhishma said,
"and I will not fight a woman. He was born
as Shikhandini, daughter of Drupada.
And in her former life, she was Amba
whom I abducted, together with her sisters,
as brides for my brother, Vichitravirya.
When Amba revealed that she was betrothed
to another suitor, I allowed her to leave.
I shall tell you what happened to her then.

"Having chosen King Shalva as her husband
before I carried her off, she traveled,
with my blessing, to his court. But he refused
to take her as his wife, regarding her
as my cast-off. Useless for her to plead
that there had never been any question
of marriage with me. He spurned her with contempt.

"Heartbroken, she sought refuge in the forest.
Brahmins advised her, 'Go back to your father,'
but she knew she would only be despised.
Then she sought out Rama Jamadagnya,
the great weapons teacher and ascetic—
he who taught me everything I know
about the arts of war. She begged him piteously
to kill me, whom she saw as the sole source
of her bitter grief. Rama ordered me
to marry her myself, but I would not break
my vow of celibacy.

                    "Furious,
Rama challenged me, and he and I
battled for many days. Each of us
invoked our powerful celestial weapons,
so that the mountains trembled and the sky
was red with boiling flame. Each of us
received agonizing wounds, but neither

could prevail over the other. Finally,
Rama's ancestors urged him to withdraw,
and he told Amba he had done all he could
and advised her to seek my protection.
But pride would not allow it. She passionately
wished me dead.

        "Meanwhile, King Drupada,
longing to avenge himself on Drona,
and having no strong son at that time, prayed
to Lord Shiva for a son. 'You shall have
a son in female form,' replied Shiva,
'and you must content yourself with that.'

"After severe austerities, and making
heartfelt pleas to powerful gods, Amba
set fire to herself and, with her final breath,
vowed that she would have revenge on me.
She was reborn as Drupada's daughter.
He and his wife named her Shikhandini
and reared her as the son they had always wanted.
She learned the skills and manners of a prince
and became accomplished in the arts of war,
taught by Drona in his weapons school.
When the time came, Drupada married her
to the daughter of the king of the Dasharnas—
whereupon she could simulate no longer.
Grossly insulted, her father-in-law sent
brahmin envoys, articulate in insults,
to challenge Drupada, giving notice
that an invading army would be dispatched
if Drupada's son was, indeed, a woman.

"What could be done? Drupada started praying.
His wife said, 'Piety is well and good
but you also have to use your wits.
Decide what you should tell your councillors,
then worship the gods to your heart's content.'

Drupada and his queen devised a plan:
the king would claim that his wife had deceived him—
only now did he know his son was a girl!

"In despair, and fearing for her parents,
Shikhandini fled far into the forest,
to starve herself to death. But a yaksha
granted her a boon—for a fixed time,
but long enough, he would become a woman,
and give her his masculine attributes.
Thus transformed, and full of confidence,
she went back to Kampilya, her father's court,
and revealed the good news to her parents.
Now, truly, she was Prince Shikhandin.

"To test the truth of things once and for all,
and meanwhile gearing up for an attack
on Panchala, the wrathful Dasharna king
brought an inspection party to Kampilya:
several gorgeous women. They were escorted
to Shikhandin's apartments. Hours later,
they emerged smiling, fully satisfied:
Prince Shikhandin was indeed a man.
Drupada breathed deeply, then ordered up
a sumptuous feast for his visitors
before they happily made their way back home,
the two kings, henceforth, on the best of terms.

"Sorrowfully returning to the forest,
the prince prepared to honor his agreement
with the helpful yaksha, and take back
his female body. But the yaksha told him
that, since they had last met, he had been cursed
by Kubera, the short-tempered yaksha king,
and must remain a woman until Shikhandin
should meet his death on the field of battle.
The prince was filled with joy and gratitude.

"Now he leads an army for the Pandavas
and has marked me as his adversary.
But, because he was born as a woman,
I will not fight him. Fate must take its course."

☙

Duryodhana had appointed generals
from among the experienced warrior kings,
and consecrated them with ceremony.
Advised by Bhishma, he had rated them
according to their skill and experience.
When it came to Karna, Bhishma judged him
as second-rate. Karna was furious,
"Left to myself, I could destroy the army
of the Pandavas in a mere five days!"
Bhishma laughed at him. "You prove my point.
You are rash and silly. Victory
can never be achieved that easily."

As brahmins performed Bhishma's consecration
bloody rain fell, and disembodied voices
were heard; jackals howled ferociously
and meteors streaked across the glowering sky.
To solicit blessings, Duryodhana
lavished gold and cattle on the brahmins,
and, strengthened by their ritual benedictions,
he marched to Kurukshetra with his armies.

There, with Karna, he measured out the camp
on the west side of the plain, on pleasant ground,
where there was easy access to fresh water.
Even the smallest details of provisioning
had been anticipated—spare axles, ropes,
banners and pennants, spades, horns, every weapon
one would expect. Even bells and rugs
had been thought of, and bunches of fresh herbs

to tie onto the chariots, to ward off evil.
With the tents erected and arranged,
the camp looked as rich as Hastinapura.

⚜

Uluka, son of Shakuni, was told
to take a message from Duryodhana
to Yudhishthira, a ritual taunt:
"Now is the time to prove yourself a man!
You lost at dice, you saw your blameless wife
dishonored, you endured long years of exile
and lost your kingdom—who would not be angry?
But angry words are one thing, courageous acts
are another. Are you brave enough
or are you impotent, you and your brothers?
Can Bhima drink the blood of Duhshasana
as he swore to do in the gaming hall?
Will you have your much vaunted revenge
or are you all hot air? Join battle with us:
either rule the earth by defeating us
or be killed and go to the heaven of heroes.

"In fact, you stand no chance—how can you beat
Bhishma, that mountain among warriors,
or Drona, master of the *Brahma* weapon?
Even though Krishna always takes your side,
even though you have the bow *Gandiva*,
I won your kingdom, and for thirteen years
I have enjoyed it. I shall enjoy it still
after I have killed you and all your kinsmen.
And when you flounder, helpless in the flood
of mighty Kauravas, when all your friends
lie dead around you, then you will regret
taking up arms against me and my brothers."

The Pandavas, hearing these boastful words,
were enraged, pacing up and down, their eyes

red with fury. Seeing this, Krishna
spoke to Uluka: "Leave this place at once,
gambler's son, and say this to Duryodhana:
'Be careful, villain! Even though Arjuna
has appointed me his charioteer,
and even though I said I would not fight,
a time may come when, as a last resort,
I shall scorch your forces like a field of straw.
Meanwhile the Pandavas are in good heart,
as you will learn tomorrow.'"

                        Arjuna,
Wearer of the Diadem, added, "Go,
gambler's son, say this to Duryodhana:
'You may think me too compassionate
to kill Bhishma, when the moment comes.
I assure you, I shall kill him first;
pelted by my arrows, he will topple
from his chariot while you look on, appalled.
And that is the start. You are about to reap
the bitter harvest of your wickedness.'"

VI

THE BOOK OF BHISHMA

32.

THE SONG OF THE LORD

"How did they fight, those ancestors of mine?"
asked Janamejaya. Vaishampayana,
with the blessing of Vyasa, told the king
how, on the eve of battle, the two sides
agreed a covenant, a code of conduct,
rules of engagement properly laid down.
Warriors should fight their counterparts—
horsemen against horsemen, infantry
against opposing infantry. Stragglers
should not be killed, nor should anyone
in retreat, or who had lost his weapon,
or one intending to surrender. No one
who was unprepared should be attacked.
Words should be fought with words. An assault
should not be made without giving due notice.
Charioteers, those engaged in transport,
those blowing conches or clashing cymbals

should not be targeted. Nor should animals
drawing chariots or carrying men.

Principle is one thing, practice another.
Soon, battle frenzy would wipe these agreements
from men's memories, but, for the present,
all were clear how to conduct themselves.

"Tell me in detail how the war developed,"
requested the king. So Vaishampayana
embarked on his narration of the conflict,
the internecine strife that shook the earth.

༄

Blind Dhritarashtra paced through his apartments
full of dread, unable to still his mind.
Now that he could not console himself
with self-deceiving hopes that his stubborn son
might yet see reason, even on the brink,
the full force of the coming calamity
was bearing down on him.

          He sought Vyasa
and sobbed to him about his son's wickedness.
"Wringing your hands is useless," said the sage.
"Time has run out for your sons and their friends.
While the fighting lasts, I can at least grant you
the gift of sight, so you can see events
as they happen."
          "Ah, no!" cried Dhritarashtra,
"I could not bear to see the gushing blood,
the mutilated bodies of my loved ones.
But I want to know how things unfold
moment by moment." So Vyasa granted
Sanjaya, the king's aide and companion,
the gift of divine vision. He would witness

all that took place on the battleground
whether by day or night, whether openly
or in men's secret hearts—there would be nothing
hidden from him. Invulnerable,
he would be present on the field of war,
everywhere at once, silent recorder
of all the joys and agonies of men,
their courage, rage, despair. And in this way,
at second hand, the king would learn everything.

"Nature is out of joint," said Vyasa.
"As witness to the coming massacre,
pigs are giving birth to foals, the trees
are weighted down with strange, unseasonal fruits.
Monsters are being born, some with two heads,
some with one leg, or none, or bloated breasts.
The very planets are engorged with blood
and fly amok, out of their natural paths."

"Without doubt," said Dhritarashtra, "fate
has designed a terrible disaster.
I have one consolation—kshatriyas
who fall with honor on the field of battle,
not dying in their beds with wasted limbs,
journey to that place reserved for heroes
where they enjoy the heavenly bliss of gods."

☙

After Vyasa had spoken and departed,
Dhritarashtra sat with Sanjaya
far into the blackest part of night
while, to calm him, Sanjaya described
the hills, plains, rivers of Bharatavarsha
and the diverse peoples of the country.
"All this belongs to the Bharatas!"
exclaimed the king. "But my misguided son

is bringing devastation to our land—
children left fatherless, wives sick with grief,
girls shorn of all hope of finding husbands!"
"You try to shift responsibility,"
said Sanjaya, "but you, too, are to blame.
You know how this will end—the Pandavas
will win for sure. Krishna is on their side,
and where Krishna is, there is victory.'

ॐ

Sanjaya departed for Kurukshetra.
All Dhritarashtra could do now was wait.
And wait. For ten long days and nights he waited,
lost in thought, all normal life suspended.
Then Sanjaya arrived at last, distraught.
"O king, the news is dreadful. The great Bhishma,
mightiest of warriors, has fallen,
defeated by Shikhandin. Now he lies
on a bed of arrows, awaiting death."

At this shock, Dhritarashtra fainted.
When he had revived, he cried aloud,
"Oh, Sanjaya! My heart must be made of stone
that it hasn't shattered at this dreadful news.
How can it have happened? Who was beside him?
Who protected him? How could he fall
when Drona was alive to stand with him?
Bhishma was like a god in strength and skill.
If he is crushed, then what hope for my sons?
Tell me who else was slain, who was victorious—
tell me all the details of the battle,
this conflict caused by my wrong-headed son."

Sanjaya said, "You should not heap all blame
on Duryodhana. But listen, O king,
and I will tell you what I have seen and heard."

And Sanjaya gave the following account,
the events leading to the fall of Bhishma.

✣

As morning broke on the opening day of war,
the rising sun streaked the sky with scarlet.
The heat slowly burned off the mist that hung
above the plain. The opposing armies,
division upon division, stretched away
as far as the eye followed the curving earth.
All was brilliant. The chariots of the princes
and of their royal allies were resplendent
with noble banners, each with its own emblem.
One king's standard carried a scarlet bull,
another, a boar on a cloth of silver,
others, bright flowers, stars, eagles, comets . . .
the sight too dazzling to be taken in.
Some kings were riding in their chariots,
others sat erect on the necks of elephants
or on spirited horses, proudly wheeling.

So much armor, on men, elephants, horses!
The brilliant gold and bronze rivaled the sun.
The mass of men and beasts, constantly moving,
was beautiful as a river thick with fish,
glittering, thousands upon thousands
all confident in prearranged formations.

With forces smaller than the Kauravas',
Yudhishthira knew a less numerous army
must mass more tightly, not be spread out wide
where men could be picked off more easily.
Arjuna said the thunderbolt formation
would serve them best, with Bhima in the vanguard
whirling his mace to dismay the enemy.
Arjuna had planned the precise position

of each Pandava and of their allies,
and placed Yudhishthira right at the center
surrounded by well-trained and furious
elephants like a range of moving hills.
Yudhishthira stood, beneath a parasol,
on his gold chariot with the golden traces,
and dozens of priests intoned prayers around him.
Dhrishtadyumna protected him from the rear.

Both forces were terrible, both beautiful.
In both, men's hearts were filled with joy and pride
at being part of it—this grand display,
this glorious event, this sacrifice,
this, the well-trained warrior's highest calling.
Fear, suffering and grief would follow later.

To see this greatest war ever fought on earth
there had gathered from all the three worlds
crowds of spectators—ordinary people,
holy men, divine beings—all assembled
to witness the spectacular clash of kin.
On rising ground that overlooked the plain,
or hovering in the sparkling air above,
they waited, jostling for the best positions.

With the two sides facing one another,
one east, one west, with ten thousand conches
blaring out in challenge, the din of cymbals
and the deep, heart-stopping throb of war drums,
Arjuna said to Krishna, his charioteer,
"Drive the chariot into no-man's-land
so I can see, before the battle starts,
the faces of the enemy I must kill."

Krishna did what Arjuna asked of him.
And there, with every soldier tense and ready,
with every horse straining at its harness;

there in the moment before hell's unleashing,
with each blade whetted, each weapon at hand;
there, in the moment when the frenzy
of preparation was over, and the din
of death not yet begun—there, at that point
in the relentless passage of events . . .

time freezes

Sanjaya continues:
Arjuna sinks down in his chariot.
His warrior's heart has failed him.
His eyes stream with tears,
his limbs tremble,
the great bow *Gandiva* drops from his hand.

Time itself holds its breath.
For Karna, Kunti, for his brothers,
for Krishna—for each differently—Arjuna
is the point, the mainspring of the action.
He is the hero on whom all the hopes
of the Pandavas are pinned; the obstacle,
above all others, Dhritarashtra's son
sees as blocking his path to victory.

Arjuna has fought scores of bloody battles,
exulting in the slaughter of enemies,
cutting them down like standing fields of grain
without regret, never looking back.
He is the supreme kshatriya;
the whole effort of his life is geared
to heroism and glorious victory.
But now he is unraveled by distress.
He gazes at the rank on rank of kinsmen.
They are so familiar—human, as he is.

How can they be stranger to him than strangers?
Death takes on new weight, sharper meaning.
Whether this war brings victory or defeat
there will be no occasion for rejoicing.

Striking his brow, he cries aloud to Krishna,
"I will not fight! A kshatriya enters battle
to preserve dharma, but how can it be right
to strike our kinsmen, coldly to kill those
who have nurtured, taught and grown with us?
Look at all our cousins standing there,
and Drona, our revered guru—and Bhishma,
Bhishma, beloved grandfather to us all!
He looks so serene, full of resolve—
has he not imagined how it will be
to aim his arrows at the hearts of those
joined to him by blood—who once were children
gathered round, enraptured by his stories?

"There are Duryodhana and his brothers,
sick with greed and anger—but should we *kill* them?
Oh, Krishna, even though they are geared for war,
even though they are blind to their own evil
and are themselves prepared to kill us—still,
how can we, who know well what is sinful,
do the same? When family is broken,
the spiritual bedrock is destroyed
leading to every kind of social wrong
and vile disorder. Chaos surely follows.

"Their force is much greater than our own—
eleven well-trained armies to our seven.
But even if we are victorious
how could we be happy at such a cost?
It would be better to let them kill us,
or to wander the world as mendicants;
better to give up the kingdom now

than gain it at the cost of so much grief.
No! I will not fight!"

Krishna says, "Friend, this is unworthy of you.
You're speaking like a feeble-hearted weakling,
not like the noble warrior you are.
Get to your feet, scourge of your enemies!"

"But how can I take aim against my elders
who deserve from me my love and reverence?
I sense already the familiar heft
of *Gandiva*, flexing to unleash death
on those I should be protecting—how can I
cut them down as though they were rank weeds?
Tell me, how, Krishna! My thoughts are scattered.
My mind is seething like a nest of hornets.
You are my guide, my greatest, wisest friend.
Help me to understand where my duty lies."

Krishna smiles, as at a foolish child.
"Son of Kunti, your doubts sound honorable
but they spring from deep misunderstanding.
You speak as if this life were all there is.
But it is just one brief embodiment
of the indestructible, eternal soul.
Bodies are born, they flourish, age, and die.
But the soul, part of that greater spirit
that infuses everything that exists,
was never born, and cannot be killed.
That soul, the witness of our every thought
and action, persists from one life to the next;
it sloughs off its old and outworn body
as one discards old clothes and puts on new.
Wise people know this, and do not lament.

"You need to refine your understanding.
In this life, nothing is permanent,

nothing can be held, or truly owned.
The individual 'I' a person clings to—
the ego with a sense of past and future,
furnished with memories and with intentions—
is illusory. Time *is* the present,
an infinite parade of present moments
to be experienced, to be endured,
misery and pleasure equally.
Beings have mysterious origins.
They emerge into the light, then disappear
into shadow. Why should this cause grief?

"Within the framework of a single life
each person has their proper course, their dharma—
the path of righteous action they should follow,
depending on the station they occupy.
Your dharma is to fight. That is your purpose.
That is what you were born for, and for that
praise-singers will extol your memory
long after you are dead. Think. To refuse
would lead to deep disgrace—people would say,
When it came to it, he was a coward.
What could be more miserable than that
for a kshatriya? Fight as a warrior should
and you cannot lose—either you are killed,
and go to heaven, or win, and enjoy the kingdom.
So gather your strength, Arjuna, stand up!

"The wise mind is as clear as pure water.
The unwise wallow in complexity;
they cast about, pursuing this practice,
that ritual, craving some benefit,
their senses agitated, minds distracted.
Often such behavior is applauded,
What a devout person, people say.

"But right understanding far outweighs
such action. Follow duty for duty's sake,

without straining after its rewards.
Do not get caught up in pairs of opposites—
pain and pleasure, failure and success—
but, rather, be strong-minded, equable.
Let your action be informed by discipline.
Practice contemplation, undiverted
by those who claim to understand the Vedas,
or by those addicted to results.
Cultivate a calm and stable mind,
your own right understanding, Arjuna.
Only then will you escape delusion."

Arjuna is still perplexed. "Tell me,
what are the qualities of a stable mind?"

"A person who possesses such a mind
is not agitated by calamity;
is free of craving and aversion, both;
is not unbalanced by the restless senses
but takes them for what they are, and is unchanged,
as the ocean receives the rippling waters
of the rivers that flow into it
and yet maintains its level. A stable mind
is free from anger; constantly serene,
filled with knowledge of the eternal Self."

"But in that case," protests Arjuna,
"why are you urging me to fling myself
into this terrible war? Why should I not
go to a forest ashram and meditate?"

"My friend, there are two paths through this world:
the path of knowledge and the path of action.
You will not attain enlightenment
by renouncing action—and indeed
you would find that is impossible.
To live out this material existence

we have to act, just to keep ourselves alive.
The question is, how to act rightly?
Right action is that which is performed
without selfish attachment to the outcome—
sacrifice offered to sustain the gods
and to maintain order in the world
is right action; not when it greedily
grasps after rewards. Through right action
gods and mortals nourish one another
and the world is held together. Remember—
action carried out in a true spirit
is the most perfect possible achievement.
It is based upon renunciation.
The divine Self informs every selfless act.

"People who are caught up in delusion
think they are sole authors of their actions
and of the consequences. So they are proud
of their success, and suffer shame or guilt
when their efforts fail. But the workings
of cause and effect are infinitely complex,
beyond the scope of human understanding,
part of the eternal cosmic dance
in which each atom mirrors every other;
unknowable and inexpressible."

Arjuna can hardly concentrate
on Krishna's words. He is preoccupied
by the enemy drawn up in front of him.
"Krishna, what impels a man to do evil
even when he receives the best advice,
even though he understands what is right—
as if some hidden force is pushing him?"

"It is desire and anger—those attachments
that cast a screen of smoke over the world.

Desire is the root, giving rise to anger.
These are the age-old enemies of wisdom.
The clamorous senses must be grappled with,
the mind must be brought under one's control.
Beyond the workings of the mind is wisdom
grounded in awareness of the infinite.
This is my yoga, the eternal way
I have taught since the human race began."

Arjuna is surprised, and mystified.
"But, Krishna, I know when you were born—
what do you mean by *since the human race* . . . ?"

"I have passed through many lives, as you have;
but I remember them, and you do not.
I am the changeless and eternal Self,
sufficient, never born, never dying.
Yet I take on a material form
whenever the world is in need of me,
to protect the good and destroy evil.
I have no personal need to act—and yet
I act, to set the world the right example,
a bulwark against ruin and anarchy.

"The spirit, the ultimate reality
that pervades the cosmos is impersonal.
You should know, I am its embodiment.
Act, and dedicate your actions to me.
Those who truly devote themselves to me,
in whatever way, will be released
from the relentless wheel of birth and death.

"You need to understand what is action
and what is non-action. It is not obvious.
Action can reside in non-action
and non-action can underlie action.
Everything depends on the state of mind.

If a person is bound up, attached
to the outcome of their action, then
that action's consequences, like a burr,
will stick to them through this life and beyond,
determining the nature of their rebirth.
That is the unshakable law of karma.
But those who do not grasp after results,
who treat success and failure as the same,
are always satisfied. Although they act,
they are really doing nothing—like a boatman
rowing with the current, at his ease.
Their actions do not stick to them, because
they are free of yearning for results.
In acting in this way, they are engaged
in one variety of sacrifice,
offering up their actions with simplicity,
relinquishing all doubt and ignorance."

&

"Krishna," says Arjuna, "I hear you praising
action, and the relinquishment of acts.
I am confused—which of these is better?"

"Both of these can lead to liberation.
Right action is the better course. And yet,
essentially, they are not alternatives.
Through either one, carried out sincerely,
one can attain the benefits of both.
Indifferent to the fruits that follow action,
those whose actions spring from the right spirit
are renouncers, since they have relinquished
attachment to everything impermanent,
seeing that these things bring no real delight.

"Such rare people see the eternal Self
everywhere—see themselves in all creatures

and all creatures in themselves; for Brahman
is one and the same in everything.
They radiate joy, exude peace and love,
knowing me as their true companion.
Understanding this is everything,
and spiritual discipline—yoga—
is the key.

       "I shall tell you what yoga is.
Yoga is austere but temperate.
It is not for the glutton, Arjuna,
but neither does it mean self-starvation.
It is not for one who lies in bed till noon,
but nor does it require sleep deprivation.

"The disciplined mind is calm, as unswerving
as a lighted candle in a sheltered place.
Not identified with suffering,
it is not shaken even by great sorrow.
That is what yoga means—yoking oneself
to true understanding; equanimity
that faces pain and pleasure evenly."

"That unswerving calm you speak of, Krishna,
seems to me impossible to attain
since the mind is obstinate and fickle,
scattered by impulse, as leaves are by the wind."

"Without a doubt, the mind is most unruly;
yet, by patient practice, by constant effort,
it can be reined in under one's control."

"But what happens to one who tries sincerely
to follow the path of discipline, yet fails?
When they die, is all their effort lost,
disintegrating like a tattered cloud?"

"No, Arjuna, no one is destroyed
who struggles to do good. They are reborn,
sustained by their efforts in previous lives,
into a family which will support
their further progress on the path to freedom."

༄

Sanjaya continues to repeat
Krishna's profound teaching: Krishna says,
"Now I shall tell you how, by practicing
discipline, counting me as your refuge,
you shall know me fully, without reserve.
For all that exists is suspended on me
like jewels on a necklace. I am everywhere.

"I am the essence of everything that is;
the cosmos is sustained by my energy.
I am the deathless radiance of the sun,
the heat of fire, the soft gleam of the moon.
I am the taste in water, son of Kunti.
I am Om, the sacred syllable.
I am the roar of the wind, the manhood of men.
I am the pure fragrance of the earth.
I am the life in all life that exists.
I am the discipline in holy men.
I am the eternal seed in all creatures.
I am the intelligence in the intelligent.
I am the brilliance in the brilliant.
I am the strength of the strong, devoid of passion.
I am the desire which is not self-seeking.
All states of being are from me alone,
facets of my all-creative nature.

"The world is caught up by appearances,
dazzled by their infinite variety,
snared by illusion, endlessly distracted,

and does not recognize me, the eternal
principle that connects the humblest flower
with the grandeur of the constellations.
It is hard to penetrate appearance;
only those who seek me pass beyond it.
Evildoers do not turn to me;
but those in distress, those who long for knowledge,
the purposeful, and those who pursue wisdom—
all these seek me out and share in me.
The afflicted world, bewildered by craving,
is blind to me, who am unborn, eternal.
But there are a few liberated souls
who know me and devote themselves to me.

"Beings are born into delusion, vision
skewed by hatred and self-centered desire.
But those that strive, through me, for liberation
even as they draw their final breath
know me as Brahman, the absolute, at last."

꙯

Arjuna says, "Please explain these matters—
say more about action, about Brahman.
Tell me, what is the true nature of beings?
How, at the point of death, can one know you?"

"Brahman is the ultimate reality,
the indestructible, unchanging Self;
it is the inherent nature of every being,
neither existent nor non-existent.
It supports all; it seems to have all senses
yet it is free of senses, unattached;
outside and inside, moving and unmoving,
distant yet near, destroyer and creator.
It inhabits every human heart.

"Action is the cosmic energy
that brings every creature into existence.
From material nature, there arise
three modes of being—purity, passion, dullness.
There is no creature in heaven or earth free
of these constituents, part of their nature.
They have diverse effects, swaying a person
this way and that. Only through detachment
can that person arrive at peace and balance.

"The state of mind that comes from purity,
based on clear understanding of the Self,
seems bleak initially, but as it grows
it reveals itself as a precious nectar.
The happiness that is based on passion
springs from sensual delight; at first
it seems like nectar, but later it turns out
to be a bitter poison. The happiness
arising out of negligence and sloth
is a dull state, lacking in energy,
a state that comes from settling for less.

"A person achieves perfection by doing
their own work, in a spirit of dedication—
better to perform one's own work poorly
than to do well the work of someone else,
for every human enterprise is clouded
by shortcomings, as fire is by smoke.
No one can go wrong if they are working
according to their station, and their nature.
Though acting in the world, they surrender
every act to me and, through my grace,
gain the eternal, imperishable home.

"But for those encumbered by desire,
consumed by appetite which knows no limits,
the world is empty. There is no sacredness,

only the frantic scramble after gain.
They tell themselves how great they are; success
is measured by their piled-up treasuries.
They despise the weak, fawn on the powerful,
grasping, grabbing, pushing, trusting no one.
Such people are reborn in degradation.
The gateway to the ruin of the soul
is built of lust, of anger and of greed.

"As cosmic day and night succeed each other,
helpless creatures take shape constantly,
and continually dissolve, perishing,
to be reborn when day comes round again.
Impartially, I witness the endless cycle.
But those who, as they die, think of me
become a part of me, be sure of that.

"Such people have gone beyond rebirth.
Casting off the body, closing the doors
of all the senses, focusing the mind
on the breath, pronouncing Om, Om,
ever absorbed in thought of the divine,
what they think, they become. Therefore, Arjuna,
think of me always. And take up your bow!"

༚

All this time, with the vision Vyasa gave him,
Sanjaya witnesses each precious word
of Krishna's great address to Arjuna.
He has already recognized that Krishna
is a divine avatar, and now
he hears his teaching with wonderment and joy;
what he is hearing nourishes his devotion.

༚

Sanjaya continues:
"Now, open-hearted Arjuna," says Krishna,
"I will reveal further secret knowledge
and wisdom which will shelter you from harm—
wisdom rooted in direct experience.
Those who turn away from this remain
shackled to the wheel of birth and death.

"In my unmanifest form, I pervade
everything that is, yet I am greater
than all appearances. For my spirit
is the source of all beings, and sustains them.
All creation manifests the divine.

"When I take human form, only a few
recognize me, and worship me with love.
I am the father of the world, the mother,
the great maintainer, the sacred hymn;
I am the goal, the lord, the upholder,
the witness, the imperishable seed;
I am the home, the refuge and the friend;
the origin, support and dissolution.
Those who devote themselves to other gods
really worship me, for I am the object
of all devotion, though they do not know me.

"I am disinterested toward all:
I feel no partiality, no aversion.
But those who truly devote themselves to me
are in me, and I am with them, always.
Offer to me everything you do—
the food you eat, the help you give a stranger,
your daily routine, even your suffering.
I accept every gift with gladness.
A humble soul may offer me a leaf
with love in their heart, and I will welcome it.
Whoever depends on me, however low,

however ignorant—without distinction
of race or gender or community—
shall attain freedom. How much more, then,
should brahmins and the highborn come to me.

"Devote yourself to me with discipline,
and you will rest in me, your final goal."

☙

"All virtuous qualities have their roots
in me, springing from the one transcendent
reality—understanding, knowledge,
freedom from confusion, patience, truth,
self-control, calmness, fearlessness,
non-violence, fairness, generosity—
all are states that come from me alone.

"Those who know this are unshakable
in their disciplined devotion. Their lives
are given up to me, and I grant them
concentration; I dispel the darkness
of ignorance with the light of knowledge."

Arjuna embraces Krishna's feet.
"I have heard wise seers acknowledge you
and call you Brahman, the eternal Self.
And now you are telling me the same.
I do not disbelieve your words—and yet
this knowledge seems remote to me. Please tell me
all the forms in which you are manifest
so I can know how to meditate on you.
Best of persons, I love to hear you speak."

"You should understand, I am everywhere,
but I shall tell you the most important forms
by which you can know me. I am the spirit

seated in the heart of every creature.
I am the death that carries all away
and I am the life of everything to come.
I am the beginning, middle, end.
Of female qualities, I am wisdom,
constancy, prosperity and patience.
Of the deities, I am Vishnu. I am Rama,
I am Shiva, I am Skanda, god of war.
Of mountains, I am Meru. Of waters,
the ocean; of wild animals, the lion.
Of birds, I am the eagle. Imagine
the greatest and the most essential form
of any class of beings—I am that, Arjuna.

"Whatever is endowed with grace and splendor,
strength and vigor, springs from a fragment of me.
But what use are all these details to you?
Enough for you to know that with a mere
fraction of myself, I support the cosmos."

"This supreme mystery you have taught me,"
says Arjuna, "your discourse on the self,
has cleared the fog of my bewilderment.
But words by themselves cannot convey
the mystery of the ineffable.
I long to witness your divinity,
to see for myself what you have described.
Great lord of all creation, I beg you,
if you think me capable of seeing it—
show me your divine manifestation."

"I will show you my hundred thousand forms,
their colors, shapes and infinite variety.
I will show you the universe in my body.
But to look at this with human eyes
would destroy you instantly, utterly.

"I will give you supernatural sight.

"NOW BEHOLD MY DIVINE POWER."

Arjuna is astounded, shivering,
bent in awe before the divine being.
He struggles to shape his vision into words,
not to be engulfed by insanity.

"Ah! Krishna, your supreme form fills the world,
with many gaping mouths and staring eyes;
with countless ornaments more beautiful
than any seen on earth; with garlands, robes,
a million arms wielding divine weapons,
dazzling, as if the light of a thousand suns
were blazing all at once, the divine form
faces in all directions, stretching out
to infinity. The whole universe
is concentrated by magnetic force
in the person of the god of gods.

"I can see . . . I can see
all gods contained within your body.
O boundless, without end, without beginning,
your innumerable arms, insatiable bellies,
all your terrible appearances.
Crown. Mace. Discus—a dazzling mass of light,
fiery brilliance.
O resting place of the universe,
Lord!
Guardian of law.
Hosts of gods enter you in procession
with folded hands, adoring, singing
hymns, praising your celestial sweetness.

"I see you stretched between sky and earth.
Lord!
I see your countless gaping mouths, terrible with tusks.
Lord!

I tremble, faint with dizziness and fear.
Now I am drawn to your glowing eyes,
I reel in terror and in rapture.
I am like a speck of dust before you,
powerless and storm-tossed.

"Now I can see Dhritarashtra's sons
with Bhishma, Drona, Karna—
and many of our foremost warriors too—
all sucked toward your fearful, flame-licked mouths,
jagged with fangs. Some are impaled, oh, their heads
crushed to pulp! As moths fly
heedless and headlong into flame and are destroyed,
so are these heroes rushing to their deaths
pouring in thousands into the flaming maw.
Oh! the devouring flames, the blood—
surely it is the end of everything.
Tell me, terrible being, who you are.
Oh, supreme god, have mercy!"

"I AM TIME, DESTROYER OF WORLDS.
Even before you act, all these warriors,
rank upon rank in the opposing armies,
are already dead. I have destroyed them.
From the perspective of eternal time,
the everlasting present,
those men you see lined up, eager for battle,
full of the vigor of their youth and strength,
are dead already.
The bodies which have known cold and heat,
pleasure and suffering, already carry
death and decomposition in their bones.

"The Pandavas will be victorious. Now
rise up, hero. Be my instrument!"

Arjuna's limbs tremble in fear. He cries,
"Praise, a thousand times praise to you!

You are all gods—the wind, the god of death,
Agni the fire, Varuna the sea god,
mighty and imperishable Vishnu.
Unceasing homage to you, supreme being.
Forgive me for the times I treated you
as my old friend and my dear companion
and spoke rashly—casually perhaps.
I knew no better. I was ignorant.
Forgive me, lord, as a father would his son,
as devoted friends forgive each other,
or a lover her beloved.
                              "I rejoice
that I have seen what was never seen before
but my heart quakes with terror—
I beg you, return to your familiar form."

ॐ

"What I have just shown you," says Krishna,
his human self again, "could not be shown
even to the most extreme renouncer.
Due to the love between us, you have seen it.
Have no more fear. Now I am the friend you know."
Arjuna breathes more freely. "Now I see you
in your beloved, gentle, human shape,
my heart is beating steadily again."

"Thinking of me, Arjuna, you will transcend
all obstacles. If, out of egotism,
you think *I will not fight,* it will be pointless;
your nature will impel you—you will do
precisely what you are trying to avoid.
My dear friend, at the heart of all beings
the Lord stands still, moving them with his power.
Turn to him with all your soul, and know peace.

"This is the mystery of mysteries
that I have taught you. Consider it—and act.

I am the love that fills the universe
and you are my beloved, Arjuna.

"My final word is this: fix your mind on me,
worship me with sincere and devoted love,
dedicate your acts to me; I promise
that I shall release you from all evils.

"You must never repeat this sacred teaching
to an audience unworthy of it.
But whoever shares this supreme secret
with the deserving shall surely be rewarded.
People who learn this dialogue of ours,
and study it with faith, and worship me,
will attain the blessed worlds of the righteous.

"Arjuna, have you listened to my words,
and have your ignorant doubts been dispelled?"

Arjuna stands, *Gandiva* in his hand.
"Krishna, they have. I have regained myself.
Through your grace, I stand, my confusion gone.
I shall do my duty, as you have shown me."

33.

THE WAR BEGINS

Time unlocks.

Sanjaya said, "O king, what I have witnessed
is so wonderful my hair stands on end.
How privileged I was to hear this teaching!
Majesty, as I keep recalling it
I tremble with a joy past all describing.

"Wherever Lord Krishna is, there, surely,
will be virtue, wisdom—and victory!"

༄

Sanjaya continued his narration:
When they saw Arjuna rising to his feet,
tall on his chariot, *Gandiva* in his hand,
a great shout exploded from the ranks
of the Pandava army. Filled with joy,
they blew their sea-born conches, clashed their cymbals,
and shouted "Jaya! Jaya!"

                    The two armies,
at a pitch of readiness, swayed and heaved,
straining to rush forward. But at the point
when it seemed they could hold back no longer,
but must break and crash on one another,

Yudhishthira, unfastening his armor,
walked toward the enemy front line.

Everyone, observing him, fell silent.
What was he doing? Had he lost his nerve?
Was he about to give up after all?
Removing their own armor and their weapons,
his brothers walked beside him. But they, too,
were surprised and bewildered. What did this mean?
"Where are you going?" they asked him as they went.
Yudhishthira walked on, not answering.
Krishna smiled. "I know where he is going,"
he said to them. "In ancient times, a warrior
sought the elders' sanction on the eve of war.
Yudhishthira is making sure that he
incurs no blame, does everything correctly."

Making his way through the bristling spears
of Duryodhana's ranks, Yudhishthira
approached Bhishma, bent, and clasped his feet.
"Great one, I salute you on the brink of war.
I have come for your permission in this matter
and for your blessing on our undertaking."

"My son," said Bhishma, "if you had not come
I would have uttered a curse for your defeat.
As it is, I am pleased with you, and wish you
victory in battle, and good fortune after.
You know the saying, *Man is the slave of wealth
but wealth is no man's slave.* I am not free,
indebted to the Kauravas as I am.
I have to fight for Duryodhana,
and I shall do my best to win for him.
But, that apart, you can ask me a favor."

"Then tell me how our forces can defeat you,"
said Yudhishthira, "you who are known to be

invincible. Say, how can you be killed?"
"No one can overpower me," said Bhishma.
"The time for me to die has not yet come.
Speak to me again." Yudhishthira bowed.

Next he went to Drona and, similarly,
sought his blessing, asking the master too
how he might be defeated. "With Krishna
on your side, you certainly will win,"
said Drona. "But I will not be defeated
unless I quit the fight; and that will be
only if a man whose word I trust
gives me heartbreaking news. I shall fight
for the Kauravas, but pray for your success."

Yudhishthira requested Kripa's blessing.
"I am as useless to you as a eunuch,"
said the old teacher. "Since I am duty bound,
by ties of obligation, to support
the Kauravas, giving you my blessing
must be a vacuous formality.
It is impossible for you to kill me.
But, best of men, I will pray sincerely,
every morning, for your victory."

Lastly, Yudhishthira sought out Shalya,
who had meant to join the Pandavas
until seduced by Duryodhana's
lavish hospitality. He confirmed
that when the time came for him to act
as Karna's charioteer, he would contrive
to undermine the nerve of the driver's son.

Krishna had a private word with Karna.
"Since you are determined not to fight
while Bhishma is alive and in command,
why should you not come over to our side?

Then, when Bhishma falls, you can go back
and take up arms for Dhritarashtra's son."
"You know that is impossible," said Karna.
"I will not cause pain in any way
to Duryodhana. I know how things will go,
but Duryodhana has been my only friend
and I will cast away my life to serve him."

Yudhishthira, his obeisances over,
called to the assembled Kaurava princes:
"Anyone who wishes to fight with us
will be made most welcome as an ally."
Scowling and shuffling among the Kauravas.
There must have been many who were tempted.
Then Yuyutsu, son of Dhritarashtra
by a vaishya woman, stepped forward, saying
"I'll fight for your cause if you will have me."
"Welcome, my friend," smiled Yudhishthira.
"Only you among your foolish brothers
will live to be a comfort to your father."

Then the Pandavas shouldered their bright armor
and returned to their lines to the beat of drums.
Everyone who had seen Yudhishthira
clasp the feet of his respected elders
shouted out, "Well done!" and "Worthy king!"
The troops approved of him; so did the audience
of gods and gandharvas who had assembled
to watch this spectacle, this war of wars.
Even those who had chafed at the delay
were moved by what he had done. Now they felt
even more fired up than they had before.

Sanjaya said:
Now nothing could hold back catastrophe.

Any weak hope that this insane conflict
might, after all, be just the stuff of games
died in the din of drums, of thundering hooves,
the clash of cymbals that forced out all thought:
pure experience without reflection.
At the deafening sound of instruments,
hoarse yells, the trumpeting of elephants,
the whinnying of thousands of fine horses,
the armies hurled themselves toward each other:
the Kauravas with Bhishma at their head,
the Pandavas with Bhima in the vanguard
roaring like a storm cloud—so terrifying
that elephants and horses pissed and shat
as though they heard a lion in the offing.

From a distance, the two armies looked
like painted figures on an immense canvas,
men running with fixed attention, while dense showers
of arrows flew all round them and above them.
The air vibrated with the thrum of bowstrings
as arrows found their mark, or fell to earth
bouncing harmlessly off casque and breastplate,
off shields and gauntlets made of toughened leather.
The battlefield was like a mighty river
with bows for crocodiles, arrows for snakes,
swords, glinting fish, and the seething infantry
tempestuous waves, churning, crashing, breaking.
The din was so great as to drive men witless,
such was the thunder of hooves, the heavy tread
of troops weighed down by armor, the clanging bells
adorning elephants, the trundling wheels.

Both men and animals had trained for this.
Yet, really, how could anything prepare them
for the sheer noise, the terror, the scale of it,
the confusion of not knowing what to do,
who was in charge. This was not an everyday

skirmish, a cattle raid, trying one's luck;
not like some exercise, some bold adventure.
But those watching saw how accurately,
how elegantly, the princes of both sides
who had been Drona's pupils used their weapons.

There were many dozens of two-man contests,
opponents well matched, marked out for each other
sustaining bitter, often fatal, wounds.
Arjuna and Bhishma fought hard and long
but, however strenuously they tried,
neither could get the better of the other.
Abhimanyu, favorite son of Arjuna,
fought powerfully with the Kosala king.
"As good as his father!" onlookers exclaimed.
Nakula fought Duhshasana; Ashvatthaman
tackled Shikhandin—but it seemed at first
that none of them was seriously determined,
none of them yet willing to deliver
a death blow—although some cut down the standards
of their opponents or slashed at their horses.

Bhishma penetrated the Pandava lines.
His oriflamme, with its palmyra emblem,
was seen everywhere and, where it flew,
men fell by the hundred. Bhishma danced
high on his chariot, powerful as a youth.

Then Uttara, King Virata's son,
whom Arjuna had forced to become a man,
riding on a great bull elephant,
charged at Shalya, making his massive mount
stamp on Shalya's horses, crushing them.
Shalya hurled an iron spear at Uttara
killing him outright; then, leaping down
from his horseless chariot, he cut off the trunk
of Uttara's magnificent elephant
which shrieked and fell down dead.

                                                Uttara's brother,
Shveta, on seeing his brother killed, flew
at Shalya, who had boarded the chariot
of Kritavarman, and, consumed with grief,
fought bitterly with Shalya, and with others
who came to his defense. These included
Rukmaratha, Shalya's beloved son
whom Shveta assailed with broad-headed arrows
and wounded fatally. A great skirmish
coalesced around Shveta and Shalya
with many warriors rushing to protect them.
Shveta battled like a man possessed,
killing hundreds. Seeing this from far off,
Bhishma rode across to join the fight,
a chaotic fray. Thick clouds of dust,
stirred up by many hooves and wheels, made seeing
difficult, so that, in the mêlée,
brother hacked at brother, father at son,
comrade blindly swung his sword at comrade.
Shveta's assault was so terrifying
that the Kauravas drew back in panic,
leaving Bhishma facing him alone.

The two fought on, mighty warriors both.
Shveta hurled a heavy mace with such force
that Bhishma's chariot was reduced to splinters.
Now both men were on foot. Bhishma aimed
but Shveta shattered his bow with one arrow,
and cut down his standard, so his troops
feared he must be dead. But no, he stood
resplendent as Mount Meru, his white hair
and upright bearing utterly distinctive,
another shining bow grasped in his hand.

Shveta flew at him, but swiftly Bhishma
mounted a nearby chariot. Then he heard
a voice from nowhere, *It has been decreed*

by the Creator that Shveta's time has come.
Bhishma, galvanized, gathered his strength
and, despite the several powerful Pandavas
rallying to brave Shveta's defense,
the patriarch nocked a single deadly arrow
and invoked the powerful *Brahma* weapon,
just one of his many celestial astras,
which, flying faster than a shaft of light,
pierced Shveta's armor, and sliced cleanly through him,
striking the earth. Just as the setting sun
carries away light from the world, so
the arrow, exiting from Shveta's body,
carried away his life. So it was
that, amid the lamentations of his friends,
a splendid warrior, rich in bravery,
rich in promise, was flung prematurely
from the world—one of a million heroes
whose early death in this cataclysmic war
would make their mothers weep; and live in legend.

This was just one fragment of the damage
Bhishma inflicted on the Pandavas
on that first day of war. With his great skill
and his mastery of celestial weapons
he was invincible, sending dense cascades
of arrows scorching through the Pandava ranks,
killing thousands. As the sun sank low
the downcast Pandavas withdrew their troops
to rest overnight. So did the Kauravas,
who came rampaging, laughing back to camp
where cooks had prepared steaming vats of food.
They drank and feasted far into the night,
exulting in their first day's victory.

In his tent, Yudhishthira was downcast,
counting the dreadful losses of the day.

"Krishna, this can't go on. Today, Bhishma
was like a raging fire fed by butter,
licking up my troops like piles of chaff.
He is unstoppable. I am not prepared
to have my loyal soldiers massacred
like helpless insects. Furthermore, Arjuna—
our only match for Bhishma, with his command
of celestial weapons—is not fighting
with genuine conviction. He saw our troops
attacked by Bhishma earlier, but did nothing.
Only Bhima fought with his whole heart
like a true kshatriya. Life is too precious
to be squandered in the dust like this.
I shall surrender, embrace a forest life!"

"Son of Kunti, you should not despair,"
said Krishna, "when so many noble princes,
allies and kinsmen, are committed to you.
Dhrishtadyumna is more than capable
as supreme commander; and Shikhandin
will certainly be the cause of Bhishma's death.
Time has decreed it." Krishna's calm confidence
allayed Yudhishthira's despondency.

Meanwhile, out on the darkened battlefield,
wounded men, located by their groans,
were carried to camp, where surgeons tended them.
Men were running to and fro, collecting
arrows and other weapons, stripping corpses
of their armor and accoutrements
to be used again. It was bloody work.
Lowborn men, whose task it was to handle
the dead, piled their carts high with bodies,
hundreds upon hundreds, some still warm,
some stiff and cold, in indiscriminate death.
They tipped them onto funerary pyres,
doused them with oil and set fire to them.
Smoke rose for hours, sullying the moon.

Throughout the night they worked. Sometimes jackals
had been there first and, as dawn approached,
crows and vultures jostled in the trees.
The workers rattled pans to scare them off.
They flapped up briefly, with complaining cries,
then settled back to their lugubrious watch.

In Yama's realm, the shades of brave warriors
were opening their eyes on another world.

34.

BHISHMA IN COMMAND

Sanjaya went on:
For a while, on the first day of battle,
the fighting had been fairly orderly
in accordance with the covenant
agreed between the sides. But very soon
rules were forgotten in the mad excitement,
the joyful surge of blood-lust, and the desperate
struggle to survive. When a leader's standard
had been cut down, or toppled, the foot soldiers
ran around like a scattered flock of geese
wildly searching for their own battalion.

Like the men, the elephants and horses
had been trained for battle. But reality,
in its terror, wiped out what they had learned.
Often they were maddened and confused.
Elephants worked well when their driver
remained in charge. But if he was wounded
and fell, then the animal was inclined
to stampede, doing enormous harm.

Day two went better for the Pandavas.
Their troops were deployed in a wide formation
resembling a crane, with wings outspread,
banners, like feathers, brilliant in the sun.
Bhishma, at the head of the Kauravas,

advanced on the Pandavas, pelting them
with streams of arrows from his mighty bow,
and soon the field was littered with the dead
and dying. But Arjuna and Krishna
rushed to confront the patriarch, and soon
cut a great swath through the Kauravas
as a violent storm flattens a field of grain,
such that Duryodhana became dismayed.
"Grandfather, I hope you have not forgotten
that it's only on account of your contempt
that Karna is not here, fighting with us,
instead of idly burnishing his bow.
So you had better see that Arjuna
does not survive the day!"

     The patriarch
well knew that Arjuna was unbeatable.
But, as he had to, he attacked the Pandava,
drawing on his preternatural prowess.
Arjuna matched his onslaught shaft for shaft,
blow for vicious blow, while all around them
soldiers fell, animals screamed and died.
When the sun set on a bloody day,
Bhishma pulled his troops back for the night.

ॐ

Sanjaya said:
On the third day, Bhishma arranged his army
in an eagle formation—himself the beak,
Drona and Kritavarman the two eyes,
the mass of troops the body and outstretched wings.
The Pandavas, arrayed in a half-moon,
vast and curving, marched steadily to meet them.
Arjuna was at the left horn, Bhima
at the right; and, between them, other generals,
each standing on his splendid four-horse chariot,

riding in the vanguard of his troops:
Yudhishthira, protected by elephants,
Virata, Drupada, Dhristadyumna,
the five sons of Draupadi, and Satyaki
(never yet defeated in single combat).
Ghatotkacha, Bhima's half-ogre son,
and other staunch allies of the Pandavas,
advanced in glittering armor, bright-hued banners
fluttering proudly above their chariots.

Like the meeting of two walls of water
rearing upward from the ocean bed,
driven by unseen forces underground,
the armies clashed and mingled with each other;
the noise of conches, drums, the marching feet
and battle cries, were enough to drown the senses
and make men mad. Earlier, back at camp,
each man had known himself a human being
with plans and passions, memories, preferences.
Now he only knew he was an atom
in a vast organism, carried forward
by the collective energy of the mass.
No place for initiative at this moment,
no room for escape. He was fired up,
seized by a frenzy larger than himself
and with a passionate desire for glory.

Dust swirled and billowed, blotting out the sun.
Men struggled to keep their bearings, to make out
which were their leaders, comrades, countrymen,
shouting names they hoped would bring an answer,
straining to catch sight of familiar standards
while, all around, tripping them, blocking them,
dead and dying men and animals
bled into the already slushy ground.
Through gashed skin the blood came spurting, leaping,
on its mending mission; blood to fill

the impossible gap, the violent breach
in the body's confident integrity;
the breach that let death enter, the spirit fly.

The great chariot warriors, well matched,
each supported by close-knit divisions,
showered each other with bright streams of arrows.
Bhishma and Drona engaged Dhrishtadyumna
and Yudhishthira in savage battle.

The Kaurava troops, getting the worst of it,
flew away in all directions, Bhishma
powerless to stop them. Duryodhana,
for whom any reverse seemed like betrayal,
reproached Bhishma harshly: "You and Drona
are allowing my army to be slaughtered
by the Pandavas. If I had known
you would be soft on them, Karna and I
would have devised a different strategy!"
Bhishma rolled his eyes to heaven in fury
and despair. "How often have I told you
that Arjuna and Krishna are invincible?
We are doing everything we can—I vow,
in front of all your kinsmen, that today
I shall hold at bay the sons of Pandu!"
At this, Duryodhana was mollified.

Bhima and Duryodhana, old enemies,
pitted themselves fiercely against each other
until Bhima, smiling wrathfully,
hurled a heavy lance with enormous force
denting the breastplate of the Kaurava
so that he sank back, fainting, in his chariot,
and was driven rapidly away.
His troops, seeing him retreat, defeated,

scattered in fear, Bhima pursuing them
with a joyful roar, killing hundreds.

Meanwhile, Bhishma, faithful to his vow,
was tearing apart Pandava divisions
like a tiger savaging its prey.
The sound of men and animals collapsing
in their armor was like an avalanche
of rocks clattering down a mountainside.
Only one Pandava was capable
of withstanding so terrible an assault.
Arjuna hated to fight the patriarch
who had loved and nurtured him from childhood.
But Krishna urged him forward, whipping up
the spirited white horses.

          That was combat
the like of which was never seen before.
Each warrior released a spate of arrows
which the other shot down with his own.
Arjuna was holding something back
although he fought with great skill and panache,
causing Bhishma to shout in admiration.
But Bhishma had made a vow, and he inflicted
such dreadful damage on the Pandava troops
that Krishna was in despair, seeing clearly
that, at this rate, a Pandava defeat
was certain. He raised his divine weapon,
his discus, *Sudarshana*, flung down the reins
and, though he had undertaken not to fight,
he ran toward the patriarch.

          Bhishma cried,
"I welcome you, lord of the universe.
What better fate than to be killed by you?
I shall be honored in all the three worlds!"
Krishna exclaimed, "It is your wrong action

that is at the root of this murderous war.
You should have prevailed on Dhritarashtra
to curb his son."

        "Krishna, I tried," said Bhishma.
"Let destiny take its course."

        As Krishna raised
the lethal *Sudarshana* to fling it,
Arjuna tore across and seized his arms.
Krishna broke free, energized by rage,
but Arjuna knocked his feet from under him
and brought him down. They glared at one another.
"Krishna, you shall not do this! It is I
who am pledged to crush the Kauravas.
You are my charioteer—that was agreed.
I will stretch every nerve to keep my word."
At this, Krishna's fury was appeased.
He mounted the chariot.

        Battle recommenced
with its cacophony, so appalling
that kites and vultures seeing, smelling flesh
were nonetheless driven to a distance
yet, then, forgetting, greedy, circled back
to hover for a time above the field.
Arjuna, lit up by new resolve,
blazed into action. His bow *Gandiva*
thrummed like thunder, shaking the very heavens.
Like a dense swarm of locusts, outstripping
the fastest wind, the Terrifier's arrows
tore into the heart of the enemy,
and none was wasted; each one found its mark.

Whatever lance or javelin or arrows
were directed at him, he intercepted
and shattered with his own unerring shafts.
Nothing Bhishma or the other Kauravas

flung at him succeeded in its aim.
He, on the other hand, devastated
the enemy. With the setting sun
about to mark an end to the day's battle,
he took the powerful *Mahendra* weapon,
invoked its power with the proper mantras,
drew back his bowstring to its full extent
and let *Mahendra* fly above the field
where it rained down showers of flaming arrows,
scorching the enemy. Those arrows stripped
men's armor from them, piercing heart and head,
or melted it on their backs, so that they died
in agonizing pain.

     "Enough! Enough!"
screamed the Kauravas. As the sun went down
on that day's victory for the Pandavas,
Duryodhana's men dragged themselves wearily
back to their camp, exhausted and downhearted.

❧

Sanjaya continued:
The fourth day of the war. The Kauravas
moved forward in a formidable array.
Elephants were adorned with dazzling cloths
in festive colors, as if this were a day
of celebration. Bhishma rode in front,
his own brilliant banner flying high.

But hearts quailed when they saw the Pandavas
marching toward them, led by Arjuna.
Their army was arranged in a vast crescent,
as the day before; four thousand elephants
on each flank, packed shoulder to shoulder,
advanced like the approach of doom itself.

Bhima was the hero of that day.
Determined to engage with Duryodhana,
Wolf-belly launched himself among the enemy,
mace whirling, roaring like a man possessed.
Alhough the Kauravas were well equipped
and organized, advancing like massed storm clouds,
Bhima, a hulking one-man war machine,
rolled on, relentless, with great loss of life.
Among the several hundred infantry
he sent to Yama's realm with his deadly mace
were fourteen of Duryodhana's brothers.

Abhimanyu and the sons of Draupadi
supported him, as he wiped out an entire
elephant division, inexorable
as death personified, his mace swinging,
dripping with blood and flesh. The dead animals
looked like a range of hills, and their riders
lay slumped over their necks, like fallen trees.
Meanwhile Dhrishtadyumna, Satyaki
and Ghatotkacha killed tough adversaries.

Then Duryodhana rallied his divisions
to attack Wolf-belly, and succeeded
in smashing him into unconsciousness.
Seeing this, the powerful Ghatotkacha
flew to his father's aid, wild with fury.
Master of sorcery, he took the form
of a monster, riding a giant elephant.
He engaged with Bhagadatta; and Bhishma,
seeing that Bhagadatta was struggling,
called a halt for the day. The Pandavas
surged back to their camp in exultation.

Dhritarashtra sighed. "Oh, Sanjaya,
you tell me constantly about the Pandavas,

how splendid their skill, how immense their courage,
etcetera, etcetera—how is it
that you never give me a grain of comfort,
never speak of my poor son's success?
Is there no end to the sorrow I must bear?
I feel as if I'm foundering in an ocean
with only my two arms to bear me up."
"Your memory is selective, majesty.
But it is true that you will have to hear
the dire consequences, as they unravel,
of your weakness, greed and faulty judgment."

Dhritarashtra was pacing up and down,
restless and fearful. At last he burst out,
"The Pandavas are indulged by the gods—
luck favors them, or perhaps it is some trick.
We have always been unfortunate."
"Not luck, not tricks," said Sanjaya, "but virtue
favors them. Simply—they are in the right.
Your sons are sinful; and victory favors
the righteous.

              "Now I shall describe to you
how the war continued. But, out of pity,
I shall spare you some of the worst details.
As the relentless killing goes on and on,
day after day, I shall conjure for you
only the main events—though I could make you
listen to stories of such suffering
as would detain us for a hundred years
and still there would be more to tell, and hear.
Think of all time's patient increments
that go to make a single human life;
and think about the casual waste of it—
that, O king, multiplied by millions,
is what your fatal failures have achieved."

☙

Duryodhana, grieving for his brothers,
went to Bhishma. "How can this have happened?
You, Drona . . . so many great warriors,
well armed, well prepared, are fighting with us—
your joint prowess is unparalleled.
Yet the Pandavas ride all over us.
Explain all this to me."
        "What is the point,"
said Bhishma, "of explaining it to you
when I have tried so very often before?
For the final time—it will be impossible
for you to overcome the Pandavas
while Krishna Vasudeva is their guide.
He is Narayana, lord of the universe,
born in human form to protect the earth,
to rid it of its demon infestation;
and Nara, his companion, is Arjuna."
Bhishma told Duryodhana the story
of how, once, in a meeting of the gods,
Brahma had begged the supreme lord, Vishnu,
to take birth in the human world, to save it
from the demons who were oppressing it.
Vishnu consented, and was born as Krishna,
Yadava prince. And Bhishma recited
an ancient hymn of praise to the supreme lord.

Duryodhana began to feel a deepening
respect for Krishna and for the Pandavas.
Bhishma went on, "He blesses his devotees.
The ignorant take him for a mere mortal.
You should know the dark one for who he is,
and realize you never will defeat him,
nor those whom he protects. Do what is right,
otherwise you will certainly be destroyed.
Truth and wickedness are at war within you.
To save yourself and all the loyal warriors
who have pledged themselves to you—pull back!

Give the Pandavas their half of the kingdom
and live in harmony."

                But Duryodhana
made no reply. To give up at this point
was impossible, however many died,
however many brothers he would lose.
However much he knew, knew increasingly,
that he could never win, Duryodhana
grimly refused to countenance this knowledge,
and banished it, like a dreaded messenger
he could bury in his mind's deepest recess.

He listened in silence. Then the two warriors
went their ways, and retired for the night.

卐

On the fifth day, Bhishma arrayed his men
into the form of a huge crocodile.
The army of the Pandavas was a hawk
with giant wings outspread. At its beak
rode Bhima. Shikhandin and Dhrishtadyumna
were its eyes, and Arjuna, with Krishna,
rode at its neck, his celestial bow
held high so his troops could see it, and take heart,
his monkey banner flying fierce above him.

At first, in the ensuing battle, Bhishma
grasped the initiative, but then the Pandavas,
led by Bhima, penetrated deep
into the mouth of the crocodile array,
inflicting horrifying casualties.
In agitation, Duryodhana called
to Drona: "Guruji! You wish me well.

Bend every effort to defeat the Pandavas—
I rely on you." Straight away, Drona
rushed at Satyaki, Krishna's kinsman,
and fought him furiously. Then Bhima joined them
and soon the greatest warriors of both sides
were drawn into a skirmish so confused
that the spectators on the nearby hill
and the gandharvas watching from the sky
could not distinguish one side from the other.
Bodies and limbs were scattered everywhere
adorned with ornaments—glittering jewels
once buried in Golconda's lavish mines
or scooped from deep under the Himalaya
now re-mingled with the reddened earth.

The choking dust cleared slightly. Arjuna
could be seen rushing against Bhishma,
with his bow *Gandiva* like a lightning flash
cutting through dark clouds in the firmament.
His arrows showered down on the Kauravas
and men and animals became confused.
Vast elephants plucked drivers from their chariots
and thrashed them against the ground repeatedly
as if they were broken branches, hair tossing
like leaves, until they were formless pulp.

Many duels between the greatest warriors
took place that day, in the midst of chaos.
Just before night, Satyaki, mighty warrior,
having killed ten thousand Kauravas,
was forced into retreat by Bhurishravas.
Immediately, Satyaki's ten sons
leapt forward to challenge him. "Bhurishravas,
fight with us now, singly or together.
Whoever wins will achieve great renown."
"I'll fight and kill the lot of you at once,"

said Bhurishravas. And, indeed, he did,
bringing burning sorrow to their father.

The day came to an end with the slaughter
of twenty-five thousand Kaurava troops.
They had been sent forward by Duryodhana
with the objective of killing Arjuna
but before they could come close enough
to aim at him, they were utterly consumed
by the scorching onslaught of the Pandava.

At sunset, fighting finished for the day
and the armies of both sides withdrew.

ॐ

During the hours of darkness, the two camps
were silent. There was no carousing now.
The men were too exhausted by their struggle,
their part in the rolling juggernaut of war
that held them in its vast machinery.
Now, they slept. Only the bark of jackals,
the muffled footfalls of the night sentries,
were heard.

But as dawn broke on the sixth day
a hum arose, that grew to busyness
and then swelled into a cacophony.
No fear, no hesitation, no dark thoughts.
Only resolve, and exhilaration
as the armies girded themselves for battle:
the clash of armor plates being fastened
around restless elephants and horses,
conches braying, cymbals, drums beating,
marching feet forming up for battle
into their vast arrays.

                    The Pandavas
formed as a crocodile; the Kauravas,
a crane. Then, with embroidered standards flying,
parasols raised over chariots,
the two armies set upon each other
and soon inflicted large-scale loss of life.

༄

All this Sanjaya told Dhritarashtra.
"How is it," said the blind king, "that our army
does not conquer easily? Our men
are excellently trained in every branch
of warfare; they are chosen for their skill,
not for their connections. They enjoy
generous pay, their families are cared for.
They are respectable, honest, disciplined—
and yet they're being killed in vast numbers.
This can only be because the gods
have willed it so. And what is ordained
cannot be otherwise."
                        "There is no need,"
said Sanjaya, "to implicate the gods.
What a man sows, he reaps, and this disaster
is the fruit of your own foolishness.
But listen to the way the day developed."

༄

Early on, heroic Bhima broke
through into the Kauravas' crane formation,
pushing deep into the enemy lines.
The Kauravas exulted, "Now we've caught him!"
But Bhima, unafraid, took up his mace
and made a dash for Duryodhana's brothers,
for he had sworn, "I will end the evil life

of every last one of Dhritarashtra's sons
who mocked Draupadi in the gambling hall."
Many of them died, and many hundreds
of the Kauravas' fiercest fighting men.

Dhrishtadyumna, fearful for Bhima's life,
plunged after him, following the trail
of elephants brought down by Bhima's mace.
When Duryodhana saw him, he cried out,
"Death to the wicked son of Drupada!"
and spurred on his men. But Dhrishtadyumna
loosed *Pramohana*, an unearthly weapon,
which took away the Kaurava troops' senses
so they fell unconscious to the ground. Drona
neutralized it with another weapon,
and the men sprang up, ready to fight again.

Drona, former guru to all the princes,
knew very well which side was in the right.
But he remembered whose food he had eaten
all these years, and what he owed the king.
With enormous energy, he attacked
the advancing Pandava battalions,
churning them up like eddies in a stream,
killing hundreds.

           Yudhishthira, anxious
for Bhima's safety, sent twelve warriors,
including Abhimanyu, Arjuna's son,
together with their divisions, to support
Bhima, who was hard pressed. The Kauravas,
seeing those strong heroes advancing on them,
stopped attacking Bhima. Then there followed
a fierce battle. The sons of Dhritarashtra
and the sons of Kunti, with their followers,
fought with all their strength, and there was no one
who did not receive many painful wounds.

Young as he was, Abhimanyu fought
with dazzling skill. His gold-flecked arrows, flighted
with the gorgeous feathers of the kanka bird,
and tipped with tempered iron, hissed like snakes
as he danced on his chariot like an acrobat.

The battlefield resembled a lake of blood
whose grayish islands were slain elephants,
whose boats were chariots, whose floating debris
were bodies without number. Remarkable
that courage never failed on either side.

Finally, as the sun was sinking, Bhima
made an all-out assault on Duryodhana.
"Your miserable life is almost over.
Now you will pay for all your many insults,
for all the sorrow you piled on Draupadi
and Kunti, for the bitter deprivation
the sons of Pandu had to endure for years.
Prepare for death!" And Bhima bent his bow
and loosed shaft after shaft like blazing lightning.
Duryodhana's standard, bearing the emblem
of a jeweled elephant, glittering,
was seen to topple, spin and fall to earth.
Then Bhima turned his bow on his hated cousin
and wounded him badly, smiling in delight.
Duryodhana's brothers had to rescue him.
But Bhishma slaughtered many Pandava troops
before both sides retired for the night.

Duryodhana was carried to his tent
bleeding and faint. He was heavy-hearted
and said to Bhishma, "Our troops are well prepared,
brave and disciplined, yet the Pandavas
made carrion of them today. Oh, Grandfather,
I am consumed with grief." Bhishma laughed
grimly. "The Pandavas and their strong allies,

Krishna above all, are tireless, mighty
in skill, and full of burning rage against you.
They will be difficult to overcome.
But I swear, I will strain every sinew
to give you victory and make you joyful,
even if I die in the attempt.
All the kings who have mustered in your cause
will do the same." Duryodhana was consoled.
Bhishma gave him a salve, and the agony
of his deep wounds gradually abated.

35.

BHISHMA IMPLACABLE

Sanjaya went on with his account:
Day followed day in carnage on a scale
that could not have been imagined. Every night,
as the sun dipped out of sight, the fighting
was suspended, and the surviving troops
plodded back to camp, spent, sorrowful.
So many corpses, heads and limbs and trunks,
so many slaughtered animals of war,
lay crushed into the mud that, with the dawn,
the armies marched out over claggy ground
buzzing with blowflies feasting on rank flesh.
Best breathe through their mouths. Best not look down,
in case the sight of sightless eyes, parched mouths,
looked too much like their own. In case they saw
the mangled breastplate of a friend or brother.
But they were kshatriyas. They had always known
that they were on the earth to fight, kill, conquer,
above all, to be brave, in certain hope
of heavenly reward. That was their dharma.

It seemed the whole world was consumed by horror.
Yet, only a short walk away, farmers
were tending fields, feeding their soft-eyed oxen,
women were cooking, babies being born.

✤

The next two days were slog and butchery,
death and heroism. In each army
hardly a man or horse or elephant
had not been wounded. Yet they battled on.
Many duels were fought, most inconclusive.
Arjuna invoked the *Aindra* weapon
and the Kauravas were put to flight,
floundering in terror and confusion
until Bhishma rescued them. The sight
of Arjuna, with his glittering diadem,
confronted by the stately Bhishma, dressed
all in white, drawn by his ice-white horses,
dazzled even the heavenly spectators.

Meanwhile, Drona went after Virata
and killed his horses and his charioteer.
Virata mounted the chariot of his son,
Shankha, and Drona, drawing back his bow,
aimed at Shankha an arrow as venomous
as a poisonous snake, striking him dead.
Virata withdrew, weeping for his son.

Yudhishthira, usually so mild, now
was incandescent with rage and energy.
His chariot seemed to appear everywhere
so that the Kaurava troops feared for their lives,
and indeed he massacred many hundreds
and wounded thousands, so that injured men,
their clothing bright with their life's blood, resembled
a beautiful forest of kimshuka trees.
Shikhandin started an attack on Bhishma,
then retreated, as Shalya defended him.
"Remember your vow!" cried Yudhishthira,
"your promise to inflict death on Bhishma."
But Bhishma, sworn not to fight Shikhandin,
instead, did battle with Yudhishthira
and his troops with dreadful effect, killing
the Pandava's fine horses.

                                    Abhimanyu
fought with great flair and ferocity
against the brothers of Duryodhana,
but did not kill them, as he knew that Bhima
had sworn he would perform that deed himself.

When the sun sank below the distant hills,
the armies halted, and walked back to their tents.
In the camps, the soldiers were well cared for.
Arrows were extracted from their bodies
and wounds were dressed. Brahmins carried out
propitiatory rites for them, and poets
sang praise-songs to their bravery and skill.

&

On the eighth day, a youth came to Arjuna.
The young man was Iravat, Arjuna's son
by Ulupi, daughter of the Naga king.
A warrior of immense abilities,
he had come to introduce himself
when Arjuna was living in Indra's realm.
Arjuna had embraced him joyfully
and asked him to support the Pandavas
in their struggle to regain their kingdom.
Now Iravat was here.

                          He set to at once,
mounted on his beautiful chariot,
and, since he was a master of illusion,
he and his troops managed to confound
the bewildered Kauravas, killing hundreds.
Duryodhana, seeing what was happening,
asked the rakshasa Alambusha,
accomplished illusionist, to intervene.
He was related to the monstrous Baka,

whom Bhima had dispatched at Ekachakra.
An extraordinary battle followed,
each fighter seeking to confuse the other
with trickery, while they went for the kill.
They were young, old, singular and many,
human and monstrous, all at different times.
At last, Iravat turned into a snake;
Alambusha, becoming a fierce eagle,
snapped him up, and quickly beheaded him.

Witnessing the death of Iravat,
Ghatotkacha cried out in grief and outrage—
roared so loudly that the ground vibrated,
deep-rooted trees keeled over, and the sky
echoed with the thunder of his cries.
The Kauravas shook at that unearthly sound.
Ghatotkacha, summoning his forces,
rushed against Duryodhana's divisions.
"Now you will pay," he cried, "for all your vileness
toward my fathers and lovely Draupadi.
Quit the field, or else endure my vengeance!"

Onslaughts of arrows followed, a deluge
pelting down onto the Kaurava army
and on Duryodhana in particular.
Bhishma, knowing the supernatural power
of Ghatotkacha, ordered reinforcements
to protect Duryodhana, and there began
a ferocious fight between Bhima's son
and the best divisions of the Kauravas.

The battle was chaotic—so many standards
were shot down, it was impossible
to tell which side was which, and in the heat
and delirium of the moment, some were felled
by the weapons of their friends and kinsmen.
Elephants, urged on to pierce the enemy,

instead ripped open the flanks of their fellows,
or became entangled. Panicking horses,
dragged down by partners slaughtered in their traces,
pawed the ground wildly, struggling to break free.

As time went on, Ghatotkacha began
to tire. Yudhishthira, observing this,
sent Bhima to his aid. The mere approach
of the mace-swinging Pandava spread terror,
and many among the Kauravas took flight
to attack the enemy elsewhere in the field.
Duryodhana blazed up with renewed courage,
and made for Bhima, fracturing his bow.
Drona, seeing the danger, rushed forward,
and instantly was pierced by Bhima's arrows
so deeply that he sank down, unconscious.
Drona's son, Ashvatthaman, threw himself
quickly into the fray, but Ghatotkacha
created the illusion of defeat,
an apparition of a million corpses,
with all the greatest warriors—Duryodhana,
Drona, Ashvatthaman, Shalya—seeming
to retreat. Seeing this, the Kauravas,
dismayed, fled away in all directions.

Hearing of the death of Iravat,
Arjuna's heart was wrenched with bitter grief.
"Oh, Krishna, how could anything be worth
this dreadful carnage of the flower of youth
by the million, for the sake of wealth?
Yudhishthira was right to try to bargain
for a mere five villages. Yet, because
Duryodhana would not even grant us that,
we are obliged to fight." He urged Krishna
to drive the chariot into the thick of battle,
and great was the damage he inflicted there.
Bhima, too, with superhuman strength,
fought, killing many of your valiant sons,

like a wolf let loose among a herd of goats.
Bhishma, rallying the Kauravas,
battled like one inspired, and instilled courage
into every man who fought beside him.

✠

When night came on, and the troops withdrew,
Duryodhana went, disheartened, to his tent.
Karna, Shakuni and Duhshasana
joined him, and they sat around discussing
the way the day had gone. Duryodhana
was in despair at the lack of progress.
The Pandavas seemed fresh and strong as ever,
and he had lost so many of his brothers
at the hands of Bhima, bent upon revenge.
"Is our army being strongly led?
Bhishma seems ineffectual. Meanwhile
our forces shrink, our weapons are dwindling.
I am wondering whether victory
can ever come our way as things are going."

"Bhishma is old," said Karna, "and every day
he shows how much he loves the Pandavas.
Besides, he enjoys the fight. Why, then, would he
do what it would take to end the war?
Ask him to withdraw. When he has laid aside
his weapons, I myself will take up arms,
and, single-handed, I will kill Arjuna,
with his friends and brothers, in front of Bhishma."
Duryodhana was fired up. "Let it be so!
Bring me fine clothes, and dress my retinue.
I shall visit Bhishma. When he consents
to my proposal, I shall come to you."

Duryodhana proceeded formally
to Bhishma's tent. Tears in his eyes, he spoke.

"When I undertook this war, I trusted
your great prowess in the martial arts.
I trusted that you could crush the Pandavas.
You promised that you would do this for me.
You have not done it. I beg you, Grandfather,
make your promise true. Or, if you love them—
or hate me—too much for that, then Karna
should fight instead. He will demolish them."

Bhishma was deeply hurt and insulted,
but did not show it. He answered quietly.
"Why do you say these things, Duryodhana,
when you know I am ready to die for you?
The Pandavas really are invincible—
I, Narada and the other sages
have told you so innumerable times.
Think about it! Think of Arjuna
and the tremendous feats he has performed,
witnessed by you. Think of the Matsya kingdom,
and how the diadem-crowned Pandava
overcame us single-handed, when we
attempted a raid on Virata's cattle.
Think of dark Krishna.

                              "You are not seeing straight.
But tomorrow, I will destroy their allies,
including Drupada's Panchalas—except
Shikhandin. I will defeat them, or, if not,
I will yield to death."

              Duryodhana
bowed his head, and went back to his tent
where he slept through the night. The next morning,
he announced that Bhishma would accomplish
the defeat of the Pandavas' strongest allies.
"But he vows that he will not fight Shikhandin.

Therefore, we must take every precaution—
protect him zealously at every turn
against attack from that effeminate prince."

ॐ

Bhishma disposed his troops in a square array,
himself in the front rank. Yudhishthira
rode at the head of the Pandava army
flanked by his brothers and by Abhimanyu.
As the armies surged toward each other
accompanied by all the din of war
dreadful portents were noticed all around:
the sun was dimmed, winds blew, huge birds of prey
hung over the field with raucous screams.
The elephants and horses, sensing menace,
rolled their eyes, and pissed and shat in terror.

Each side longed for today to be decisive;
they were sick of deadlock. Abhimanyu,
with all the energy of youth, sprang forward
and, like a swimmer entering the ocean,
plunged deep among the Kauravas, advancing,
dealing death on every side of him.
All who saw him marveled at his skill.
Duryodhana sent in the rakshasa
Alambusha to attack the sons of Kunti.
The Pandavas severely wounded him
so he became unconscious for a while.
But, recovering, the ogre roared with pain
and rage, swelling to twice his normal size,
and destroyed the bows, standards and chariots
of many of the Pandava ranks, forcing
their withdrawal. Swiftly, Abhimanyu,
slim and agile, challenged the bulky monster
and the fight that followed was like the one

between the gods and demons in ancient days,
illusion pitched against celestial weapons
and sheer martial skill.

           At last, Alambusha,
pierced with many arrows, created darkness,
reducing the whole field of men to blind,
stumbling impotence. Calm and undeceived,
Abhimanyu invoked the solar weapon,
bringing brilliant sunlight. Then the ogre,
his tricks exhausted, gave up the fight and ran.
Exhilarated, Abhimanyu turned
back to attack the Kaurava battalions,
killing men by the thousand.

                Now, Drona
and Arjuna were fighting one to one.
How could they do this with a firm intent,
summon the resolve to inflict harm,
when they had been so dear to one another?
The warrior code was paramount, outweighing
every tie of loyalty and love.
So it was that they perfectly displayed
the highest pinnacle of martial craft,
and each admired the skill shown by the other.

Meanwhile, Bhishma was heavily engaged
with waves of Pandavas, whom he dispatched
with ease, though Virata and Drupada
pierced him with many arrows. Dhrishtadyumna
also wounded him, and then Shikhandin
shot more than twenty arrows into him.
Bhishma's blood flowed, but though he destroyed
Drupada's bow and wounded Dhrishtadyumna
he ignored Shikhandin. Duryodhana
ordered reinforcements to shield Bhishma—
thousands of horsemen led by Shakuni—

which, wounded though he was, enabled him
to inflict more harm. In the general battle
which followed, bewildered men and animals
ran around, aimless, looking for direction,
as bodies were dashed, bleeding, to the ground,
heaped up, to be crushed by chariot wheels
and trampled by milling troops. It was soon clear
the Pandava force was disintegrating
under Bhishma's strong, relentless onslaught.

Krishna cried to Arjuna: "Your vow!
The time has come for Bhishma to be killed,
before he utterly destroys your army.
Make your words true!" Arjuna looked anguished.
"The alternatives seem terrible to me—
to end up in hell, or win the kingdom
by killing those whom I should honor most.
Nevertheless, guided by you, I'll do it."
Krishna drove the chariot forward. Bhishma
let loose at Arjuna a stream of arrows
and Arjuna aimed, deflecting all of them
and splitting Bhishma's bow. The patriarch
quickly strung another, but Arjuna
smashed that one too. "Very well done!" cried Bhishma,
and taking another finely crafted bow,
he rained Arjuna's chariot with arrows.
Krishna, with great skill, avoided them
as he steered the horses round in circles.
The exchange continued, more like a display
than a fight to the death. Keen-eyed Krishna,
perceiving that Arjuna was holding back
while Bhishma was so ruthlessly attacking
the Pandava troops, could no longer bear it.

For the second time, leaping from the chariot,
whip in hand, only bare arms for weapons,
Krishna rushed furiously toward Bhishma

and all who saw him gasped, as if Bhishma
were dead already. Krishna looked beautiful,
his yellow silk robes streaming out behind him
as he ran, his smooth skin dark and glowing
like lapis lazuli. When Bhishma saw him
he raised his bow and, with a fearless heart,
said, "I am ready. Strike me down in battle
and I shall die in tranquillity and joy."
But Arjuna grabbed Krishna and held him back,
seething as he was with rage. "Stop, Krishna!
I will not let you make your vow untrue—
this burden is mine, and mine alone.
I swear I will do whatever it may take
to destroy the enemy." Without a word,
angry still, Krishna remounted the chariot.
Bhishma resumed his battle with the Pandavas,
inflicting death on an enormous scale,
creating panic and the wildest chaos
until, as evening came, they fled the field
like confused cattle, floundering in mud.
The troops found no protector on that day.

❧

In the Kaurava camp, there was rejoicing.
Bhishma was worshiped for his feats. Calmly
he retired to his tent in solitude.
The Pandavas had been put to rout. Grieving
at the loss of so many brave warriors,
Yudhishthira called his generals together.
All were despondent at the day's events.
Yudhishthira was in despair. "Oh, Krishna,
I am the cause of all these tragic deaths.
Bhishma is unbeatable—he crushes men
as an elephant tramples a bamboo grove.
He is like a fire licking up dry grass.
I value life; I am wasting it.

Tell me what I can do, within the bounds
of the duty laid upon me by my rank."

Krishna said, "I understand your sorrow.
But Bhishma is not invincible. Arjuna
has greater skills in war than other men;
he can kill Bhishma if he will decide to,
or, if he is reluctant, I will do it.
I am your friend and kinsman—natural, then,
that I should fight for you. But Arjuna
swore to us in Upaplavya, that he
would kill Bhishma—the time to act is now,
if he wishes not to be called a liar.
It is a question of resolve, not skill."

Yudhishthira agreed. "But listen, Krishna,
I do not want to be responsible
for causing you to break your vow. Your presence
is priceless to me. You will not need to fight.
Before the beginning of this dreadful war,
Bhishma told me he could not fight for me,
but he could advise me. The time has come
to speak to him again. He was our father
when we came fatherless to Hastinapura.
Even now, I believe he wishes us well."

After divesting themselves of their armor,
Yudhishthira and his brothers, with Krishna,
walked to Bhishma's tent. Bhishma received them
lovingly, and with the greatest joy,
asking them in what way he could serve them.
Yudhishthira said, "Grandfather, you know
everything. You stand high on your chariot
radiant as the sun. Today, your skill
brought devastation to our troops. Tell me,
how may we defeat you?"

                              "While I am alive,"
said Bhishma, "you cannot obtain victory,
so you should strike me down without delay
and save yourselves days of useless carnage.
This is what you must do. I will not fight
in inauspicious circumstances, therefore
I will not fight Shikhandin, for the reason
that you know. Let Arjuna advance
toward me, with Shikhandin in front of him.
He may then attack me—I shall be defenseless.
Then, only then, your victory will be certain."

Grateful, sorrowful, the Pandavas
returned to their own camp. The Terrifier
felt even more tormented than before.
To be responsible for Bhishma's death
on the advice of the old man himself
seemed to him unbearable. "I remember
how I used to climb onto his lap
and dirty his clothes in my thoughtlessness,
yet he never said a reproachful word.
I used to call him *Father,* and he would say,
Not your father, child, but your father's father.
How can I kill this man who nurtured me,
who is so dear to me? I cannot do it!"

"You have to do it, Arjuna," said Krishna.
"You made a vow—you must do your duty
as a kshatriya, acting without malice
and without grief. Besides, all these events
are preordained. Bhishma himself knows this."

36.

THE FALL OF BHISHMA

Sanjaya described the tenth day of the war:
Soon after dawn, O king, the Pandavas
advanced toward the enemy, to the din
of drums and trumpets, shouts, the bray of conches:
the sounds of warriors thirsting for the fight.
Shikhandin rode out in front, ably guarded
on either side by Arjuna and Bhima.
Close behind came rank upon rank of warriors,
men in their thousands, armor flashing fire,
formed into well-disciplined battalions.
The Kauravas were led by mighty Bhishma,
protected by the sons of Dhritarashtra.

Battle was joined, a vigorous attack
from each side, leaving many hundreds dead
within the first half hour. The Pandavas
seemed at first to have the upper hand
but Bhishma, full of energy, then launched
a savage onslaught, scorching the division
led by Shikhandin, who in turn let fly
dozens of arrows, many piercing Bhishma.
Bhishma laughed, "You can do what you like,
I will never fight you. You may call yourself
a warrior, but be sure I know you still
as the woman the Creator made you!"
Shikhandin, mad with rage, replied, "Bhishma,

fight me or not, I swear to you this day
will be your last!" Saying this, he pierced
Bhishma in the chest with five straight arrows.
But the noble son of Ganga merely shrugged.

"Shikhandin, you must strain every sinew,"
cried Arjuna, "or you'll be a laughingstock!
You *must* kill Bhishma. I will keep at bay
the great Kaurava chariot warriors
coming to his defense. Do it now!"

♣

Arjuna led the Pandavas in aiming
a storm of arrows at where the Kauravas
were least well protected. Many thousands
were cut down, and others put to flight,
scattering randomly across the field.
Duryodhana, in great distress, cried out,
"Bhishma! My troops are flying like headless birds,
despite your skill. You are their only hope."
"Listen," said Bhishma, "I made you a promise
that I would kill ten thousand Pandava men
every day. This I have done. Today
either I myself will die in battle,
or I will slaughter the brave sons of Pandu.
Either way, I will discharge my debt
for the food I have consumed at your expense!"

Bhishma renewed his attack like one inspired,
like one who had cast off his life already.
The arc of his bow was a perfect circle.
He shone, resplendent as a smokeless flame,
seeming to be everywhere at once,
dazzling all who saw him. Hundreds and thousands
of the Panchalas led by Drupada
fought their last fight. Elephants and horses
by the thousand were reduced to carcasses.

Arjuna advanced toward Bhishma,
Shikhandin in front of him—but then was stopped
by Duhshasana. They fought. Your son
was a worthy match for Arjuna. Both men
are great chariot warriors and, at first,
Duhshasana held back the Pandava
as a cliff might stand against the raging sea.
He wounded the son of Kunti in the head.
Furious, Arjuna split your son's bow,
then hit him with a torrent of sharp arrows.
Duhshasana fought like a true hero
despite his many wounds, but Arjuna
beat him back, and at last he retreated
to help protect the patriarch's chariot.

The day wore on. There were many duels
between opposing heroes. Abhimanyu,
dark like his uncle, tall as a shala tree,
launched a fierce assault on Duryodhana.
Nakula did battle with Vikarna,
the two warriors fighting as furiously
as two bulls horn-locked over a herd of cows.
Bhima fought with Shalya, and with many
valiant heroes of Duryodhana's force.
His roars terrified the troops.

                    Drona,
skilled in the art of reading omens, knew
this day was inauspicious. He had heard
the jackals howling, seen the sun obscured
by a dull crimson mist. The Kauravas
would not have fortune on their side that day.
Sensing that Bhishma was in serious danger
from Arjuna and Shikhandin, Drona sent
his son and other heroes to protect him.

Bhishma was fighting like a man possessed;
his chariot was like a blazing fireball,

unleashing devastation near and far.
He was not giving up his power; it must be
taken from him. His nemesis, Shikhandin,
managed to wound him, but not mortally;
he was too well defended. Bhishma laughed.
He invoked a fiery celestial weapon
and aimed it at Arjuna, but Shikhandin
rushed between them, and Bhishma called it back.

༄

Several times Arjuna, with Shikhandin,
tried to move closer to the patriarch.
Each time, he was deflected by a challenge
from a formidable Kaurava warrior.
Bhishma battled on but, more and more,
he felt how futile was the woeful slaughter
he was engaged in. He was prepared for death.
Seeing Yudhishthira nearby, he said,
"This body has become a burden to me.
If you love me, see that Arjuna
attempts to kill me soon." Yudhishthira
mobilized his forces to converge
entirely on Bhishma. The Kauravas
did the same, and the ensuing battle
was the most terrible of the war so far.

How did it end? Bhishma knew the Pandavas
could not be killed with Krishna to protect them.
Otherwise, he could have used such skill
as would have defeated them single-handed.
He thought of the boon given him by his father
many years before: that he would not die
except by his own decision—he would choose
the moment of his death. Now, Bhishma thought,
the proper time for him to die had come.

He heard the voices of celestial beings
—Vasus, his brothers—calling from above.
"Do as you have decided, best of Bharatas;
withdraw your mind from violence." A shower
of fragrant flowers rained down on Bhishma's head
as if to show the approval of the gods.

The sun was sinking in the western sky.
Bhishma told his charioteer to drive
straight into the heart of the Pandava force.
There he stood, tall, calm and beautiful,
hands together, bow unflexed by his side.
He was smiling. Duhshasana was with him.
Ambidextrous Arjuna, half sheltered
by Shikhandin, shot with either arm,
inflicting massive damage. Shikhandin, too,
shot many arrows into the patriarch
and destroyed the large and lovely standard
that, all along, had inspired the Kauravas.

Bhishma murmured to Duhshasana,
"I feel the arrows traveling toward me
in one straight stream; these are not Shikhandin's.
My vital organs are being pierced, as if
by a bolt from heaven—not by Shikhandin.
These shafts that cut me like the cold of winter
must come from Arjuna, not from Shikhandin.
Only he can inflict such pain on me."

Now Bhishma, as if in a final gesture,
as if he could not bring himself to die
passively, despite his resolution,
hurled a spear at Arjuna, who blocked it
and cut it in three pieces. The old warrior
took up a sword and gold-edged shield, and started
to climb down from his chariot. Arjuna
smashed the shield to fragments. Then it seemed

that the entire army of the Pandavas
was shouting joyfully and vengefully,
"Throw him down! Capture him! Cut him to pieces!"
shooting at Bhishma an arrow shower so dense
that soon his body was entirely hidden
by arrows sticking out at every angle.
His chariot was awash with blood. He staggered.
He toppled over, headlong, to the ground,
his head toward the east and, as he fell,
the earth shook, and everyone who saw him
screamed, "Bhishma the invincible has fallen!"
Trumpets and conches blared from your nephews' side.

Seeing him fall, the hearts of everyone
lurched with him. His body did not touch earth
but was suspended, as if on a bed,
by his exoskeleton of arrows.
A shower of rain refreshed him, and he heard
voices lamenting. Rishis disguised as geese
flew overhead, crying to one another,
"Why should this mighty, great-souled warrior
die here, now, at this inauspicious time?"
"I am alive," whispered Bhishma through his pain.
"I know the sun is on its journey southward.
I will postpone my death."

                A strange sound
filled the battlefield—the sound of stillness,
of nothing happening. All stood motionless,
having no appetite for battle now.
Some wept, some fainted, some extolled Bhishma,
some cursed the order of kshatriyas.
The Pandavas were glad, relieved, and yet
the disappearance of the patriarch
seemed unthinkable. He has been present
all their lives—affectionate, wise counselor,
principal link with the ancestral past.

☙

When news of Bhishma's fall reached Duryodhana
he was stunned beyond all telling, deathly pale.
Drona could hardly catch his breath, and fainted,
falling, unconscious, from his chariot.

Warriors on both sides laid down their weapons
and clustered around Bhishma. He greeted them,
then asked that a headrest be found for him—
his head was hanging down uncomfortably.
Many fine, luxurious pillows were brought
but he refused them all. "These are too soft.
I need a pillow for a hero's head.
Arjuna, find me something suitable."
Arjuna took up his bow *Gandiva*,
consecrated it, and shot three arrows
into the ground, at just the right height
to hold up Bhishma's head. The patriarch
was pleased, "This is a pillow for a warrior!
This is how a fallen kshatriya
should be supported on the field of battle.
I will rest until the sun is journeying
toward the north, after the winter solstice.
Then I will relinquish my last life-breath."

Surgeons came, skilled at removing arrows.
Bhishma honored them, but then dismissed them.
"I am content. I have reached the highest state
available to a kshatriya. In time,
I wish to be placed on a funeral pyre
and burned with these arrows still in my body."

Later, Krishna spoke with Yudhishthira.
"I rejoice that fortune has favored you,"
said Krishna. "It is through you and your grace,"

answered Yudhishthira, "that we succeed.
With you as our refuge and our guide, nothing
is impossible!" Krishna smiled at him.

ॐ

The following morning, there was no battle.
Both Pandavas and Kauravas attended
the son of Ganga. Around his bed of arrows
throngs of people jostled—the kind of crowd
that might be gathered at a holy site—
pushing for a glimpse of the great man.

The pain from Bhishma's wounds was agonizing,
and he burned with fever. "Water! Bring water!"
Pots of cooling, citrus-flavored water
were brought at once, but Bhishma rejected them
and called for Arjuna. The Pandava
took his bow and, consecrating it,
shot into the earth a well-aimed arrow.
Up gushed a fountain of pure, sparkling water
of heavenly scent and taste. All who saw it
trembled in awe.

     Bhishma quenched his thirst.
He praised Arjuna, so that Duryodhana
heard every word. "Most excellent of warriors,
performer of feats of which the very gods
are incapable. Just as the eagle
is to other birds, as Mount Himavat
is to mountains, so are you to archers."
Then he said to your son, "Listen to me—
you'll never defeat this man; even the gods
together with the asuras could not do it.
I beg you—make peace with the Pandavas.
Divide this prosperous kingdom as before.
Too many brave men have already died;
think now of the thousands upon thousands

who could still return to their far-flung homes,
seeing their wives and children lit by joy,
who otherwise will sleep their final sleep
here in the choking mud of Kurukshetra."

Having said this, Bhishma became silent.
To rise above the torture of his wounds,
he closed his eyes and moved into a state
of profound meditation. Duryodhana,
having heard him, frowned, turning away
like a dying man refusing medicine.

൸

Later, when the crowds had dispersed, Karna
went to where Bhishma lay, and sat quietly
at the patriarch's feet. Apprehensive,
choked with tears, he spoke. "Best of Bharatas,
I am Karna, son of Radha—Karna
whom you have always looked upon with hate."

Slowly, Bhishma opened his clouded eyes
and reached out to Karna like a father.
"Come, my young rival, I know who you are—
Vyasa told me. You are not Radha's son,
but Kunti's. I feel no hatred for you.
If I have been harsh, dismissive even,
it was because you were so full of pride,
so scornful of true worth. I know your virtues,
your military prowess, your devotion
to truth, your generosity with alms,
your loyalty—though it is unfortunate
that you attached yourself to such company,
becoming hard and envious yourself.
You set your face against me—that is why
I have been harsh. And also to avert
family discord. But all that is over;
now I feel only goodwill toward you.

I only wish that you could find it in you
to join with your true brothers, the Pandavas."

"Bhishma," said Karna, "that is impossible.
Having for so long enjoyed the wealth
and friendship of Duryodhana, I cannot
betray him now. For him, I will abandon
my wife, my children, everything I own,
my life itself. Besides, I have done so much
to antagonize the Pandavas,
and I am incapable of giving up
my fierce hostility to Arjuna.
I know he is invincible, and yet
I am resolved to conquer him in battle.
With a cheerful heart, I shall go to fight him.
I ask your approval for my enterprise,
and beg that you forgive me for anything
I may have said to you—whether from anger,
brashness or a lack of due respect—
that gave offense. I beg you, pardon me.

"Death is not the worst. A kshatriya
should not die feebly, stewing in his bed.
I must do what is right."

                    "Go then," said Bhishma.
"You shall have my blessing on your choice.
For years, I have done all within my power
to prevent this futile war, and I have failed.
Fight your necessary fight with Arjuna.
Fight him calmly, with no pride, no anger.
Through him, you will certainly attain
the afterlife a kshatriya deserves
who dies in battle, firm of heart and mind."

Karna knelt to receive Bhishma's blessing.
Then he went back to Duryodhana.

VII

THE BOOK OF DRONA

37.

DRONA LEADS THE KAURAVAS

Janamejaya said:
"After the great Bhishma was cut down
and the news was carried to Dhritarashtra,
how did the blind king survive the sorrow?
Tell me in detail, Vaishampayana."
Vyasa's disciple spoke:

Hastinapura. Endless days of waiting.
For the blind king, life seems to be suspended
as he sits and waits, waits for Sanjaya
to come with further news from Kurukshetra.
He mourns the bitter loss of the great Bhishma—
how can the Kauravas prevail, deprived
of the patriarch? They must be floundering.
But even now, even though Bhishma lies
dying on his painful bed of arrows,

Dhritarashtra entertains some hope
that his son will yet defeat the Pandavas.

At last Sanjaya arrives with recent news
and the news is worse than nightmare—great Drona,
who had succeeded Bhishma as commander,
has been struck down. The master is no more.

☙

When Dhritarashtra heard from Sanjaya
of the death of the supreme weapons master
his limbs turned to water and he fell
fainting to the ground. The women with him
rushed to lift him up, and gently placed him
on the throne, weeping, fanning him
until he began to move. When he revived
he cried to Sanjaya, "Dead? Impossible!
Greatest of warriors, the man who taught
generations of fine kshatriyas
everything they know of the arts of war
cannot be dead! It must have been some chance,
some freak accident. Oh, Sanjaya,
I foresee a time when you and I
will have to kneel before Yudhishthira
as abject supplicants with our begging bowls.
It is clear that, struggle as we may,
the gods' design, pitiless time, propels us
where it will. It is as if I too am dead,
as if Mount Meru had collapsed, the sun
fallen from the firmament . . .

                              "But tell me
how it came to this. Who brought himself
to kill that peerless brahmin? Dhrishtadyumna?
But why was he not stopped? Why was Drona
not protected by his friends and allies?

Yet—who could stand against the might of Krishna
and those he protects, for he and Arjuna
are Nara and Narayana incarnate,
one divine soul split between two bodies.
Oh, how is my son bearing this disaster?
What's to be done? Who has replaced Drona?"

Seeing that, even now, Dhritarashtra
was hoping for victory for the Kauravas,
Sanjaya described the dire events
that culminated in the death of Drona.

❦

When Bhishma lay down on his bed of arrows
never to rise again, the Kauravas
were utterly bereft. They were like a boat
foundering far from land on violent seas.
Their thoughts turned to Karna—he was the hero
who could save them from terror and defeat!
"Karna! Karna!" they cried. The driver's son
came to them at once. The time had come
for him to play his part. He addressed the troops.

"The Kauravas have lost their great protector,
their pinnacle. If the patriarch, towering
like a mountain, can be thrown like this,
should we not reflect on the impermanence
of all things? Surely all of us are drifting
toward the jaws of death, all transient.
Considering this, all that remains is duty.
Why should we be afraid? I am ready
to take up the burden left by Bhishma.

"Bring my bright armor, sparkling with gold and gems;
heft it onto my shoulders. Bring my fine bow,
my quivers, my belt patterned like a serpent.

Bring out my horses, my well-fashioned chariot,
my standard, adorned with blue lotus flowers.
I will fight with all my reserves of strength
in the cause of noble Duryodhana.
I shall crush his enemies, or else
I shall sleep soundly on the field of battle.
Either is honorable." When they heard this
the Kauravas, heartened beyond measure,
sent up a great cheer.

         Then Karna went
back to the place where Bhishma lay, his eyes
closed in meditation. A small awning
had been erected over him, to shield him
from the sun's relentless rays. Karna wept
to see that paragon of mind and spirit,
that prince of warriors, foremost Bharata,
reduced to this. Karna approached him humbly
with joined palms. "It is I again, Karna,
come to seek encouragement. I know
the power residing in the Pandavas.
Who could defeat Arjuna if you,
with all your skill, all your celestial weapons,
could not prevail? Yet I must believe
that I can kill him. Give me a word of comfort."

"My child," said Bhishma, "your great loyalty
to your friends is legendary. In warfare,
remember all you have achieved till now—
the kingdoms conquered for Duryodhana.
The Kambojas, the Kiratas, the Kalingas
and many other clans were brought by you,
by fearlessness and through sheer martial skill,
into the fold of our expanding kingdom.
Be to your friends as Vishnu to the gods.
Firm of purpose, be an inspiration,
lead them on the path which you have chosen."

Karna, cheered by these auspicious words,
stooped to touch the feet of the patriarch.
Then he rode back to the Kaurava camp.

Duryodhana drew great reassurance
from Karna's firm resolve. He told himself
that Bhishma's heart had been with the Pandavas—
that was why he had not defeated them.
But Karna was a warrior whose loyalty
was beyond question. He asked his friend's advice:
"Now that Bhishma is no longer with us,
who should take his place as supreme commander?"
Karna replied, "There are many great contenders
but the one who stands above them all
is Drona, the wise teacher. He should be asked.
Only he can command the confidence
of every warrior in your fighting force."

Humbly, and with lavish words of praise,
Duryodhana approached the old master
and, to the frenzied cheering of the troops,
appointed him to lead the entire army.
"I am honored," he said. "The Pandavas
will find it difficult to fight with me.
But I cannot kill Dhrishtadyumna,
son of Drupada; that man is destined
to be the death of me. Now, you should say
what is the outcome that would please you most,
and, if I can, I shall accomplish it."

"Well then," said cunning Duryodhana,
"I want you to seize Yudhishthira alive
and bring him to me." Drona was astonished.
Did Duryodhana perhaps intend,
after all, to give up half the kingdom?
"But why do you not seek his death?" he asked.
Duryodhana smiled. "If Yudhishthira dies,

I can't win. Arjuna would never rest
until he had slaughtered every one of us.
But as my prisoner, saintly Yudhishthira
can be enticed into another dice game,
which he will lose, and off he'll have to go
back to the forest, and his brothers with him.
There we are! The kingdom remains mine."

Drona disliked this plan, but he had promised
to do his best to fulfill the prince's wish.
"I can attempt so bold a capture only
if Arjuna can somehow be drawn away,
leaving Yudhishthira without protection."
"You had better succeed," said Duryodhana,
suspecting him of partiality
toward the Pandavas. He then ensured
that Drona's promise was made known to all,
so he could not renege—with the result
that Yudhishthira came to know of it.
Arjuna promised he would be protected.

༄

With ceremony and with great rejoicing
the army witnessed Drona's consecration.
Then he ordered the troops into battle lines
with Karna leading the chariot warriors.
The driver's son, though he was now deprived
of the breastplate and earrings he was born with,
glowed with a golden light, tall and beautiful,
and all who saw him felt their hearts lift, thinking,
"Bhishma is lost to us, but we have Karna;
Karna will save us from catastrophe."

Staring at him across no-man's-land,
Arjuna stood resplendent on his chariot,
Gandiva at his side, the monkey banner

fluttering above him. At the reins
was Krishna, with his discus, *Sudarshana,*
a luminous circle hanging in his hand
as though he held the wheel of time itself.
Karna, Arjuna: perfectly matched archers,
each with the other's death within his sights.
Which would inflict defeat upon the other?

As the armies surged across the field
the earth shuddered and, from the glowering sky,
a torrent of blood and bones poured down, and vultures,
jackals and other scavengers appeared,
circling greedily, howling, screeching.

White-haired Drona, as though a youth again,
scorched the well-trained Pandava divisions
like whirling fire consuming a great forest,
his reserve of celestial weapons raining
death onto the struggling enemy.
His bow was like a bolt of monsoon lightning
flashing amidst dark clouds of deadly arrows.
The ground was slippery with blood, and marrow
oozed from the mangled bodies of the dead—
numberless heroes now already traveling
to Yama's realm. Soon it was a crimson
river of blood, swirling with severed limbs
and broken chariots.

                Careful Yudhishthira,
mindful of the plan to capture him,
asked Arjuna to stay close. The Terrifier
assured him the stars would tumble from the sky
before Duryodhana would have his way.
"It's true that I would rather lose my life
than fight Drona, to whom I owe everything.
But my promise to you stands—I have never
made a vow and left it unredeemed."

☙

Watching from some vantage point, O king,
a connoisseur of horses could have counted
horses dappled like the antelope,
horses pale as the moon, pale as milk,
pigeon-colored horses, dark blue stallions,
horses the color of fresh mustard flowers,
horses red as the red deer, with flashes
of startling white on their chests and necks,
dark spotted horses, others honey brown,
still others black as impenetrable night,
beautiful cream horses with black manes,
glossy chargers gleaming like polished wood;
delicate Sindhu horses, dusky as smoke—
so many lovely ones, thousands and thousands,
many decorated with gold chains,
yoked to splendid chariots.

    And above them
flew the gorgeous individual standards
of each chariot warrior: Drona's, black
deerskin, emblazoned with a water vessel.
Bhima's bore a gigantic silver lion,
its eyes picked out in lapis lazuli;
Yudhishthira's had a golden moon device
with planets circling it; Sahadeva's
bore a silver goose, and Abhimanyu's
a sharngaka bird, bright as beaten gold.
On Ghatotkacha's standard was a vulture,
and his enchanted horses were capable
of flying through the air as he commanded.

But in the desperate battle, there was no time
for appreciation. There was only
confusion, fear, anger, mad excitement

and savage joy as arrows or spears sank home
and enemies fell, wounded, dead or dying."

Countless heroes engaged in single combat—
Bhima inflicted wounds on Vivinshati;
Shakuni felled Sahadeva's charioteer;
Shikhandin, adept at all types of weapon,
pierced Bhurishravas with ninety shafts,
causing him to tremble and retreat.
Shalya hit his nephew Nakula,
smiling as if it were a joke. Nakula,
furious, shot Shalya's bow out of his hand.

Abhimanyu, Arjuna's heroic son,
alight with zeal, fought like one inspired,
leaping from ground to chariot and back
like a gymnast, wielding bow and sword.
Shalya fought with Bhima. They resembled
two massive elephants, circling each other,
each with a hefty mace. Sparks flew up
as their weapons clashed like thunderbolts.
They hit each other simultaneously
and both were stunned. Then Kritavarman hauled
Shalya into his chariot and drove him off.
At the sight of this retreat, the Kauravas
felt despondent—and indeed, the tide
was turning in favor of the Pandavas.

Drona made more than one attempt to reach
Yudhishthira, but he was beaten back
and hit with many arrows. Then, in rage,
he advanced toward Yudhishthira's chariot
looking like all-destroying Death himself.
All the Pandavas who saw him coming

cried in alarm, "Yudhishthira is lost!"
But Arjuna, seeming to spring from nowhere,
killing men by the hundred as he came,
covered Drona's troops with a shower of arrows
so dense, the sky turned black. And in due time
the sun itself was setting. Drona ordered
withdrawal for the night.

                     He was cast down.
He had fought hard, had inflicted damage,
forcing an opening through the Pandavas,
yet he had been unable to deliver
Yudhishthira as Duryodhana had asked.
He knew the prince was likely to suspect him
of lacking determination. "I told you,"
said Drona, "that to take Yudhishthira
would be impossible with Arjuna by.
Tomorrow, if Arjuna can be distracted,
I'll lay hold of Yudhishthira—you'll see."

The Trigartas, who hated Arjuna
for past humiliations, volunteered
to challenge him to combat at a place
a little distance off. They were five brothers,
brave kshatriyas and skillful fighters,
whose frequent and abundant gifts to brahmins
assured them of good fortune in the field
or, if not, in the afterlife. They led
a strong alliance—brave, committed forces.
Priests presided over a consecration
and the Trigartas swore a solemn vow
to conquer, or to die in the attempt.
"Arjuna will never refuse a challenge.
If we retreat, may we share the fate
of the most heinous sinners in the world.
Let the earth be rid of Arjuna,
or let it see the death of the Trigartas!"

✥

Sanjaya continued:
As they had predicted, Arjuna
was fired up by the prospect of the fight.
Yudhishthira was worried, but Arjuna
assured him that Satyajit, Drupada's son,
would surround him with a large defensive force.
"But if Satyajit should be killed in battle,
then you should quit the field immediately."

Then, with a picked band of champion fighters,
Arjuna rode out after the Trigartas
like a hungry lion, avid for the kill.
Sighting him, the Trigartas raised a cry,
exultant and threatening. Arjuna smiled.
"Listen to them," he said to dark-skinned Krishna,
"shouting with joy when they should be terrified.
But, after all, perhaps they should be joyful,
bound for a place where no fool can pester them."

Though the Trigartas and their men were full
of resolution, at the dreadful sound
of *Devadatta*, Arjuna's conch, they froze
as if in thrall, deprived of all volition.
Recovering, they loosed a rain of arrows
which Arjuna intercepted in mid-flight.

There followed a tremendous battle. Krishna
drove the chariot swiftly, skillfully,
and wherever Arjuna advanced,
hundreds died. At the same time, the Trigartas
unleashed such a punishing storm of arrows
that Krishna and Arjuna could hardly see
and were wounded countless times. The Trigartas,
counting on victory, were overjoyed,

cheering, waving their garments in the air.
But Arjuna employed the *Tvashtri* weapon
to create illusion, so Trigartas
fought Trigartas thinking they were killing
Arjuna. Men, mounted or on foot,
scattered like rats fleeing a hungry hound.

But the Trigartas were not beaten yet.
In fury, they kept fighting back, releasing
torrents of arrows and razor-edged spears.
Then, with broad-headed shafts, Arjuna
dispatched thousands of the enemy,
slicing off their helmeted heads, their hands
still grasping weapons. Billowing clouds of dust
stirred up by the frenzy of the battle
were turned to mud by copious showers of blood
spilled by Arjuna. So terrifying
was his assault on the Trigarta troops
that at one point they started to retreat
in fear, until their king exhorted them:
"Are you deathless heroes—or are you cowards?
Have you not sworn to conquer or to die?
Return! Redeem your pledge, no matter what!"

So it was that the Trigartas fought
on and on, until the land was littered
with mutilated bodies, dead and dying
jumbled one on another. The air rang
with a cacophony of groans and cries.
The blood-soaked earth resembled a broad field
of poppies, stretching out in all directions.

౼

Anxious for Yudhishthira, Arjuna
and Krishna turned toward the main battle.
There, Drona, bent on seizing Yudhishthira,

led his men in an eagle formation—
the wings outstretched, the back made up of hosts
of foot soldiers, chariots, elephants.
At the tail rode Karna, tall, magnificent,
leading his troops, allies, friends and kinsmen.
Kings, warriors, were glorious in the sun,
their banners flying, armor flashing light;
some rode high on mountainous elephants.
The entire army was in fighting fettle,
mad with lust for blood and victory.

Seeing them advance like a tidal wave,
knowing their whole intent was to capture him,
Yudhishthira turned to Dhrishtadyumna. "Friend,
you should do whatever is necessary
to prevent my being taken prisoner."
Drupada's son reassured him. At once
he shouted to his charioteer to gallop
straight for Drona. The teacher's heart quaked,
knowing that Dhrishtadyumna would bring his death.
But one of your valiant sons, Durmukha,
rushed to his defense, and fought so fiercely
with Dhrishtadyumna that Drona got away
and began to slaughter the Pandava army
in huge numbers. Soon any resemblance
to two disciplined forces disappeared.
Each man lashed out wildly, with no regard
for battle etiquette or decency.
To spectators looking down on them
the scene was like the panic-stricken stampede
of cattle when a tiger comes among them,
trampling each other in blind desperation
to survive.

Sighting Yudhishthira,
Drona made toward him, but at once
a warning cry rose from a thousand throats

as the Pandava forces saw the danger.
Satyajit, as he had promised Arjuna,
loosed a powerful weapon spiked with venom.
Drona's charioteer fell senseless. Next,
the horses were attacked, and Satyajit,
circling Drona, cut down his fine standard.
Drona resolved that this would be the last
battle for Satyajit, and though that hero
fought courageously and skillfully,
at last his head was severed from his shoulders,
earrings flashing as it fell to earth.
Then Yudhishthira turned his chariot
drawn by superb horses, and retreated.

Drona focused on the Panchalas.
He and his forces set about destroying
everything in their path. As a thunderstorm
pelts the helpless earth with vicious hailstones
so he assaulted the Panchala divisions.
Seeing it, Duryodhana laughed with joy
and said to Karna, "Look at the devastation
our forces are inflicting on the allies
of the Pandavas—falling by the thousand!
They can never recover after this."

Karna was less confident. "The Pandavas
will not collapse so easily. Look there—
Bhima is surrounded by our warriors.
It may look hopeless, but with his huge strength
he has killed hundreds of our men already.
You can be sure that he is remembering
the wrongs he and his family have suffered
because of us—Ekachakra . . . Draupadi . . .
We should provide Drona with reinforcements."

๛

Duryodhana clashed with Bhima, each leading
an elephant division, the animals
splendidly decked out, their curving tusks
filed to cruel points. Huge as hills, cheeks trickling
with juices, the Kaurava beasts were quickly
mangled by Bhima's arrows, and swerved away,
spurting blood. Then Duryodhana struck Bhima,
and Wolf-belly, eyes glowing red with rage,
released a shower of arrows in return,
hoping to send his cousin to Yama's realm.

Bhagadatta, King of Pragjyotisha,
long-standing ally of Duryodhana,
renowned elephant warrior, joined the fight.
He advanced on Bhima riding his elephant,
a battle-hardened monster of great cunning,
rolling its eyes, eager for the kill.
Bhima was, by this time, on the ground
and, rather than trying to escape, he ran
under the beast's body, and began
to slap it with fierce blows, which made the creature
turn like a wheel to face the Kauravas,
menacing his own side, mad with musth.
As he emerged, Bhima was nearly strangled
by the elephant's trunk, but wrestled loose
and ran away to safety.

             Bhagadatta
then began to attack Yudhishthira.
High on his elephant, he was besieged
by Pandava forces, blasted by an onslaught
of well-aimed arrows. But his elephant
trampled hundreds of horses and infantry,
and he broke free. Just as the scorching sun
sheds its rays on everything around,
so Bhagadatta, on his monstrous mount,
sprayed lethal arrows on his enemies.

Terror spread among the Pandavas
and they scattered. No one could withstand
this champion of elephants and his master,
the best elephant warrior in the world—
except Arjuna.

It had struck Karna
and Duryodhana that the son of Kunti,
faced with the choice between Bhagadatta
and the Trigartas, would very likely choose
the latter—the men who had challenged him.
Now, as Arjuna and Krishna traveled
to rejoin the main battle, they heard, far off,
distinctive sounds, and guessed that Bhagadatta
and his elephant were wreaking havoc.
But Arjuna was torn. He heard behind him
the thundering hooves of the Trigarta horses—
the survivors, pursuing him to the end.
He turned and, concentrating on the mantra,
he unleashed the deadly *Brahma* weapon,
filling the air above the pursuing troops
with white-hot arrows, trailing flashing fire,
annihilating hundreds, like men of straw.
Even the solid block of infantry
cracked apart like an overheated vessel
faced with his unearthly energy.
Krishna raised his hands in admiration.
"Quick! Drive to Bhagadatta," cried Arjuna.

ॐ

The encounter between Bhagadatta
and Arjuna was fierce in the extreme.
Bhagadatta had a height advantage
and could rain down arrows by the hundred.
But Arjuna deflected them. Krishna whirled
the chariot round to the rear of Bhagadatta
where Arjuna could have killed him easily,

but the Pandava held back, respecting
the rules of fair fight.

        Bitter and prolonged
was the struggle between those fine warriors,
with many wounds inflicted on both sides,
and many deadly darts and spears deflected.
Hard pressed and desperate, Bhagadatta hurled
straight at Arjuna's chest an iron hook
charged with the celestial *Vaishnava* mantra.
Krishna swiftly stepped in front of his friend
and the weapon, striking him instead,
turned into a garland of lovely flowers,
blue lotuses, glowing with tongues of flame.
Arjuna complained, "You should keep your word
and drive the chariot. I can defend myself."
But Krishna told him Bhagadatta's weapon
could not be survived by anyone but him.

Arjuna raised his bow and, with great force,
struck the forehead of the elephant
with a long, thick arrow. As lightning
can split a mountain, so the arrow drove
deep into its head. Though Bhagadatta
urged it on, the beast fell, paralyzed
and, trumpeting its last cry of distress,
it died. Quickly, Arjuna let loose
a crescent-headed spear at Bhagadatta.
Arrows and bow fell from the king's hands.
His world became a mesh of darkness, heart
skewered by Arjuna's unerring weapon,
and the celebrated warrior, wreathed in gold,
slid from the elephant, his gorgeous headdress
unraveling as he plummeted to earth.

With the death of mighty Bhagadatta
the Kauravas, in anger and dismay,

thirsted for revenge against Arjuna.
Two of Gandhari's brothers, skilled archers
standing side by side in their chariot,
let fly shaft after shaft. But very quickly
Arjuna pierced them with a single arrow
and, as one body, they fell to the ground.
Then their brother Shakuni, the gambler,
took on Arjuna by means of sorcery.
Spiked clubs, iron balls, daggers, tridents, spears,
rocks, scimitars and snake-headed shafts
began to fall on Arjuna and Krishna.
Hordes of wild and hungry animals
appeared all around them, baying and snarling.
Laughing, Arjuna countered all of this
by wielding well-chosen celestial weapons.

Next a thick and choking fog engulfed them
and, after that, huge waves of foaming water
which Arjuna dispelled. Then Shakuni,
seeing that his tricks were ineffective,
fled the battlefield like a craven coward.

With *Gandiva*, Arjuna released
his arrows like a humming flight of locusts
and each one found its mark in man or beast.
Panic surged through the Kaurava divisions
as fighters, desperate to save themselves,
abandoned kin and comrade, left their horses
and trampled on the wounded as they ran.
"Help, Lord help me!" Everywhere were heard
cries of the dying, untended and alone.

Meanwhile, to the south, Drona was leading
a furious assault on the Pandava force
led by Dhrishtadyumna. Extensive damage
was sustained by both sides, and the Pandavas

lost Nila, one of their greatest bowmen.
Karna fought with Satyaki, a duel
that ended with each wounded, but intact.
Arjuna and Krishna joined them, killing
three of Karna's brothers. So it went—
an ecstasy of violence and rage,
until night fell, and the two sides withdrew.

On the whole, it seemed the Kauravas
had come off worst from the day's events.

38.

THE DEATH OF ABHIMANYU

Sanjaya continued:
Morning broke over the dismal plain.
From the vast carnage of the days before,
the jumbled bodies, limbs and carcasses,
too numerous now to be attended to,
littered the field as far as the eye could see.

Reviewing the events of the previous day,
Duryodhana concealed his boiling rage
as he addressed Drona before the troops.
"Drona," he said, "you made me a promise
which, it seems, you conveniently forgot,
since you failed to seize Yudhishthira.
He was within your grasp; you did not grasp him.
I am wondering whose side you support."

Despite the fact that he had made every effort,
Drona was ashamed. "I promise you:
before the sun sinks on another day
I will put in place a battle formation
so large, so tight, so intricately designed
that no man will escape—a trap for heroes!
And I swear to kill a prominent warrior
from among the Pandavas. But, once again,
you have to entice Arjuna away
from the main action. He is invincible."

༄

That thirteenth morning, there was no eagerness
for what was coming. For the weary troops,
despite brave words and boastful declarations,
endurance was the order of the day,
not confidence.

        The hot-blooded Trigartas,
as had been planned, challenged Arjuna
to fight them in the southern part of the field.
Drona directed ten thousand of his men
into the wheel formation, a rotating,
winding, circular shape, impossible
to penetrate, save by a very few.
This was a hand-picked and experienced force
who had solemnly sworn never to break ranks.
They had smeared themselves with sandal paste
and, terrible to see, all wore red robes
with gold ornaments, and scarlet banners.
Ten thousand trained, courageous warriors,
yet they advanced as one, shoulder to shoulder,
shields edge to edge, standards overlapping—
a sight to strike fear in all who witnessed it.

At the front rode Drona, and behind him
were proud Jayadratha with Ashvatthaman.
Duryodhana, shaded by his parasol,
was flanked by his greatest chariot warriors—
Karna, Kripa, Duhshasana among them.

The Pandavas met Drona's force head on.
A fierce battle followed, with many hundreds
massacred or wounded mortally.
The wheel was unassailable, and from it
a storm of missiles rained on the Pandavas

who could make no headway, but instead
time and again took dreadful punishment.
Yudhishthira drew Abhimanyu aside.
He was still a boy, but in accomplishment
and in beauty he rivaled his great father.
All the virtues, all the martial skills
of the five sons of Pandu, and of Krishna,
were united in him. Abhimanyu
was admired and loved by all who knew him.

Yudhishthira addressed him. "With your father
engaged elsewhere, you are the only one
who knows how to break into the wheel.
Child, for the sake of all of us you must try
to penetrate what Drona has constructed
or else, when Arjuna returns, he'll blame us."
Abhimanyu was fired up with zeal.
"Today, the world will witness my great feats;
I shall slaughter all who challenge me
or I'll not call myself Arjuna's son!
Only—my father taught me how to enter
the wheel, but not how to come out again."
"Once you have broken in," said Yudhishthira,
"you will force a path for us to follow.
Never fear, we shall be close behind you
and we can smash it open from within."
"Then," said Abhimanyu, "I will fly
like a mad moth into a searing fire!"

Hearing what Abhimanyu had in mind,
his charioteer was woebegone, fearful
that the task was far too dangerous.
"You have scant experience of war;
Drona with all his skill will surely crush you."
But Abhimanyu, full of cheerfulness,
said, "Oh, Sumitra! It will be glorious!
Who is Drona? Is he omnipotent?

Even if I were to face my father
or my uncle on the battlefield
I should not be afraid. Now, driver—drive!"

Thus Abhimanyu, dressed in flashing armor,
tall and beautiful as a flowering tree,
standard flying over his splendid chariot,
urged his driver on. The Kauravas
rejoiced to see him coming to the trap.
The Pandavas followed closely in his wake.

Mocking catcalls, whistles, ululations
reached him from the jeering Kauravas
but Abhimanyu was the first to strike
hard and precisely, like a human scythe
shearing a field of grass. First, he lopped off
arms by the hundred still grasping spears and bows.
Then Kaurava heads were rolling on the ground
surprised by death, fine turbans still intact
adorned with precious jewels. Single-handed,
the boy brought chaos to his adversaries.

Duryodhana advanced to engage with him.
At once, at Drona's urging, the best warriors
moved forward to protect your noble son,
courageous as he was, and Abhimanyu
was forced to back off, roaring like a lion
whose prey has been denied him. Savagely,
he hurtled through your son's brigades, dispatching
countless men with his swift-flying arrows,
feats so dazzling that even the Kauravas
shouted in admiration.

                    Fighting free
of this initial skirmish, Abhimanyu
managed to break open the wheel formation
and entered. At once, he was surrounded.

The Pandavas were following hard behind
but, before they could enter, they were blocked
by Jayadratha. Violent and rapacious,
the powerful king of Sindhu had long harbored
bitter hatred toward the Pandavas,
ever since Bhima had prevented him
from abducting Draupadi in the forest,
and savagely humiliated him.
After he had engaged in austerities
great lord Shiva had granted him a boon—
that at the crucial time he would have the power
to hold in check the might of the Pandavas.

Now, that time had come. The Pandavas,
try as they might, could not penetrate the wheel.
Jayadratha held them off with ease,
smashing their weapons in their helpless hands.
Soon, the route by which Abhimanyu entered
closed again, as elephants, troops and chariots
rearranged themselves. The young prince stood
quite alone, surrounded, unprotected
before the legions of the Kauravas.

O majesty, what followed will be sung
as deathless legend, generations hence.
The young hero gathered his resources
and demonstrated his unearthly skill
and courage. Many great Kaurava warriors,
the best there were, died at his hands that day.
Beautiful as a flame in a dark place,
it was as if this were a delightful game.
A kind of joyful calm pervaded him.
He crowed in exultation as he aimed
unfailingly with arrows and with spear,
with sword and mace—with every kind of weapon,
earthly and celestial.

> He received
many painful wounds, and still he fought,
inflicting thousands more on his opponents.
He fought like a young god, and all who saw him
would remember it to their dying day.
Drona rejoiced that his favorite pupil
had passed on all his prowess to his son.

He killed Karna's brother, and he slew
Lakshmana, Duryodhana's cherished son.
He caused many strong, courageous fighters
to fall back. Wave after wave of warriors
rushed at him; and he repulsed them all,
slicing off hands, arms, ears, so that the ground
was an altar sluiced with sacrificial blood.
And yet, because of his respect for kindred,
Abhimanyu battled with restraint;
as Drona remarked, he often chose to wound
rather than kill. "Ah," sneered Duryodhana,
"our Drona has a soft spot for the princeling;
if he wanted, he could finish him,
master that he is; yet he does not do it."

For hours, Abhimanyu appeared tireless.
Although the Pandavas could not reach him,
they saw his amazing deeds and cheered him on
until the dust of battle hid him from them.

ૐ

How could it not end in tragedy
when no help was at hand for Abhimanyu?
One by one, his weapons were destroyed,
his bow broken, his chariot smashed, his spear
splintered. Finally he fought on foot,
only a mace to defend himself, for now
he was the target more than the attacker.
As cowardly wolves prefer to hunt in packs,

six of the most powerful Kauravas—
Drona, Karna, Kripa, Kritavarman,
Ashvatthaman and Duhshasana's son—
set upon the exhausted Abhimanyu.
These were great warriors; they knew full well
that a mob attack on a lone opponent
was contrary to dharma. Yet they did it.
Duhshasana's son delivered the final blow
with a mace, smashing the young hero's head
as, already down, he tried to rise.
Abhimanyu, Arjuna's best beloved,
beautiful in death as he was in life,
fell to earth, and did not move again.
It was as though the full and luminous moon
had fallen from the sky to the black earth.
The Kauravas, a much depleted army,
whooped with delirious joy.

                It was dusk.
The last fiery filaments of the sun
streaked the sky over the western hill.
The warriors surveyed the devastation,
the battlefield resembling a sacked city.
Scavengers were gathering already
to feast on the abundant human flesh:
crows and ravens, jackals, kanka birds
ripping at the frail skin of the fallen
to drink their fat, lick marrow from their bones,
guzzle their blood.

               These were fallen comrades,
brothers, sons, fathers reduced to this
welter of mere matter, food for birds.
Unable to perform the proper rites,
the living felt defiled, grief unresolved.
The somber troops slouched silently to their tents.

☙

The Pandavas were overwhelmed with sorrow
for Abhimanyu. Yudhishthira could see
that his men had lost all zest for battle.
"We must not grieve," he told them, "we should rather
follow Abhimanyu's great example.
Today, he slaughtered countless Kauravas.
That hero is in heaven; if we stand firm,
we shall defeat our enemies for sure."

But privately, Yudhishthira was crushed
by grief for his brave and beloved nephew.
He sat in his tent, weeping bitter tears,
blaming himself entirely. "Oh, Abhimanyu!
It was for me that you risked everything.
For me you battled with such bravery.
Eager for victory, I urged you on.
How shall I face Arjuna? How will Subhadra
bear to live without her precious son?
And Krishna—how will he find consolation
now that his nephew, little more than a child,
has left the earth?"

                    At this point, Vyasa
appeared, to give comfort. For Yudhishthira
in the face of this catastrophe,
it was as if the fact of death had struck him
for the first time. "What does it mean," he said,
that men are born, are nourished by their mothers,
nurtured with care, have rich experience,
learn the ways of human intercourse,
love, create, take pleasure in the world,
acquire a warrior's skills, respect dharma—
what does it mean that such men can ride out
in the morning, courageous, full of hope,
and by evening are mere carrion
for crows to feast on? Why? What is death?"

"Death takes everything that lives," said Vyasa,
"there is no exception." And he told

the story of the lady Death herself,
and how Brahma, creator of the worlds,
sent her out to achieve his purposes,
so his created worlds would not become
overburdened. "For creatures—even for gods—
death is part of life, that is the law,
and everything that lives carries the germ
of its own destruction. Understanding this,
a wise person does not grieve, Yudhishthira."
Yudhishthira took comfort from this story,
and Vyasa told him many other tales
of kings whose sons were taken away by Death.

Vyasa said to him, "Abhimanyu
lived his life fully, although he was so young.
He will be in heaven; and those who taste heaven
never prefer this world to that bliss."

త

Arjuna had won a splendid victory
over the forces that had sworn to kill him,
but at nightfall, riding back with Krishna,
he was seized with a dreadful premonition.
The camp was silent; no one greeted them.
He had heard of Drona's wheel deployment
and, knowing that Abhimanyu had not learned
how to exit it, he hoped and prayed
that his brave son had not been entrapped.
On every side, he noticed ashen faces.

Hearing the truth, he thought he would die of grief.
He sank down, sighing, face awash with tears.
"Krishna, Subhadra will not survive this news.
Oh, my beloved boy, I remember
how I and your mother held you in our arms.
My glorious son, the joy of all who knew you,

witty, courageous, generous and kind—
if I will never see your face again
how can I live? In that dreadful wheel,
standing alone, you must have thought that soon
your father would arrive to rescue you.
But no, you would have focused on the fight
and nothing else—a hero to the end."

Arjuna was gripped by deep despair.
Krishna gently spoke to him. "My friend,
bear this with fortitude. You are not the first,
nor will you be the last to lose a loved one.
Abhimanyu has gone to the realm for those
who meet death courageously in battle,
with a cheerful heart. We are warriors;
for us, this is how it has always been."

"How did it happen?" asked Arjuna, grim-faced.
"Tell me exactly. How could Abhimanyu
die with my great brothers to protect him?
Sons of Pandu, sons of Drupada,
what were you doing!? Do you carry weapons
merely as ornaments? Did you cowards watch
while my brave boy fought overwhelming odds?"

When he heard the facts, grief turned to rage
at wicked Jayadratha. He swore an oath:
"Before darkness falls tomorrow night,
I will cut off Jayadratha's head,
unless he comes and begs on his knees for mercy.
If I do not, may I never enter heaven,
but may I meet the hideous fate of those
who kill their parents, who cuckold their teachers,
defile women, betray the innocent trust
of those who depend on them. If I do not,
if, tomorrow night, Jayadratha
still struts the earth, breathing our common air,
I shall enter a blazing fire and die!"

In the opposing camp, the Kauravas
picked up a chilling sound on the night breeze,
faint at first, then swelling ever louder,
a sound to shake the world to its foundations:
Devadatta, Arjuna's great conch,
sounding out a challenge and a threat,
followed by furious shouts from the Pandavas.

Jayadratha knew it was meant for him.
Gripped by fear, he had a sense that death
was rushing to meet him. "Ah! What can I do?
Shall I escape at once, fly home to Sindhu?"
"Take heart, calm your fear," said Duryodhana.
"Who could harm you, when you will be surrounded
by our bravest, most accomplished warriors?
And you yourself are a tiger among fighters."
His spies had told him about Arjuna's oath
and, craftily, he thought if Jayadratha
could be protected until the sun went down
Arjuna would fail and, bound by honor,
he would have to immolate himself.

Slightly reassured, Jayadratha
went to Drona's tent, and knelt before him.
"Master, will you tell me Arjuna's secret,
how his arrows fly so fast, so far, so deep?"
"Son," said Drona, "Arjuna's skill has been
honed in the crucible of suffering.
No one can defeat him. But take heart,
I will protect you. You should fight tomorrow;
be true, follow your kshatriya dharma."

Through spies, the Pandavas were given news
of the elaborate arrangments planned

to guard the Sindhu king. Krishna, concerned,
wished that Arjuna had been less hasty
in uttering his vow. But the Terrifier
was scornful. "I assure you, Jayadratha
is already on his way to Yama's realm.
Tomorrow, he and his ill-fated friends
will have cause bitterly to regret the day
they wallowed in the sin of child murder!"

At Arjuna's request, Krishna visited
Abhimanyu's mother, Krishna's sister,
who was with Draupadi and Uttaraa,
the young hero's even younger wife.
Krishna told them of Abhimanyu's feats,
assuring them he was certainly in heaven.
"Alas!" cried Subhadra, "O my child,
my beautiful one, deserving of the best
this earth can give, how can you be sleeping
now on the cold ground, your lovely body
punctured by arrows! O son, O sinless one,
this world is desolate without you in it!
My little boy, my arms ache to hold you,
I long for the smell of your skin, your hair.
Oh, I am hungry for the sight of you.
That you could die with Krishna to protect you
is proof of fate's unfathomable ways."

Uttaraa and Draupadi, Abhimanyu's
second mother, paced wildly in their grief,
weeping without cease, inconsolable.
Krishna told them of Arjuna's vow, and how
Abhimanyu's death would be avenged,
but still they wept; the most extreme vengeance
could not restore to them their beloved boy.

Krishna returned to camp in sorrow. That night
no one slept well. They thought of tomorrow

and what had to be done to bring success.
What if Arjuna should fail? What then?
What if he were killed? How could Yudhishthira
pursue this war without him? What would he do?
Throughout the Pandava army, every man
prayed that Arjuna's mission would succeed.

Before he retired to rest, long-haired Krishna
walked out onto a small rise in the land
and sprinkled it with water. Immediately
lush grass covered it, and fresh-sprung flowers.
He laid out objects for the night offering
to the gods, and Arjuna came to join him.
Learned priests consecrated the Pandava
and Arjuna felt his heart become lighter.
He hung fragrant garlands round Krishna's neck
and gave him the ritual night-offering.

At the darkest hour, Krishna left his tent
and sought out Daruka, his charioteer.
"Tomorrow, we have the greatest challenge yet.
Arjuna swore this oath impulsively
without consulting me. I fear the worst.
Even the son of Kunti cannot kill
a man whom Drona has promised to protect.
Duryodhana will summon every means
to thwart Arjuna's intentions. I want you
to bring my chariot and all my weapons
and follow us, so I can support him
if things go wrong. Oh, Daruka, Arjuna
is more dear to me than all the world.
I could not bear this life if he were dead."

Restless on his bed, Arjuna wondered
how he would be able to keep his vow
if Jayadratha skulked behind a stockade
of chariots assembled by the Kauravas.

He slept at last, a sleep riven by nightmares.
Then he dreamed Krishna came to comfort him
and told him not to despair. "All that exists
rests in the lap of time. Despair is the foe
that robs you of the energy to act.
You must obtain the weapon, *Pashupata,*
from Lord Shiva. Fasten your mind's eye
on him. When you have found him, be silent.
Then honor him, devote yourself to him
and, by his grace, he will give you *Pashupata.*"

Arjuna sat down in meditation
and it seemed he was traveling through the sky
with Krishna, over beautiful terrain,
over the snowy slopes of Himavat,
over the remotest mountain regions,
over the pleasure gardens of Kubera,
over groves where apsarases played.
They paused on a mountain peak to view the earth
shimmering gold beneath them, with its cities
and lakes scattered like the loveliest flowers.

At last, they reached the home of Lord Shiva.
The god was sitting, huge and awe-inspiring,
glowing with his own fire, trident in hand.
Parvati, his wife, was by his side.
Arjuna and Krishna bowed before him
and sang a hymn of praise, "O Lord Shiva,
to you who are the soul of the universe;
to you the unconquered, the all-merciful;
to you who have a thousand thousand eyes;
to you whose name is Death, lord of creatures,
all-powerful, and all-compassionate,
we join our hands in homage and devotion."

"Welcome, Nara and Narayana,"
said the god, smiling. "Tell me what you desire

and I will grant it." Arjuna looked deeply
into the flame that is the mighty god
and saw there the ritual night-offering
he had given Krishna earlier.

Shiva granted them the powerful weapon,
showed them where to find it, and how to use it.
Thus, for the second time, the son of Kunti
received the terrifying *Pashupata*.
Joyfully, the heroes worshiped Shiva
and returned to earth, and blissful sleep.

39.

IN PURSUIT OF JAYADRATHA

"Tell me, Sanjaya," said Dhritarashtra,
"after they had slaughtered Abhimanyu
so contrary to dharma, so unfairly,
how could our warriors hold up their heads?
And when they heard the great conch *Devadatta*,
how could they march out to face Arjuna,
grim as all-destroying Death himself?
I fear what you will tell me. Oh, my friend,
I wish we had made peace with the Pandavas.
If only we had taken heed when Krishna
came as their envoy. But Duryodhana
was foolish and stubborn, and this holocaust
is the result."

     "You should blame yourself,"
said Sanjaya. "You had a hundred chances
to guide your son with a restraining hand.
You pandered to his greed—your lamentations
are like the hollow clank of empty vessels,
and come too late. What is done is done.
If you had set your son on the right path,
if you had heeded wiser heads than yours,
this disaster never would have happened.
O king, prepare yourself—your misery
has only just begun. Now I shall tell you
what happened on the fourteenth day of war."

ॐ

Arjuna woke refreshed and confident.
He took his bath and performed his devotions.
Yudhishthira was woken by the sound
of his musicians welcoming the dawn.
After his morning rituals were over
he held a meeting of his greatest warriors.
Turning to Krishna in deep respect, he begged
that he would do all he could for Arjuna.
Krishna reassured him. "Arjuna
will certainly fulfill his vow this day."
Arjuna, worried for Yudhishthira,
asked Satyaki, that undefeated warrior,
to make all efforts to protect the king.

Everything that could be done was done:
horses fed and harnessed, the chariots
and weapons checked and blessed, well-fitting armor
carefully tied on. Last, the great standard
bearing the emblem of the divine monkey
was fixed in its socket. With a last embrace
between the brothers, the fighting day began,
a day of make or break, a day of truth.

The blare of conches, the relentless beat
of numberless war drums struck the Kauravas
like a summons to eternity.
More than any of them, Jayadratha
was trembling with terror and dismay.
But as Drona laid out his battle plan,
and as he blew his conch with confidence,
the Sindhu king started to take heart.
Drona had mobilized his divisions
into a complex wheeled cart formation;
behind it, an impenetrable lotus

and, inside that, a strong needle array.
All these forces, well trained and determined,
stood between Jayadratha and his fate.

Arjuna, at the vanguard of his army,
where the densest arrow showers would fall,
was imposing—tall, muscular and graceful,
with shining eyes. Driven by dark-skinned Krishna,
he stood high on his gleaming chariot
upright, his black hair streaming out behind him.
His armor glittered. He was garlanded,
and on his head was the dazzling diadem
given to him by his father, Indra.
His jeweled earrings sparkled in the sun.
Relaxed, alert, he grasped his bow *Gandiva*,
while, above him, the great ape on his standard
bared its teeth and snarled at the enemy.

Battle began. Arjuna's whole effort
must be to penetrate the Kaurava force
to reach Jayadratha. He told Krishna
to drive at your son Durmashana, the prince
positioned in the vanguard of your army.
The onslaught was devastating, and broke up
the front ranks of the Kauravas, who fled
under the fury of his attack. Heads
by the hundred were severed in a flash
of well-aimed arrows, and tumbled to the ground
like heavy fruit, while, for a short moment,
headless trunks fought on before they fell.
Duhshasana's strong elephant division
joined the battle then, but did no better
and retreated, bristling with arrows.

Now, Arjuna formally approached Drona.
He joined his hands in respect. "Master," he said,
"as your pupil, I claim your protection.

Look upon me as if I were your son.
Allow me to put the Sindhu king to death
as he deserves, and as I have sworn to do.
Help me keep my word."

      Drona smiled slightly.
"If you want Jayadratha, take me first!"
and he pelted Arjuna with arrows,
wounding his horses, severing his bowstring.
Arjuna fought back, volley for volley,
weapon for weapon, white horses against red.
This was a contest between the most skilled warriors,
a demonstration of most dazzling prowess.
But as the sun climbed higher in the sky,
Krishna urged Arjuna to leave the duel
and keep his mind fixed on the main objective.
"What?" cried Drona, "Are you giving up
on an opponent who is not yet beaten?"
"You are not my opponent," said Arjuna,
turning away from him, "but my dear master."

Mounting an assault on Drona's forces,
Arjuna released a thousand arrows
in the time a normal fighter would fire ten.
Kauravas fell by the hundred. Pandavas
also suffered losses. And Arjuna
was knocked senseless by a well-aimed lance
flung by Shrutayus. Quickly recovering,
he invoked the *Shakra* weapon, which spewed out
many thousands of straight and speedy arrows,
and the Kauravas were washed glistening red
as bloody fountains sprang from elephants,
horses and men, splashing to the ground.
Gaining, yard by yard, Krishna drove forward
until at last they broke through Drona's lines
and shattered the well-planned lotus formation
as the Kauravas scattered in disarray.

❧

Horrified, Duryodhana rushed over
to where Drona stood. "It's a disaster!
Arjuna is scorching our infantry
like a raging fire consuming tinder.
It is as if my troops were feeble children!
How long have you eaten at my table?
I have pampered you in every way,
yet I know your heart is with the Pandavas—
I was a fool to trust you!" Drona sighed.
He was expecting this; Duryodhana
could not bear things not to go his way
and had to find somewhere to pin the blame.
The tantrum soon passed. "Forgive me, Drona—
put it down to rage and disappointment.
We must at all costs guard Jayadratha.
What hinders you?"
                              "It's the sheer speed," said Drona.
"Those horses are the finest in the world,
and Krishna drives with supernatural skill,
swerving, dodging through the smallest gaps.
I am not young, pace is not my strength.
I propose that you protect Jayadratha,
block the Pandava from getting near him,
while I attempt to seize Yudhishthira."

"But how can I do that," groaned Duryodhana,
"when even you have failed? The gods themselves
couldn't stop him."
                              "I have a solution,"
said Drona; and he gave Duryodhana
a gleaming, finely wrought golden breastplate
and fastened it on, chanting secret mantras,
tying it with sacred *Brahma* strings.
Pausing only to receive Drona's blessings,

Duryodhana, restored to confidence
and followed by the hosts of the Trigartas,
set out to do battle with Arjuna.

&

Bent on capturing Yudhishthira,
Drona turned to the front of the array
where he sought to hold back Dhrishtadyumna,
advancing at the head of a vast force.
Drupada's son aimed to divide and conquer.
Drona tried to stop him, but repeatedly
the Kauravas were split in three. One part
gravitated toward Kritavarman,
hotly harassed by Yudhishthira;
another coalesced round Jalasandha,
chased by mace-wielding Bhima; while a third,
harried by the brilliant Dhrishtadyumna,
gathered around Drona. Fighting was fierce;
shafts of sunlight struggling through clouds of dust
made seeing difficult, but showers of arrows,
loosed with no special target, found a mark
in man and beast alike.

                             Dhrishtadyumna
urged his charioteer, "Quickly! Approach
Drona, that boastful warrior, that great teacher,
that brahmin traitor to his natural calling!"
Then the two accomplished fighters clashed.
It was a spectacle—all around them
other fighting stopped, so men could watch
the consummate display of archery,
the two well matched, making little headway
against each other. Then Drishtadyumna
rashly leapt up onto Drona's chariot,
poised on the backs of his rust-red horses
to fight him hand to hand. It was a feat

to remember. But Drona knocked away
his sword, wounding him in many places
and, if Satyaki had not rescued him,
and himself taken on the fight with Drona,
it could have been the end for Dhrishtadyumna.

Satyaki and Drona fought like gods—
fiercely, but with finesse and self-possession.
The sky grew overcast as clouds of arrows
blotted out the sun, and soon they both
ran with blood. Each hoped for victory,
and other warriors stood around, watching,
gripped by such astounding mastery.
(At heart, Drona, too, applauded Satyaki,
noting that he had learned from Arjuna
skills Drona himself had taught the Pandava.)
Both were masters of celestial weapons,
and each of them could neutralize the other.
Neither won. Eventually, Yudhishthira
called his troops to arms, and general battle
was resumed.

❦

　　　　　Now the white sun had started
on its inexorable downward course
toward the outline of the Asta hills.
Krishna and Arjuna, with their divisions,
forced a passage through the Kaurava ranks,
their sights set steadfastly on Jayadratha.
Arjuna, with his limitless supply
of iron-tipped arrows, inflicted dreadful harm,
but the Kauravas had too much at stake
to slacken their resolve.

　　　　　So did Arjuna.
The going was hard. The chariot maintained

enormous speed, and still the Terrifier
was killing men a league ahead of him.
No chariot had moved as fast before.
It moved with the speed of imagination,
the speed of thought, the speed of rapt desire.
But the horses were becoming tired.
Krishna was concerned. "We must unyoke them,
remove their arrows, give them time to breathe.
And they need to drink, but there is no water."
Arjuna shot an arrow at the ground
and at once a sparkling lake appeared,
with water birds and dense, shade-giving trees.
Then he made a shelter out of arrows
and, while he held back the Kauravas,
Krishna led the horses under it
and calmly unyoking them from the chariot,
rubbed and stroked them with an expert touch
so they revived from their fatigue and wounds.
To unyoke horses in the midst of battle!
Such a thing had never been done before.

Seeing this, at first the Kaurava troops
roared in triumph; surely now they had him,
heroic Arjuna, on foot and alone!
But, calm and focused, the great Pandava
raked your forces with his powerful weapons.
"Just our luck!" groaned some of them. "Duryodhana
has set us up as sacrificial sheep.
He doesn't seem to understand that no one
can defeat Arjuna. King Jayadratha
is a dead man already. Duryodhana
should make arrangements for his funeral rites."

Now, with the horses rested, Krishna drove
furiously forward, sweeping aside
all attempts to block their headlong progress.
The two heroes shone like twin dazzling suns.

At last, they caught a glimpse of Jayadratha
with Duryodhana protecting him.
Joy seized them. Now Arjuna roared in rage
and exultation. "Even Indra himself
with all the celestials could not save him now!"
They advanced all the faster, hooves thundering,
terrible ape banner striking terror
into the heart of the cowering Sindhu king.

"Attack Duryodhana!" shouted Krishna.
"It's time to kill that wicked ill-wisher,
that greedy villain!"
                              "Drive on!" cried Arjuna,
remembering his cousin's many wrongs.

Duryodhana jeered, "Come on, son of Pandu,
fight me if you dare! Show everyone
if this great prowess people talk about
is real heroism, or empty talk!"
Arjuna took aim and loosed his arrows
at Duryodhana, who stood there, laughing
as the shafts bounced harmlessly off his armor
time after time. Krishna was astonished.
Arjuna realized: "The villain's armor
must have been tied onto him by Drona.
But I know a mantra that will make him
vulnerable again, a powerful weapon."
He invoked that weapon, but before
it reached Duryodhana, it was deflected
by Drona, from a distance. If Arjuna
had invoked the weapon a second time
it would have killed his own troops, and himself.
Instead, he used his ordinary skill
to kill Duryodhana's charioteer and horses
and smash his chariot. He then shot off
your son's leather gauntlets, and pierced his hands.
Krishna blew his conch *Panchajanya*,

Arjuna gave a blast on *Devadatta,*
and the Kaurava forces stood stupefied.

Meanwhile Drona tried again to capture
Yudhishthira, but the king was whisked away
on Sahadeva's chariot. Alambusha
now lusted to avenge his monstrous brother.
Ghatotkacha advanced to fight with him.
He plucked him from his chariot, whirled him round
as though he were a doll, and flung him down
onto the ground where, like a brittle pot,
he was dashed to fragments.

Yudhishthira
had picked up the sound of conches blown
by Krishna and Arjuna, and he was fearful
for their safety. He spoke to Satyaki,
consumed by anxiety, tears in his eyes,
and told him to go to Arjuna's defense.
Satyaki, fast as lightning in the field,
was slow in his reactions otherwise.
Arjuna had told him to guard his brother
and guard Yudhishthira he must. Desperate,
Yudhishthira was forced to press him hard:
"Arjuna may be in mortal danger
floundering in an ocean of Kauravas!
You, Satyaki, have always been our mainstay,
second only to Krishna in weaponry.
You must obey me." Satyaki was perplexed
since he owed obedience to Arjuna,
his teacher, just as he did to his leader;
and Arjuna had said . . . So the conundrum
went round and round in poor Satyaki's mind.

At last, reluctant, he agreed to go,
but only after repeating once again
Arjuna's parting words to him; and after
assuring Yudhishthira that Arjuna
was bound to be quite safe, and did not need
rescuing by him. "And another thing,
who will protect you from Drona while I'm gone?"
Yudhishthira assured him Dhrishtadyumna
and Bhima would be constantly at his side.

"Very well, I'll go," said Satyaki.
"Let no one think me slow to obey orders.
I have your interests constantly before me
as I do Arjuna's. I'll follow him
and battle by his side until he slaughters
Jayadratha. I shall scourge the Kauravas.
Like fire, I shall certainly destroy them.
But please arrange to have the proper weapons
placed in my chariot in the correct places—
in fact, let five times as many weapons
as usual be provided." Then Satyaki
went to his tent and took a ritual bath,
changed his clothes, drank honey for energy,
gave gifts to brahmins to secure good fortune
and, saying goodbye to Yudhishthira,
was finally off. The sun was sinking fast.

Following the route blazed by Arjuna,
Satyaki sliced through the Kaurava lines,
killing hundreds. Again, he encountered Drona,
but wasted no time fighting him. Instead
he told his charioteer to find a passage
between the separate divisions led
by Drona and Karna.

                Now he had set his mind
on his objective, all his mastery

and his celestial weapons came into play.
At one point he dueled with Duhshasana
but with restraint, remembering Bhima's oath.
Duhshasana ran for Drona's protection.
"Why are you fleeing from the fight, my son?"
asked Drona scornfully. "You were brave enough
when you insulted Draupadi. Where now
is your pride and insolence? What will you do
when you are up against real opposition,
faced with Arjuna the invincible?
If you are that frightened, urge your brother
to make a just peace with the Pandavas."

Once again, Drona and Dhrishtadyumna
met in battle. They wounded each other badly,
but neither of them could get the upper hand.
Drona, white-haired, eighty-five years old,
fought like a youth. In fact, the rumor spread
that this was Indra himself, armed with thunder.

Yudhishthira was desperate to know
what was happening to Arjuna.
Again he heard Krishna's conch, and was afraid—
suppose it meant his brother had been killed?
He said to Bhima, "I'm seeing Arjuna,
seeing him in my mind—his tall, straight form,
his shining hair and dark skin, his strong arms.
I cannot see his standard, so I fear
he has been overwhelmed. And Satyaki—
what has become of him? You, my Bhima,
must go and find out. Dhrishtadyumna here
can certainly protect me from abduction."

Bhima set off, though with some reluctance,
and found that Arjuna was fighting strongly.
He uttered a great roar, and Yudhishthira,

hearing it, was reassured. Then Karna,
that hero endowed with preternatural skill,
desiring battle, his first formal duel
of the war, mounted an assault on Bhima.
What a fight that was! The two great warriors
fought differently—Karna graceful, subtle,
Bhima more dependent on sheer strength,
but accurate for all that. Each let loose
hundreds of arrows. Roaring still, Bhima
bisected Karna's bow, then wounded him
with ten straight shafts. Seizing another bow,
Karna shot a lightning cascade of arrows.
Bhima blocked them. Then, with broad-headed shafts,
he killed Karna's charioteer and horses,
and all the while he smiled and roared with pleasure.
Karna quickly mounted his son's chariot
and fought on; but, mindful of the promise
he had made to Kunti, he fought with restraint.

Soon, the heroes were bristling with arrows
sticking out all over, like porcupines,
and blood flowed down over their golden mail,
rendering it coppery. They exchanged
insults: "You contemptible driver's son!"
"Eunuch! You lumbering half-wit! You glutton!"
Seeing Karna hard pressed, Duryodhana
sent one of his brothers, Durjaya,
to support him. It was not long before
Bhima sliced his head from his body. Later,
after Karna had twice more had his chariot
smashed to bits beneath him, another brother,
Durmukha, came—and met with the same fate.
Then Duryodhana sent several more
of your sons, each of whom was felled
by the furious Bhima. Karna, grieving
and feeling responsible for all these deaths,
withdrew from the fighting for a while

and ritually walked around each body
out of respect for these fallen princes
who for years had been like his own brothers.

꣸

Dhritarashtra interrupted Sanjaya:
"Something in your tale is disturbing me.
Duryodhana pins all his hopes of victory
on Karna. This war was only started
because the driver's son assured my boy
that he could annihilate the Pandavas.
But (as you have told me) he has promised
that he will not kill Kunti's other sons,
only Arjuna. I am wondering, then,
how can Karna, with his heart divided,
act completely for Duryodhana's good?

"But these things are beyond my comprehension.
It is time, after all, that will decide."

꣸

Sanjaya continued:
Bhima began to make his way to where
Arjuna and Krishna could be found.
But Karna followed him. Breathing hot sighs,
keen to avenge the dead Kaurava princes,
keen, too, to prove his worth to Duryodhana,
Karna shot a cloud of golden arrows
radiating in a shining blur
like the sun itself. So many were there
it was as if they sprang not just from his bow
but from all round his chariot. The arrows,
beautifully fletched with peacock feathers,
were like a flight of the most lovely birds.
And he himself was radiant: tall, handsome,
crowned with a chaplet of blue lotuses.

Bhima, remembering his former wrongs,
eagerly responded. A roaring tempest,
he scattered the discouraged Kauravas
like fragile leaves sent flying in the wind.
Soon his arrows were drinking Karna's blood,
and thirty-one of your sons, O majesty,
died in that fracas.

    Now Duryodhana
remembered how wise Vidura, his uncle,
had warned him that events in the gaming hall,
the insults suffered by the Pandavas,
would bear bitter fruit. But this recall
did not set him on a saner path
though, even now, he could have stopped the war
by acting rightly.

    Bhima roared with joy,
gladdening the heart of Yudhishthira
as he launched his troops against Drona
some way off. Bhima's duel with Karna
became a spectacle, with celestial beings—
rishis, siddhas and gandharvas—applauding
and showering the combatants with petals.

Bhima, though full of rage, knew that Arjuna
had Karna marked out as his own opponent,
so aimed to hurt, rather than to kill him.

Finally, Bhima's weapons were used up.
Karna harried him and struck him senseless.
Recovering, he seized what came to hand—
chariot wheels, elephants' severed limbs—
and flung them at his opponent.

      "You're a child!"
jeered Karna, "What do you think you're doing?
Children don't belong on the battlefield.

Go to the woods! Gather fruits for your dinner."
and he touched Bhima lightly on the chest
with his bow-end. Bhima laughed scornfully.
"Haven't I always got the better of you,
you wicked bastard?" And he turned away.

⚜

"Satyaki is approaching," said Krishna.
"Yudhishthira must have ordered him
to join you; as he comes, he is dispatching
Kauravas by the hundred. Satyaki,
your friend and disciple, is truly great."
Arjuna was not pleased. "My instructions
were to guard Yudhishthira. Now Drona,
like a circling hawk, will swoop on him.

"And look—you can see Satyaki's in trouble:
he is tired, his weapons all but spent,
and now he is being attacked by Bhurishravas,
that formidable fighter! This is too much!
Yudhishthira was wrong to send him here.
Now I have to worry about him
and about Yudhishthira, *and* somehow
slaughter Jayadratha before sunset!"

Bhurishravas, strong and menacing,
advanced on Satyaki. "Today, my friend,
prepare to die. The wives of all those heroes
whom you have killed will rejoice, I promise you."
"Save your breath," scoffed Satyaki. "Stop boasting,
you bag of wind!" With that, they launched themselves
with great energy, wounding each other
with showers of arrows, so that their blood flowed.
They ended up on foot, circling each other
with naked swords, grasping their bull-hide shields.
They roared and grunted like two elephants,

sometimes thrusting, sometimes head-butting,
rolling on the ground, wrestling, no holds barred.

Bhurishravas looked likely to be victor
since Satyaki, who had never known defeat,
was exhausted and was lacking weapons.
Sooner than see Satyaki broken now,
Arjuna chose a razor-headed arrow
and sliced off the arm of Bhurishravas,
the sword still in its hand. The warrior
cried to him in wrath. "Oh, Arjuna,
this is a sinful act, cruel and heartless—
I was not fighting you. Were you not taught
the rules of righteous conduct? Shame on you!
You have been keeping sinful company;
no doubt that's why you've left the path of virtue."

"Self-defense is not a sin," said Arjuna,
"and Satyaki is like a part of me—
my dear disciple and my honored kinsman.
You had your sword poised to cut his throat—
it would have been a sin just to stand by."

Bhurishravas, now useless as a warrior,
vowed to die by fasting unto death,
and sat meditating upon mantras,
senses withdrawn, in great tranquillity.
But Satyaki still wanted to dispatch him,
remembering the pain he had inflicted
in killing Satyaki's beloved sons
earlier in the war. He raised his sword
and, with one blow, beheaded his enemy.
"Alas! Shame! Shame!" cried the Kauravas.
Satyaki snapped back, "What's your complaint?
This man has been killed in the press of battle.
Wicked Kauravas! Where was your sense of shame
when you set upon an unprotected boy

like a pack of slavering hyenas?
Where was *shame* then? I see you do not answer!

"I have it on reputable authority
that men should always act to accomplish that
which gives the most grief to their enemies—
even women were killed in the old days.
In killing this man, I acted lawfully."

No one there applauded him, however,
neither Kaurava nor Pandava.

ॐ

Time moved relentlessly, marked by the sun
indifferently sailing through the heavens,
dropping westward. No earthly thing would make it
slow its course, however high the stake,
even if Arjuna should lose his life
for want of a few extra, dawdling, minutes.
The Pandava was desperate. "Speed on!
Speed on the horses, Krishna, outstrip the sun!
Make my vow true!"

              Duryodhana was tense;
the Pandava chariot was approaching fast.
"Karna, take up arms against Arjuna.
Look at the sun! We only have to stop him
briefly and the world will belong to us.
Without him, the Pandavas are finished."
Karna, in great pain from his fight with Bhima,
said, "Fate will decide, but I will do my best."

For this last-ditch defense, the Kauravas
mobilized their most accomplished fighters:
Ashvatthaman, Kripa, Duhshasana,
Karna and his son Vrishasena,

Shalya the Madra king, Duryodhana . . .
But even as they grouped themselves for battle
in a cordon around the Sindhu king,
and as the sun was throwing streaks of flame
across the sky, Arjuna was already
laying waste to the Kaurava defense.

Then followed the most fierce and bitter fighting
of the whole war so far. Great Arjuna,
whose thoughts were never far from Abhimanyu,
massacred by the men before him now,
fought like a god. A hundred of his arrows
pierced Karna, bathing him in blood. Karna
in return pelted him with arrows;
Arjuna cut them all off in mid-flight,
then sent a special shaft—which Ashvatthaman
intercepted, knocking it to earth.
Arjuna killed Karna's four fine horses
and his charioteer. Ashvatthaman
hauled Karna up onto his own chariot
and the fight continued, others weighing in.

Such was the damage dealt by Arjuna
that the Kaurava troops began to falter
as they stumbled over the mangled bodies
of their comrades, who formed a jumbled mound
at least three deep. Strewn with dead elephants,
with horses missing heads or hooves, with men
whose wounds were like gaping mouths, gouting blood,
some moving still, some screaming and pleading,
the scene was a truly horrifying hell.

The chariot was mud-caked and obstructed
but Krishna, with preternatural skill, managed
to steer a course nearer, ever nearer
to Jayadratha. Suddenly it was clear
that between the Sindhu king and death

stood only a handful of exhausted troops,
defeated and disorganized.

But look!
Only the barest sliver of the sun
could still be seen above the Asta hill
and Jayadratha himself, fresh and rested,
fought Arjuna, with everything to gain.
To and fro went the advantage. Kaurava
warriors rallied now to Jayadratha
and surrounded him. "Arjuna," said Krishna,
"I will resort to yoga to make it seem
as if the sun has set. Do not yourself
be deceived. Thinking he's safe, Jayadratha
will relax his guard—and you can finish him."

The sky grew dusky. The Kauravas sent up
a cheer of relief, and dropped their vigilance.
"Arjuna!" cried Krishna, "Now is the moment!
But be careful. The Sindhu king carries
a dangerous protection. Whoever causes
his severed head to fall upon the ground,
that person's own head will disintegrate
into a hundred pieces. The time has come
for you to invoke the marvelous *Pashupata*."

Arjuna, with the mantras he had learned,
aimed *Pashupata* at Jayadratha.
His head flew off and, carried by the weapon,
traveled to where the Sindhu king's old father
was sitting in profound meditation.
Down fell Jayadratha's head, landing
in the lap of his own father. Oblivious,
old Sindhu did not notice and, when he rose,
it fell onto the ground, and his own head
exploded in a cloud of fragments.

"Shame!"
cried the outraged Kauravas. "What wickedness!
Arjuna has flown in the face of dharma
and killed the Sindhu king when day was over."
"The dust got in your eyes, that's all," said Krishna.
"Rub them and look again—it's not yet sunset."
And now, gazing at the western sky,
everyone could see the crimson segment.
It was still only late afternoon.

⚜

"I still cannot grasp," said Dhritarashtra,
"how we could fail against the Pandavas
when our forces are so well prepared,
so numerous. What can it be but fate?"

"Perhaps," said Sanjaya, "our forces know
the cause they are supporting is unrighteous.
The kings who make up Duryodhana's army
are his vassals—they are obliged to fight.
Perhaps the allies of the Pandavas
are fighting from conviction, confident
that their cause is just."

"How can we know?"
said the blind king. "Destiny plays with us;
it will always have the final word.

"But tell me, Sanjaya, what happened next?"

40.

BATTLE AT NIGHT

Sanjaya went on:
"Arjuna," said Krishna, "you have triumphed!
No other warrior in all the three worlds
could have done what you have done today,
alone and unsupported."

                        "Beloved Krishna,"
Arjuna replied, "this vow of mine
has only been fulfilled by virtue of
your skill, your power, above all, your wisdom.
This victory is yours." Krishna smiled.
He cast his eyes over the battlefield.
He saw brave kshatriyas by the thousand
lying dead or dying, some at peace,
some clutching at the earth like a loved woman.
He saw their muddied banners; their bright jewels,
collars of gold and ornaments, adorning them
even now. In this sea of carnage
it was still possible to notice beauty.

It was for this these men had lived—for glory,
a hero's heaven. For their place in legend.
Yet how many would have their story told
in poetry or song? How many of them
would have a hero's stone raised in their honor;
how many be expunged, obliterated
from Earth's memory, as though they had not lived?

❧

Arjuna and Krishna brought the good news
of Jayadratha's death to Yudhishthira,
who wept tears of joy. "By good fortune
our enemies flounder in a sea of grief!"
And, recognizing Krishna's divine aspect,
he gave thanks to him as the eternal Lord,
as well as the Pandavas' most cherished friend.
Bhima and Satyaki arrived; Yudhishthira
joyfully embraced them and praised their courage.
It was a splendid moment—catastrophe
decisively, heroically averted.

The sun had set. But the savage battle
continued, so fired up were the two sides
with hostility toward each other.
Arjuna, glorious in his diadem,
energized by success, fiercely fought
the attacking Kauravas, and put to flight
his old teacher Kripa, and Ashvatthaman.
Those of your sons who were still alive
skirmished with Satyaki, but the Vrishni hero
did not kill them, though he smashed their chariots.
He left them to be finished off by Bhima.

Wolf-belly had complained to Arjuna
of how Karna had insulted him,
treating him like a child, not a worthy foe.
Going up to Karna, Arjuna
spoke scornfully. "Driver's son, you should know
that Bhima could have killed you easily
but held back so I can fulfill my vow
and slaughter you myself. Your empty boasts
and sinful insults will be avenged by me;
Duryodhana will weep over your body.

Further, there's your part in the shameful murder
of Abhimanyu. For that, I swear to you,
I will kill your own son, Vrishasena,
before your eyes!" Karna walked away.

༄

In Duryodhana's camp the mood was somber.
The thwarted Kaurava wept bitter tears
for the devastation of his army
and the death of Jayadratha. As he wept,
he remembered how he had believed Karna
when he proclaimed he could kill the Pandavas.
Because he longed for that, because he wanted
to believe in his friend's martial greatness,
he had refused to yield. Yet now he saw:
with Krishna, Arjuna was invincible;
Karna was not.

Heaving deep sighs, the prince
went to Drona and poured out his sorrow.
"Master, no one can protect my army.
Jayadratha is dead despite our efforts;
so many allies who trusted me are dead
and it is my fault. My greed and anger
have brought this about. Even a hundred
horse sacrifices could not wipe out my sin.
I cannot annul my debt to my dead friends—
it is for me alone that men have died
who otherwise would be enjoying their lives
in tranquillity. I should find a hole
and bury myself in it! Failing that,
the only way I can have peace of mind
is to destroy the Pandavas and their allies
or myself be killed, and join my friends.
Yes, I shall lose . . . and that is not surprising
when the great Drona, chief of the whole army,
deals gently with the Pandavas—Arjuna

is your disciple and you favor him.
That's it—you have decided that we will lose
and are bringing it about by skillful means!
And we took you for a friend! It seems
that only Karna wants victory for me."

Drona was desolate. "Oh, Duryodhana,
you know better! Was it not you who failed
to protect the luckless Jayadratha
despite celestial armor? I always told you
that Arjuna will never be defeated.
Even so, I have done my best for you.
This tragedy began in the gaming hall—
Shakuni threw the dice to favor you,
but now it seems as if those dice were arrows
sent speeding down the years for your destruction.
Vidura warned you of it at the time.

"Both the armies are geared up to fight
throughout the night. Prepare yourself for that.
Look—the Pandavas and the Panchalas
are rushing toward me, thirsting for my death.
I vow that I shall not remove my armor
until I have wiped out the Panchalas
or died trying. Tell my son, Ashvatthaman,
to live in righteousness, as I have taught him."
With that, Drona drove off into battle.

Duryodhana went to Karna for comfort.
"Drona is siding with the Pandavas.
If he had fought for us wholeheartedly,
Jayadratha would be living now."
"Drona is doing his very best," said Karna,
"but he is old, and Arjuna is outstanding.
We ourselves failed to protect the Sindhu king.
In my view, it is fate that governs things.
All our plans to harm the Pandavas
have failed, one by one, baffled by time.

Destiny never sleeps; we can't evade it.
All we can do is summon all our courage
and fight with resolution, following dharma."

✣

As night fell, the Pandavas advanced;
the Kauravas stormed out to meet them, fired
by a burning thirst for retribution—
elephant divisions against elephants,
foot soldiers clashing with their counterparts.
Soon it was too dark to see—only
men calling out their names made it possible
for the two sides to know friend from enemy;
quite soon, the general uproar prevented
even that. Chaos and carnage followed.
Men lashed out wildly, horses stampeded,
nocturnal scavengers were on the prowl.
Then blazing flambeaux, fixed to chariots,
illumined scenes resembling hell itself.

✣

"Tell me what happened next," said Dhritarashtra.
"Which well-armed warriors fought against each other?"

"Many were the duels that took place
in that infernal night," said Sanjaya.
"Suffice it to tell you that, before the sun
cast cruel light on the fifteenth day of war,
valiant Ghatotkacha, Bhima's son,
huge as a hill, loved by all who knew him,
of supernatural strength and bravery,
clever conjuror of occult illusions,
was killed by Karna. This is how it happened:"

✣

In the general battle, Ghatotkacha's son
was killed by Ashvatthaman. Enraged by this,
Ghatotkacha, with other rakshasas,
set on Ashvatthaman, who invoked
celestial weapons, of which he is a master,
and wounded Ghatotkacha, rendering him
unconscious. Dhrishtadyumna gathered him up
and had him placed on another chariot.

Meanwhile Yudhishthira, like one inspired,
fought off yet another attempt by Drona
to capture him. The Pandava troops, heartened,
pressed hard on the Kauravas, pushing them back.
Duryodhana appealed to Karna. "Friend,
you must save our troops—they are surrounded
by hostile forces." Karna reassured him:
"Arjuna is the linchpin of the Pandavas.
I plan to kill him with the fatal spear
I obtained from Indra—I am saving it
for him. All the other Pandavas
and their allies will collapse without him.
When I turn them into porcupines
with my onslaught of arrows—I shall give you
the entire earth and everything that's on it."

Kripa, overhearing, ridiculed him.
"If words were weapons, Karna, Duryodhana
would have in you a wonderful protector!
But words are what give brahmins their distinction;
kshatriyas become heroes by force of arms,
not by building chariots in the air!
The fact is, driver's son, you have never fought
the Pandavas and beaten them. Your boasting
is like the roaring of dry thunderclouds.
Your roars will soon stop when you meet Arjuna."

Karna met this provocation calmly.
"True heroes always roar like clouds in autumn

and, like a seed dropped on the earth, in season
they deliver fruit. You should understand
that boastful speeches on the eve of battle
are the way a hero prepares himself,
having agreed to a great undertaking.
They are part of mental resolution,
inviting destiny to lend him strength.
These boasts of mine are never mere hot air,
but quite intentional. As for you,
you are old, unskilled—and a brahmin.
Furthermore, you love the Pandavas.
You extol their achievements, but our troops
have slaughtered their divisions by the thousand."

At this, Ashvatthaman, a brahmin too,
and furious at the insult to his uncle,
drew his sword and started to threaten Karna,
until Duryodhana intervened: "Come, friends,
forgive each other. We need you to focus
on the task ahead."

                At the braying challenge
of the Pandava conches, and the shouting,
"Where is Karna? Come on! Fight with us!"
Karna went out calmly, and alone.
There followed spectacular feats of skill
on Karna's part. Against the Pandava host
he held his own, and dispatched many hundreds,
splitting apart divisions, so men wandered
hither and thither, aimless as stray cattle.

Seeing his troops afflicted, Arjuna
entered the fray, skirmishing with Karna,
killing his four horses and his driver.
Karna jumped up onto Kripa's chariot,
but the Kaurava troops started to withdraw,
smelling defeat, and fearing Arjuna.

Duryodhana cried to them, "Defend Karna!
Don't run away, you cowards! I'll fight myself
to show you how to challenge Arjuna!"
And he prepared to rush into the fray.

Kripa called to Ashvatthaman, "Stop him!
He's like an insect flying into flame.
Don't let him get anywhere near Arjuna
or he'll be burned to ashes!"
                              "It isn't right
that you should expose yourself to the enemy,"
said Ashvatthaman. "Let me fight instead."
Duryodhana turned on him, in a frenzy:
"You and your father love the Pandavas—
is that why you never do me good?
Maybe you have a fondness for Draupadi!
But what can I do but rely on you?"

"It's true, the Pandavas are like my brothers,"
said Ashvatthaman. "But I know my duty—
this is war, and I am a warrior
in your service. Battle is my calling.
Today, seeing my feats, Yudhishthira
will think the whole world filled with Ashvatthamans!"
"Go then," said your son, "and do your best."

꧂

Bhima came face to face with Duryodhana,
both full of wrath. It was a short encounter.
Bhima aimed a blazing spear; the Kaurava
cut it in three as it sped toward him.
Then Bhima hurled his mace with ferocious force,
smashing Duryodhana's horses and chariot,
pulverizing them, so the troops who saw it
dimly, in the murkiness of night,
thought Duryodhana himself had met his end.

Karna fought a duel with Sahadeva.
The Pandava, desperate for glory,
gave the battle everything he had,
using every weapon and, when they ran out,
hurling anything that came to hand
in a furious onslaught. All of this
Karna deflected easily. Then he said,
"You should fight your equals, Pandava.
Go and join your brother over there.
Or perhaps you would be better off at home."
He touched Sahadeva lightly with his bow.
Sahadeva wept with humiliation.

In the darkness, it was difficult to tell
what was happening. But courageous Karna
acquitted himself with honor. He defeated
Dhrishtadyumna after a long fight
and made deep inroads into the Pandava troops.
His bow glowed in a shining blur of arrows,
as he almost danced on his chariot platform
like the chief of the celestials.

Arjuna, thwarted by the lack of progress,
said to Krishna, "I should confront Karna
and fight him to the death—his or mine."
"No," said Krishna, "that time has not yet come.
Karna carries the celestial spear
Indra gave him. He's reserving it for you.
Let ferocious Ghatotkacha fight him.
You apart, he is the only one of us
who can stop Karna. He is superbly skilled;
he has celestial and magic powers—
and ogres' strength is quadrupled at night."

Ghatotkacha, his blood-red eyes alight,
slavered at the prospect of the kill.

"I shall easily dispatch Karna
and my fame will be sung till the end of time!"
He was an awesome sight, gargantuan
with pointed teeth, skin bristly and colored
blue and red. He wore a diadem
of jewel-encrusted gold, and on his chariot,
drawn by fierce, impatient demon horses,
a hundred bells tinkled merrily.

With zest, he rushed at Karna, and there followed
such a combat, such a thrum of bowstrings,
such a wielding of celestial weapons,
such an invocation of illusions
that men in the two armies, witnessing,
thought they had never seen such a display.
The two were matched so evenly that neither
could gain the upper hand. Ghatotkacha
assumed many forms—sometimes a mountain,
then a thumb-sized creature, or many-headed
monster. Every time he changed his shape
Karna saw through the trick, and launched at him
torrents of spears and arrows, both man-made
and celestial. The courageous rakshasa
shattered Karna's bow, but he seized another.
Ghatotkacha turned into a thundercloud
and rained down stones, which Karna pulverized
as they fell. He conjured the illusion
of demon hordes, fierce as hungry tigers,
but Karna destroyed them all. And so the duel
went on and on, wonderful to behold.

Meanwhile, the rakshasa Alayudha
approached Duryodhana with a large force,
to offer his support. He had waited years
to avenge his monstrous kinsmen, Baka
and Hidimba, dead at Bhima's hands.
Now he saw his opportunity.

Duryodhana was, of course, delighted,
and the ogre troops heartened the Kauravas
with their loud roars and wildly clattering chariots.

Then, it seemed, every man on the battlefield
flung himself into the fray with curdling cries
as if this battle could decide for good
the outcome of the whole disastrous war.
Sparks from clashing weapons lit the darkness,
revealing for a moment the expressions
of rage and anguish. Some men carried torches
which threw garish light, making more profound
the pitchy blackness that surrounded them.

Alayudha made his way to Bhima
to settle scores with him. The two fought
ferociously, with great resourcefulness,
but blow by blow, illusion by illusion
the rakshasa was gaining the advantage.
Krishna spoke urgently to Arjuna:
"We're in great danger. Ghatotkacha now
should leave Karna, and lend support to Bhima.
Meanwhile, let Dhrishtadyumna and Shikhandin
take Ghatotkacha's place and harass Karna.
Nakula and Sahadeva should focus
on killing as many ogres as they can.
You and I should concentrate on Drona
and his divisions."

Ghatotkacha flew
to his father's aid, and the two monsters,
covered with wounds, clashed against each other
like two great storm clouds, raining sweat and blood.
Then Ghatotkacha, whirling a razor-sharp
scimitar, sliced off Alayudha's head
and flung it down at Duryodhana's feet.
The Pandavas beat gongs and blew their conches,

and Duryodhana started to believe
that Bhima's vow to kill him and his brothers
was already as good as accomplished.

☙

Now came radiant Karna's finest hour.
Once he had been unbeatable, but now,
deprived of the protection he was born with—
the earrings and cuirass he had relinquished
to Indra—he had only the deadly spear
the wily god had given him in exchange:
a lopsided bargain.

    But he also had
his courage, and his extraordinary skill.
He fought the Pandavas and the Panchalas
in a manner that took the breath away.
He stormed the enemy with whetted spears.
Handsome as a god, he loosed a torrent
of superb arrows, each finding its mark.
He cut off in mid-flight the stream of weapons
aimed at him. He seemed unreachable.
So quick were his movements, no one could see
when he touched his quivers, drew out the arrows,
when he nocked those arrows to the bowstring,
when he raised his fine bow and released them.
They only saw that the dust-filled night sky
was darkened even further by the cloud
of Karna's well-aimed and death-dealing shafts
that slaughtered Pandava forces by the hundred
and made them flee in utter disarray.

Ghatotkacha, maddened by the sight,
advanced again at Karna—the rakshasa
roaring like an angry lion; Karna
silent, focused, graceful, dignified.

Neither of them could gain the advantage.
Each supremely skilled, they were like dancers
engaged in a miraculous performance.

Ghatotkacha beheaded Karna's driver
and killed his horses. Then he disappeared
and, drawing on his powers of sorcery,
set the sky alight with flaming clouds
and pelted down onto the Kaurava troops
a cascade of missiles of all kinds
so that hundreds of men and animals
were massacred where they stood, powerless
to fight back. "Oh, Karna," cried the soldiers,
"save us, for pity's sake! Kill the rakshasa!"

Karna knew he had few means to defend
his forces, who were crying out to him.
Calmly, he thought; and knew what he must do,
although he clearly saw the consequences.
With resolution, he took out the spear
Indra had given him, the divine missile
he had reserved for Arjuna, the weapon
he had long counted on. He raised it high.
The spear destroyed the power of trickery
and Ghatotkacha, now visible,
terrified, began to run away.
Karna hurled the spear. That dreadful dart
blazed as it flew, hissing like a snake,
and plunged into the heart of Bhima's son,
felling him instantly. As he died, he shone
like Himavat illumined by the sun.
Then proud Karna walked away in silence.

The Pandavas had loved Ghatotkacha
and saw their forces, grim and demoralized,
shed tears of grief. But Krishna was exultant,
laughing with delight, embracing Arjuna.

"How can you be happy," asked Arjuna,
"at such a time?"
                    "I'll tell you why," said Krishna.
"With this death, our victory is certain!
If Karna still possessed the sacred spear
even you could never cause his death.
Karna is a very great hero,
greater than you know. Generous, kind
even to enemies, devoted to truth—
and a warrior of consummate skill.
There was a time when even the gods themselves
could not have defeated him. That was before
he gave away the breastplate he was born with
and the earrings that made him invincible.
The spear of Indra was his last advantage
and now it has been spent! Ghatotkacha
was created to be the instrument
of Karna's downfall. But make no mistake,
it will not be easy to overcome him
even now. You must do as I tell you:
there will come a moment, as you fight him,
when his chariot wheel will stick in the ground.
Disregarding all the rules of warfare,
you must kill him when I give the sign.

"By means of stratagems like this, I have worked
for your good, and for the good of Earth,
killing Shishupala, Jarasandha,
and Ekalavya—supremely skilled warriors
who would have taken Duryodhana's side.
The rakshasas must also be removed,
inimical to dharma as they are.
So Hidimba died, Baka, Alambusha . . .
If Karna had not killed Ghatotkacha
I would have had to contrive his death myself."

Yudhishthira, furious and grief-stricken
at the death of Ghatotkacha, started

to rush at Karna, but island-born Vyasa,
suddenly appearing, stayed his hand:
"If Karna had not used his celestial spear
on Ghatotkacha, it would certainly
have found its mark in Arjuna. In fact,
Ghatotkacha was killed by Death himself,
making Indra's spear his instrument.
Divest yourself of grief and anger, Pandava;
practice forgiveness with a cheerful heart.
Five days from now, the kingdom will be yours."

ॐ

"Tell me, Sanjaya," said Dhritrashtra,
"why did Karna waste the spear of Indra
on Ghatotkacha? Why did he not hurl it
at Arjuna or Krishna—surely, then,
my son would have gained the victory?
As it is, benighted Duryodhana
is on a direct course for Yama's realm."
"That is true," said Sanjaya. "Each night,
returning from the battle, everyone
urged Karna, 'Tomorrow, use your spear,
your never-failing weapon, on Arjuna.'
And that had always been Karna's intention.
Yet, in the event, divine illusion
confused his understanding. It was Krishna
who muddied Karna's mind, to help Arjuna."

41.

DRONA AND ASHVATTHAMAN

Sanjaya continued speaking:
Into the very blackest hours of night
fighting continued. Yudhishthira ordered
his best foot soldiers to converge on Drona
together with elephants and cavalry.
The battle was fierce at first, but gradually,
having been in the field throughout the day
and into the night, both armies lost their verve
and were drooping with weariness, staggering
blind with sleep around the field. Arjuna
decided that the Pandava troops should rest
and Drona called a halt for the Kauravas.
Some lay down on the backs of elephants,
some on chariots, but most collapsed
on the bare ground, sleeping like the dead,
or as if they lay upon their lovers' breasts.

The full moon rose, cool as a white lily,
casting a silver light, dispelling darkness.
Misty at first, its light grew ever brighter
until the field stood out in stark relief.
It woke the troops, who stretched their limbs, yawning,
then made ready to resume the fight.

Duryodhana was tense and discontented.
He spoke to Drona in a peevish tone:
"We should have attacked while they were sleeping
but you were kind to them, and now—you'll see—
they'll rise up even stronger. You always act
for their benefit, and not for mine.
With your mastery of celestial weapons
you could finish off their entire army
at a stroke; and yet you favor them."
Drona grew angry. "It would be ignoble
to use such weapons on the rank and file,
yet even this I am prepared to do
for your sake. But you forget Arjuna.
You forget that, once he is roused to fight,
no one can overcome him."

                    "That's fear talking,"
scoffed Duryodhana. "Karna and I
together with Duhshasana and Shakuni
will kill Arjuna today."

                  "Good luck!"
said Drona scornfully. "Only a fool
would talk as you do. But by all means try it!
Fight with the foremost hero of the Pandavas
and die as a virtuous kshatriya."

ॐ

Dawn was breaking on the fifteenth day.
The opal sky was reddening in the east
and soon the sun, like a great copper disc,
lifted itself above the far horizon
and cast its image on the nearby river,
the river that reflects experience
in its quiet waters, that witnesses
joys and tragedies, triumphs and horrors,
and keeps them to itself, flowing onward
imperturbably toward the sea.

Sunlight fell on the carnage of the night,
on bodies pitiful in death, their attitudes,
even their faces, strangely similar
as if, already, they had been reduced
to mere substance, meat for scavengers.

Sunlight fell on Karna's radiant face
while he stood deep in prayer, as every morning.
Now he knew who his true father was
he worshiped him with even more devotion.

Sun fell on the diminished infantry
as each man too, his hands joined together,
made obeisance to the lord of light.
Hungry, thirsty, they rubbed their aching limbs
and grumbled to each other. Yet already
they were looking round for their commanders,
shouldering their weapons, their blood stirring
in anticipation of heroic deeds.

ༀ

Useless to list each and every duel.
It was as if the war was a kind of dance
where partners changed in endless combinations
and squared up to each other, jeering, wounding,
but often with an inconclusive outcome.

Drona focused on the Panchalas
and killed three of Drupada's brave grandsons.
Enraged, Drupada, backed by Virata,
unleashed an assault on his old enemy.
With a couple of well-directed arrows,
Drona killed them both. Then Dhrishtadyumna,
shaking with grief and rage, uttered this vow:
"May the merit of all my piety

be lost to me; may I be consigned to hell
if I do not send my father's murderer
to the realm of Death before this day is out!"

A major battle centered around Drona
with Dhrishtadyumna leading the Pandavas
and Drona reinforced by Duhshasana.
It was a fair fight; no improper means
were used on either side—no poisoned arrows,
or ones with rusty tips, or barbs, or ones
with many-pointed heads, or made of bone,
or arrows that pursued a crooked course,
awkward to extract. Bhima grew angry
at the lack of progress, and he charged
through the enemy lines, making for Drona
although he was protected.

                      Duryodhana,
seeking to give support to Drona, joined in
and was about to fight with Satyaki
when a sudden memory struck him—childhood,
when he and Satyaki were the dearest friends.
They paused and gazed at one other, smiling.
"A curse on war, my friend," said Duryodhana,
"a curse on anger, folly, greed, revenge!
We were dear friends once, yet here we are,
aiming our deadly weapons at each other."
"That was then," said Satyaki with a laugh.
"We are no longer playing around in school;
we're warriors now."
                     "Where did those times go?"
said Duryodhana, "and how did this war
overtake us? It seems we can't escape
the web of time."
                 "That's how it's always been,"
Satyaki said. "We are kshatriyas
and warfare is our way. If I am dear to you

kill me at once, and I shall happily
proceed to the realm where virtuous warriors go.
I do not like to see this tragedy—
friends murdering friends." Then the Vrishni
launched into an attack on Duryodhana.
The two wounded each other bitterly
yet still they smiled, and still they fought each other.
Karna rushed to support Duryodhana,
but Bhima blocked him.

                   Then Yudhishthira
urged the Panchalas and the Matsyas
to attack Drona together. They fought hard
but Drona so fiercely staved off their attack
that soon they had to go on the defensive,
struggling against defeat. Arjuna,
who could have pressed his teacher hard, held back
from fighting all-out with him.

                   "Come, Arjuna,"
said Krishna, "things are serious. What we need
is rather less scruple, much more stratagem.
Drona cannot be overcome in battle
but if his son were dead, then, I think,
he would not fight. Therefore, let someone tell him
that Ashvatthaman has been overcome."
Neither Yudhishthira nor Arjuna
liked this plan. But Bhima took his mace
and killed a mountainous bull elephant
named Ashvatthaman, with one blow to the head.
"Ashvatthaman has been killed!" he yelled.
Drona heard, and his head swam with the shock.
But then he thought, "This must be a false report.
Ashvatthaman is too skilled a warrior
to be overcome." And he renewed
his powerful assault on Dhrishtadyumna,
though without success.

                              He was desperate
to obliterate the Panchalas.
He invoked the *Brahma* weapon, becoming
a whirlwind of destruction, killing thousands
of Panchalas with that celestial astra.
To direct a weapon of mass destruction
at ordinary mortals was unrighteous,
as Drona knew. There appeared before him
a group of rishis from the celestial realm
who censured him. "Drona, you are a brahmin,
well versed in the Vedas, devoted to truth.
It ill becomes you to act so cruelly.
Your time on earth is very nearly over;
lay down your weapons."

                         Drona was chastened.
He thought again of the voice he had heard shouting
in triumph: "Ashvatthaman has been killed!"
Knowing Yudhishthira would not speak untruth,
he called to him, "Tell me, is my son no more?"
Krishna spoke quietly to the Pandava:
"Drona is quite capable of destroying
your entire army. To prevent that
you know what you must say. To speak untruth
in order to save lives is not a sin.
Do it, Yudhishthira!" Reluctantly,
but earnest in his longing for victory,
Yudhishthira called back, "Ashvatthaman
[the elephant] is indeed dead!"

                              Until now,
Yudhishthira's chariot had always glided
a handsbreadth off the ground. After this deceit
it became earthbound.

                         Drona was seized
by profound despair. He felt ashamed

of what he had done with the *Brahma* weapon.
Now, he almost lost his mind with grief
at the loss of Ashvatthaman. Dhrishtadyumna,
who had long thirsted after Drona's life
to avenge the insult to his father,
rushed forward with his blazing bow drawn back
and aimed at Drona. "Yield, wicked brahmin,
I was born to kill you!"

     Drona rallied
to resist the Panchala, but his weapons
would not obey him as before. Nonetheless,
he tried. He still had much of the old skill,
and made things difficult for Dhrishtadyumna.
The battle became general. But the Panchala,
with fixed resolve, was dodging around Drona,
sword in hand, now leaping on his chariot shafts,
now darting beneath the horses—a marvelous
sight to see.

     Drona was reckless now.
He rushed into the thick of the Pandavas
knowing that he would die, indifferent,
inflicting enormous harm on all around.
And always Dhrishtadyumna followed him,
mounted on Bhima's chariot. "Quick, my friend,"
said Bhima, "no one but you can kill the teacher."
Then Bhima, grabbing Drona's chariot shaft,
said, "Drona, you have abandoned dharma.
Although you are a brahmin, you have pursued
the calling of a kshatriya, for gain,
and for your only son—who now lies dead
somewhere on the field. You should be ashamed.
Because of men like you, kshatriyas
are being exterminated."

     Hearing this,
Drona laid down his bow and other weapons

and, seated on his chariot, composed himself
in yoga, in profound meditation.
As he sat, seemingly still alive,
his soul was liberated from his body
and traveled to the domain of the blessed.
Some men saw his spirit flying upward
like a meteor, merging with the firmament.

Dhrishtadyumna, unaware of this,
took his sword and raised it high in triumph.
Although the Pandavas cried out in horror,
he hauled the seated Drona from his chariot,
grabbed the old man's hair, cut off his head
and flung it on the ground contemptuously
in front of the Kauravas, who backed away
in dread. And when they looked for Drona's body
they could not find it among the headless trunks
lying in their thousands all around.

Bhima roared and slapped his arms like thunder.
Leaderless, the Kaurava foot soldiers,
seized by terror, weeping, fled the field,
scattering like a flock of frightened birds.
Each intent on saving his own life,
men stumbled wildly over one other,
and animals, infected by the panic,
stampeded, so that many men were trampled
or crushed, or sliced in half by chariot wheels.

Many crowded round Duryodhana
seeking direction, but he was so shocked
he was incapable, and turned away.
Even Karna and Shakuni took flight.
"The Kauravas are totally destroyed!"—
that was the cry everywhere. The troops
dropped their weapons and armor as they ran,
convinced they would not now be needing them.

In a far part of the field, Ashvatthaman,
fighting still, caught sight of the main army
fleeing headlong, and he was astonished.
He ran to Duryodhana. "What's happening?
I've never seen the men behave like this."
Duryodhana could not bear to tell him.
Kripa, weeping, forced himself to speak.
"Ashvatthaman, your father is no more.
He was fighting against the Panchalas,
and his troops were suffering many casualties.
So then Drona invoked the *Brahma* weapon
and killed the enemy by the thousands—
he was fighting like a fit young warrior,
not like the ancient brahmin that he was."
Then Kripa told him the entire story.

Ashvatthaman almost lost his senses
with grief and rage. He cursed Yudhishthira
for his duplicity. Then he attempted
to console himself, knowing that his father
was now certainly in the heavenly realm.
Then he became distraught again, to think
that Drona had died undefended, while he,
the son who should have been his father's mainstay,
his principal protector, was elsewhere.
But he railed most against Dhrishtadyumna:
that he, a former pupil of his father,
could have treated Drona so brutally.
He swore revenge on all the Panchalas.
He swore revenge on all the Pandavas.
He swore that he would use celestial weapons,
of which he, like his father, was a master,
to grind his enemies into the dust.
Hearing these brave words from Ashvatthaman,
the Kauravas were heartened, and began
again to gather weapons, fasten armor,
harness horses to the chariots, prepared
to rally to the banners of their chiefs.

At a distance, the Pandavas picked up
the sounds of battle-readiness, and wondered
who would lead the Kaurava forces now.
"It must be Ashvatthaman," said Arjuna.
"Protecting Dhrishtadyumna will be hard,
but we must try. The brahmin must have heard
how his father was unrighteously killed
after he had laid aside his weapons.
Dhrishtadyumna was wrong. I tried to stop him
but not hard enough, and for this fault
I'm overcome with shame." Bhima was furious,
"You sound like a hermit living in the woods,
or like some priest! You are a kshatriya!
The task of a kshatriya is to rescue
others from harm. That means he must also
protect himself. You sound like an ignoramus.
You have done nothing you should be ashamed of.
Fix your mind on all the humiliations
we endured at the hands of Duryodhana.
We went into this war to be avenged,
yet now you seem half-hearted, almost scared
of what Ashvatthaman can throw at us.
Well, *I* am not afraid. If necessary,
I can destroy that brahmin single-handed!"

Dhrishtadyumna, too, vented his anger
at Arjuna. "Answer me this! Name me
the six duties of a brahmin. I'll tell you—
performing sacrifices, teaching, giving,
assisting at sacrifices, receiving gifts,
and study. Which of these did Drona follow?
He was too occupied with martial skills
to observe the dharma of his own order.
He himself acted shamefully; he was killed
by trickery—what's wrong with that? I killed him,
but I was born expressly to avenge

the insult that man offered to my father.
He used the *Brahma* weapon improperly.
Why should he not be killed by any means
available to us? Why, you killed Bhishma
through strategy. You should be offering
congratulations, not reproaching me.
I have only one regret—that I did not,
instead of throwing his gray head on the ground,
toss it among the dead untouchables!"

There was a shocked silence. No one spoke.
Then Krishna's cousin Satyaki burst out,
"Is no one going to strike this evil man
for what he just said? As if his sinful act
were not bad enough! You say that Bhishma
has been killed by Arjuna. But in fact
Bhishma's death will be of his own choosing,
and Shikhandin was the true instrument.
Wretched Panchala! Just let me hit you
with this mace, and you can return the stroke—
if you're still standing!"

          Dhrishtadyumna smiled.
"Strong words, Satyaki, but I forgive you.
Reflect on all the wrongs the Pandavas
have suffered at the hands of the unrighteous
Duryodhana. Just think about the death
of Abhimanyu. On this side of the balance
there is Drona and, yes, the defeat of Bhishma.
But sinfulness cannot always be countered
by narrow virtue. Ends justify means.
Being yourself unrighteous, nonetheless
you would rebuke those of us who are honest.
You are a sinful wretch from head to toe.
What about your slaughter of Bhurishravas
after Arjuna had cut off his arm,
and as he was sitting fasting unto death?

Was that a righteous act? And yet you dare
to censure me! Not one more word from you!"

Hearing this, Satyaki's eyes bulged red.
He seized his mace, and started to rush over
to Dhrishtadyumna, with murderous intent;
but Bhima leapt up and, planting his feet,
wrapped his arms around the furious Vrishni
and held him fast. Sahadeva spoke,
"We are all friends here, and have been for years.
Surely this hostility makes no sense.
What quality is better than forgiveness?"
But the two strong antagonists continued
roaring at each other like raging bulls.
Finally, only Krishna could calm them down.

ॐ

The Kauravas were in good heart again,
encouraged by the sight of Ashvatthaman.
He invoked the weapon called *Narayana*,
more damaging than any so far seen.
It released into the sky thousands of arrows,
razor-edged discuses, and iron balls
which in turn exploded into hundreds
of metal darts, spraying down like rain
over a wide area, piercing thousands.
Once in the body, the darts bent and twisted
inflicting terrible internal wounds.
Those who were able started to run away
and Yudhishthira, shocked at the fierceness
and scale of the attack, was in despair,
and was ready to surrender.

                    But Krishna
halted the fleeing troops. "Stop, all of you.
Lay down your weapons, leave your chariots
and stand still. Do not let yourselves even
imagine fighting. In this way, *Narayana*

will not harm you." The troops obeyed. But Bhima,
full of swagger, proposed that, single-handed,
he would resist the *Narayana* weapon
and overcome it. He started to attack
and was overwhelmed immediately.
Only because Arjuna intervened,
using his *Varuna* weapon to neutralize
Narayana, did Bhima survive. Krishna
rebuked him, and made him cast away his mace.
All at once, everything was calm;
sweet breezes blew, birds sang, men and animals
became cheerful, and geared up once more
for battle.

       "Use *Narayana* again!"
cried Duryodhana. Ashvatthaman answered,
"That is impossible. This is a weapon
that cannot be used twice." With normal weapons,
Drona's son rode out against the Pandavas,
and many warriors were severely wounded.
Arjuna, cast down by what had happened,
lashed out at Ashvatthaman. "You are proud
of your accomplishments, proud of your love
for the Kauravas, of your hatred for us.
Dhrishtadyumna who has killed your father
will follow that by crushing your pride too!"
Ashvatthaman, hurt and furious, invoked
the incendiary *Agneya* weapon. At once,
a choking darkness blotted out the field,
and blazing arrows rained down, burning all
they touched. A fiercely scorching wind blew, hotter
and hotter. The clouds rained blood. Desperate beasts
bucked and stampeded, breathing in great drafts
of burning air. Men's cries were pitiful.
It was the stuff of nightmares, multiplied.

The watching Kauravas began to cheer
to see their enemies so afflicted,

but before they could draw a second breath,
Arjuna invoked the *Brahma* weapon
to neutralize the terrible *Agneya*.
Instantly, darkness lifted and cool winds
began to blow. Now the devastation
could be seen—burnt bodies everywhere;
one complete division had been reduced
to a single welded mass of blackened flesh.
But there was joy, too, at finding how many
warriors had survived. Krishna and Arjuna
blew their conches in triumph and relief.

Ashvatthaman was disconsolate
and, laying down his bow, he left the field
and ran off aimlessly. As he wandered,
he met Vyasa. Ashvatthaman's voice
was choked with grief. "O wise sir, is there no truth
anywhere? How can this have happened?
How did my great weapon become powerless?
No one in the three worlds is capable
of baffling the *Agneya* weapon, and yet
only one enemy legion was destroyed
before it petered out. And Arjuna
and Krishna are still alive! Was there some fault
in the way I summoned up *Agneya*?"

Vyasa explained. "Mighty Narayana
in a previous existence, long ago,
as a reward for disciplined devotion
to Lord Shiva, was granted boons by him.
Nara was born as his close companion,
and each of them would be invincible.
In this earthly life, they have taken
the human forms of Krishna and Arjuna.
You too have a divine origin.
You are a portion of the great Lord Shiva.
Honor Krishna, whom Shiva greatly loves."

Calmed by these words, Ashvatthaman did so,
and called a halt to fighting for the day.

Then Vyasa visited the Pandavas.
Arjuna spoke with him. "Master, tell me
what this strange thing means: several times,
as I have gone into battle, I have seen,
gliding in front of me, a shining figure,
lance in hand, whose feet do not touch the ground.
He never throws the lance but, at his approach,
the enemy forces break. People think
I have destroyed them, but they have already
been destroyed by him, as if a thousand
lances issue from the lance he holds."

"It is Lord Shiva you have seen," said Vyasa,
"lord of the universe, all-powerful god,
the deathless deity of many names.
He is acting for you. Go forth, Arjuna.
With Krishna as your counselor and friend,
be confident that victory will be yours."

VIII

THE BOOK OF KARNA

42.

KARNA IN COMMAND

Two days later, Karna, now appointed
the next supreme commander, met his death,
cursed and alone, at the hands of Arjuna.

Sanjaya brought the news to the blind king,
sparing him nothing, and reproaching him.
"Knowing that this disaster is the outcome
of your own failings, do you not despair?
Thinking of the loss of the greatest heroes—
Bhishma, Drona, Karna . . . do you not despair?
Remembering the words of your counselors
which you ignored, do you not despair?"

"If the blind king," said Janamejaya,
"hearing of Bhishma's fall, then Drona's death
and now the death of Karna, his great hope—
if the old king did not die of sorrow,
then that is remarkable indeed."

༄

Dhritarashtra fainted, as did Gandhari
and the other women. Every last hope
for Duryodhana's victory had been pinned
on Karna. Now the old king feared the worst.
"I do despair," he groaned. "I cannot believe
that such invincible heroes could be dead!
And what of my son—is he also dead?"
His legs buckled under him; he burned with grief.
"Duhshasana is dead," said Sanjaya;
"Duryodhana still lives." Dhritarashtra,
slightly recovering, begged Sanjaya
to tell him exactly how Karna had died.

"I will," said Sanjaya, "but a wise man
does not despair, since the gods determine
whether or not effort is rewarded."
"You are right," said Dhritarashtra. "I will not
despair over-much. Now, tell me everything."

༄

After Drona's brutal, unlawful killing,
the Kauravas spent the night in misery.
Duryodhana and his main advisers
sat together, hour after hour, talking.
Sleep eluded them. They kept reflecting
on all their crimes against the Pandavas,
knowing that they were unforgivable.
Ashvatthaman urged Duryodhana

to appoint Karna as supreme commander,
praising his great prowess. Before dawn
the appropriate rites were carried out.
Karna was consecrated with sacred water.
Luxurious gifts were lavished upon brahmins
so they would pray for victory, and everyone
felt somewhat comforted.

      Yudhishthira
and Arjuna surveyed the battlefield
and looked at their own forces forming up.
"How few men are now left in both our armies,"
said Yudhishthira. "A few short days ago,
our ranks stretched further than the eye could see,
yet now they look so pitiful. Today,
I pray you will dispatch Karna, the sole
great warrior among the Kauravas."

Conches announced the start of the day's battle.
Fierce fighting began. Although Arjuna
thirsted to kill Karna, repeatedly
he was drawn away by the Trigartas,
whose dedicated mission was to slay him.
They kept provoking skirmishes, like horseflies
stinging a stallion, and although they suffered
devastating losses, they persisted,
squad upon relentless squad of them.

☙

Later, Arjuna fought Ashvatthaman,
who inflicted painful wounds on him.
Suspecting restraint, Krishna was impatient.
"Arjuna, why are you not finishing him?
Ashvatthaman is immensely dangerous
and, just as a disease, if left untreated,
will cause more trouble later, so it is

with him." Arjuna increased his efforts.
But Ashvatthaman, knowing that Arjuna
and Krishna were invincible, withdrew.

Karna was whirling round the battlefield
standing high on his chariot, armored in gold
like the sun himself. He was formidable,
attacking the Panchalas and Srinjayas
like a lion savaging a herd of deer.
He killed hundreds, and mutilated more,
while Ashvatthaman pursued the Pandyas.
The field was littered with the jeweled limbs,
heads and trunks of numberless fallen heroes.

Karna fought a duel with Nakula.
Onlookers might have thought them evenly matched,
but Karna could have killed the younger man
with little effort, had he not borne in mind
the solemn promise he had made to Kunti.
Nakula sustained only slight wounds
and was withdrawing when Karna, with his bow,
hooked him back as if he were a fish.
"Just stick to your equals," he said, laughing,
and let him go. Nakula shook with rage
and humiliation.

                    Yudhishthira
fought with Duryodhana, while their forces
battled around them. The fight was long and hard
although eventually Yudhishthira
got the better of it, and could have killed
his opponent. But Bhima, seeing this,
reminded him that he himself had vowed
to send Duryodhana to the afterlife.
So Yudhishthira withheld his weapons,
and your son, in great pain and enraged,
limped back to camp, face like a thundercloud.

☙

The sun had almost set. But now, at last,
Karna and Arjuna met face to face—
the greatest warriors in all the world!
For each, the other was the ultimate,
the glorious partner, destiny incarnate.
Almost like lovers, ardent and obsessed,
they rushed eagerly toward each other.
Only one would walk from Kurukshetra;
the other's blood would feed this tragic soil.

But this was not the final act, not yet.
This was not a duel between two heroes
but a fierce battle between the armies
which the heroes led. And Arjuna,
piloted by Krishna, did most damage,
thickly raking the Kauravas with arrows
without respite, so that the battle seemed
to be raging under a mesh of shafts.
Battered and wounded, hurled out of their vehicles,
crushed by their own elephants, stripped of armor,
weapons spent, the exhausted Kauravas
had never been more grateful for the dusk.
Joyless, they limped and straggled back to camp.

☙

Late that night, in Duryodhana's tent,
Karna took stock. "No doubt Arjuna
is a redoubtable and skilled opponent.
His bow *Gandiva* is celestial,
but my bow is finer—the great *Vijaya*
given to me by my respected teacher.
My prowess as an archer surpasses his.
No one has more courage than I do.

My will to win is absolute. But he has
Krishna—that is what makes him formidable.
Krishna advises him. Krishna inspires him.
Krishna is an unearthly charioteer,
weaving and dodging with the speed of light.
Then, too, Arjuna's horses are immortal
and swift as thought; chariot, impregnable.

"Nevertheless, I have vowed to kill him.
Tomorrow, he will die, and I will give you
victory over all the world, or else
I myself will die attempting it.
To redress the balance of advantage,
I would like Shalya as my charioteer—
no one exceeds his expertise with horses.
If he will do it, nothing on earth can stop me."

Knowing Shalya would certainly take umbrage
at being asked to drive for a driver's son,
Duryodhana spoke to him with honeyed words.
When he heard your son's proposal, Shalya
was incandescent with hurt pride and anger.
"I am a king, a distinguished warrior!
I could split the earth with my bare hands—
see the muscles on these arms of mine!
The driver's son is vastly my inferior;
how can you ask me to be his underling?
This is an insult! I will not fight at all.
Farewell—I shall depart for my own kingdom."

"It is an unusual request, I know,"
said Duryodhana. "I realize
that those belonging to the driver caste
should be the servants of kshatriyas,
not the reverse. And you are a great warrior,
ruler of the Madras, virulent dart
in the contemptible skin of your enemies.

But Karna was a foundling, as you know.
Look at him, his stature, his massive chest;
think of the natural armor he was born with—
how could he really be of inferior birth?
Would his guru have taught celestial weapons
to one whom he regarded as unworthy?

"Arjuna is able to crush our forces
only because Krishna is his driver.
You are the only warrior we have
who can be compared in skill with Krishna.
Just as Karna is greater than Arjuna,
so your skill with horses is superior
by far to Krishna's. Agree to this, my friend,
I beg you; help Karna crush the Pandavas."

Reluctant, but flattered, Shalya acquiesced—
but specified that he would speak to Karna
as he felt inclined, not with deference.
Duryodhana, relieved, reminded him
that in the war between the gods and demons,
great Brahma acted as the charioteer
of Shiva, who was able to destroy
the triple city with a single arrow.

❧

It was the seventeenth morning of the war.
The armies, much reduced, were riding out
to meet each other. The Kauravas rejoiced
to see Karna, resplendent on his chariot,
brilliant as the lord of light himself,
driven by Shalya. Impervious to fate,
full of cheerful trust and optimism,
they did not pay attention to dire portents—
thunder in a cloudless sky, fierce winds,
a shower of bones tumbling around them.

Karna's horses stumbled as they set out
to tumultuous cheering from the ranks.

As they traveled, Shalya bore in mind
the promise he had made to Yudhishthira
that he would say and do all in his power
to shake Karna's resolve and confidence.

"Do not think, Shalya, I am afraid to die,"
said Karna. "Simply, I cannot tolerate
any harm coming to Duryodhana.
Among his warriors, only I am able
to protect him and deliver victory.
With my beautiful bows, my blazing sword,
in my gorgeous chariot draped with tiger skins,
I will, today, send Arjuna to the realm
of Yama—and if all the celestials
were to combine forces to protect him,
with you as my driver I would vanquish them!"

Scornfully, Shalya laughed at him. "Stop now!
Stop these empty boasts, driver's son," he said.
"Think of the many brave and marvelous feats
Arjuna has performed. Remember how
he burned the Khandava Forest; how he snatched
Krishna's sister as his bride; how he rescued
Duryodhana from the gandharvas; recall
how he beat off the Kaurava cattle raid,
sending you scurrying for safety! Why
did you not defeat him on that occasion?
Arjuna and Krishna are unsurpassed.
Stop your bragging, if you have any sense."

"Enough! Enough!" cried Karna, full of rage.
"Time enough, when I have fought the Pandava,
to know if your taunts are fair, or puffs of smoke.
Now, charioteer, rouse up my splendid horses!
Make haste! Let us ride in search of Arjuna."

As they went he made a handsome offer
to all the Pandava soldiers whom they met:
riches for anyone who would point out
where Arjuna could be found. Shalya sneered.
"No need to waste your wealth. For sure, Arjuna
will be easy enough for you to find.
When you are face to face with him, you'll soon
regret your foolish boasts and windy speech
and long for the protection of your troops.
You'll wish you'd searched for him without success.
In your longing to engage with Arjuna
you are like a jackal, rash, deluded,
who dreams of killing a ferocious tiger.
Arjuna is a tiger; and you, my friend,
are a mere jackal, and you always will be."

"I think you are a foe in friend's clothing!"
exclaimed Karna, furious and insulted,
"but you will not succeed in weakening me.
The Madras are known as an outlandish race,
unclean in their habits and appearance.
Your women are promiscuous and uncouth,
they scratch their arses and piss standing up.
Your people drink spirits and eat disgusting,
impure substances. They commit robbery
and procure abortions—horrible!
Fickle, disloyal, unreliable,
there is no sin a Madra won't embrace.
You're clearly a stooge for the Pandavas,
planted to discourage and alarm me.
But no one will deflect me from my task.
Out of respect for Duryodhana
I hold my peace. But if you carry on
I'll separate your vile head from your shoulders."

"It is the backward citizens of Anga,"
retorted Shalya, "who are the sinful ones—

it's said they even sell off their own children.
That is the kind of people you rule over.
Still—good and bad are found in every country.
It's easy to condemn the faults of others.
What I am saying should not make you angry."

"I know better than you do," said Karna,
"the qualities of Arjuna and Krishna.
But it is neither helpful in you, nor kind,
to gloatingly remind me of them now.
I shall fearlessly fight the Pandava.
It's true, I am troubled by the double curse
I bear. But if my celestial weapons
prove ineffective, my enemy will learn
that I have many others. Just as the land
resists the mighty pounding of the ocean
so will I stand up to Arjuna
with calm and hopeful heart. I know my skill;
my gifts as an archer are at least as great
as his. And if I boast, it is because
boasting is fitting conduct for a warrior
on the brink of battle—quite deliberate,
not mindless bragging. Now, let us drive on.
I entrust myself to the gods' will."

༄

No sooner had the two armies engaged
than the Trigartas, always in the offing,
with Arjuna their solitary target,
attacked him like a swarm of killer bees.
He made short work of them, but close behind
came the legions of the Kaurava allies,
and soon the battle became more general.
Meanwhile, Karna was fighting the Panchalas
and others among the Pandava allies,
accompanied by three of his valiant sons,
and they killed dozens of leading warriors.

Grieving for Ghatotkacha, killed by Karna,
Bhima cut off the head of Karna's son,
Satyasena, beautiful as the moon.
He took aim at another son, Sushena,
but Karna blocked his arrow, and then injured
Bhima with several swift shafts of his own.
Then, in an even more violent assault,
he slammed seventy arrows into Bhima.

So it continued. Karna, as if inspired,
struck his enemies so fast and furiously
that no one could make out how he took aim,
only the blur of his strong arms in motion.
He found himself confronting Yudhishthira.
He destroyed the Pandava's bow, and then,
with ninety almost simultaneous arrows,
stripped off his armor, bright with precious jewels
like the night sky glittering with stars.
Yudhishthira, enraged, fought back with lances
and wounded Karna, who quite soon, however,
deprived him of all weapons. Yudhishthira
began to withdraw, but Karna laid a hand
on his shoulder and, mindful of his promise,
merely spoke to him. "Have you forgotten
how a kshatriya should conduct himself?
Leaving the battle to save your craven life,
you are behaving like a timid brahmin.
I would not stoop to kill one such as you."
Your nephew turned, pale with humiliation.

He shouted to his troops, "Exert yourselves!"
The Pandava troops then flung themselves against
the Kauravas, who returned their vicious blows,
yelling wildly with a savage joy
until the earth was littered with the limbs
of heroic combatants, drunk with battle.

The sound of music coming from the sky
was heard above the din, as apsarases

greeted heroes newly arrived in heaven.
That sound made those still battling below
more careless of their lives, anticipating
the pleasures that awaited them. They fought
like men possessed; if they lost their weapons
they tore at one another with their nails,
punched, bit each other, dragged at each other's hair,
hurled themselves into the lake of blood
that grew ever wider.

              Bhima had seen
Karna inflict shame on Yudhishthira
and was as eager to avenge his brother
as Karna was keen to re-engage with him.
"Truly," said Shalya, seeing Bhima coming,
"I never saw Bhima look so menacing.
He looks as if he could dispatch the creatures
of all three worlds together!" Karna laughed.
"Quite right," he said. "But if I can wound Bhima,
or destroy his chariot, then Arjuna
will come for me. And that is what I want—
have wanted all my life." Shalya drove
at Bhima, and the two great warriors clashed.
Painful wounds were inflicted by each of them,
arrows thudding into each other's body,
ripping through armor, taking the breath away.
At last Bhima, drawing his bow right back,
loosed an arrow straight at Karna's heart
with such deadly force that Karna fainted,
and Shalya drove him out of shooting range.
Exhilarated, Bhima then attacked
and killed many more of your brave sons.

ॐ

Karna, recovered, went back to the assault
against Bhima, and destroyed his chariot.

Bhima jumped down and, brandishing his mace
like Indra destroying mountains with his thunder,
charged the Kaurava elephant division,
felling hundreds. He seemed superhuman,
tackling Kaurava riders by the thousand,
smashing a hundred of the foremost chariots
and several hundred foot soldiers.

                              Meanwhile,
Karna had returned to Yudhishthira,
again succeeding in making him retreat,
and killing his charioteer. Hour after hour
battle raged between the two great armies.
To and fro went the advantage, like the sea's
shifting tides under the governing moon.
And still Karna had not come face to face
with Arjuna. Almost like one who knows
his true place is with his absent soul mate,
he longed for him. Only when they met,
weapon against weapon, body for body,
would his life achieve its resolution.

But Arjuna was fighting the Trigartas
yet again. This time, he and Krishna
blew on their conches, and while the enemy
was confused by the immense and brutal din
which scrambled the brain, Arjuna invoked
the *Naga* weapon, to paralyze the limbs
of his enemies. Each of them found
his legs encircled with strong writhing snakes,
hampering his movement. Then Susharman,
king of the Trigartas, mobilized
the *Sauparna* weapon, which brought flocks of birds
to gorge themselves, feasting on serpent flesh.
The Trigartas went back to the attack,
wounding Arjuna. Then he invoked

the *Aindra* weapon, slaughtering many thousands,
but still your son's staunch allies would not give up;
only the death of Arjuna, or their own,
could fulfill their vow.

      Karna, now,
fought like a celestial incarnate.
Wherever he was, the sun seemed specially bright.
None who saw him balancing on his chariot,
armored all in gold, could ever forget him.
Years afterward, survivors telling children
tales of their heroic past might say,
"I saw Karna fight at Kurukshetra,
mowing down the Pandavas like grass
and with extraordinary grace and beauty,
radiant as the sun. I can assure you
the world will never know his like again."

☥

The day wore on. If you could have looked down
on the battlefield from a great height,
it might have seemed an altar, with offerings
of all the precious wealth of the whole world.
The altar cloth was red, of varied shades
from poppy scarlet through to almost black.
It looked like a tapestry without design
(or, if there was one, it was not apparent)
and on it were objects, some moving, some still,
gray mounds, shining shapes, glittering colors,
gold and precious jewels without number.
What deity could ask such hard-won riches?
Who was entitled to such sacrifice?

☥

Krishna scanned the field. "I fear Yudhishthira
must be badly wounded. I cannot see

his standard anywhere, and the Panchalas
are rushing forward, as if to rescue him."
Arjuna urged Bhima to find their brother
but Bhima was reluctant, fearing to seem
as though he was avoiding Karna. Krishna
urged on the horses, and he and Arjuna
hurried to Yudhishthira's tent, and found him
lying on his bed, hurt but alive.
Joyfully, he greeted Arjuna.
"Your coming must mean Karna is no more!
All these years, the thought of him, the dread,
has never left me. And since he overcame me
yet let me go, my rage and shame have burned me
with unbearable pain. Tell me everything!
Tell me how you fought and slaughtered him."

"I had to fight again with the Trigartas,"
said Arjuna. "Karna was terrorizing
our troops, and I was just about to find him
to send him flying to the realm of Death
when I heard that you were injured, perhaps killed,
so I hurried here at once." Yudhishthira
was angry and disappointed. "Arjuna,
this is dishonorable! You made a promise
that you would kill Karna, that wicked soul.
Even at your birth, it was predicted
that you would vanquish all our enemies.
How is it that you have fallen so short?
Your bow *Gandiva* is all-powerful,
you have the blessed Krishna for your driver.
The divine monkey adorns your banner.
If, despite all this, you can't succeed,
give *Gandiva* to another warrior
and let him finish off that villain Karna!"

Arjuna blazed with anger. He drew his sword
and would have killed Yudhishthira if Krishna
had not held him back. "Arjuna! Stop now!

You came here to check on Yudhishthira;
you have seen him. Why are you so angry?"
"I made a secret promise to myself,"
said Arjuna, "that I would kill anyone
who told me I should pass *Gandiva* over
to someone braver."

         "That is no excuse,"
said Krishna. "You have violated dharma.
To draw your sword when not engaged in battle
is wrong; to draw it on your elder brother
is a deep outrage. That vow you made
was foolishness. And Yudhishthira spoke
in pain from his wounds, without reflecting."

"Oh, Krishna," said Arjuna, "you always speak
wisely. But now how can I do what's right?
If I were to kill my beloved brother
I would commit the most appalling sin.
But if I break my word, I shall be unrighteous
according to the scriptures. What's to be done?"
Krishna replied, "Scripture is well and good,
but it does not provide for every case.
Sometimes we have to use our powers of reason.
Remember the example of Kaushika:

"THERE WAS ONCE an ascetic called Kaushika, who lived
in an isolated spot at the confluence of many rivers. He
was not very well educated in the Vedas, but he made a vow
that he would always speak the truth, and became famous in
those parts as a truth-teller.

"One day, some fugitives ran past his house, being pursued by robbers, and they entered a nearby wood. Soon afterward, the robbers arrived. 'Holy one, which way did those
people go?' they asked. 'We know you always speak the truth.'

" 'They ran among the trees, over there,' replied Kaushika.

"Off rushed the robbers; they caught up with their quarry
and killed them all. And foolish Kaushika was consigned to
deepest hell.

"So, Arjuna, you must understand:
dharma is about doing the least harm—
you decide, therefore, what you should do."

Arjuna remained perplexed. "Well," said Krishna,
"I suggest you could fulfill your vow
by doing harmless harm to Yudhishthira.
You could address him disrespectfully—
that could be seen as symbolizing murder.
After that, prostrate yourself before him,
touching his feet. And, in that way, honor
on your side and on his will be satisfied.
You will avoid both fratricide and falsehood.
Then, apply yourself to fighting Karna."

A chastened Arjuna obeyed: "Yudhishthira,
what you have said to me, even if prompted
by pain and disappointment, is most unfeeling.
If Bhima had addressed me in this way,
I could have taken it, since he tirelessly
pits himself against the enemy.
But you are constantly away from battle,
protecting yourself, or else being protected.
Everything we do, the risks we take,
all the searing wounds inflicted on us,
are for your good. And the only reason
that we are here, rather than enjoying
a life of pleasant ease in Indraprastha,
is your love of gambling, nothing else.
For this alone, millions of brave men
have lost their lives, condemning wives and children
to a bereft and comfortless existence."

Having spoken, Arjuna was appalled
at what he had just said. He drew his sword,
this time to kill himself. Krishna stopped him.
"How impetuous you are, Arjuna.

Kill yourself, and you certainly will go
to the vilest hell imaginable.
Say something now to praise your own merits—
that will be tantamount to suicide."
Arjuna boasted of his accomplishments,
after which he put away his sword
and asked his eldest brother for forgiveness.

But Yudhishthira had taken Arjuna
seriously and, rising from his bed,
lamented, blaming himself bitterly.
"Bhima should be king instead of me!
I should retire to the farthest forest
in penance, for the remainder of my days."

"Yudhishthira," said Krishna, "please forgive me.
It is my fault that Arjuna was moved
to speak the way he did. Now, let all this
be forgotten. Today, without a doubt,
Karna will be killed by Arjuna."
Yudhishthira became relieved and cheerful.
"What would we do without you? You always
guide us wisely when we lose our way!"

Yudhishthira and Arjuna embraced,
weeping, comforting each other. Arjuna
bowed to his brother, clasping his two feet.
"Today, I shall kill Karna. Until I do,
I shall not return. When you next see me
it will be as Karna's conqueror."

43.

TRAGIC KARNA

As Arjuna and Krishna traveled back
to the battlefield, Arjuna grew worried
about the task ahead—to kill Karna.
Krishna spoke words of calm encouragement.
"Think about it. He has long supported
your cousin's wicked acts—and, but for him,
Duryodhana would not have risked this war.
He is much at fault—not from self-interest,
but from devotion to Duryodhana,
and from abiding rivalry with you.
He wants to give Duryodhana the world.
Without doubt, Karna is a towering force,
but even he is not invincible.

"On your cousin's side, five great warriors
remain—Ashvatthaman, Kripa, Shalya,
Kritavarman and Karna. You may well
be reluctant to kill Ashvatthaman
out of your old devotion to his father,
your beloved teacher. You possibly
feel the same for Kripa, your first guru.
Shalya and Kritavarman are your kinsmen
on your maternal side. That may mean
that you will shy away from harming them.
But you should have pure enmity for Karna,
as he does for you. Your noblest duty

is to kill him—kill him today, Arjuna;
redress the wrongs against the Pandavas!"

A new zeal took hold of Arjuna.
"Today, killing Karna in single combat,
I vow to free us from the grief we've harbored
for all these years, and bring joy to my brothers.
I shall pay my debt to the Panchalas,
honor the memory of Abhimanyu
and all our fallen heroes, and prove myself
worthy to possess the great *Gandiva*!
Today, Draupadi will be avenged!"
He bent his bow, and wiped the bowstring clean.

"Arjuna has returned to join the battle!"
shouted Wolf-belly's driver. Bhima's relief
was so great, he rewarded his charioteer
with twenty chariots, fourteen villages
and a hundred female slaves! Sadly,
the man did not live to enjoy these riches.

In the desperate assault that followed
huge losses were inflicted by both sides,
mainly achieved by Karna and Arjuna
although the two did not come head to head.

In a slight lull in the hostilities,
Arjuna came within sight of Karna.
Like a swollen river in full spate,
Karna was laying waste to the enemy
and warriors' bodies, chariots, animals
were scattered all around, like fallen trees.

Then the thunder of Arjuna's chariot
was heard, coming closer. "Karna," cried Shalya,
"the man you're seeking is approaching fast.

Attack! No one else can overcome him.
Summon your great skill."

                     "Ah," said Karna,
"for the first time, I feel you are on my side.
I shall strain every nerve to kill Arjuna.
I know the son of Pandu has no equal.
He can shoot a dozen arrows in the time
another man shoots one. And he has Krishna.
Seeing them advance toward me, I sense
my skin grow cold, my hair standing on end.
But I also feel a calm resolve.
My whole life has prepared me for this battle.
If I fail, I shall sleep on the black earth.
Either way, I shall achieve my purpose."

The Kaurava army was now breaking up
in dismal disarray, deserting Karna,
cowed by the force of Arjuna's attacks.
But Karna, with unruffled authority,
rallied them to come to his protection.
He was like a rock to which they clung.
Karna's son, Prasena, lost his life,
and Karna, in furious revenge, renewed
his onslaught on the Panchalas, killing
Dhrishtadyumna's son, wounding Shikhandin.

Meanwhile, Duhshasana was fighting Bhima.
The mortal enemies wounded each other
with arrows; then Bhima took up his mace.
"Today, wicked soul," he roared, "I shall drink
your pulsing blood, as I have sworn to do."
He hurled the mace with such force Duhshasana
was knocked the distance of at least ten bow-lengths
and lay writhing in agony on the ground.
Bhima saw, in vivid memory,
this man assaulting blameless Draupadi
in the gaming hall. He sprang forward,
planted his foot on Duhshasana's throat

and, ripping his chest open with his sword,
drank the warm blood from his still-beating heart,
gulping it down with relish. "This blood tastes
better than honey, better than mother's milk!
Soon I will also end Duryodhana's life,
honoring the second vow I made."

All who witnessed this were terrified.
Bhima's sheer animal ruthlessness
appalled Karna. "Take heart," said Shalya, "focus
on Arjuna; he's your only business now.
And here is your eldest son, Vrishasena,
rushing to your support."

                    Vrishasena,
seeing that his father was set back
by Bhima's act of butchery, launched himself
against the Pandavas. He mangled Nakula,
then vented his anger against Arjuna,
lodging arrows in him, and in Krishna.
The Kauravas were joyful. But wiser heads
knew that these great warriors would swat him
as if he were an irritating fly
whenever they saw fit. Indeed, Arjuna
wrathfully called to Karna, "I know that you,
together with other wicked Kauravas,
killed my son, courageous Abhimanyu,
when he was unprotected and alone,
contrary to all the rules of war.
For that I have vowed to kill this son of yours,
and after that, send you to Yama's realm!"

Then, with ease, Arjuna took his bow
and with a few razor-headed arrows
cut off the arms and head of Vrishasena
who, like a lovely flowering tree that's stricken
by a bolt of lightning, fell to earth.

Karna, scorched by grief, rushed at Arjuna.
"Keep a cool head," said Krishna. "Our brave army
is breaking up in terror at the sight
of Karna galloping full tilt toward us."
"Our victory is assured," said Arjuna.
"Contemptible Karna is already dead!"

❧

Even at this late hour, Ashvatthaman
approached Duryodhana, arguing for peace.
"Listen to me, you know I am your friend.
Stop the fighting. Arjuna and Krishna
are impossible to beat. The Pandavas
never wanted war for its own sake—
you forced it on them. If now you offer them
half the kingdom, I know they will agree.
Offer peace, and regain their goodwill.
The whole kingdom will be better off.
I will be the go-between in this,
and I will speak to Karna."

                         Duryodhana
was silent. He considered. Then he sighed.
"What you say is good sense, Ashvatthaman.
But think how Bhima killed Duhshasana
as though he were a beast. And the Pandavas
will never trust me, thinking of the ways
I have made them suffer. How can there be peace?
Arjuna is tired from his many battles—
Karna still has a chance of killing him.
I know you're speaking with the best intentions
but—no. Now, hurry back to the front line."

❧

The time had come. This would be the duel
that would decide the outcome of the war.

It struck onlookers that the two combatants
looked surprisingly alike: both tall,
broad-chested, well-proportioned, beautiful,
both god-like in their energy and strength.
Among the demons and celestial beings,
some supported Arjuna, some Karna.
The sky was for Karna, the earth for Arjuna.
Vaishyas, shudras and those of mixed descent
cheered for Karna, while Arjuna was the hope
of the higher orders.

                The gods themselves
were divided between the two heroes.
Indra supported his son, Arjuna,
while Surya sought victory for Karna.

Karna asked Shalya, "Tell me, if I am killed
what will you do then?" Shalya replied,
"I will myself kill Krishna and Arjuna."
Arjuna asked Krishna the same question.
"Arjuna," said Krishna, smiling, "the earth
will split into a thousand jagged fragments
before Karna will succeed in killing you!
If it did happen, it would be a sign—
the last days of the world would be approaching,
and I would kill both Karna and Shalya
with my bare hands!" Arjuna was joyful.
"Today I shall grind Karna in the dust,
and make sorrowing widows of his wives.
Today, Abhimanyu's grieving mother
will receive some comfort, and today
Kunti will receive the news she longs for."

To the deafening sound of drums and conches,
the two great heroes closed on one another
like two clashing banks of rain-filled cloud,
or like two maddened elephants in season.

Although each warrior was supremely skilled
at cutting the other's arrows in mid-flight,
soon blood was flowing freely on both sides.
Bhima, thinking Karna was doing better,
squeezed his hands in rage. "Come on, Arjuna,
how can you let your arrows miss their mark!
Think how this wretched man insulted us!"
And Krishna, too, reproached him. "Arjuna,
the Kauravas are cheering as though they think
Karna has won. Take *Sudarshana*,
my razor-headed discus, and separate
Karna's head from his contemptible body!"

Arjuna braced himself for greater effort.
He invoked the lethal *Brahma* weapon,
but Karna, smiling, baffled it in mid-flight,
rendering it harmless. Arjuna
called up other celestial weapons, able
to inflict huge damage. So did Karna.
He fought with such panache, such superb skill,
it looked as if he would certainly prevail
as arrows poured in torrents from his bow.
The watching Kauravas yelled with delight.

But the battle was not over. The fine bodies
of both great warriors were slick with blood
but both had plentiful reserves of strength,
courage and energy. Karna released
five arrows like snakes, piercing Krishna
and passing through him to sink into the earth.
In fact, these were snakes indeed, related
to one Arjuna had killed at Khandava.
Incensed, Arjuna cut up these arrows,
and sent them winging back with such force
that Karna, deeply wounded, trembled in pain.
Then Arjuna sprayed the surrounding Kauravas
with such a dense onslaught of darts and arrows

that the sky turned black. They fled in terror.
Unsupported, Karna felt no fear
but rushed at Arjuna with a joyful heart.

O king, never before has there been seen
a duel between such transcendent warriors.
Having many weapons of different kinds
at their disposal, the two fighters displayed
miraculous and beautiful maneuvers;
and the celestials, watching from the sky,
shouted in admiration, sprinkling
the heroes with cool, perfumed sandal-water.

Ashvasena, Arjuna's snake enemy,
managed to insinuate himself
into Karna's quiver, where he took shape
as a blazing arrow. Nocked on the bowstring,
he caused the sky to shimmer with evil portents—
thunderbolts and fiery meteors.
"Use another arrow," shouted Shalya,
"that one will not have the effect you want."
But Karna rejected the advice, and loosed
the awe-inspiring arrow. It seemed to carve
a channel in the firmament as it flew
straight for Arjuna's head. Calmly, easily,
Krishna pressed down the chariot with his feet,
causing it to sink. In this way, the arrow
did not behead Arjuna, but merely knocked
his lovely jeweled diadem to the ground.
The Pandava bound his hair with a white cloth.

The snake hissed at Karna, "When you shot me
you did not aim with care. That is why
I was unable to decapitate him."
"Who are you?" asked Karna.
                              "I am a hater
of Arjuna, my mother's murderer.
Shoot me again, and you will quickly see

his head knocked from his shoulders." Karna said,
"Karna will not win through another's power;
and I will not shoot an arrow a second time."
"As you please," hissed the snake, and he aimed himself
straight at Arjuna—who sliced him up
in mid-flight, and sent him writhing, spinning
to earth.

        Krishna righted the chariot
and, as he did so, Karna attacked.
Arjuna, with several well-judged shots,
penetrated Karna's armor; exultant,
Karna struck him back, laughing aloud.
Arjuna, with preternatural skill,
stripped Karna of his beautiful gold headdress,
his jeweled earrings, and his shining armor,
then wounded him so deeply and severely
that Karna gasped, staggered, streamed with blood.

The driver's son set down his bow and quiver,
thus signaling a respite. Arjuna,
observant of the rules, let fall his bow,
but Krishna urged him on. "Don't let up now!
Karna is your hate-filled enemy.
Kill him while you can—as Indra did
when he slaughtered the demon Namuchi.

Arjuna obeyed, and soon Karna
was spiked with arrows all over his body.
But, rallying, he snatched up his fine bow
and pelted Arjuna with fiery shafts.
Now he struggled to recall the words
of the mantra for the highest *Brahma* weapon,
but his mind was blurred; he could not grasp them.
His inner light was wavering in him.

The hour of Karna's death was fast approaching.
Time itself, whispering in his ear,

told him that Earth was starting to devour
his chariot wheel. The chariot lurched, tilted
and stuck fast in the ground. His lovely bow
fell from his hand. Mortally wounded now,
wringing his hands in despair, Karna cried,
"I have followed dharma, but righteousness,
after all, does not protect the righteous.
Instead, righteousness is destroying me!"

As Krishna and Arjuna closed in on him
Karna climbed down from his chariot
and struggled to release his mud-bound wheel.
"Hold off!" he cried. "Only a coward strikes
when his opponent has laid down his arms.
Arjuna, you are a man of principle,
you observe dharma—do what you know is right!"

Krishna shouted, "It is well and good
for you to plead dharma when you're in trouble.
Where was dharma when you outraged Draupadi?
Where was it when you helped Duryodhana
to plot the murder of the Pandavas?
And where, when you connived in their exile?
And when young Abhimanyu was outnumbered,
where was dharma then?"

                        Karna bowed his head.
He picked up his bow. Then Arjuna destroyed
Karna's glittering bejeweled standard,
symbol of Duryodhana's ardent hopes.
Seeing that, a shocked lament arose
from all the watching Kauravas. Arjuna
took out his hefty arrow *Anjalika*
with blade as broad as two hands joined together
and, placing it in his bow *Gandiva*,
he prayed that it would find its rightful mark.
And aimed. *Anjalika*, flaming like a comet,

flew with unearthly speed, straight and true,
and struck off Karna's head. It fell to earth
as the red disc of the sun drops at sunset.
It was afternoon.

         As Karna's head and trunk
fell, still lovely, glistening with blood,
the light that always seemed to shine from him
left his body, and rising through the sky,
traveled to the sun, and merged with it.
Everyone saw that. Karna's fallen head
lay like a quenched fire after a sacrifice,
or like a boulder loosed from a mountainside
by a violent storm.

         When Karna fell,
the rivers ceased to flow, the sun turned pale,
the planet Mercury seemed to change its course
and the earth trembled.

ॐ

         It is said by some
that as Karna's spirit left his body,
he saw a brahmin (Krishna in disguise)
who asked him for gold. Having none to give,
with a stone, Karna knocked out his own teeth,
with their gold caps, washed them, and offered them.
Then Krishna granted him the supreme vision
of his divine self, riding on Garuda,
and promised him whatever boon he wished.
Karna considered choosing victory
for Duryodhana. But he asked, rather,
that Kunti should be brought news of his death.
He knew she would then come to the battlefield
and tell his brothers who he really was.
He asked a second boon. In his life,

he had been unable to gain the merit
of feeding others, since no one would want
hospitality from a driver's son.
He asked Krishna that in his next birth
he should have that chance. Krishna blessed him
and granted his wish.

Sanjaya went on:
When Karna fell, the fighting was suspended
and warriors of both sides gathered round
in disbelief. Some of them were awestruck,
some were fearful, others sorrowful,
sobbing in grief, according to their natures.

The Pandavas were wild with exultation.
They blew their conches, shouted, waved their arms
and flapped their garments, dancing in delight.
Bhima roared and slapped his arms in triumph.
Arjuna, his vow fulfilled, relinquished
hostility for Karna. Yudhishthira
felt he had been reborn, and had to look
and look again at the body of the man
he had so long feared. "What good fortune,"
he exclaimed, "has today delivered
victory! Krishna, today I have become
king of the earth, together with my brothers,
and it is thanks to you."

Duryodhana's troops,
in disarray, milled around aimlessly
like horses without riders, or like boats
bobbing directionless on a choppy sea.
Grim, sorrowful, Shalya drove Karna's chariot,
now freely moving, away from the scene of death.
Duryodhana was shocked past all expressing.

Tears poured from his eyes. But seeing his men
leaderless, he gathered his resolve
and rallied them. Then, for a little while,
battle resumed between the two armies.
Many of the warriors fled the field.
Duryodhana fought bravely, and attempted
to bring them back. "What is the use of running?
The Pandavas will pursue you everywhere.
Better to fight bravely and die with honor."
Reluctantly, with faces pale as ash,
the men turned, and obeyed your son's command.

Shalya turned Duryodhana's attention
to the hideous sights of the battlefield:
the bloody corpses of men and animals,
the chaos of war's paraphernalia.
"You yourself are the cause of all this horror.
The sun is hanging low over the hills;
let the troops retire for the night."

Later, Duryodhana gave way to grief.
"Alas, Karna! Alas!" he cried, and stood
weeping beside his friend, who lay surrounded
by hundreds of gently glowing oil-filled lamps.

IX

THE BOOK OF SHALYA

44.

DEFEAT FOR DURYODHANA

"Tell me what happened after the death of Karna,"
said King Janamejaya. "I never tire
of hearing of my ancestors' great deeds."
Vaishampayana continued to recite
island-born Vyasa's epic poem.

After hearing of the death of Karna,
Dhritarashtra spent his time in dread,
braced for the most crushing news of all.
It was not long coming. Sanjaya arrived
stumbling, trembling, weeping as he approached,
to tell him, first, of the deaths of Shalya
and Shakuni. Then, that his last son,
his cherished Duryodhana, his first-born,
had fallen, felled by Bhima!

So appalling,
so harrowing was the news that the whole court
collapsed unconscious from the shock of it—
as if they themselves, in sympathy,
embraced Earth in the final swoon of death.
Slowly, they revived, speechless with distress.
"Ah!" wept Dhritarashtra, "this heart of mine
must be made of adamantine rock
that it does not shatter in my breast!
But I always knew this day would come,
cursed with the eyesight of insight as I am.

"When sly Shakuni tricked Yudhishthira,
trapped in the ill-fated gambling match—
then, Sanjaya, I lost hope of victory.
When Draupadi was dragged into the hall
and treated like a common prostitute—
then, Sanjaya, I lost hope of victory.
When I heard that Arjuna had obtained
the *Pashupata* weapon from Lord Shiva—
then, Sanjaya, I lost hope of victory.
When I was told that Duryodhana
had been saved from gandharvas by Arjuna—
then, Sanjaya, I lost hope of victory.
When I heard that Krishna was supporting
the Pandavas in this horrific war—
then, Sanjaya, I lost hope of victory.
And when I heard that Bhishma had fallen—then,
then, Sanjaya, I lost hope of victory.

"And yet, Duryodhana, my most loved boy,
how confident you were of victory.
You described to me our powerful allies,
how they would dedicate their lives and wealth
to your cause. How Krishna would not fight.
How the Pandava force was dwarfed by ours.

So I imagined the Pandavas would die.
Now, thinking of the death of all our heroes,
and all my sons—what can this be but fate?

"Oh, come back to me, my Duryodhana,
prince of princes, so loving, so proud-hearted!
How could you abandon me in my blindness?
Who will be my refuge in my old age?
Who will greet me when I wake, calling me
'lord of all the world'? Who will embrace me,
who will love me now? How could you die
with so many strong kings to protect you?
So many brave men slaughtered for your sake,
and all five Pandavas alive, unharmed!
What else can this be but the work of fate?
There is nothing left for me in this life
but to pass my last days in the forest.

"Tell me how it came about, Sanjaya.
What happened after Karna had been killed?"

Sanjaya continued his narration.

ॐ

In the evening of the seventeenth day,
a deputation went to Duryodhana
led by Kripa, urging the stubborn prince
to sue for peace. Duryodhana refused.
"I understand you speak to me as friends,
but your suggestion is impossible.
What we have done to harm the Pandavas
has lit a fire that cannot be extinguished
while I live. How can they forgive us?
Even if they could (I know Yudhishthira
is compassionate), how could I exist
beholden to the Pandavas? I have lived

as a prince on my own terms; I have ruled
righteously—my household is well cared-for,
I have been generous and just. I have conquered
many kingdoms. Now nothing remains
but to die fighting gloriously in battle—
an end befitting a kshatriya.
Only through death can I discharge my debt
to those brave warriors who have died for me.
I cannot preserve my life fully aware
that they have given theirs to serve my cause.
And what kind of life could I enjoy,
bereft of brothers, kinsmen, friends, my kingdom—
knowing that every breath I draw, I owe
to Yudhishthira? No! I who have been
lord of the earth will make my way to heaven
by fair fight. It will not be otherwise."

༄

At dawn next day, Shalya was consecrated
as commander. He mounted his chariot,
its battle standard bearing a golden furrow,
and made a speech to his diminished forces.
The Kaurava troops cheered and beat their drums.
Compared with the uproar on the war's first day,
the warriors' shouts rang thin and pitiful.
But still, those who were left were in good heart.
The two armies marched out. Battle began.

Unnecessary for every dreadful detail
to be rehearsed in full. I need only say
that, by the time the sun had reached its zenith,
the war that pitted cousin against cousin
was at an end. Almost every Kaurava
was stretched out dead or dying on the field.

At first, Shalya had seemed unbeatable,
a powerhouse of destruction. But Yudhishthira,

having the end securely in sight, perhaps,
fought the Madra king ferociously
and after a lengthy duel, fairly fought,
he cut down Shalya. This was the opponent
Krishna had marked out for him to kill,
his personal share of the victory.
The ruler of the Madras, arms outstretched,
fell facedown, embracing his own shadow,
clinging to the earth like a dear beloved.
The Pandavas cheered, "Now that Shalya's dead
Duryodhana's fortune has deserted him!"

The Kaurava troops fled; the Pandavas
flew after them. Then turning, rallying,
the Kauravas fought back. Duryodhana
was backed by Shalva, chief of the mlecchas,
who inflicted damage on the Pandavas,
mounted on a great war elephant
of quite exceptional strength and bravery.
The elephant attacked the chariots
of many warriors, snatching them up like toys,
dashing them onto the ground in splinters.
But Satyaki, with Bhima and Shikhandin,
managed to head it off, and Dhrishtadyumna
gave it the coup de grâce with his heavy mace
and then cut off the head of the beast's master.

❧

Dhritarashtra and Gandhari listened,
their faces drawn, their eyes brimming with tears
as Sanjaya described what happened next.

Duryodhana fought with despairing courage,
the way a man fights standing on the brink
of oblivion. Almost all his brothers
had been killed by now. His remaining wish
was for this catastrophe to finish,

but finish in a blaze of bravery.
Arjuna, too, was eager for the end.
He still marveled that Duryodhana
had chosen war, despite the good advice
he had received from all his counselors,
listening instead to Karna—as if born
to bring about the destruction of the world.

Now, hurling himself into the midst
of the enemy, Arjuna fought on.
He encountered the rump of the Trigartas
and killed them all, with their king, Susharman.
Sahadeva slaughtered Uluka, then
Uluka's father, Shakuni the gambler,
after a bitter fight with every weapon,
parting his head cleanly from his shoulders.
His troops fled in confusion, but Duryodhana
shouted, "Turn back! Face the Pandavas!"

Bhima attacked your few remaining sons
until Sudarsha, the ninety-ninth brother,
was felled. Duryodhana's great fighting force
was finished, almost down to the last man.
Just three great chariot warriors remained—
Kripa, Ashvatthaman and Kritavarman.

☙

"How many were left of the Pandava force?"
asked the blind king.
                    "Two thousand chariots,
seven hundred elephants, five thousand horses
and ten thousand troops, led by Dhrishtadyumna."

"And what did my Duryodhana do then?"

Sanjaya went on:
Duryodhana, his chariot smashed beneath him,

took his mace and fled on foot toward
a lake some distance off. The lake was called
Dvaipayana. The words of Vidura
came back to him—his wise uncle had known,
long ago, how events would turn out,
even before the fateful, fatal dice game.
He was blind with tears. I followed him
but, on the way, encountered Satyaki
and Dhrishtadyumna. "No point in sparing this one,"
said the Panchala, jeering. Satyaki
raised his sword and was about to kill me
but Vyasa appeared and stayed his hand.
After I had given up my weapons,
Satyaki, laughing, sent me on my way.

I hurried after Duryodhana
and found him weeping. "Sanjaya," he said,
"tell my father that I have nothing left,
nothing in the world worth living for.
I shall immerse myself in this deep lake."
Then, by enchantment, making himself a space
deep within the lake, and sealing the surface,
Duryodhana sank and disappeared from view.

Presently, I encountered Kritavarman
approaching with Kripa and Ashvatthaman,
bringing their horses to the lake to drink.
I told them what Duryodhana had said
and pointed out the place where he had vanished
beneath the water. "Alas!" sighed Ashvatthaman,
"Perhaps he did not know we were still alive.
The four of us could have fought on, even now."

⚜

The three companions and I went back to camp.
The whole place was in panic. In muddled haste,

everything was being dismantled—tents
taken down, equipment roughly bundled
and loaded onto carts. Duryodhana's wives,
sobbing and terrified, were setting off
back to the city with their aged servants.
Scared by rumors of Pandava reprisals,
even local farmers left their fields
and hurried toward the city for protection.

Yuyutsu, who had fought for the Pandavas,
now set off to return to Hastinapura,
anxious for your welfare. He met Vidura,
who was overjoyed to see him. "Thank the gods,
Dhritarashtra has one son still alive
to give him comfort in his terrible grief!"

Duryodhana's three remaining friends
hid beside the empty Kaurava camp,
and watched as Yudhishthira and his brothers
came looking for Duryodhana, searched the site
but, failing to find him, went to their own camp.
Once the Pandavas had gone, the three men
hurried to the lake, and called the prince.
"Come out, Duryodhana, and fight the Pandavas.
The four of us can take them by surprise
and quickly overcome them." Duryodhana
answered from the depths of the lake. "My friends,
I thank you, but this is not the time to fight.
You are tired, and I am badly battered.
Tomorrow, for sure, we'll fight the enemy."
Ashvatthaman tried to change his mind.
"If I do not kill our enemies
this very night," he cried, "then may I never
enjoy the fruits of my pious sacrifices."

It happened that some hunters were nearby,
men who had been bringing Bhima baskets
of fresh meat every day. They overheard
the conversation and, anticipating
a fat reward, they approached the Pandavas.
Bhima and his brothers were delighted
and relieved to have news of Duryodhana.
Word spread quickly, and Yudhishthira,
with a group of followers, rode out
toward the seemingly deserted lake.
Their chariot wheels caused the earth to tremble
and Duryodhana's three friends, in alarm,
knowing the prince was safe, crept quietly
behind a tree a little distance off,
where they settled down to rest for a while.

The Pandavas arrived at the lakeshore.
"That wretch is skulking underneath the water
by some trickery," said Yudhishthira.
"No one can reach him. But he won't escape me!"
"Ways and means," said Krishna. "Against tricksters
you have to use trickery of your own—
that is how the gods themselves have conquered
slippery enemies. Nothing wrong with that."

"Duryodhana!" Yudhishthira called out,
"Why are you hiding like a low criminal?
Because of you, an entire generation
of noble warriors has been wiped out,
yet you seek to preserve your worthless life.
Come out and fight! You are a kshatriya!
Furthermore, you are a Bharata.
People speak of you as a great hero—
you've always boasted of your bravery.
But here you are, lurking in fear, avoiding
the battle you yourself have brought about.

All these days, you have seen your friends and kinsmen
slaughtered in your cause, yet you thought yourself
immortal. How little you understand!
Where is your pride? Where is your courage now?
Do your duty, man, come out and fight."

Duryodhana replied from the lake's depths.
"You are wrong. I am not afraid of you.
I did not leave the battle to save my life.
I was alone, wounded, without a chariot,
deprived of driver, weapons, followers.
For this reason only, I wanted rest—
not from fear, or grief, only fatigue.
Why don't you yourselves rest for a while.
Then I shall certainly rise up from this lake
and fight—and destroy every one of you!"

"We have rested enough," said Yudhishthira.
"Come out and fight! Either win the kingdom
or else die honorably at our hands
and pass on to the realm reserved for heroes."

Duryodhana's voice rose from beneath the water.
"Without my friend and brothers to share it with,
the kingdom of the Bharatas means nothing.
Without heroic kshatriyas to enjoy her,
Earth is like a widow—you can take her.
I still, however, wish to crush your pride,
bring low the Pandavas and the Panchalas.
Take the kingdom! Enjoy it if you can,
stripped as it is of warriors, all its wealth
devoured by devastating war. As for me,
I no longer wish to live. I shall retreat
to a life of contemplation in the woods."

"I do not pity you," said Yudhishthira.
"You may well, now that everything is lost,
be willing to give up the kingdom to me.

But the kingdom is no longer yours to give.
And how can you think I would accept
a gift from you, when you refused to cede
even as much terrain as would be covered
by a needle's point?! Do you not see
that if both of us remain alive,
no one will understand who won this war?
You cannot choose to live. I could choose
to let you live; but I will not do so.
Come out of there and fight!"

                    Duryodhana,
unused to being talked to in this way,
was mortified, and sighed like a hissing snake.
"This is unfair—there are so many of you,
all well equipped and in good health, while I
am stripped of everything, badly wounded;
and I am all alone. Nevertheless,
if you agree to fight one at a time,
I shall kill each one of you with my mace.
I am not in the least afraid of you.
Today I shall discharge my debt to my friend,
my brothers and those kings who died for me."

"I see you now remember what is due
from a kshatriya," said Yudhishthira.
"A pity your sense of what is a fair fight
deserted you when you and your companions
killed Abhimanyu, tearing at his flesh
like a pack of wolves. Every one of you
was a trained warrior; you were all steeped
in the protocols of war! Nevertheless,
I agree that we will fight you singly.
So come out. Prepare to meet your death!"

Hearing this, Duryodhana stirred the water
and struggled, dripping, from the lake, his body

streaked with blood. His mace was in his hand.
"Shoulder this armor," said Yudhishthira,
"and bind your hair; here is a well-made helmet.
Furthermore, you may choose your opponent.
And if you win, then you shall have the kingdom."

"I am prepared to fight each one of you,"
roared Duryodhana, "and I shall kill you
one after another. No one can match me!"

While Duryodhana boasted in this way,
Krishna took Yudhishthira aside.
He was alight with anger. "You are mad!
By letting him decide his adversary
and promising the kingdom if he wins,
you're gambling with your future—it's as if
you're back in the gaming hall, taking a chance!
Who but a fool would risk losing the kingdom
when it's within his grasp? Duryodhana
is a master with the mace. All those years
when you were exiled in the forest, he
practiced every day against a statue
shaped like Bhima.

                    "Bhima's your only hope.
He has enormous strength and stamina
but Duryodhana has the greater prowess,
and prowess always wins. None among you
is capable of beating Duryodhana
in a fair fight. We are in great danger,
thanks to your stupid gesture. It seems to me
the Pandavas were born to live in exile!"

Duryodhana chose to fight with Bhima,
the man he hated most in all the world.
Having heard Krishna reprove his brother,

Bhima said, "Krishna, you should not despair.
I have waited thirteen years for this,
living in torment, knowing that vile villain
was enjoying every luxury, while we
wandered in deerskins in the wilderness.
Duryodhana may have practiced with his mace,
but I have practiced with my mind, reliving
every iniquity that wretch committed.
Be happy, brother, today I shall regain
your kingdom—and restore my peace of mind."

Krishna applauded him, "That is heartening talk!
But in fighting Duryodhana, take care
not to rely on strength and rage alone;
you will need all the skill at your command."

The two cousins squared up to one another.
But at that very moment, Balarama,
Krishna's older brother, was seen approaching.
A great mace warrior, he had been the teacher
of both Bhima and Duryodhana.
Before the war, rather than take sides,
he had gone on an extended pilgrimage
to the sacred fords. Now he had returned.
He suggested that the fight take place
at Samantapanchaka, part of the field
which was revered, in the domain of gods,
as the sacred northern altar of Lord Brahma.
Whoever died in battle there was certain
to go straight to heaven, to dwell with Indra.
The group set off, Duryodhana ill at ease
walking with his hated enemies.

The auspicious place chosen by Balarama
was beside the river. The ground was firm,
trees grew on the slope, providing shade
for the spectators. Then a formal challenge

was issued by Duryodhana, and all noticed
disturbing portents—fierce winds skittering
pebbles along the ground, clouds of dust,
thunder rumbling in a clear blue sky.
Bhima exulted, "This is a sure sign:
today Duryodhana will be defeated!
Today he will rest his head on the bare earth;
never again will he see his loving parents,
never enjoy the company of women.
Today the sufferings of the Pandavas
will be requited!"

　　　　　Then the fight began.
Never were combatants more furious.
Half a lifetime's hatred and resentment
went into every blow. They were well matched,
and each took special pleasure in the knowledge
that he was pitched against a worthy foe.
Both were beautiful in their massive strength,
their graceful footwork as they made their moves
dodging, defending, attacking, circling
in intricate maneuvers. When they clashed
sparks flew, the ground shook with the force of it.
Body blows drew torrents of blood, and made
the fighters reel and stagger; but that served
only to reinforce their strength of purpose.

"Who is doing better, in your view?"
Arjuna asked. "Bhima has strength," said Krishna,
"but he will never win in a fair fight;
indeed, I see that he is struggling now.
He must bend the rules—especially
since Yudhishthira has been so foolish."

Standing to Duryodhana's left, Arjuna
slapped his own thigh. Bhima saw the sign.
Soon Duryodhana, to avoid a blow,
jumped—and Bhima, seizing his chance, smashed

his mace full strength against the Kaurava's thighs,
breaking both instantly. Duryodhana
crashed to the ground groaning. The Pandavas
were filled with joy. Bhima had won. The war
was over!

       Bhima strode round Duryodhana
and scuffed his head with his foot. "Not boasting now?
Where is your scorn, your dirty tricks, you wretch?"
Many onlookers were scandalized
by Bhima's behavior to a dying man
and Yudhishthira reproved him, "Bhima,
stop now! You have fulfilled your vow at last.
For all his evil actions, Duryodhana
is a Bharata, our kinsman. You must not
touch a kinsman with your foot." He approached
Duryodhana, with streaming eyes. "Oh, cousin,
it is your own folly and wickedness
that have brought you to destruction. Destiny
cannot be averted. But I envy you.
Heaven will welcome you as a brave hero;
we must face the widows' bitter grief."

Balarama was extremely angry.
"Shame on you, Bhima! All the treatises
are clear that in a fight, no blow must strike
below the belt. Surely you know that!"
The furious Balarama rushed at Bhima,
but Krishna wrapped his powerful arms around him
and stopped his brother in full flight. "Come now,"
he said, "the Pandavas are our friends and kin.
Bhima was fulfilling a vow he made
when Duryodhana insulted Draupadi.
The rishi Maitreya cursed Duryodhana
himself, saying Bhima would break his thigh.
And we have now entered the age of Kali;
breaches of dharma are to be expected."

Upright Balarama was unconvinced
by his brother's fraudulent reasoning.
"Bhima will be known as a crooked fighter.
Duryodhana, on the other hand, acted
with propriety, and will go to heaven.
His blood is a libation on the ground
of this auspicious place."

                Krishna spoke
to Yudhishthira, reproving him.
"Why did you do nothing when Bhima kicked
Duryodhana in the head?" Yudhishthira
was unhappy. "I don't approve that action
but, remembering all Bhima has endured,
I felt he should be forgiven for that act,
righteous or otherwise." Half-heartedly,
Krishna said, "So be it," and turned away.

Bhima bent before Yudhishthira
with joined hands, lit up with happiness.
"Today, O king, the earth, restored to peace,
is yours. May you rule justly and well."
With a grateful heart, Yudhishthira thanked him.
Bhima was reveling in the victory,
rejoicing in the rout of his enemies.
All his friends and allies gathered round
to wish him well, shouting, blowing conches,
twanging their bowstrings, dancing in delight.
"Bhima, your fame will spread throughout the world,
bards will sing of you, eulogists praise you
for defeating the wicked Kaurava.
Jaya! Jaya!"
                Krishna upbraided them.
"It is not right for one who has been slain
to be slain a second time with cruel words
and triumphant glee."

Meanwhile, your son
was lying on the ground in agony.
Raising himself painfully on his elbows
he spoke to Krishna. "Don't think I don't know
that Bhima recalled his vow to break my thigh
only because of you. That is just one
of many devious and sinful actions
perpetrated by you in this war.
But for you, Bhishma would be uninjured,
Bhurishravas and Drona would be alive.
And the virtuous and mighty Karna
would still be by my side to comfort me.
Only because you acted wickedly
the Pandavas, who should have lost this war,
have won."

"Son of Gandhari," Krishna said,
"virtue has won. Your defeat, and the killing
on this bloody field of Kurukshetra
are due to you alone, and your sinful envy.
Bhishma and Drona are dead because of you.
Karna is dead because he followed you,
so are your brothers. I tried to counsel you.
Your father, Bhishma, Vidura and Drona
all tried. Enslaved by all-consuming greed,
you would not hear the wisdom of your elders.
Now, bear the consequences."

Duryodhana,
sweating with pain, replied, "Listen, Krishna,
I have followed the duties of my order;
I have ruled well, have given generously;
I have governed the wide world, and her riches—
who is more fortunate than I? I have fought
as a kshatriya should, and fallen gloriously.
I have enjoyed the pleasures of the gods—
who is more fortunate than I? Today

those I love most will welcome me in heaven—
who, then, is more fortunate than I?
As for you and the cheating Pandavas,
you must live on in this unhappy world,
bereaved, burdened by sorrow and regret."

After he spoke, a shower of fragrant flowers
fell from the sky, and voices were heard singing—
celestial beings, praising Duryodhana,
lamenting the unrighteous deaths of Bhishma,
Drona, Bhurishravas and Karna.

At this, the Pandavas became ashamed
and wept, their previous joy contaminated.
Krishna spoke to them in a voice like thunder.
"Listen to me! Each of those mighty warriors
was unbeatable by lawful means.
Knowing that righteousness was on your side,
I arranged that you would overcome
those great opponents. If I had not done this,
victory would never have been yours;
war would have dragged on indefinitely.
The same applies to Duryodhana's death.

"In war, faced with defeat, foul means are fair.
When the enemy has superior numbers
any stratagem is permissible.
The gods, in their battle against the demons,
trod the same path, and what the gods think fair
men can surely emulate. Now, friends,
go back to your tents for well-earned rest."

Much cheered, the Pandava party returned
to their camp. But the five sons of Kunti
went with Krishna to the Kaurava camp,
riding on Arjuna's great chariot.
As soon as they arrived, and had stepped down,
the splendid vehicle, with its monkey standard,
turned into a ball of flame. In no time,

it was just a pile of ash. Earlier, Drona
and Karna had destroyed it, but Krishna's power
had stopped it from imploding until now.

They contemplated Duryodhana's tent,
now stripped of its luxurious appointments,
dismal, like a festive amphitheater
when the audience and players have departed.
They found large boxes full of gold, silver
and precious jewels: Yudhishthira's by right.

Krishna advised them not to go back to camp.
To mark the new reign, it would be auspicious
to spend the night, together with Satyaki,
beside the sparkling river Oghavati
that formed one boundary of the battlefield.
Once settled there, Yudhishthira asked Krishna
to travel on his behalf to Hastinapura
and speak with you, his cousin's grieving parents.
He is on his way here as I speak.

⚜

"Explain to me," said Janamejaya,
"why the Dharma King requested Krishna
to go to Hastinapura. Why did he
not come here himself?"
　　　　　　　　　"Yudhishthira knew,"
said Vaishampayana, "that Queen Gandhari
had spiritual powers, which she had earned
by her great austerities. He was afraid
that if he went himself to visit her
she would curse him to burn up on the spot,
blaming him for the death of all her sons.
Krishna would be able to console her
with wise words."

⚜

Arriving in the city,
Krishna hurried to where Dhritarashtra
and Gandhari sat, despairing, desolate.
He bent before them and addressed the king.
"Sir, you understand the workings of time.
You know the complete history of the conflict
between the sons of Pandu and your own.
Yet, it seems, fate can stupefy even those
who understand it—so when I came to you
to broker peace, despite the best advice
of Vidura and all the other elders,
you failed to curb your son. Whether from love
or avarice, you acted foolishly.
Defeat is the result. I beg you, therefore,
not to blame the Pandavas, who behaved
righteously, courageously. The future
of the Bharata line now rests with them.
Yudhishthira has nothing but goodwill
toward you and his aunt. He grieves for you."

Turning to Gandhari, Krishna said,
"Best of women, remember your own words
in the assembly: 'Foolish Duryodhana,
the course that you propose is not virtuous,
and victory will be where virtue is.'
Thinking of this, let your heart be steady.
Do not wish destruction on the Pandavas."

"You are right," said Gandhari. "This dreadful news
made me blaze with fury. But now I am calm.
My husband is like a child—may the Pandavas
and you, Krishna, be a refuge to him,"
and Gandhari was overcome with sobs.

Dhristarashtra said, "I cannot believe
that my son, strong as ten thousand elephants,
could have been cut down. Oh, what misery!

How will we two, an aged couple, live
destitute of children? And how will I,
who have been king myself, now bend the knee
as a mere lowly slave to Yudhishthira?"

Krishna became aware, through intuition,
that Ashvatthaman, still alight with anger
at the manner of Drona's death, was plotting
an attack on the Pandavas and their friends.
He took hasty leave of the royal couple
and quickly traveled back to the battlefield,
to join his cousins on the riverbank.

⚜

After Krishna's departure, Dhritarashtra
turned to Sanjaya. "What did my son say
after he had fallen to the ground,
felled by Bhima?"
                "Sir," said Sanjaya,
"he asked me to tell you, his sorrowing parents,
that he regrets nothing. He has lived his life
as a kshatriya should; and he has died
in unfair fight, and in full confidence
of heavenly reward. He feels for you
and for his sister, and fears for your fate."

"Tell me what happened then," said Dhritarashtra.
"Your son's surviving friends," said Sanjaya,
"learned that Duryodhana was lying helpless.
Quickly, they came to him, and were enraged
and grief-stricken to hear how he had been
cut down unrighteously. Writhing in pain,
drenched in blood, that tiger among men
looked like a wounded beast, dusty, disheveled.
Ashvatthaman broke down in tears to see him.
'Death comes to us all,' whispered Duryodhana.

'Do not grieve for me. I am fortunate.
I have never swerved from the true path
of a kshatriya. I shall be rewarded.
You all strove to your utmost, but destiny
cannot be thwarted.'

"Ashvatthaman cried,
'It is not over! The dastardly Panchalas
murdered my father. But, even more than that,
I burn with rage at what has been done to you.
I swear that before dawn, in Krishna's presence,
I will send your enemies to Yama's realm.
Bless my intention, Duryodhana.'

"Your son, highly pleased, asked for water
and had Kripa consecrate Ashvatthaman
as commander. Drona's son embraced
Duryodhana, and the three survivors—
Kripa, Kritavarman and Ashvatthaman—
left him lying there to pursue their mission."

X

THE BOOK OF
THE NIGHT ATTACK

45.

MASSACRE BY NIGHT

Sanjaya continued:
The three companions set out toward the south.
The sun was low, the air slowly cooling,
and as they neared the enemy camp, they heard
sounds of rejoicing and loud merriment,
raucous singing, and the bray of trumpets
that froze their hearts with dread. Probably
Dhrishtadyumna, Drona's murderer,
was drinking with his friends.

                      Night came on.
The firmament was luminous with stars,
like an expanse of beautiful brocade.
Skirting the camp, they found a gloomy wood,
dense with tangled vines, and hid in it
to rest in the shelter of a banyan tree.

Wounded and exhausted as they were,
they lay down to sleep. But Ashvatthaman
could not settle—not for the hard ground,
but for thinking about Dhrishtadyumna,
and of the manner of Drona's cruel death.
He, Ashvatthaman, had unfinished business:
to avenge the father who had given him life.
The Panchala's death should be his by right.

Anger was a tight knot in his chest.
Looking around, he saw a nearby tree
where a gang of crows was roosting, huddled up,
their heads under their wings. Then, silently,
a huge, yellow-eyed owl glided down
and set about killing the sleeping birds
(for owls are the mortal enemies of crows),
tearing off wings, snapping necks and legs,
so bloody fragments splattered on the ground
encircling the tree. The monstrous owl
appeared well satisfied with the night's work.

Ashvatthaman, struck by what he saw,
began to think what he might learn from it.
Surprise was everything. Those crows felt safe,
sleeping on their perches. Ashvatthaman
knew there was no possibility
that he could overcome his enemies
in a fair fight—if he attacked openly
he would be foolish as a mindless insect
cremating itself in a candle flame.
Yet—if he could catch them unawares . . .

He woke his uncle Kripa, and Kritavarman
and explained his plan—to kill the enemy
as they lay sleeping. "That would only be
the natural consequence of what they've done,

grossly flouting dharma, and now—hear that—
carousing in their camp without a care!"

Kripa replied, "I've listened to what you say;
now hear what I think. All outcomes are produced
both by divine will and human effort.
Success does not come through the gods' will alone,
nor by effort only, but both together.
We work to till the soil and plant the seed
and heaven sends rain—or else it does not.
Some foolish people, seeing a well-tilled field
parch for lack of rain, conclude that effort
is a waste of time. The wise know better—
effort usually bears fruit, but sloth
never does. The man who prepares the ground
and then worships the gods, seeking their blessing,
cannot go wrong.

        "The wise also know this:
that a man who consults his elders, listens,
and follows their advice may well succeed.
One who, moved by his desires and passions,
ignores the elders often comes to grief.
That is what happened to Duryodhana;
he would not drop his stubborn sinfulness
and now we all suffer. This calamity
has stupefied my mind. I think we should ask
Dhritarashtra, Gandhari and Vidura
their view of your proposal. We should follow
their advice—and if we should not succeed
in whatever course they set us on,
then it must be the gods who will decide."

Ashvatthaman answered impatiently:
"When we are young, matters look different
from how they seem in old age. Surely, then,
all we can do is follow our own judgment,

shaped by the circumstances of our lives.
I was born a brahmin, but through ill fortune,
and the decisions taken by my father,
I find myself living as a kshatriya.
I cannot go back. I have to take the path
my father—and you, uncle—trod before me.

"I am proud to be a warrior, and tonight
I shall carry out my plan. Before long
the Panchalas, with wicked Dhrishtadyumna,
will have shed their armor, unyoked their horses,
and settled to what they think is well-earned sleep.
I shall kill them all!"

                    "Wait until morning,"
urged Kripa. "I am very glad to hear you
so set upon revenge. But at daybreak,
when we are rested, all three of us can rise,
don our armor and attack the Panchalas.
I have celestial weapons; so do you.
We'll have the great advantage of surprise
and, united as we are, we shall surely win
and you will dance like the blessed Indra
after his slaughter of the asuras!
But for now, we should bide our time and sleep."

Ashvatthaman's eyes were red with anger.
"How? There are four impediments to sleep—
rage, grief, desire and an overactive mind.
Any one of these will baffle sleep;
I suffer from all four! No, I've decided.
I cannot bear another hour lying here,
my guts twisting, thinking of my father,
and of Duryodhana, so vilely killed.
My plan is good, and I shall act on it."

"It is my view," said Kripa, "that a person
in the grip of passion is in no state

to understand what's right and wrong behavior.
Listen to me, son, do not act rashly.
Slaughter of sleeping persons is unrighteous.
The same applies to those who are unprepared
for battle, who have laid aside their weapons.
So far, your life has been exemplary;
if you commit this shocking act, it will be
like a splash of blood on pure white cloth."

"You may be right, uncle," said Ashvatthaman.
"I want to act well, but the Pandavas
have made a mockery of righteousness
time after time. Why don't you censure them?
My mind's made up. And if I am reborn
as a worm, or some other lowly creature,
so be it. Dhrishtadyumna slew my father
as if he were a sacrificial beast.
Today I'll do the same to him—in that way
he'll not attain the heaven reserved for heroes
who die in battle."

                    Having little choice,
his two companions fastened on their breastplates
and followed Ashvatthaman toward the camp.
As they walked along, their doubts dissolved
and they began to glow with rage and fervor
like ritual fires well nourished with ghee.

ॐ

Arriving at the camp gate, Ashvatthaman
saw a towering figure in the way,
a terrifying vision. He blazed with light,
and round his hips was draped a tiger's hide
dripping with blood. For his upper garment
he wore the skin of a black antelope.

A snake was wound around his upper arm.
Thousands of lovely eyes adorned his face
and flames seemed to be leaping from his mouth
from which sprang innumerable Krishnas
each holding a conch, a discus and a mace.
The whole sky seemed imprinted with his image.

Fearless Ashvatthaman shot showers of arrows
at the being and, finding those useless,
continued his attack with spear and sword,
with mace and dagger—struggling, battling
with every ounce of strength, until at last
all his weapons were exhausted. Still
the huge presence barred his way, unmoved.
Panting with impotent rage, mystified,
Ashvatthaman thought of Kripa's words.
Perhaps this was a sign that if he blundered
off the path of dharma, he would become
lost in a trackless wilderness of sin.
Perhaps the gods would frustrate all his efforts.
"Yet I have also heard, the worst misery
afflicts a man who, out of fear, abandons
a great goal he has set out to achieve.
On the other hand, would this apparition
be blocking me unless I were meant to fail?
What can I do? I can't fight divine will."
He walked about, despondent, indecisive,
until at last his mind turned to Lord Shiva
and he resolved to seek the god's protection.

He stood, hands joined in reverence, head bowed,
and prayed to Shiva, speaking his many names.
A golden altar sprang up in front of him
on which a blazing fire crackled and spat,
a fire that seemed to spread across the sky
and fill the universe. And then a vision
of every kind of creature, every species

of unearthly being seemed to appear,
some terrible, some lovely beyond words—
headless monsters, rough-skinned pachyderms,
malevolent sprites, and female deities
so beautiful it made him gasp to see them.
These beings roared, muttered, groaned, and sang
hymns of surpassing sweetness, praising Shiva.
They had come to honor Ashvatthaman,
to test the quality of his resolve—
and to be present for the coming carnage.

Ashvatthaman faced the flaming altar.
"O Lord Shiva, accept me as sacrifice,"
he prayed, "accept my most sincere devotion!"
And the son of Drona walked into the fire.

A tremor in the air, a rushing wind,
and the great god Shiva stood before him,
smiling. "None is dearer to me than Krishna.
For him, I have protected the Panchalas.
But their time has now run out." And with that,
Shiva gave a sword to Ashvatthaman
and entered his body. At once, the brahmin
was filled with energy. There was nothing
he could not accomplish!

                    Kritavarman
and Kripa were waiting for him. They agreed
that Ashvatthaman would enter the camp alone
while the other two would guard the gates,
killing anyone who sought to flee.
Unafraid, but walking cautiously,
Ashvatthaman stole into the camp.
All was silent. It was the darkest hour.
Knowing where to go, inspired by Shiva,

he found his way to Dhrishtadyumna's tent.
Before him lay the prince of the Panchalas,
sprawled on linen sheets scattered with fragrant flowers.
He woke him with a kick, and Dhrishtadyumna
knew him at once. Ashvatthaman seized him
by the hair, wrenched his head back and ground his throat
beneath his foot. The Panchala fought, struggled,
tearing at Ashvatthaman with his nails,
but the brahmin's arms were the arms of Shiva.

"Kill me with a weapon!" cried Dhrishtadyumna,
"so I can reach the heaven reserved for heroes."
"Villain! There is no heaven for such as you,
one who kills his teacher!" And Ashvatthaman,
with naked strength alone, butchered his victim
as a sacrificial animal is killed.

The violent noise woke Dhrishtadyumna's guards
but they froze, appalled at what they saw.
At the sound of screams and women's shrieks,
the whole camp was thrown into a panic,
men shouting, running wildly in the dark
not knowing where the danger was, or who—
man or ogre—was attacking them.
Elephants ran wild, horses stampeded
raising dust, deepening the darkness.
Some men grabbed swords and, seized by mortal terror,
lunged at anything that moved. In this way
Panchala caused the death of Panchala.

Ashvatthaman stalked along the paths
and alleys of the camp, entering tents,
swiftly slaughtering every warrior
he found, with the sword Shiva had given him.
Many hundreds died. Drona's vengeful son,
emissary of death, showed no mercy.
The flaming energy and fiery zeal
of fire-born Dhrishtadyumna had entered him.

More than a man, more, even, than a god,
it was violence personified that whirled,
howling in triumph, through the camp that night.

Learning of the death of Dhrishtadyumna,
the five courageous sons of Draupadi
were amazed. "This never could have happened,"
they exclaimed, "if our fathers had been here!"
They tracked down Ashvatthaman, and began
to shower him with arrows. Drona's son
rushed at them with his celestial sword
and killed all five, one after another,
with hideous disfigurements. Shikhandin
pierced Ashvatthaman in the forehead
and was rewarded by being split in two.
Next, all the young Panchala princes
were massacred with Shiva's blazing sword,
among them, Drupada's remaining grandsons.

Some men, by chance, managed to reach the gateway
and ran out, sobbing with relief—to find
Kripa and Kritavarman ready for them.
Most were unarmed, having sprung bewildered
from their beds. They quickly met their deaths.
The assassins lit fires in three places,
which quickly spread, encircling the camp
with flame, making it even easier
for Ashvatthaman to do the thorough work
of the sacrifice, mad with blood-lust.

Violence and time. This holocaust
was like the entire Kurukshetra conflict
compressed. On many nights during the war
men had dreamed they saw a dark-skinned crone,
embodiment of all-destroying time,
smeared with red, her mouth agape, her eyes
seeping blood. In her hand she held a noose,
or halter perhaps, for leading men away.

This dreadful goddess now appeared to them
in solid form. They knew her for what she was:
their hideous escort to the afterlife.

The sky began to lighten. In the east,
streaks of orange and red grew ever brighter.
At last the camp was hushed, inhabited
only by corpses and by carrion-eaters
slinking among the shadows, getting bolder.
Ashvatthaman walked out of the gate,
his clothes caked with blood, and the bloody hilt
of Shiva's great sword stuck fast to his hand.
He was at peace. At last he had assuaged
the wracking grief he had felt for Drona's death.
He joined his two companions. They exulted
at their good night's work.

                              In that moment
they felt that the achievement was all theirs.
Yet, in truth, only because Lord Shiva
had made them his instrument; only because
Krishna had allowed it, had they succeeded.
Effort had joined hands with the gods' design.

"But," asked Dhritarashtra, "if Ashvatthaman
was capable of such an outstanding feat,
why did he wait until the war was lost,
and my son lying helpless on the ground?"
"It was because he feared the Pandavas,"
said Sanjaya. "Had your nephews been present
this great slaughter never could have happened."

Sanjaya continued:
The three hurried back to Duryodhana

and found him lying as before, attempting
to repel rapacious carnivores that sidled
ever closer. His groans of agony
were fainter now, blood frothing from his mouth.
The three men wept with pity and outrage
to see him, wept for you, his bereaved parents,
who soon would have no sons left in the world.
"Oh, woe," said Kripa, "even this great warrior
is brought down by time. Look, his golden mace
that has never failed him, that was his friend
in every battle, is now lying by him
as a loving wife lies down beside her lord
when he prepares for sleep. Alas, this prince
to whom brahmins could always look for food
will soon himself be food for scavengers."

They wiped his bloody face with their bare hands.
Then they told him all that they had done
and made him happy. "Blessings on you all!
You have achieved what even my great Karna,
even Bhishma, even your own father
could not accomplish. We will meet in heaven."

Having spoken, he gave up his life.
And at that moment, best of Bharatas,
the power which, for eighteen endless days,
enabled me to witness every detail
of the war, and bring you news of it—
my divine vision—was suddenly withdrawn.

Dhrishtadyumna's driver was the only man
who had escaped the carnage, slipping past
Kritavarman in the dark; and he it was
who brought the dreadful news to Yudhishthira.

The Pandava fell to the ground in shock.
The five brothers huddled together, weeping,
lamenting the loss of all their stalwart sons,
Draupadi's children. "Ah!" cried Yudhishthira,
"if our kinsmen had only been more watchful
Ashvatthaman never could have breached
their guard, to murder them so savagely.
So brave they were! And such outstanding warriors
that they survived all eighteen days of war—
only to perish now like helpless sheep.
They are like travelers who, having sailed
the treacherous oceans and come back to port
without mishap, drown in a shallow stream.

"Now we who were victorious have been vanquished,
and our defeated enemy has conquered.
What does victory mean if what it brings
is the searing loss of all we cherish most?
Is it not just defeat by other means?
And how will our beloved Draupadi
bear this bereavement? How can she survive it?
Her father already killed; now two brothers
and all her beautiful, courageous sons!"

Yudhishthira sent Nakula by chariot
to Upaplavya, to fetch Draupadi.
Then, with his other brothers and Satyaki,
he went to the camp. Seeing crows and vultures
tearing at the bodies of their children,
they all collapsed, fainting, on the ground.

When Nakula brought Draupadi, next morning,
she hurried to the place where her five sons
lay lifeless and, crouching, cradled in her arms
each bloody, mutilated boy in turn.
"O my precious one, how can I live
and never see your handsome face again;

never hear your laughter in the distance;
never feel the warmth of your strong arms
as you embrace me?" She rocked to and fro,
then she, too, collapsed, undone by grief.

Bhima lifted her. Weeping, shaking,
she addressed Yudhishthira in anger.
"I hope you are happy with your victory,
your capture of the earth. I hope you enjoy her
after the slaughter of our shining sons,
the flower of youth, heroic kshatriyas.
Perhaps you will sleep undisturbed by thoughts
of Abhimanyu and these other children.
But I tell you now, Yudhishthira,
if you do not make Ashvatthaman pay,
if you do not rip his life from him
together with the lives of his wicked friends,
then, starting now, I shall sit and fast to death!"

"Draupadi," said Yudhishthira, ashen-faced,
"all your sons have lost their lives with honor—
even now, they must be enjoying heaven.
You should not grieve. You understand dharma.
You know that the life of a kshatriya
is shaped for war from earliest infancy.
As for Ashvatthaman, our spies tell us
he has fled into the forest, like a cur.
We shall pursue him with all possible speed,
but if he is caught and killed as he deserves,
how shall we prove to you that he has perished?"

"I have heard," said Draupadi, "that Drona's son
was born with a jewel on his forehead.
When you bring me that jewel, when I place it
on your own head, Yudhishthira, only then
will I decide to live." She turned to Bhima,
"Bhima, you have always been our refuge—

think of Hidimba, and the time you saved me
from that lustful wretch in Virata's city.
Now, wreak vengeance on wicked Ashvatthaman!"
Bhima seized his bow, mounted his chariot
driven by Nakula, and galloped off
along the route taken by Ashvatthaman.

&

When Krishna learned of this, he was dismayed
and said to Yudhishthira, "You should realize
that you have put your brother in great danger.
Ashvatthaman has a deadly weapon,
capable of destroying the whole world—
the *Brahmashiras* weapon. Years ago,
Drona gave that weapon to Arjuna,
knowing he could be trusted. Ashvatthaman
was jealous, and kept pestering his father
to give it to him too. Drona, reluctant
because he knew his son lacked Arjuna's
calmness and discipline, at last gave in.
'But,' he warned, 'it never must be used
against human beings.'

        "Some years later,
during the time of your forest exile,
Ashvatthaman came to see me. 'Krishna,'
he said, smiling at me, 'I have the weapon
called *Brahmashiras*. I will give it to you.
Please give me your discus in exchange.'
He had no idea what he was asking.
I told him to keep his weapon, but to take
whatever of mine he wanted. Delighted,
he seized my discus—but he could not lift it,
try as he might. Then I said to him,
'Ashvatthaman, even Arjuna,
foremost of warriors, wielder of *Gandiva*,

he who is my dearest friend on earth,
he to whom there is nothing I would not give,
even my wives and children—Arjuna
has never asked of me what you just asked.
My precious son Pradyumna, my dear brother
Balarama, my cousins, my close kin
have never asked of me what you just asked.
Tell me—what use would you make of it
if I gave you my discus?' He replied,
'I was going to fight you with it—then
I would be the world's greatest warrior.'
That's how wrongheaded Ashvatthaman is!
He is very cruel, impulsive, angry—
and he has the *Brahmashiras* weapon.
Bhima must be protected."

                Immediately
Krishna leapt onto his chariot, yoked
to superb horses garlanded in gold.
Above him flew his celestial standard,
bright with gems, depicting the fierce eagle,
Garuda, enemy of snakes. Arjuna
and Yudhishthira sprang up beside him.
This swiftest of all chariots caught up
with Bhima, but failed to stop him charging
toward Ashvatthaman.

             Drona's son
had sought refuge in Vyasa's hermitage.
The Pandava party tracked him down at last
sitting piously beside the Ganga
dressed from head to foot in brahmin's garb,
surrounded by Vyasa and other seers.
Bhima roared, "Stand up and fight, you villain!"
and the ground shuddered as he advanced.
Ashvatthaman quickly called to mind
his dreadful weapon. He picked a blade of grass

and inspired it with the proper mantras.
"For the destruction of the Pandavas!"
he cried, and then the blade of grass became
a raging furnace.

             "Arjuna," urged Krishna,
"it is time to use that celestial weapon
given by Drona, to neutralize all weapons."
Arjuna jumped down, lifted his bow,
and, speaking softly, wished well to Drona's son
as well as to his brothers and himself.
With his mind on the welfare of all beings,
he prayed aloud: "May Ashvatthaman's harm
be neutralized by this!" He loosed his weapon.

It seemed as though the entire universe
was consumed by flame; thunder roared
and meteors crashed to earth. The whole world trembled.
Then the great rishis Narada and Vyasa
spoke up angrily. "What kind of rashness
is this?" they exclaimed. "Bhishma and Drona,
who knew such weapons, never mobilized them
in battle, even when faced with their own death."

Arjuna agreed to withdraw his weapon.
"But if I do, Ashvatthaman's weapon
will destroy us and the three worlds. O rishis,
you must find some way to protect us all."
To withdraw such a powerful weapon
was almost impossible. Only one
who had observed extreme austerity,
who had gone through the discipline and vows
of a devout ascetic, had the power.
Arjuna was such a man; he withdrew
his weapon. Ashvatthaman could not do it.
His weapon was directly dedicated
to the destruction of the Pandavas.

Vyasa reproved him, "Although Arjuna
could have used his weapon before this,
he has never done so, out of concern
for the innocent who would be harmed by it.
You must call your dreadful weapon back.
And give that jewel of yours to the Pandavas
that they may spare your weak, misguided life."

"This jewel," said Ashvatthaman, "is more precious
than all the combined wealth of the Bharatas.
He who wears it will never suffer fear.
Holy one, although I hate to lose it,
I will obey you. But I am powerless
to stop the *Brahmashiras*. All I can do
is to redirect it into the wombs
of the Pandava wives, killing their offspring
and making them barren."
                              "Then you must do it,"
said Vyasa.

              Krishna addressed Ashvatthaman.
"Once, a brahmin at Virata's court
told Uttaraa, Abhimanyu's widow,
that she would bear a son, called Parikshit,
a son to carry forward the Bharata line."
"That will not happen," shouted Ashvatthaman,
"however much you love the Pandavas!"
"I assure you, this will indeed come true,
despite your weapon. I shall see to it,"
said Krishna. "As for you, accursed wretch,
you will bear the fruit of your sinful acts.
Infamous as the murderer of children,
for three thousand years you will walk the world
a joyless outcast, afflicted by disease,
with no soul to talk to, passing your days
in gloomy forests and dreary desert tracts.
Parikshit, well schooled in the Vedas,

practicing pious vows, skilled with all weapons,
will rule in righteousness for sixty years."

"Let it be so," said Vyasa. "Ashvatthaman,
this is what comes of living out your life
as a kshatriya, despite your brahmin birth."

Grim-faced, Ashvatthaman gave his jewel
to the Pandavas. Without a word, he turned
and slowly walked away among the trees
to begin his solitary banishment.

The Pandavas rode back to Draupadi
where she sat, fasting. Bhima said to her,
"This jewel is yours. The murderer of your sons
has been defeated. Grasp life again. Recall
kshatriya dharma. Think of those words of yours
when we were in the forest, how you said,
'Since the king wants peace, I have no husband.'
You wanted war, you thirsted for revenge.
Now we have slaughtered every Kaurava.
I have drunk Duhshasana's blood, avenging
that villain's act in violating you.
We have exacted full dues from our foes.
We let Ashvatthaman keep his life,
out of respect for our teacher, his dead father,
and because he is a brahmin. But that life
will hardly be worth living."

                Draupadi said,
"I only wished for adequate revenge
for all our injuries; that we have obtained
in full measure—and at terrible cost.
Now, despite my grief, I shall cease my fast.
I wish well to the teacher, and his son.
Bind this gem on your head, Yudhishthira."
The king did so, seeing it as a gift
from his dead teacher.

Later, he asked Krishna,
"How could our sons, mighty kshatriyas,
have been easily killed by Ashvatthaman
whose skills were much inferior to theirs?
And valiant Dhrishtadyumna? And Shikhandin?
How could that have happened?" Krishna explained
that Shiva had afforded his protection
to Ashvatthaman. "Those who died perished
through Shiva's power; they were the great god's share
of the sacrifice that was the bloody war
of Kurukshetra." And he then described
Shiva's contribution to creation.

Their talking went on far into the night.

XI

THE BOOK OF
THE WOMEN

46.

DHRITARASHTRA'S GRIEF

"After all was lost," said Janamejaya,
"what did Dhritarashtra do? And what
did wise Sanjaya say to the blind king?"
Vaishampayana said, "I will tell you . . ."

Having lost all who were dearest to him,
what could the father of a hundred sons
do now? What kind of life remained to him?
So rich in children only a month before,
his line secure, a treasury of sons
to keep his memory alive, he now
stood destitute, as though they had never lived.
He was reduced to a stupor of distress.
His blind eyes leaked and dripped like a cracked cistern;
his soft hands trembled uncontrollably.

Sanjaya was stern. "Why do you sit there
self-absorbed, weltering in misery?
Grief, feeding greedily on itself,
never brought any good. Do something useful—
see that all those fathers, husbands, sons,
all those kings and followers whose flesh,
thanks to you, now mixes with the mud,
at least receive the proper funeral rites.
Enough self-indulgence!"

                    "Unfeeling man,
you are too severe!" moaned Dhritarashtra.
"I'm like a husbandman who has long watched
his orchard grow, mature and bear ripe fruit,
who now has all his sturdy trees destroyed
by lightning and the howling desert wind.
Oh, I am like a blasted tree myself,
one that in its scanty sap preserves
a longing for the green that once played round it.
I shall be broken-hearted until death.

"And, in addition, I have lost my kingdom.
How can you expect me not to grieve?
I had the best advice—I took no notice.
Now I have paid. A curse on my bad judgment.
I must have done great wrong in previous births—
I don't remember. I suppose it's fate.
Was ever a man more unfortunate?"

Sanjaya was unmoved. "Never mind 'previous'—
you've had enough shortcomings in this life
to explain your woe. When Duryodhana
swaggered about in his youthful pride
you offered him encouragement, not sense.
You failed to show him the path of principle.
Nothing but war would do for that foolish man.
Seduced by the splendor he had promised you,

you were greedy, too avid for gain.
Blind as you are, unfit for a warrior's life,
perhaps the glamour of war excited you,
that glorious ideal. However it was,
you were too fond of Duryodhana
and loved to please him. You yearned for the kingdom
to belong to the Kauravas alone,
and you were blind to dharma. But now regret
is useless. Rather, seek for understanding."

❧

Vidura, too, exhorted Dhritarashtra
to put aside self-pity. "We all die.
Death seizes us, heroes and cowards both.
A man may fight, and live; or stay at home
and die anyway. Time cannot be cheated.
You should not mourn your sons who fell in battle.
They all died facing forward. Heaven receives them
even without rituals; they are fortunate.
Remember, once they did not exist for you;
now, again, they inhabit a different world.
Like clouds, your lives overlapped, then parted.
They did not belong to you, nor you to them.
There is nothing to lament. Listen:

> *"In our rebirths—hundreds of children,*
> *mothers, fathers, brothers.*
> *Which are ours? To whom do we belong?*
>
> *The foolish allow grief and fear*
> *to torture them dozens of times a day.*
> *The wise do not.*
>
> *A person in the grip of greed or pride*
> *is happy to tell others how to live,*
> *but does not want to learn himself.*

Time treats everyone alike:
the lowest outcast, the greatest king.
No one can negotiate with time.

Nothing, and no one, lasts;
our lives are inscribed on a flowing stream.
The wise do not grieve over this.

Heartache does not leave
the man who dwells on it; it settles in
and makes itself at home.

Knowledge is for this:
to fight disease with medicine
and misery with wisdom.

We cannot escape the fruits of our deeds;
like burrs that we have brushed past thoughtlessly
they cling to us everywhere we go."

Dhritarashtra sighed. "These words of yours
are no doubt full of wisdom. But please tell me,
how do the wise avoid being made unhappy
by what they cannot have, and by affliction?"

"By meditating on impermanence,"
said Vidura, "until awareness of it
is experienced with every breath,
not just with the head. Our bodies are houses
that fall apart in time, but the soul inside
is ageless and beautiful and, in time,
is born again. We act, we speak, we think,
we make our own misery and happiness
and come to heaven or hell as we deserve."

Then Vidura told the blind king this story:

"A BRAHMIN CAUGHT in an endless cycle of rebirth finds himself in a thick forest, full of terrifying animals and other creatures. He is lost, and runs here and there, searching for a way out, or at least some place of safety from the dangers that surround him at every turn. In the heart of the wood is a hidden well, overgrown with vines, and the brahmin falls head-first into it, and hangs there, upside down, struggling, unable to get free. A fierce elephant waits at the top of the well shaft, to attack him in case he does happen to escape. Black and white rats gnaw busily at the roots of the vines.

"A bees' nest on an overhanging branch is letting fall a continuous stream of honey. Surrounded by dangers of every kind, he nevertheless avidly sucks at the honey—he can't get enough of it. In this way, pleasure distracts him, even though the rats will eventually gnaw through the roots of the vine, and he will fall to his death."

"Ah! the poor man!" exclaimed Dhritarashtra,
"I'd like to rescue him."
                              "It's just a story,"
explained Vidura, "an allegory.
We get caught up in pleasures and desires,
and we ignore the rats of time, working
for our destruction. The wise, who understand
the wheel of death and rebirth, cut the ties
that bind them to the wheel.

                    "Think of it this way:
The body of a person is a chariot,
the mind the charioteer, and the senses
are the horses. The unskillful mind
lets the horses career round in circles,
plunging after this or that attraction
in the cycle of rebirth. When the senses
are schooled in renunciation of desire,
the person is undistracted, free from fear
of death. That way salvation lies."

Alas,
such lessons are not easy to absorb.
Dhritarashtra was seized anew with pangs
of longing for his sons, and fell, fainting.
When he revived, he became agitated;
he cursed this human life, and was resolved
on suicide. Vyasa came to him—
that seer with access to the world of gods
as well as that of men—and pacified him.
"Listen to me. Once when I visited
the realm of Indra, I found the gods and seers,
headed by Narada, talking together.
Earth had come to them with a request
to rid her of her burden—too many people
had swelled her population, bad kshatriyas
had overrun the world, and she was suffering.
Vishnu, greatest of beings, smiled and told her
Duryodhana would resolve her problem.
Because of him, a great war would take place
at Kurukshetra, and kshatriyas by the million
would be killed. This I heard with my own ears.

"Dhritarashtra, try to accept this:
your son was an embodiment of Kali,
discord incarnate, born to bring destruction.
He was willful, angry, unforgiving.
His brothers copied him. His friends and allies
played their part in the celestial plan.
You should not weep for them; they were at fault.
They died because of their own wickedness.
These events were ordained by the gods
and could not have been otherwise. Knowing this,
might you come to find your life worth living?
And might you find it possible to feel
some love for the Pandavas? My son,
try to move beyond this searing pain:
quash your sorrow each time it arises."

"I have been struggling in a net of anguish,"
said Dhritarashtra. "My mind was not my own.
But, having heard your story, I will live,
I will try not to drown in misery."

After this, Vyasa disappeared.

卐

Later, Dhritarashtra stirred himself.
He ordered chariots, and asked Vidura
to assemble all the women of the court,
Gandhari and Kunti first among them.
They would travel to the battlefield.
Sunk in despair, but glad to be occupied,
Gandhari and all the royal women
joined the king and, hollow-eyed and drawn,
rode out of the city. They were watched
by all Hastinapura, all bereaved.
It seemed that every house contained a widow,
a sister or a weeping mother; women
whose normal lives were lived in strict seclusion
ran into the streets with hair unbound,
dressed in simple shifts, screaming, wailing,
as if all sense of modesty was lost.
Artisans, merchants and laborers
streamed from the city behind the royal party.

卐

Yudhishthira, too, went to Kurukshetra,
taking Draupadi and the other women.
Each woman on that field, of either side,
was engulfed in the most vivid grief,
screaming, sobbing, almost mad with horror
at witnessing the hideous devastation.
Nothing their anxiety had imagined—

not descriptions, not their restless dreams—
had prepared them for this.

                      Yudhishthira
looked for his aunt and uncle in the crowds
of women rooting among mangled bodies
and body parts for someone they recognized:
their man, among these thousands of mere things,
beloved flesh among the mounds of corpses.
Craving a face, an amulet, a ring,
anything familiar, they searched, keening
like ospreys calling for their mates at dusk.

Hundreds of women mobbed him, crying out,
"How can a king claiming to know dharma
kill his kin so cruelly? Can you stay sane
after killing your teacher? Your grandfather?
How will you rule without your kin around you?
Shame! Oh, shame on you, Yudhishthira!"

In dread, Yudhishthira and his brothers
announced themselves to their aunt and uncle
and paid them homage. Dhritarashtra managed
to embrace Yudhishthira, but when it came
to Bhima, lawless killer of his dear son,
rage welled up in him like molten lava.
Summoning all his power, he made to crush
his nephew, but Krishna, knowing the king's mind,
pushed Bhima to one side and quickly shoved
an iron effigy into the old man's arms.
Dhritarashtra pulverized it, injuring
his own chest in the process. He fell, bleeding,
crying, "Oh! Bhima!" And all-knowing Krishna,
seeing that the king's anger had subsided,
told him he had only crushed a statue
and counseled him:

"Try to call to mind
the times when you betrayed the Pandavas
although they were blameless. You know the Vedas,
you know how a righteous king should act,
yet you followed your own stubborn path,
were deaf as well as blind. Because your son,
among his many wrongs, insulted Draupadi,
Bhima vowed to kill him. It was deserved.
Try to understand your own part in this."

"It is as you say," said Dhritarashtra.
"Love for my son undermined my judgment.
With all my sons dead, only the Pandavas
will give us consolation. Who else is there?
Who else will protect us in our old age?"
Weeping, and with trembling arms, he embraced
Bhima and his brothers, blessing them.

Then the Pandavas approached Gandhari,
standing tall and silent. In her agony
over her lost sons, she was at first
inclined to curse Yudhishthira. But Vyasa,
reading her thoughts from far off, instantly
appeared. "Excellent woman, this is no time
for curses—rather, this is the time for peace.
Eighteen days ago, when Duryodhana
asked for your blessing on his enterprise,
you said, 'Whoever is in the right will win.'
And so they did—you always speak the truth.
Restrain your anger now."

"Blessed one,
I have no animus toward the Pandavas.
I have no quarrel with what was done in war—
I know how war is, I know kshatriya dharma.
But when, afterward, Bhima killed my son
by striking him below the waist—it's that

I find inexcusable. And when, earlier,
he gulped the blood of my Duhshasana—
that was how a barbarian would act!
How could Bhima, who knows dharma, do it?"

Bhima said, "I did not drink his blood—
it did not pass my lips. I smeared my face
and bathed my hands in it—so all would think
I had fulfilled that solemn vow I made
when your son dragged Draupadi by the hair
to the gaming hall. As for Duryodhana,
you know that I had vowed to punish him
for exposing his thigh to Draupadi.
I realized, as we fought, I could not win
by fair means—he was too skilled for me.
Rather than lose everything we'd fought for
I did what I did. Please forgive me for it."

Gandhari understood. "But oh, Bhima,
could you not have spared us just *one* son,
one who had offended only slightly,
one who would live to comfort our old age?
Even in the bedlam of battle,
could you not have thought of us, and left
just one of them? Where is Yudhishthira?"

Grim-faced, Yudhishthira approached his aunt.
"I am the killer of your sons, great lady,
I have caused devastation on this earth;
I am not fit for wealth, not fit to govern.
Curse me, for I deserve to be cursed."
And, though he was afraid of his aunt's wrath,
Yudhishthira prostrated himself before her.

Gasping with rage, Gandhari looked down
and glimpsed the tips of Yudhishthira's fingers
below her blindfold. Instantly, his nails

shriveled and turned black. Nervous, Arjuna
moved away, but Gandhari's anger
had spent itself. She blessed the Pandavas.

Having observed the proper etiquette,
the Pandavas could now go to their mother,
Kunti—the mother none of them had seen
since they left Hastinapura to begin
their long exile. Imagine with what joy
they held each other now; what scalding tears
streamed from their eyes. But Kunti did not forget
Draupadi, whose sons would never again
embrace their mother, and who now was crouching
on the unyielding earth. "Oh, Kunti," she cried,
"where are your grandsons, all my lovely boys
and Abhimanyu? What use is the kingdom
now that my courageous sons are dead?
For years, in the affliction of our exile,
the thought of them was a bright talisman
I kept safe in my heart. Now they are gone.
What was it all for?"

                    Kunti raised her up
and comforted her. Then they went to join
Gandhari. Together they stood, trying
to console each other. "We must accept it,"
said Gandhari. "We have to think this carnage
was the will of the gods. It had to happen."

47.

GANDHARI'S LAMENT

Acknowledging her spiritual strength,
Vyasa gave a gift to Gandhari:
standing where she was, blindfolded still,
she could now see the entire battlefield,
distant and close, by means of divine vision.
Her inner eye was opened. She exclaimed
to Krishna at everything she saw and heard.

"Ah! I can see this sweeping, blood-drenched plain
of Kurukshetra, in all its dreadful detail.
Everywhere is chaos, mangled flesh,
the aftermath of massacre. Everywhere
I look, in all directions, countless bodies
lying in abandon, heads and limbs
at sickening angles, mouths gaping as if
their final cry should still be reaching us.
Eyes that shone with every heartfelt passion
now are empty pits, cleaned out by crows.
Gashes and holes in the silk of skin
show where a cunning spear has found its way
between the panels of bright, well-wrought mail.
Some wear their armor still, and seem unscathed
as if lapped in the luxury of sleep,
while others are half-naked, stripped of all
that marked them out from the mire they're made of.

"Krishna, who am I now? I am Gandhari,
childless mother of a hundred sons.
But is there no word for women such as I,
a word like 'widow,' another word for 'empty'?

"Look at these fine young men, embracing Earth
as if discovered in the act of union
with a beloved bride—arms spread, their faces
oblivious to everything but this.
Oh, Earth has stolen them! Earth has triumphed
over all of us, defeated women.

"What priceless wealth is scattered all around—
crowns, jeweled bracelets, ropes of gold
twisted round the muscled upper arms
of so many heroes; anklets, torques,
all the regalia of rank. How useless
is that wealth—why, it could not protect them
from the smallest dart; and it cannot keep
monsters and other scavengers from feasting
on their fat and flesh. Look at those kanka birds,
tall as men, looking so disdainful,
picking their way among the piled-up corpses,
yet ripping flesh from bone with cruel beaks
as ruthlessly as any rakshasa.

"A month ago, who could have imagined
that men who loved the music of the bards
would now hear only the despairing cries
of their beloved wives. They who slept soft
now lie uncushioned on the filthy ground.
Men who plunged deep in the sumptuous flesh
of women now lie, torn, gnawed by jackals,
their rigid arms locked hard around a mace.

"Oh, these poor women! Some are mute with shock;
most are wailing, shivering in their pain.

They call like cranes for mates that will never come.
Some try to find the body that belongs
with the head they love, then they realize
it is not his. Some fail to recognize
the face of their own brother.

                "And, Krishna—
there is Duryodhana! Oh! my tragic son,
caked in blood, your strong legs smashed, distorted,
your breastplate still in place. I remember
how you looked when you asked for my blessing,
full of pride and foolish hope. I knew then
it must end in defeat. All I could manage
were lukewarm words—not what you most wanted,
not the heartfelt prayer for victory
men need from women when they go to war.

"Time turns. You died a hero, Duryodhana.
Devoted women once fanned you to sleep;
now only the urgent wings of hungry birds
make a breeze around you. Here's your poor wife,
Lakshmana's mother, weeping for her son,
and for you. That broad-hipped, lovely girl
is huddling in the crook of your strong arm.
No more good times for her; disregarded,
she'll spend her life alone.

                "So many women,
trying to wash blood off their men's dead faces;
others whirling, screeching like lunatics
at vultures circling on creaking wings.
What must we have done in a past life?
What sin could have deserved this utter horror?

"And look at my other fine sons! There they lie;
distinct in life, with differing looks and gifts,
each with his individual voice, his laugh,
now meat for undiscriminating crows.

"There is Abhimanyu, still beautiful,
that brilliant warrior who outshone even
his father. And there is Uttaraa, his wife,
crouched beside him, kissing his cold face.
Now she has undone his gilded armor,
stares intently at his wounds, and cries,
'Oh, Abhimanyu, my beloved husband,
my world, soul of my soul, how your injuries
gape for all to see. My heart, too, is pierced
by death's pitiless darts, but invisibly.
You were like Krishna in your strength and courage,
so alive. Yet now you sleep too soundly.
Your skin is soft, delicate as a girl's;
isn't the rough ground grazing you? Your arms
flung wide, you sprawl as though you are exhausted
by grinding labor. Rest, my love.'

                  "She cradles
his head in her lap and strokes his tangled hair.

" 'Where were their hearts, those Kauravas who trapped you,
a solitary boy? Where were your uncles,
your natural protectors? How can a kingdom,
however rich, however well deserved,
be worth your life, my prince, my precious one?
I wish I too could die. I long to join you!
But no one dies before the gods decide.
You are no more; I have my wretched life.
In that world you've gone to, will there be
a woman to caress and laugh with you
as if she were me? Oh, my Abhimanyu,
be happy in your heaven, but remember
what I was to you, how we loved together!'

"Her father's wives are pulling her away
from Abhimanyu's corpse. Now they themselves
collapse. They have seen Virata's body—

and that of Uttara, the bragging boy
whom Arjuna transformed into a man.

"There is Karna. His wives are sitting round,
their hair in disarray, crying miserably
for him, and for their courageous sons.
So many heroes looked upon his face
as the last they saw on earth, until Arjuna
cut him down. He was the most loyal friend
to Duryodhana, most brave, most steadfast.
Firm as the Himalaya, brilliant as fire,
unforgiving, stern, that great warrior
lies like a tree felled by a tornado,
ruined, defaced, unrecognizable.

"Look at Jayadratha. Puffed with pride,
full of uncalled-for animosity
toward the Pandavas, now he is laid low,
dragged into a ditch by growling beasts,
though his weeping wives tried to guard his body.
The Pandavas might have killed him when he tried
to abduct Draupadi, but they refrained
out of consideration for my daughter.
If only they could have thought of her grief now.
She runs this way and that, quite distracted,
searching, searching for Jayadratha's head.

"And there lies Shalya, complicated man.
We never knew whose side he really took;
perhaps, in the end, he didn't know himself.
Now it is all the same—and, look, two crows
are pecking at his lolling, facile tongue.

"Bhishma, on his tormenting bed of arrows,
is still alive. He looks like the sun itself,
fallen to earth. That man is a hero
like no other. Skilled in warfare, steeped
in wisdom and dharma—what other warrior

would have told Yudhishthira how to kill him!
Who will there be as a bright lodestar
for the Bharatas, once Bhishma is no more?

"And Drona, the great teacher—all those weapons
acquired from the gods were useless in the end.
Kripi, his loving wife, sits, eyes downcast
beside his body. His bow still in his hand,
gauntlet and greaves in place, it almost seems
that he could rise and resume the fight. But look,
his feet, honored by so many pupils,
are gone, already gnawed by scavengers.

"There is Somadatta's sorrowing widow,
lamenting for their son, Bhurishravas:
'Oh, husband, fortunate that you cannot see
our son—his arm, his lovely arm, hacked off.
His wife is bathing it with her hot tears,
mourning the hand that lately would have loosened
her clothing, stroked her breasts, caressed her face.
Lucky that you cannot see his parasol
broken, splintered, lying across his chariot.'

"Her bereaved daughters-in-law are shrieking
and crying, a pitiful thing to witness.
Arjuna acted wickedly. Still more
horrible was Satyaki's sinful act—
killing him as he sat in meditation.
The world will censure you for allowing it,
Krishna. I'd like to think you are ashamed.

"So many shields strewn on the bloody field
like fallen moons; and scattered spears and bows
shining like shafts of sunlight in the gloom.
Look at Shakuni, fallen where he belongs,
that mischief-maker. This war was his doing.
I warned my son—told him that his uncle
walked with death. He it was who stirred up

the quarrel, as he loved to do. He hated
the Pandavas. What a barbed tongue he had.
But he died in battle; the heroes' heaven
awaits him, as it does all my brave sons.
He cared for no one, not even himself.

"There are the womenfolk of old Drupada
killed by Drona, his lifelong enemy,
as an elephant is savaged by a lion.
He was a heroic warrior. See, Krishna,
his beautiful white parasol is gleaming
in the light. His body is already burned.
His grieving wives and daughters-in-law circle
the pyre clockwise, heads covered, sobbing softly.

"Oh, so much sorrow! It is women's fate
to love and lose, love and lose again.
What joy it is to give birth to healthy sons,
to play with them, sing to them, to see them
grow in strength, acquire a warrior's skills
ready to take on a world of enemies.
What's wrong with us? Why do we not start weeping
as soon as we see our newborn is a boy?
But no, we glow with pride—as if this creature,
these perfect arms and legs, this lusty voice,
this future food for crows, were an achievement.
Broodmares for corpses—that's what women are
if they are born unlucky kshatriyas!"

❧

Gandhari sank down, broken, desolate.
"Krishna, when your peace mission failed, and you
returned to the Pandavas, then my poor sons
were as good as dead. You could have done more
to save them, but this was what you wanted,
this war, and all my precious sons are lost.
I curse you, Krishna! For presiding over

this tragic conflict, kinsman against kinsman,
a time will come when you will pay in kind.
In thirty-six years' time, having killed
your sons, brothers, cousins, you will meet
an ignominious end. And then your own
womenfolk will weep and tear their hair,
as inconsolable as these women now."

Krishna smiled. "Excellent Gandhari,
you give words to what I already know.
I, and I alone, shall destroy the Vrishnis,
and your curse will help me carry out that task.
When the time is right, they will kill each other;
I shall decide.

    "But don't give way to anguish.
Grief breeds grief; you are wise enough to know that.
You yourself are by no means blameless.
You thought too well of Duryodhana
and tolerated his pernicious acts.
Now you see the tragic consequence."

ॐ

Dhritarashtra asked Yudhishthira
for the facts—how big were the armies
and how many were killed? Yudhishthira
gave numbers more vast than the mind could hold.
"And what has become of them, Yudhishthira—
you who know everything?"

     "The afterlife
is proportioned to the way a man has lived
and how he died—how courageously.
The highest realms welcome those who fight
like true kshatriyas, who stubbornly
battle on even when they are wounded,
when they have lost their chariot, when lesser men

have fled the field. They go to the seat of Indra.
Lower realms receive cautious warriors,
those who fight with qualified commitment.
Those who desert meet suffering after death."

"How do you know all this?" asked Dhritarashtra.
"I sat at the feet of many holy men
when we were in exile in the forest.
There I practiced the yoga of knowledge,
and I made extended pilgrimages
to sacred sites and holy bathing places."

Dhritarashtra urged Yudhishthira
to arrange that rituals for the dead
be performed, especially for those who lay
neglected on the field, with no relations
to mourn their passing—those whose loving kin
perhaps had heard no news, and were still praying
for their menfolk's safe return.

                              Yudhishthira
ordered retainers and priests to see to it.
They summoned sandalwood and precious aloe,
sesame oil, ghee and fragrant herbs.
Warriors' bodies were heaped up by the thousands.
High piles were made of the smashed chariots
and other wood, corpses wrapped in cloth
and burned with all appropriate ritual,
the fires fed with ghee and perfumed oil.

Then all went in procession to the river.
The Bharatas gathered at the water's edge,
the serene Ganga, fringed with lovely trees.
The mourning women shed their ornaments
and, entering the water, poured libations.

Suddenly, Kunti, weeping, speaking quietly,
said to her sons, "You should take special care

that you perform the proper rites for Karna."
Yudhishthira was surprised. "That hero Karna,"
said Kunti, "whom you thought the son of Radha,
whom you despised as a driver's son—that man
who was unrivaled in integrity—
pour libations for him. He was your brother."

Yudhishthira stared at her, uncomprehending.
"I bore him by the sun god, Surya,
secretly, when I was very young,
too young to understand what was happening.
I was beside myself with fear and shame.
Secretly, I stowed him in a casket,
carried him to the river—and gave him up,
watched my son float away."

        Yudhishthira's
heart pounded; he shook, his face turned dark.
"Mother! How can this be? All these years!
How—oh, *how* can you have hidden from us
that Karna was our brother? That towering hero,
so brave, so skillful it took Arjuna—
and then only with Krishna's help—to kill him!
If Karna had been our acknowledged brother,
surely the war never would have happened.
This news is like a death to me, far worse,
even, than the loss of all our sons!"

Yudhishthira then sent for Karna's wives
and joined them in performing funeral rites
with Vedic hymns and solemn incantations,
relinquishing to sacred mother Ganga
the hero he had never known as brother.

As the tranquil water flowed around him,
Yudhishthira stood silent and alone.
Then, his mind boiling in confusion,
he stepped out of the river onto the bank.

XII

THE BOOK OF PEACE

48.

YUDHISHTHIRA, RELUCTANT RULER

After the funerary rites; when silence
had fallen on the plain of Kurukshetra,
the Pandavas remained outside the city
of Hastinapura, dwelling by the river
for a month, to purify themselves
from the pollution brought about by death.
Learned brahmins gathered, to provide
help and consolation; foremost of them
were Vyasa and Narada.

              Yudhishthira
was sunk in deepest sorrow. Narada said,
"Son of Pandu, why are you not rejoicing?
You have won the earth by force of arms
and won it righteously. Surely, now
you can put grief behind you, and be glad."
"I have, indeed, conquered the whole earth,"

said Yudhishthira, "through the strength of Krishna
and Arjuna. But since I have destroyed
so many of my kin, and other warriors
from far and wide; since I have caused the death
of Abhimanyu and Draupadi's five sons,
this victory tastes as bitter as defeat.
It is because I coveted the kingdom
that Subhadra's tears flow constantly.
And how can Draupadi ever cease grieving?

"But most of all, Narada, I am bowed down
with sorrow over Karna. He had no equal.
I think of him constantly, how generous,
how tall and straight he was, his golden color,
the way he swayed like a lion as he walked.
Honest, learned, firm in his resolve,
skilled in all weaponry, wonderfully brave—
no greater soul has ever walked the earth.
Yet Kunti waited until he was dead
to tell us that he was her son, our brother!
He knew it. Kunti went to him, and begged him
to alter his allegiance and fight with us.
But he was loyal to Duryodhana,
and he did not want it said he was afraid
of fighting Arjuna, his arch-enemy.

"'After the war,' he told her, 'when I have fought
Arjuna, when I have taken his life,
then I will make peace with the Pandavas.'
He promised her that, even if confronted,
he would not kill her other sons. That hero
kept his promise, as he always did.

"I remember—at the fateful dice game,
when Dhritarashtra's sons were taunting us,
I happened to glance at Karna's feet, and saw
they were like Kunti's! It struck me very much

but I could never explain it to myself.
I can't forget that I have caused his death.
I burn with regret that we were never friends.
Together, brothers reconciled, united,
the Pandavas could have fought the very gods!
Why was Karna so unfortunate?"

Narada told Yudhishthira the story
of Karna's birth and thorny path through life.
Then Kunti spoke coaxingly to her son.
"You should not grieve for him, Yudhishthira.
Grief is not wisdom, and Karna has surely gone
to Indra's heaven. I tried to persuade him
to reveal to you that you were brothers.
So did the sun, his father. But he was set
on his chosen course. I could not prevail."

Yudhishthira flared up in rage. "If only
you had not kept that secret to yourself
for all these years. Ah! I curse all women—
may they be unable to keep secrets!

"If only we had given up ambition—
lived, say, on charity in Dvaraka—
we never would have done this dreadful harm.
Ambition, an abiding sense of grievance
and greed for power brought us to this point.
Much better are self-control, sincerity
and harmlessness, the traits of forest dwellers.
Now, our kinsmen and our friends are dead.
I know Duryodhana always hated us;
he wronged us many times; we responded.
We were like dogs fighting for a bone
and both dogs died. For neither of us has won.
Millions of men, too young to have enjoyed
the pleasures of the world, now never will,
because of us.

        "But evil can be annulled
by the merit flowing from renunciation.
I am going to give up the kingdom,
take my leave of you, and live in the forest
without possessions. Then I shall be free.
Arjuna, you must rule instead of me.
The kingdom is yours; I wish you joy of it."

Arjuna was furious. "What nonsense!
What feeble self-indulgence! Having won
the kingdom through enormous sacrifice,
do you think you can just walk away?
Someone who lives on handouts ought to be
really poor, not playing at what he's not.
Poverty degrades a man. Wealth is the key
to respect for men like us. One without wealth
cannot follow kshatriya dharma, cannot
pay for the proper sacrificial rites.
The seers will tell you—even the gods themselves
achieved their power through force. And force brings wealth.
You should perform the horse sacrifice
for which you will need wealth—that is the way
to make atonement after a great war."

"No!" said Yudhishthira, "listen to me.
The road one treads alone is a peaceful road.
I shall live in the woods with the animals,
eating roots and berries, wearing rags,
my hair piled on my head. Enduring heat
and cold, harming no one, meditating
on the Vedas, I shall live alone.

"Or perhaps I shall smear myself with ashes
and wander from place to place, living on alms,
taking what comes, good and bad alike,
with equanimity. I shall have no wishes,
no possessiveness. I shall neither

want to live nor want to die; pleasure
and pain will be the same to me. Free
from attachment, free also from aversion,
I shall drift like the wind about the world
until the dissolution of this body."

"King," said Bhima, "your judgment has been addled
by all that learning, parroting the Vedas
mindlessly, by rote. What was the point
of crushing the Kauravas if you were set
on a life of idleness, turning your back
on duty? 'Harmlessness'! 'Non-attachment'!
If we had known your mind was heading that way
we could have caved in to Duryodhana
and lived a quiet life. But we went to war
because it was right to regain our kingdom.

"What you are proposing is as if
a hungry man refuses food, or as if
a virile man obtains a gorgeous woman
and turns her away. We obey you, brother,
because you're the eldest; but if the eldest
happens to be a eunuch, then we become
eunuchs too, objects of ridicule.
You maintain that you understand the Vedas
but you have picked up false interpretations
from witless renouncers."

Arjuna broke in.
"On my travels, I was told a story
about this very point:

"A GROUP OF BRAHMINS, hardly out of school, resolved on a
life of renunciation and, abandoning all family respon-
sibilities, took to the forest to lead an ascetic life, living on
scraps. Indra saw them and, taking the form of a golden bird,
flew down to talk to them.

" 'Those who eat scraps,' he said, 'do something that is very hard for humans. Their life is truly praiseworthy.'

" 'That's us!' said the brahmins, pleased with themselves. 'We are following the highest path.'

" 'No, not you, you dust-smeared idiots. Real scrap-eaters are not like you at all.'

" 'Oh,' said the brahmins, crestfallen. 'Teach us what is good.'

" 'Good for brahmins is not good for all,' said the bird. 'And what is good for one stage in life is not good for every stage. Taking to the forest is the path for those whose social duties have been accomplished. The world depends on ritual action to maintain order. The householder is the true scrap-eater—he who eats what is left only after he has done his duty by his family, guests, the gods and his ancestors, adhering to the proper observances. His is the really difficult path.'

"Understanding now, the young brahmins returned to their families, and followed the dharma appropriate to their station."

Nakula, who rarely spoke, spoke now,
blushing a little. "Brother, the priests tell us
that the path of ritual action is the highest.
For kshatriyas, and specially for a king,
that type of renunciation is the best
which gives generously, dispensing riches,
lawfully acquired, to the deserving.
The kind of renunciation you propose
involves unbalanced human attributes—
an inappropriate want of energy.
Merit is the fruit of righteous action,
not the result of chasing after it.
Having fought this grievous war, and won,
you should use your victory to good effect,
not run away from responsibility.
Seeking your own spiritual advancement
is not renunciation, but selfishness.
Use your wealth to pay for sacrifices—

that is the virtuous way. Renunciation
is a state of mind, not a facile gesture.
To live in the world, accepting its fruits
without attachment—that is renunciation;
not giving up and heading for the woods."

Sahadeva said, "Nakula is right.
True renunciation is not a greedy
craving for perfection of the spirit,
however strictly one may mortify
the flesh, and give up ordinary comfort.
You could renounce all wealth and seat yourself
beneath a tree with nothing but a loincloth,
but if you think 'This is my tree,' well, then
your detachment would be lost. Oh, brother,
forgive me if I'm speaking foolishly.
I only say these things out of love for you."

Yudhishthira was silent. Draupadi spoke.
Sometimes in the past she had addressed him
harshly, and was inclined to be disdainful,
deeply conversant with dharma as she was.
Now she spoke in sorrow. "Yudhishthira,
your brothers are crying in the wilderness
for all you care. They have suffered badly;
you could make them happy. Don't you remember
what you said when we were in the forest
undergoing every deprivation:
'After we have conquered our enemies
we shall enjoy the earth, offer sacrifices
and give abundantly to brahmins'—your words!
How can you disappoint your brothers now,
when they have risked their precious lives for you?
A eunuch gains no riches. A eunuch
does not wield the rod of punishment.
A kingdom whose king shrinks from exercising
due authority can never prosper.
Harmlessness, study, asceticism—all these

are a brahmin's business, not a king's.
A king's duty is to protect the pious,
punish the wicked, and stand firm in war.
A king knows both fear and fearlessness,
anger and patience; he knows when to give
and when to take. You did not win this war
through holy learning, nor through moderation,
certainly not through cowardice. You won it
through prowess and bravery, against a force
stronger than yours in numbers. And you crushed them!
The whole world honors you—yet you're not happy.
Don't snatch defeat from the jaws of victory!

"Kunti told me, when you married me,
'Yudhishthira will bring you great happiness.'
She was wrong—your mind is out of joint,
and when the eldest in a group is mad
the rest follow. If your brothers had their wits
they would clap you in shackles, and rule the earth!
A man who behaves like you needs medicine—
ointments, inhalations, poultices,
whatever it takes! Oh, Yudhishthira,
even though I have lost my precious children—
after our sufferings, I want to live!"

She sat down, and Arjuna spoke again.
He spoke about the role of punishment,
how without it, or the threat of it,
no one would behave as the law requires,
horses and dogs would be ungovernable,
children would boldly disobey their parents,
people would grab each other's property—
the world would be a terrifying place.
"Someone has to wield the rod of punishment;
that person is the king, Yudhishthira."

Bhima was getting more and more impatient.
"Yudhishthira—we try to understand you

but you're a mystery. How can a king
who has studied all the learned treatises
be as confused as any ignoramus?
Listen to me now—I have an argument
to convince you that you must be king.
If it is your nature to hark back
constantly to what is past, consider
the time when we were nearly burned to death,
the time when Draupadi was roughly treated,
the years when we were homeless refugees—
so many other times when we have suffered.
That should remind you why we fought the war
and make you see why we should enjoy the kingdom
and you should rule it. Now that the war is won
you need to turn to the battle for your mind."

Yudhishthira reflected. When he spoke
it was as if he were wrestling with himself:

> *"You desire the kingdom*
> *because you're in the grip of evil passions—*
> *greed, agitation, pride, a lust for power.*
> *Desire feeds on itself, insatiable,*
> *so conquer desire.*

"Conquer desire
by enjoying the earth that you have won;
that is the highest good.

> *"The highest good*
> *comes only after death, in the afterlife.*
> *That is not reached through riches.*

"The kingdom's harmony, its peace and wealth
depend on how you rule.

> *"Free yourself*
> *from that heavy burden—renounce this world.*

"The tiger has one belly, but what he kills
feeds many creatures that depend on him.

"A wise man shrinks the scale of his desires;
a king wants conquest, and is never satisfied.

"Those who eat only leaves, drink only water,
and consume only wind, are miserable.

"Those who see the many as the One
gain the freedom that comes from understanding.
Renounce wishes, have no sense of 'mine.'
They who set no value on possession
cannot lose, and will grieve for nothing.
Janaka, looking at his royal city,
said, 'If Mithila were engulfed by fire
nothing of mine would perish in the flames.'"

"Yes," said Arjuna, "I know the story
of how King Janaka renounced his kingdom
and became a beggar—thought himself a saint;
his wife thought otherwise! Hear what she said:

"'LOOK AT YOU! Sitting there with shaven head, a grain of wheat in one hand, holding your rags together with the other. Once, you were a source of nourishment to family, guests, priests, the gods. Now you beg from them!

"'What about those who depended on you? What can I, your lawful wife, expect from you, now that you are selfishly pursuing your own advancement? I have no husband, and yet he walks the earth, doing nothing. Hypocrite! You say you are free of possessiveness. Would you truly be indifferent if someone stole your robe and broke your water pot? I don't think so. As a king, you installed the ritual fires, supported holy men by the thousand. Why could you not cultivate non-attachment while living in the world? Do you have to act out

this pantomime? King Janaka did good to the whole community. Janaka the beggar contributes nothing!' "

"Arjuna, you just don't understand,"
said Yudhishthira. "I know the Vedas;
I know the arguments around these issues.
You have lived your life as a warrior
and have not thought about the subtleties
as I have. While I was sitting in the forest
discussing with the seers, you were away
on other business. But you mean well, I know,
and I appreciate your sincerity."

"I still maintain that a life of action,
of deeds that make a difference in the world,
is better than passivity," said Arjuna.
"And to be effective, you need wealth,
whether it be for ritual purposes
or to sustain those who depend on you.
To rule the kingdom and dispense your wealth
with wisdom is the highest possible good."

"But wealth brings evil," said Yudhishthira.
"Men invariably want more and more.
Craving, aversion—these are the great causes
of suffering. They bind us to the wheel
of endless birth and rebirth. A wise man knows,
true freedom comes from renunciation."

49.

YUDHISHTHIRA LISTENS
TO THE SEERS

At this point of impasse, the great ascetic
Devasthana entered the discussion.
"Arjuna is right to defend wealth,
but one must understand its use correctly.
You know that a man's life should have four stages:
first a student, then a householder,
next a forest hermit, and finally
a renunciant, wandering the world.
A life is like a ladder to be climbed
step by step, in the correct manner.
You should not try to leap to the top rung
before you have attained the previous three
with due regard to the conduct right for each.
You have won the earth, Yudhishthira,
and won it lawfully. You should not now
simply renounce it—that would be misguided.

"As a king, you are a householder.
Your task is the support of your dependents
and providing wealth for sacrifices
to sustain the gods. Wealth was created
to support such ritual sacrifice,
and by making offerings in this way
people acquire merit. With wealth, also,
they make donations to those who deserve them,
especially priests—and true wisdom resides

in judging who is worthy and who is not.
By this means, through sacrifice and gifts,
a man at the householder stage of life,
living without anger, fear or greed,
may be content. So you, Yudhishthira,
should cast aside your grief, and do your duty
as a king and householder, devoted
to the protection of your subjects, free
of negative emotions."

                    "Only listen,"
said Arjuna, "to this excellent advice
and shed your misery. All those we killed
died as warriors, and are in heaven now;
knowing this, why should you grieve for them?
Think of Indra—he killed his wicked kinsmen
and is honored for it throughout the three worlds."

Vyasa agreed: "What if all and sundry
took to the forest just as they felt inclined
before they reached the proper stage in life?
You must exercise authority
as King Sudyumna did in ancient times."
"Tell me about that king," said Yudhishthira.

"TWO BRAHMIN BROTHERS, Shankha and Likhita, were
living a life of abstinence, each in his own hermitage
beside the lovely river Bahuda, down in Panchala country.
One day, Likhita went to visit Shankha but found he was not
at home. While he waited, Likhita idly picked a ripe fruit and
was eating it when his brother returned.

"'Where did you get that fruit?' asked Shankha angrily.
'Who gave you permission to pick it? You have committed
theft. You should denounce yourself to the king, and ask him
to punish you.'

"Likhita went to King Sudyumna, who knew him well,
and told him what he had done.

"'If I am the agent of punishment,' said the king, 'I also

have it in my power to pardon you—which I hereby do, knowing you to be a man of scrupulous conduct.'

"Likhita was pleased, but he insisted on his punishment,
so the king had his two hands cut off.

"In great pain, Likhita went back to his brother. 'Blessed
one,' he said, 'I have borne my punishment. Now, please forgive me.'

" 'I am not angry with you, brother,' said Shankha. 'You
have atoned for what you did. Now go quickly to the river and
pour libations to the gods and the ancestors.'

"Likhita waded into the water and, as he tried to pour
water in the prescribed manner, his two hands reappeared,
whole and perfect. He was amazed.

"Shankha said, 'I performed this miracle with my ascetic
power.'

" 'But if you could do this,' exclaimed Likhita, 'why did
you not purify me of my sin before?'

" 'It was not my dharma to inflict punishment on you.
That is the king's task and, through performing it, he has
gained merit, and so have his ancestors. You, too, have been
purified by it.'

"You should follow the ancient king's example,
Yudhishthira. Listen to Arjuna.
Wielding the rod is right for a kshatriya;
shaving the head is not. And, furthermore,
you owe it to your brothers and Draupadi,
after so many years of deprivation,
that they should enjoy life as they did before."

"To rule can bring me only misery,"
said Yudhishthira. "I am tormented
by the terrible laments of those poor women
whose main purpose in life is now denied them—
to be loving mothers, sisters, wives."

Vyasa said, "You feel responsible,
but to think that these events were your doing

is arrogant, my son. Nothing occurs
unless the time has come around for it;
those of perfect understanding know this.
Only time governs our lives' events,
whether they be tiny or momentous;
the shallowest breath, the greatest massacre—
both are produced by time. What happens happens.
To resist, or to recriminate
and wish it had been otherwise, to yearn
for another chance, another life, is fruitless;
craving is the source of suffering.
Happiness and sorrow, pain and pleasure—
both pairs of opposites bring suffering
if one engages with them. Better by far
to accept what time delivers, knowing
that there is nothing changeless but change itself."

But Yudhishthira was still unconvinced.
He hardly took in what Vyasa said,
so gripped was he by grief. "Abhimanyu,
just a child! And all Draupadi's sons!
Bhishma—that dear man who was so kind to us
when we came as boys to Hastinapura.
My mind is haunted by the memory
of how he staggered as if struck by lightning
under the onslaught of Arjuna's arrows.
And the lie I told to our great teacher,
Drona, making him lose his will to fight,
causing him such grief! And most of all
our brother Karna, who always fought fairly—
all those great men would be among us still
but for my hunger to possess the kingdom.
Knowing this, I cannot live. Farewell.
I will sit in this place, and fast to death."

"This is very wrong," said Vyasa sternly.
"Your grief is self-indulgent and excessive.

You have not heard what I have been telling you
so I will repeat it, in another way.
Please pay attention." And Vyasa spoke again
about the wheel of time, and how it brings
both pleasure and pain to everyone on earth.
"We are born; we die. And in between
we briefly act. We are like transient bubbles
arising on the surface of a stream:
not here, then here, and then again not here.
All that happens, everything we do,
is conditioned by unfolding time.
We make plans, choices, we act well or badly,
and think the outcomes are of our own making.
But it is time, working through our actions,
that shapes events. This war, Yudhishthira,
that gives you so much pain, was predetermined;
every death was unavoidable,
no matter how it seems."

         The Pandava
was silent. Then Arjuna asked Krishna
to speak to the downcast king. Yudhishthira
had loved his cousin since they had first met,
more deeply, even, than he loved his brothers.
Krishna held his hand and, speaking gently,
told him he should not grieve, emphasizing
everything that Vyasa had said before him.
As he spoke, he glowed with a gentle light.
"Those who were killed on the field of battle
are like figures in our dreams. We have awoken;
they are no more. You should not weep for them.
They all died fighting bravely, as true heroes."

Vyasa spoke again. "Any kingdom
needs a ruler to enforce the law,
to punish those who act improperly.
That is what you did by waging war

against Duryodhana and his supporters.
You set out to protect the social order;
you acted righteously."

        "But it was greed
that motivated me," groaned Yudhishthira,
"and, but for that, millions of brave men,
prematurely swept to Yama's realm,
would be here now."

        Vyasa shook his head.
"Your cousin sinned against morality.
To have refrained from punishing transgression
would have made you complicit in that sin.
Therefore, the war you fought was justified.
You did your duty as the Dharma King.
As for responsibility—consider
who is the doer. It may be human beings,
it may be the gods, it may be chance, it may
be karma, the consequence of previous actions.
Where the gods act through a human instrument
they are accountable—just as, if a man
chops down a lovely tree, we blame the man
and not the ax he uses. You may object
that even if the gods determine deeds,
the people who perform them are responsible
if they intend them for their own purposes
and desire their fruits. But this is not correct.
The gods are still finally accountable.
No one can escape what is ordained.

"But even when someone commits wrongdoing
on their own initiative, it can be
expiated by subsequent good acts.
If you believe that acts arise randomly
by chance, then good and bad do not exist;
the world is mere chaos. But that will not do.
People want to distinguish good from bad

and the most perfect guide to that is dharma.
Furthermore, actions have consequences
for the one who performs them—that is karma.

"So you should be confident, Yudhishthira,
that you have rightly followed kshatriya dharma.
But in atonement for the suffering
the war has brought, you can ensure your conduct
is exemplary from this time onward."

"My guilt is too appalling to be expunged
by mere good deeds. Only the most severe
ascetic discipline will do. Please tell me
of hermitages that will meet my need."

Vyasa said, "Sometimes, Yudhishthira,
right looks like wrong. That's how it is with you.
You have acted rightly, as was ordained,
yet, blind to this, you burn with wrongheaded guilt.

"The solution I prescribe for you
is to perform a great horse sacrifice.
That sacrifice will require huge resources
of energy and wealth. It will be hard.
Start by going in turn to all the kingdoms
whose kings you killed in battle. Make peace with them
with soothing words. Appoint their sons or brothers
as successors, and have them consecrated.
If there is no one left in the male line,
have queens or princesses appointed ruler.
After encouraging those territories
in this way, return to Hastinapura
and prepare for the horse sacrifice.
In that manner, even though the war
was ordained by the gods, you will atone
for any shameful motive you may have had."

For the first time, Yudhishthira was hopeful.
He began to see a way to conquer grief.
He asked Vyasa to explain more fully
right and wrong action. Vyasa answered him,
then suggested that Yudhishthira
should go to Bhishma for more profound teaching
before the patriarch gave up his life.

"I am not worthy," said Yudhishthira,
"to approach Bhishma, guilty as I am
of his great suffering on his bed of arrows."

"Nonsense!" said Krishna. "Stiffen your resolve
and do what Vyasa tells you. He knows best.
The whole kingdom is waiting for you—please
make us all happy."

                    Yudhishthira stood up.
He had put aside his spiritual torment
and found some peace of mind. The time had come
for the Pandavas to enter the city.

After worshiping the gods, Yudhishthira,
radiant as the moon in the firmament,
mounted a gleaming chariot, draped with the skins
of antelopes. It was drawn by sixteen
auspicious white cattle, driven by Bhima.
Arjuna grasped the dazzling white parasol;
the twins held ceremonial yak-tail whisks.

The rest of the royal party followed—
a line of chariots, carts and palanquins
scattered with fragrant flowers and perfumed powders,
escorted by huge elephants, foot soldiers,
horses, and musicians blowing trumpets.

The streets of Hastinapura were close-packed
with joyful citizens. The royal cortège

processed through the decorated entrance
and up the King's Way hung with welcoming flags
and swagged with fragrant garlands. On each side
of the broad thoroughfare stood splendid mansions,
and women leaned from every balcony,
waving and singing praises. At the far end,
in the vast and well-proportioned square
stood the royal palace, festooned with flowers.

Yudhishthira descended from his chariot
and paid reverence to the effigies
of the gods, scattering them with petals.
After he had honored Dhritarashtra
and Dhaumya, the household priest, Yudhishthira
bestowed many lavish gifts on brahmins—
sweets, gold, jewels, cattle, clothing—
and they loudly blessed him and sang his praises.

When the noise died down, one Charvaka
approached Yudhishthira, to speak with him.
Disguised as a brahmin, he was in fact
a rakshasa, a friend of Duryodhana.
"All these brahmins," he said, "have entrusted me
to speak for them. They wish me to say this:
'May evil come to the Pandavas. Curses
be upon you for slaughtering your kin!'"
The brahmins howled him down. "You wicked monster,
you do not speak for us. We bless the king!"
Then, simply by chanting "hum," the brahmins
burned up the rakshasa. All were relieved.

After the brahmins left, Krishna said,
"I always honor brahmins. They can kill
through their ascetic power, but at the same time
they are easy to please. Now, Yudhishthira,
be cheerful! Be glad of your good fortune,
kill your enemies, protect your subjects,
honor brahmins—and do not be weak!"

❧

"Tell me what Yudhishthira did then,"
said Janamejaya, "once he regained
the kingdom." Vaishampayana continued.

❧

The royal son of Kunti shed his grief.
He sat enthroned, surrounded by his household,
and held an audience for his subjects,
who brought him gifts according to their means.
Dhaumya lit a sacred fire on the altar
and assembled all the objects he would need.
Then, with Draupadi seated by his side,
Yudhishthira was duly consecrated
king of the Bharatas. And so it was
that the Pandava took back his kingdom
in the presence of those who wished him well.

❧

Yudhishthira ordained that Dhritarashtra
should be treated by all with deep respect,
as he had been before. Vidura,
Sanjaya and Yuyutsu should attend
the aged king. Yudhishthira installed
Vidura as his own adviser. Bhima
was heir apparent, and worthy Sanjaya
was put in charge of records and revenues.
Nakula was made head of the army.
Arjuna was to ensure public order
and look out for subversion in the kingdom.
The king required sweet-natured Sahadeva
to be his personal bodyguard at all times.

The first shraddha rites were carried out
for the Pandavas' kinsmen killed in battle.
Dhritarashtra made lavish donations
to brahmins, in memory of his sons.
No one was forgotten, and the king
was specially solicitous to women
who had lost all their male relatives,
guaranteeing them royal protection.
He made sure the poor were well provided for.

❧

The next morning, Yudhishthira's first act
was to design a system of rewards
appropriate to every class of person
who was dependent on him. In doing so
he laid down a ground plan for the way
the kingdom would be run. This calmed his mind.

Then he went to Krishna. The dark-skinned one
was sitting in deep meditation. Dressed
in yellow silk, seated on a fine couch,
he looked like a rare jewel set in gold.
The king greeted him; he did not reply.
Yudhishthira marveled at how still he was.
He bowed to Krishna as the blessed Lord
and gave voice to his devotion, speaking
his many names. "O origin of all things,
changing and unchanging, without beginning
and without end, ruler of all the worlds,
I worship you. I submit to your will."

Krishna stretched his limbs and smiled at him.
"Bhishma is meditating on me—my mind
had gone to be with him. When he is no more,
the earth will become like a starry sky
without its moon. Yudhishthira, you should go

and seek teaching from him, otherwise
his profound wisdom will vanish with him."
"I will," said Yudhishthira, "and Bhishma needs
to see you." Krishna's chariot was made ready
and they set off for the field of Kurukshetra
together with a mounted retinue.

"Look there," said Krishna, "over to the right
are the lakes that Rama Jamadagnya filled
with kshatriyas' blood, when he destroyed them
twenty-one times over."
                              "Then how was it,"
asked the king, "that kshatriyas survived
to perish in such numbers at Kurukshetra?"
As they traveled, Krishna told the story.

"LONG AGO, when people lived for thousands of years,
the earth was tyrannized by violent kshatriyas, burning and looting, persecuting brahmins, causing mayhem
everywhere. Some of them killed the seer Jamadagni, and
in revenge, his son, the fiery-tempered Rama Jamadagnya,
swore to rid the earth of kshatriyas. Twenty-one times he
almost succeeded, slaughtering men and boys by the million. But each time, a few survived. Some were secretly protected by their mothers, or not yet born when the massacres
took place. Others were hidden by seers, or by cows, monkeys, bears, or by the ocean.
   "Eventually, Rama offered the earth to the seer and
ancestor, Kashyapa, who banished Rama to a distant spot, in
order to preserve the remnant of kshatriyas. The earth was
in a state of anarchy because there were no kings to enforce
order. The goddess Earth pleaded with Kashyapa to create
kings, in order that she would not be continually ravaged,
and she nominated kshatriyas who were particularly heroic.
Kashyapa appointed kings from among them, and they
founded lineages. The Pandavas and other royal kshatriyas who live today are their descendants. As for Rama, he

devoted himself to becoming a great master of weaponry. He
was the teacher of Bhishma, and of Karna—with the tragic
results we know about. He has always retained his hatred of
kshatriyas."

Now they were getting close to where Bhishma lay.
The field was still a monument to death—
the ground a mess of bones and hair and hides;
millions of skulls gathered up in heaps
waiting to be dealt with. The remains
of funeral pyres were everywhere. Mountains
of arrows, axes, maces, swords lay rusting.

The patriarch lay with great seers in attendance—
Narada, Vyasa, Devasthana . . .
His eyes closed, he was engaged in praising
Krishna, the supreme deity.

                    "O Lord,
the unmanifest within the manifest;
the knower of the field, the supreme witness;
light of the world, lord of all creation;
whose fiery brilliance is greater than the sun;
lord of all that moves, and everything
that is still; the eternal irreducible;
who is the embodiment of perfect freedom;
whose hair is the rain clouds, in whose limbs
run the life-giving waters; who is time
and beyond time; who is the supreme Self;
who is the maker and who is the destroyer—
I devote myself to you. Help me to see
the path to blessedness in the world hereafter."

So prayed Bhishma in his hymn of praise.
He was like the sun, and his many arrows
were its rays. Krishna greeted him gently.
He could see the patriarch's strength was fading.
"I hope your mind is clear, O Bharata.

I hope you are not in unbearable pain.
Most excellent man, no one surpasses you
in wisdom and ascetic discipline.
Here is the virtuous King Yudhishthira.
The Pandava is struggling with searing grief
after the death of so many of his kin.
Please speak to him. Help him to understand
the dharma of kings; resolve his perplexity."

Krishna conferred a blessing on the patriarch,
and Bhishma witnessed, with his inner eye,
the divine manifestation of Vishnu—
in the past, the present and in time to come—
a revelation granted to very few.
He raised his voice in wonder, joy and praise.

"Bhishma, in the days remaining to you,"
said Krishna, "please instruct Yudhishthira
in all he should know." Bhishma joined his hands.
"My mind is foggy—pain from all my wounds
is sapping my energy. My speech is slurred.
And how can I lay claim to wisdom, Krishna,
when you are here? I would be ashamed—
it would be like a pupil holding forth
in the presence of his revered master."

"Greatest mainstay of the Bharatas,
your wisdom is legendary," replied Krishna.
"But I can ease your physical distress.
You will have no more pain or tiredness,
your mind will be clear, and you will remember
all you ever knew. With your celestial eye
you will see the truth of things entire,
as if watching fish in limpid water."

The sun was dropping behind the western hills.
All took their leave and left Bhishma to rest.
The royal party rode back to the city.

卐

In the morning, Yudhishthira decided
he would go back to Bhishma with no escort,
only Krishna and his family.
They found the seers around him, as before.
Yudhishthira could not bring himself to speak,
so Krishna approached. "How is it with you?
I hope you are comfortable." Bhishma replied,
"Thanks to you, all my pain has left me,
my mind and understanding are diamond clear.
But why, tell me, do you not yourself
teach Yudhishthira?" Krishna answered him,
"I wish to do you good. What you teach the king
will become known throughout the three worlds,
bringing you great glory. The Pandavas
are here. Please speak to them like a father;
they trust you utterly."

             "Let Yudhishthira
question me," said Bhishma. "That son of Pandu
is scrupulous in his respect for dharma,
self-controlled, truthful and devout.
He worships the gods and respects his elders,
is gracious to guests, and generous to brahmins—
Yudhishthira should say what he wants to hear."

"He is too full of shame to approach you,
aware of having harmed you, and so many
other outstanding men. He fears a curse."

"Krishna," said Bhishma, "as you know, the scriptures
have laid down that warfare is to kshatriyas
what piety and study are to brahmins.
A kshatriya should always be prepared

to kill even his kin in a just cause.
Yudhishthira has acted honorably."
Hearing this, Yudhishthira drew near
and clasped Bhishma's feet. "Welcome, my son,"
said Bhishma. "Be seated, do not be afraid.
Whatever you desire to know—ask me."

50.

THE EDUCATION OF
THE DHARMA KING (1)

Now came a time when King Yudhishthira,
with his family and Krishna listening,
sat, day after day, at Bhishma's feet
receiving knowledge and the profound wisdom
gained in a life of dedicated service
to the house of Bharata.

                         The new king
had spent all he had to gain the kingdom
and now, even though he had found peace
from the worst pangs of self-doubt and remorse,
he suffered still. Restless, he paced his rooms
night after sleepless night. How could he ever
be a ruler great enough to justify
the enormity of what the throne had cost:
the frightful slaughter, all the broken lives—
children who would not, now, have a father
to launch them in the world; nubile women
whose beds would be perpetually cold.

Although he yearned to have no part of power,
longed for the solace of renunciation,
he had accepted that there was no escape
from royal obligation. In that spirit,
therefore, he had come to learn from Bhishma.

Whatever questions the young king put to him,
all his fears, all his perplexities,
the patriarch had patient answers for him.
And, to breathe life into the dry bones
of abstract principle, he told stories
of brahmins, gods, of legendary rulers
and of mythic animals and birds.

༄

"All-wise Grandfather," said Yudhishthira,
"people say kingship is the highest calling.
To me, it is a burden—yet I know
that for a people to pursue in peace
the goals of merit, wealth, and enjoyment
their king must perform his royal duties.
If he does not, the kingdom will be ravaged
by evil and confusion. A king's rule
acts like the tether that keeps an unschooled horse
from running wild. So please enlighten me—
what are the crucial duties of a king?"

"My son," said Bhishma, "first you must understand
that only a man devoted to the gods
and generous to brahmins will succeed
in following the dharma of a king.
But do not suppose that supernatural help
will be available if you yourself
do not engage in energetic effort.
Both these are necessary: human striving
and blessings from the gods. But of these two
effort is most crucial—when informed
by a strong, unwavering devotion
to the highest reality.

      "The brahmins
are the most important people in this world.

They are the guardians of timeless wisdom
acquired through study and through lifelong practice
of meditation and austerities,
as well as through their virtuous former lives.
They should be treated with the highest honor
as their attainments benefit us all.
At each important moment of our lives,
at times of change, of joy and desolation,
at our point of entry into the world
and at our leaving it, the ancient prayers
and rituals the brahmins perform for us
ease our spiritual pilgrimage
through this world and the next.

        "With that support
the king can function as a man of action.
From time to time, this question is debated:
does the age produce the king, or the reverse?
Have no doubt—the king creates the age.
When a king rules following his dharma,
wielding the rod of royal authority,
society runs smoothly, as it should.
The gods are worshiped properly, the crops
are plentiful, the people are contented.
All is harmonious in heaven and earth.

"A bad or foolish king will bring about
an age inferior in every way:
sinful, confused, tormented by disasters.
A good king makes the world a better place
in small ways, and in great. His righteousness
sustains morality; the rituals
which he supports construct and integrate
the very cosmos. For him, the right path
is not pursuit of personal liberation
and does not lead to renunciation.
Rather, it takes him to the heart of conflict

and complexity, where those he governs
depend on him for justice and protection.
That is your lonely path, Yudhishthira.

"I know the memory of war still haunts you
and that inclines you to be lenient
toward your subjects. Yes, you can by all means
cherish your people. But you should be careful—
kindness is not always the best policy.
Kindness to one person may directly lead
to suffering for another. Never think
only of your personal inclination,
but of how you are seen—of how the office
of king is served, or not, by your decisions.
The king's every action will be assessed
by the people, according to their lights.
Be guided by the Vedas; royal justice
should neither be too harsh nor too indulgent
but should strike a balance between the two,
moderate, as the sun is in the spring.
In that way, you will earn respect and honor.

"Brahmins will help you; seek out their advice.
But you must be aware—not every brahmin
is what he seems, or what he ought to be.
Some may be deviant, seek to undermine
your authority and harm the kingdom.
Such men should not be physically chastised,
but should be banished to some distant spot,
cut off from the temptations of intrigue.
A king should punish all, even his teachers,
who work against his interests and act wrongly.

"A king's servants cannot be his friends.
Do not allow familiarity,
joking, and so on. They should never think
it is their place to question your decisions

or offer opinions. If they do, then soon
they will be running things at court their way
and boasting that the king seeks out their views.
Then they'll start stealing from the royal coffers,
riding the king's horses, wearing his clothes,
resenting his orders—imagine where it ends!
Clear boundaries make everyone contented.

"A good king sustains the social order
and he judiciously administers
the public purse. He ought to recognize
his people's right to property, and should not
high-handedly deprive them of it. That way
they will respect him. A good king is steady,
free from fits of anger or despair.
He is self-disciplined, fair in his dealings.
His people move in safety round his kingdom
as children do within their father's house.
Protection is the principal advantage
every subject looks for in their ruler.

"If he is to carry out his duties
the king has to survive, and that entails
a sharp awareness of his enemies,
both those who may surround him every day
and those in other kingdoms with an interest
in attacking his. While avoiding
morbid distrustfulness, he should be watchful,
astute; never underestimate
the harm that can be done by hostile men.
Even a weak ill-wisher can do damage,
as a small fire can become an inferno.
Think ahead, listen to your spies, store up
provisions against hard times. Gain support
among the people through your virtuous conduct.
A kingdom is a complex entity;
maintaining it will call for every shred
of energy and judgment you can muster."

"Bravo! Bravo!" cried the assembled seers
sitting around Bhishma. But Yudhishthira,
as evening fell, was serious and sad.

༄

Early the next morning, Yudhishthira,
after performing his prayers and ablutions,
sat again at Bhishma's side.

                    "Grandfather,
explain to me: how is it that one man,
whose body is the same as other men's,
who is no more noble or accomplished
than many others, who is born and dies
as they do—how is it that this one man
is called 'king,' and must protect the earth,
is respected above other men
and treated like a god?"

                    Bhishma replied,
"There was a time in the history of the earth
when there were no kings, and no use of force
or punishment; all people lived in peace
with one another, honoring the law.
But then greed arose, lust and anger,
and people grabbed what did not belong to them,
fought each other, and forgot morality.
Their ritual obligations were neglected.
All was chaos; the people were desperate,
lacking any source of authority.

"The gods hurried in distress to Brahma,
lord of creatures. 'Blessed one,' they cried,
'we are afraid. The natural reverence
accorded us by humans has broken down.
These days, they no longer honor us

and we no longer shower them with favors.
Our divine status, which derives from yours,
is disappearing.' Brahma thought long and hard
and composed the Group of Three, the goals
all men should follow to avert chaos:
virtue, wealth and pleasure. And he specified
a further, spiritual, goal: moksha—
release from the ceaseless round of birth and death,
merging the self with the absolute.

"He composed a hundred thousand lessons
addressing every aspect of earthly life.
The gods were satisfied. They asked Vishnu
to nominate a leader, one superior
to other human beings, a person worthy
to implement the teachings of Lord Brahma.
After some setbacks, and with difficulty,
the seers identified a virtuous man,
respectful of the gods, and of brahmins,
imbued with the spirit of Vishnu himself.
His name was Prithu, and the seers were sure
he would be attentive to the brahmins' views,
and enforce the law. They consecrated him.
The populace welcomed him as their ruler.
That was the origin of kingship. Soon
order and prosperity returned,
the earth flourished and men and gods were happy.

"Of course, not every king since those distant days
has defended virtue as he should.
But the ideal is there; all recognize
and love a worthy king when they see him,
and without a king all would be chaos,
evil would prevail throughout the land."

"What causes evil?" asked Yudhishthira.

"Greed is the ultimate root of every evil.
People who covet what they do not have

are prone to anger, and become obsessed.
They are mean-spirited, enslaved by wanting.
Those who pile up wealth for its own sake
are often ruthless and contemptuous,
despising those less well off than themselves.
Lust comes from greed. Dishonesty, ill will,
envy, ruthlessness—every kind of sin
starts with desiring more than one possesses.

"Ignorance springs from the selfsame root.
Greed spreads its branches and the mind grows dark,
unable to judge clearly. Even the wise,
skilled in offering advice to others,
are rarely free, in their secret hearts,
of craving, lust, jealousy, and longing
for an existence free from every hardship.

"Yes, greed is the worst vice. To escape its grip
one must cultivate that self-control
which is the scaffolding of every virtue.
With self-control come patience, moderation,
gentleness and generosity.
Some people might take self-control for weakness
but it is really tolerance, openness
to all experience, a non-judgmental
acceptance of all that life may send our way.
A person does not need a forest ashram
if they can exercise such self-control
while engaged fully in the daily round."

༄

Yudhishthira asked about the four classes
in society, and about the four stages
through which a man may pass during his life.
Bhishma gave details of the many virtues
that all four orders should pursue in common.
He emphasized the close connectedness

between the different classes, how they depend
one on another; but how each has its own
distinct dharma laid down for its members;
and how the king must uphold the distinctions
and not permit the blurring of boundaries.

"As for a king," said Bhishma, "his first duty
is to his subjects, caring for their welfare
like that of his children. If they are virtuous
the king shares in the merit of his people.
He must be generous, without self-seeking.
He should worship the gods with sacrifices,
but not officiate; recite the Vedas
but not teach them. He should defend the land
bravely against marauding enemies.
To this end, he must acquire wealth
and rule the kingdom on enlightened lines.
He must use wisdom in choosing ministers
and advisers. They must be honest, able
and sincere, but the king should never
trust them entirely, nor confide too much.

"The key to all this is authority:
the power to use the rod when necessary.
A king should never act with cruelty
but he must not hesitate to punish
wrongdoers, in proportion to their crime.
Without the use of proper punishment
the kingdom will become demoralized,
there will be mayhem, and the old and weak
will become the helpless victims of the strong
as, in nature, big fish gobble small ones.
The king protects against the law of fishes.
Judicious use of royal discipline
ensures that every subject knows their place
and knows the conduct suitable for them
within the scheme of things. But if the king

applies authority erratically,
and only partially ensures fair treatment,
then, correspondingly, there will develop
all manner of ills—famine, epidemics
and breakdown of the basic forms of life.

"A king's strength derives from a well-trained army
which can protect the kingdom against attack,
and in turn can conquer other kingdoms.
In this way, wealth can be accumulated.
Conquest can be achieved by other means,
by cunning for example. He must send spies
into the territory of his enemy;
there they can use bribery, sow discord
and send key information back to him.
But constant vigilance is necessary
for the enemy can do the same to him!"

"What should be the personal qualities
of a good king?" asked Yudhishthira.

"A king should be the master of himself
before he seeks to impose his will on others.
More than this, there are many attributes
a king should cultivate—remember these:

He should do his duty without resentment.
He should be cheerful and affectionate.
He should pursue wealth without cruelty.
He should be brave without being boastful.
He should be generous, but not foolhardy.
He should not ally himself with evil men.
He should not engage in war against his kin.
He should not use dishonest men as spies.
He should avoid acting under duress.
He should not trust an irreligious man.

He should not betray confidences.
He should never kill a messenger.
He should not get angry without good reason.
He should work hard and conscientiously
and never be unmindful of the moment.
He should enjoy his pleasures moderately.
He should guard his wife, but without jealousy.
He should not act hypocritically.
He should not live too ostentatiously.
He should be thoughtful in everything he does.

"Whoever cultivates these kingly virtues
will be fortunate in this life and the next."

"Grandfather," Yudhishthira asked Bhishma,
"being a king is such a heavy burden,
so much responsibility. How can he
avoid being continually anxious?
With such opportunity for error,
how can he ever sleep at night?"

       "My son,"
replied Bhishma, "you should surround yourself
with virtuous brahmins, and with ministers
who are the wisest and best-qualified
men you can find. In choosing them, be guided
not by personal preference or love,
still less by pressure to confer favors,
but rather by your own considered judgment
of their abilities and character.
They should be men whose interests coincide
with yours, men innocent of secret motives.
Be ready to suspect your ministers.
Beware of any person who would profit
either from your misfortune or your death.

"The brahmins you invite to live at court
must be learned in the Vedas, and devoted
to right action. Support them generously;
their prayers and wisdom will console you daily.
Surrounded by such men, anxiety
will be kept at bay. In particular,
your court priest will be a refuge for you."

But Yudhishthira was once again
overwhelmed by doubt: "I have never yearned
to be king, not for a single minute!
I agreed because everyone around me
persuaded me it was the right decision.
But it seems that there is no 'right' in kingship.
It is impossible to be a king
without engaging in immoral actions.
I'll have none of it! I renounce the throne
and the royal rod of force that goes with it.
I'll go to the forest, live on roots and berries,
and live a life of prayer and meditation."

"But you *are* a king, Yudhishthira,"
said Bhishma patiently. "If you retreat
to the woods, renounce the world, to follow
your own spiritual path, you will be
a king reneging on his kshatriya dharma,
behaving like a brahmin, or like someone
in the final phase of life. I know you value
gentleness, and shrink from the exercise
of forceful authority. But the fact is
nothing great has ever been achieved
by gentleness alone. Your forebears knew this,
they knew their duty was to protect their subjects,
and what they knew should be good enough for you.
The proper dharma of a king is action;
for a kshatriya, nothing is more evil

than inertia. Your parents' greatest wish
was always for you to embrace your duty."

"But is it never right," asked Yudhishthira,
"for a person to follow the life path
of an order other than their own?
After all, some brahmins become warriors."

"They do—but they are rarely right to do so,"
replied Bhishma. "It is the king's duty
to correct brahmins who have veered away
from their proper calling—those, for instance,
who live as merchants or farmers. It may be
that they do so out of hardship. Then the king
should provide them with adequate support,
so they return to their appropriate dharma.
Brahmins who are ignorant of the Vedas,
and make their living in a different way,
should be taxed like other citizens.

"It is the role of brahmins and kshatriyas
to support one another. To that end
the two orders should remain distinct,
each pursuing its appropriate path."

"That sounds straightforward," said Yudhishthira.
"The Vedas tell us we should give to brahmins,
but where does giving end? It seems the scriptures
make no allowance for a king's resources.
What about periods of scarcity?
The Vedas say, trust in the sacrifices
the brahmins carry out on our behalf.
But how can we trust, when all we can give
is scraps and scrapings from our empty coffers?"

"You should not have such disrespectful thoughts,"
said Bhishma, "nor should you insult the Vedas.

Gifts to brahmins are part of sacrifice;
you give what you can."

        "But aren't those gifts
merely a transaction, a form of payment
for the merit the sacrifice produces?
Rather than such ritual sacrifice,
one's body can be a sacrificial vessel
in ascetic practice. In my view
asceticism is better than sacrifice."

"Listen to me, O learned one," said Bhishma.
"Asceticism withers up the body—
what merit lies in that? True self-denial
consists in kindness, self-control, compassion,
truthfulness—wise people know that these
are true asceticism. Doubting the Vedas,
our timeless spiritual authority,
is to abandon any absolutes—
that way destruction lies. No more foolishness!"

⚜

Yudhishthira asked Bhishma every question
he could think of, relating to the duties
of a king. When his attention focused
on the particulars of governance
it seemed to steady him, and calm his doubts.
They discussed strategies for protecting
a great city, and how to make provision
for possible emergencies. "The city,"
said Bhishma, "should be strongly fortified,
and there should be capacious granaries
and other stores inside the city walls.
Life should be pleasant for all citizens,
with shady courtyards, fountains and broad streets.
The buildings should be gracious and strongly made,

the markets well supplied, and there should be
fairs, festivals and temples where the gods
can be honored. Treasury and armories
should be well stocked. Experts in every art
coming from far and near should be welcomed in.
The city is like a living organism
with different parts working in harmony.
The king should take a hand in everything,
be aware of every activity,
so no intrigue can flourish behind his back.

"The countryside that lies around the city
is its source of sustenance, and must be milked
as if it were a cow—but not so much
that it becomes exhausted. Country dwellers
must feel fairly treated, their lives secure
against marauders. As for paying tax,
which no one likes, the king should make it clear
that they are living under constant threat
of aggression by invading hordes
who will certainly lay waste to the land
and rape the women if not beaten back
by a strong army—for which tax is needed.
Tax is the king's wealth, but if the burden
is felt to be oppressive and unjust,
rich cattle owners may migrate elsewhere.
A wise king encourages the wealthy
since their wealth will benefit the kingdom.
It is impossible to treat all alike.
The king should cultivate the powerful
and ensure the compliance of the rest.
But the rich should not despise the poor,
nor must the strong take advantage of the weak.

"The kingdom must be run on moral lines.
Taverns and whorehouses should be suppressed,
and begging banned, except in times of famine.
Robbery should not be tolerated.

"A king should be impartial—never swayed
by prejudice. Always observing dharma,
he should live soberly, and shun excess,
arrogance, falsehood and anger. Women,
except his wives, are to be avoided.
He should make certain that intermarriage
between one social class and another
does not muddy the waters of his kingdom;
that will be the best way to ensure
dutiful conduct within the family."

☙

They talked at length about war: how to tell
right from wrong action, how to discriminate
between appropriately war-like acts
and dishonorable trickery.
"I hate kshatriya war," said Yudhishthira,
"so many lives are lost by it—for what?"

"War can bring prosperity," said Bhishma,
"as well as rewards in the afterlife.
A kshatriya is born for the battlefield.
Suppose he goes to war to defend brahmins—
a worthy cause, a response to evildoing—
there could be no more glorious sight on earth
than a brave warrior offering his body
as sacrifice, his bright blood flowing freely
over his limbs. The gods rejoice to see it.
And when that kshatriya dies, washed clean of guilt,
in the fullest flower of his manhood,
he heads for heavenly bliss. It is most shaming
for warriors to meet death in their beds,
coughing feebly, moaning and shivering.

"Nevertheless, a king should avoid rashness.
If a stronger kingdom threatens his,

he should bide his time, not start a battle
he is bound to lose. He should be like
the reeds that grow beside a swollen river
which, bending flat with the powerful current,
only stand up when the time is right.

"But a flourishing kingdom does not spring
from war alone. A king should first secure
his base at home, by good governance.
A strong base comes from contented subjects
in both the city and the countryside.
The people should be plump and prosperous,
the army in good heart, and those at court
busy and purposeful. This comes about
when the king is mindful of right action,
when he is solicitous for his subjects,
is moderate, generous and energetic.
Of life's three goals—merit, wealth and pleasure—
pleasure should come last for him. His people
will see how he works hard on their behalf
and will love and honor him.

        "Only then,
when all is well at home, should the king think
of reaching for the wealth of other kingdoms
by well-planned attack. He should invite them
to submit to his authority,
promising that he will rule them fairly.
If they are reluctant, he should seek
to offer payments and conciliate.
Only if they refuse should he make war,
and then using the least possible force,
with due respect for the rules of chivalry.
Having conquered, he should pay attention
to winning hearts and minds in his new lands
through gifts and friendly speeches. Punishment
should not be used on men whose sole offense

is having fought against him. Treated well,
his new subjects may not feel inclined
to forge alliances with his enemies.

"But do not discount humiliation.
To be defeated is a bitter thing
for a proud people; memory is long
and there will always be brave young hotheads
who wish to have revenge, and prove themselves.
So the king must always be vigilant
against conspiracy, and train his spies
to be his eyes and ears."

       "Revered Grandfather,"
said Yudhishthira, "explain to me
how republics work. Without a king,
why do they not split apart?"
       "Quite often
they do," said Bhishma, "when they have become
demoralized by greed and selfishness.
A republic's strength lies in the way
an individual's effort is amplified
by being joined to that of the whole group.
When collective loyalty is uppermost
in people's minds, when scrupulous attention
is paid to justice, fairly administered
by the wisest men, so corrupt influence
does not take hold, well, then a republic
will flourish. But when conflicting interests
are not resolved, then fissures will appear
and the weakened polity will fall victim
to the predations of its enemies."

51.

THE EDUCATION OF
THE DHARMA KING (2)

"How very many points," sighed Yudhishthira,
"have to be borne in mind by any person
who sincerely seeks a virtuous life!
Is there one precept, above all the others,
one should not forget?"

                    "In my view," said Bhishma,
"nothing is more important than honoring
one's parents and one's teachers; they should always
be obeyed and treated with deference.
Mother, father, teacher—they are the three worlds,
the three sacrificial fires. Their needs
should never be neglected. There is no one
in the world more wicked than a person
who harms any of these, by word or deed.
Of these, the teacher is the most important.
The two parents create the child's body
which grows, strengthens, withers and grows old.
But one is born again through the instruction
the teacher offers. That teaching is divine,
timeless, and never decays with age."

Yudhishthira was struggling with confusion.
Though Bhishma talked of honoring one's parents
above all others, the Dharma King remained

angered and shocked by what Kunti had done
in covering up the truth of Karna's birth.

"How can a man go on?" he cried to Bhishma.
"I want to live virtuously, but how to tell
right from wrong, when truth and falsehood seem
so intertwined? What *is* truth, what is falsehood?
And should one always speak the truth, regardless?"

"There is nothing higher than truth," said Bhishma.
"But sometimes truth is false, and falsehood true.
A simple person clings to the literal;
wisdom brings deeper discrimination.
The law on what is right is intended
for the good of creatures, avoiding harm.
So, on occasion, lying may be right—
think of simple-minded Kaushika.

"There are many circumstances when the truth
may not be what it seems, and nor may lying.
Someone who witholds the truth, while not
directly lying, is committing falsehood.
Someone who lives by dishonesty
is a liar, and should certainly be punished.
But one who lies in order to support
a virtuous outcome is acting as they should.
And one who kills a hypocrite acts rightly
since, in fact, that sinner is already
killed by their own behavior. Remember too—
to act toward a person in the way
that they themselves have acted is to choose
right conduct.

            "You look downcast, Yudhishthira.
All you can do is live as best you can—
do your duty as you understand it,
enjoy your pleasures, but in moderation,

worship the gods, and devote yourself
to Narayana above all others."

"But tell me, Grandfather," cried Yudhishthira,
"how can a king possibly be happy?"
"He must cultivate his higher faculties,"
replied Bhishma, "and act with energy,
never opt merely for an easy life.
Let me tell you the story of the camel.

"LONG AGO, in a previous age, there lived a camel. He was a great ascetic and scrupulously obeyed his vows. Lord Brahma was pleased with him, and granted him a wish. 'Blessed one,' said the camel, 'I would like a neck so long that I could graze all around without having to move from place to place.' Brahma granted his wish, and life was then so easy for the camel that he became lazier and lazier and hardly stirred himself at all. One day, during a violent storm, rather than looking for proper shelter, he poked his head into a nearby cave to keep it dry, and his head got stuck. A jackal who had taken shelter in the cave started to eat the camel's neck. Try as he might, the camel could not escape, and that was the end of him. The story teaches us two lessons: do not become lazy; and—be careful what you wish for!"

ॐ

"I worry about how to choose officials
and retainers," said Yudhishthira.
"A king cannot rule by himself, that's certain,
so what qualities should I be looking for
in my staff? What background should they come from?
I understand what you said earlier—
the king should not be swayed by favoritism—
but how can I be sure to make wise choices,
of people I can trust?"

Bhishma replied,
"You should choose men from good families
who observe dharma, and who are rich enough
not to be corrupted. They should be
well educated and intelligent,
good at analyzing situations,
and astute at understanding people
and relationships. They should be capable
of planning ahead, practical, far-sighted
and meticulous in all their dealings.

"The most important guiding principle
is that they should be well qualified
for the posts they occupy. They should not be
promoted inappropriately. On this point
a story comes to mind:

"IN A REMOTE FOREST lived a seer, practicing extreme austerities and living on roots and berries. The animals of the forest regarded him as their friend and they would visit him to pass the time of day. One animal stayed with the seer all the time—a lanky dog, who ate the same food as his master and was calm and devoted.

"One day, a hungry leopard came that way, a large and cruel beast, and it stalked the dog with a view to eating him.

" 'Help me, blessed one,' cried the dog to the seer, 'a leopard wants to eat me, please rescue me.'

" 'Don't worry,' said the seer, and he turned the dog into a golden leopard. The dog-leopard was delighted, and cavorted around in the forest without fear.

"Then a hungry tiger saw the dog-leopard and thought he would make an excellent meal. The affectionate seer turned the dog-leopard into a tiger. The dog-tiger was delighted. But, now he was a tiger, he had no taste for roots and berries, and regularly preyed on the smaller animals in the forest.

"One day, the dog-tiger was sleeping off a large meal when he was woken by a shadow falling across his face. A gigantic elephant in rut was looming over him, about to attack. Once again, the seer rescued him, turning him into an elephant so large that his rival trundled off between the trees, grumbling. The dog-elephant was delighted to be an elephant, and joyfully plundered the lotus ponds and groves of frankincense.

"Another time, the seer rescued him from a lion by turning him into a lion fiercer than any other. The dog-lion was delighted to be a lion. But the gentler animals which previously had visited the seer were now too nervous to approach.

"You might think that no creature could frighten the dog-lion now. But one day an eight-legged sharabha, a horrific beast, approached the dog-lion. Again, the seer rescued him by turning him into an even fiercer monster of the same kind. The dog-sharabha was delighted to be a sharabha, and preyed on every kind of creature, so that all other animals and birds fled from that part of the forest, and the air was silent. Food became scarce, and one day, the dog-sharabha's lust for meat was such that his thoughts turned to attacking and eating the seer, his benefactor. But the holy man perceived this with his inner eye, and said to the dog-sharabha, 'Because of my affection for you, I changed you into fiercer and fiercer creatures. But now you want to attack me, ungrateful one! For this, you must return to your true nature.'

"The dog-sharabha, who had become so corrupted by advancement that he eventually wanted to turn on his benefactor, became a dog again. And the seer expelled him from the forest.

"Bear this tale in mind, Yudhishthira,
when you are choosing men as your officials.
Never appoint them to a post beyond
their natural station and capacities."

"Grandfather, what should be a king's public face?"

"The king is first and foremost a protector,
as I have said before," answered Bhishma.
"How should he go about it? He should learn
from the peacock's example. The peacock's tail
has very many colors. In the same way
the king should have a repertoire of styles
at his disposal. Sometimes he will be stern,
sometimes devious, brave, compassionate,
and so on—drawing on these various modes
at will, according to the circumstances.
Master of moods, effecting subtle changes,
he will manage even difficult matters.

"Just as a peacock is silent in autumn
the king will guard his intentions to himself.
He will keep his balance on slippery ground
as the peacock does at the edge of waterfalls;
and as the peacock relies on the blessed rain,
the king depends on blessings from the brahmins.

"As the peacock sports in the lush forest
and dances for its mate, so at night,
in private, the king's wives and concubines
will take pleasure in his virility.

"The king should gather wisdom where he can
as the peacock snatches tasty flying insects.
Just as a peacock frequents shadowy places,
the king should make alliances in secret,
taking care not to display his weaknesses.
Like the peacock, he should steer clear of snares.
His eyes should be as wary as a peacock's
when it looks out for poisonous snakes, and kills them.

"The king should be alert to all that happens
within his realm, moving among his people

as a peacock flies from one tree to another.
And, as a peacock cleans itself of vermin,
the king should shed attachments by performing
selfless deeds. Last, as the brilliant colors
and splendid outline of the peacock's tail
inspire the gorgeous flowers of the forest
to put forth their best blooms, so the king,
by dint of his exemplary behavior,
teaches his subjects to live virtuous lives."

ॐ

"Now I wish to know," said Yudhishthira,
"about the kingly rod of force, the *danda*.
You have often talked of its importance;
I am convinced that it is necessary.
But what form does it take? Does it mean
more than a suitably severe response
to acts of wickedness?"

                    Bhishma replied,
"The rod of force has many embodiments.
In concrete form, every single weapon
can exemplify it. More symbolically,
it is Lord Vishnu himself, and the goddess
Lakshmi, Brahma's daughter, and Sarasvati . . .
indeed, the rod of force takes many forms,
divine, mortal, public, private—too many
to list them all.

                "It is the origin
of the three fundamentals of a good life:
merit, wealth and enjoyment. It underlies
judicial process, whereby a wrongdoer
is fairly tried and punished equitably.
In a peaceful kingdom, there may seem no need
for correction. People live in harmony

with their fellows. But if the rod of force
did not exist, social cooperation,
and all it means, would not be possible.
Without the fear of punishment, the strong
would terrorize and kill the weak, and slaughter
each other.

       "The rod of force does not depend
on the whims and preferences of the king.
It is greater than any king, impersonal,
which is why it is held in such high regard.
It is an overarching principle
which protects us all."

       "Tell me, Grandfather,"
said Yudhishthira, "merit, wealth, enjoyment,
or the lack of them, are critical
in all we do. What is the origin
of these important elements of dharma?
And how are they connected?"

       Bhishma answered,
"When people can be cheerful faced with death,
that is because these vital elements
dwell in them harmoniously, in proportion.
A person's body derives from the degree
of merit earned in past and current lives.
So, too, does wealth—riches follow virtue—
and pleasure is said to be the fruit of wealth.
All of them are grounded in desire
based on the senses. Wealth is desirable
for the sake of doing meritorious deeds
which will lead to a fortunate rebirth.
A virtuous life consists in the right balance
between these three, and each should be pursued
with thoughtfulness, and in moderation.
Absolute freedom, permanent release

from the painful cycle of birth and death,
comes from going further than these three:
withdrawal from attachment to the senses."

Yudhishthira asked how one can acquire
habitual inclination toward dharma,
and Bhishma told him of a conversation
between Duryodhana and Dhritarashtra
when the envious Duryodhana
had just returned home from Indraprastha
after Yudhishthira's great consecration.

"Duryodhana was wracked by misery,
and his anxious father questioned him:
Why was he so distraught, when he enjoyed
the best of everything—friends and relatives
who obeyed him, fine clothes, spirited horses—
what could he wish for, more than he possessed?

"The prince told him about your assembly hall,
the beauty of which surpassed any other.
He told him about your enormous treasure
which he had seen with his own eyes. 'Oh, Father,
ten thousand brahmins eating from golden plates!
Exquisite jewels, gorgeous palaces,
coffers full of gold! My enemies
enjoy greater wealth than Indra himself!'
'My son,' said Dhritarashtra, 'if you want
wealth on the scale of Yudhishthira's, then
you must become habitually virtuous,
as he is. You must not indulge in anger.
You must restrain your passions and your senses
and cultivate wisdom. You must look kindly
on all beings, in thought, word and deed
and never desire something for yourself
that does not bring some benefit to others.
Wealth comes to the virtuous. If people

get rich while living contrary to dharma,
then they will not enjoy those riches long;
very soon, their actions will destroy them.'
That is what Dhritarashtra told his son.
We all know how he paid attention to it!"

"It still grieves me," said Yudhishthira,
"that Duryodhana could not be brought round.
Right up to the brink of war, I hoped
he would draw back, do what he knew was right.
I was foolish, but optimism is boundless.
It seems we all, at times, harbor great hope
despite the evidence. Why do we, Grandfather?"
Yudhishthira wept as though his shoulders carried
the weight of the world.

Bhishma told him this:

"ONCE THERE WAS a wise king called Sumitra. Hunting one day, he shot a deer, but not fatally, and the deer ran off, jinking and feinting and occasionally stopping to look back, as if playing with the king. He shot arrow after arrow, and some of them pierced the deer's hide, but still it ran, and still the king hoped to kill it.

"Eventually it entered a thick forest. The king pursued it, but lost it among the trees. Frustrated and disappointed, he came to a clearing where a number of seers were assembled. He told them who he was, and how his hopes had been dashed. 'Tell me, blessed ones,' he said, 'which is greater: the great bowl of the sky, or boundless hope? I have lived on this earth for many years, and I have never come to the end of hope.'

"One of the seers, Rishaba, spoke up. 'I will tell you of something I witnessed for myself when I was visiting Nara and Narayana. Walking near their retreat, I came across an ascetic so skinny that his body was the width of my little finger. I bowed before him and, as we were talking, a king came by with a large retinue, searching for his only son, whom he had lost in the forest. The king had been rushing here and there, always thinking that any moment he would find the boy, but he had got to the point where hope was a torment, for he knew it was likely that the child had been killed by wild beasts.

" 'It so happened that, sometime in the past, the skinny ascetic had asked this king for a golden jug, and some strips of bark for clothing, and had been insulted. He had vowed there and then to undertake extreme austerities to shrink his hopes, and this he had done. The king did not recognize him, and asked, in his anguish, "Can hope be made to shrink? Is there anything in this world more difficult to achieve?"

" 'The ascetic reminded him of their previous encounter, and told him of his austerities. The king was amazed. "Can anything in this world be more shrunken than you?"

" ' "When a father with just one son searches and searches and cannot find him—his hope is slimmer than I am," answered the ascetic.

" 'The penitent king prostrated himself, asked for forgiveness and begged the ascetic to bring his son back to him. This he did, through the great power of his spiritual accomplishment, and the king was overjoyed. The ascetic scolded the king for his past meanness, and then revealed himself as Lord Dharma himself.'

"When Sumitra heard this story, he immediately let go of his very slim hope of catching the deer.

"Yudhishthira, you should learn from this,
and be immovable as the Himalaya,
not allowing hope to bring you grief."

52.

DHARMA IN DIFFICULT TIMES

One day, Yudhishthira remarked to Bhishma,
"It seems to me that it is hard enough
for a king to live a life of righteousness
when times are good. How much more difficult
if his allies have turned their backs on him,
his treasury is exhausted, his army
is in disarray. Suppose his ministers
are corrupt, disorder plagues the land
and enemies are massing at the borders.
He would be too hard pressed to conduct himself
as you advised. What should the king do then?"

Bhishma looked grave. "This question goes beyond
what I agreed to talk to you about.
Dharma is subtle; what is right and wrong
is hard to speak about in general.
In such a case, a king who has been virtuous
will find within himself the moral judgment
to make the best decisions. He should be
pragmatic, and do what seems necessary
as a temporary expedient,
even if it does not lead to merit.
Only afterward will it be clear
whether that was the wisest course of action.

"This advice should not be heard as meaning
that anyone can bend the rules of dharma

when they like, to make life easier.
But a kshatriya, still less a king,
should never sink into ruin. If his wealth
is spent, the king must do what it may take
to replenish his empty treasury.
That is his duty since, lacking riches,
he can accomplish nothing. If ruthlessness
is needed, he must not hesitate. Later,
he can again become compassionate.
There is one law for normal times, and one
for times of crisis. He may have to take
riches even from brahmins, though normally
that would be a vile abomination.
But brahmins, too, if they are in dire straits,
must survive in whatever way they can,
trading, for example, or working the land—
reprehensible in normal times.

"The people should rally to the king's support.
If, in times of famine, he has given
his wealth to keep his subjects from starvation,
they should help him now—if they do not,
he is justified in using force.
For this is clear: a poverty-stricken king
is weak, and cannot benefit his subjects.
The king needs wealth not only for his army,
not only to maintain the royal household,
but to finance the sacrificial rites
that bring good fortune to the entire kingdom.
The sacrifices he makes possible
have cosmic consequences—as I have said,
the king creates the times, not the reverse.
Much depends upon the king's intentions.
To acquire wealth is his crucial duty,
but for general good, not for private greed."

"Meanwhile," asked Yudhishthira, "how should the king
deal with the enemy states that threaten him?"

"If the enemy is reasonable
and honest," said Bhishma, "then the king should seek
to conclude a treaty with them, even if
that involves restrictions on himself.
There may be circumstances where he must
flee the kingdom to avoid capture,
in the hope that, later, he will return.

"On the other hand, he may decide to fight
even if the odds are piled up against him.
It may be that he will be victorious
with even a small force of fighting men
who are passionately devoted to him.
But even in defeat he will win glory
from death in battle, and go to Indra's realm."

"In the worst of times," said Yudhishthira,
"when the rules that make a kingdom stable
are disregarded, and families are broken;
when wrong becomes right; when laws are despised;
when the religious principles of life
are treated with contempt—what should one do?
And worthy brahmins? How can they survive
when dharma is disintegrating, when
the land is scorched by evil?"

　　　　　　　　Bhishma answered,
"In such a case, the king has to rely
on his best judgment, and on that of brahmins.
In this world, brahmins provide the standard
for what is right. Whatever they may do,
if they are pure-minded, counts as dharma.
We all rely on their discrimination,
though we may not always agree with them.
Listen to this story of Vishvamitra:

"MANY YEARS AGO, there was a terrible drought that lasted twelve years. Rivers and lakes dried up, and crops failed. People starved, and the normal social activities of buying and selling, singing, worshiping stopped completely. People were so desperate that they roamed the countryside eating each other, stronger adults eating old people and children. Everyone feared everyone else.

"The wise seer Vishvamitra, with nothing to sustain him, wandered through the forest in search of food, and came across a run-down village where chandalas lived. He begged for food, but no one had anything to give him. In his extreme weakness, he lay down on the ground. Then he noticed, inside one hut, a rope on which a haunch of butchered dog-meat was hanging. He decided to wait until night, and then steal it.

"When it was dark, and all was quiet, Vishvamitra crept into the hut and was about to seize the meat when the chandala leapt from his bed crying out, 'Who is pulling at my rope and stealing my meat? I will kill you for this!' The seer replied, 'I am Vishvamitra.'

"The chandala knew him, and folded his hands in respect. 'What in heaven's name were you trying to do?' he exclaimed.

" 'I am starving,' said Vishvamitra. 'I have found no food anywhere, and I am near to death. I know it is stealing, and I am well aware of the dietary rules, but I have decided to eat the haunch of the dog that is hanging there.'

"The chandala was horrified. 'Great seer—the dog is the lowest of all animals, and its backside is the lowest part of all. And how can a brahmin steal from a chandala—it's grotesque! Rather than doing this, you would be better off going away and dying quietly.'

" 'My friend,' said Vishvamitra, 'life is better than death. Only by living can I engage in virtuous behavior. My body is a brahmin body, and I am devoted to it. I should do anything necessary to preserve its life. Besides, a dog is pretty similar to a deer, so I am justified in eating its rear end, which I am sure will taste delicious.'

"'Well,' said the chandala, 'do as you see fit, of course. But if everyone broke the rules when it suited them, where would we be?'

"'The body is different from the mind,' said Vishvamitra. 'My mind is pure, so even if I eat the dog's rear end, I won't turn into someone like you.'

"But the chandala had another thought, and kept a firm hold on the dog meat. 'No—I cannot collude in your behaving so unlawfully. If I allow you to steal from me, I shall be tainted by your sin as well.'

"'Of course, there is wrong on both counts,' agreed Vishvamitra. 'But wrong can be permitted *in extremis*, and I can atone for it afterward.'

"The chandala handed over the meat, and the seer ate it. Soon afterward, the rains came and the land became fertile again. Vishvamitra expunged his sin through extreme asceticism, and achieved spiritual perfection.

"This story teaches us that, in a crisis,
one may lawfully depart from dharma
just to keep going, to preserve one's life."

"That is horrible!" cried Yudhishthira.
"I am appalled. I don't agree with you
that Vishvamitra acted properly."

"Remember Vishvamitra's state of mind,"
said Bhishma. "If he had been driven solely
by lust for food, then you would have a point.
But he had weighed up the precise nature
of the wrong he was committing, and he knew
that he was doing wrong for the right reason
and could atone for it in the long run.

"In hard times, the king, too, must be pragmatic,
rather than sticking mindlessly to dharma.
He must gather wisdom from here and there,

and use his own best judgment. Yudhishthira—
be practical! You were made for fierce deeds."

"Is there any rule one should not violate?"
asked Yudhishthira, almost despairing.

"Respect and nurture brahmins, and attend
to what they say. Your strength will come from that.
Their wisdom nourishes; they are the guardians
of our sacred heritage, our social wealth.
Brahmins are like nectar when well treated,
but if you anger them, they are like poison."

⚓

"I am perplexed," said Yudhishthira.
"A kingdom is surrounded by other kingdoms.
How can the king decide which are his friends,
and which his enemies?"
                         "Here too," said Bhishma,
"you should be pragmatic. Alliances
cannot be expected to last for ever,
but should be made according to strategy.
Your allies will be those whose vital interests
coincide with yours—for the moment.
There is a story which illustrates the point.

"AT THE FOOT of a beautiful banyan tree, there lived
a mouse. Higher up in the branches lived a cat and,
higher still, flocks of birds and other creatures made their
home. The mouse was a survivor, and had built a burrow with
a hundred exits, to avoid being caught by any of his upstairs
neighbors, especially the cat, who was always on the lookout
for a juicy mouse.

"A lowborn hunter who lived in the nearby town came
every night to the banyan tree and set a snare. Every morn-

ing, after a good night's sleep, he would return and collect any animals or birds which had become caught in his net.

"One night, through carelessness, the cat became caught in the snare, held fast by the cleverly woven strings. The mouse saw this and rejoiced. He sauntered around at his ease, feeling much safer than he normally did. He climbed up on top of the snare to eat the piece of meat that the hunter had put there as bait. Gleefully, he pranced about on the net while he ate the meat but, as he chewed, he happened to look down, and he saw that another of his mortal enemies was waiting on the ground, licking his lips: a mongoose with eyes so red that it looked like the god of war himself.

"The mouse looked up, and saw that someone else was looking at him—an owl with a cruelly sharp beak, who lived in a high hollow of the tree. The mouse started to panic. It seemed that whichever way he moved, some creature would make a meal of him. But then he thought to himself, 'Surely there is a way out of this spot of trouble.'

" 'Cat,' called the mouse, 'I am speaking to you as a friend. I'm sorry to see the predicament you're in, but I see a way to free you; and it so happens that what is best for you is best for me too on this occasion, all things considered. That mongoose and that owl are out to get me, and they're making me nervous. Suppose I climb down to you, and you agree to protect me from the mongoose and the owl. I'll undertake to bite through the bonds that tie you, if you agree not to kill me. I save you, and you save me—how about it?'

"The cat looked at the mouse, his green eyes shining. 'What a clever mouse you are,' he purred. 'I agree to your excellent suggestion, and put myself entirely at your disposal.'

"So the mouse climbed down and snuggled comfortably on the bosom of the cat, whereupon the mongoose and the owl got bored and started to look around for faster food. Then the mouse started to gnaw through the strings of the snare, very, very slowly. The cat became more and more impatient. 'Why are you being so slow? Get on with it, before that cat-eating barbarian turns up!'

" 'What's your hurry?' said the mouse. "We both know how time operates. If I free you before the hunter arrives, then why would you not eat me there and then? I plan to gnaw through the last cord at the precise moment when I see him approaching—the moment when the danger is identical for both of us, and when your main concern will be to scramble up the tree out of his reach.'

" 'Why don't you trust me?' said the cat reproachfully. 'I know I hunted you before, but now we are friends for life. I will always honor and respect you, and so will all my relatives.'

" 'Listen to me,' said the mouse. 'Between the weak and the strong there can be no real friendship, let alone for life. There are only linked interests. Friendship and enmity are the product of the situation. Unlike the bond between brothers, neither trust nor sentiment comes into it.'

"At dawn, they heard the hunter's footsteps approaching, and the mouse quickly cut the last cord. The cat rushed up the tree, and the hunter went home disappointed.

"In this way, Yudhishthira, through the use
of his intelligence, a beleaguered king
can make use of a much more powerful ally
and outmaneuver him."

"But surely, Bhishma,
without trust, a king cannot operate.
How can he feel at ease with anyone?"
said Yudhishthira unhappily.

"It is enemies, actual and potential,
that you should never trust," replied Bhishma.
"Of course, you must have trust in ministers
and other staff whom you yourself have chosen
with utmost care. And you can be confident
in trusting brahmins who depend on you,
since their prosperity is linked to yours.
But trust must always be provisional.
Consider the story of the bird Pujani.

"PUJANI WAS a wise and learned bird who lived in the women's quarters of King Brahmadatta's palace. She and the king were friends, and often conversed together. Pujani gave birth to a beautiful son and, around the same time, the queen also produced a son. The two young creatures grew up playing together.

"One day, Pujani flew to a place near the ocean where wonderful fruits were hanging from the trees. She brought back one for her son, and one for the little prince. The fruit tasted delicious and was so nourishing that it brought an instant increase of strength. When the prince ate it, he jumped from his nurse's arms, grabbed the young bird and killed it.

"When Pujani saw her cherished son lying cold and still she was consumed by grief. She wept copious tears, and cried, 'Kshatriyas are heartless, incapable of friendship! This king's son has killed the one who ate and played with him, the one who should have enjoyed his protection.' She went to the prince and put out his eyes with her talons. Then she prepared to leave the king's court.

"King Brahmadatta tried to persuade her to stay. 'We have injured you; you have avenged the injury. Surely now we are even, and our friendship can continue as before?'

" 'Friendship between one who has committed injury and their victim can never be repaired. We both know that in our hearts. We two could never trust one another again.'

"And Pujani flew away."

❦

"How does one uphold the way of dharma
when villains are a power in the world?"

"There is no simple rulebook for a king;
he must use his mental faculties
and garner his ideas and policies
from a wide variety of sources.

A king who rules with scrupulous attention
to dharmic principles is justified
in doing all that is needed to maintain
prosperity, and his hold on the kingdom.
He should be ruthless with his enemies,
smashing them when the time is right—as one
might dash a clay vessel against a rock.
He should seek out an enemy's weak points
but hide his own, as a turtle hides its limbs.
Studying the example of the animals,
he should watch and wait like the crafty heron;
he should attack as boldly as the lion;
he should display the savagery of the wolf;
and, when he needs to, he should run away
like the rabbit. Remember, the rod of force
should always be ready at the king's right hand.
The threat of force is a great persuader
both at home, and toward rival kingdoms.

"There are those who twist the learned teachings,
who deplore the use of force by anyone.
They are people of weak understanding,
blind to practical necessity.
Others mock morality, and declare
that dharma is no more than what people do.
They too are ignorant and self-serving.
Dharma is highly complex, and a king
should be guided by those who know it best
through many years of devoted study.
The abstruse details are not his business.
He has been created to enforce
correct behavior throughout his kingdom."

❧

"What is the king's responsibility,"
asked Yudhishthira, "toward those who flee

into his kingdom—refugees escaping
persecution perhaps? Does he gain merit
by offering sanctuary?"

"He gains great merit,"
answered Bhishma. "Listen to this story:

"THERE ONCE WAS a wicked hunter, who made his living
by killing beautiful wild birds and selling them for
meat. No decent person would have anything to do with him,
so repugnant was his occupation. One day, in his wanderings
through the forest, he was caught in a violent storm which
flooded the forest and left him without shelter.

"In misery, and shivering with cold, the hunter stumbled
about until he came to a towering tree, and since he was far
from home, he decided to take shelter for the night under
its branches. Joining his hands, he addressed the tree: 'May
whatever gods live here protect me.' Then he lay down on a
pile of leaves, with a stone for a pillow, and tried to sleep.

"In that tree there lived a handsome pigeon. His wife had
been gone all day and had still not returned. 'Ah!' he sighed,
'some terrible harm must have come to my dear one. She is
so beautiful and so loving. I cannot live without her.' And he
called out in distress.

"His wife, who was caught in one of the hunter's snares,
heard her husband crying. 'Listen, beloved,' she called, 'this
hunter has sought refuge with you, and we know that great
sin accrues to one who refuses help to such a person. Treat
him with respect, therefore, and do everything you can for
him. Since your duties as a householder are completed, and
our children have flown, you should serve him even at the
cost of your life. If you do, you will certainly be rewarded in
heaven.'

"The pigeon's eyes filled with tears at hearing his wife's
wise words.

'Welcome,' he called to the hunter, 'you have taken refuge
in my house, and I wish to do what I can for you.'

" 'I am freezing to death,' said the hunter. 'Save me from the cold.' The pigeon collected leaves, flew to a nearby charcoal-works for the means to kindle a fire, and soon the hunter was warmed and revived.

" 'I am very hungry,' said the hunter. The pigeon thought hard. He had no food available that he could give the man—except himself. He walked three times around the fire and entered into the heart of it.

"When he saw this, the hunter was appalled, and consumed with shame and pity. 'This kind bird's death is my fault! His dutiful action has taught me a great lesson. From now on I shall follow an ascetic's life.' Then he set aside his snares, released all the birds he had captured, and left.

"The pigeon-wife flew up to the tree, and wailed in grief. 'Oh, my perfect husband!' she cried. 'He was always kind to me. He wooed me with his sweet songs; I remember how we made love in the treetops, how we swooped through the sky together. My life is empty without him.'

"Then she flew down and entered the fire herself, and as she did so she saw her husband in heaven, garlanded, riding in a beautiful chariot, honored by all, and waiting for her to join him.

"The hunter, looking up, saw the birds in paradise and he yearned to follow them. He resolved to begin his final journey, eating nothing but the wind, wandering from place to place, free of all personal possessions. Eventually he came to a forest which was on fire. He was overjoyed, and ran to the place where the fire burned most fiercely. There, his body was consumed, and his sins with it.

"So, Yudhishthira, a person's sins
may be expiated by devotion
and extreme austerity. But the sin
of spurning one who seeks out your protection
is dreadful, and can never be wiped clean."

☙

Yudhishthira derived great consolation
from Bhishma's teachings, which appeared to him
like a draft of purest nectar.

"Grandfather,
I hear brahmins talk about 'the Real.'
What is its nature? And how may it be known?"

"It is the all-pervading Brahman, essence
of everything that is, the entire cosmos.
In every object, every living being,
it is the atman, the true self, the soul.
We know it in meditation, when we see
there is no 'me' or 'mine' specifically—
that 'I' am part of everything that is.
When we hear the chanting of the Vedas
the Real is given expression in those sounds.

"The Real is that which every living person,
from the most accomplished sage right down
to the lowest sweeper, has in common.
It is impersonal. And it is changeless.
It manifests itself in human virtue."

⚜

Yudhishthira turned to the other Pandavas
and his uncle Vidura, who had been listening,
and asked them this: "I want you to think about
the three great goals of life. First, there is virtue,
law or dharma; then there is wealth, or profit;
finally there is pleasure, love, enjoyment.
Which of these three is the most important?
Which of them is the key to the other two?"

Vidura spoke first. "It is virtue
on which the other two always depend.
Think about it. Dharma encapsulates

the best of which mankind is capable—
learning, asceticism, renunciation,
unstinting faith, sacrificial rites,
compassion, truthfulness and self-restraint.
These are the perfections of the spirit;
practicing these, a person will be calm
and all their life's endeavors will be blessed.
Those will include wealth. As for pleasure,
that is the least of the three goals of life."

Arjuna sprang up. "This is a world
made up of action, and wealth is at its heart.
There are no activities that do not aim
at profit in some way. The holy scriptures
say that law and pleasure could not happen
without profit; profit makes all possible.
The wealthy man is able to follow dharma
and to enjoy pleasure. There are some—
mendicants, rattling their begging bowls—
who claim to have renounced pursuit of wealth
in favor of devotion to 'higher' goals.
But the test is in their state of mind.
Are they covetous? Are they in the grip
of attachment? If so, they are no less
involved in profit than a wealthy man,
while the latter may be indifferent to wealth,
seeing it as a means and not an end.
But I see Nakula and Sahadeva
wish to speak."

            The twins spoke hurriedly:
"Profit is the fruit of virtuous action;
and wealth makes pursuit of pleasure possible.
No merit: no wealth. No wealth: no pleasure.
So the three goals are inseparable."

Bhima joined in. "It's obvious that pleasure
and love are the key to every part of life

because they mean desire. Without desire
why would one pursue either wealth or virtue?
Why would one even rise up from one's bed?
Desire is at the heart of every action.
It takes many forms—enjoying, for instance,
delightful dalliance with seductive women
gorgeously dressed, murmuring sweet endearments . . .
If all men valued pleasure as I do
the world would be a kinder, more peaceful place!"

Yudhishthira smiled. "I'm glad to hear your views;
now, this is what I think. Someone who strives
after none of these; who can regard
good and evil with a dispassionate eye;
gripped neither by aversion, nor by craving,
free from fear of death—such a person
has gone beyond distinctions. All attention
is fixed on liberation, perfect freedom
beyond the endless round of death and rebirth.
That person knows the gods direct all beings,
that what has been ordained will surely happen.
Even without pursuing all three goals
one may attain moksha, absolute release,
the final object of a virtuous life."

The brothers praised Yudhishthira for his speech,
and he turned back to Bhishma, to question him
about the way that freedom can be achieved.

53.

THE PATH TO ABSOLUTE FREEDOM

Day by day, almost imperceptibly,
the year was moving onward toward winter.
The early mornings had a chill to them,
the sun swung lower through the midday sky.
Everyone around the patriarch
knew—though no one spoke of it—that soon
the winter solstice would arrive and, with it,
Bhishma's chosen time to leave the earth.

Soon—but not yet. Still he lay serenely,
free of pain, benevolent, alert,
answering Yudhishthira's every question.
Seated round him, listening in reverence,
were distinguished seers, gathered from far and wide.
They seated themselves around the patriarch
and began discussions among themselves,
praising Bhishma in the highest terms,
so that the old man thought himself in heaven.
Then they made themselves invisible,
their concealed energy lighting up the sky.

"Grandfather," said the eldest Pandava,
"now that you have taught me a king's duties
my mind is turning to immortal matters,
matters of the soul. How should one live
as a person in the world? How can the soul

obtain final release from the drear cycle
of birth, death and rebirth? And how can one
overcome the perennial pain of loss,
whether of possessions, or of loved ones?"

Bhishma replied, looking at him fondly,
"The virtuous life has many entrances.
To carry out your worldly obligations
at every stage of life will bring you merit
and is never wasted. But ultimate freedom
is of a different order. To approach it
a person must learn to release their grasp
on all that's dear to them, whether objects,
parents, children—or a cherished idea.
Of course, when these are lost one feels great sorrow,
but then, with the aid of meditation,
one should seek to let that sorrow go,
let it float free, like a passing cloud,
learning detachment, equanimity,
as King Senajit did in the old story:

"KING SENAJIT was burning with grief after the death of his son. A visiting brahmin found him prostrate with sorrow, and reprimanded him.

"'Use your intelligence. Who do you know who does not, at some time, become an object of grief for others? Include yourself in this; include me. We all return to the place we came from—there are no exceptions. Simply, this is what happens. You should not grieve about it.'

"'What you say is rational,' said the king, 'but, all the same, how does your heart not break when you know that someone who was the light of your life will never come to you again?'

"'My heart does not break,' said the brahmin, 'because I regard nothing as specially mine, not even my own self. I see the whole world as mine, everything as equally precious. By clinging to one son in a world of sons, you bring yourself nothing but suffering, lurching between joy and sorrow. Everything that happens is influenced by destiny, and only wisdom can bring understanding of the world. Friends, wealth, victory, love, hardship—those things we think responsible for our happiness or misery—they all pass. Only wisdom endures, and only the wise person lives at their ease. Such a one fears no one and is feared by no one; they wish for nothing and avoid nothing, but are in control of their senses. That, O king, is wisdom.'

"Hearing this, King Senajit cast aside his grief and again found purpose in his life."

"We humans live in very diverse ways,"
said Yudhishthira. "How can someone
who lacks the wealth to pay for sacrifices
find happiness in this world, or the next?"

"There is no need for costly sacrifice
for one who seeks ultimate salvation.
Sacrifice sustains the ancestors
in the heavenly realms, and it makes easier
one's own passage in the afterlife.
It can prolong one's stay in heavenly comfort
before one is reborn. But liberation
from the cycle of rebirth depends, rather,
on a person's spiritual achievements.

"Equanimity, not grasping after
this result or that; truthfulness;
absence of attachment to 'me' and 'mine'—
these are the qualities that bring happiness
and lead to liberation. A poor person
who travels through the world without possessions,
taking life as it comes, envying no one—
such a one sleeps peacefully at night
with his arm for a pillow. But the rich
ache with anxiety—with every breath

they dream their wealth is being snatched from them.
They wake, calculating how they may
acquire still more. Wealth makes people stupid,
muddy-minded. And consider parents
who see their children as their property,
clutching them close in the name of love!

"Everything comes and goes, ceaselessly changing
according to its nature. Time is a river
that carries us, and all phenomena,
ever onward. Every coherent thing
tends inherently toward dissolution.
How futile, then, to crave and cling. Far better
to accept that life is sometimes hard,
sometimes good, and welcome both equally,
knowing that nothing lasts, riding serenely
on the tide of change toward oblivion."

ॐ

"In what does human greatness most reside?"
asked Yudhishthira. "Is it in wealth
or kin, or doing good deeds, or in wisdom?"

"Wisdom is much the greatest attribute,"
Bhishma replied; and he went on to tell
the story of Indra and the rishi's son:

"KASHYAPA, THE SON of a rishi, a man of sober, pious
habits, was mown down by a chariot driven by a prosperous merchant, driving dangerously, full of his own importance. Kashyapa, badly hurt, lay on the ground and cried
out, 'I've had enough of life! A poor man's life is worth nothing in this world!' And he prepared to die.
    "As he was lamenting in this way, a jackal came by who was
really the god Indra in disguise. He rebuked Kashyapa. 'All
inferior beings envy the life of a human; you are a human.

And, among humans, everyone envies the life of a brahmin; you are a brahmin. Your life is an achievement, and you are foolishly proposing to give it up! Actually, you are motivated by greed—if you can't have everything your way, you want to turn up your toes. Consider this—you have hands. What wouldn't I give for a useful pair of hands! Without them, I can't extract this thorn from my body, or crush the biting insects that are driving me mad. With hands, there is so much you can do—build shelters, make clothes, construct a delightful bed to sleep on. Think yourself lucky that you are not a jackal or a frog. Or a worm—imagine that!

"'I don't give up on life just because I have no hands. When I look around me, I consider a jackal to be rather well off. But how few creatures are content! Human beings are never satisfied with what they have. They become wealthy—and they want power. They achieve earthly power—and they want to be gods. The thirst for gain is inexhaustible. But even the most miserable pauper rarely wishes to embrace death. If you recover from your injuries, pull yourself together and lead a virtuous life. Apply yourself to studying the Vedas, pass your time cheerfully, and you will win very great happiness. In my previous life, no one gave me such good advice. I insulted the Vedas and created mayhem—that is why I have been reborn a jackal.'

"Kashyapa was astonished at the creature's wisdom, until the jackal dropped his disguise and revealed himself as the great Indra himself. Kashyapa rose up and worshiped him. Then he limped home, a wiser man."

༄

Yudhishthira asked how gifts and penances
have beneficial outcomes for the giver.
Bhishma taught him the subtleties of karma.
"All a person does throughout their life
sticks to them as their shadow does, including
actions they would wish to be forgotten.

Each act is pregnant with its consequences.
Just as a plant develops flowers and fruit
at the proper time, without effort,
according to its nature, so the actions
of this life give rise to future outcomes
in the next. A person must live out
those consequences, whether good or bad,
until they are spent. But when one dies
some residue of merit and demerit
always remains, to be carried forward
and to determine the form of the next birth—
unless, through extreme austerities
and discipline, a person has achieved
final release, and union with Brahman,
the ultimate, eternal reality."

Bhishma went on to speak of many matters
relating to the state of being human.
"The human being is made of the elements:
earth, space, water, fire and wind.
Individuals combine these elements
in different proportions. The sense of hearing
springs from space or air; touch from wind;
sight is the attribute of fire, energy;
taste comes from water, and scent from the earth.
The more specific human attributes
are the mind, the understanding and the soul.

"With the five senses, we perceive the world.
Mind, confused, creates uncertainty.
Understanding clarifies perception.
And soul is the witness, which sees everything,
present in every atom of the person.
It is a fragment of the supreme Soul,
that universal spirit which infuses
the entire universe, all that exists.

"Three qualities in particular pervade
created beings, part of their inborn nature.
In human beings everywhere are found
complex strands of darkness, passion and goodness.
These govern our material existence.
Darkness includes anger, lust and hate;
passion means love, and all forms of attachment;
goodness embraces the higher moral sense.
Consciousness is made up of these three.
From goodness comes joy, from passion, misery,
and delusion is the fruit of darkness.

"The freedom-seeker must pursue goodness.
One in whom goodness is dominant
moves through the world as a swan does through water,
never drenched or dragged down, but rather
buoyant, tranquil, treating all experience
equally. That person generates
virtue as a spider spins its threads.
Such a person knows true happiness.

"The whole cosmos, threaded with desire,
turns and turns. Its revolutions sweep
the unwise person into its delusions,
into its giddy and frenetic dance.
Only one who sees with a clear eye,
who sees how craving feeds upon itself
and is never satisfied, will take the path
that leads to ultimate release—moksha."

༄

"Tell me about spiritual observance,"
said Yudhishthira. "I have encountered
silent reciters of the sacred Vedas.
What do they attain by such a practice?
What path are they following?"

Bhishma told him,
"It all depends upon their state of mind.
First they should strictly practice all the virtues,
subduing the senses, celibate, austere.
They should live alone, concentrating
on meditation and on non-attachment.
Using their mind, they should meditate
on mind itself, reducing their dependence
on all things external, all things internal.
In this way, the world of opposites—
self and other, joy and misery—
becomes increasingly unreal to them.
As they silently recite the Vedas,
they sit, meditating upon Brahman
—Brahman the formless, the One, the infinite—
losing all sense of distinctiveness
until only awareness itself remains.

"If they recite without any desire
for favorable outcome, they attain
the highest reward, complete liberation.
If they retain desire for the reward
of their pious practice, then they go
to the realm of one god or another,
or even to hell. There they experience
the attributes of that particular sphere.
Only if they relinquish all attachment
can they go beyond, and merge with Brahman."

Then Yudhishthira asked to be told
about the different spiritual routes,
the paths of understanding, and of conduct.
"If one's aim is spiritual release,
is it best to focus on observance,
fulfilling every ritual obligation
to the letter? Or should one, rather, follow

an inner journey—prayer and meditation—
toward enlightenment and final freedom?"

Bhishma said, "Acting scrupulously
in line with ritual and moral precepts
is always right, and leads to happiness.
But happiness is not the highest goal,
and a person who seeks it for itself,
gripped by craving, will find themselves in hell
tortured by suffering, a burning sense
of separation from the eternal One.
Only by true indifference to results
can action lead to liberation—union
with the divine, the inexpressible,
the being with no attributes, neither
male, female, nor neuter, neither existent
nor non-existent, beyond categories.
It is akin to the dark side of the moon—
we know it exists, though we are unable
to perceive it with our mortal senses.

"The path of understanding is austere.
It is the apprehension of the soul
by the soul itself. Devoted study
leads to great learning, but learning alone
will not reveal Brahman. Just as we may wait
for the moon to emerge from its shroud of mist
to light us on our way, so, patiently,
we wait for the One to manifest itself.
Only then can we come to experience
our own being as part of the divine.

"For this, we should detach ourselves from sorrow
and from every sensual impression.
We should not yearn for what is transitory
as a child runs here and there after a toy.
We should not say, 'Why me?' at our misfortunes,

but see that sorrow knocks at every door.
Cultivating true understanding,
we move beyond sensory experience,
beyond distinctions, beyond attributes,
even beyond language, into the radiance
of a clearer, more far-sighted vision.
In this way, our soul becomes prepared
to recognize that it has always been
continuous with the eternal Self.
The clouds disperse. We see. Only illusion
has kept our true nature hidden from us.
Those who are obsessed by earthly things
will never understand reality."

ॐ

"Grandfather, please tell me more of Vishnu,
the uncreated Creator of all that is."

"Vishnu is the highest of all beings,"
said Bhishma. "He created the elements
and the earth, and then he laid himself
floating on the surface of the waters.
He made consciousness, which infuses
all created things. And as he lay
on the waters, a most beautiful lotus
grew from his navel and gave birth to Brahma.
From the surrounding darkness, there then sprang
Madhu, a demon, bent on killing Brahma.
Brahma called on Vishnu to protect him
and instantly, Vishnu destroyed the demon;
that is why he is called Madhusudana,
'Slayer of Madhu,' among his many names.

"Vishnu then created day and night,
the seasons, and all temperaments of weather.
In Brahma's line, sons were born, and daughters,

and from them came animals and demons
and gods, to populate the three worlds.
Next he created the four human orders.
From his mouth, he created brahmins;
from his arms, kshatriyas; from his thighs,
he made vaishyas; and, lastly, from his feet
he brought lowly shudras into being.
He appointed gods to be responsible
for diverse aspects of the heavens and earth
and to guard the cardinal directions.
He made Brahma lord of created beings.
He appointed Yama ruler of the dead;
Kubera was lord of treasures; Varuna,
lord of the waters and of aquatic creatures.

"At first, there was no fear of death—people
lived as long as they chose. There was no sex.
Children were conceived by touch alone.
Only in a later age did people
feel the need to marry and live in pairs.
And only later, too, did warfare start."

"Tell me how Lord Vishnu saved the world
the first time, by taking animal form."

"This is how it was told to me," said Bhishma,
"in the hermitage of Markandeya:

"MANY YEARS AGO, the earth was overrun by demons.
They had become very powerful and arrogant and,
rather than being content with their earthly riches, they cast
their eyes up to heaven, and were envious of the prosperity
of the gods.

"The other inhabitants of the earth, minor deities and
their offspring, were oppressed and grief-stricken, and came
to Brahma in great distress. He reassured them. 'The fate of
those wretches has already been decided. They do not know

that the invincible Vishnu has assumed the form of a boar, and is out to destroy them for their pride and wickedness.' The petitioners were overjoyed.

"As Brahma had said, Vishnu, in the form of Varaha, burst into the place under the ground where the demons had congregated. Astonished, the foolish demons tried to fight the animal, seizing it and trying to drag it down. But however hard they tried, and whatever weapons they used, the boar remained unharmed. At this they became afraid. Then the boar started to give voice to roars so loud and terrifying that they resounded over the entire earth and through the heavens as well. The demons fell to the ground, unconscious, and the boar pierced them with its hooves, tearing the fat and flesh from their bones.

"At the tremendous sound, the gods ran to Brahma in confusion. He told them the world had been put to rights again by the great Vishnu—Creator, all-destroying Time, Ordainer, Upholder of the world. And he told them that, from time to time, when the earth was oppressed, Vishnu would incarnate himself, in order that balance and order could be restored. And so it happens that, in our day, he has taken birth as Krishna, for the good of all humanity."

This account was so wonderful, the listeners
were moved to tears, and gave heartfelt thanks
that they were living at this historic moment
when Vishnu walked among them on the earth.
The story was familiar but, somehow,
in the telling, it became news again.

"What are the faults a person should avoid,"
asked Yudhishthira, "if they hope for freedom?"

"Avoid those qualities that are born of passion
and darkness," warned the patriarch, "such as greed,

lust, anger, cruelty, procrastination,
laziness and self-indulgence. The person
whose soul is purified by austerity
will see these tendencies for what they are.
But those caught in illusion will meet sorrow.

"From the very moment we inhabit
a body, in the womb, sorrow begins.
We all have to be born from a woman's womb,
defiled by blood, phlegm, urine and excreta
which give rise to evil tendencies.
Women are primal substance; men are souls.
Wise men should keep well away from women;
they are the eternal embodiment
of the senses, and give rise to trouble.
Leading the fascinated mind to follow
as a child chases a dazzling butterfly,
they draw a man from his spiritual path.
A student at the start of life, practicing
celibacy, should avoid all contact,
even the most mundane, with any woman.
If semen spurts out of him as he dreams,
he should immerse himself up to the chin
in water, and remain there for three days.
If this fails, he should abandon sleep,
that forest of illusory delights,
and use the long hours of the night for study.

"Later, because the man desires a woman,
children arrive who undermine his quest
for wisdom. 'These are my children,' he will say.
But they no more belong to him than vermin
born on his body; he should shake them off
as he would fleas and mites. The man of wisdom
should avoid becoming attached to them.
He will find the practice of yoga useful
in harnessing the restless, possessive mind."

So said Bhishma, lifelong celibate.
And if Yudhishthira gave any thought
to Draupadi, sitting among the listeners,
and wondered what she felt, we will never know.

"A clear mind is the way to liberation.
Even compassion, since it is prone to lead
to attachment, will hold a person back
by focusing attention on particulars.
One cannot know the universal soul
if worldly concerns clutter up the mind
with material issues and distinctions."

☙

Day after day Bhishma shared his wisdom.
There seemed to be no end to the king's questions.
He asked how happiness could be achieved,
how fear could be avoided. What penances
were most appropriate; and whether people
really were the authors of their actions.

"On this last point," said Bhishma, "there is a tale
of the visit Indra paid to Prahlada:

"PRAHLADA, CHIEF of demons, had fallen on hard times, defeated by the gods, his enemies. Indra came to visit him, intending to gloat over his vanquished opponent, expecting to find him crushed and humiliated. But far from being cast down, the demon was living in tranquillity, seated in an empty room, meditating, observing stringent vows, and indifferent equally to praise and blame. A clod of earth and a heap of gold were just the same to him. He wished for nothing and avoided nothing.

" 'How is it,' asked Indra, 'that you are apparently so unaffected by the misfortunes that have come your way? You have lost everything, and yet you seem happy and serene.'

"Prahlada smiled. 'It is because I understand that every

event, every entity, comes into existence and then ceases to exist in accordance with its own nature. No personal effort is required to bring this about; it is simply what happens. I have been defeated; in time, you will meet the same fate. Time is the agent. Most people do not see it that way. They struggle to achieve a goal and, because they regard themselves as the doer of acts, they suffer torment when their actions fail to produce the desired results. They may blame themselves for not trying hard enough, or for not having acted cleverly. But they are the person nature has made them, and they act accordingly. A person engages in activity, of course, and the soul is the silent witness. It is foolishness for a person to feel proud of their talents, or to feel ashamed of their shortcomings. Even final release arises from nature, not from human effort by itself. Understanding this, I am incapable of grieving.'

"'How did you arrive at this understanding?' asked Indra.

"'I observe how nature works,' said Prahlada, 'how everything rises and falls. I pass my time very happily. I am obedient to my teachers and I listen to those who are old and wise. Watching the play of phenomena as they appear and disappear, I am without craving or hope, without affection or aversion, without fear or anger. I do not yearn for this world or the next.'

"Indra was profoundly impressed, and went thoughtfully back to his own domain."

☙

"Grandfather, is dharma meant for this world,
or the next?" asked Yudhishthira.
"It is meant for both worlds," answered Bhishma.
"Observance of the rules of dharma leads
to happiness in this world and beyond.
Each class should follow its own dharma.
Vaishyas should labor to create wealth;
kshatriyas should fight to protect it; brahmins

should spend the wealth appropriately; and shudras
should do the work that sustains the others.

"Everyone honors dharma—including those
who do not follow it. Even the thief
who wickedly robs others will appeal
to the king to enforce the rules of dharma
when he himself is robbed of his possessions."

"Is it possible," asked Yudhishthira,
"for a man to attain liberation
while still living as a householder?
Can a reigning king achieve moksha?"

In reply, Bhishma told him the story
of Janaka and the yogi Sulabha:

"MANY YEARS AGO, there lived King Janaka, who
claimed to have attained a state of liberation while
still remaining ruler of his kingdom. He was greatly revered,
and his fame spread far and wide.

"A female ascetic, Sulabha, heard the story of his achievement, and wanted to find out for herself whether it was true.
Through her yogic power, she took on the disguise of a beautiful woman, and presented herself at the king's court.

"Janaka, struck by her beauty, welcomed her and offered
her lavish hospitality. 'Who are you, and to whom do you
belong?' he asked her. As they sat, in the midst of an assembly of learned men whom Janaka had gathered around him,
Sulabha opened up the topic of liberation, asking the king
to tell her if he was, indeed, enlightened. She gazed into
Janaka's eyes, her yogic powers enabling her spirit to enter
his, and there ensued a conversation between them, both
occupying the same body.

"Janaka told Sulabha what he had learned about enlightenment. 'My guru, Panchashikha, stayed with me for four
months during the rainy season, and I was able to learn

from him all I needed to know. As a result, I have reached a state of equanimity. I regard all things as having equal value. I am free of attachment—I neither love my wife nor hate my enemies. I have learned that, by following the path of knowledge, it is possible to arrive at an exalted spiritual state. It is said that a king cannot achieve liberation; for that, one should renounce all earthly ties. But I have shown the contrary.

" 'Of course, I have to wield the rod of authority and distinguish between the law-abiding and the delinquent. But mendicant renouncers, too, reward and chastise people as they see fit. And many mendicants, while showing all the outward trappings of renunciation, have by no means achieved a state of non-attachment, as I have. My circumstances are affluent, I have great wealth, but liberation does not depend on whether one is rich or poor; it depends on knowledge.

" 'Madam, I have taken a liking to you. But I have to say that I regard it as very deceitful of you to enter my body with a view to testing me. It is also contrary to dharma. You are a brahmin woman, I am a kshatriya. By entering my body you have mixed the social orders in an inappropriate manner. Perhaps you have a husband somewhere? If so, you have committed the additional sin of adultery. You are living the life of a renouncer; I am a householder. So by entering me you have committed a third sin: the mingling of differing modes of life. It may even be that we belong to the same line of descent, in which case you have committed the further sin of incest! It seems to me that you must have an evil nature—otherwise, you would not be roaming around the country by yourself. And you would not be attempting to prove yourself the superior of a man. I suspect you wish to show your superiority to my whole court, and humiliate these learned men. But now that I have assured you that I have achieved liberation, you should tell me who you are, what is your background, and what is your purpose in coming here.'

"Sulabha replied, 'Being made of ever-shifting particles, the human being changes constantly, as the liberated person knows. By asking me who I am, and whose, you show that you are still mired in the illusion of distinct identity, seeing the world in terms of dualities. If you were truly liberated, you would see that there is no difference between me and others, or between me and you. The self is neither male nor female. If you were truly liberated, I could not have wronged you by entering your body with my mind.

" 'You speak of "having" great wealth. A liberated person does not speak of "me" and "mine." Of course, a king must worry about wealth, and must defend his kingdom. He has to live in a world of dualities. That is why he cannot attain enlightenment so long as he remains a king.

" 'As for your gross accusations—I have not touched you with any part of my body. How, then, could I be guilty of mixing social orders? My soul, which has entered you, is the same as your soul. What have I done, then? You have insulted me by uttering your crude accusations in front of the whole court. In fact, I am a kshatriya like you, a descendant of a royal sage. No suitable husband could be found for me, so I have devoted myself to the study of liberation, and am firm and steady in my vows. I came here in a spirit of inquiry. Tonight, I shall stay inside you, as if you were my chamber— an empty chamber, since I find that it is devoid of under- standing. Tomorrow, I shall leave your court.'

"King Janaka was silent, lost for a suitable reply."

⚜

"Which deity above all other gods
should one worship to obtain release?"
asked Yudhishthira. "The Lord Narayana,"
Bhishma replied. "Listen to this story:

"ONCE, IN the Krita age, the seer Narada was address- ing the divine seer Narayana, who was engaged in performing austerities. 'Since you are yourself the uncre- ated creator,' said Narada, 'whom do you worship as divine?'

Narayana replied that he worshiped the indestructible origin of all, the universal Self which infuses all beings.

"Then Narada, desiring to see the highest lord with his own eyes, traveled to the White Island, where those devoted to Lord Narayana, the supreme being, live in an exalted state, beyond the senses, motionless, pale and spectral as the moon. Narada performed extended acts of devotion, knowing that only those people may see Lord Narayana who have been devoted to him with their whole being, for a great length of time. He had practiced the most severe austerities, but not everyone who had done so, and who had traveled to the White Island hoping to see the lord, was blessed with that supreme vision.

"Narada sang a great hymn of praise to the god—that being without attributes who is the essence of all virtuous qualities—recounting his many forms and legendary deeds. Lord Narayana appeared before him, in indescribable bodily form, having something of fire about him, and something crystalline, something of gold, and something of the deepest lapis lazuli. He was enormous, with a thousand arms, and utterly beautiful. The god offered Narada a boon. 'O Lord, to have seen you with my own eyes is the greatest possible boon!' exclaimed Narada.

"Then he made his way back to the hermitage of the divine seers, Nara and Narayana. 'And have you seen the highest lord, the universal Self?' asked Narayana. 'I have,' replied Narada, 'and when I look at you and Nara, I see him still.' Then Narada remained at the hermitage for a thousand years, worshiping the supreme lord with all his heart and soul.

"Yudhishthira, you should remember this—
only those who are free of greed and passion,
only those who are devoted to him
with their entire being, will see the Lord.
In him are contained all other gods,
the Vedas, sacrifices, austerities . . .

To worship the highest lord, and him alone,
to be granted the unspeakable joy
of seeing him in his unearthly form
is all that is required for liberation.
From age to age, the Lord becomes incarnate
to protect his creation. Many tales
are told of his wonderful interventions
but, in the end, all the tales are one.
What I have told you is the essence of them
and, listening, your soul is purified."

Then the patriarch, in a fading voice,
yet ecstatic in his love for Krishna,
extolled his many marvelous attributes,
intoning his thousand names—a poem of praise,
a sublime hymn that is still recited
by devotees of Vishnu to this day.

Having heard Bhishma's inspiring words
Yudhishthira and his brothers all became
devotees of lord Narayana.

☙

Hearing all this from Ugrashravas,
the holy men of the Naimisha Forest
were eager to know more, and the bard told them
that Janamejaya had also asked
many questions of Vaishampayana.
How was it, he had wondered, that the gods
pursue the path of action in all the worlds
rather than the path to liberation?
"We pupils asked Vyasa the same question,"
said Vaishampayana. "He explained to us
that after the gods and seers had been created,
and after they had performed sacrifices,
Brahma assigned to them their diverse duties

to sustain the worlds—some to engage
in action, others to be disengaged.

"And remember," said Vaishampayana,
"Krishna's great teaching to Arjuna
when he was crushed by doubt on the battlefield.
The lord himself has revealed to mortals
the path of devotion, which can be pursued
in the midst of action and engagement.
I learned this from the great Vyasa here."
And Vaishampayana extolled Vyasa,
calling him the son of Narayana.

"Why do you call him that?" asked Janamejaya,
"when previously you have referred to him
as the island-born son of Parashara?"
Vaishampayana explained, relaying
what he had learned from Vyasa: "This creation
is only the most recent one of many,
stretching back through all eternity.
When Narayana stirred, and began to form
this world and its creatures, he created
a great seer named Apantaratamas
whose given task was to divide the Vedas
and make them known. Pleased with the seer's work,
Narayana told him he would be reborn
as the son of the rishi Parashara,
and would beget, in the line of Bharata,
a race of mighty princes, who would quarrel
and destroy each other—this being
Narayana's intention for the world.

"That is Vyasa, and those are his origins
—and who else but a portion of Narayana
could have composed the Mahabharata?"

XIII

THE BOOK OF
INSTRUCTION

54.

THE TEACHING CONTINUES

Even after all Bhishma had taught him,
all his exhortations, all his stories,
Yudhishthira had not gained peace of mind.
"How can I be tranquil," he cried out,
"when I see your body, blood-encrusted,
covered with running sores? When I see you
skewered on those flesh-tormenting arrows
and know your cruel suffering is my fault,
mine and Duryodhana's? That wicked soul
has never had to face what he has done
to you, and to so many brave warriors;
never had to sit here, watching you,
our blameless and beloved grandfather,
endure a living hell because of us.
How I wish a hero's death had saved me
from this relentless misery and remorse!"

Bhishma replied, "How can you still suppose
the slaughter was your fault? You were the channel
for forces much more powerful than yourself.
If you search for the causes of events
you should look beyond your blinkered mind.
Listen to this story:

"A BRAHMIN WOMAN called Gautami, who had seen a
great deal of life and had attained peace of mind, found
one day that her son had been killed by a snake. A hunter
caught the snake and brought it to Gautami, all trussed up
with string so that it could not move.

"'Here is the culprit!' exclaimed the hunter, dangling the
snake from his fist, 'and now I shall kill it for you. How would
you like it done? Shall I hack it to pieces? Throw it on the
fire? It's up to you—this creature has made you suffer, and
now I shall show it what suffering is!'

"'Let the snake go,' said Gautami. 'Killing it will not bring
back my boy, and you will only incur sin yourself by doing so.
I understand the difference between what can be changed
and what is inevitable, and true understanding enables one
to pass over life's waters as a ship sails over the ocean.'

"'What you say is all very well for an enlightened person,'
said the hunter. 'But for someone down-to-earth such as
myself, only revenge will bring comfort—so I'm going to kill
this evil serpent. To kill one's enemies is a virtuous act, after
all—and this snake is your enemy, so by allowing me to kill
it, you will acquire merit in the hereafter.'

"'You are wrong,' replied Gautami. 'What good can come
from tormenting an enemy? Rather, good comes from not
acting cruelly to one who is in our power.'

"The argument continued, to and fro, between them;
and the snake remained painfully tied up, listening, and
sighing to itself. Finally it said, 'You stupid hunter—I did not
choose of my own free will to kill the child. Death told me
to do it. I killed the boy, yes; but I am not an independent

cause. Cause and effect are highly complex. You should not be blaming me.'

" 'Well,' said the hunter, 'even if you aren't the only cause of the child's death, you are *a* cause, and you're the one we've got our hands on—so you should be killed.'

"Just then, Death himself appeared. 'It's true that I told the snake to kill the boy, but I was prompted by Time. So neither I nor the snake is to blame—we are not free agents. Time appointed us to do his work.'

"Then Time, too, arrived. 'Neither I, nor Death, nor the snake is the ultimate cause of the boy's death. That cause is the karma of the boy himself—his deeds in his previous lives. Karma is the cause no one can escape, no matter who, or what, delivers its effects.'

" 'What you say is right,' said Gautami. 'My son must have died as the result of his own karma—and my grief at his loss is the result of mine.'

"Gautami found comfort in this thought,"
said Bhishma, "as should you. Neither your cousin
nor you was author of this massacre.
A person's karma shapes their life and death.
And, beyond that, there is the cosmic plan,
the grand design constructed by the gods."

"Are we just trapped, then?" asked Yudhishthira.
"Just acting out a part provided for us,
a part we play in ignorance, until
Death comes to claim us? Tell me, Grandfather,
has anyone who leads a normal life
(not a renunciant practicing austerities)
ever defeated Death through their devotion
to dharma, through unwavering resolve?"

"Very few," said Bhishma. "A householder,
of whom a king is the supreme example,
has to deal with so many distractions,

temptations, compromises. But there was
Sudarshana, son of the fire god . . .

"Sudarshana had determined to conquer Death while living as a householder. He and his beautiful wife, Oghavati, lived a simple life—here at Kurukshetra, in fact. Sudarshana always impressed upon Oghavati that, for a householder, honoring a guest is the highest duty. 'No matter what a guest asks for, we must vow always to give it—even our own bodies.' Death, ever-watchful, was sure that, sooner or later, this vow would be broken, and then he would seize Sudarshana and carry him off.

"One day, when Sudarshana was out collecting firewood, a brahmin called at the house. Oghavati welcomed him with every attention and, after washing his feet with perfumed water, asked him why he had come, and what she could do for him. 'I have come because I am drawn by your great beauty,' said the brahmin. 'I want you to take off your clothes and surrender yourself to me.'

"Oghavati was utterly dismayed, and tried to interest the brahmin in other gifts. But he would not be put off. Remembering what her husband had told her, she took the brahmin to her bed.

"When Sudarshana returned with the wood, he was surprised not to be greeted at the door by his wife, and even more surprised when he called her and there was no reply. Locked in the brahmin's arms, Oghavati was too ashamed to speak. Instead, the brahmin called out, 'I came to your house as a visitor, and your wife is giving me what I asked for—though she did try to offer me other things instead. I am very much enjoying her hospitality, and you can do what you like about it!'

"Death, hanging around in the shadows, was certain that Sudarshana would now break his vow, and was ready to strike him down. After all, no more painful test than this could be imagined. But Sudarshana called back, 'Please enjoy yourself. You are my honored guest, and anything I have is yours.'

"At that, the brahmin emerged from the bedroom and

revealed himself to be Dharma himself, the embodiment of duty. He praised Sudarshana and Oghavati for their great virtue and told them that Oghavati, whose devotion had protected her from being defiled, would be transformed. Half of her would become the river Oghavati—which flows through Kurukshetra to this day. The other half would accompany Sudarshana to heaven, which he would enter in his bodily form, since he had conquered Death. Meanwhile, Death, frustrated, went off on other, more fruitful, business."

Then Bhishma spoke at length about the duty
of care and generosity to brahmins.
"If someone breaks a promise to make gifts
to a brahmin, then all their previous merit,
all their good deeds and ritual observances,
will be canceled out. To invite a brahmin
and then to give him nothing is an act
as serious as if one had murdered him."

☙

"I have often wondered," said Yudhishthira,
"whether men or women enjoy sex more.
How could one ever know?"

　　　　　　　　Bhishma replied,
"Only a person who had changed their sex
could know for sure. On this, there is the story
of King Bhangashvana and the god Indra.

"THERE ONCE LIVED a king called Bhangashvana. He was upright and virtuous and was known as a royal sage. But he had no children. He resolved to perform the fire sacrifice, which he hoped would bring him children; and, in due course, a hundred sons were born to him.

"Indra was infuriated by this ritual, which involved exclusive sacrifice to Agni, the fire god. He felt slighted and, from then on, looked for ways to punish Bhangashvana. Sometime later, the king went on a hunting expedition. Seizing his opportunity, Indra plunged him into a state of confusion, so that he wandered aimlessly in the thick forest, faint from hunger and thirst.

"At last he came to a beautiful lake. He immersed himself and drank deeply—and when he emerged, he found that he was now a woman. The king was appalled at the loss of his manhood. How could he explain this transformation to everyone who knew him? How would he even be able to mount his horse? He managed, however, with difficulty, and rode home, embarrassed. He—now she—told her wives and sons what had happened and, leaving the kingdom to her sons, she retired to the woods and lived as the wife of an ascetic. By this man, she bore a hundred sons.

"When the time was right, she took these hundred sons to the court and asked her previous sons to share the kingdom with them, as children of the same parent. This they did, and the two hundred sons and their families lived harmoniously together.

"Seeing this, Indra was mortified. 'It seems that, intending to punish Bhangashvana, I have done him nothing but good!' He took on the appearance of a brahmin and went to the court. There he spoke to the first hundred sons. 'How has this situation come about? Even brothers of the same father often quarrel, yet here you are, sharing the kingdom with the sons of an ascetic, letting them enjoy *your* inheritance.'

"His words had the desired effect. The two sets of brothers began to distrust one another and, very soon, they came to blows, and they did not stop fighting until all of them lay dead.

"When the news reached Bhangashvana, she was overcome with grief, and poured out her lamentations to a passing brahmin, telling him the whole story. The brahmin then revealed himself as Indra, and explained that she, when she was king, had insulted him by her exclusive worship of the fire god. Bhangashvana knelt before him. 'Please forgive me,' she begged. 'It was only my great longing for children that led me to perform that ritual. I had absolutely no wish to offend you.'

"Indra was mollified and granted her a boon: one of her sets of sons would be brought back to life. 'Which sons shall I revive,' asked Indra, 'the first-born, or the ones born to you as a woman?'

"'The second-born,' replied Bhangashvana. 'Women are more loving, and so I am more attached to those younger sons of mine." Indra was impressed by her answer, and told her that he would bring all two hundred sons back to life.

"'I will give you another boon,' he said. 'You can choose whether to remain a woman or to resume the male sex you were born with.'

"'I choose to remain a woman,' said Bhangashvana. Indra was amazed, and asked her to explain. 'Because women enjoy sex far more than men do,' replied Bhangashvana.

"That is how we know the answer to your question."

As Bhishma waited on his bed of arrows
for the appointed moment of his death,
Yudhishthira continued with his questions.
"How can a person become a brahmin
when they are born in a different order?
I know that the kshatriya Vishvamitra
became a brahmin through his austerities."
Bhishma told him, "That is true, but generally
such an achievement is impossible
within one lifetime. Only through the process
of multiple rebirths, acquiring merit
lifetime after lifetime, can it be done.
The story of Matanga bears this out.

"A BOY, Matanga, brought up as a brahmin, was sent on an errand by his father. He traveled on a cart drawn by a donkey which, being young, kept veering off the track, seeking to rejoin its mother. Matanga beat it savagely.

"Seeing this, the donkey's mother said to her offspring,

'Never mind, son. What more can you expect from such a fellow. No brahmin would have beaten you so cruelly. I happen to know that this boy is really a chandala, born of a lustful brahmin woman by a shudra hairdresser.'

"Matanga rushed back to his father and told him what the mother donkey had said. 'How can I be happy with such a history!' he lamented. 'I shall go to the forest and undergo severe austerities to rid myself of this impurity.' This he did, enduring every sort of privation, with the aim of attaining brahmin status. His efforts came to the attention of the gods, and Indra appeared to him. 'Why are you doing this, my boy, refraining from every human pleasure when you should be enjoying yourself? Tell me what you want and I shall grant you a boon.'

" 'I wish to become a brahmin,' said Matanga. 'That is the purpose of my privations, and when I attain my goal, I shall return home.'

" 'That is impossible,' said Indra. 'Chandalas can never become brahmins no matter what rigorous practices they perform. You are wasting your time—you will die at this rate. Better to go home to your father.'

"But Matanga ignored this advice and proceeded to stand on one foot for a hundred years. Indra appeared to him again, and was stern with him. 'What you are trying to do simply cannot be done,' he said. 'A four-legged creature, having spent many lifetimes in exemplary service to human-kind, might eventually succeed in being born as a chandala. A chandala, after many lifetimes as a chandala, might be reborn as a shudra. So it goes on. You can see how many virtuous lifetimes it would take to be born as a brahmin—and longer still to be born as the kind of brahmin who is learned in the scriptures and recites the Gayatri mantra. It is for this reason that brahmins are so highly honored—because of all the accumulated virtue lodged in them. So give up your foolishness, and let me give you a boon by way of consolation.'

"But, again, Matanga refused to listen. He went away and stood on one foot for one thousand years, in deep meditation. Then, still disappointed, he stood on his toes for a hundred years, until his legs became knotted and swollen and his body was no more than a skin-covered skeleton.

"Indra came to him again, and Matanga spoke bitterly to him. 'It seems that destiny is very cruel. A man may be born a brahmin and receive respect even if he behaves badly, while I, who have strained every sinew and have behaved righteously, am doomed by my mother's fault to inferior rank. Well, let me have a boon from you then. Let me be able to take on any form at will. Let me be adored by brahmins and kshatriyas. Let me enjoy any pleasure I wish for. And let my fame live for ever.'

" 'I will grant you this,' said Indra: 'Your name will be celebrated by poets. You will be adored by women. And you will be famous throughout the three worlds.'

"So you see, Yudhishthira," said Bhishma,
"only in the cycle of rebirth
can a person's place in the social order
be transformed. Matanga could not succeed.
Each person should pursue their own dharma
in the hope of better future lives.
And brahmins should be honored above all—
worshiped for their piety and knowledge.
For, whether they are virtuous or not,
they have earned their station in their former lives.
Feed a brahmin and you feed the gods.
Furthermore, they have particular powers
and can be dangerous if they are crossed.
Yes, you should always honor brahmins:
'Protect them like sons, respect them like your father.'
That is the golden rule to bear in mind."

"Please speak of compassion," said Yudhishthira.
"When we are faced with others' suffering
what should we feel?"

         Bhishma told this story:

"THE GREAT RISHI Chyavana, who was benign and loved by all, decided to undertake the discipline known as Udavasa: for twelve years, he would immerse himself in water. He took himself off to Prayaga, the place where the river Yamuna meets the Ganga. At that spot, the surging waters of the two great rivers combine forces in their rush toward the sea. Chyavana braced himself against the mighty current, but the river, out of respect, flowed past him and left him undisturbed. He stood like a block of wood, contemplating the changeless, ever-changing river. Sometimes he lay down in the water and slept peacefully.

"The fishes and other creatures that lived in the river became his friends and nuzzled him as they swam around. In time, his skin became overgrown with river moss, his hair and beard matted and green with algae. Freshwater molluscs made their home on his body as if it were a rock.

"One day, a group of poor tribal fishermen came to the river and, casting wide their net, they pulled in hundreds of fishes, and Chyavana among them. The rishi was grief-stricken at the slaughter of so many fishes, and sighed repeatedly. The fishermen were astonished to find him in their net and instantly saw that this was a holy man. They prostrated themselves before him. 'We never meant to disturb you, O great one. Tell us what we should do to make amends.'

"Chyavana, sitting in the midst of the dead fishes, said, 'These fishes were my companions—we belong together. So either kill me too, or sell me with them.'

"The fishermen were horrified and hurried off to consult the king. With his ministers and his priest, the king came to the riverbank and bowed in reverence before Chyavana. 'Holy one,' he said, 'tell me what I can do for you—anything at all.'

"'These fishermen have worked hard,' said the rishi. 'I want you to pay them a proper price for the fishes, and for me. You must decide what that price should be.'

"The king told his priest to pay the fishermen one thousand coins for Chyavana. 'That is not the right price,' said the rishi.

" 'A hundred thousand coins, then,' said the king.

" 'That is not the right price,' said Chyavana. 'You should consult your ministers.'

" 'Ten million coins!' cried the king in desperation. 'Half my kingdom—or even the whole of it!'

" 'Half your kingdom, or even the whole of it, is not the right price,' said Chyavana.

"The king was completely at a loss, and went back to his palace, sighing. He knew that if the rishi was not treated well he had the power to destroy the three worlds.

"An ascetic who lived in the woods not far from the palace came to see the king, and offered a solution. 'There is no wealth that can be set against the value of a rishi,' he said. 'Cows are also priceless—therefore the right price for Chyavana is one cow.'

"The king hurried back to the river. 'Holy one,' he said, 'I think the right price for you is one cow.' And he held his breath.

" 'Yes!' said Chyavana, 'that is the right price indeed.' And he discoursed for some time on the qualities, significance and virtues of cows.

"The fishermen received the cow as payment, and begged the rishi to accept it from them, as a gift. For this, Chyavana blessed them, and told them that they were absolved from their sins and would go immediately to heaven, along with the fishes.

"And so they did."

55.

THE DEATH OF BHISHMA

Bhishma had recounted a wealth of stories
in answer to Yudhishthira. But once more
the Pandava was suddenly assailed
by despair and doubt. "Somehow, these tales
seem a distraction. The hard fact remains
that millions of men have died because of me;
millions of wives and children are bereaved.
I shall surely go to the deepest hell."

Yudhishthira's mind was turning yet again
to renunciation and a hermit's life.
Bhishma did not argue but, instead,
talked at great length to him about the ways
a king and householder can make amends
for his previous actions. He described
the many kinds of gifts he could bestow.
"Take reservoirs, for instance. A well-built tank
is a delight to gods and men alike.
It furthers dharma, wealth and pleasure—all three.
The king who builds such tanks acquires the merit
equivalent to many sacrifices.
In making the gift of water to his kingdom
he gives the very means of life itself.
People, cattle and diverse lovely creatures
will come to drink, thanks to his generous act.
In the same way, the gift of fruit-bearing trees,

offering shelter from fierce midday sun,
will bring great rewards.

                    "As for penance,
one who abstains from sensual excess,
who fasts and lives a life of strict discipline,
who embraces hardships and privations,
will atone for shortcomings in this life
and be well repaid in the life hereafter.
All this can be done, while at the same time
living as an active and potent ruler."

Yudhishthira tried to stiffen his resolve.
Turning to his brothers and to Draupadi
who sat nearby, he told them he no longer
hankered for a life of renunciation,
but was reconciled to being the king.
They applauded him, relieved and joyful,
shouting, "Yes, Yudhishthira! Well done, brother!"

ॐ

"Which is the best of gifts," asked the king,
"which gift brings the greatest benefits
in the next life?"
                    "Without doubt," said Bhishma,
"giving to the destitute is highly praised.
But you should also give in the right spirit
to avoid attachment to possessions.
Make sure the act of generosity
is accomplished before the gift is given.
Above all, give to brahmins, for they are
the most precious beings that walk the earth."

"Do all the virtuous go to the same heaven?"
asked Yudhishthira. "No, there are many heavens
just as there are many hells," said Bhishma.

"People go to the afterlife they deserve."
Then he told the story of Gautama.

"THE SAGE GAUTAMA came across a baby elephant that
had lost its mother and was wandering about, hungry
and bereft. Gautama, full of compassion, took it home and
reared it as if it were his own son. In time it became full-
grown, huge as a hill.

"One day, the god Indra, assuming the form of King Dhritarashtra, seized the elephant and made off with it. Gautama
pursued him. 'Please don't rob me of my elephant. I have
brought it up as my own child and now it renders me useful
service, fetching wood and carrying water for me. It is very
dear to me.'

"'I'll give you a thousand cattle in exchange, and a hundred maidservants and five hundred gold pieces. What is
a brahmin doing with an elephant anyway? Elephants are
meant to belong to kings, so I am entitled to take it.'

"'You can keep your cattle and maidservants and gold,'
said Gautama. 'What use is wealth to such as I? If you don't
give back my elephant I shall pursue you, even to Yama's
realm, where the virtuous live in joy and the wicked in misery,
and I shall take him back from you.'

"'You won't find me there,' laughed Dhritarashtra, 'I shall
be going to a higher realm than that.'

"'Then I shall pursue you to that heaven for the blessed,
where gandharvas and apsarases dance and sing for ever;
and there I shall force you to give me back my elephant.'

"'That is a delightful place indeed,' said Dhritarashtra,
'but I am destined for a higher realm.'

"'I shall pursue you to the heaven bright with flowers and
lovely woods, where those who are learned in the scriptures
go; and there I shall force you to give up my elephant.'

"'Such a place must be extremely beautiful, but I shall be
going to a higher realm than that.'

"Gautama named and described one heaven after another
but, each time, Dhritarashtra gave the same answer.

"Finally, Gautama realized. 'Oh! You are not Dhritarashtra
at all! I think you are the great god Indra who likes to roam
through the entire universe and play tricks on people—I
hope I have not offended you by not recognizing you before.'

" 'I am very pleased that you have recognized me at all,'
said Indra. 'Not many people do. You can ask a boon of me.'

" 'Then please give me back my elephant. He's only young,
and very attached to me. He is the son I have never had.'

" 'Take him,' said Indra. 'And because of your goodness
and integrity, you and he shall come to heaven with me without delay.' And Gautama and his elephant were taken up into
Indra's chariot, and seen no more on earth."

"How can we know," asked Yudhishthira,
"where we will go to in the afterlife?
And when, at death, we leave our lifeless body
as though it were a lump of wood, or clay,
who goes with us into the unknown?"

Bhishma said, "This is the greatest mystery.
But here comes the revered Brihaspati,
preceptor to the gods. You should ask him.
No one is more knowledgeable than he is."

Brihaspati had come to pay respects
to Bhishma. Yudhishthira touched his feet
and put his question. The holy one replied,
"One is born alone, and dies alone, O king.
And whether life brings ease or difficulty,
one faces it essentially alone.
Our righteous conduct is our sole companion,
our only friend in this life, and in death.

"Those who love us weep when we are dead,
then they turn away to their own concerns.
Our former deeds govern our destination.
For a while, a person goes to heaven

or to misery in hell. Then the time comes
for them to be born again in a new body.
Their good or evil deeds accompany them
and they are born appropriately—blessed,
or in an inferior position.
This is the inexorable law
of the cosmos."

        "But can a sinful person
not redeem themselves?" asked Yudhishthira.
"If one suffers an agony of remorse,"
replied the sage, "the consequence of sin
may be avoided. Remorse must be sincere,
and must be declared in front of brahmins.
Then one must fix one's heart, with complete focus,
on rapt contemplation of the divine.
If this is done with single-mindedness
one can be cleansed of sin. Furthermore,
a person seeking merit should make gifts
to worthy brahmins, especially gifts of food."

"Which of the virtuous observances,"
asked Yudhishthira, "carries greatest merit?"
The sage replied, "Non-harming, meditation,
obedience to teachers, self-control—
all these are part of dharma. But most precious
is non-harmfulness, because it springs
from compassion for all beings. People
who see all creatures as themselves, sharing
the joy and grief of every other being,
follow the highest dharma. Such a one
is at home everywhere, and walks the earth
weightless as a feather in the wind,
leaving no footprint. For violence brings
violence in return. Kindness breeds kindness."
And with that, having said everything
he thought was beneficial, Brihaspati

turned away, and disappeared from sight,
returning to the heaven from whence he came.

"I am confused," said Yudhishthira.
"We have just been told that the highest good
is non-violence, yet to perform the rites
for ancestors, animals must be slaughtered
and then the meat is eaten. Tell me, Bhishma,
what are the rights and wrongs of eating meat?"

"In my view," said Bhishma, "to take the life
of a fellow creature just to gratify
the palate is a very heinous sin.
Meat is addictive. One who has eaten it,
and then gives it up, acquires great merit.
The seers have debated this, and all agree
one should abstain from meat—though it is argued
there are exceptions. Meat killed for sacrifice
has been called pure. And deer hunting is normal
for kshatriyas. But nevertheless,
complete non-harming is the highest dharma,
and heaven awaits those who practice it."

⚜

"Faced with a threat," asked Yudhishthira,
"which is more effective—conciliation,
or to placate the enemy with gifts?"
"There is no general rule," answered Bhishma,
"it depends. But here is an example
of when conciliation can be best:

"A LEARNED BRAHMIN was traveling through a forest when he was waylaid by a ghastly-looking ogre, gaunt and pale. 'I shall eat you presently,' said the terrible creature, 'but if you can tell me why I am so pale and thin, I shall let you go.'

"The brahmin kept calm and considered his options. He could try to escape, but he knew the monster could run faster than he could. He could try to bargain for his life, but he had no possessions that he could offer. Instead, with a tranquil mind, he gazed into the ogre's eyes, as one creature gazing at another, and he read there the whole history of the monster's pain.

" 'You are living alone in this forest, without the company of your family and friends; that is why you are pale and thin. You treat your friends well, but still they are hostile to you, because they are mean-spirited. Although you try your best, you see others effortlessly rising in the world, while you are stuck here. Others look down on you and show you no respect. That is why you are so pale and thin. You have tried to steer others away from wrongdoing, but they simply despise you for it. You have worked hard, only to see others profit from your efforts. You cannot always find the right words, and that makes you ashamed and angry. You know how you would like to live, but cannot see how to achieve it. That is why you are so pale and thin, O rakshasa.'

"The ogre was nourished by this answer. The brahmin, by giving words to his condition, had made it more bearable. He praised the brahmin and let him go on his way."

ॐ

Yudhishthira asked Bhishma to recite
the names of Shiva. "I am not competent
to do so," replied the dying patriarch,
and he requested Krishna to reply.
Krishna described his journey, some time before,
to snowy Himavat. There, he had worshiped
Shiva, who had granted him a son
named Samba, born from his wife, Jambavati.
He had learned the thousand names of Shiva,
at the lovely hermitage of Upamanyu.
Now he recited them, to the great benefit
of all who were attending upon Bhishma.

&

In question after question, the Dharma King
sought to plumb the depths of Bhishma's wisdom:
What benefits may be obtained by fasting?
What consequences flow from hurting brahmins?
What gifts should be offered at ceremonies?
What is the origin of the shraddha rites?
And many more. It was as though he heard
in his mind's ear a clamorous call for answers,
a longing for wise guidance, in the voices
of those who would come after, down the ages.

The patriarch was tired. Day after day
Yudhishthira had put to him his questions
and his doubts. Now the time was approaching
for Bhishma to depart. But, while there was time,
the king raised the few remaining matters
that most concerned him.
                              "Please tell me," he said,
"how to reconcile the authority
of the Vedas with practical experience.
When should one rely on one's own reason,
when be guided by others' example,
and when seek out the counsel of the wise?
How can there be one dharma when there is
more than one source of authority?"

"Only fools rely on their own experience,"
replied Bhishma. "The deepest understanding
of the true reality that underlies
all that is, the one and formless Brahman,
comes only from protracted meditation.
You should carry any doubts you have
to those immersed in knowledge of the Vedas."

"It seems," said Yudhishthira, "that outcomes
cannot be guaranteed. Some villains prosper;

some virtuous people struggle to succeed
and still may fail."
               "Unless the seed is planted
there can be no crop," said Bhishma. "Time
determines everything and, in the end,
time protects dharma from wickedness.
Be steadfast and, to keep on the right path,
recite the names of the gods, at dawn and dusk."

After this, Bhishma became silent
and, around him, the circle of his listeners
fell silent too, seers and Pandavas,
motionless as figures in a painting.
Vyasa told him that Yudhishthira
had now been restored to his own best nature,
and suggested Bhishma should dismiss him.
With a few last words of good advice,
Bhishma told Yudhishthira to go
back to Hastinapura, to take up
the reins of kingship. But he should return
immediately after the winter solstice.

꧁

When the pale and gentle winter sun
had turned toward the north, Yudhishthira
and the whole court arrived at Kurukshetra.
They had with them materials they would need
for Bhishma's funeral rites—silk cloth, flowers,
ghee, fragrant sandalwood and dry tinder.
Many priests accompanied them, carrying
sacrificial fires. They found Bhishma
attended by Vyasa and Narada,
and some kings who had survived the war.

Yudhishthira approached the bed of arrows
where the patriarch lay with his eyes closed.

"If you can hear me, Grandfather," he said,
"I want you to know that I am here
and so are all your kin."

                  "Ah," said Bhishma,
opening his eyes. Yudhishthira
cradled Bhishma's withered hand in his.

The dying man addressed Dhritarashtra.
"My time has come. So many days have passed
while I have lain here. It seems a century.
I want you to stop grieving for your sons.
What has happened was long preordained
and could not have been other than it was.
Treat the Pandavas as your own sons
as, morally, they are. They will protect you."

Then Bhishma worshiped Krishna, the supreme
creator, the divine, the eternal Soul.
He asked permission to give up his life.
"I give you leave, great Bhishma, blameless one,"
replied Krishna. Then Bhishma asked permission
of the Pandavas. Tears streamed down their faces
as they consented.

                  Bhishma spoke no more.
With yogic concentration, he withdrew
the vital force from each part of his body
and, to the amazement of all who watched,
the dreadful wounds shrank and disappeared.
His whole body healed, despite the arrows.
Then his remaining life-breath exited
through the crown of his head, and flew to heaven
like a great meteor. Celestial drums
were heard, and beautiful and perfumed flowers
rained down. Bhishma, the great patriarch,
was dead.

The Pandavas and Vidura
wrapped the body in a cloth of silk
and placed it on the pyre. Brahmins made
oblations and chanted Vedic hymns. The pyre
was doused with sandalwood oil and black aloe.
The fragrant fuel was lit, and the remains
flared up, glowed, then were reduced to ash.

The party walked together to the Ganga
and poured water libations for the goddess,
Bhishma's mother. They saw her rise up, weeping,
lamenting for her son, remembering
his great achievements. "Yet my illustrious son,
proud, unbeaten, was killed by Shikhandin!"
"Not so," said Krishna. "It was Arjuna,
shielded by Shikhandin, who killed your son.
No one but Arjuna was capable,
and then only because Bhishma allowed it.
But since he was no ordinary mortal,
but one of the Vasus, cursed to be born human,
now he has gone to the heaven where he belongs."
Ganga was consoled. The royal party
paid tribute to the goddess, and she blessed them.
Then they traveled back to Hastinapura.

XIV

THE BOOK OF THE
HORSE SACRIFICE

56.

KING YUDHISHTHIRA
TURNS TO THE FUTURE

Bhishma was no more. After the rites
were over, and libations had been poured,
Yudhishthira sank down on the riverbank.
Seeing him despondent, his brothers too
sat gloomily beside him on the ground.
Dhritarashtra tried to encourage him.
"Come now, it is Gandhari and I
who should be crushed by grief. Have we not lost
a hundred sons, as if they were never born?
You have gained all you were fighting for."

Krishna, too, rebuked him. "This is feeble!
There is a world of tasks awaiting you."
"Krishna," said the king, "you have always loved
and supported me. Let me now retreat

to a life in the forest. I find no peace,
thinking of the horrors of the war
fought for my sake." Vyasa spoke sternly to him.
"Yudhishthira, you are acting like a child.
Are we wasting our breath when we remind you,
over and over, of your proper duties,
when we speak of destiny's part in this?
It is as if you are mired in ignorance
despite your long days sitting at Bhishma's feet,
despite what Krishna and I have said to you.
If you're incapable of being convinced,
then assuage your unnecessary guilt
by performing the horse sacrifice."

"How can I?" replied Yudhishthira. "The war
completely drained the coffers of the state.
That sacrifice requires enormous riches."
Vyasa said, "I know where there is treasure.
On the snowy slopes of the Himalaya
vast quantities of gold were once buried
by King Marutta, after a sacrifice.
That treasure is still there."
                                    Yudhishthira
was astonished. "How did that come about?"
Vyasa told him:

"KING MARUTTA wanted to perform a great sacrifice—a
sacrifice on such a vast scale that no ordinary priest
could perform it. He approached Brihaspati, priest to the
gods, who lived in Indra's realm. At the prompting of Indra,
who was envious of Marutta, Brihaspati refused. 'I certainly
cannot act as priest for a mere mortal,' he said. 'Find someone else.'

"Marutta approached Brihaspati's brother, Samvarta.
The two brothers were bitter rivals. Samvarta had left Indra's
realm because he could no longer bear his brother's jealous
behavior, and Indra always took Brihaspati's side. Marutta
found him living simply in the forest, and made his request.

"Samvarta told Marutta he would do it. 'But you will need vast wealth,' he said, and advised Marutta to apply to Lord Shiva. 'Only he can provide the wealth you need. But if you are successful, and my brother comes to hear of it, he and Indra will be very angry, and will seek to do you harm. You will require the utmost steadiness of mind.' Marutta understood.

"'High in the beautiful Himalaya,' said Samvarta, 'Shiva lives with his consort, Uma, engaged in the constant practice of austerity. You must go there.'

"Marutta did so, and sat in meditation for days and weeks, contemplating the many names of Shiva. At last Shiva rewarded him by granting him quantities of gold the like of which had never been seen on earth.

"Brihaspati, hearing of this, was eaten up with rage and jealousy, thinking of the splendid gifts his brother would receive. He grew emaciated, and Indra was concerned about him. Indra sent the fire god, Agni, as messenger to Marutta, offering him immortality if he would take Brihaspati as his priest for the sacrifice.

"'Greetings to Indra. I hope all is well with him,' said Marutta, 'but Samvarta will be my priest for the sacrifice. Please tell Brihaspati that, since he has acted as priest to no less a being than the great Indra, it would certainly demean him to serve a mere mortal.' Agni pestered and cajoled until finally Marutta grew angry. 'Go away at once, or I will burn you with my evil eye acquired through austerity!' Agni fled.

"Indra sent a gandharva to Marutta, armed with a thunderbolt, by way of persuasion. Marutta refused to change his mind, and Samvarta protected him from the force of the thunderbolt and the howling winds and rain that Indra flung at him in his wrath.

"Then Marutta had the wise idea of inviting Indra to attend the sacrifice. The god came, and was delighted with everything. The sacrifice was a great success. Marutta gave away gold by the sackful to all the brahmins present, and there was still a great deal left. This he buried, and it is that gold I am advising you to find. When you bring it back to Hastinapura, you will be able to hold the horse sacrifice."

⚜

Yudhishthira, recovering his spirits,
consulted his ministers. But Krishna saw
that the king was not yet firm of purpose.
"My friend," he said, "your war is not yet finished.
Your understanding is still clouded over
by complicated doubt. That is an illness
akin to bodily disease. Enmeshed
in memory and regret, you make yourself
weak and ineffective—as a tiger
caught in a net struggles this way and that
but gets nowhere. You have been victorious
in the war with weapons. You cannot bring back
the men who left their bones on the battlefield.
Now you must win the war within yourself
and seek right understanding. That is the war
that all must fight alone. There are no weapons,
no friends and allies, no supporting troops,
only your own strength. Be vigilant.
Know that craving takes many subtle forms,
and can wear the mask of righteousness.
It fritters energy; it is the broad road
to destruction. Know it for what it is.

"Persistently you long for the forest life
of renunciation. You deceive yourself.
Renunciation is a state of mind
you can achieve anywhere. You do not need
extravagant gestures, outward show, bringing
grief to those whose welfare you should cherish.

"You might say desire informs all action,
but craving, grasping, is a different matter.
To lead a life of action, without craving,
as a river flows naturally to the sea

acting simply according to its nature—
that is the highest dharma, Yudhishthira.
Discipline your mind. Start preparation
for the horse sacrifice, and let it be
the most magnificent ever seen on earth.
Acquire great merit in the eyes of the gods!"

Arjuna and Krishna spent some time
traveling together in the countryside,
enjoying mountain scenery and woods,
swimming in cool lakes and bracing streams,
seeing holy places. They visited
Indraprastha, passing happy hours
in repose and reminiscence, soul mates
delighting in each other's company.

Their talk returned often to the war.
The loss of Abhimanyu was a sorrow
Arjuna bore always, an aching wound.

"Krishna," said Arjuna, "on the brink of war
you revealed to me your celestial form
and showed me many truths. Unfortunately
my memory is poor—I have forgotten
what you said then. Please teach me again."

Krishna said, "I am disappointed in you.
If you had understood what I taught you,
when I had entered an exalted state,
you would have retained it. As it is,
I cannot now repeat to you in detail
that most sacred teaching, which concerned
yoga and the spiritual path.
But I will recount to you the story
of a profound discussion I once had

with a brahmin who came from the heavenly realms
to visit us at Dvaraka. I asked him
to speak to us about enlightenment.
I shall give you the essence of what he said:

"WE COME into the world carrying the fruits of our
deeds in former lives, whether good or bad. This
is a world of action, and as we act we exhaust our previous
deeds and accumulate the fruits of new ones—which in turn
accompany us into our next rebirth. Through living virtuously, we spend some time in heaven and eventually enter
a more fortunate rebirth than before. But virtuous action
alone cannot permanently release us from the cycle of death
and rebirth. Only yoga, spiritual discipline, can do that.

"To obtain release, one must practice concentration and
meditation, freeing oneself of all passions, all preferences,
all sense of 'I.' Through these practices, even women, and
even the lowborn, can achieve freedom."

Then Krishna told the story of the exchange
between an enlightened brahmin and his wife:

"'HUSBAND,' said the brahmin's wife, 'I notice that you
no longer perform sacrifices to sustain the gods.
Since a woman takes on the merits and demerits of her husband, what chance is there that I shall attain the heavenly
realms if you are not following brahmin dharma?' Her husband replied, 'I am engaged in an internal sacrifice, the
sacrifice of yoga, in which craving and sensual indulgence
are symbolically committed to the flames. I have no need of
empty rituals.'

"The brahmin told his wife how the various creatures
of the earth had once approached Brahma, lord of created
beings, to be taught. Brahma pronounced to all of them the
sacred syllable 'Om,' and when the creatures went back to
their homes they interpreted the sound in their own ways,
according to their natures. The snakes understood it as an
injunction to bite, the demons to practice deceit, the gods to

be generous, and the seers to control their senses.

" 'As a creature acts,' said the brahmin, 'so it becomes. I have undergone every human experience. I have been caught up in lust and anger, and my sins have led to many miserable births. I have sucked at many breasts. I have been both blessed and cursed. I have been wounded and humiliated. I have been afflicted by disease. I have acquired great wealth and lost it all. At last, in great distress, I turned my back on the world of joy and sorrow and took refuge in the formless Infinite. Through austerity and meditation, I have followed the path to ultimate liberation. I shall suffer no more rebirths.

" 'Wife, you need have no anxiety. As I move through the world, I am part of everything that is, and it is part of me. I am everywhere, creator and destroyer. Through your devotion to me, you will come to me in the world hereafter.'

" 'I can hardly grasp what you are telling me,' said the wife. 'I am in need of further explanation.' The brahmin gave her further teachings, speaking to her about the nature of Brahman, the supreme Self, and she herself became enlightened.

"Arjuna," said Krishna, "understand
that in this parable I am the teacher,
the mind is my pupil, the brahmin's wife,
and I am the Soul pervading all that is.
It has been taught that life is like a wheel
which only the wise can truly understand.
Non-harming, serene, free from all attachment,
such a person reaches a state of mind
beyond self, and beyond all suffering.
Remember my words, Arjuna. Follow them,
and you will reach moksha, perfect freedom."

༄

The time came for Krishna to depart,
to return to Dvaraka, his sea-girt city.
The Pandavas were sorrowful. Farewells

were said, the chariot loaded, and Krishna,
with Subhadra, and Satyaki, his kinsman,
set off. Once out of sight of Hastinapura,
Krishna told his charioteer, Daruka,
to urge the horses on, and the chariot,
charged with celestial power, flew like a comet.

On their way, traveling through the desert,
they came upon Uttanka, an ascetic
who knew Krishna of old. They spoke together.
Uttanka, a man of reclusive habits,
had not heard about the war. "Tell me,"
he said, "did you succeed in reconciling
the Kauravas and the Pandavas? I'm sure
you must have brought peace, powerful as you are."
"I tried," said Krishna, "but Duryodhana
refused to listen to advice—from me,
or from the elders. Now the Kauravas
are guests of Yama in the realm of death,
together with countless thousands of brave men.
Only the Pandavas remain. You know well,
there is no way of evading destiny."

Uttanka's eyes grew wide in shock and outrage.
"But you are Krishna! You could have prevented
such carnage, so much catastrophic waste.
Many of those heroes were dear to you
and yet you let it happen. I shall curse you!"

"Uttanka, in your life of discipline
you have acquired much spiritual merit.
I should hate to see that merit canceled
by an ill-judged curse—which, in any case,
would be ineffective."

                    "Well," said Uttanka,
"tell me more about your part in this.
Then I will decide whether to curse you."

"Know me, then," said Krishna, "as the source
of all that is, and of all that is not.
I am sacrificer and sacrifice.
I am the heart of every righteous act,
the hymn of praise, and also the object
of adoration. In all the three worlds
I am known as Vishnu, Brahma, Shiva.
I am the creator, the preserver
and the destroyer. In every age
I am the supporter of righteousness.
In every realm I take birth differently,
and I act in the manner of that realm.
Among gandharvas, I am a gandharva.
Among the Nagas, I take a Naga form.
Born now in the realm of humankind,
I take on fully human qualities.
In that form, I appealed to Duryodhana.
Finding him obdurate, I even revealed
my divine nature. But being sunk in sin,
he was not changed. War was the result.
Time overtook him."

                    "Now I understand,"
said Uttanka, and he begged to witness
Krishna's divine form, whereupon,
the curse forgotten, he bent and worshiped him
as the supreme Lord. Krishna gave him a boon:
wherever Uttanka was, needing water,
if he thought of Krishna, he would find it.

৬

Uttanka wandered on into the desert.
Soon he became thirsty, and thought of Krishna.
A naked chandala appeared, caked with dirt

and followed by fierce dogs. A stream of urine
was flowing from his penis. "Drink," he said,
"I can see you are thirsty."

                    "I am indeed,"
said Uttanka, appalled, "but not that thirsty!"
and he sent the chandala on his way.
Presently, Krishna appeared before him.
"That was a test," he said. "It was to see
if you could look beyond appearances.
You failed." Uttanka was bitterly ashamed.
Krishna consoled him, "You shall still have your boon.
When you are thirsty think of me, and clouds
will instantly appear and drop sweet water.
Those rain clouds will be known as Uttanka clouds."
And so they are, up to this very day.

༺༻

In Hastinapura, there was an air of waiting.
Uttaraa was far gone in pregnancy
but still deeply grieving for Abhimanyu
and refusing food. "Please eat," begged Kunti,
"or you will harm your baby." Wise Vyasa
arrived to give reassurance: "This new child
will be a great hero and rule the earth.
It has been foretold. Meanwhile, O king,
you should turn your mind to preparations
for the horse sacrifice."

                Yudhishthira,
together with his brothers, started off
on the journey north to the Himalaya
in search of gold. They took along with them
substantial forces—soldiers, retainers, priests
and men possessing all the varied skills
needed to sustain their enterprise.

As the procession left, citizens gathered
to wish them well. With his white parasol
held over his head, the king was radiant.

After much traveling, the party reached
the lower mountain slopes. Vast dazzling peaks
soared above them. "This is the place," said Vyasa.
Yudhishthira ordered that they should pitch camp,
and the party settled for the night, fasting.
Next morning, priests made offerings to Shiva—
flowers, meat and various kinds of grain—
and ghee was poured on the sacrificial fire.
Kubera, god of wealth, was also worshiped.
The ground was measured and marked out in squares
and the great excavation was begun.

After some time, glints of gold were seen.
Stashes of gold coins, vessels and objects
of various kinds, some small, some very large,
all gold, were brought out of the ground. Digging
took several weeks. Then the gold was hefted
into large panniers, and onto the backs
of thousands of pack animals. At last
the caravan lumbered off toward home,
traveling very slowly, so laden was it.

☙

Krishna's kinsfolk welcomed his return
with joy and celebration. As it happened,
a festival was in full swing, with flags
and floral garlands adorning every house,
and singing in the streets. Of course, his father
knew about the war, but not the details,
and Krishna told him—though selectively,
not wanting to break bad news all at once.

"Tell him!" cried Subhadra. "Tell our father
about Abhimanyu," and she fell down
in a faint. The king, too, lost consciousness
when he heard of Abhimanyu's death
but, recovering, wanted to know more,
longed to hear how his beloved grandson,
beautiful as Krishna, brave as Arjuna,
could have met his death. Krishna told him
how courageously Abhimanyu fought,
how sinfully he was surrounded. He spoke
of the grief of all the women, of how Uttaraa
was carrying his child. And the king,
summoning his strength, and comforted
by the certainty that Abhimanyu
had reached the highest heaven, set in train
elaborate funeral ceremonies.
Krishna performed shraddha rites, and made
rich gifts to the officiating brahmins.

The weeks passed pleasantly. But Krishna knew
that Uttaraa's due time had nearly come.
Subhadra had already made the journey
back to Hastinapura, to be with her.
Krishna thought of the lethal *Brahma* weapon
and of Ashvatthaman's curse. The whole future
of the Bharatas now rested on him.
After loving farewells to his parents,
he set out in his wonderfully made chariot
driven by Daruka, fast as the wind.

༈

When Krishna arrived at Hastinapura
the Pandavas were still away from home
in the Himalaya. He found the women
tense with expectation; Uttaraa,
scarcely emerged from childhood herself,

was in labor. The whole city held its breath
and then the cry went up, "A boy! It's a son!"
and there was cheering, drumming, serenade—
until the bulletin that quickly followed,
"The baby is born dead!" Catastrophe!
Every face was slippery with tears,
every house loud with lamentation,
knowing that the dynasty's last hope
was now extinguished.

     Through the palace halls,
through courtyards, corridors and colonnades
strode Krishna, his yellow silk robe streaming
behind him, his dark features purposeful.
At the entrance to the women's quarters
Kunti met him. "Krishna! You must help us!
Fulfill your promise now. Don't let my sons
die unmourned by heroes after them."
She collapsed in grief, and so did Draupadi,
Subhadra and the other weeping women.

Krishna entered the room where Uttaraa lay.
Midwives and physicians were in attendance,
silent and helpless. The room was orderly
with rows of water pots, flowers and fragrant
burning wood. Uttaraa was prostrate,
convulsed with tears, crying, shrieking aloud
like a madwoman, with all the other women
weeping in sympathy. All her kin were dead;
now her lifeless baby was in her arms.
Then sitting up, trying to calm herself,
she rocked her infant son, and murmured softly,
the baby lying inert as a swaddled doll.
"O my dear one, just wake for a moment
to see the mother of your grandfather
plunged in sorrow. Pity us, my son.
But if you cannot live, go to your father,

tell him how my life is pointless now;
I should be dead myself!"

                Krishna listened,
then he poured a few drops of fresh water
into his right hand, and touched with it
the infant's lips, nostrils, both ears, both eyes,
drawing out the toxic *Brahma* weapon.
"I have never spoken an untruth;
I have never turned away from battle;
I have never failed to support brahmins.
By the merit of those acts of mine,
may this child live." Silence in the room.
Then, almost imperceptibly at first,
the child began to stir.

                What thankfulness!
What joy sprang up! It was a great explosion
that burst from the women's quarters into all
corners of the palace, and out, out
among the disbelieving citizens
of Hastinapura. Then, tumultuous joy
seized them like a fever, and all night long
with celebration, feasting and loud music,
the city was ablaze with noise and light.

Next day, Krishna announced the infant's name:
Parikshit, born to save his failing line.
He would go on to rule for many years,
after the Pandavas had left the earth.

About a month after the baby's birth
news came that the Pandavas were approaching,
bringing with them unimaginable
quantities of wealth. All the townsfolk,

of every station, crammed the thoroughfares
as the great caravan, groaning with gold,
trundled slowly toward the treasury.
Entering the city, the royal party
was greeted by cheering crowds. Their success,
and the horse sacrifice it made possible,
would bring blessings to the entire kingdom.

57.

THE HORSE SACRIFICE

The birth of Parikshit changed everything.
Despite the victory of the Pandavas,
Ashvatthaman's awful invocation
of the *Brahma* weapon had cast dragging doubt
on the future of the Bharatas, planting
a seed of hopelessness in every heart.
But now it seemed the dynasty was safe.

One of King Yudhishthira's first acts
was to consult Vyasa. Touching his feet,
formally he sought the seer's permission
to conduct the horse sacrifice. "Excellent!"
said Vyasa, "I myself will play a part
in the ceremony, according to your wishes.
This great sacrifice will absolve all sin.
See to it that you please the deities
by making abundant gifts."

                          Yudhishthira
also sought consent from Krishna, who
rejoiced at the prospect of the great event.
"Let your brothers, too, be sacrificers,"
he said. Then Vyasa was asked to name
the best time for the ceremony which must
inaugurate the sacrificial process:
the initiation of the Dharma King.

He ordered that the ritual implements
and other objects should be made of gold.

Planning began for the great event.
A superb stallion would be selected
and then let loose to wander the land at will.
The horse would be protected by the army
led by a distinguished kshatriya,
and in whatever kingdom it might roam
that land would be claimed for King Yudhishthira.
Any ruler who put up resistance
would be subdued. Then he would be invited
to Hastinapura, as a welcome guest
at the splendid sacrifice, when the time came.
After a year, the horse would find its way
back to the kingdom of the Bharatas,
and then the great ceremony would be held.

On Vyasa's advice, Yudhishthira
designated strong-armed Arjuna
to be protector of the horse, saying,
"As you progress, when hostile kings come out
to oppose you, and resist our rule,
try to avoid battles, and above all
avoid killing warriors whose kindred
met with death on the plain of Kurukshetra.
Be friendly. Invite them to the sacrifice.
Consecrate the sons of fallen heroes
—or daughters, if there are no surviving sons."

A most beautiful piebald horse was chosen
and kept in readiness. From near and far,
guests arrived for the initiation
of King Yudhishthira, the first ritual step.
He was resplendent in red silk, with gold
accoutrements. Staff in hand, wearing
a soft black deerskin for his upper garment,

the king shone like a star in the firmament.
Priests performed the rites; then it was time
for the magnificent horse to be let loose.
As it began to wander on its way
from Hastinapura, an exuberant crowd
pressed and jostled to get sight of it,
shouting, "Farewell, Wealth-winner, return safely!"
and Arjuna, accompanied by priests,
soldiers and retainers, began his journey.

⚜

Through the months that followed, Arjuna,
riding a chariot drawn by fine white horses,
followed the stallion as it made its way
on a meandering route through many lands.
Despite his brother's hopes, there were fierce fights.
Men who had lost most at Kurukshetra
were often just the ones who wanted battle,
thirsting for revenge. Thus it happened
that the horse crossed into Trigarta country,
the kingdom whose men had harried Arjuna
so tenaciously on the battlefield.
Now they came out in strength, intent on capture.

Mindful of the king's request, the Pandava
tried to make peace. "Do not attack, you villains.
Life is precious, as you should know by now!"
The Trigartas took no notice, but let fly
a cloud of arrows which, flexing *Gandiva*,
Arjuna deflected in mid-flight.
Bitter conflict followed. Arjuna
was wounded in the hand by a young warrior
whose outstanding skill he much admired
and whom, for that reason, he refrained from killing.
Instead, he slew a host of his companions.
Eventually the rest threw down their weapons

and formally acknowledged Yudhishthira
as their ruler. Arjuna invited them
to be present at the horse sacrifice.

This was the shape of many more encounters.
The horse wandered up hills, into valleys,
across desert terrain. Sometimes the rulers
of these lands met Arjuna's conditions,
sometimes they resisted. A great engagement
took place between Arjuna and the Sindhus.
Jayadratha (husband of Duhshala,
sole sister of the hundred Kauravas)
had been their king, and they were full of wrath
at the way Arjuna had slaughtered him.
They launched a blistering attack against
the sacrificial horse and its protector.
In the savage fighting, Arjuna
was badly wounded, and lost consciousness.
Celestial rishis revived him with their prayers,
and he fought on. Remembering Yudhishthira,
he called to his enemies, "We are intent
on your surrender rather than on slaughter."
But, unpersuaded, the Sindhu forces hurled
their spears and arrow showers ever more fiercely.

They were losing ground when Duhshala,
their interim ruler, approached, carrying
her infant grandson in her arms. Weeping,
she told the Pandava the baby's father,
Jayadratha's son, had been in mourning
for his father when he heard that Arjuna
had arrived to subjugate the kingdom—
at which he died of grief and fear. She begged
her cousin to take pity on the baby,
and sued for peace, ordering her warriors
to lay down their weapons. Arjuna,
seeing that the Sindhus posed no threat,

embraced her warmly, and expressed the hope
that she would come to the horse sacrifice.

⚕

The horse came to the kingdom of Manipura
ruled by Arjuna's son by Chitrangadaa,
Babhruvahana. The stalwart youth
rode out to meet Arjuna, carrying gifts,
loth to fight his father. But Arjuna,
thinking his son must be a feeble coward,
shouted at him, pricking him with insults.
"Are you a woman? I have come to fight,
not to chat with you. You're a kshatriya,
so fight like one!" Then the young man's stepmother,
Ulupi, daughter of the Naga king,
beautiful, sinuous, rose up through the ground
and urged her stepson to acquire merit
by fighting the world's greatest warrior.

Reluctant though he was, Babhruvahana
called for his armor and his chariot,
having first captured the sacrificial horse.
He flew toward his father, and loosed a stream
of arrows, piercing him badly in the shoulder.
Arjuna was shocked, but gratified
by his son's skill. A heroic fight followed,
son against father, a dazzling display
delighting both, one of those rare moments
when war is the best of games. It did not last.
Soon both warriors were severely wounded;
then the son, letting fly an iron arrow,
deeply pierced Arjuna through his breastplate,
shearing it off his body. Penetrated
through lungs and heart, Arjuna fell, lifeless.
Babhruvahana, too, fell to the ground
fainting from his wounds, and from the shock
of seeing his father killed—and he the killer!

News of the event reached Chitrangadaa.
Shocked, she ran to the scene lamenting loudly,
and seeing Ulupi there, she turned on her.
"How could you do this! How can you stand, dry-eyed,
when my son, whom you encouraged, has just killed
your husband and mine? Was it jealous spite?
You must know it is entirely proper
for men to marry more than a single wife.
Oh, revive him! I know you have the power.
I have released the sacrificial horse.
It is right for a son who kills his father
to die; but this great Bharata, this hero
on whom Yudhishthira utterly depends,
should not be lying here. O Ulupi,
if you do not bring him back to life
I shall end my own life before your eyes!"

Babhruvahana stirred. Seeing Arjuna
lying lifeless on the bloody ground,
he wished to die himself. What earthly penance
could expiate the sin of patricide?
Hopeless, he sat down to begin a fast
to death.

      Ulupi summoned a powerful gem
frequently used by snakes to counter death.
"Son, you need not grieve. You have done no wrong.
Your father challenged you—and it was because
I knew that he had come wanting to test you
that I spurred you on. And I created
the illusion of his death. This mighty Arjuna
has divine origins—he cannot be killed
by ordinary mortals. To revive him,
place this gem on his breast." The young man did so.

As if roused from a deep, refreshing sleep,
Arjuna opened his eyes and looked around.
He was surprised to see the women there.

Ulupi said, "Listen—I have acted
entirely for your good. A while ago
I heard a conversation. The Vasus
had gone to Ganga, goddess of the river,
mother of Bhishma, and complained to her
that you had killed their brother unrighteously,
shooting him under cover of Shikhandin.
For this, they proposed to place a curse on you.
Ganga consented. I was horrified
and hurried to my wise, compassionate father.
To protect you, he implored the Vasus
to offer a concession. They relented.
'When Arjuna is struck down by his own son
our curse will end. He will have made amends.'"

Arjuna was profoundly grateful. His son
and Chitrangadaa were relieved. They asked him
to spend the night in their palace. Arjuna
declined. "This horse is wandering at will
and I must follow. It is not permitted
that I stop anywhere." But he invited them
to Hastinapura for the sacrifice,
and they assured him that they would attend.

༄

The sacrificial horse meandered on
over the earth, between one mighty ocean
and the other, from the palm-fringed shores
of the south to the sparkling Himalaya.
It moved among the ebony Dravidians,
among the green-eyed warriors of the north,
among the war-like and the peaceful peoples
of the Western Ghats.

          Inevitably,
there were battles. The ruler of Magadha
rode against Arjuna with enthusiasm.

Very young, unskilled in weaponry,
he nonetheless aspired to heroism
as a kshatriya. At first, Arjuna
was easy on him, and the boy felt proud
of his achievements, and wounded Arjuna.
At that, Arjuna destroyed his bow,
killed his horses, smashed his other weapons
and called on him to surrender. The young man
was glad to do so, and happy to accept
the invitation to the horse sacrifice.

In the land of Chedi, Shishupala's son
fought, and then conceded to Arjuna,
as did the rulers of many other kingdoms.
With some, the battles were mere token fights
for the sake of self-respect. But the nishadas,
led by the son of Ekalavya, fought
furiously before they were defeated.
So did the vengeful son of Shakuni,
king of the Gandharas, Arjuna's cousin.
He seized the horse, then launched a fierce attack
and would not give up, even after dozens
of his soldiers, horses and charioteers
had been killed. Arjuna spared his life
because the two were kindred, and because
Shakuni's wife came out to intervene
and had the sacrificial horse set free.

&

At last, the horse turned toward Hastinapura.
Yudhishthira's sources of intelligence
brought him the news, and he was overjoyed
to know that he would soon see Arjuna.
Bhima consulted brahmins and engineers,
and supervised construction on a site
marked as auspicious for the sacrifice.
Roads were built, and ample living quarters

to accommodate the many thousands
of guests who were expected. Bhima sent
messengers near and far, in all directions,
to tell royal guests when to arrive.

In the days preceding the sacrifice,
people started to assemble. They brought gifts—
jewels, horses, weapons, female slaves.
When they looked around, they were amazed.
Everywhere they turned was luxury;
every object their eyes fell upon
seemed to be made of gold. Some remembered
the rajasuya rite at Indraprastha;
this was even more magnificent.
Krishna arrived with his relatives,
gorgeously adorned, and he brought news
of Arjuna, and of his many battles.

"Why is it, Krishna," sighed Yudhishthira,
"that Arjuna is so unfortunate?
Through what fault of his has he undergone
so many tribulations for my sake?"
"I see no reason," Krishna said, "except—
perhaps his cheekbones are too prominent."
Draupadi frowned. She could not tolerate
the slightest criticism of Arjuna
even as a joke.

For the great event,
Bhima had thought of everything, providing
food on an enormous scale. Thousands
of brahmins, and a comparable number
of vaishyas, were fed in relays. Vats of rice,
tanks of curd, many delicious dishes
and expensive sweets were served by attendants.

☙

A messenger arrived from Arjuna—
within two days, he would be there in person!
The city buzzed with anticipation
and at last, after his long journey,
the Wealth-winner, lean and battle-scarred,
walked into the city, the horse beside him.
After greeting his loving family
he went to bathe and restore his energy,
sleeping like a man thrown onto shore
as sole survivor of a storm-tossed voyage.
Meanwhile Chitrangadaa and Ulupi
had arrived with Babhruvahana,
and were warmly welcomed, for Arjuna's sake,
by Kunti, Draupadi and Subhadra.
Beautiful and rare gifts were exchanged.

Three days later, Vyasa told the king,
"The signs are favorable; the constellations
have been scanned by the astrologers.
The time is right to start the sacrifice.
Distribute at least three times as much gold
as is customary. In that way
you will earn great merit, and any sorrow
remaining from the Kurukshetra war
should finally be lifted from your shoulders."

Huge crowds of the king's subjects, from the city
and all around, had gathered. All was ready.
Stakes had been erected made of wood
of diverse kinds, as detailed in the scriptures,
but decked with gold for the beauty of it,
and adorned with rich and lovely flags.
Gold bricks were brought to build a fire altar
four tiers high, shaped like Garuda.
Three hundred sacrificial birds and beasts
were bound to the stakes on the sacred ground.

Many distinguished seers thronged the enclosure.
The rites, conducted by the most learned priests

guided by the Vedas, took several days.
Soma was pressed and drunk, and in between
the ceremonies, dancing and sweet music
were performed by accomplished gandharvas.
Birds and animals were killed and cooked,
each dedicated to a specific god.

The sacrificial horse was brought, then stifled.
As chief queen, Draupadi lay beside it.
Then it was dismembered, and its entrails
were roasted on the fire. The rising smoke—
that smoke capable of cleansing sin—
was eagerly inhaled by the Pandavas,
to the great joy of Yudhishthira.

When the sacrifice was over, it remained
for the Dharma King to distribute riches.
Now he was ruler of the earth, he offered
that earth to Vyasa, as the chief priest.
Vyasa returned it, asking for its equivalent
in wealth, which Yudhishthira duly gave.
This was divided among brahmins. Giving
was expiation for Yudhishthira.
The brahmins shared the artifacts between them:
gold bricks from the altar, the stakes, the arches.
Yudhishthira then, in order of precedence,
loaded his guests with gold, jewels, treasure.
Vyasa gave his share of wealth to Kunti,
for her to use in charitable acts.

Just when everything seemed to be over,
and all involved were greatly satisfied,
a large, blue-eyed mongoose approached the priests,
one side of its body shining gold.
In a booming voice, it said, "This sacrifice,
grand as it was, was not nearly the equal

of the coarse barley given by the brahmin
of Kurukshetra." The priests were astounded
and quite indignant. Speaking all at once,
they enumerated all the rituals,
all the procedures, scrupulously observed,
the gifts distributed, the benefits . . .
How could this sacrifice possibly have been
bettered? "Let me tell you," said the mongoose.

"IN KURUKSHETRA, there lived a devout brahmin, committed to a gleaning lifestyle. He subsisted on the grains of barley he gathered from the ground, after the harvest had been gathered in. He lived with his wife, son and daughter-in-law, and their existence was a happy, if frugal one.

"It happened that famine came to the land. The small store of grain the family had put by dwindled, and then was almost gone. They suffered. Day after day they went hungry as the brahmin found almost nothing to glean from the fields. One day, he managed to gather enough barley to make a small meal for the four of them. They ground the barley and made a porridge from it; then they sat down to eat. At that moment, an unexpected guest presented himself at their door. They greeted him warmly, and invited him to sit down with them.

"The guest was obviously hungry, and the brahmin gave him his own share of the barley porridge. The guest ate it, and still looked hungry. 'Let him have my share,' the wife whispered to her husband. But the brahmin was unhappy with this suggestion, knowing that his wife was reduced to mere skin and bone, and faint from hunger. 'My duty is to sustain you to the best of my ability,' he said. 'I cannot bear to see you giving up your meal.' 'But I have joined my life to yours,' she answered. 'You have given me all you have—and you have given me our beloved son. In return for so many favors, let me give you my share of porridge and you can give it to our guest.' So another portion of porridge was set before the guest. But his appetite was still not satisfied.

" 'Father,' said the son, 'please give our guest my portion.' The brahmin was reluctant to accept. 'I brought you into this world; it is only right that I look after you to the best of my ability.' 'As your son, I am part of you,' said the young man, 'and I should serve you in whatever way I can. I know that you will suffer greatly if you cannot perform your duty as a host. Please take my share.' So the brahmin accepted, and gave the porridge to the guest. He ate it, and was still hungry.

"Seeing this, the brahmin became sad and thoughtful. Then his daughter-in-law said, 'Father, take my share. Through your son—and therefore through you—I shall obtain a son. Thanks to you I shall know great happiness. Please take my porridge and give it to our guest.' The brahmin, seeing the girl wasted and weak, was very unhappy at this suggestion. But she persuaded him that, by accepting, he would be enabling her to obtain great merit. So he took her meal and gave it to the guest.

"The guest then revealed himself to them as Dharma, the god of righteousness. 'I am delighted with you,' he said, 'and so are the deities in heaven. With a pure heart, you have given me everything you have. Such a gift is worth far more than many a lavish consecration ceremony and horse sacrifice, because it is your entire wealth, and is offered without reserve. Your hard life on this earth is over. By your kindness to me today, you are assured of heaven.' Then flowers rained down from the sky, and the brahmin family ascended into heaven.

"All this," said the mongoose, "I witnessed from my hole in the ground. When the family had gone to heaven, I came out; and what with the flowers, and the water the guest had been given to wash his holy feet, and what with the scraps of barley, and the scent of sanctity, my head and half my body turned to gold. Ever since, I have been attending hermitages, pilgrimages, and sacrifices, in the hope of finding an example of devotion to match that of the brahmin family. In that way, the rest of my body could be changed to gold. That is why I came to this horse sacrifice, having heard of

King Yudhishthira's devotion to dharma. But I have been disappointed."

Having spoken, the mongoose disappeared
and the brahmins, astonished and impressed,
made their way in silence to their homes.

⚜

On hearing this story, King Janamejaya
was perplexed. "It is well known," he said
to Vaishampayana, "that sacrifices,
properly performed by learned priests,
bring great benefits. Why, then, did that mongoose
treat Yudhishthira's great horse sacrifice
with such contempt?"
                              "Millions of ascetics,"
replied Vaishampayana, "have attained
heaven through practicing renunciation,
self-control, compassion and truthfulness,
without the need to take the lives of creatures.
Sacrifice is not so wonderful."

"Who was the half-gold mongoose?" asked the king.
Vaishampayana told him this story:

"ONCE THE SEER Jamadagni collected milk from his cow,
to use in a shraddha ceremony. To test the seer's forbearance, Anger spoiled the milk. But Jamadagni, staying
calm, sent Anger to see the ancestors, since it was they who
had been deprived of the milk.

"The ancestors cursed Anger to take the form of a mongoose. He would only become free of the curse by censur-
ing dharma. Through his condemnation of Yudhishthira's
sacrifice, the curse was lifted, since Yudhishthira was the
Dharma King."

XV

THE BOOK OF
THE HERMITAGE

58.

THE RETREAT OF THE ELDERS

Hastinapura. Life at court took on
a pleasant pattern. The horse sacrifice
had helped to reconcile Yudhishthira
to his royal burden, and he soon became
a most judicious ruler, compassionate
even to enemies. Always in his mind
were Bhishma's teachings.

                      He never forgot,
for a single day, the harrowing price paid
for the great kingdom that he now possessed.
The searing loss endured by Dhritarashtra
and Gandhari could never be repaired.
But the king made sure as far as possible
that the aged couple should enjoy a life
similar to the one they led before.

Yudhishthira consulted Dhritarashtra
on many affairs of state. The old man
had Vidura, Sanjaya and Yuyutsu
as his frequent companions. And Vyasa
would visit him, reciting many stories
about the rishis back in ancient times.
At the king's request, his younger brothers
would very often sit with Dhritarashtra,
showing him their respect. And their mother,
Kunti, with Draupadi and Subhadra,
waited on Gandhari with great devotion.

Vidura was now Yudhishthira's steward
and managed his dominions with such skill
that they prospered, and his subjects too.
Dhritarashtra took it upon himself
to dispense royal pardons to prisoners
who were condemned to death, and Yudhishthira
did not interfere with him in this.
The king ensured that the most delicious
food and drink, the most comfortable apartments,
were made available to the old couple.
In short, Yudhishthira and his brothers
behaved toward them like devoted sons—
in fact with more devotion than their own sons
had ever shown. Yudhishthira forbade
any mention of Duryodhana
and his wickedness. On the surface, then,
happiness prevailed on every side
and, in this way, fifteen years went by.

But all was not exactly as it seemed.
Dhritarashtra felt only affection
and gratitude to four of the Pandavas.
But he could not banish from his mind
the way Bhima had killed Duryodhana.

It rankled still. And Bhima, for his part,
still resented Dhritarashtra's role
in the disastrous dice game, and afterward.
Bhima knew the king would not permit
any overt insult to their uncle.
But he found ways of making the old man's life
miserable—for instance, causing servants
to disobey him. And, within the hearing
of the old couple, he would boast and swagger
to his friends, "Do you see my powerful arms?
These are the arms that sent Duryodhana,
that brute, together with his sons and brothers,
to their deserved destruction!"

              Dhritarashtra
suffered this in silence, and Yudhishthira
never came to hear of it. But in time,
the old man became more and more despondent.
One day, he summoned his nephews. "We all know
how the great destruction at Kurukshetra
was brought about. I take the blame for it.
All my advisers gave me the same counsel:
'Control Duryodhana.' But you see
I loved him, and that overrode my judgment.
Bitter remorse has gnawed me ever since.
Although it was the working out of time
that brought the destruction of kshatriyas
as was ordained, still, I regret my part.

"Now, after many years, I have resolved
to expiate my sins with renunciation.
Only Gandhari knows that, for some time,
I have eaten little, and have slept
on the bare ground. So has Gandhari.
Though we have lost a century of sons
we no longer grieve for them. They all died
as true kshatriyas." He turned to the king.

"Yudhishthira, you have behaved toward us
as if you were our son. We have been happy.
But now we have decided to retreat
into the forest, wearing bark and rags,
and there, blessing you, eating little,
we shall end our days. Our austerity
will be to your benefit, since kings enjoy
the fruits of acts performed within their kingdom,
auspicious and inauspicious. Sanjaya
and Vidura will go with us. Now we come
to ask you to release us."

              "Oh no, uncle!"
cried Yudhishthira, "I thought you were content!
I have neglected you—I did not realize
that you were practicing such self-denial
and had these plans in mind. You need not go—
I myself will retreat to the forest
and your son Yuyutsu can rule the kingdom,
or you can rule, or anyone you choose.
Or if you insist on leaving here, then I
will go with you." In this way, the king
flailed around in his shock and grief.

Dhritarashtra, exhausted by his fast,
was fainting, and unfit for more discussion.
"I will make no decision," said the king,
"until you agree to take a little food."

Vyasa appeared then, and urged the king
to let Dhritarashtra and Gandhari go.
"It is appropriate," he urged. "The old king
should not die a demeaning death at home.
If not in battle, then he should be able
to acquire merit through renunciation
like many kings of old. For kings are like
exalted householders, and it is right

that, after their royal duties are completed,
they should embark on the third stage of life,
asceticism." The king said, "So be it."

Over the next days and weeks, well-wishers
came from far and wide to pay respects
and say their last farewell to Dhritarashtra.
A great crowd, citizens of every class,
congregated in the assembly hall.

In a failing voice, the old king spoke to them.
"Like my brother Pandu in his time,
I ruled you fairly. So did Duryodhana.
Through his wicked pride, he caused great bloodshed,
and paid for it with his life. That did not mean
that he neglected you. Now, for some years,
Yudhishthira has held the reins of kingship,
supported by his brothers, and he has been,
and will remain, an outstanding ruler.
I urge you to look after him with your lives
as he protects you. Now he has allowed me,
together with my respected wife, Gandhari,
to leave the court and spend what life is left
in renunciation. I ask you, too,
the people, to favor me with your consent."

There was silence. All assembled there
were deeply moved, their eyes streaming with tears
at their old king's humility. Then a buzz
of discussion arose, and they appointed
a learned brahmin to speak on their behalf.
"Sir, I speak for all of us. We honor
your decision. Everything you have said
is true. The house of Bharata has always
ruled us well and fairly. Duryodhana
never harmed us. The terrible events
that took place on the field of Kurukshetra

were not your fault, nor were they brought about
by Duryodhana, nor by heroic Karna.
That tremendous slaughter could not have happened
if the gods had not intended it.
We therefore, in your presence, absolve your son,
who now dwells in the heaven fit for heroes.
And we pledge our deep loyalty to the king."
At this, the crowd shouted their approval,
and the old king joined his hands and honored them.

ॐ

The date for the departure of the elders
was to be the day of the full moon.
Meanwhile, Dhritarashtra spent much time
with Yudhishthira, advising him.
Although the Dharma King had already ruled
for fifteen years (and long before, had reigned
in Indraprastha), he listened patiently
and welcomed his old uncle's homilies.

In his last days at court, Dhritarashtra
sent Vidura to ask the king a favor:
would Yudhishthira give him the means
to carry out large-scale memorial rites
for his sons, and for all the other heroes
who were killed, even Jayadratha,
and including Bhishma? Yudhishthira
and Arjuna were pleased with this proposal,
but Bhima frowned. Arjuna said to him,
"Brother, do not begrudge our uncle this.
Look at the way time turns things upside down.
Once, we were begging him to favor us;
now, by good fortune, he is the supplicant."
Bhima burst out, "It isn't right! Why should he
perform rites to sustain his wicked sons,
gladdening his heart? They should be left

to make their own way in the afterlife.
Of course, rites should be carried out for Bhishma,
and Kunti can make offerings for Karna.
But it should be *we* who provide the gifts,
not Dhritarashtra. He and his wretched sons
subjected us to twelve long years of exile.
Where was his affection for us then?
What did he do to protect Draupadi?
How—" But then Yudhishthira cut him short
and rebuked him.

          The king turned to Vidura.
"Please tell Dhritarashtra that my treasury
is at his disposal. Let him make gifts
to gratify the priests. And kindly ask him
to forgive Bhima his lack of charity.
Our years of exile still afflict his heart."

Vidura went back to Dhritarashtra
with the king's message. The old man was pleased
and set about arranging a huge event
to take place on the day of his departure.
There would be enormous gifts of wealth
made to brahmins, and to the assembled guests.
Yudhishthira collaborated fully
and decreed that the money spent on gifts
be multiplied tenfold.

          The day arrived.
After the elaborate shraddha rites,
Dhritarashtra and his three companions,
dressed in deerskins, started on their journey.
The entire court and the citizens
came out into the streets, and sorrowfully
escorted their old king out of the city.
Then, slowly, they turned back toward their homes.
Kunti did not turn back. She had decided

to accompany the others to the forest.
Yudhishthira was shocked; so were his brothers.
Together they begged Kunti to change her mind.
"Mother, you cannot go," said Yudhishthira.
"It was you who urged us to fight for justice,
you who said the kingdom should be ours.
How can you leave us now, abandon us
when we have gained the fruits of your advice?
Show some compassion; please do not deprive me
of your wisdom in my difficult calling."
But Kunti continued walking.

                    Bhima said,
"We were born in the forest; it was you
who brought us as children to this city.
Do not reject Yudhishthira's achievement.
It is unnatural for you not to share it—
and, you can see, the twins are heartbroken."

"I have made up my mind," replied Kunti.
"This is no quick decision. My heart is burdened
by sorrow and guilt at the death of Karna.
I was very wrong not to reveal
the truth about his birth, and now I grieve
bitterly every hour of every day
for the man who was, and was not, my son.
All I can do is seek to expunge my sin
by penances. True, I encouraged you
to fight for the kingdom that was yours by right.
You are kshatriyas, and of royal birth.
It was for this I brought you from the forest,
to acquire a warrior's skills, a noble heart.
I owed your father that. Otherwise,
I could have climbed on his pyre, as Madri did,
and enjoyed heaven with him.

                    "I saw you grow
into fine young men. I stayed with you

through hard and dangerous times. I prayed for you
through all the dreary years of your long exile,
never knowing if you were alive or dead.
Then I urged you to fight. I understood
that only victory or death in battle
could bring you honor, and give any meaning
to all your sufferings. Only the deaths
of Duryodhana and Duhshasana
could avenge their insult to Draupadi
and give her peace.

     "For the last fifteen years
I have devoted my life to Gandhari
whom I revere, both for her great virtue
and as the wife of Pandu's older brother.
I have watched you and your brothers flourish.
But now my task on earth is at an end.
The fruits of sovereignty are yours, not mine.
I do not want them. I now wish to attain,
through penances, and through obedient service
to the wise Gandhari and Dhritarashtra,
happiness with Pandu in the next world.
So you must let me go, Yudhishthira."

The king was now ashamed, and stopped protesting.
He understood.

     "Take care of Sahadeva,"
said Kunti. "He is the most attached to me.
Remember Karna; make generous gifts for him.
Take care of your brothers. And let your mind
always be steeped in righteous understanding."
With those last words, Kunti turned away,
following Gandhari into the trees.

༺

Dhritarashtra and his fellow elders
made their new home deep inside the forest
close beside the shining river Ganga,
where they quickly settled to a life
of abstinence, austerity and prayer
in the hermitage of the sage Shatayupa.
They were visited by many seers,
Narada and Vyasa among them.
Narada had just been visiting
the realm of Indra. There, he had seen Pandu,
who was always thinking of his brother,
and who would help him in the afterlife.
Kunti would join Pandu in Indra's heaven.

Narada foretold that Dhritarashtra,
with his wife, would fly to Kubera's realm,
after three more years of earthly life
burning away his sins through austerity.
Dhritarashtra rejoiced at this fine prospect
after a lifetime's sorrow and wrong turns.

⚜

As time went on, there was much speculation,
a buzz of talk in street and marketplace.
How were the old people managing?
They must be finding life extremely hard.
Was Kunti pining for her family?
Might they perhaps return?

                    The Pandavas
were sorrowful. They found no consolation
in anything—not hunting, wine or women,
not even in the study of the Vedas.
This loss of the older generation
brought back to them the pain of other losses:
their kinsmen and their sons. Especially,
they thought of Karna, their lost, unknown brother,

of how they might have loved him. Only the sight
of young Parikshit, so like Abhimanyu
in skill and beauty, gave them any joy.

Night and day, they worried about Kunti
and the other elders, ill-equipped
for life far from the luxuries of court.
How would their emaciated mother
be able to find strength to serve Gandhari?
What were they eating? Were their lives in danger
from wild beasts?

    At last, Sahadeva,
echoed by Draupadi, convinced the king
to organize a journey to the forest
to reassure themselves that all was well.
Members of the court and citizens
would be welcome to join the expedition.
At once their spirits rose. Yudhishthira
arranged that the party would leave the city
almost at once.

    Arriving at the Ganga,
they knew they must be near their destination.
Dismounting, the brothers went ahead on foot
and soon came to the elders' hermitage.
On the riverbank, they saw their mother
and others collecting water. Sahadeva
rushed to embrace Kunti, weeping profusely,
and she gathered her darling in her arms,
then cried aloud with happiness to see
her other sons and Draupadi.

    What joy!
The king presented to the old, blind couple
the entire stream of visitors—kshatriyas,
brahmins, women, soldiers, citizens—

and everyone rejoiced. A large number
of holy hermits, who lived in the forest,
gathered to see the famous Pandavas
and their companions; Sanjaya pointed out
each one of them, naming their attributes.

"That one with the nose of an eagle,
with wide and eloquent eyes, with golden skin—
that is the king himself. The one whose tread
shakes the ground like a massive elephant,
whose skin is fair, whose arms and legs resemble
tree trunks, is Bhima, scourge of the Kauravas.
That is Arjuna, with the dark complexion
and curling hair—he is the great bowman,
courageous as a lion. He is unbeaten
and unbeatable. See, over there,
sitting beside their mother are the twins;
no men in all the world are more beautiful
nor more loving and sweet-natured. See
the way they look at Kunti. Over there
is Draupadi, the queen. Look—even now
she is the loveliest woman on this earth,
resembling a goddess, with her smooth skin
and shining eyes. All those other ladies
with their hair scraped back, dressed all in white,
are the widows of the hundred Kauravas.
Many of them lost their sons as well."
And Sanjaya went on to itemize
every member of the royal household.
Thoroughly awestruck and well entertained,
the ascetics thanked him and took their leave.

"Where is Vidura?" asked Yudhishthira,
looking all around and not seeing him.
Dhritarashtra said, "My beloved brother
has gone further in extreme self-denial
than the rest of us. He eats only air

and no longer speaks." Just then, Yudhishthira
caught a glimpse of Vidura in the distance
and pursued him, calling. He followed him
to a remote clearing deep in the forest
and found him standing, leaning against a tree.
He was almost unrecognizable—
filthy, skeletal, his mouth filled with stones,
his hair matted and dusty. Yudhishthira
paid him homage, and Vidura stared at him
with a luminous gaze. As he did so,
his life-breath left him and, with yogic power,
entered Yudhishthira. Each of these two men
was an aspect of the god of righteousness,
Dharma. Now they were one. Yudhishthira
felt himself increase in inner strength
and was aware of an expanded wisdom.
His mind turned to arranging the last rites
for his beloved uncle, whose lifeless body
still leaned against the tree. But then he heard
a voice from heaven say, *Do not cremate
the body of this man called Vidura.
Your body is in his. Do not grieve for him;
he has gone to the regions of the blessed.*
Full of wonder, Yudhishthira went back
and told Dhritarashtra what had happened.

༄

Dhritarashtra said, "It makes me happy
to have you all around me, those I love.
My strict penances and your presence here
have consoled me. I am confident
that I shall have blessings in the afterlife.
But my mind never ceases to be tortured
by memories of the many wrongful acts
my foolish and misguided son committed.
When I think of how many brave men

died because of him, and because I
indulged his wickedness, well, then I burn
and know no peace, either by night or day."

"My husband speaks the truth," said Gandhari,
"and we all suffer—all who are bereaved—
even though sixteen long years have passed
since those terrible events. The worst
is wondering what has happened to them now,
all our fallen sons, brothers, husbands."
She turned to Vyasa, who was visiting.
"O rishi, you are capable of wonders.
If you could enable us to see them
as they are now, in the afterlife,
then I think we would find peace at last."

Vyasa said, "It is with this in view
that I have come to see you. When night falls,
if you go down and stand beside the river
you will see them rising up like swimmers
from their far dwellings in the afterlife.
They all met death as true kshatriyas;
all of them fulfilled their destiny.
Each one of your kin contained a portion
of some god or demon. They were on earth
to accomplish a celestial purpose."

Just as, in the aftermath of the war,
Vyasa had enabled wise Gandhari,
through the gift of divine sight, to see
all that took place on the battlefield,
so, now, he granted her and Dhritarashtra
the power of vision. As the daylight faded
and the sun dipped low behind the trees,
Vyasa conjured up a miracle.
This is what Gandhari saw, speaking
silently to herself as it occurred:

"The air is growing cooler. All of us
have come to stand beside the river Ganga
and we are waiting. Time drags. No one speaks.
Slowly, the forest birds are falling silent.
Our hearts are pounding—with dread? With excitement?
How will it be? Will we know what to say?
Soon, through Vyasa's power, Dhritarashtra
will see the sons he has never seen before!
Will he know them? I believe he will.

"The light is fading. There is mist, floating
over the water. Silence. Vyasa stands
in the shallows, erect, his lips moving.
Now, a murmur from the river, becoming
an immense rushing, a roar. Oh wonderful!
The water is churning, heaving, and the warriors
I last saw on the field of Kurukshetra,
broken and torn apart, are rising up
from the depths of the Ganga in their thousands.

"Their lovely heads and bodies are unblemished,
whole again, as when their womenfolk
gave them a last embrace before the battle.
Their graceful robes are shimmering with color
and they are all wearing auspicious jewels—
they must be gifts, blessings from the gods.

"Oh, but this sight defies the power of language
to describe! The most splendid celebration
ever seen must have been dull, compared with this.
All the different celestial realms
have yielded up their dead inhabitants
for this one night, and bitter enemies
are embracing now—Drona with Drupada,
brave Abhimanyu with Jayadratha,
Ghatotkacha with Duhshasana . . .

"Friends parted by death embrace each other—
Karna and Duryodhana, Bhishma and Drona . . .
Dhritarashtra has copious tears of joy
flowing down his cheeks, and how I tremble
with gladness to see all my beloved sons
without their hideous wounds, their faces, too,
unmarked by their suffering.

                "Vyasa said
destiny had decreed these savage losses.
It is as if fate was the puppet master,
and these brave men were galloped off to war
on invisible strings, their faces lit
by foolish happiness and warrior's pride.
Now, fate is satisfied; the gods, whose wishes
are opaque to us, have had their way
and, by the grace of Vyasa's yogic power,
have released our heroes. For this one night,
they can again be loving, open-hearted;
they are perfected, cleansed of the human stain
of hatred.

         "Now they are turning to us, our men,
and we, the living, take them in our arms
and sink in their embrace. All these widows,
whose shrieks I last heard on the battlefield,
are screaming now with joy and recognition
and something more. The Pandavas, with Kunti,
meet Karna and are reconciled with him
in perfect understanding. And now they rush
to embrace their beloved Abhimanyu,
and Uttaraa, too, is blissfully united
with the husband whose son now looks like him.
Dhritarashtra clasps Duryodhana,
as I do, and we have all passed beyond
any need for words . . ."

❦

Dawn began to turn the treetops red.
At a gesture from Vyasa, the warriors
began to plunge into the rippling Ganga
and were gone, back to their heavenly homes.
Vyasa spoke. "Any widow who wishes
to join her husband in the afterlife
should quickly plunge into the holy Ganga."
So many women, released from their bodies,
regained the companionship of marriage
in celestial worlds.

     Vyasa promised
that any person, at whatever time
and in whatever place, who heard the story
of how the dead were brought back to this world
to bring joy to the living, would be changed,
consoled by it. And you have heard it now.

❦

Having seen his sons for the first time,
and the last, Dhritarashtra shed his grief
and returned, content, to his retreat.
"My son," he said to King Yudhishthira,
"the time has come for you to leave this place.
Through your visit, and through the miracle
summoned by Vyasa, I have achieved
perfect equanimity. I must resume
my penances without any distraction.
And the kingdom needs you." Sahadeva
longed to stay with Kunti, sharing her life
of self-denial. "No, you must leave, my son,"
she said. "Seeing you daily, my affection
would undermine my vow of non-attachment."

So Yudhishthira and his family,
knowing that this parting would be final,
sadly took their leave, and made their way
back to the City of the Elephant.

❦

Two years later, Narada visited.
Eagerly, Yudhishthira asked for news
of the elders. "After you saw them last,"
said Narada, "the revered Dhritarashtra,
with his companions, moved his sacred fire
deeper into the forest. There he practiced
more severe austerities than ever,
holding only pebbles in his mouth,
not speaking, and wandering randomly
through the woods. Gandhari and Kunti
starved themselves too, and drank very little.

"One day, a forest fire sprang up, creeping
closer and closer to where the elders sat.
Sanjaya urged his master to escape,
since this fire had not been sanctified,
but Dhritarashtra refused, confident
in the power of his penances—and indeed,
he was too weak to run from the hungry fire.
Sanjaya escaped, and has made his way
to the high Himalaya. But your uncle,
Gandhari and your mother were burnt to death.
You should not grieve for them—it was their will
that they should die like this."

The Pandavas
were heartbroken, and felt like dying themselves.
"How could the god of fire be so ungrateful,"
cried Yudhishthira, "after Arjuna

went to his aid all those years ago
in the Khandava Forest! Had he forgotten?"
"In fact," said the seer, "this was no ordinary
inferno. The conflagration had been sparked
by the elders' own sacrificial fire,
left carelessly unguarded by assistants—
so they died in a sacred fire, after all."

Gradually, the wisdom of Narada
calmed the brothers' horror and desolation.
Every apt ceremony was performed
and they spent a month living simply
outside the city walls, undergoing
purification. Then the Pandavas
re-entered Hastinapura and, grieving still,
resumed the heavy burden of government.

XVI

THE BOOK OF
THE CLUBS

59.

KRISHNA'S PEOPLE

Thirty-six years after Yudhishthira
had come into his kingdom, strange portents
began to trouble him. His reign had been
largely without incident, prosperous
and peaceful. But now he felt uneasy.
Strong winds howled through the streets, scattering stones.
The great rivers flowed backwards to their source.
The sun and moon were cloaked in angry colors,
partly obscured by fog and framed in black.

Then came dreadful news: Krishna's people,
the Vrishnis, had been violently destroyed,
killed by an iron bolt, through a curse inflicted
by outraged brahmins. It seemed that only Krishna
and his brother, Balarama, had escaped.
The Pandavas cried out in bleakest grief.

Janamejaya asked Vaishampayana,
"How could all those warriors have been killed,
slaughtered in front of Krishna's very eyes?
I want you to explain to me in detail."
Vaishampayana did as he was asked.

One day some Vrishnis tried to play a trick
on a distinguished group of brahmin sages,
including Narada, who were visiting.
They dressed Krishna's son, Samba, as a woman
and called out to the sages, "Hey, rishis,
this is the wife of Babhru. As you can see,
this lady is expecting—can you tell her
if her offspring will be male or female?
She really wants a son." The holy brahmins
were not deceived, and they took great offense.
"Wicked and cruel louts, drunk with pride!
This son of Krishna's will certainly give birth,
but to an iron club, which will bring destruction
and death to the entire race of Vrishnis."
The sages traveled on to visit Krishna
and told him what had happened, and of their curse
on his crass relatives. This would fulfill
his own purposes; he would not intervene.

As was foretold, Krishna's son gave birth
to an iron bolt, a messenger of death.
The king, Krishna's father, in great distress
decreed that the bolt should be ground up small,
reduced to powder, and the powder then
be scattered in the sea. He issued orders
that no intoxicants of any kind

should be manufactured. The frightened people
obeyed, hoping to avert disaster.

In the sea-lapped city of Dvaraka,
Time stalked the streets in an embodied form,
a bald and monstrous figure. Few could see him
though his relentless tread was heard by many.
Cooking pots cracked; cats were born from dogs,
elephants from mules. All was awry.
Dharma began to be disregarded.

Krishna knew the signs, and as he watched
his Vrishni people wallowing in sin,
Gandhari's old curse came into his mind.
He knew catastrophe was in the offing,
and that his time on earth was almost over.
He would see Gandhari's words made true.

Signs of doom and decay were everywhere.
Rats and mice infested every house
and ate men's hair and nails while they were sleeping.
Freshly cooked food rotted instantly.
There were unceasing cries of raucous birds.
People became deranged, wives attacked husbands,
fathers killed their children. Priests and elders
were treated with contempt. Witnessed by all,
Krishna's discus rose into the air
and flew back up to those celestial regions
from whence it came. His splendid horses fled,
pulling his divine chariot behind them,
galloping over the surface of the sea.

Krishna summoned his kinsfolk and explained
Gandhari's curse. They were filled with fear.
Knowing events would take their predestined course,
he told them to undertake a pilgrimage
along the coast, to bathe in the sacred ocean.

A huge expedition was prepared
with an armed guard and wagons of food and drink,
and the Vrishnis set off, with their families,
to Prabhasa, on the rocky coast,
where the sacred Sarasvati joined the sea.

Rather than a sober pilgrimage,
this was a bacchanal. There was loud music,
actors and acrobats entertained them,
trumpets blared and, as the sun went down,
men became more and more intoxicated.
Food that had been cooked specially for brahmins
was doused in alcohol and given to monkeys.
Krishna joined the party, silently.

Satyaki started taunting Kritavarman
for his involvement in the night attack
on the Pandava and Panchala camp.
"What kind of a kshatriya are you,
slaughtering sleeping men, put up to it
by a perverted brahmin! Shame on you!"
His friends clapped and cheered uproariously.
"What right have you to take the moral high ground?"
shouted Kritavarman, pointing the finger
of his left hand in disrespect. "Call yourself
a hero? You cut down Bhurishravas
despicably, when he had lost his arm
and had withdrawn from battle." Krishna frowned
at Kritavarman.

                    The quarrel escalated.
Satyaki leapt to his feet in a fury.
"I swear," he shouted, "you're about to join
Draupadi's sons, and those other heroes
you cruelly killed, you coward!" And with that
he rushed at Kritavarman and cut his head
from his body. Then Kritavarman's friends

attacked Satyaki with any implement
that came to hand, and soon the entire party
were striking one another viciously.
Krishna watched calmly, knowing what must happen,
but when he saw his son Pradyumna killed,
then his son Samba, and Satyaki his friend,
Krishna became angry and snatched up
a handful of the coarse eraka grass
that grew there on the shore. In his hand
it became a massive, lethal club, transformed
by the powdered iron—the brahmins' curse.
Others copied him. Each blade of grass
became a deadly weapon, capable
of penetrating the impenetrable.
Inflamed by wine, the fighters soon became
indiscriminate, father attacking son,
brother killing brother. Before long
there were few survivors, and those few
were killed by Krishna, instrument of fate.
The moon rose on mound upon mound of corpses.

What would happen, now, to all the Vrishni
women and children—no men to protect them
against brigands? "Daruka," said Krishna
to his charioteer, "go quickly now
to Hastinapura and seek out Arjuna.
Give him the news; tell him he should come
without delay. He will know what to do."
Daruka flew off. Then Krishna noticed
one Vrishni hero, Babhru, was still alive.
Krishna sent him running to the city
to report, and to protect the women.
But Babhru too had been a reveler
and the sages' curse caught up with him:
a massive club hurled by a hidden hunter.

Krishna perceived that his earthly power
was waning. He told his brother Balarama

to go to the forest and wait for him there.
First, he himself must return to Dvaraka.
Already news had reached the bereaved city,
and the streets echoed with the sounds of sorrow,
fear and confusion. Krishna reassured
the women, "Arjuna will soon be coming;
Arjuna will protect you." Then he went
to see his aged father for the last time.
He bent his head to touch Vasudeva's feet.
"Father, this slaughter fulfills the sages' curse.
The holocaust that has destroyed our people
is akin to the deaths at Kurukshetra:
it had to happen. Now my time on earth
is almost over, and I wish to spend it
in yoga with Balarama in the forest.
You must guard the city, until Arjuna
arrives to take command, as I have asked him.
Arjuna and I are a single being."
Vasudeva assented, broken-hearted.

Krishna found Balarama among the trees
sitting in meditation. From his mouth
a huge, white, red-eyed serpent was emerging,
the celestial snake which had inhabited
Balarama's body until then.
The snake made its way toward the ocean
and many distinguished creatures honored it—
highborn members of the Naga people.
Then it slithered into the sea and vanished.
Thus Balarama shed his earthly life.

Krishna wandered in the peaceful forest
in profound meditation. He reflected
on Gandhari's curse of long ago, and knew

the time had come for him to leave the world.
Now, all his tasks had been accomplished.
He lay down on the ground, closed his eyes,
and withdrew his senses. A passing hunter,
taking him for a deer, shot an arrow
and pierced him in the foot. Running up,
the horrified hunter saw what he had done.
No deer lay there, but a dark-skinned man
in a yellow robe. Krishna blessed him.
"It was meant to be," he said—and died.

The immortal spirit of the blessed Lord
rose swiftly, lighting up the firmament,
passing through heavens, worshiped by the gods,
until he reached his own celestial region,
inconceivable, ineffable.

ॐ

As soon as Arjuna received the summons
from Daruka, he started off at once
for Dvaraka. He found the place desolate,
unnaturally silent. The streets and squares
of the noble city, formerly vibrant
with song and color, were empty and forlorn,
like a lotus pool in the depths of winter.

Krishna's sixteen thousand wives and concubines
were beside themselves. When Arjuna saw them,
and when he learned that his dear friend was no more,
he moaned with grief, and sank down on the ground.
Two of Krishna's most important wives,
Rukmini and Satyabhama, raised him
and made him sit, while the women gathered round
talking, praising their beloved Krishna,
finding solace in sharing their distress.

He went to see his uncle, the old king,
and the two men wept together. "Arjuna,
I have lived too long," cried Vasudeva.
"Krishna could have acted to prevent
the sinful self-destruction of our people—
was he not Vishnu, lord of the universe?
He refrained from canceling the curses
uttered by Gandhari and by the brahmins.
The Vrishnis, influenced by Satyaki
and Kritavarman, brought it on themselves.
Now that you have arrived, I can abdicate.
Food and drink will no longer pass my lips.
I will withdraw my senses. My earthly life
is over." And he closed his eyes for good.

Arjuna could not imagine living
in a world that had no Krishna in it,
but he knew that he must not give way.
He called a meeting in the assembly hall
for city dwellers, brahmins and ministers.
The despair in that hall was palpable.
"We must act," said Arjuna. "The sea
will soon engulf Dvaraka. Everyone
should gather all their portable belongings
and prepare the women for departure.
I will lead you all out of the city
and escort you to Indraprastha. There
you may live in safety. Krishna's descendant
Vajra will be your king." Just then a cry
went up from the king's palace: Vasudeva
was dead.

Arjuna ordered that, straight away,
the king's funeral should be carried out.
Vasudeva had been greatly loved
and the whole city followed behind his bier
as it was taken to the cremation ground.

Shraddha rites were performed for Krishna,
Balarama and all the dead Vrishnis.

A few days later, the much diminished clan
set off in slow procession from Dvaraka—
thousands of wagons, chariots, elephants
and well-loaded oxcarts. Women traveled
in covered carriages with the children
and old people. To protect the procession,
the remnant army provided outriders.

No sooner had the last cart left the city
than the ocean breached the sea defenses.
The sky grew black and seemed to be torn in two.
The planet Mercury swung from its usual course
and a tempest plowed the foaming ocean
into troughs and mountainous peaks of water.
The sea retreated from the land, then, rearing,
seemed to hang, impossibly still, before
it crashed forward, a voracious beast
savaging the city with watery claws,
devouring streets, squares, palaces and gardens,
indiscriminate in its appetite.
The houses of the poor dissolved instantly.
The mansions of the rich took little longer;
soon every one of the well-constructed buildings,
every tower and pinnacle, was drowned.
It was as if Dvaraka had never been.
The people stared. Then they turned their backs
in resignation. The past closed up behind them.

❧

The stream of sad and weary refugees
traveled slowly. Each night, they made their camp
by a source of water, in some pleasant spot.
Arjuna was vigilant. He made sure

that scouts went forward, to spy out the land
while watchmen were on guard throughout the night.
At first, all went well. But then they crossed
into the country of the Abhiras,
a barbarian land swarming with bandits.
Sighting the procession, guessing its riches,
and seeing that Arjuna was the only bowman,
the army feeble and demoralized,
the brigands struck. Yelling spine-chilling threats,
hundreds of ruffians swept down on the party,
armed with sticks.

          Arjuna, confident
that he could see them off with his great bow,
tried to string *Gandiva.* He only managed
with a huge effort. Then he tried to summon
his celestial weapons, but the mantras
would not come to mind. He loosed some shots
from his bow, but quickly all his arrows
were gone. The inexhaustible supply
had failed. He stared at his empty quivers, then
lashed out at the robbers with the bow,
using it as a club. But he watched, helpless,
as the brigands helped themselves to chests of gold
and seized many of the women; others
went with the bandits of their own accord.

Arjuna understood that his loss of power
was the work of destiny. The diminished group
made its way to the city of Indraprastha.
Many of Krishna's wives went to the forest
to end their days in prayer and penances.

Now that Arjuna had done all he could
for Krishna's people, he went to see Vyasa

in his forest ashram. He broke down in tears.
Vyasa was brisk with him. "What is the matter?
Have you killed a brahmin? Have you had sex
with a woman at the wrong time of the month?
Why do you look so wan and woebegone?"
Arjuna told him everything (although
Vyasa must have known it all already):
the destruction of the Vrishnis, the death
of the old king, the drowning of the city,
his own defeat at the hands of the robber band.
But, most of all, Arjuna talked of Krishna.
"How can I live without my friend?" he wept.
"The world is flat and colorless without him,
devoid of meaning. What should I do now?
Tell me, Vyasa!"

                    "All this, Arjuna,"
said Vyasa gently, "is the fruit of time.
The man, Krishna, was the incarnated
Vishnu himself, born in time to accomplish
his divine purpose. Now his work is done
he has returned to his celestial region.
You and your brothers were also born on earth
to play your part in the grand cosmic plan.
This you have done. Your celestial weapons
have withdrawn their power. Time provides,
and time takes away. Time is indeed
the driver of the universe. And now
the time has come for you to leave the world.
That will be best for all of you, Arjuna."

Arjuna returned to Hastinapura
and told Yudhishthira all that had happened.

THE BOOKS OF THE FINAL JOURNEY and THE ASCENT TO HEAVEN

60.

THE FINAL JOURNEY

Janamejaya said:
"Now Krishna was no more, now he had returned
to his heavenly realm, what did my ancestors
do then, deprived of their most cherished friend?"
"I will tell you," said Vaishampayana,
"and we are nearly coming to the end
of great Vyasa's monumental poem."

Having heard Arjuna's tale, Yudhishthira
proposed to all his brothers and Draupadi

that they renounce the kingdom and the world.
"Time," he said, "cooks all things in its cauldron.
We have achieved all that was preordained;
now there is nothing for us to do on earth."
They all agreed. The king sent for Yuyutsu.
He consented to be the guide and helper
of Parikshit, who would be the new king.
With Vajra as the ruler of Indraprastha,
Yudhishthira felt confident of peace
and prosperity throughout the kingdom.
Indeed, in future times, it would be told
how, under Parikshit, the kingdom prospered.

Lavish shraddha rites were undertaken
for Krishna, Balarama, Vasudeva
and all dead kinsmen of the Bharatas.
Brahmins were fed, and given generous gifts.
Kripa was installed as revered guru
to Parikshit, who would be his disciple.

When the people heard of the king's decision
they were distressed and tried to change his mind,
but he was firm, and managed to convince them
that it was for the best. Then he turned his thoughts
to departure. On the appointed day,
the five Pandavas and Draupadi,
clothed in garments of bark, and having fasted,
left Hastinapura. They were reminded
of the time so many years before
when they had left the city in bark clothing
after the defeat in the gambling hall.
Then, they were entering miserable exile;
now, quitting Hastinapura for ever,
they were at peace, feeling only joy.
Some citizens escorted them on their way,
still hoping to persuade them to return.
But failing, and bidding them a last farewell,

they turned back to the city, and their new king.
Only a stray dog stayed with the Pandavas,
trotting along behind them, keeping pace.

Traveling on foot, for many months
they circumambulated the whole land
of Bharatavarsha, through varied terrain.
Living austerely, they first turned eastward
toward the rising sun and the eastern mountains,
following the course of the mighty Ganga
to where its waters flow into the sea.
Arjuna still carried his bow *Gandiva*,
and his quivers, once inexhaustible.
They were useless to him now, but still
he was attached to them, as to old friends.

As they approached the coast, a tall figure
appeared in front of them. "I am the fire god,
Agni," he said. "It was I who burned
the Khandava Forest all those years ago.
Arjuna, I gave you *Gandiva* then,
procured from Varuna, the god of waters,
and now it is time to give it back to him.
It will return to earth in another era.
Like Krishna's discus, it will be taken up
to benefit the world." Then Arjuna,
standing on a rock, threw his weapons
out into the ocean, where they sank.

The Pandavas went on toward the south
following the shore by the Eastern Ghats.
Next, they went west and north through many kingdoms
that once had owed them fealty, unnoticed
and unrecognized. Eventually,
they reached the coast where Dvaraka once stood,
radiant jewel of the western sea
now submerged beneath its crashing surf.

The travelers turned inland, heading northeast,
and still the scruffy dog was at their heels.
At last, they sighted the majestic outline
of snowy Himavat, the king of mountains
dazzling in the sun, known as the source
of the sacred Sarasvati. They climbed upward,
ever higher, through the sparkling air.
In the distance, they could hear the roar
of rivers tumbling down over the rocks
through deep ravines. During their twelve-year exile,
when they had spent time in the high mountains
consoled by the peace and beauty of the place,
Yudhishthira had promised to return
at his life's end, as a penitent.
Now, as they walked in a state of meditation
they passed through groves of flowering plants, surrounded
by the singing of innumerable birds.

But they did not stay. Steadfastly they journeyed
onward toward the pure land of Mount Meru,
greatest of mountains, home to the mightiest gods.

Then, as they walked in single file, Draupadi
fell down, lifeless. "Brother," exclaimed Bhima,
"why has she died now, she who was blameless,
who never did a sinful act?" Yudhishthira
thought, then said, "She was wife to all of us,
but she has always favored Arjuna.
Perhaps that was her sin."

                      They traveled on
and, after some time, Sahadeva fell.
"Why?" asked Bhima.
                        "Perhaps he was too proud
of his wisdom," said Yudhishthira.

Nakula fell next. "He was righteous
and intelligent," said Yudhishthira,
"but he thought that none could rival him
in beauty. I suppose that is the reason
why he has fallen now."

Then Arjuna
fell to the ground and gave up the breath of life.
"Why Arjuna?" asked Bhima. "I cannot think
of any time when he spoke untruthfully,
even as a joke."
"He was too proud,"
replied Yudhishthira. "You remember—
he boasted that he would defeat our foes
in a single day. He was contemptuous
of other archers. That is why he has fallen."

Then Bhima fell to the ground. "Why me?" he cried,
"I want to know." Yudhishthira replied,
"You were a glutton; you failed to attend
to the wants of others. And you were a boaster,
proud of your mighty arms. But for all of us,
our death is preordained." And he walked on
without looking back, accompanied
only by the dog.

After Yudhishthira
had trudged on through the snow for many days,
his gaze fixed steadily upon Mount Meru,
he was exhausted. There was a rushing wind
and Indra appeared to him on a fine chariot.
"Climb on," he said, "and come with me to heaven."
But Yudhishthira stayed where he stood,
looking back down the mountain. "My brothers
and Draupadi must go with me," he said.
"I do not want to be in heaven without them."
"Do not grieve for them, Bharata," said Indra.

"They have all reached heaven ahead of you,
having cast off their bodies. It is ordained
that you should reach heaven in bodily form."

"This dog must come with me," said Yudhishthira.
"Through our entire journey, he has walked
beside me loyally, sharing all hardships."
"Impossible. Heaven is no place for dogs,"
said Indra. "You have won the supreme reward
by your virtuous life—there is no sin
in abandoning the dog."
                              "I cannot do it,"
said Yudhishthira. "It would be wicked
to cast aside one who is so devoted
from a selfish desire for the joys of heaven."
"But you have renounced all other ties,"
said the god. "You left your wife and brothers
lying on the ground. Why is this dog different?"
"They were already dead. There was nothing more
I could do for them. This dog is alive.
To abandon him would be equivalent
to the worst sins—slaughtering a woman,
theft from a brahmin, injuring a friend.
I have never done such a sinful deed,
and I never will, so long as I have breath.
Indra, I cannot, and I will not do it."

Suddenly, the animal was transformed
into the god of righteousness himself:
Dharma, father of Yudhishthira.
He was delighted with his virtuous son.
"This compassion is a supreme example
of your righteous mode of life. There is no one
in all the worlds more virtuous than you."

Yudhishthira was taken up to heaven
by Indra, accompanied by other gods
and celestial beings. The seer Narada

was one of many there who welcomed him.
He told Yudhishthira that no one else
had ever had the privilege of earning
heaven while they were in their earthly body.

Yudhishthira thanked the gods. "But now," he said,
"I wish to go to that realm where my brothers
and Draupadi have gone. I want to join them."

"You have earned a special place," said Indra.
"Why do you still cling to your old attachments?
Your four brothers and Draupadi have reached
happiness. You should stay here with us—
enjoy your great success."

    But Yudhishthira
insisted that he wanted to be only
where his brothers and his wife had gone.

"Open your eyes, Yudhishthira," said Indra.
Yudhishthira looked around—and what he saw
was Duryodhana! The Kaurava
was seated on a splendid throne, surrounded
by gods and many heavenly attendants,
together with the other Kauravas.
Yudhishthira, shocked and outraged, turned his back.
"How can this be! This wicked cousin of ours,
this man, driven by greed and bitter envy,
was responsible for the deaths of millions
and the desolation of millions more.
It was due to him that the blameless Draupadi
was humiliated; due to him
that we endured those thirteen years of exile,
suffering privation—yet here he sits
enjoying the rewards of Indra's heaven!
I do not even want to look at him.
Let me go to where my brothers are."

"This response is wrong, Yudhishthira,"
said Narada. "Heaven knows no enmity.
You should put all these concerns behind you.
I know Duryodhana behaved wrongly
to the Pandavas, but by the sacrifice
of his body on the field of battle,
and by his courage, he has pleased the gods.
He never ceased to follow kshatriya dharma.
He never fought unfairly. You should approach him
in a spirit of goodwill."

           Yudhishthira
looked away. "I do not see my brothers,
or any of the heroes who fought with us;
nor do I see Karna. Ever since
my mother told me that he was our brother
I have longed for him, both night and day.
When I noticed, in the gaming hall,
that Karna's feet so much resembled Kunti's,
I should have realized. I should have spoken.
I wish to go to him, and to the others,
my other brothers and faithful Draupadi.
Where my loved ones are—that is heaven.
For me, this place is not heaven at all."

The gods ordered a celestial messenger
to escort Yudhishthira to his kinsfolk.
The messenger went first, to show the way
over rough terrain. It was treacherous,
mushy with flesh and blood, bones, hair,
and stinking of the cadavers that lay
all around, swarming with flies and maggots
gorging on the decomposing bodies.
The way was lined with fire, and it was jostling
with crows and other scavengers, their beaks
iron-hard and cruel. Dark spirits lurked there
with needle-sharp incisors and hideous claws.

They passed a river, boiling and foul-smelling,
and a stand of trees whose every leaf
cut like the keenest blade. Worst of all,
people on every side were enduring
the most dreadful torture imaginable.

"How much further?" asked Yudhishthira.
"What is this place? And where are my brothers?"

The messenger stopped. "My instructions are
that I should come this far only. If you wish,
you may return with me." Yudhishthira
was suffocated by the dreadful stench
and stifling heat. His courage was failing him.
He turned round to follow the messenger.
But then he heard piteous voices, calling out,
"Son of Dharma! Royal sage! Great Bharata!
Pity us! As long as you are here
a fragrant breeze is bringing us relief.
Please stay, even for a little while."

"Ah, how terrible!" exclaimed Yudhishthira.
The voices seemed familiar. "Who are you?"
he called to them. He heard the voices answer,
clamorous with pain—
"I am Karna!"
"I am Bhima!"
"I am Arjuna!"
"I am Nakula!"
"I am Sahadeva!"
"I am Draupadi!"
"I am Dhrishtadyumna!"
"We are the sons of Draupadi!"

Yudhishthira, horrified and bewildered,
could not understand. It seemed to him
that everything he knew, and had believed

throughout his life, had been turned upside down.
"What madness is this?" he asked himself.
"What have these beloved people done
that they should be consigned to hell like this?
It makes no sense at all that Duryodhana
should be enjoying every luxury
while these dear ones, who have been most scrupulous
in observing dharma—and all these months
have been steadfast in yoga—are suffering.
Am I dreaming, perhaps? Is this delusion?"
Yudhishthira began to blaze with anger.
"What kind of beings are the gods we worship
with such devotion? What is dharma worth
if these good souls can be so cruelly treated?"

He spoke to the messenger. "I shall stay here.
How could I enjoy gross privilege
in heaven, having seen what you have shown me?
My presence here seems to bring some relief
to these dear people. Therefore, I shall remain
to comfort them. This is where I belong."

The messenger went away. But in no time
the gods appeared, with Indra at their head,
and, among them, the lord of righteousness.
Immediately, the scene changed completely.
Dark became light. The dreadful sights and smells
disappeared. A gentle, fragrant breeze
blew all around. There were no tortured beings,
no rotting corpses, no lacerating trees.

"Yudhishthira," said Indra, "do not be angry.
You will suffer no more of these illusions.
Hell has to be witnessed by every king.
Whoever first encounters heaven will afterward
experience hell. He who endures hell first
will afterward see heaven. Sinful people
enjoy the fruits of their good actions first,

spending some time in heaven before hell.
For those whose lives were mainly virtuous
it is the opposite. Because you tricked Drona
by letting him believe his son was dead,
you, through a trick, had to spend time in hell.
It was the same for your brothers. Illusion
caused them to suffer, just for a short time.
Now that is at an end. Shed grief and anger.
Your brothers and your kinsfolk have now gone
to those realms where they enjoy happiness."

Lord Dharma spoke. "My son, I am highly pleased.
You have passed all the tests I set for you.
By the Dvaita lake, you answered my riddles.
You showed loyalty even to a dog.
And here, out of compassion, you chose to share
the suffering of others. There is no one
in all the worlds more virtuous than you.
You must now bathe in the celestial Ganga
where you will cast off your human body."

This Yudhishthira did. And, with his body,
all resentment, grief, hostility
also fell away. Then the gods took him
to the place where everyone he loved,
as well as all the sons of Dhritarashtra,
were enjoying bliss. There he saw Krishna
in his divine form; and each of his brothers
transformed by splendor, yet recognizable,
associating with the gods, their fathers.
He saw Karna, with Surya, the sun god.
He saw Draupadi, radiant with light,
accompanied by all her royal sons.
He saw Abhimanyu. He saw Pandu
reunited with Kunti and Madri.
He saw Bhishma, Drona . . . so many heroes
it would take an eon to name them all.

Epilogue

"Now," said Ugrashravas, "I have related
the story of the Pandavas and Kauravas
in its entirety." The bard fell silent.
Then he rose, preparing to take his leave,
but the Naimisha Forest seers detained him,
clamorous for more: "What happened then
at King Janamejaya's snake sacrifice?
What did the king say when Vaishampayana
had finished telling Vyasa's epic tale?"

"He too wished to know what happened next
(since no one wants a great story to end),
bombarding Vaishampayana with questions:
Did the heroes enjoy heaven for ever?
Did they attain freedom from death and rebirth?
What about those who had not been mentioned—
Ghatotkacha, say, and Jayadratha?

"So, with the approval of Vyasa,
his disciple answered the king's questions.
'When a person goes to Indra's realm,
spending time in heaven and in hell,
not all the fruit of their actions on earth,
their karma, is used up. In the course of time,
they are reborn in whatever body
they deserve, according to the balance
of the good and bad deeds that still cling to them.

Those who have no remaining karma
are not reborn, and reach absolute freedom.
'For most of the heroes whose earthly deeds
are told in Vyasa's epic poem—whose names
we do not even know—it is not revealed
what was their journey in the afterlife,
nor what was the nature of their next rebirth.
But some of those whose parts in the great events
were most significant were incarnated
portions of gods and other divine beings.
After their task in this world was accomplished,
they returned and fused with those deities.'
And Vaishampayana listed by name
the demons, rakshasas and deities
associated with each character
in the great narrative."

        The forest seers
urged Ugrashravas to tell them more
(as the king had urged Vaishampayana)
concerning the creation of the cosmos,
and how it happened that the first king, Prithu,
was appointed. What was it that caused
the battle between gods and demons, leading
Vishnu-Narayana to descend to earth?

They asked the bard to tell what he had heard
about the life of Krishna Vasudeva
and his people, the Vrishnis and Andhakas.
Ugrashravas described the early life
of Krishna and Balarama, their childish pranks
among the cowherders, and Krishna's part
in the Vrishnis' migration to Dvaraka.

Many tales were told, but at last the bard
turned to leave the forest and travel on.

No one knew where next he might relate
the marvelous story.

　　　　　These were his parting words:
"What is found in the poem I have recited—
concerning dharma, riches and enjoyment,
as well as the path to final liberation—
may be found elsewhere. But anything
it does not contain will be found nowhere.

"It is sacred, equal to the Vedas.
It should be heard by everyone on earth,
the most exalted as well as the most humble.
To read it brings enormous benefit.
To recite it spreads enlightenment,
for whoever gives voice to these teachings
takes on the mantle of the wise Vyasa.
It is said that the day's sins may be dissolved
by listening to a part of it at night
in a joyful spirit, with a trustful heart,
with a perfect quality of attention.

"Just as Himavat is a mine of jewels,
the Mahabharata is a fathomless
mine of wisdom, precious gems of knowledge
for anyone receptive to the truth.

"We are born, we live our lives, we die;
happiness and grief arise and fade.
But righteousness is measureless, eternal."

So ends the matchless Mahabharata,
composed by Vyasa, for the good of all.

AFTERWORD

The Poetry of the *Mahabharata*

VINAY DHARWADKER

Dites, qu'avez-vous vu?
Tell us, what have you seen?

CHARLES BAUDELAIRE, *Le Voyage* (1857)
ROBERT LOWELL, *Imitations* (1961)[1]

O NE OF THE pleasures of Carole Satyamurti's retelling of the *Mahabharata* is that it pursues a variety of goals and accomplishes them with seemingly effortless skill. It is a contemporary poem in English that seeks to stand aesthetically on its own, to be valued for its craft, thematic significance, and imaginative scope and depth. At the same time, however, it is overwhelmingly concerned with representing another poem as transparently as possible, even though the latter is remote in time and place as well as language and culture, and embodies a very different set of shaping principles. On a different plane, Satyamurti's poem sifts through the numerous interwoven stories of the original in order to fashion a cogent storyline, and creates a narrative momentum that will hold our interest continuously. But it also pulls us in other directions, as it flexibly accommodates a mass of material from Sanskrit, and

1. Robert Lowell, *Imitations* (1961; New York: Farrar, Straus and Giroux, 1990), p. 68.

absorbs an abundance of unfamiliar terms, concepts, and qualities. Even as it maintains balance and restraint, the book takes some remarkable risks: adapting iambic pentameter and English blank verse to its practical tasks, it achieves a monumental size of almost 27,000 lines and 200,000 words. More than two and a half times the length of Milton's *Paradise Lost* and over three times the length of Wordsworth's 1850 *Prelude*, it emerges modestly as the longest successful experiment in English narrative poetry in modern times.

Astonishing as Satyamurti's technical accomplishments are, however, it is her desire to re-narrate an ancient Indian poem that defines her primary purpose in these pages. But what kind of work is the *Mahabharata* itself, and what are its attributes that a modern version ought to represent? How does this English poem actually relate to its largely inaccessible Sanskrit source? And what sort of world do the original *Mahabharata* and this innovative retelling open up for us, as cosmopolitan readers here and now? Wendy Doniger's Foreword and Satyamurti's Preface offer two kinds of answer to these and related questions; in this Afterword, I would like to explore a third angle of vision that complements their perspectives.

TEXTUAL FORMATION[2]

The *Mahabharata* became a subject of international interest beyond the borders of Asia almost two hundred and fifty years ago, when the typographer and philologist Charles Wilkins, working in Calcutta under the patronage of Warren Hastings, then governor-general of the East India Company's Indian territories, started to translate it from Sanskrit into English. Like most other translators who have followed him, Wilkins was unable to complete the project, but he did publish his rendering of one part of

---

2. Detailed information on the epic's textual history, print publication, and critical edition appears in the general introduction to *The Mahabharata*, vol. 1: *The Book of the Beginning*, translated and edited by J. A. B. van Buitenen (Chicago: University of Chicago Press, 1973), pp. xiii–xliv; see especially pp. xxiii–xxxix.

it, the *Bhagavad Gita*, in 1785, which proved to be both popular and influential in Europe.[3]

Ever since then, scholars and commentators have been divided into two main camps about the form and classification of the *Mahabharata*, especially in literary terms: one camp essentially views it as a "library," or a loose-leaf "encyclopedia" at best, whereas the other regards it, first and foremost, as a particular poem in Sanskrit, with a well-defined structure and definite aesthetic properties. It may be difficult to pinpoint the work's authorship, or to fix its date, place, and process of composition the way we can for modern works, but uncertainties of this kind do not deprive it of specificity as a Sanskrit poem. The poem's unifying principle does not lie in a "coherent point of view" or a fixed set of themes on the surface, but lies instead, as A. K. Ramanujan also argued in the 1980s, in a multilayered integration of shape and substance, sources and ends, at a deeper level of organization.[4] The aesthetic and imaginative aspects of the *Mahabharata* are vital factors in its reception in world literature today.

Around the turn of the twentieth century, Indian and Euro-American scholars came to generally agree that, given the complexity and importance of the *Mahabharata*, it was essential to establish a definitive text in its original Sanskrit form. After some delay, a team of Indian Sanskritists, led mainly by V. S. Sukthankar, took up the task independently at the Bhandarkar Oriental Research Institute at Poona (now Pune). They collated and calibrated 1,259 surviving manuscripts, from different parts of the subcontinent, and rigorously evaluated every word and every line in more than 89,000 verses attributed to the poem, before publishing its critical edition in 21 volumes between 1919 and 1969.[5] In the course of the past eight decades, the international community of Sanskrit scholars has arrived at a clear consensus that the Poona critical

3. J. J. Clarke, *Oriental Enlightenment: An Encounter between Asian and Western Thought* (New York: Routledge, 1997), pp. 58–59 and 85.
4. On classical arguments and his own position, see Ramanujan's "Repetition in the *Mahabharata*," in *The Collected Essays of A. K. Ramanujan*, edited by Vinay Dharwadker (New Delhi: Oxford University Press, 1999), pp. 161–83, especially p. 163.
5. V. S. Sukthankar et al., Critical Edition of the *Mahabharata*, 21 vols. (Poona, Maharashtra, India: Bhandarkar Oriental Research Institute, 1919–69).

edition gives us the best version of the *Mahabharata* as a poem that possibly can be reconstructed in modern times.

AUTHORSHIP

All the information we can gather and all the inferences and assessments we can make indicate that the poem reconstructed in the critical edition was composed collectively in a preclassical variety of Sanskrit by successive generations of poets between about 400 BCE and 400 CE, on the Gangetic plains in north India, mostly under imperial regimes.[6] However, in view of the astonishing connectedness, consistency, and cogency the poem achieves on such a temporal and textual scale, it is conceivable that, at the end of the compositional cycle, the text may well have been assembled, edited, and integrated by a single group of poets, possibly working under one master editor, on the eve of India's classical age (which runs roughly from 400 to 1200 CE). Given our bias as modern readers—that a poem is "never finished, only abandoned"—it is plausible that the canonical Sanskrit form of the *Mahabharata* that we have today is the form in which that final editor or group of poets "abandoned" it to the future accidents of history some sixteen hundred years ago.

The text itself says that it is the work of a *rishi*, or visionary sage, of brahmin patrilineal descent named Krishna Dvaipayana, whose extraordinary life span stretches across several generations of principal characters in the poem, and who is an eyewitness to its events as well as a seminal participant in them. Krishna Dvaipayana—not to be confused with Lord Krishna, the very different divine-human character—is also addressed as "Vyasa" (literally, redactor or editor), and appears forty-four times in the poem's action. Once he has completed his great poem, Vyasa teaches it to others, including his preeminent pupil, Vaishampayana, who becomes its principal transmitter. Vyasa's text is broadcast for the first time in his

---

6. The case for multiple authors of the *Mahabharata* is made in van Buitenen, op. cit., "Introduction."

presence and under his supervision, when he authorizes Vaishampayana to recite it in its entirety to King Janamejaya, at a "snake sacrifice," a Vedic ritual of cosmomoral significance, which the latter sponsors in order to set the world in order early in his reign.

Among those attending this public event is a bard named Ugrashravas, whose father, Lomaharshana (literally, "the teller of hair-raising tales"), is the most famous bard of the times. Ugrashravas carries the vast narrative Vaishampayana delivers at King Janamejaya's sacrifice to another notable event, a conference of all the hermits who live in Naimisha Forest—a region that, famously, is as much a spiritual and ecological retreat from worldly human society as a sequestered celestial zone of magic and fabulation. At the invitation of the hospitable hermits, who are eager to hear his "tales of wonder," Ugrashravas recites the text he had heard from Vaishampayana; and, as the *Mahabharata*'s opening chapter informs us, Ugrashravas's renarration in the enchanted forest—at two removes from Vyasa—is the version that reaches the rest of humanity as the canonical form of the poem. Thus, unlike the Homeric epics, which offer barely a glimpse of the supposedly blind poet of Greek antiquity, the Sanskrit poem provides us with a full metanarrative about its origins and transmission.

A BASIC POETICS

What makes the *Mahabharata* a poem, and how is it put together? If we were to answer this question as fully as possible, we would arrive at an account of the Sanskrit work that would serve a purpose similar to that of Aristotle's *Poetics*,[7] which is concerned with poetry in the ancient Greek world, especially in the genre of drama and the subgenre of tragedy. In order to explain—theoretically and practically, descriptively and prescriptively—how tragic drama is composed and how it works in the theater, Aristotle breaks it down into six constituents and their mutual relations and func-

7. Aristotle, *Poetics*, edited and translated by Stephen Halliwell, Loeb Classical Library 199 (Cambridge, Mass.: Harvard University Press, 1995), pp. 47–55.

tions in an artistic whole. These six components are *muthos*, plot, narrative; *ethos*, character and its environment; *dianoia*, thought, theme, meaning; *lexis*, language, diction; *opsis*, spectacle onstage; and *melopoeia*, melodic composition, lyric set to musical accompaniment. For the *Mahabharata*, we have no such formula or ready-made analytical framework for a comprehensive explanation. However, keeping Aristotle's paradigm in mind, along with a range of premodern Indian and modern Euro-American literary scholarship, we can formulate a basic poetics of the Sanskrit poem, by focusing on four of its aesthetic elements: its handling of characters and characterization; its method of emplotment, of plotting its multiple storylines; its treatment of narrators, narration, and narratives; and its conceptualization of its own form and genre.

CHARACTERS AND CHARACTERIZATION

The *Mahabharata* probably has more than five hundred human characters who appear as distinct, active figures in its narrative. The majority of them have names and play well-defined roles in the action, even if they appear only briefly; scores of them are one-dimensional and unnamed, and serve mainly as functional devices to get the story told. This rough estimate does not include the unspecified members of groups, assemblies, entourages, communities of slaves and servants, and gathered armies described or invoked in the text; nor does it include the numerous personages who are mentioned by characters and narrators in passing, but who do not participate in the action. The estimate also excludes all non-human characters or participants; if we count the many gods, celestial beings, mythological figures, anti-gods, demons, subhuman creatures, supernatural animals, and creatures belonging to other categories and to mixtures of categories, who have names and play specific roles in the narrative, then the final number would be much higher. As the foregoing catalog indicates, the *Mahabharata* is a cosmic poetic tale in which almost everything in the human and natural orders is interconnected (and also transmuted in various ways), and both are intimately related to the underworld as well as the world of the gods. The size and spread of this elaborate cast of characters have several consequences for the poem, for its architecture as well as its meanings.

Perhaps the most striking consequence of such a large, variegated roster of characters is that, unlike other epics from the ancient world, the *Mahabharata* is not centered on a singular hero. It is fundamentally a narrative poem with a disorientingly large group of protagonists and antagonists—twenty-four to be exact—none of whom can be omitted without altering the tale significantly.

PLOT AND EMPLOTMENT

The reason the *Mahabharata* has two dozen leading characters at its core lies in the magnitude of its action, and in the fact that its action is manifold. From the verbal surface as well as the organization of the Sanskrit poem, it is evident that it seeks to develop a comprehensive account of all the events in its narrative, making them plausible and explicable at one level and emotionally and imaginatively resonant at another. The events it represents span the space, time, and causal structure of the cosmos. It uses this enormous scaffolding to narrate the history of the race of its heroes (the Bharatas), together with the history of their land (*Bharata-varsha*). For its poetic potential and explanatory power, the war of succession to the throne of Hastinapura is the defining moment in both these histories, and it also becomes the master-node upon which the diverse quests and destinies of all the protagonists and antagonists converge.

In the case of an Athenian tragedy, Aristotle's *Poetics* conceives of *muthos* or plot as a single, continuous, and plausible order of events, with secondary episodes integrated with the main developments, and the whole adjusted in scale for representation on the stage. In this conception, the plot is a concrete sequence of events as a spectator perceives it in the course of a performance, from a vantage point "outside" the depicted characters. Simply because of its scope, the action of the *Mahabharata* cannot be treated on a par with action represented in an amphitheater: if chanted by a relay of reciters at a steady rate of two verses per minute for about eight hours a day, the text of the critical edition would take nearly seventy-five days to deliver in full. But the Indian poem also does not fit into Aristotle's prescription for the epic—which is supposed to offset the magnitude of its action ("unlimited in time span") with an "unchanging meter"—because its Sanskrit text does not use prosodic uniformity to contain thematic diversity. To explain how the *Mahabharata* actually manages its narratives, it therefore may be more productive to turn to the *Natyashastra*, the earliest work on poetics in the Sanskrit tradition, which began to circulate in India around 300 CE and provides an alternative account of plot.[8]

In one of the *Natyashastra*'s perspectives, every character in a narrative is motivated by a desire to attain a specific goal or set of goals; and the character's actions in pursuit of those goals, at particular times and in particular places and situations, constitute his or her distinctive plotline, which has the shape of a quest. In a work's overall narrative, each significant character has a specific plotline with a beginning, a middle, and an end determined by the origin, evolution, and conclusion of a quest, and especially by his or her point of view on the quest's stages and progress. The reader or spectator views this quest empathetically from the character's point of view, and not from some disembodied or impersonal vantage point "outside" the action. The aggregate plot of a poem, then, is the intertexture of the individual plotlines that unfold in the fictional lives of its principal characters—however many they may be—with each evolving plotline viewed from the "inside," as it were. The *Natyashastra* complicates this picture by arguing that a character's quest and motivation emerge from an initial situation, a *bija* (seed or germ) that serves as an origin, and whose offshoots comprise the primary and secondary strands in a plotline; and that the offshoots spreading out from the germ are brought into line by a *bindu*, a "centering principle" that ensures structural as well as discursive

---

8. Manomohan Ghosh, trans., *The Natyashastra*, vol. 1: chaps. 1–27 (Calcutta: Royal Asiatic Society of Bengal, 1950). Plot and emplotment are covered in Chapter 21, pp. 380–400. Ghosh's translation is unfortunately opaque on this topic; my overview uses the Sanskrit text.

cohesion. Moreover, a narrative germ produces a plotline in which a thesis gives way to an anti-thesis, and both yield to a synthesis; the synthesis then bundles the various offshoots of the initial situation into a decisive moment of crisis and a subsequent resolution.

In the case of the *Mahabharata*, the large roster of protagonists and antagonists means that the poem's overall emplotment has some two dozen distinct plotlines, each centered on a particular character pursuing a distinctive set of goals in interaction with other characters. Readers and listeners who grow up with the *Mahabharata* in their inherited cultural environment learn, from others around them, to imaginatively traverse the poem's aggregate plot many times over, and to grasp the totality of the represented action from the different points of view of different principal characters. Thus, on one occasion, one may follow Kunti's plotline from beginning to end, and grasp the epic as a whole from her point of view as Pandu's wife and widow, as the biological mother of Yudhishthira, Bhima, and Arjuna and of Karna (each fathered on her by a different god), as the foster mother of Nakula and Sahadeva, as Draupadi's mother-in-law, and as Duryodhana's, as well as Lord Krishna's, aunt; and on another occasion, one may view everything afresh through the eyes of, say, Karna or Duryodhana or Arjuna, and discover how different that character, as well as the whole epic, looks. Many Indians, perhaps the majority of those familiar with the *Mahabharata*, internalize this (non-Aristotelian) process of shifting interpretation over a lifetime, and hence entertain multiple perspectives on the characters, events, and meanings of the epic. Given the range of characters and the number of protagonists and antagonists, as well as the scope of the represented action, no one character's quest, point of view, or plotline defines a true or complete interpretation. That is, the absence of an omniscient narrator and of an absolute frame of reference in the *Mahabharata* implies that the coexistence of multiple perspectives in a multiplex plot is fundamental to its poetics. At the same time, the protagonists' and antagonists' divergent quests and points of view are held together by the *bija*, or germ, from which all of them spring (who should inherit the kingdom, under what conditions and why), by the progression from thesis to anti-thesis to synthesis in this central emplotment (from dishonorable disinheritance to failed diplomacy to inescapable war), and by the establishment of a just society and kingdom in the war's aftermath.

NARRATION AND NARRATIVE

If the action represented in the *Mahabharata* is inherently manifold, and its emplotment in the poem is necessarily multiplex, then the technical challenge facing the poets who finalized the Sanskrit text had to be the same that still faces every storyteller in modern times: since no story is ever one story only, and the telling of one story always spills over into the telling of other stories, what is the most efficient and effective way to tell *multiple stories together*? Historically speaking, even though the *Ramayana* had experimented earlier with an answer on a moderate scale, and the Buddhist *Jataka* moral tales and the Hindu *Panchatantra* animal fables had developed basic strategies for short narratives, the *Mahabharata* was the first work in world literature to confront this technical problem head-on, and to invent a solution that remains the most comprehensive one to this day.

The *Mahabharata*'s strategy for multiple narratives and narrations is to maximize the possibilities opened up by the device of narrative framing. At its simplest, a narrative frame is defined by a narrator and his or her narration and narrative; whenever a narrator is explicitly identified in a poem, and relates a particular emplotted sequence of events, the resulting narrative defines the extent of his or her narrative frame. If a narrator stops narrating events, and a different narrator takes up the narrative (or starts a different one), then the poem changes its narrative frame, and we, the audience, adjust our expectations and interpretive procedures accordingly. A poem with multiple framed narratives has to employ devices that inform its audience about who the narrator is at any given moment, what his or her *ethos* or character and setting are, and what we may expect from him or her; about the junctures at which a particular narrator's narrative begins and ends, or various narrative frames open and close; and exactly what the structural relationships are between one frame and another, and among all the frames and narrators that may be housed inside an aggregate plot.

The *Mahabharata* exploits the potential of the last of these devices fully, by employing all the vital relationships among narrative frames, and all their variations and combinations. One closed frame may be fully contained inside a larger one; one frame may be contiguous with another, so that the latter opens as soon as the former closes; one larger frame may contain two or more closed frames that are not contiguous with each other; and in the most complex interrelation, two frames may significantly overlap, so that a new frame opens well before—and continues well after—the previous one closes. Moreover, the epic does not hesitate to superpose these structures of containment, contiguity, discrete serialization, and intersection upon each other, or to use them in tandem. The variety of frames and framings produces the thick interweave that constitutes the actual text of the Sanskrit poem.

The *Mahabharata* as a whole is solidly encased in three outer narrative frames, nested successively inside one another, that are never dislodged over its entire length. For us, as an audience, the outermost frame always belongs to the "voice" that tells *us* the story, in a recitation or on the page, here and now; inside this anonymous frame is Ugrashravas's frame, retelling the epic to the sages gathered in the Naimisha Forest; and inside that frame is Vaishampayana's frame, in which the latter recites the entire *Mahabharata* at Janamejaya's snake sacrifice. All the events we read about or hear being narrated in the epic are always *inside* Vaishampyana's frame—except for the meta-events that reach us from Ugrashravas's outer frame. My rough estimate is that, inside the three outermost frames, we encounter some four hundred distinct narrative frames that fall along a spectrum, one end of which is marked by narrators who appear many times, and the other end by narrators who appear only once each, to convey a single fable, explanation, vignette, or thumbnail sketch.

This vast structure of emboxed narrative frames—conceptually resembling a set of Russian dolls or Chinese boxes, fitting snugly one inside another—allows the *Mahabharata* to create the most compact configuration for the integrated narration of multiple stories, in which both the causal interrelations among events and the mimetic force of their representation in the poem are articulated clearly. The tightness of this structure in each recension, as in the critical edition of the poem, cannot be overemphasized. In the various Sanskrit recensions we have inherited, each narrative frame is duly opened and closed, and the poem stands consistently as a well-crafted whole, its great diversity of themes held together by the underlying grid of narrative frames.

FORM AND GENRE

The *Mahabharata* derives one kind of structural integrity from its scaffolding of framed narratives, but its poetic qualities depend as much on what it communicates as on its mode or manner of communication. What, then, is the text's shaping principle with respect to its raw material, and what kind of poem does it become in the process of representing its content? In the past two centuries, Euro-American scholars have often found it difficult to respond to the Sanskrit work as an aesthetic object; as a consequence, they generally have ignored its structural integrity, and have focused instead on its uses as a religious text and its usefulness as a cultural document for outsiders, especially as a source of information about ancient Indian society, religion, politics, law, and morality. For a much longer time, Indian audiences have also turned to the *Mahabharata* primarily for its content, and perhaps secondarily for its aesthetic qualities—but this is so because, in the practice of Hinduism, the Sanskrit text has the status of scripture or quasi-scripture, next in spiritual authority only to the four Vedas. As a "fifth Veda" or body of authoritative knowledge and discourse, it is valued for its guidance on duty and ethics, its teachings about right and wrong, its arguments about the human self and the ends of life, its analysis of war and justice, and its vision of a good ruler and a good society. At the same time, however, the subcontinent's artists have long affirmed the epic's power as a work of beauty and imagination—not apart from, but in addition to, its power as a text linked to scripture revealed in "the language of the gods."[9]

Nevertheless, just as the *Mahabharata* provides a picture of its author, its authorship, and its transmission, it also offers commentary on its form and genre. One of its classifications of itself is as an *akhyana*, which identifies its mode of presentation and its poetic function. This label means that the poem sees itself as a telling, a narration, or an informative communication; that what it relates is specifically an old tale or a legend; and that its preferred mode of delivery is speech or oral performance rather than writing. The Sanskrit text also describes itself as an *upakhyana* which, as a nuance of *akhyana*, means that it is a retelling, rather than an original narration, of a tale heard earlier from others.

When the *Mahabharata* uses a different self-descriptive label, *samvada*, it characterizes its own form as dialogue. This is a precise specification because, in recitation and on the printed page, the Sanskrit text presents itself, from beginning to end, as a vast dialogue involving primary and secondary (and sometimes also tertiary) characters, nested inside and outside its numerous narrative frames. The poem, in fact, is fundamentally dialogic, not only in the sense of being cast in the form of a verbal exchange, but in the more robust sense of belonging to "the dialogic mode."[10] In Bakhtin's theory, this is the mode in which individuals exist in human society in constant interaction with others, so that any one person's thought and speech on any given occasion are always already "in dialogue with" some other—or someone else's—prior thought and speech. The poets of the *Mahabharata* explicitly understand and acknowledge dialogism as the shaping principle of their poetry, and they systematically flesh out the entire poem as a vast, multivoiced, ongoing *samvada* about everything on earth and in the universe, inside as well as outside the borders of human experience, so that, as they claim, "Whatever is found here may be found somewhere else, but what is not found here is found nowhere else." As

9. "The language of the gods" translates an ancient epithet for Sanskrit as a sacred medium.

10. See M. M. Bakhtin, *Dialogic Imagination: Four Essays*, edited by Michael Holquist (Austin: University of Texas Press, 1981), pp. 426–27.

a dialogic poem that goes well beyond the surface form of verbal exchange, the *Mahabharata* is an active response to the states of affairs it depicts, and its narrative therefore is always a multifarious modification of plain mimetic representation.

Finally, the Sanskrit poem also describes its genre in terms of its theme or content. Almost two millennia ago, the poets who finalized its text cast it as an epic, but they did not have a label for their enterprise. *Itihasa* was the everyday word they adopted to name the genre with which they could represent the absolute past of the people and the land of which they were the imaginative inheritors. At least two thousand years old, the word *itihasa* literally means "thus it was" or "so it happened," and is the exact Sanskrit precursor of the German phrase *wie es eigentlich gewesn ist*, "as it has been actually." By claiming to be an *itihasa*, the *Mahabharata* seems to assert its function as a mimetic representation of events past. Following this implication, Indian as well as Euro-American scholars since the nineteenth century have tried to interpret the *Mahabharata* as history—often too literally, and usually with absurd outcomes. Any encounter with the *Mahabharata*'s narrative, however, indicates immediately that the poem does not define itself as a history in the modern sense. Its poets are under no illusion that they somehow are composing a factual, empirically verifiable, or documentary account of the past, and they do not wish to impose any such illusion on their audience. Instead, they seem to focus on events that are long over, even for them, to which they themselves no longer have any real access (through direct experience or personal memory or reliable eyewitness reports), and which they know they can memorialize only *poetically*—events that can be "recovered" solely by imagining and reimagining, narrating and renarrating what Goethe, with a fellow poet's acuteness, called "the absolute past."

Bakhtin, again, explains what this means in a way that fits the *Mahabharata* with surprising precision. The genre that is designed to represent the absolute past is the genre that we now designate as the epic which, for the Russian theorist, has "three constitutive features": it seeks to represent the "epic past" of a nation; it draws on "national tradition" for its narrative, and not on its author's "personal experience and the free thought that grows out of it"; and, in "Goethe's and Schiller's terminology," it establishes and works across "an absolute epic distance" between "the time in which the singer . . . lives"—or the worlds in which the author and his audience exist—and "the epic world" that it depicts. These three features, Bakhtin argues in his emphatic style, are interrelated:

> The world of the epic is the national heroic past: it is a world of "beginnings" and "peak times" in the national history, a world of fathers and founders of families, a world of "firsts" and "bests" . . . The epic was never a poem about the present, about its own time . . . [It] has been from the beginning a poem about the past, and the authorial position immanent in . . . and constitutive for it . . . is [that] . . . of a man speaking about a past that is to him inaccessible, the reverent point of view of a descendant . . . Both the singer and the listener, immanent in the epic as a genre, are located in the same time and on the same evaluative (hierarchical) plane, but the represented world of the heroes stands on an utterly different and inaccessible time-and-value plane, separated by epic distance. The space between them is filled with national tradition. To portray an event on the same time-and-value plane as oneself and one's contemporaries . . . is . . . to step out of the world of epic into the world of the novel.[11]

The *Mahabharata* displays all the characteristics that Bakhtin attributes to an epic. It combines the epic mode with myth and romance, allegory and high mimeticism; and it perfects the method of narrative framing, using it to contain multiple plotlines and divergent points of view, as each of its main characters pursues his or her own quest. It is at once a telling and a retelling, a dialogue and a history—but it is especially a poem on a grand scale about a clan divided by hatred, a queen molested and avenged, a just war against an unjust disinheritance, a victory that is indistinguishable from defeat, and the death of an old order and the birth of a new one.

11. Bakhtin, ibid., pp. 13–14.

RETELLING THE *Mahabharata*

Satyamurti, an established British poet with a connection to India, approaches the *Mahabharata* as a modern poet responding poetically to an ancient poem. In its most direct form, her objective is to understand the Sanskrit work, to capture her understanding of it in a poem of her own, and to place her text before contemporary readers in English—for whom it then becomes a means to experience the poetry of the *Mahabharata*, though necessarily at a remove. Her concern is with poetry at every stage in an idealized circuit: as an object of understanding, as a mode of understanding, as a medium of expression, as a vehicle of communication, and as an outcome of the process as a whole. Poetry thus becomes a seamless continuum enveloping her enterprise, an analogue of the Irish poet W. B. Yeats's "hermetic egg," which needs nothing outside itself in order to give birth to new life.

There is, however, one practical rupture in this continuum. Whenever a modern work sets out to represent an older work, it can only do so in a genre that shades off into other genres performing similar functions but in other ways. A text that represents another text may be a translation ("faithful"), an adaptation (somewhat "loose"), a retelling (relatively "free"), or even a reworking ("creative"). In the past two decades, literary theorists have argued persuasively that all these categories can be placed on a single conceptual gradient called "translation" in the broadest sense, which moves from the most literal rendering of a text at one end to the most approximate at the other. In the late seventeenth century, John Dryden suggested brilliantly that the three defining positions on this spectrum be labeled "metaphrase," which is a word-for-word or interlinear version; "paraphrase," which deviates from the letter of a text, but not its spirit; and "imitation," which ignores the letter, and also merely "strives after" its spirit. In general, translators may pursue any of these shades of rendering legitimately, provided they identify the genre of their output without ambiguity—that is, as a translation, a paraphrase, an adaptation, an imitation, and so on. For whichever genre they practice, translators can choose one of two overall methods: the direct method, where the translator adequately knows and uses both the languages involved, the one from and the one into which she is translating; and the indirect method, where she knows only the language into which she is translating, and has access to the original text solely through preexisting intermediary renderings and other resources.

In Satyamurti's project, the break appears at the link of genre of representation and choice of method. On the general spectrum of translation, her retelling can be seen as a paraphrase. Her method, however, is the indirect method, because she is not a scholar of the Sanskrit language, and has access to the original text of the *Mahabharata* only through intermediary English translations and commentaries. Since her poetics of retelling rests on the assumption that her English poem is a reliable representation of the Sanskrit poem, she has to ensure that her intermediary resources are as trustworthy as possible. Her version of the epic therefore is based on the most literal and scholarly renderings available in English, together with the most dependable and informative commentaries, selections, and condensations.

In its practical application, Satyamurti's indirect method is as elaborate and systematic as it is fine-tuned. Her retelling is not a mere versification of an existing prose translation or someone else's gloss or crib. Depending on the material and her selection, she chooses to narrate some parts in detail, some in a condensed form, and some only in brisk summary. The Sanskrit original and its prose metaphrases in English may handle a given episode in uniform depth, but Satyamurti omits some parts altogether and treats other parts differently, guided by her sense of their poetic value and meaning, their significance in the larger narrative, and their potential imaginative impact on her readers. Even as she goes by the emotional flow of sounds, rhythms, images, characters, and events in her own verse, however, she works strictly within the limits of her intermediary resources, which determine the reliability of her rendering. Given the meticulousness of her craft and her strong sense of balance and proportion, restraint and understatement, her retelling emerges as a neatly scaled "miniature representation" of a gargantuan whole.

The proportionality that Satyamurti is able to maintain follows largely from her strategies and decisions at the level of craft. For one, she pays close attention to the poetic organization of the *Mahabharata*. She keeps all 18 major books in her version, but she treats them astutely as "accordion structures" that can be expanded and compressed to fit narrative exigencies; she represents the minor books as "chapters," and reduces their number to 60. Each of her chapters corresponds to one or more minor books and, within its framework, she carefully selects the characters, episodes, stories, and themes that will advance the narrative effectively. For whatever she chooses to highlight in a chapter, she usually combines detailed narration with condensation and précis to keep up the proportionality between retelling and original. Her poem is only one-twelfth the size of the *Mahabharata*, but it still gives us a detailed and balanced picture of the whole.

For another input at the level of craft, Satyamurti brings extraordinary discipline and inventiveness to her versification. Unlike the *Iliad* and the *Odyssey*, each of which is composed uniformly in a single meter, the *Mahabharata* is a composite poem in Sanskrit. In its critical edition, the text contains 73,821 numbered units; almost 99.5 percent of these are in verse, while 385 of them are prose passages, the latter being distributed over 12 "cantos" in 6 minor books. Of the 73,436 units in verse, 4,426 are composed in meters belonging to the *trishtubh* class, whereas 68,858 verses are in meters of the *anushtubh* class. The common form of this last category is the *shloka*, which consists of 32 syllables arranged in two equal "lines," each divided at its midpoint by a caesura; structurally, we can view the *shloka* as either a couplet (with 16 syllables per line) or a quatrain (with 8 syllables per line). In Sanskrit, a "verse" is syntactically closed, so it ends in a period; the end of a "line" coincides with a syntactic break, and hence coincides with the end either of a clause or of a sentence; and a caesura within a line, whether in a symmetrical or an asymmetrical position, coincides with the end either of a phrase or of a clause but not of a sentence. The short and long pauses around the middle and at the end of a line, and the long pause at the end of a verse, reinforce the rhythm arising from the metrical pattern, which gives the verse an incantatory or lyrical quality. One consequence is that, whenever a Sanskrit text composed in verse is delivered orally, it is not merely recited or read aloud, it is either chanted or sung. The conceptions involved here, especially of lyricism, differ from those in a language such as English, because Sanskrit verse forms do not require end rhyme or internal rhyme. The convention of chanting and singing applies as much to a short poem, a ritual mantra, and a philosophical treatise, as to an epic. Given the general prosodic features of Sanskrit, and given that the bulk of its text (about 75 percent) is composed in the *shloka* verse form, the *Mahabharata* appears to graft a "lyrical" texture onto a metrically variable narrative of massive size.

Satyamurti makes no attempt to reproduce or even approximate this system of versification, which is impossible in any case because of fundamental differences in phonology, syllabification, and prosody. Instead, she chooses boldly to invigorate English blank verse, developing a flexible line of nine to eleven syllables, with an average of five stresses. She brings it forward into the twenty-first century, not only by reducing its mechanical quality, but specifically by blending its metrical pattern with the syntax and vocabulary of contemporary "middle diction." Satyamurti's blank verse avoids poeticisms as well as archaisms, syntactic inversions as well as semantic simplifications, without becoming prosy or prosaic. Her sentences flow smoothly through enjambments and shifting caesuras, providing a medium for the narrative that is both transparent and dynamic—as amenable to the conversation of the gods and the fury of battle, as to philosophical disquisition, theological debate, deathbed speech, domestic vignette, emotional outburst, and evocation of landscape. A light and elastic surface of this kind stands in contrast to the *Mahabharata*'s verbal texture, but it is the ideal vehicle in English for a multiplex narrative that stretches out to 27,000 lines. It transports us back to a past that is cut off from us, as in an epic, but it also brings that past alive, here and now, as though it were a novel in finely crafted verse.

Acknowledgments

In approaching the *Mahabharata* as a non-specialist, I have, throughout, had the benefit of advice from Dr. Simon Brodbeck, Sanskrit scholar and Reader in the School of History, Archaeology and Religion at Cardiff University (UK). Many specialists would have been dismissive of an attempt by a non-Sanskritist to render the epic for the general reader. Simon's support for the project has been unwavering, and the value to me of his expert and detailed knowledge and deep understanding of the epic is impossible to overstate. He was unfailingly tolerant of my errors and wrong turnings, and generous in sending me useful articles, referring me to others, and lending me books. His own books and articles on aspects of the *Mahabharata* were among the most illuminating. I cannot thank him enough. Needless to say, any errors are mine alone.

I am extremely grateful to Professor Vinay Dharwadker of the Department of Languages and Cultures of Asia, University of Wisconsin–Madison, for his positive and scholarly response to the way I have attempted to render the *Mahabharata*; for his suggestions for improvement; for his very interesting Afterword; and for his help with ancillary materials, including the Glossary.

The team at Norton has done a wonderful job in producing a beautiful-looking book. My editor, Jill Bialosky, has been of immense help over the years it has taken me to complete it. I am grateful to her for her confidence in the project, her patience, and for her steady hand on the tiller, steering it through the publication process. Her colleagues, Rebecca Schultz and Angie Shih, have also been a great support. My copyeditor, Amy Robbins, did remarkable work on my enormous typescript, combining meticulousness with sensitivity. I very much appreciate her contribution.

Many thanks to the following friends and relations who read and commented on parts of the text, and whose response was encouraging: David Black, Robert Chandler, Patrick Early, Judy Gahagan, Mimi Khalvati, John Mole, Vaughan Pilikian, James Redmond, Emma Satyamurti, Manou Shama-Levy, Nancy and Al Stepan, Gregory Warren Wilson, and Martin Wilkinson.

I particularly want to thank Susanne Ehrhardt for her careful reading of my entire text, for her detailed comments and suggestions, and for her enthusiasm.

Thanks are due to the editors of *Modern Poetry in Translation, New Walk,* and *Poetry Review,* in which sections of this work have appeared.

I am grateful to Arts Council England for a grant which enabled me to concentrate on this project.

Genealogies

GENEALOGY ONE

The Older Generations

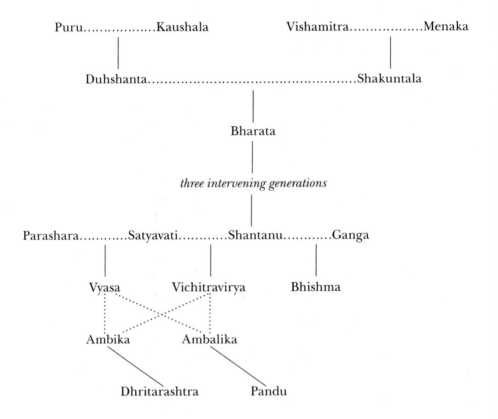

Simplified lines of descent for important characters spanning nine generations preceding the Pandavas and Kauravas, with characters only in six generations shown selectively. Each dotted line represents a marriage or sexual relationship; each continuous line descends from biological parents to offspring. More than one dotted line leading from or to a name indicates more than one relationship for that person; multiple relationships may be serial or simultaneous.

Parashara and Satyavati engender Vyasa before Satyavati becomes Shantanu's queen and engenders Chitrangada (not shown) and Vichitravirya with the latter; Shantanu engenders Bhishma with Ganga before marrying Satyavati. Thus, both Bhishma and Vyasa, in that chronological order, are Vichitravirya's elder half-brothers from different parents. Vichitravirya marries two sisters, Ambika and Ambalika, but dies without producing children. Satyavati, his mother and queen, then invokes the "law of levirate" to continue the royal line. Bhishma cannot participate because he has taken a vow of celibacy; so Vyasa steps in, and fathers Dhritarashtra upon the elder widow, Ambika, and Pandu upon the younger, Ambalika. Ancient Hindu levirate broadly resembles biblical levirate, as in Deuteronomy 25.

GENEALOGY TWO

The Younger Generations

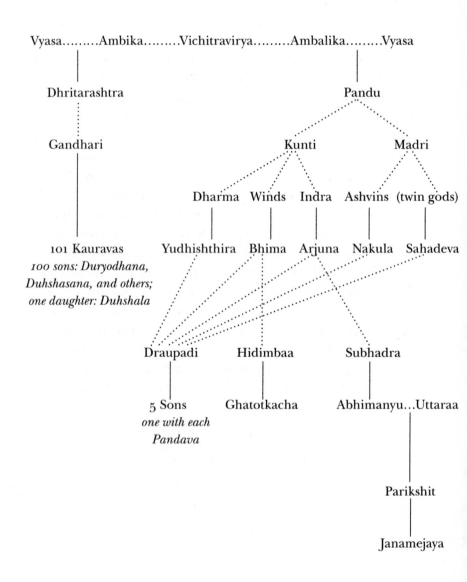

Lines of descent for select characters in six generations, with two generations preceding and three generations succeeding the Pandavas and Kauravas. Each dotted line represents a marriage or sexual relationship; each solid line connects biological parents to offspring. More than one dotted line leading from or to a name indicates more than one relationship for that person; multiple relationships may be serial or simultaneous.

Dhritarashtra is in a monogamous marriage with Gandhari, whereas Pandu is in a bigamous marriage with Kunti (elder wife) and Madri; both families, however, have difficulty procreating. Gandhari, in a single supernatural pregnancy, conceives and gives birth to 101 children, of whom Duryodhana is chronologically the first. Kunti invokes three gods to father three biological sons, whereas Madri invokes twin gods to produce two; after Pandu's and Madri's deaths, Kunti raises the Pandavas as a widow.

Draupadi is married polyandrously to all five Pandavas simultaneously. In the course of that marriage, Bhima also marries the metamorphosing female demon Hidinbaa; with her, he fathers Ghatotkacha, who is raised in the Pandava household. While in the polyandrous marriage with Draupadi, Arjuna also polygamously marries and has children with other women (not all shown). Among the latter is Subhadra, Krishna's biological sister, with whom Arjuna has Abhimanyu. When the young Abhimanyu is killed in the war at Kurukshetra, his bride Uttaraa is pregnant with Parikshit, who inherits the Pandava kingdom later, and passes it on to his own biological son, Janamejaya.

Suggestions for
Further Reading

TRANSLATIONS

I HAVE DRAWN on a number of translations of the *Mahabharata*. The only complete one, to date, is that by K. M. Ganguli, published at the end of the nineteenth century, (*The Mahabharata of Krishna Dvaipayana Vyasa*, republished by Munshi Manoharlal Publishers Pvt Ltd, 4th edition, New Delhi, 2008). This translation is also available online (in the "Internet Sacred Text Archive"). Ganguli's work predates the Sanskrit Critical Edition (1933–66), and is based on sources which differ from that work in some respects. But it is regarded by contemporary scholars as broadly accurate, and although the language is rather archaic, as one would expect, his often waspish footnotes about interpretations other than his own are a delight.

The University of Chicago Press has, since 1973, been bringing out a new translation, based on the Pune Critical Edition. The translators are, first, J. A. B. van Buitenen (Books 1–5) and, more recently, James Fitzgerald (Book 11 and part of Book 12). More volumes are to come. Apart from the texts themselves, the Notes and Introductions are very useful.

The Clay Sanskrit Library (published by New York University Press) has produced a number of volumes in parallel text, covering the war books in particular. Vaughan Pilikian's translation of part of the Book of Drona is especially vivid.

John Smith's abridged translation, *The Mahabharata* (Penguin Books, 2009), is an invaluable resource. It alternates passages of full translation with abridged passages. Apart from its intrinsic merits, it will enable any reader embarking on the vast ocean of Ganguli's cumbersome prose to navigate far more easily.

W. J. Johnson has translated the *Bhagavad Gita* and *The Saupti-kaparvan of the Mahabharata: The Massacre at Night* as separate volumes, both published by Oxford World's Classics, and both containing useful Introductions.

SECONDARY SOURCES

For an account of the history of ancient India, see Romila Thapar, *Early India: From the Origins to AD 1300* (Berkeley: University of California Press, 2003).

There is a wealth of scholarly books and articles on the *Mahabharata*. Below is a short selection of books which I, as a non-specialist, have found interesting, and which will begin to open up, for the general reader, some of the main issues raised by the *Mahabharata*.

Brockington, John. *The Sanskrit Epics.* Leiden: Brill, 1998.

Brodbeck, Simon. *The Mahabharata Patriline: Gender, Culture and the Royal Hereditary.* Farnham, U.K.: Ashgate, 2009.

Brodbeck, Simon, and Brian Black, eds. *Gender and Narrative in the Mahabharata.* London: Routledge, 2007.

Das, Gurcharan. *The Difficulty of Being Good: on the Subtle Art of Dharma.* Delhi: Penguin Books, Allen Lane, 2009.

Dhand, Arti. *Woman as Fire, Woman as Sage: Sexual Ideology in the Mahabharata.* Albany: State University of New York Press, 2008.

Fitzgerald, James L. "Mahabharata." In *The Hindu World*, edited by Sushil Mittal and Gene Thursby. New York: Routledge, 2004.

Hill, Peter. *Fate, Predestination and Human Action in the Mahabharata.* Delhi: Munshiram Manoharlal, 2001.

Hiltebeitel, Alf. *The Ritual of Battle: Krishna in the Mahabharata.* Ithaca, N.Y.: Cornell University Press, 1976.

———. *Rethinking the Mahabharata: A Reader's Guide to the Education of the Dharma King.* Chicago: University of Chicago Press, 2001.

Hopkins, E. Washburn. *The Great Epic of India: Its Character and Origin.* New York: Scribner, 1901.

Karve, Irawati. *Yuganta: The End of an Epoch.* Hyderabad: Orient Blackswan, 1969.

Katz, Ruth C. *Arjuna in the Mahabharata: Where Krishna Is There Is Victory.* Columbia: University of South Carolina Press, 1989.

Lipner, Julius, ed. *The Fruits of Our Desiring: An Enquiry into the Ethics of the Bhagavadgita for Our Times.* Calgary: Bayeux Arts, 1997.

Matilal, B. K., ed. *Moral Dilemmas in the Mahabharata.* Delhi: Motilal Banarsidass, 1989.

McGrath, Kevin. *The Sanskrit Hero: Karna in the Epic Mahabharata.* Leiden: Brill, 2004.

Sen, K. M. *Hinduism.* London: Penguin Books, 2005.

Sharma, Arvind, ed. *Essays on the Mahabharata.* Leiden: Brill, 1991.

Sullivan, Bruce. *Seer of the Fifth Veda: Krishna Dvaipayana Vyasa in the Mahabharata.* Delhi: Motilal Banarsidass, 1999.

Sutton, Nicholas. *Religious Doctrines in the Mahabharata.* Delhi: Motilal Banarsidass, 2000.

Woods, Julian F. *Destiny and Human Initiative in the Mahabharata.* Albany: State University of New York Press, 2001.

Glossary

T HE FOLLOWING ALPHABETICAL list identifies the principal characters in the narrative, and provides basic explanations of the Sanskrit terms that appear in the text. Among the headwords, characters' names are given in bold roman type, whereas other terms are in bold italics.

Each headword is followed by a brief annotation in square brackets. For most headwords, this information consists of the syllabification of the term, its scansion in English, and its scansion in Sanskrit, in that order. The syllables in a word are separated by dots; thus, "Abhimanyu" is broken up into four syllables as A·bhi·man·yu. The English scansion is specified using s for a stressed syllable and u for an unstressed syllable; the metrical pattern of A·bhi·man·yu is thus displayed as susu. The sound pattern of Sanskrit words is measured in "duration" rather than stress; L represents a short or "light" syllable, and H represents a long or "heavy" syllable. The scansion of A·bhi·man·yu in the original language is LLHL, which is different from the susu pattern in English.

In some instances, the annotations identify the grammatical gender or number of a term. Whenever the syllabification of a headword involves significant differences between the English spelling and the original Sanskrit spelling, both spellings are provided. For example, for the word *"danda,"* the entry in square brackets gives us "dan·da, su; *dan·da*, HL"; the (latter) Sanskrit spelling indicates that both *n* and *d* are retroflex sounds in this instance, as in English *den*t. Readers will find the annotations in square brackets useful for the pronunciation of unfamiliar terms.

In many cases, the English spelling provided here reflects the

Sanskrit pronunciation quite accurately. Sometimes, however, diacritical marks have to be added to it in order to capture the original spelling or pronunciation. The transcriptions in square brackets use a simplified system of essential diacritical marks.

BASIC PRONUNCIATION OF
SANSKRIT TERMS

The common vowels in Sanskrit are consistently transcribed and pronounced as follows: *a* as in "*a*bout"; *ā* as in "f*a*ther"; *i* as in "b*i*t"; *ī* as in "b*ee*t"; *u* as in "p*u*t"; *ū* as in "b*oo*t"; *e* as in "th*ey*"; and *o* as in "g*o*." Three other vowels can be approximated thus: *r* as in "*ri*g"; *ai* like the *i* in "h*i*gh"; and *au* like the *ou* in "h*ou*se." When no ambiguity is involved, the long *ā* is represented in the English spelling of a word as *aa*.

The majority of Sanskrit consonants can be pronounced as they appear in English. The unusual consonants are represented or simplified as follows: *ch* as in "*ch*ew"; *t* as in "bu*t*"; *d* as in "*d*o"; *n* as in "ti*n*t"; *t* as in French "*t*u" or in Italian "pas*t*a"; and *d* like the *th* in "*th*ou" or "*th*ough."

Sanskrit distinguishes between two sibilants, both of which are simplified here to *sh*, as in "*sh*ip." Hence, the main text uses "Shiva" and "Vishnu" as the Anglicized names of these gods, and the Glossary adds "Vish*n*u" as the more precise transcription of the latter (with the *n* as in "ti*n*t").

Whenever *a* appears at the end of a Sanskrit word, it should be pronounced as a short vowel (as in "*a*bout"), and not as a long *ā*. Sanskrit distinguishes clearly, for example, between "Krish*n*a"/"Krishna" (short *a* at the end) and "Krish*n*ā"/"Krishnaa" (long *ā* at the end). Likewise, the language distinguishes between "Chitrāngada"/"Chitraangada" and "Chitrāngadā"/"Chitraangadaa."

Whenever an *h* appears after a consonant, the sound of the latter is aspirated (pronounced with an accompanying expulsion of air from the mouth). Thus, *t* is pronounced as at the end of "goa*t*," whereas *th* is pronounced as the conjoined *th* in "goa*th*erd." Hence, "Dhrish*t*adyumna" and "Yudhish*th*ira."

Abhimanyu [A·bhi·man·yu, SUSU; LLHL]: son of Arjuna by
   Subhadra, Krishna's sister

Adhiratha [A·dhi·ra·tha, SUSU; LLLL]: adoptive father of Karna

Agastya [A·gast·ya, USU; LHL]: a great seer

Agni [Ag·ni, SU; HL]: god of fire

ahimsa [a·him·saa, USS; LHH]: non-harmfulness

Ajatashatru [A·jaa·ta·shat·ru, USUSU; LHLHL]: "unrivaled," a
   name of Yudhishthira

Alambusha [A·lam·bu·sha, USUU; LHLL]: rakshasa killed by
   Ghatotkacha

Alayudha [A·la·yu·dha, UUUU; LLLL]: rakshasa killed by
   Ghatotkacha

Amba, Ambika, Ambalika [Am·baa, SS; HH. Am·bi·kaa, SUS;
   HLH. Am·baa·li·kaa, USUS; HHLH]: daughters of the king of
   Kashi, abducted by Bhishma as brides for Vichitravirya

Anga [An·ga, SU; HL]: kingdom given to Karna

Apantaratamas [A·paan·ta·ra·ta·mas, USUUSU ; LHLLLL]: seer;
   previous incarnation of Vyasa

apsarases [English plural; singular: ap·sa·ras, SUU;
   HLL]: beautiful celestial nymphs

Arjuna [Ar·ju·na, SUU; HLL]: third son of Pandu and Kunti;
   fathered by the god Indra

ashrama [aa·shra·ma, SUU; HLL]: one of the four approved life
   paths

Ashvapati [A·shva·pa·ti, SUSU; HLLL]: king of the Madras,
   father of Savitri

Ashvasena [Ash·va·se·na, SUSU; HLHL]: son of Takshaka, the
   snake king

Ashvatthaman [Ash·vat·thaa·man, SUSU; HHHL]: son of Drona

Ashvins [English plural; singular: Ash·vin, SU; HL]: twin
   deities, fathers of Nakula and Sahadeva

Astika [Aas·ti·ka, SUU; HLL]: snake-brahmin, savior of the
   snakes at Janamejaya's sacrifice

astra [as·tra, SU; HL]: supernatural weapon

asura [a·su·ra, SUU; LLL]: demon

atman [aat·man, SU; HL]: human self or soul; an aspect of
   Brahman

Babhru [Ba·bhru, SU; HL]: a Vrishni warrior

Babhruvahana [Ba·bhru·vaa·ha·na, SUSUU; HLHLL]: Arjuna's
son by Chitrangadaa

Baka [Ba·ka, SU; LL]: rakshasa killed by Bhima

Balarama [Ba·la·raa·ma, UUSU; LLHL]: Krishna Vasudeva's
older brother

Ballava [Bal·la·va, SUU; HLL]: Bhima's alias at Virata's court

Bhagadatta [Bha·ga·dat·ta, SUSU; LLHL]: an ally of the
Kauravas

Bhangashvana [Bhan·gaash·va·na, USUU; HHLL]: king who
becomes a woman

Bharadvaja [Bha·rad·vaa·ja, UUSU; LHHL]: seer; father of
Drona

Bharata: (1) [Bhaa·ra·ta, SUU; HLL] lineage of both the
Pandavas and the Kauravas; (2) [Bha·ra·ta, SUU; LLL] king,
founder of the royal lineage

Bharatavarsha [Bhaa·ra·ta·var·sha, SUUSU; HLLHL]: ancient
name for India south of the Himalaya

Bhargavas [English plural; singular: Bhaar·ga·va, SUU;
HLL]: brahmin descendants of Bhrigu

Bhima [Bhee·ma, SU; HL]: (1) second of the five Pandava
brothers; fathered by Vayu, god of the wind; (2)
Damayanti's father

Bhishma [Bheesh·ma, SU; HL]: son of Shantanu and Ganga;
Bharata patriarch

Bhrigu [Bhri·gu, SU; HL]: a seer

Bhurishravas [Sanskrit singular; Bhoo·ri·shra·vas, SUSU;
HHLL]: an ally of the Kauravas

Brahma [Brah·ma, SU; HL]: god of created beings

Brahma's Head [Brahma as above]: powerful celestial weapon,
also known as *Pashupata*

Brahmadatta [Brah·ma·dat·ta, SUSU; HLHL]: king; friend of the
bird Pujani

Brahman [Brah·man, SU; HL]: universal soul; essence of all that
is

brahmins [as in English; SU]: highest class in the social
hierarchy; priests, guardians of the Vedas

Brihadashva [Bri·ha·dash·va, UUSU; LLHL]: a sage

Brihannada [Bri·han·na·daa, USUU; *bri·han·na·dā*, LHLH]: Arjuna's alias at Virata's court

Brihaspati [Bri·has·pa·ti, USUU; LHLL]: preceptor/priest to the gods

Chandalas [English plural; singular: Chaan·daa·la, SSU; *chān·dā·la*, HHL]: a lowborn and despised community

Charvaka [Chaar·vaa·ka, SSU; HHL]: a rakshasa posing as a brahmin

Chekitana [Che·ki·ta·na, SUSU; HLLL]: Vrishni warrior; ally of the Pandavas

Chitrangada [masculine; Chi·traan·ga·da, USUU; HHLL] elder of Shantanu's two sons by Satyavati

Chitrangadaa [feminine; Chi·traan·ga·daa, USUS; HHLH] mother of Arjuna's son Babhruvahana

Chitrasena [Chi·tra·se·na, SUSU; HLHL]: king of the gandharvas

Chitravahana [Chi·tra·vaa·ha·na, SUSUU; HLHLL]: king of Manalura

Chyavana [Chya·va·na, SUU; HLL]: a great seer

Damayanti [Da·ma·yan·tee, UUSU; LLHH]: wife of Nala

Danavas [English plural; singular: Daa·na·va, SUU; HLL]: a type of demon

danda [dan·da, SU; *dan·da*, HL]: rod of royal authority

Daruka [Daa·ru·ka, SUU; HLL]: Krishna's charioteer

Devadatta [De·va·dat·ta, SUSU; HLHL]: Arjuna's conch

Devasthana [De·va·sthaa·na, SUSU; HHHL]: a great ascetic

Devavrata [De·va·vra·ta, SUSU; HHLL]: Bhishma's original name

dharma [dhar·ma, SU; HL]: righteousness; right conduct

Dharma [as above]: god of righteousness; Yudhishthira's father

Dharma King [as above]: a title for Yudhishthira

Dhaumya [Dhaum·ya, SU; HL]: the Pandavas' household priest

Dhrishtadyumna [Dhrish·ta·dyum·na, SUSU; *dhrish·ta·dyum·na*, HHHL]: Panchala warrior; son of Drupada; brother of Draupadi

Dhrishtaketu [Dhrish·ta·ke·tu, SUSU; *dhrish·ta·ke·tu*, HLHL]: ally of the Pandavas

Dhritarashtra [Dhri·ta·rash·tra, SUSU; *dhri·ta·rāsh·tra*, HLHL]: blind king of the Bharatas; son of Vyasa; father of the Kauravas

Draupadi [Drau·pa·dee, SUU; HLH]: daughter of Drupada; wife to the five Pandavas

Drona [Dro·na, SU; *dro·na*, HL]: great brahmin weapons teacher

Drupada [Dru·pa·da, SUU; HLL]: king of Panchala; father of Draupadi, Dhrishtadyumna, and Shikhandin

Duhshala [Duh·shaa·laa, SSS; HHH]: only daughter of Dhritarashtra and Gandhari

Duhshanta [Duh·shan·ta, SSU; HHL]: father of Bharata, founder of the Bharata lineage

Duhshasana [Duh·shaa·sa·na, SSUU; HHLL]: second son of Dhritarashtra and Gandhari

Durjaya [Dur·ja·ya, SUU; HLL]: one of Dhritarashtra's sons

Durmashana [Dur·ma·sha·na, SUUU; HLLL]: one of Dhritarashtra's sons

Durmukha [Dur·mu·kha, SUU; HLL]: one of Dhritarashtra's sons

Durvasas [Sanskrit singular; Dur·vaa·sas, USU; HHL]: a seer

Duryodhana [Dur·yo·dha·na, USUU; HHLL]: eldest son of Dhritarashtra and Gandhari; leader of the Kauravas

Dvaipayana [Dvai·paa·ya·na, USUU; HHLL]: (1) a name for Vyasa; (2) lake where Duryodhana hides at the end of the war

Dvapara age [Dvaa·pa·ra, SUU; HLL]: second-worst of the four ages; also personified as an evil being

Dvaraka [Dvaa·ra·kaa, SUU; HLH]: Krishna's city

Dyumatsena [Dyu·mat·se·na, SUSU; HLHL]: Savitri's father-in-law

Ekalavya [E·ka·lav·ya, SUSU; HLHL]: a tribal youth, son of the king of the nishadas

Gandhari [Gaan·dhaa·ree, SSU; HHH]: Gandhara princess; wife of Dhritarashtra; mother of the hundred Kauravas

gandharvas [English plural; singular: gan·dhar·va, USU; HHL]: celestial musicans and accomplished fighters

Gandiva [Gaan·di·va, SUU; *gān·di·va*, HLL]: Arjuna's bow

Ganesha [Ga·ne·sha, USU; *ga·ne·sha*, LHL]: elephant-headed god; scribe of the *Mahabharata*

Ganga [Gangaa, SU; HH]: (1) sacred river; (2) goddess of the river

Garuda [Ga·ru·da, SUU; *ga·ru·da*, LLL]: celestial eagle

Gautami [Gau·tam·i, SUU; HLH]: a wise brahmin woman

Ghatotkacha [Gha·tot·ka·cha, USUU; *gha·tot·ka·cha*, LHLL]: half-rakshasa son of Bhima and Hidimbaa

ghee [as in English]: clarified butter, used in rituals

Govinda [Go·vin·da, SUU; HLL]: a name for Krishna

Granthika [Gran·thi·ka, SUU; HLL]: Nakula's alias at Virata's court

Hanuman [Ha·nu·maan, UUS; LLH]: divine monkey

Harishchandra [Ha·rish·chan·dra, USSU; LHHL]: an emperor of previous times

Hastinapura [Has·ti·naa·pu·ra, SUSUU; HLHLL]: City of the Elephant; the capital of the Bharata kingdom

Hidimba [Hi·dim·ba, USU; *hi·dim·ba*, LHL]: rakshasa killed by Bhima

Hidimbaa [Hi·dim·baa, USS; *hi·dim·bā*, LHH]: Hidimba's sister; wife of Bhima; mother of Ghatotkacha

Himalaya [Hi·ma·la·ya, USUU; LHLL]: great mountain range in the north of Bharatavarsha

Himavat [Hi·ma·vat, SUU; LLL]: Himalaya

Indra [In·dra, SU; HL]: powerful god; father of Arjuna

Indraprastha [In·dra·pras·tha, SUSU; HHHL]: beautiful city created by the Pandavas

Iravat [I·raa·vat, USU; LHL]: Arjuna's son by Ulupi

Jaimini [Jai·mi·ni, SUU; HLL]: one of Vyasa's disciples

Jalasandha [Ja·laa·san·dha, USSU; LHHL]: a son of Dhritarashtra

Jamadagni [Ja·mad·ag·ni, UUSU; LLHL]: seer of ancient times; father of Rama Jamadagnya

Jambavati [Jam·ba·va·tee, SUUU; HLLH]: one of Krishna's wives

Janaka [Ja·na·ka, SUU; LLL]: a king claiming to have achieved moksha

Janamejaya [Ja·na·me·ja·ya, UUSUU; LLHLL]: king, descendant of the Pandavas, to whom the Mahabharata is recited

Jarasandha [Ja·raa·san·dha, USSU; LHHL]: king of Magadha, killed by Bhima

Jarita [Ja·ri·taa, SUU; LLH]: bird, wife of Mandapala

jaya [ja·ya, SU; LL]: victory

Jayadratha [Ja·yad·ra·tha, SUSU; LHLL]: Sindhu king; husband of Duhshala

Jayatsena [Ja·yat·se·na, USSU; LHHL]: ally of the Pandavas

Jimuta [Jee·moo·ta, SSU; HHL]: wrestling contestant at Virata's court

Kailasa [Kai·laa·sa, SSU; HHL]: northern mountain, home of gods

Kali age [Ka·li, SU; LL]: worst of the four ages; worst throw at dice; personified as an evil being

Kampilya [Kam·pil·ya, USU; HLL]: capital of the Panchala kingdom

Kanika [Ka·ni·ka, SUU; LLL]: Dhritarashtra's minister

Kanka [Kan·ka, SU; HL]: Yudhishthira's alias at Virata's court

Kanva [Kan·va, SU; HL]: seer; adoptive father of Shakuntala

karma [as in English]: natural law whereby acts have consequences for the doer

Karna [Kar·na, SU; HL]: premarital son of Kunti by the sun god; friend of Duryodhana

Kashyapa [Kash·ya·pa, SUU; HLL]: a rishi's son

Kauravas [English plural; singular: Kau·ra·va, SUU; HLL]: descendants of Kuru; name given to the hundred sons of Dhritarashtra and Gandhari

Kaushika [Kau·shi·ka, SUU; HLL]: an ascetic

Khandava Forest [Khaan·da·va, SUU; *khān·da·va*, HLL]: forest tract destroyed by Arjuna and Krishna

Kichaka [Kee·cha·ka, SUU; HLL]: Virata's general; would-be seducer of Draupadi, killed by Bhima

Kirmira [Kir·mee·ra, USU; HHL]: rakshasa killed by Bhima

Kripa [Kri·pa, SU; HL]: Bharata princes' first weapons teacher

Kripi [Kri·pee, SU; LH]: sister of Kripa; wife of Drona

Krishna Dvaipayana [Krish·na Dvai·paa·ya·na, SU SSUU; *krish·na dvai·pā·ya·na,* HL HHLL]: a name for Vyasa

Krishna Vasudeva [Krishna as above; Vaa·su·de·va, SUSU; HLHL]: avatar of Vishnu; cousin and supporter of the Pandavas

Krishnaa [Krish·naa, SU; *krish·nā,* HH]: "the dark one," name of Draupadi

Krita age [Kri·ta, SU; LL]: first and best of the four ages of the world; best throw at dice

Kritavarman [Kri·ta·var·man, SUSU; LLHL]: Krishna's kinsman; ally of the Kauravas

kshatriyas [English plural; singular: Ksha·tri·ya, SUU; HLL]: the ruling class; warriors; second-highest class in the social hierarchy

Kubera [Ku·be·ra, USU; LHL]: god of treasure

Kunti [Kun·tee, SU; HH]: first wife of Pandu; mother of Karna, and of the five Pandavas; sister of Krishna's father

Kuntibhoja [Kun·ti·bho·ja, SUSU; HLHL]: adoptive father of Kunti

Kurukshetra [Ku·ru·kshe·tra, SUSU; LHHL]: "Kuru's field," the plain on which the great war is fought

Lakshmana [Laksh·ma·na, SUU; *laksh·ma·na,* HLL]: son of Duryodhana

Lapita [La·pi·taa, SUU; LLH]: bird in the Khandava Forest

Left-handed Archer: name for Arjuna

Likhita [Li·khi·ta, SUU; LLL]: brahmin brother of Shankha

Lomapada [Lo·ma·pa·da, SUUU; HLLL]: a king of Anga

Lomasha [Lo·ma·sha, SUU; HLL]: a seer

Madhu [Ma·dhu, SU; LL]: demon killed by Vishnu

Madhusudana [Ma·dhu·soo·da·na, SUSUU; LLHLL]: "killer of Madhu," a name for Vishnu

Madras [English plural; singular: Ma·dra, SU; HL]: a people

Madri [Maa·dri, SU; HL]: Pandu's second wife; mother of Nakula and Sahadeva

Mahabharata [Ma·haa·bhaa·ra·ta, USSUU; LHHLL]: the present epic poem

Maitreya [Mai·tre·ya, SUU; HLL]: a great sage

Malavi [Maa·la·vee, SUU; HLH]: mother of Savitri

Mandapala [Man·da·paa·la, SUSU; HLHL]: bird in the Khandava Forest

Mandhatri [Maan·dhaa·tri, SSU; HHL]: a great archer and king

mantra [as in English, SU]: powerful incantation

Manu [Ma·nu, SU; HL]: the first man

Markandeya [Maar·kan·de·ya, SUSU; *mār·kan·de·ya*, HHLL]: a great seer, famously long-lived

Marutta [Ma·rut·ta, USU; LHL]: an ambitious king

Matali [Maa·ta·li, SUU; HLL]: Indra's charioteer

Matanga [Ma·tan·ga, USU; LHL]: boy who tried to become a brahmin

Matsya [Mat·sya, SU; HL]: land ruled by King Virata

Maya [Ma·ya, SU; LL]: demon architect

Mlecchas [English plural; singular: Mle·chchha, SU; HL]: barbarians

moksha [mok·sha, SU; HL]: final release from the cycle of birth and death

Mudgala [Mud·ga·la, SUU; HLL]: devout gleaner

muni [mu·ni, SU; LL]: a holy man

Naga [Naa·ga, SU; HL]: snake deity

Nahusha [Na·hu·sha, SUU; LLL]: Pandavas' ancestor, who turned into a serpent under Agastya's curse, and resumed his human form when saved by Yudhishthira

Nakula [Na·ku·la, SUU; LLL]: one of the Pandava brothers; twin son of Pandu and Madri; fathered by the Ashvins

Nala [Na·la, SU; HL]: husband of Damayanti; obsessive gambler; victim of Kali

Namuchi [Na·mu·chi, SUU; LLL]: demon killed by Indra

Nara [Na·ra, SU; LL]: deity/seer associated with Arjuna; companion of Narayana

Narada [Naa·ra·da, SUU; HLL]: a great seer, traveler in the three worlds

Naraka [Na·ra·ka, SUU; LLL]: a demon

Narayana [Naa·raa·ya·na, SSUU; *nā·rā·ya·na*, HHLL]: (1) a name for Vishnu; (2) a divine seer

Narayaniya [Naa·raa·ya·nee·ya, SSUSU; *nā·rā·ya·nī·ya*, HHLHL]: devotional hymn to Narayana

Nila [Nee·la, SU; HL]: ally of the Pandavas

nishadas [English plural; singular: ni·shaa·da, USU; LHL]: a forest tribal people

Nivatakavachas [English plural; singular: Ni·vaa·ta·ka·va·cha, USUSUU; LHLLLL]: demon enemies of Indra, defeated by Arjuna

Oghavati [O·gha·va·tee, SUUU; HLLH]: (1) river at Kurukshetra; (2) Sudarshana's wife

Paila [Pai·la, SU; HL]: one of Vyasa's disciples

Panchajanya [Paan·cha·jan·ya, SUSU; HLHL]: Krishna's conch

Panchala [Paan·chaa·la, SSU; HHL]: (1) kingdom ruled by Drupada; (2) the people of that kingdom

Pandavas [English plural; singular: Paan·da·va, SUU; HLL]: the five sons of Pandu; also their forces in the war

Pandu [Paan·du, SU; *pān·du*, HL]: brother of Dhritarashtra, fathered by Vyasa; father of the five Pandavas

Pandyas [English plural; singular: Paand·ya, SU; *pānd·ya*, HL]: allies of the Pandavas

Parashara [Pa·raa·sha·ra, USUU; LHLL]: a seer; father of Vyasa by Satyavati

Parikshit [Pa·rik·shit, USU; LHL]: heir to the Bharata kingdom after Yudhishthira; father of Janamejaya

Parvati [Paar·va·tee, SUU; HLH]: wife of Shiva

Pashupata [Paa·shu·pa·ta, SUSU; HLLL]: supreme celestial weapon

Pradyumna [Pra·dyum·na, USU; LHL]: Krishna's son

Prahlada [Prah·laa·da, SSU; HHL]: wise chief of demons

Prasena [Pra·se·na, USU; LHL]: Karna's son

Prithu [Pri·thu, SU; LL]: the first king

puja [poo·jaa, ss; HH]: act of worship

Pujani [Poo·ja·nee, SUU; HLH]: a wise bird

Purochana [Pu·ro·cha·na, USUU; LHLL]: Duryodhana's agent in the burning of the lacquer house

Pushkara [Push·ka·ra, SUU; HLL]: Nala's brother

Radha [Raa·dhaa, SU; HH]: Karna's adoptive mother

rajasuya yajna [raa·ja·soo·ya yaj·na, SUSU SU; HLHL HL]: imperial consecration sacrifice

rakshasa [raak·sha·sa, SUU; HLL]: ogre

Rama [Raa·ma, SU; HL]: hero of the *Ramayana*

Rama Jamadagnya [Raa·ma Ja·mad·aag·nya, SU UUSU; HL LLHL]: brahmin warrior; great weapons teacher

Ravana [Raa·va·na, SUU; *rā·va·na*, HLL]: demon abductor of Sita in the *Ramayana*

Rishabha [Ri·sha·bha, SUU; LLL]: a recluse

rishi [ri·shi, SU; LL]: sage

Rishyashringa [Ri·shya·shrin·ga, SUSU; LHHL]: an innocent brahmin youth

Rukmaratha [Ruk·ma·ra·tha, SUUU; HLLL]: Shalya's son

Sahadeva [Sa·ha·de·va, UUSU; LLHL]: twin son of Pandu and Madri; one of the five Pandavas; fathered by Ashvin

Sairandhri [Sai·ran·dhree, SSU; HHH]: Draupadi's alias at Virata's court

Samba [Saam·ba, SU; HL]: Krishna's son

Samvarta [Sam·var·ta, USU; HHL]: brother of Brihaspati

Sanatsujata [Sa·nat·su·jaa·ta, USUSU; LHLHL]: wise ancient youth

Sanjaya [San·ja·ya, SUU; HLL]: Dhritarashtra's aide and companion; witness of the entire Kurukshetra war

Sarasvati [Sa·ras·va·tee, USUU; LHLH]: river

Satyabhama [Sat·ya·bhaa·maa, SUSU; HLHH]: Krishna's wife

Satyajit [Sat·ya·jit, SUU; HLL]: son of Drupada

Satyaki [Saat·ya·ki, SUU; HLL]: Krishna's kinsman; ally of the Pandavas

Satyasena [Sat·ya·se·na, SUSU; HLHL]: Karna's son

Satyavat [Sat·ya·vat, SUU; LLL]: Savitri's husband

Satyavati [Sat·ya·va·tee, SUUU; HLLH]: second wife to Shantanu; mother of Vyasa, and of Chitrangada and Vichitravirya

Savitri [Saa·vi·tree, SUU; HLH]: virtuous wife of Satyavat, who wins him back from Death

Senajit [Se·naa·jit, SSU; HHL]: king, bereaved father

Sita [See·taa, SU; HH]: wife of Rama in the *Ramayana*

soma [so·ma, SU; HL]: sacred drink, a Vedic sacrificial offering

Somadatta [So·ma·dat·ta, SUSU; HLHL]: father of Bhurishravas

Subhadra [Su·bhad·raa, USU; LHH]: Krishna's sister; Arjuna's wife

Sudarsha [Su·dar·sha, USU; LHL]: one of Dhritarashtra's sons

Sudarshana [Su·dar·sha·na, USUU; LHLL]: son of the god of fire

Sudarshana [Su·dar·sha·na, USUU; LHLL]: Krishna's discus

Sudeshna [Su·desh·naa, USU; *su·desh·nā*, LHH]: Virata's wife

Sudyumna [Su·dyum·na, USU; LHL]: king of Panchala in ancient times

Sulabha [Su·la·bhaa, SUU; LLH]: female ascetic; interrogator of King Janaka

Sumantu [Su·man·tu, USU; LHL]: one of Vyasa's disciples

Sumitra [Su·mi·tra, USU; LHL]: a king who lives in hope

Sunda [Sun·da, SU; HL]: demon; brother of Upasunda

Surya [Soor·ya, SU; HL]: sun god; father of Karna

Susharman [Su·shar·man, USU; LHL]: king of the Trigartas

Sushena [Su·she·na, USU; *su·she·na*, LHL]: Karna's son

sutas [English plural; singular: soo·ta, SU; HL]: inferior social group of mixed brahmin and kshatriya or kshatriya and vaishya descent; traditionally employed as drivers and bards

svayamvara [Sva·yam·va·ra, USUU; LHLL]: bridegroom choice ceremony

Shakuni [Sha·ku·ni, SUU; LLL]: Gandhari's brother; close supporter of Duryodhana

Shakuntala [Sha·kun·ta·laa, USUU; LHLH]: mother of Bharata

Shalva [Shaal·va, SU; HL]: (1) Amba's chosen bridegroom; (2) demonic king of the flying city of Saubha, defeated by Krishna; (3) Mleccha chief

Shalya [Shal·ya, su; hl]: literally, "dart"; king of Madra, uncle of Nakula and Sahadeva, who fights for the Kauravas

Shankha [Shan·kha, su; hl]: (1) son of Virata; (2) brother of Likhita

Shantanu [Shan·ta·nu, suu; hll]: Bharata king; father of Bhishma; husband of Ganga and Satyavati

Sharadvat [Sha·rad·vat, usu; lhl]: father of Kripa and Kripi

Shatayupa [Sha·taa·yu·pa, usuu; lhll]: a sage

Shaunaka [Shau·na·ka, suu; hll]: brahmin who accompanies the Pandavas into exile

Shibi [Shi·bi, su; ll]: devout king tested by the gods

Shikhandin [Shi·khan·din, usu; *shi·khan·din*, lhl]: son of Drupada; reincarnation of Amba

Shishupala [Shi·shu·paa·la, uusu; llhl]: king of Chedi, killed by Krishna

Shiva [Shi·va, su; ll]: powerful god

shraddha [shraad·dha, su; hl]: ritual offering to nourish the ancestors

Shri [Shree, s; h]: goddess of royal fortune

shudras [English plural; singular: shoo·dra, su; hl]: servants, peasants, etc., lowest of the four main classes in the social hierarchy

Shuka [Shu·ka, su; ll]: Vyasa's son

Shveta [Shve·ta, su; hl]: Virata's son

Takshaka [Ta·ksha·ka, suu; hll]: king of snakes

Tantipala [Tan·ti·paa·la, susu; hlhl]: Sahadeva's alias at Virata's court

Terrifier: name for Arjuna

Tilottama [Ti·lot·ta·maa, usuu; lhlh]: woman created by Vishvakarman to test Sunda and Upasunda

Treta age [Tre·taa, su; hh]: second-best of the ages of the world; second-best throw at dice

Trigartas [English plural; singular: Tri·gar·ta, ssu; hhl]: a people sworn to kill Arjuna

Ugrashravas [Sanskrit singular; Ug·ra·shra·vas, ssuu; hhll]: a

bard; narrator of the *Mahabharata* to seers in the Naimisha
Forest

Uluka [U·loo·ka, USU; LHL]: Shakuni's son

Ulupi [U·loo·pee, USU; LHH]: snake princess; wife of Arjuna

Upasunda [U·pa·sun·da, UUSU; LLHL]: demon; brother of
Sunda

Urvashi [Ur·va·shee, SUU; HLH]: an apsaras

Uttanka [U·tan·ka, USU; LHL]: an ascetic tested by Krishna

Uttara [masculine; Ut·ta·ra, SUU; HLL]: son of Virata

Uttaraa [feminine; Ut·ta·raa, SUU; HLH]: Virata's daughter;
wife of Abhimanyu

Vaishampayana [Vai·sham·paa·ya·na, SUSUU; HLHLL]: Vyasa's
disciple; reciter of the *Mahabharata* to King Janamejaya

vaishyas [English plural; singular: vai·shya, SU;
HL]: merchants, artisans, etc; third-ranking class in the
fourfold social hierarchy

Vajra [Vaj·ra, SU; HL]: Krishna's descendant; designated ruler
of Indraprastha

Varaha [Va·raa·ha, USU; LHL]: boar incarnation of Vishnu

varnas [English plural; singular: var·na, SU; *var·na*, HL]: social
categories; precursors of caste divisions

Varuna [Va·ru·na, SUU; *va·ru·na*, LLL]: god of the waters; one
of the world guardians

Vasus [English plural; singular: Va·su, SU; LL]: eight celestial
beings born as mortals; Bhishma is an incarnation of the
eighth

Vasudeva [Va·su·de·va, UUSU; LLHL]: Krishna's father

Vasudeva [Vaa·su·de·va, SUSU; HLHL]: "son of Vasudeva," one
of Krishna's names

Vasuki [Vaa·su·ki, SUU; HLL]: Naga king

Vayu [Vaa·yu, SU; HL]: god of the wind; Bhima's father

Vedas [English plural; singular: Ve·da, SU; HL]: the most holy
scriptures, orally transmitted by brahmins

Vibhishana [Vi·bhee·sha·na, USUU; *vi·bhī·sha·na*, LHLL]: king of
Lanka

Vichitravirya [Vi·chi·tra·veer·ya, USUSU; LHLHL]: son of
Shantanu and Satyavati

Vidura [Vi·du·ra, suu; lll]: son of Vyasa by a maidservant; brother of Dhritarashtra and Pandu

Vikarna [Vi·kar·na, usu; *vi·kar·na*, lhl]: son of Dhritarashtra

Virata [Vi·raa·ta, usu; *vi·rā·ta*, lhl]: king of Matsya; host to the Pandavas in exile

Vishnu [Vish·nu, su; *vish·nu*, hl]: supreme deity

Vishvakarman [Vish·va·kar·man, susu; hlhl]: divine craftsman

Vishvamitra [Vish·vaa·mit·ra, susu; hhhl]: a seer

Vivimshati [Vi·vim·sha·ti, usuu; lhll]: son of Dhritarashtra

Vrishasena [Vri·sha·se·na, susu; hlhl]: Karna's son

Vrishni [Vrish·ni, su; *vrish·ni*, hl]: Krishna's clan, a subdivision of the Yadava people

Vyasa [Vyaa·sa, su; hl]: seer; author of the *Mahabharata* and major participant in the events; a.k.a. Krishna Dvaipayana

Wealth-winner: a name for Arjuna

Wearer of the diadem: a name for Arjuna

Wolf-belly: a name for Bhima

Yadavas [English plural; singular: Yaa·da·va, suu; hll]: "descendants of Yadu," a people to whom Krishna belongs

Yaja [Yaa·ja, su; hl]: priest who brings Dhrishtadyumna and Draupadi into being

Yakshas [English plural; singular: Yak·sha, su; hl]: earth spirits serving Kubera

Yama [Ya·ma, su; ll]: god of death

Yamuna [Ya·mu·naa, suu; llh]: major river of northern India

yoga [as in English]: spiritual discipline

Yudhishthira [Yu·dhish·thi·ra, usuu; *yu·dhish·thi·ra*, lhll]: eldest of the Pandava brothers; the Dharma King

Yuvanashva [Yu·va·naash·va, uusu; llhl]: king, father of Mandhatri

Yuyutsu [Yu·yut·su, usu; lhl]: son of Dhritarashtra by a vaishya woman; ally of the Pandavas in the war

About the Authors

Vinay Dharwadker is Professor in the Department of Comparative Literature and Folklore Studies at the University of Wisconsin–Madison. He translates from Hindi, Marathi, Urdu, Punjabi, and Sanskrit, and his *Kabir: The Weaver's Songs* won India's national translation prize in 2008. He is the South Asia editor of the *Norton Anthology of World Literature*, third edition (2012).

Wendy Doniger (O'Flaherty) received her PhD from Harvard University and her DPhil from Oxford University. She teaches at the University of Chicago and is the author of over thirty books, from *Siva: The Erotic Ascetic* (1973) to *The Bedtrick: Tales of Sex and Masquerade* (2000), *The Woman Who Pretended to Be Who She Was* (2005), *The Hindus: An Alternative History* (2009), and *On Hinduism* (2013).

Carole Satyamurti is a poet and sociologist. She has published several books of poetry with Oxford University Press and Bloodaxe, of which the most recent are *Stitching the Dark: New and Selected Poems* (2005) and *Countdown* (2011). Her poetry has received many awards and has been widely anthologized.